# Understanding Business Markets: Interaction, Relationships and Networks

# Understanding Business Markets: Interaction, Relationships and Networks

Second Edition

The Industrial Marketing and Purchasing Group

*Edited by*

David Ford

**The Dryden Press**

*Harcourt Brace & Company Limited*

London Fort Worth New York Orlando
Philadelphia San Diego Toronto Sydney Tokyo

The Dryden Press
24/28 Oval Road,
London NW1 7DX



**A catalogue record for this book is available from the British Library**
ISBN 0-03-099-053-X



Typeset by Mackreth Media Services, Hemel Hempstead
Printed in Great Britain at WBC Book Manufacturers, Bridgend, Mid Glamorgan

# Contents

## PART III: DEVELOPING MARKETING STRATEGY

## PART IV: DEVELOPING PURCHASING STRATEGY



## PART V: TECHNOLOGY AND NETWORKS

# Introduction: The Interaction Approach

*David Ford*

The main aim of the second edition of this book is to help students and managers to make sense of what happens in complicated business markets. The book brings together a number of previously published articles by the IMP (Industrial Marketing and Purchasing) Research Group and some of our co-workers in a form that provides students, practitioners and academic colleagues with an overview of the group's work. The book presents a comprehensive coverage of what has become known as the *Interaction Approach* to understanding and managing in business markets.

It is perhaps a good idea to start by outlining the development of the interaction approach and why it seems to be useful for students who are trying to understand business markets and for managers who must try to make profits in them. This introduction may also help readers to relate some of the ideas in the book to what is found in more general marketing texts. It will also provide a background to show how the readings that follow are related to each other and are part of a continuing attempt to understand business markets.

## THE TRADITIONAL APPROACH TO MARKETING

The traditional approach both to understanding and to managing a company's marketing activities had its roots in consumer marketing, particularly in the marketing of fast-moving, non-durable goods, such as personal care products. This approach was built around a core of the marketing mix, or the relatively small set of variables considered to be available for the marketer to manipulate – the "4Ps"; the product itself; the price charged for it; the way it was promoted and the distribution methods used (or "place" in which it was sold). Marketing within companies was organized around the management of individual brands and the creative task for each brand manager was to manipulate the mix for that brand, to achieve growth in market share and profitability. At the same time, academic debate continued about whether there were really only four "Ps" that marketers could manipulate, or whether other "Ps" such as the "People" involved in the process should be added to the list. Meanwhile, marketing research centred on two aims. The first was to gain a greater understanding of the effectiveness of different approaches within each mix variable, such as the ways in which companies determined their prices, or the promotional techniques that would bring the best response from the market. The second area of research was to understand consumers better and, in particular, the processes by which they responded to the mix and eventually came to choose a particular brand and make a purchase. Researchers were also interested in the differences between the behaviour and choice criteria of different groups of consumers within the market. We can summarize this approach to marketing as follows.

First, the approach said that marketing is what marketers *do*. In particular it is what manufacturers do. By implication, retailers were seen as people who simply provide shelf-space after they have been selected by the manufacturer to be part of its mix. A side-effect of this is that the marketing literature still tends to downplay the importance of marketing *by* retailers, despite the fact that many of them are major brands in their own right, who often develop innovative products, who have promotional budgets that dwarf those of most manufacturers, who determine the price paid by the consumer and who, of course, distribute products.

Secondly the approach, it said that the seller is the active party in the process of marketing, with the task of assembling the mix – to *do* the marketing. Each customer was considered to be individually insignificant and part of a relatively homogeneous market, or at least part of a segment within that market. The role of the customer was seen as passive and limited to choosing to respond or not to respond to the mix that the manufacturer launched at the market as a whole.

## BUSINESS MARKETS

Now the story gets slightly more complicated because this same approach was also followed when marketing researchers turned their attention to the way in which companies marketed to other companies in business or industrial markets. Most marketing textbooks had chapters on business marketing, which was regarded as some sort of special case of "normal" marketing. Academics also tried to map the purchase processes that companies went through, which seemed to be even more complicated than those of consumers. The researchers categorized the different types of purchases, different types of customers and who was influential in taking purchase decisions. They also tried to find out what were the most effective mixes that a seller could use to obtain the desired response from the market. These mixes for the business marketer also seemed to be more complicated. Instead of an emphasis on advertising, the promotional element was more likely to favour personal sales effort and somewhere in the 4 "Ps" it was necessary to find room for things like after-sales service, etc.

But this way of looking at and doing business marketing had three even more significant characteristics:

- It was based on the separate analysis of the marketing and purchasing process.
- It concentrated on the purchase process for a single purchase.
- It carried over from the consumer–marketing literature of the time the implicit view that buyers were individually insignificant, passive and part of a relatively homogeneous market.

Of course, this way of seeing business markets did not exist just in the academic literature. This was the way in which it was taught to those who were to become business marketers, although paradoxically it did not coincide closely with what experienced practitioners were actually doing in the real world.

## THE INTERACTION APPROACH

The development of the interaction approach to understanding business markets started because of a realization that the prevailing literature did not seem to relate closely to what really happened in business markets. In particular, business markets do not consist of a large number of individually insignificant customers. Customers vary widely in size and requirements: some of them are bigger than their suppliers and marketers seem to talk about them individually so that each seems to be more or less important to the seller.

Business markets do not consist simply of active sellers and passive buyers. Often, a buying company, faced with a particular requirement, has to seek out suitable suppliers, assess them and even sometimes persuade them to meet those requirements. This task is difficult if the buyer's requirements are hard to satisfy or the potential purchases are small. More generally, what is supplied and bought is not a fixed, standard product determined by the seller. The product is often modified or even designed specially at the customer's request. It may also be manufactured in a particular way, perhaps even in a purpose-designed plant. It may be delivered on a mutually agreed schedule and at a price that is individually negotiated. Lots of people from different functional areas in both companies are likely to be involved in the process, not just marketing, sales and purchasing staff, but also people from engineering, production and finance, etc.

*This means that the process is not one of action and reaction; it is one of interaction.*

Furthermore, sales and buying people in business markets do not simply meet, do a deal and then never see each other again. Sometimes, there may be a long period before the first purchase, involving lots of interaction – months of initial meetings, product and production development, and negotiation. More importantly, this first purchase may be the forerunner of others. At one extreme, deliveries are likely to be continuous in the case of production components, perhaps over many years. For capital equipment each customer may make a purchase only infrequently. But each time, it will remember its previous purchases and what the pattern of interaction was like with the successful and unsuccessful suppliers before, during and after the purchase. Some other purchases will be less important to either of the parties involved and the interaction between them may be limited to a phone call each time a product is required. Even here, each purchase will be influenced by what has happened before and each in turn will influence what happens the next time a similar purchase takes place.

All of this means that each business purchase is just a single *episode* among many in a *relationship* between the two companies, and each purchase can only be fully understood within the context of that relationship. Each episode, whether it is the exchange of product, service, finance or even a social interaction, is affected by the relationship of which it forms part, and each interaction, in turn, affects the relationship itself. These business relationships have a life of their own, which is separate from the companies that are part of it. To understand business marketing and purchasing we must understand business relationships, and many of the papers in this book look at ways to do that.

Many, perhaps most of the relationships in business markets are close, complex and long term, like that for a middle-aged married couple. But, just as with a married couple, this does not mean that the parties know everything about each other, or indeed that they always act in each other's best interests. Other relationships centre on a single transaction, like that for the purchase of a major piece of capital equipment, which could take months or years in gestation. Some business relationships are characterized by domination by one or other of the partners, or by conflict and deceit. Some relationships between companies simply lose their reason for existence and become inert or end in divorce. Others are short term, such as when one of the parties seeks to take advantage of the other. Perhaps the buyer will seek to exploit the technical resources of the seller with the implied promise of a long-term relationship that it has no intention of fulfilling. Here again there is a close analogy with the relationships that can exist between people. Yet other relationships are more distant and the only contact between the two companies is impersonal, by advertising or mail. In this way they approximate to the situation in many consumer markets.

## RELATIONSHIPS

Early work by the IMP group took the *relationship* as its unit of analysis, not an individual purchase or the marketing company itself. This approach was not just an academic device: it was based on the belief that the critical task for the business marketer is the development and management of its relationships with its customers. This, in turn led to two further elements of the group's approach.

First, the task of managing a buyer–seller relationship is essentially similar for both of the companies involved: both buyer and seller companies enter a relationship for their own ends and seek to achieve them through that relationship, sometimes at the expense of the other party and sometimes in co-operation with it. Both companies bring resources to their relationship and will use these to design, manufacture and transfer products between themselves and onwards to other companies. Both companies will have to take decisions about how much to adapt their products, processes or administrative procedures to suit the requirements of the other company. This view of the similarity of the task for the buyer and the seller influenced our research process, because we believed that it is possible to make sense of what happens in business markets only by simultaneously studying *both* sides of a relationship. Also, we were struck by the fact that the value of a company's purchases often accounts for 60–80% of its cost-of-goods sold. This means that the purchasing function makes a major contribution to cost reduction and profit enhancement.

Perhaps even more importantly, purchasing is the function that is concerned with using the skills and resources of supplier companies to achieve positive competitive advantage. Despite this, purchasing continues to be viewed as a relatively low-status, routine, non-strategic and efficiency-oriented function. It is under-researched, under-funded and misunderstood. For this reason, studies by the group have taken a strong interest in purchasing management itself.

Second, the relationship management task is not confined to a single relationship. Instead, each company has a *portfolio* of buying and selling relationships in which it is enmeshed and it must manage that portfolio. For example, a marketing company will see some of its customers as sources of future profits and will be likely to commit considerable resources to meet their requirements. Other customers may have particularly demanding technical requirements and the company may see these as an opportunity to develop its technology, which can then be applied elsewhere in the company's portfolio. Similarly, a buying company may differentiate between companies it sees as the source of its next generation of requirements and share information and joint development resources with them. It may characterize others solely as suppliers of more standardized products and hence as companies that are a more easily replaceable part of its portfolio. This introduces another important point.

*Our work has increasingly been based on the idea that close or co-operative relationships are not always a good thing.*

It may well be in a company's best interests to keep its distance when dealing with some counterparts, perhaps because it doesn't trust them or perhaps because there are simply no advantages in getting close. Similarly, co-operating with another counterpart may not be in the company's best interests and it may be better to seek advantage at the expense of the other side, even to the extent of exploiting it for short-term gain – after all, it's a hard world out there! On the other hand a company would have to be aware of the effects of its actions with any one company on the feelings of others in its portfolio.

## SOME PROBLEMS WITH THE INTERACTION APPROACH

The interaction approach to the study of business markets provided a different perspective when compared with previous studies, but inevitably it had drawbacks.

The first is that some of the early writings by the group seemed to indicate that business relationships were closer and more co-operative than is always the case. Perhaps the reason for this was that the writing was reacting to the prevailing culture. This culture was (and largely still is) that business purchasing is about seeking advantage over suppliers and playing one off against the other for short-term price reduction. Faced with this, the marketing task was commonly seen as being to win sales and achieve short-term reward from the market. After all, this was how the two disciplines were taught. It was only as our ideas on relationships and portfolios developed that it became clear that it was *not* always sensible for buyer–seller relationships to evolve in the direction of closeness and co-operation. Paradoxically, as studies started to emphasize the full range of variation that should exist in relationships, the business press has become full of articles arguing that close relationships are something to be strived for *in almost all circumstances.* This has led to a number of simplistic prescriptions for such things as "partnership purchasing", which often bear scant resemblance to the complexity of the situation facing both marketers and purchasers.

Nevertheless, whether they are close, distant, co-operative, conflictful, predictable or wildly fluctuating, relationships between companies *exist.* "Relationship" is not a dichotomous variable and a company cannot choose to have or not have one with a particular customer or supplier. Instead, the issue is what the nature of that relationship will be. This will not be determined by one side, but by both. Relationships are not just important: a company's relationships with others effectively *define* its existence and without them it has no meaning. When these relationships are good they are major assets, when they are bad they are liabilities, but whatever they are, they have to be managed.

The second shortcoming of many of the earlier works by the group was that they attempted to mirror the complexities of business markets by examining sales and purchases within the context of a *single* relationship and a portfolio of other relationships. But this level of analysis is in itself insufficient to give a realistic picture of what happens in business markets. Each business company is enmeshed in an even more complex *network* of relationships. This network consists of the direct relationships that the company has with its suppliers and customers as well as with other organizations such as financial institutions and research houses. The network also consists of the relationships that these counterpart companies have with other suppliers or customers. For example, a major supplier to the "focal company" will probably also have relationships with other customers. What the supplier does in these relationships will also affect what happens in its relationships with the focal company. This can be because of what it learns in those relationships and the way it uses its resources in them, or how it regards its relationship with the focal company in comparison with them. The network surrounding the company also consists of the pattern of indirect relationships between companies with which the focal company has no contact, but which can affect its way of doing business. For example, these indirect relationships can be between two companies that also supply one of the focal company's customers. What happens in this distant relationship could well affect this customer's requirements from the focal company or its attitude towards it. Similarly, a technology or pattern of contact that is developed between two companies elsewhere in the network could lead to a change in the thinking of the focal company's suppliers.

These networks of relationships have their own dynamic and each company and its relationships are part of the pattern of influence and change that flows through them. Sometimes, a company will seek to influence many of the companies around it and try to alter its position in the network, such as in the case of a powerful retailer that seeks to affect the operations of its product suppliers, and also of *their* suppliers. More commonly, the state of a network and the direction of its evolution is the result of the actions and motivations of many different companies, some acting alone and some together. In the same way that a company cannot unilaterally design or control its relationships with others, it is even less likely to be able to design or control the wider network that surrounds it.

To understand what goes on inside a business company we need to try to understand its relationships. To understand what goes on inside a company's relationships we need to try to understand the network of which they form part. It is for this reason that the later research within the interaction approach has moved from the study of business relationships to a wider, network, perspective.

## RELATIONSHIP MARKETING

Recently, ideas on *relationship marketing* have come to prominence within the consumer marketing literature and it is worthwhile to distinguish these from the work within the interaction approach. These ideas on relationship marketing have two main origins. The first is a realization that consumer marketing, just like business marketing, is about repeat purchases – there really is little profit to be had in getting someone to buy a particular brand of coffee on just one occasion. The second origin is in the direct marketing literature. For a long time direct-marketing practitioners have emphasized the difference between customers who buy once and clients who buy frequently. The growth in the technology of what became known as database marketing meant that practitioners were able to know much more about the attitudes, lifestyles and purchase habits of people overall and not just narrowly about the products with which they were currently involved. This led to a change in emphasis amongst practitioners from the task of constructing a good offering and a suitable message, to the task of maximizing the company's return on its client base, over time, and by a succession of different offerings. Hence the term "relationship marketing". However, relationship marketing is still largely a one-sided process with an active seller and a passive buyer. The major difference between it and conventional consumer marketing is that its emphasis is on repeat purchases by an identifiable customer. Relationship marketing may be perfectly appropriate in those consumer markets where it is used, but is inappropriate as a description of what happens in business markets. In this book we are concerned with marketers and purchasers who are *both* active within relationships.

## ABOUT THE BOOK

The first edition of this book was intended to introduce some of the IMP group's work within the interaction approach to a wider audience of academics. The book was adopted as course text on a considerable number of courses on relationship management, networks, and business marketing and purchasing. This showed that there is clearly a need to provide a straightforward introduction to the interaction approach and its application in business marketing and purchasing. Because of this, the articles and extracts selected for this edition are not necessarily those that are the "cleverest", in terms of conceptual complexity or research methodology, although some of them are pretty fine. Instead, I have tried to include readings that give a clear exposition of the various concepts and issues involved in understanding business markets. Also included are a number of readings that illustrate the *reality* of business markets and which have an international perspective. This has meant leaving out a number that either develop concepts much further than would perhaps interest the average reader or which contain a mass of detailed data analysis.

The book also includes work by a number of people who are not part of the original IMP group, but who we have met over the years and from whom we have learned a great deal during the course of work together, such as Jim Anderson, Geoff Easton, Lars-Gunnar Mattsson, Jim Narus, Ian Wilkinson, Dave Wilson and Louise Young. There are also pieces in here from some second- or even third-generation researchers within the overall interaction approach, who have developed some basic ideas much further. As always, there are many readings that could well have been included, but are not, and perhaps a few that are here but should not be. Despite this, we hope that the book will be of value.

*David Ford*
*University of Bath,*
*March 1996*

*On behalf of the IMP group*

# Some Previous Books by IMP Group Members and Co-workers


Axelsson, B. and Easton, G. (eds). *Industrial Networks: A New View of Reality.* Routledge, London (1992).

Ford, D. (ed.). *Understanding Business Markets.* Academic Press, London (1990).

Ford, D. and Saren, M. *Technology Strategy for Business.* Thomson International Press, London (1996).

Forsgren, M. and Johanson, J. (eds). *Managing Networks in International Business.* Gordon and Breach, Philadelphia, PA (1992).

Gross, A. C., Banting, P. M., Meredith, L. N. and Ford, D. *Business Marketing.* Houghton Mifflin, Boston (1993).

Håkansson, H. (ed.). *International Marketing and Purchasing of Industrial Goods.* John Wiley, Chichester (1982).

Håkansson, H. (ed.). *Industrial Technological Development: A Network Approach.* Croom Helm, London (1987).

Håkansson, H. *Corporate Technological Behaviour: Co-operation and Networks.* Routledge, London (1989).

Håkansson, H. and Gadde, L.-E. *Professional Purchasing.* Routledge, London (1992).

Håkansson, H. and Snehota, I. (eds). *Developing Relationships in Business Networks.* Routledge, London (1995).

Lundgren, A. *Technological Innovation and Network Evolution.* Routledge, London (1995).

Sharma, D. D. *Advances in International Marketing.* JAI Press, Greenwich, Connecticut (1993).

Turnbull, P. and Cunningham, M. T. *International Marketing and Purchasing.* Macmillan, London (1981).

Turnbull, P. and Paliwoda, S. (eds). *Research Developments in International Marketing.* Croom Helm, London (1986).

Turnbull, P. and Valla, J.-P. (eds). *Strategies for International Industrial Marketing.* Croom Helm, London (1986).

Wilson, D. and Möller, K. *Business Marketing: An Interaction and Network Perspective.* Kluwer Academic Publishers, Boston (1995).

# Part I

## Interaction and Relationships in Business Markets

The first section of the book introduces ideas on how the interaction approach can help us to understand business or industrial markets. The first reading is taken from the initial book by the IMP group, edited by Håkansson in 1982. It presents a general model of buyer–seller interaction and contrasts this approach with earlier literature and other approaches. The reading uses a number of the basic ideas that are developed further in other readings in this book and that we have referred to in the introduction: both industrial marketing and purchasing people are seen as active participants in the market who take part in an often complex series of "episodes" in exchanging product or service, information, money and sociability. These episodes are part of a relationship between the two companies and this relationship provides the "atmosphere" within which interaction takes place. The second reading, "Influence tactics in buyer–seller processes" by Håkansson, Johanson and Wootz (all founder members of the IMP group), is the earliest one in the book and is one of the precursors of the interaction approach. It illustrates the reality facing many firms in industrial markets with a limited number of large customers, which they have to deal with individually. The reading illustrates one of the fundamental requirements for any company operating in a business market, whether as buyer or seller, which is the need to get "inside the head" of their counterpart. In this case, the reading describes the problems or uncertainties faced by buyers in business markets and how these uncertainties can be influenced by a seller company to its advantage.

The third reading, by the editor, continues to develop the idea of business marketing as a process between individual companies and introduces ideas on the relationships that exist between buying and selling companies. It suggests that buyer–seller relationships develop through a series of stages and points to some of the managerial tasks involved in these relationships. The fourth reading, "How do companies interact?", looks at the interaction between companies in more detail. It uses the concepts of "mutuality", "particularity" and "inconsistency" to show the nature of the choices open to business marketing managers in their relationships with customers. The reading is interesting, not just because of the possible usefulness of the concepts to assist managers in developing and explaining their ideas, but also because it is an example of an attempt to develop and modify some of the earlier concepts within the interaction approach.

Reading number five also appeared in the first edition. Ford and Rosson explore particular types of buyer–seller relationships not covered elsewhere in the book. These are the relationships between exporters and their overseas distributors. As well as examining an interesting and important area, the paper shows how problematic is the development of relationships between companies and how they can readily fail or become inert. The reading thus forms an interesting contrast to the earlier Ford reading on the development of buyer–seller relationships, which concentrated on relationship development as a somewhat deterministic process over time.

The final paper by Wilkinson and Young also shows how concepts can be refined over time. This article appeared 15 years after reading number three on developing buyer–seller relationships and shows how ideas have developed over that time. In particular, it emphasizes the nature of both co-operation and conflict in buyer–seller relationships. The reading also uses the metaphor of different types of dances to describe what goes on between companies in their relationships and contrasts this with the view that sees buyer–seller relationships as being rather like marriages.

## CONTENTS

# 1

# An Interaction Approach

*IMP Group*

## INTRODUCTION

In a joint research project with several researchers with different backgrounds there are always problems in developing a common theoretical framework. This was further complicated in this project by differences in language, approach and emphasis between the researchers. We were however fortunate in having similar *basic* approaches to the analysis of Industrial Marketing and Purchasing.[1] Extensive discussion within the project group led to the discovery of important concepts and assumptions which were shared by all. It is on this theoretical basis that the design and the methodology are built. These concepts and basic assumptions are now presented in this chapter.

## RELATIONS TO PREVIOUS RESEARCH

Our theoretical framework can be traced back to two major theoretical models from outside the marketing literature. These are Inter-organizational Theory and the New Institutional Economic Theory. At the same time it is possible to relate our approach to earlier thinking in marketing and purchasing as well as some emerging trends in the marketing and purchasing literature.

### Inter-organizational Theory and Marketing Literature

Much of the work in Inter-organizational Theory involves attempts to apply theory and concepts from intra-organizational studies to problems where several organizational units are involved. Here the focus of attention is on relationships between those organizations rather than within each individual organization. Works

Reprinted by permission of John Wiley and Sons Limited, An Interaction Approach by the IMP Group from *International Marketing and Purchasing of Industrial Goods*, pp 10–27.

in this area can be classified into three groups, based upon differences in the relation between the organization and its environment as proposed by Van de Ven *et al.* (1975). It is also possible to classify marketing literature along similar lines, again depending on the perspective of researchers when dealing with organization–environmental relationships. Such a categorization of the marketing literature has been presented by Sweeney (1972). We will consider the categorization of the inter-organizational literature and the marketing literature in parallel:

*(a) Organization based studies.* The environment is seen as an external limitation for the organization in this group of studies. Inter-organizational studies which can be included in this group are those which examine the internal organization based on an open systems approach. Here, the organization is seen as being dependent on its environment, for example in obtaining access to certain inputs. At the same time the organization seeks to manipulate or control parts of its environment. Because of this, the characteristics of the environment will influence the shape of the internal organization structure. This organization–environment connection is central and is analysed in many studies.[2]

The predominant current viewpoint in marketing shares this perspective. It is characterized by Sweeney as the "organizational system perspective", and is exemplified in the so-called "managerial approach" to the study of marketing. In this, marketing researchers are concerned with techniques for the development and management of product, price, distribution, and promotional strategies to optimize desired market response. The boundaries of marketing are defined as those "publics" which have a "... potential impact on the resource converting efficiency of the organization" (Kotler and Levy, 1969). It is implicit in this approach that buyers are passive and only react to the stimuli of the seller by buying or not buying. The selling firm is the active partner in the buyer–seller relationship. Further, this relationship is largely seen to be between the seller, and some generic "market", rather than with individual customers.[3]

It is worth noting at this stage that a side effect of this approach to the study of marketing has been that the study of buyers has developed along somewhat separate lines from the study of sellers. Here, researchers have analysed the factors which affect both the individual and company buying processes, e.g. previous purchase experience, the importance of "task" and "non-task" variables, the effect of different organizational forms and the degree of formality in hypothesized decision-making processes. These analyses have concentrated on the stages in a *discrete* purchase. Thus, there has been an emphasis in the industrial buyer behaviour literature on single rather than continuing purchases from a particular supplier. Additionally, the study of the buying process has taken place with relatively scant regard to the influence of the selling firm in that process.[4]

Thus, the first group of studies includes two distinct and *separate* approaches to the study of what occurs in industrial markets. On the one hand, there is an analysis of the manipulation of marketing variables by the seller to achieve a desired market response. On the other hand, there is the separate analysis of a single buying process and the factors which affect that process, from which lessons can be drawn for marketing.

*(b) Studies based on several organizations.* In this second group of inter-organization studies, the organization is seen as part of a group of interacting units. Studies within

this category are often based on the dependence between the particular organization and its environment as defined by studies from category (a). In order to obtain necessary resources, the organization is seen to develop relations with a number of other organizational units and thus it enters into a network of relationships.

Two aspects of this network have mainly been studied. Firstly, the characteristics of the different organizations have been investigated as they relate to the other organizations within the same network. Secondly, the links between the units have been analysed in terms of, for example, formalization, intensity, and standardization.[5]

The parallel to these studies in the marketing area are those from a "distribution system perspective". In this, the field is viewed as a system of interconnected institutions performing the economic functions required to bring about exchange of goods or services. This perspective is, of course, broader than the organizational system perspective. The boundaries of marketing at this level of aggregation include those institutions involved in the distribution of goods within the society. The focus is on the nature of the functions being performed by the system and on the structure, performance and inter-relationships of the institutions which comprise the system. Aspects of these areas which have received study are the division of roles and responsibilities between different members of a manufacturing–distribution channel, the conflicts between different levels and within levels in the channel as well as the patterns of power and communication which exist between them.[6] During recent years, a number of works on more general aspects of marketing and purchasing have appeared which fit within this group.[7]

*(c) Studies of the organization in a societal context.* In this third category, the organization is seen as an integrated part in a larger social system. In order to describe and understand how a certain organization functions it is necessary, according to this approach, to see the organization in relation to the larger system. The organization is part of what some authors call "inter-organization collectives" and these groups influence to a large extent the actions of the organization.[8] The view of marketing from a "social system perspective" sees it as a social process which evolves to facilitate the society's needs for efficient and effective exchange of values. There is a clear distinction between this approach and its emphasis on analysis of the exchange process, and the organizational system approach which is concerned with the technology employed to execute that exchange process.

The view of marketing from a social system perspective is little developed. The majority of the marketing literature can be classified into group (a) above, while our approach belongs to group (b). There are also some minor attempts in our study to go in the direction of the works in group (c). However, the major focus of our attention is on the units (the buying and selling firms) and the link between them (the process of interaction).

## The New Institutionalists

The second theoretical area outside the marketing literature that we have built upon has been characterized by Williamson (1975) as "the New institutionalists". This line of thought within micro-economic theory is based on a criticism of certain aspects of traditional economic theory. Williamson discerns two alternative ways in which the exchange (transaction) may be handled between technologically separable units in a production or transformation process. Firstly, the transaction can take place within a market setting. On the other hand it can be internalized in one organizational unit (a hierarchy), i.e. two successive stages in the production process are vertically integrated in a hierarchically built organization. There are certain deficiencies in markets that favour the internalization of transactions. Similarly, there are also deficiencies in the way organizations function that operate in favour of keeping the transactions in the market, i.e. keeping the successive production stages under separate control and reaching agreements on buying and selling, through, for example, negotiated contracts.

Williamson argues that many transactions which are internalized in one organization could be carried out by separate organizations, from the point of view of technological separability. However, the co-ordination of these units by means of market relations involves disadvantages. Markets may be considered to operate inefficiently in certain instances, due to human and environmental factors. When the environment is characterized by complexity and uncertainty, then the bounded rationality of man makes it very costly to design and negotiate viable contracts. An example would be between two subsequent stages in a steel mill. Furthermore, the parties to such transaction may become very dependent on each other. This evolves into a small-numbers bargaining relation. Although the parties in a formal sense retain the option of selecting partners in the market, this is not a viable alternative due to transaction costs. Thus it will be very costly to design and negotiate contracts with new partners. This is because it is often difficult for one party to achieve information parity with the other party, which is necessary for a "fair" deal. Man is not just characterized by bounded rationality but also by opportunism ("self-seeking interest with guile"), and this makes markets operate inefficiently when there is an imbalanced dependence between the parties.

The high transaction costs that would be associated with operations in markets of the atomistic kind provide incentives for the internalization of such expensive transactions in vertically integrated units. Conflicts are considered to be settled in a more efficient and less costly way within an organization (by fiat rather than by haggling), and sequential, adaptive decision-making is facilitated. Opportunism is checked by control and audit.

However, there are also conditions counteracting the internalization of transactions. Firstly markets often do not operate as rigidly, and organizations do not operate as smoothly as depicted in the idealized extreme models (internal control is made more difficult as organizations grow in size), and thus transaction costs increase. Also there are checks on the opportunism in markets, e.g. courtesy, the interest in establishing conditions for future business and the effects of the firm's reputation on business deals with others. Imbalances are not always exploited in the short term in a way that increases transaction costs. Secondly, transactions do not take place in an attitudinally neutral setting. The establishment of satisfying exchange relations (an "atmosphere") modifies and is modified by the transactions.

Thus there are several factors that influence transaction costs and there are also intermediary settings for the exchange relations. Many industrial markets can be seen as such intermediary forms. Here we find such market characteristics as established small-numbers bargaining relations and lack of information parity. There are also organizational characteristics such as checks on opportunism due to established social relationships. Often a specific atmosphere has evolved that is characterized both by environmental and human factors.

Our theoretical framework is closely related to both "inter-organizational theory" and the "new institutionalists". At the same time it is directly related to evolutions in the literature of marketing, and particularly to the emphasis on inter-company relationships. This has emerged from those studies having a distribution system perspective and more recently from those empirically based studies which have emphasized the importance of inter-company relations.

## OUTLINE OF THE MODEL

Our approach to industrial markets – *The Interaction Approach* – is based on the theoretical idea described earlier. It is also built on a number of factors which our earlier empirical studies indicate are important in industrial markets and which appear to have been largely neglected in previous research:

Firstly, that both buyer and seller are active participants in the market. Each may engage in search to find a suitable buyer or seller, to prepare specifications of requirements or offerings and to manipulate or attempt to control the transaction process.

Secondly, the relationship between buyer and seller is frequently long term, close and involving a complex pattern of interaction between and within each company. The marketers' and buyers' task in this case may have more to do with maintaining these relationships than with making a straightforward sale or purchase.

Thirdly, the links between buyer and seller often become institutionalized into a set of roles that each party expects the other to perform, for example the division of product development responsibility, or the decision as to who should carry inventory and test products. These processes may require significant adaptations in organization or operation by either or both companies. Clearly, these relationships can involve both conflict as well as co-operation.

Fourthly, close relationships are often considered in the context of continuous raw material or component supply. However, we would emphasize the importance of previous purchases, mutual evaluation and the associated relationship between the companies in the case of infrequently purchased products. Further, we are concerned in this research with the nature of the relationship between a buying and selling company which may be built up during the course of a single major transaction.

Our focus is generally on a two party relationship, but the approach can be applied also to a several party relationship. This, indeed, may be necessary to accommodate the study of the simultaneous interactions between several buying and selling companies in a particular industry. The main components of our approach are illustrated in Fig. 1.

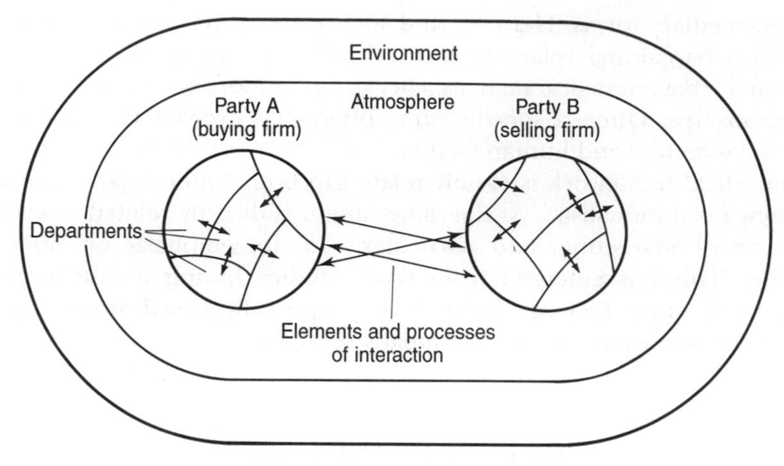


Fig. 1. Main elements of the interaction model.

In the figure we identify four groups of variables that describe and influence the interaction between buying and selling companies:

1. Variables describing the *parties* involved, both as organizations and as individuals.
2. Variables describing the *elements and process of interaction.*
3. Variables describing the *environment* within which the interaction takes place.
4. Variables describing the *atmosphere* affecting and affected by the interaction.

The approach does not only involve an analysis of these groups of variables but it also includes the relations between them.

## THE INTERACTION MODEL

The marketing and purchasing of industrial goods is seen as an interaction process between two parties within a certain environment. Our way of analysing industrial marketing and purchasing has four basic elements which in turn are sub-divided. These are:

1. The interaction process.
2. The participants in the interaction process.
3. The environment within which interaction takes place.
4. The atmosphere affecting and affected by the interaction.

In this section we will describe each of these four basic elements more extensively. The major focus here is on *description* of buyer–seller relationships and interactions. Only secondary emphasis is placed here on the interplay between the separate elements which we discuss. These interrelationships are developed later in the book.

## The Interaction Process

We have already noted that the relationships between buying and selling companies in industrial markets are frequently long term. Thus, it is important in our analysis to distinguish between the individual "Episodes" in a relationship, e.g. the placing or delivering of a particular order, and the longer-term aspects of that relationship which both affects and may be affected by each episode. We shall consider these individual episodes, first:

### *(a) Episodes*

The episodes which occur in an industrial market relationship involve exchange between two parties. There are four elements which are exchanged:

(i) Product or service exchange;
(ii) Information exchange;
(iii) Financial exchange;
(iv) Social exchange.

*(i) Product or service exchange.* The exchange of product or service is often the core of the exchange. As a result, the characteristics of the product or service involved are likely to have a significant effect on the relationship as a whole. For example, one major aspect of the product or service which seems important is the uncertainty with which they are associated. The exchange process will be quite different depending on whether or not the product is able to fulfil a buyer need that is easy to identify, and for which the characteristics of an appropriate product are easy to specify. It will also be important whether either buyer or seller is uncertain as to the requirements or resources of their opposite number.[9]

*(ii) Information exchange.* Several aspects of information exchange are of interest. The content of information is, of course, important. This can, for example, be characterized by the degree to which technical, economic, or organizational questions dominate the exchange. Furthermore, the width and depth of the information for each of these groups of questions should also be of importance. Information can be transferred between the parties by either personal or impersonal means. Impersonal communication is often used to transfer basic technical and/or commercial data. Personal channels are more likely to be used for the transfer of "soft data" concerning, for example, the use of a product, the conditions of an agreement between the parties, or supportive or general information about either party. Finally, the formality of the information exchange is important. The degree of formality may depend on wider organizational characteristics which can affect the nature of the interaction process and the relationship between the companies as a whole.

*(iii) Financial exchange.* Money is the third element. The quantity of money exchange is an indicator of the economic importance of the relationship. Another important

aspect is connected with the need to exchange money from one currency to another and the uncertainties in these exchanges over time.

*(iv) Social exchange.* Social exchange has an important function in reducing uncertainties between the two parties (Håkansson and Östberg, 1975). This is particularly significant when there exists spatial or cultural distance between the two parties or where the experience of the two parties is limited. Social exchange episodes may be important in themselves in avoiding short term difficulties between the two parties and in maintaining a relationship in the periods between transactions. However, perhaps the most important function of social exchange is in the long term process by which successive social exchange episodes gradually interlock the two firms with each other. Many aspects of the agreements between the buying and selling firms are not fully formalized nor based on legal criteria. Instead the relationship is based on mutual trust.[10] Building up this trust is a social process which takes time and must be based on personal experience, and on the successful execution of the three other elements of exchange. Furthermore, the need for mutual trust and the requirement of social exchange varies with differences in the elements exchanged in different relationships. Examples are variations in the amount of money exchanged, in the need for large amounts of informational exchange or in the complexity of the product exchanged. However, the development of trust is also dependent upon experience in exchange of the other three elements.

### *(b) Relationships*

Social exchange episodes are, as has been described above, critical in the build up of long-term relationships. Exchanges of product and service (which can be in both directions) and of the other elements of money and information can also lead to the build up of long-term relations. The routinization of these exchange episodes over a period of time leads to clear expectations in both parties of the roles or responsibilities of their opposite numbers. Eventually these expectations become *institutionalized* to such an extent that they may not be questioned by either party and may have more in common with the traditions of an industry or a market than rational decision-making by either of the parties (Ford, 1978).

The communication or exchange of information in the episodes successively builds up inter-organizational contact patterns and role relationships. These *contact patterns* can consist of individuals and groups of people filling different roles, operating in different functional departments and transmitting different messages of a technical, commercial, or reputational nature. These patterns can interlock the two parties to a greater or lesser extent and they are therefore an important variable to consider in analysing buyer–seller relationships. It is important to note that information and social exchange between parties can continue for a considerable time without there being an exchange of product or money. Thus, literature, specification development, and visits between companies can occur before the first order is placed or between widely spaced individual orders.

Another important aspect of the relationship is the *adaptations* which one or other party may make in either the elements exchanged or the process of exchange.

Examples of this are adaptations in product, in financial arrangements, in information routines or social relations. These adaptations can occur during the process of a single, major transaction or over the time of a relationship involving many individual transactions. The benefits of these adaptations can be in cost reduction, increased revenue, or differential control over the exchange. Adaptations in specific episodes may also be made in order to modify the overall relationship. Thus one party may make a decision not to offer special products to a customer out of a wish to be more distantly involved with that customer, rather than being closely involved and or heavily dependent on it.

The manipulation of different aspects of adaptation is of course a critical marketing and purchasing issue. Although adaptations by either party can occur in an unconscious manner as a relationship develops, it is important to emphasize the conscious strategy which is involved in many of these adaptations. Thus, modifications to product, delivery, pricing, information routines and even the organization itself are part of the seller's marketing strategy. Similarly, the buying organization will consider adaptations in its own product requirements, its production methods, the price it is prepared to accept, its information needs and the modification of its own delivery or stocking policies in order to accommodate the selling organization.

### The Interacting Parties

The process of interaction and the relationship between the organizations will depend not only on the elements of the interaction but also on the characteristics of the parties involved. This includes both the characteristics of the two organizations and the individuals who represent them. The organization factors include the companies' position in the market as manufacturer, wholesaler, etc. It also includes the products which the selling company offers, the production and application technologies of the two parties and their relative expertise in these areas. Below, we will discuss some of the major factors in more detail:

*(a) Technology.* Technical issues are often critical in buyer–seller interaction in industrial markets. The aims of the interaction process can be interpreted as tying the production technology of the seller to the application technology of the buyer. Thus the characteristics of the two technological systems and the differences between them give the basic conditions for the interaction. These basic conditions influence all the dimensions of the interaction processes: for example, the requirements for adaptations, mutual trust and contact patterns. Similarly, if the two organizations are separated by a wide gulf of technical expertise then the relationship between them can be expected to be quite different from a situation where the two companies are close in their level of expertise. Technology will be one of the variables which are in focus in the rest of this book. It will be further discussed in the methodological chapter, then in relation to the company cases and finally as a separate theme.

*(b) Organizational size, structure, and strategy.* The size and the power of the parties give them basic positions from which to interact. In general, a large firm with

considerable resources has a greater possibility of dominating its customers or suppliers than has a small firm. The structure of each organization and the extent of centralization, specialization and formalization influence the interaction process in several ways: this influence is seen in the number and categories of persons who are involved. It also affects the procedure of the exchange, the communications media used, the formalization of the interaction and the substance of what is exchanged – the nature of product or service and the finance which is involved. In the short term, organizational structures can be considered as the frameworks within which interaction takes place. In the longer term, it is possible that these organizational structures may be modified *by* the emerging interaction process or indeed by individual episodes.

The strategies of the parties are, of course, important influencing variables on the relationships. Later on we will describe how strategies can be formulated and analysed in relation to our theoretical approach.

*(c) Organizational experience.* A further factor is the company's experience not only in the relationship but also its experience and activities outside it. This experience may be the result of many other similar relationships and will equip the company with knowledge about the management of these kinds of relationships. It may also affect the level of importance attached to any one relationship, and hence the company's commitment to that relationship.

The variables which we will discuss in the next section under the title of The Interaction Environment will be mediated by the experience of specific individuals in a company as well as by the more generalized "experience" of a company. Thus the company's experience in particular markets will enable it to be more or less fitted for dealing in that market. Similarly, its experience of international operations will affect its willingness and ability to establish international relationships.

*(d) Individuals.* At least two individuals, one from each organization, are involved in a relationship. These are usually a buyer and a salesman. More commonly, several individuals from different functional areas, at different levels in the hierarchy and fulfilling different roles become involved in inter-company personal interactions. They exchange information, develop relationships and build up strong social bonds which influence the decisions of each company in the business relationship.

The varied personalities, experience, and motivations of each company's representatives will mean that they will take part in the social exchange differently. Their reactions in individual episodes could condition the ways in which the overall relationship builds up. Further, the role, level, and function of central persons in the interaction affect the chances of future development occurring in the relationship.

Individual experience may result in preconceptions concerning certain suppliers or customers, for example those in a certain country. These will affect attitudes and behaviour towards those buyers or suppliers. The process of learning from experience on both an individual and corporate level is communicated to and affects detailed "Episodes" in interaction. Additionally, the experience gained in individual episodes aggregates to a total experience. Indeed, the experience of a single episode can radically change attitudes which may then be held over a long period of time.

**The Interaction Environment**

The interaction between a buying and selling firm cannot be analysed in isolation, but must be considered in a wider context. This wider context has several aspects:

*(a) Market structure.* Firstly, a relationship must be considered as one of a number of similar relationships existing either nationally or internationally within the same market. The structure of this market depends in part on the concentration of both buyers and sellers and the stability or rate of change of the market and its constituent members. It also consists of the extent to which the market can be viewed as strictly national or needs to be thought of in wider international terms. The extent of buyer or seller concentration determines the number of alternatives available to any firm. This has a clear bearing on the pressure to interact with a certain counterpart within the market.

*(b) Dynamism.* The degree of dynamism within a relationship and in the wider market affects the relationship in two ways that are opposite to each other. Firstly, a close relationship increases the knowledge of one party of the likely actions of the other party and hence its ability to make forecasts based on this inside information. Secondly, and conversely, in a dynamic environment the opportunity cost of reliance on a single or small number of relationships can be very high when expressed in terms of the developments of other market members.

*(c) Internationalization.* The internationalization of the buying or selling market is of interest as it affects either firm's motivations in developing international relationships. This in turn may affect the company's organization, in needing sales subsidiaries or overseas buying units, the special knowledge it may require, e.g. in languages and international trade and its more general attitudes.

*(d) Position in the manufacturing channel.* A further aspect of the environment which must be brought into consideration is the position of an individual relationship in an extended "channel" stretching from primary producer to final consumer. Thus, for example, manufacturer A may sell electric components to manufacturer B, who then incorporates these components into actuators that are sold to manufacturer C, who adds them to valves. These valves, with many other products, may form the stock of distributor D and so on. The marketing strategy of A may thus be influenced by and directed at several markets at different stages in the channel. Clearly his relationship with buying company B will be affected by both A's and B's relationship with C and other subsequent organizations.

*(e) The social system.* As well as the effects of both horizontal market and vertical channel influences on a relationship, we must also consider the characteristics of the wider environment surrounding a particular relationship – the social system. This is particularly relevant in the international context where attitudes and perceptions on a generalized level can be important obstacles when trying to establish an exchange process with a certain counterpart. An example of this is nationalistic buying practices or generalized attitudes to the reliability of buyers or customers from a

particular country. Other aspects of these general influences concern regulations and constraints on business, for example exchange rates and trade regulations. There are other, more narrow social system variables which will surround a particular industry or market. For example, a supplier who has not previously delivered to a certain type of customer, e.g. in the automobile industry, has to learn both the "language" and the rules before it will be accepted in that industry.

## The Atmosphere

The relationships between buying and selling firms are dynamic in being affected by the individual episodes which take place within them. At the same time they have the stability which derives from the length of the relationship, its routinization and the clear expectations which become held by both parties. The relationship is influenced by the characteristics of the parties involved and the nature of the interaction itself. This in turn is a function of the technology involved and the environment within which the interaction takes place. Organizational strategy can also affect both the short-term episodes and the long-term relationships between the parties. One of the main aspects of the relationship which may be affected by conscious planning is the overall atmosphere of the relationship. This atmosphere can be described in terms of the power–dependence relationship which exists between the companies, the state of conflict or co-operation and overall closeness or distance of the relationship as well as by the companies' mutual expectations. These variables are not measured in a direct way in this study. Instead the atmosphere is considered as a group of intervening variables, defined by various combinations of environmental, company specific, and interaction process characteristics. The atmosphere is a product of the relationship, and it also mediates the influence of the groups of variables. There are reasons for the buying and selling firm to both develop a high degree of closeness with their counterpart as well as to avoid such closeness. There are both advantages and disadvantages connected with different atmospheres. We can analyse the reasons involved with regard to an economic (cost–benefit) dimension and a control dimension.

*(a) The economic dimension.* There are several types of cost that can be reduced for a firm by a closer interaction with a buying or selling firm. One of these costs is that which Williamson (1975) describes as the transaction cost. A closer connection means that it may be possible to handle distribution, negotiations, and administration more efficiently. Another type of cost which may be reduced is the production cost. A close relationship gives opportunities to find a more optimal division of the production process between the supplier and the customer. The supplier and buyer may reallocate some production processes between each other or co-operate in the design so as to make the product easier to produce or for the customer to develop further. There are also increased revenues which can be gained by a closer interaction. Both sides may achieve positive gains by better use of the other's competence, facilities, and other resources. New products can be developed together or old products may be redesigned. Furthermore, the parties can also often give each other valuable technical and commercial information.

*(b) The control dimension.* Another important reason for closer connection with a counterpart can be to reduce the uncertainty associated with that input or output by increasing its control over the other company. Such an increase in control improves the firm's chances of forecasting and determining that part of its environment. The ability to control a relationship is related to the *perceived* power of the two parties. Perceptions of power are likely to be unclear in the early stages of a relationship and one of the key functions of initial exchange episodes will be to enable each party to come to an understanding of each other's power. Even so, perceptions of power may change over the life of a relationship. They will, in turn, be related to the resources perceived to be possessed by each party as well as to their relative dependence on this individual relationship. Inter-organizational power will depend on the ability of either party to reward or coerce each other through exchange, or their relative expertise and access to information, as well as on their referent power, i.e. the value which one party places on association with another because of its wish to learn from and act similarly to the other.

The power of organization A over B is directly related to the dependence of B on A. The dependence on any one relationship by an organization is a major element in the wish to restrict interaction. Investment of time and resources in one relationship has an opportunity cost related to the value of those investments in another relationship. Also, the level of dependence on one relationship affects the vulnerability of an organization to the exercise of power by its opposite number. In everyday terms this is exemplified by a selling company which has a large proportion of its sales to one single buying company. It is the management of the closeness of the relationship, with its associated power and dependence, which is perhaps a crucial aspect of many industrial marketing and purchasing strategies.

Summing up this discussion of the reasons for a close interaction, we can conclude that relationships are established and used in order to gain economic benefits, lower costs, higher profits, and/or improving the organization's control of some part of its environment. A critical aspect of the management of these relationships is the extent to which the firm can balance its inter-dependence with others. The firm must seek to balance the advantages of a close relationship, perhaps in terms of cost reduction and ease and speed of interaction against the opportunity costs of that single relationship and the dependence which it involves.

## SUMMARY

In Fig. 2 we have tried to illustrate the different variables which have been presented here. The model shows the short-term and long-term aspects of the "Interaction Process" between buying and selling companies A and B. The short-term "Exchange Episodes" involve product–service, financial, information, and social exchange. These are separated from the longer term processes of "Adaptations" and "Institutionalization".

Both the short- and long-term aspects of the interaction are considered as being influenced by the characteristics of the organizations and individuals involved (circles A and B). Additionally, we see the interaction taking place within an

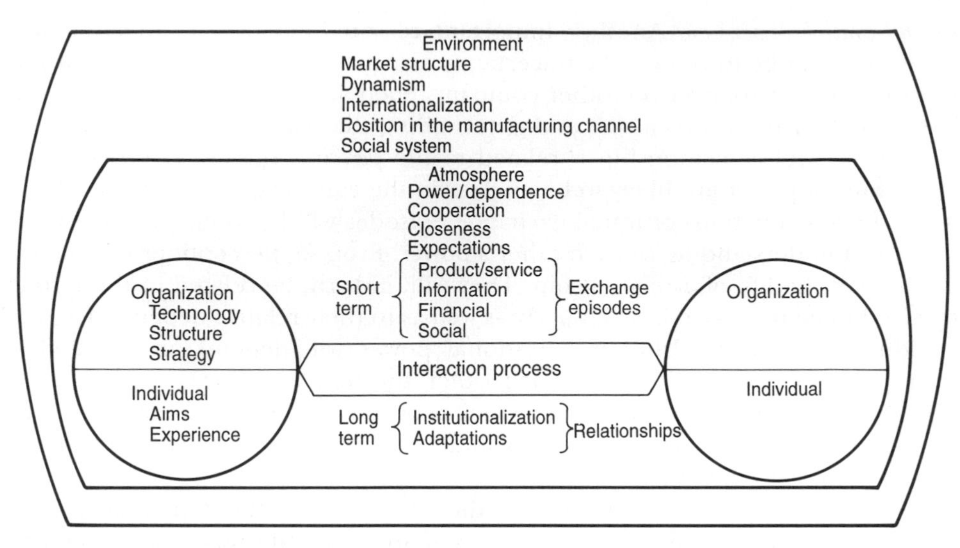


Fig. 2. An illustration of the interaction model.

"Environment" consisting of the vertical and horizontal market structure and general social influences.

Finally, we include "Atmosphere". As the company's relationship develops so the parties' views of their relative power may change. Previous research has shown quite clearly that the interaction between buying and selling companies is conditioned by a clear and commonly held view of the relative power of the parties to the interaction and the areas to which this power extends. At the same time we have noted that conflict can characterize these relationships as well as co-operation. Thus it is quite possible for a company to have one relationship with a particular buyer–seller which is characterized by co-operation. It is also possible for the company to have a relationship with another company which is characterized by co-operation on the *minimum* level, in order for transactions to take place but thereafter is marked by frequent conflict over means and allocations of resources. Thus the detailed interaction process is subject to the perceptions of both parties of the overall state of relations between them – power–dependence and conflict–co-operation.

The figure shows that it is possible to identify and study connections between the variables on different levels. Firstly, at the most general level, one variable group can be related to another, for example it is possible to relate the parties in the exchange process to the interaction environment. Secondly, it is possible to investigate the linkage between variables in one variable group, for example between the elements of exchange and the process of exchange. Thirdly, it can be valuable to explore the relation between the variables within a sub-group. An example of this is the connection between the characteristics of the product and the characteristics of the information which is exchanged. Some of the relationships between the variables mentioned above are more obvious and are documented in other studies. Others are more hypothetical and have never been studied systematically. Furthermore, the whole picture has never been studied as a totality. Our approach is to select combinations of variables from the environment, company, and interaction categories. This provides a number of "interaction atmospheres", within which different linkages are studied as well as systematic comparisons made.

## IMPLICATIONS FOR MANAGEMENT

Before starting to discuss how our theoretical model has been used in this project we would like to briefly indicate the kind of help this model can give practitioners. The practical use of a theoretical model is, of course, that it helps to structure the "world" and thereby the problems. A new model can as a consequence give new opportunities because problems which were neglected earlier may be identified and solved. We shall now give some examples of problems that can be identified for managers of marketing or purchasing departments in firms working in certain industrial markets. We shall start with the marketing side.

### Marketing Management

The key problems in marketing according to the marketing mix model are (1) allocation of resources and (2) design of individual competitive means.[11] In the same way we can use the interactive model and identify two groups of important problems. These groups have been named (1) limitation and (2) handling problems.[12]

Two different kinds of limitation problems can be specified. The first problem concerns the marketing firm's overall limitation of its activities in certain types of relationships. This must be achieved because the demands on its technology, organization and knowledge, etc., are closely related to the type of relationships. For example, it is very difficult for a seller to have customers with very high demands on the quality and performance of the product *and* customers which just want a standard quality as cheaply as possible. The marketing firm, thus, has to limit itself to be an efficient counterpart in a certain type of relationship and to design its technology, organization, and knowledge in accordance with this.

The second type of limitation problems for the marketing firm are concerned with its individual counterparts. The question is, should customers be treated in a uniform way, or should some customers get special treatment? Normally there is a very clear difference between how those "special" customers – often those who buy most – get special services, extra attention and so on. The customers are in other words often dealt with quite differently and it is therefore necessary for the marketing firm to develop a policy on these questions.

The handling problem concerns both the long-term aspects of the relationships as well as the short-term exchanges of different elements. The long-term problems concern handling the power–dependence and the co-operation–conflict aspects of the relationships. The aim is to have a controlled development of the relationships. This can sometimes mean closer co-operation and sometimes the opposite. The short-term problems are primarily related to attaining an efficient way of handling the elements (the different exchange processes) with individuals as well as groups of customers. One problem area, is, for example, to design one's own adaptations and to influence the counterpart's adaptations in order to make exchange processes easier. The way of solving the short-term handling problems affect, of course, the long-term problems. Adaptation is an example of one aspect of the power–dependence relationship. This means that the long- and short-term problems in a relationship cannot be divided; they can better be seen as short- and long-term effects of all of the activities which constitute the relationship.

### Purchasing Management

The key problem in purchasing that can be identified using the interaction model are (1) to develop an appropriate structure of suppliers and (2) to handle each relationship in an efficient way. The second group of problems are the same as the handling problems for the marketing side and we, therefore, can leave them aside and concentrate on the first group.

A supplier can be seen as an external resource by the buying firm. The buyer's aim in relationships is to use these external resources in an efficient way. But in order to be attractive as a counterpart, the purchasing firm has to have some internal resources. One strategic purchasing question, therefore, is to find and maintain a balance between the external and the internal resources. The problem in the short term can be formulated as using these external resources as much as possible given the internal resources of the buying firm.

Another problem is that suppliers can be used in different ways. In some situations the purchasing firm may want to use a supplier's ability to develop and design a special product, while in other situations it may just want to use the supplier's ability to produce a standardized product at low cost. The counterparts are used in different ways and a problem is then to find the right combination of suppliers, i.e. to develop an appropriate external resources structure.

## NOTES

1. The background of the research teams can be seen in the following references: Cunningham and White (1974), Cunningham and White (1973/6), Cunningham and Kettlewood (1976), Cunningham and Roberts (1974), Ford (1976), (1978), Håkansson and Wootz (1975a), (1975b), (1975c), (1975d), (1979), Håkansson, Johanson, and Wootz (1977), Håkansson *et al.* (1979), Håkansson and Östberg (1975), Johanson and Vahlne (1977), Johanson and Wiedersheim-Paul (1975), Kutschker (1975), Kutschker and Roth (1975), Kirsch, Lutschewitz, Kutschker (1977), Lutschewitz and Kutschker (1977), Kirsch and Kutchker (1978), Kutschker and Kirsch (1978), and Valla (1978a), (1978b), (1978c), (1978d), and (1978e).
2. Important works within this category: Dill (1958), Burns and Stalker (1961), Thompson (1967), Emery and Trist (1968), Aiken and Hage (1968), and Hall (1972).
3. Important works within this area are textbooks such as Kotler (1976) and McCarthy (1978). These deal mainly with consumer marketing but these and similar works have formed a basis for the development of literature in the industrial marketing field. Examples within industrial marketing which share this approach are Corey (1976), Hill *et al.* (1975), Hill (1972), and Wilson (1972) and (1973).
4. Important works regarding purchasing using this approach are textbooks such as England (1970), Lee and Dobler (1971) and Westing, Fine, and Zenz (1976) and research oriented

books like Buckner (1966). Robinson and Faris (1967), and Webster and Wind (1972a). The two most well-known models of purchasing are Webster and Wind (1972b) and Sheth (1973).
5. Important works within this category: Levine and White (1961), Litwak and Hylton (1962), Evan (1966), Warren (1967), Marrett (1971), and Aldrich (1972).
6. See for example Rosenberg and Stern (1970), Little (1970), Heskett, Stern, and Beier (1970), El-Ansary and Stern (1972), Hunt and Nevin (1974), Angelmar (1976), and Reve and Stern (1979).
7. Examples are Blois (1975), Guillet de Monthoux (1975), Mattsson (1975), Jarvis and Wilcox (1977), Melin (1977), Webster (1979), and Arndt (1979).
8. Important works are: Levine and White (1972), Warren (1973), Van de Ven *et al.* (1975), Zeitz (1975), and Aldrich (1979).
9. Need uncertainty has for example been used as a variable by Håkansson, Johanson, and Wootz (1977) in order to describe this aspect.
10. See for example Macaulay (1963).
11. See IMP Group (1982).
12. This section builds on Håkansson, Johanson, and Wootz (1977), and Håkansson and Wootz (1979).

## REFERENCES


Aiken, M. and Hage, J. Organizational interdependence and intra-organizational structure. *American Sociological Review*, **33:6**, 912–30 (1968).

Aldrich, H. E. Cooperation and conflict between organizations in the manpower training system: an organization–environment perspective. In Negandhi, A. R. (ed) *Conflict and Power in Complex Organizations: An Inter-Institutional Perspective.* Kent State University Press, Kent, Ohio (1972).

Aldrich, H. E. *Organizations and Environments.* Prentice-Hall, Englewood Cliffs, New Jersey (1979).

Angelmar, R. Structure and determinants of bargaining behaviour in a distribution channel simulation: A content analytic approach. *Unpublished Ph.D. Dissertation.* Northwestern University, New York (1976).

Arndt, J. Toward a concept of domesticated markets. *Journal of Marketing*, **43**, (4), 69–76, (1979).

Blois, K. J. Supply contracts in the Galbraithian planning system. *Journal of Industrial Economics*, **24**, (1), 29–39 (1975).

Buckner, H. *How British Industry Buys.* Hutchinson, London (1966).

Burns, T. and Stalker, G. M. *The Management of Innovation.* Tavistock Publications, London (1961).

Corey, E. R. *Industrial Marketing: Cases and Concepts*, 2nd ed., Prentice-Hall, Englewood Cliffs, New Jersey (1976).

Cunningham, M. T. and Kettlewood, K. Source loyalty in freight transport buying. *European Journal of Marketing*, **10**, (1), 60–79 (1976).

Cunningham, M. T. and Roberts, D. A. The role of customer service in industrial marketing. *European Journal of Marketing*, **8**, (1), 15–28 (1974).

Cunningham, M. T. and White, J. G. The determinants of choice of supplier. *European Journal of Marketing*, **7**, (3), 189–202 (1973).

Cunningham, M. T. and White, J. G. The behaviour of industrial buyers in their search for suppliers of machine tools. *Journal of Management Studies*, **11**, (2), 115–128 (1974).

Dill, W. R. Environment as an influence on managerial autonomy. *Administrative Science Quarterly*, **2**, (4), 409–443 (1958).

El-Ansary, A. I. and Stern, L. W. Power measurement in the distribution channel. *Journal of Marketing Research*, **9**, 47–52 (1972).

Emery, F. G. and Twist, E. L. The causal texture of organizational environments. *17th International Congress of Psychology*, Washington, DC (1968).

England, W. *Modern Procurement Management: Principles and Cases.* 5th ed., Irwin, Homewood, Illinois (1970).

Evan, W. M. The organization-set: toward a theory of interorganizational relation, in Thompson, J. (ed) *Approaches to Organizational Design.* University of Pittsburgh Press. Pittsburgh, Philadelphia (1966).

Ford, D. I. An analysis of some aspects of the relationships between companies in channels of distribution. *Unpublished Ph.D. thesis.* University of Manchester, Manchester (1976).

Ford, D. I. Stability factors in industrial marketing channels. *Industrial Marketing Management,* **7**, 410–422 (1978).

Guillet de Monthoux, P. Organizational mating and industrial marketing conservation – some reasons why industrial marketing managers resist marketing theory. *Industrial Marketing Management,* **4**, (1), 25–36 (1975).

Håkansson, H., Johanson, J. and Wootz, B. Influence tactics in buyer–seller processes. *Industrial Marketing Management,* **5**, 319–332 (1977).

Håkansson, H. and Wootz, B. Supplier selection in an international environment – an experimental study. *Journal of Marketing Research,* **12**, (February), 46–51 (1975a).

Håkansson, H. and Wootz, B. *Företags inköpsbeteende* (Buying Behaviour of the Firm). Studentlitteratur, Lund (1975b).

Håkansson, H. and Wootz, B. Risk reduction and the industrial purchaser. *European Journal of Marketing,* **9**, (1), 35–51 (1975c).

Håkansson, H. and Wootz, B. *Changes in the Propensity to Import – An Interaction Model on the Firm Level.* Department of Business Studies, University of Uppsala (1975d).

Håkansson, H. and Wootz, B. A framework of industrial buying and selling. *Industrial Marketing Management,* **8**, 28–39 (1979).

Håkansson, H., Wootz, B., Andersson, O. and Hangård, P. Industrial marketing as an organizational problem. A case study. *European Journal of Marketing,* **13**, 81–93 (1979).

Håkansson, H. and Östberg, C. Industrial marketing – An organizational problem? *Industrial Marketing Management,* **4**, 113–123 (1975).

Hall, R. H. *Organization, Structure, and Process.* Prentice-Hall, Englewood Cliffs, New Jersey (1972).

Heskett, J. L., Stern, L. W. and Beijer, F. J. Bases and uses of power in interorganizational relations. In Bucklin, L. P. (ed) *Vertical Marketing Systems.* Scott, Foresman, and Company, London (1970).

Hill, R. M., Alexander, R. S. and Cross, J. S. *Industrial Marketing.* 4th ed., Homewood. Irwin, Illinois (1975).

Hill, R. W. *Marketing Technological Products to Industry,* Oxford, UK (1972).

Hunt, S. D. and Nevin, J. R. Power in a channel of distribution: sources and consequences. *Journal of Marketing Research,* **11**, 186–193 (1974).

Jarvis, L. P. and Wilcox, J. P. True vendor loyalty or simply repeat purchase behavior? *Industrial Marketing Management,* **6**, 9–14 (1977).

Johanson, J., and Vahlne, J.-E. The internationalization process of the firm – a model of knowledge development and increasing foreign market commitments. *Journal of International Business,* **8**, (1), 23–32 (1977).

Johanson, J. and Wiedersheim-Paul, F. The internationalization of the firm – four Swedish case studies. *Journal of Management Studies,* **2**, (3), 305–322 (1975).

Kirsch, W. and Kutschker, M. *Das Marketing von Investitionsgütern – Theoretische und empirische Perspektiven eines Interaktionsansatzes.* Verlag Gablers, Wiesbaden (1978).

Kirsch, W., Lutschewitz, H. and Kutschker, M. *Ansätze und Entwicklungstendenzen im Investitionsgütermarketing – Auf dem Wege zu einem Interaktionsansatz.* C. E. Poeschel Verlag, Stuttgart (1977).

Kotler, P. *Marketing Management, Analysis, Planning, and Control.* 3rd ed. Prentice-Hall, Englewood Cliffs, New Jersey (1976).

Kutschker, M. *Rationalität und Entscheidungskriterien komplexer Investitionsentscheidungen – ein empirischer Bericht.* Aus dem Sonderforschungsbereich 24 Der Universität Mannheim, Mannheim (1975).

Kutschker, M. and Kirsch. W. *Verhandlungen auf dem Markt für Investitionsgüter.* Plannungs – und Organisationswissenschaffliche Schriften, München (1978).

Kutschker, M. and Roth, K. Das Informationsverhalten vor industriellen Beschaffungsentscheidungen. *Veröffentlichung aus dem SFB 24 der Universität Mannheim.* (1975).
Lasswell, H. D. and Kaplan, A. *Power and Society*, Routledge, London (1952).
Lee, Jr. L. and Dobler, D. W. *Purchasing and Materials Management: Text and Cases.* 2nd ed. McGraw-Hill, New York (1971).
Levine, S. and White, P. Exchange as a conceptual framework for the study of interorganizational relationships. *Administrative Science Quarterly*, **5**, (4), 583–601 (1961).
Levine, S. and White, P. The community of health organizations. In Freeman, H. E., Levine, S. and Reader, L. (eds) *Handbook of Medical Sociology*, Prentice-Hall, Englewood Cliffs, New Jersey (1972).
Little, R. W. The marketing channel; who should lead this extra-corporate organization. *Journal of Marketing*, **34**, 31–38 (1970).
Litwak, E. and Hylton, L. F. Interorganizational analysis: A hypothesis on coordinating agencies. *Administrative Science Quarterly*, **6**, (4), 395–420 (1962).
Lutschewitz, H. and Kutschker, M. *Die Diffusion innovativer Investitionsgüter – Theoretische Konzeption und empirische Befunde.* Verlag Kurt Desch, München (1977).
Macaulay, S. Non-contractual relations in business: a preliminary study. *American Sociological Review*, **28**, (1), 55–67 (1963).
Marrett, C. B. On the specification of interorganization dimensions. *Sociology and Social Research*, **61**, 83–99 (1971).
Mattsson, L.-G. System interdependencies – A key concept in industrial marketing? *Proceedings from the Second Research Seminar in Marketing as Senanque.* Fondation Nationale pour l'Enseignement de la Gestion des Entreprises (1975).
McCarthy, E. J. *Basic Marketing* 6th ed. Irwin, Homewood (1978).
Melin, L. *Strategisk inköpsverksamhet – organisation och interaktion.* (Strategic Purchasing Actions – Organization and Interaction) (with summary in English). University of Linköping, Linköping (1977).
Reve, T. and Stern, L. W. Interorganizational relations in marketing channels. *Academy of Management Review*, **4**, (3), 405–416 (1979).
Robinson, P. J. and Faris, C. W. *Industrial Buying and Creative Marketing.* Allyn and Bacon Inc. and the Harbeling Science Institute, Boston, Massachusetts (1967).
Rosenberg, L. J. and Stern, L. W. Toward the analysis of conflict in distribution channels; a descriptive model. *Journal of Marketing*, **34**, 40–46 (1970).
Sheth, J. N. A model of industrial buyer behavior. *Journal of Marketing*, **37**, 50–56 (1973).
Thompson, J. *Organizations in Action.* McGraw-Hill, New York (1967).
Valla, J.-P. Basic concepts in industrial marketing: Specificities and implications. *Institut de Recherche de l'Entreprise.* Editions Verve, Lyon (1978a).
Valla, J.-P. Strategies in Industrial Marketing. *Institut de Recherche de l'Entreprise.* Editions Verve, Lyon (1978b).
Valla, J.-P. Organization and Structure in Industrial Marketing. *Institut de Recherche de l'Entreprise.* Editions Verve, Lyon (1978c).
Valla, J.-P. Information and Communication Systems in Industrial Marketing. *Institut de Recherche de l'Entreprise.* Editions Verve, Lyon (1978d).
Valla, J.-P. Implementing the marketing concept in the industrial firm: problems and possible solutions. *Institut de Recherche de l'Entreprise.* Editions Verve, Lyon (1978e).
Van de Ven, A. H., Emmit, D. C. and Koenig, R. Frameworks for interorganizational analysis. In Negandhi, A. R. (ed) *Interorganizational Theory.* Kent State University Press, Kent, Ohio (1975).
Warren, R. The interorganizational field as a focus for investigation. *Administrative Science Quarterly*, **12**, 396–419 (1967).
Warren, R. The interactions of community decision organizations: some conceptual considerations and empirical findings in Negandhi, A. R. (ed) *Modern Organization Theory.* Kent State University Press, Kent, Ohio (1973).
Webster, Jr., F. E. *Industrial Marketing Strategy.* John Wiley and Sons, New York (1979).
Webster, Jr., F. E. and Wind, Y. *Organizational Buying Behavior*, Prentice-Hall, Englewood Cliffs (1972a).

Webster, Jr., F. E. and Wind, Y. A general model for understanding organizational buyer behavior. *Journal of Marketing*, **36**, 12–19 (1972b).

Westing, J. H., Fine, I. V. and Zenz, G. J. *Purchasing Management: Materials in Motion.* John Wiley and Sons, New York (1976).

Wilson, A. *The Marketing of Professional Services*, Publications Service, New York (1972).

Wilson, A. *The Assessment of Industrial Markets.* International Publications Service, New York (1973).

Zeitz, G. Interorganizational relationships and social structure: A critique of some aspects of the literature. In Negandhi, A. R. (ed) *Interorganization Theory.* Kent State University Press, Kent, Ohio (1975).

# 2

# Influence Tactics in Buyer–Seller Processes*

*H. Håkansson, J. Johanson and B. Wootz*

## INTRODUCTION

The industrial goods producer, like the consumer goods producer, uses various means of competition in his marketing activities. The standard literature offers chapters on advertising, sales promotion, personal selling, technical service, delivery, quality and price.[1]

When marketing a product or a service it is assumed that the firm combines these means of competition in a marketing mix. Much of the literature is devoted to decisions concerning the optimal combination and the contents of these competitive means. This approach seems appropriate in situations where the firm has many customers who can be treated in a standardized way. These situations also imply that the customers in relation to each competitive mean can be described by an average response curve. In many producer markets, however, the selling firm has a limited number of big customers who are in consequence very important and must be handled individually. The relations to these customers are often complex, involving several departments and decision-makers on both sides in order to solve technical, commercial and delivery problems. In these situations it is altogether meaningless to base the planning of marketing activities on average response curves and therefore there is a need for another approach. The aim of this chapter is to discuss such an approach and illustrate its usefulness for practical decision-making.

In this chapter the relation between the buying and the selling firm is seen as an interaction process between two active components.[2] In the first two sections we discuss this interaction process from the buying and the selling firm's point of view respectively. Our purpose is to find descriptive variables appropriate to increase our understanding of industrial markets.

---

*The authors are grateful for the constructive comments of Lars Hallén, Lars-Gunnar Mattsson, Ivan Snehota of the University of Uppsala, Ove Brandes and Leif Melin of the University of Linköping. The study has been financially supported by the Svenska Handelsbanken Foundation for Social Science Research.

Reprinted by permission of the publishers from Influence Tactics in Buyer–Seller Processes by H. Håkansson, J. Johanson and B. Wootz, *Industrial Marketing Management*, Vol. 4, No. 6, pp. 319–332.

In the third section attention is focused on some specific activities of the selling firm. These concern the selling firm's way of influencing the buyer – its influencing tactics. Three examples of influencing tactics used in reality are described in the last section in order to illustrate our theoretical model.

## THE INTERACTION PROCESS FROM THE BUYING FIRM'S POINT OF VIEW

In the interaction processes with suppliers the buying firm strives efficiently to secure the supply of needed products and services. In some situations this is a very simple task – when there is no doubt about the firm's needs and there are several reliable suppliers on the market. Then the buyer can choose the supplier offering the lowest price among those which fulfil all the functional requirements. Other situations may be more troublesome. The need may be difficult to determine and specify for example when it is impossible to measure its characteristics. Another situation raising problems is when the market is heterogeneous and/or dynamic. A third type of situation which is difficult for the buyer to handle is when he does not completely trust the seller's reliability, or when there are problems of coordinating the actual transaction with own production or with other transactions. These three types of situation can in general terms be described as having different degrees of uncertainty in the need, the market and the transaction respectively.

In order to characterize the interaction process from the buyer's point of view, we can use these three uncertainty variables. To a certain extent the uncertainty emanates from the actual situation, but it can also be dependent on the interaction process itself. It is important to understand how the uncertainty in these three dimensions increases or decreases during different interaction processes. The three variables are presented in more detail below.

### Need Uncertainty

There are often difficulties in interpreting the exact nature of the needs for materials, machines, tools, services, etc., in the firm. The buyer's perceived need uncertainty is a function of these difficulties in combination with the importance of the actual need. If for example production will be stopped due to an unsuitable product the need uncertainty will be perceived as considerably higher than if it only affects a minor aspect of production.

It is important to realize that the need uncertainty can be both increased and decreased during an interaction process with a supplier. He may, for instance, have knowledge of factors not previously considered by the buying firm which will increase the need uncertainty. On the other hand the seller may know some way of interpreting the need more exactly and this will probably decrease the buyer's need uncertainty.

The need uncertainty is not directly related to the technical complexity of the product. The exact nature of the raw materials required in some production processes, as for example pulp used for producing high quality paper, may be very difficult to interpret and the buying situation for these products can consequently be characterized as having high need uncertainty. Other products with high technical complexity are standardized in terms of output and can therefore be said to have a low need uncertainty. These examples illustrate that there is no direct or clear-cut relation between the degree of need uncertainty and the technical complexity.

### Market Uncertainty

Market uncertainty is related to suppliers perceived by the buying firm as source alternatives. The degree of market uncertainty depends on the degree of difference between the suppliers (heterogeneity) and how these differences change over time (dynamism). The problem from the buying firm's point of view is that by working up a relation with one supplier they will lose the chances of exploiting the differences and changes. In other words, there is an opportunity cost depending on whether the degree of heterogeneity and dynamism is large or small. When the heterogeneity and dynamism are both large the opportunity cost is large and there are in consequence reasons for caution in developing extensive relations.

### Transaction Uncertainty

The transaction uncertainty has to do with problems of getting the product (physically, legally, on time, etc.) from the seller to the buyer. There are for example differences in the degree to which the delivery of the needed product must be coordinated in time with other events (production schedules, delivery of other products, etc.). Another important aspect of the transaction uncertainty is related to the "difference" between the buyer and the seller. When there are differences in language, culture, technology, etc., there are further obstacles to the two parties' understanding of each other. The initial difference between the two may, however, be reduced during the interaction process, which in other words can be seen as a learning process.

A third factor influencing the transaction uncertainty is the degree to which trading procedures of a certain product are standardized. The less standardized these procedures are, the greater the complexity of the discussions and negotiations will be and the greater the transaction uncertainty.

### The Buying Firm's Behaviour in Response to the Three Uncertainty Dimensions

The organizational buying model presented here was developed and tested by the authors of this chapter. In order to exemplify the theoretical discussions above we summarize some of the main results. These were presented earlier in: Håkansson and Wootz (1975a), Håkansson and Wootz (1975b), Håkansson and Wootz (1975d), Håkansson (1975) and Wootz (1975).

In situations characterized by high need uncertainty decision-makers in the buying firm:

- Are relatively more concerned with functional and quality than price aspects;
- Prefer to interact with suppliers in countries with a small cultural distance;
- Choose to interact with suppliers which have been used earlier (high source loyalty);
- Form a more complex internal communication structure which often involves different kinds of specialists in the decision-making unit;
- Form a more complex external communication structure which often involves different kinds of specialists in direct contact with the supplier;
- Have relatively more contacts with the supplier which also means a more time consuming decision process.

High market uncertainty means that decision-makers in the buying firm:

- Have contacts with a relatively greater number of suppliers;
- Are specialized in relation to these high uncertainty markets.

High transaction uncertainty means that decision-makers in the buying firm:

- More often strive to find parallel suppliers;
- Are more concerned with delivery questions;
- Have relatively more contacts with the supplier before making the final decision.

## THE INTERACTION PROCESS FROM THE SELLING FIRM'S POINT OF VIEW

In the long run the seller's goal in the interaction process is to make profits by selling his product or service at a price which exceeds his costs. In order to make the buyer pay this price the seller must be able to solve some of the problems of the buying firm. Primarily the ability concerns the degree to which the seller can satisfy important aspects of a certain need, and secondly, the degree to which the seller can transfer the solution to the buyer. We label the first problem the seller's need solving ability and the second the seller's transfer ability. The need solving ability includes both the ability which is built into the product (function, quality, etc.) and the services which are given in combination with the product. It covers for example the seller's ability to understand and interpret the buyer's need and find suitable solutions.

The transfer ability concerns the capacity and reliability of the deliveries and also the extent to which problems related to the negotiations can be solved.

The selling firm's resources in terms of equipment, technical and economic knowledge, organization, etc., determine the total "stock" of both need solving and transfer abilities. The seller's total stock, i.e. its ability profile, can therefore only be increased through changes in these strategic means. Thus the ability profile cannot usually be changed by for example an advertising campaign. The ability must be demonstrated in practice before the customer's perception of the profile really can be assumed to have changed.

Of the means mentioned above only the organization is not a traditional means in marketing. Our way of analysing industrial marketing problems implies that the organizational design is of critical importance in the interaction process, where the seller is assumed to demonstrate his need solving and transfer abilities. If, for example, a firm wants to demonstrate a high need solving ability, it must be so organized as to make contact with customers easy in both depth and breadth. The authors' practical experience suggests that the strategic importance of the organization as a means in industrial marketing is underestimated. This probably means that a great number of firms have an inadequate balance between investments in equipment, knowledge and organization.[3]

The higher the ability the firm wants to attain, as regards both need solving and transfer abilities, the more resources must be invested in knowledge, equipment and organization. As a consequence the firm will finally arrive at a higher cost level. On the other hand the buyer values these abilities positively and will be prepared to pay a higher price for them only in situations where he perceives uncertainty to a particular degree. It is assumed that the higher the uncertainty, the more the buyer values the corresponding ability. Therefore it is important for the selling firm to adapt its abilities to the perceived uncertainty of the buying firm.

From a marketing point of view the above description of the seller raises two very important questions.

The first question pertains to how much of the total ability of the firm should be "offered" to each buying firm (the limitation problem). Selling firms normally do not distribute their efforts to all customers in a uniform way. Some customers, important in one way or another, are given special treatment. Technical adaptations of products are for example sometimes offered to some customers, whereas other firms can only buy from a standard product range. The relation to a certain buying firm is, as we mentioned earlier, built up successively. Often there are some kinds of self-generated aspects in the process which means that it develops in both volume and stability. The process must therefore be controlled in order to avoid binding the seller to inappropriate buying firms. For the seller the solution of this problem is therefore not to make one or a few decisions regarding the customers with whom he will interact and the level of interaction, but more or less continually pay attention to this matter and analyse the nature of the interaction process with different customers.

The second question concerns the handling of each relationship (the handling problem). Here it is important to regard both social and physical exchange. Social exchange relates to the creation of confidence.[4] One aspect here is to give customers information about important conditions of the seller's own firm and obtain information about the customer. If, for instance, a firm wants to demonstrate a high need solving ability, its marketing department must be competent to handle technical questions up to a certain level and also have routines for involving technical experts in the interaction when its own technical competence is inappropriate. A firm which tries to demonstrate a high transfer ability must have a broad experience in transport economies, logistics, and so forth.

Arrangements like these are thought to give high social exchange which implies an efficient physical exchange (e.g. regarding deliveries of actual products, financial arrangements, etc.).

Physical and social exchange are also related to each other in such a way that a more complex physical exchange must be combined with a more extensive social exchange.

The discussion up to this point identified two important aspects of industrial marketing – need-solving ability and transfer ability. In relation to these aspects the industrial goods producer is confronted with two problem areas – the limitation problems and the handling problems. Both of these problem areas ought to be a focus for further research. In this chapter we now limit the discussion to a specific aspect of the handling problems – the seller's possibilities of influencing decision-makers in the buying firm. We call this aspect the seller's influence tactics. The seller always has the ability of changing the buyer's perception of a certain situation. This does not mean that the seller tries to communicate inadequate information because professional buyers will in the long run see through such a ploy. Instead the seller should try to adapt the buyer's perception to what he believes is a reasonable assessment of the situation. The next section will be devoted to this question.

## ALTERNATIVE INFLUENCE TACTICS

In accordance with the introductory discussion each customer is assumed to be more or less unique in industrial markets. In an analysis of the influence tactics of an industrial goods purchaser it is consequently inappropriate to start the analysis with an average picture of the customers. Instead the starting-point should be the relationship with the individual customer. In some situations, however, several customers can be influenced in the same way, making aggregations possible. Irrespective of this fact we define the influence tactics in relation to the individual customer. Thus an industrial goods producer will have a number of tactics which are similar in some respects and different in others.

The theoretical argument is supported by the empirical fact that industrial goods producers often have specialized organizational units which are responsible for activities directed toward more important customers.

By influencing the perceived uncertainty of the buyer in different ways it will be possible for the selling firm to bring about various types of behaviour effect. The perceived uncertainty can be either increased or decreased depending on the contents of the influence tactics. In different marketing situations different combinations of increases and decreases in the three uncertainty dimensions discussed earlier are more or less efficient. Before discussing various combinations in detail, i.e. influence tactics with various contents, we treat each uncertainty dimension separately.

By giving the buyer new technical information the seller may modify the buyer's actual perception of the product and increase his perceived need uncertainty. In consequence decision-makers may try to broaden the decision base internally, and interact with firms which can be expected to fulfil the increased functional demand.

A seller can also try to reduce the perceived need uncertainty of a buyer by emphasizing that the problems to be solved are not as complex as the buyer believes. From an influence point of view it is, in other words, possible both to increase and to diminish the perceived need uncertainty. Probably it is much more difficult to achieve the latter in practice.

If the seller can give such information that the buying firm perceives greater differences and or greater changes on the market than was previously the case, the perceived market uncertainty of the buyer increases. The buyer's attention will consequently be focused on the market and he will make more extensive comparisons between prices, qualities, payment conditions, and so forth. On the other hand, if the seller provides information which emphasizes the uniformity of the market the opposite effect will probably be achieved. In this case the buyer does not conceive the idea of broadening his knowledge of the market situation.

The seller may also emphasize the abilities of the firm to carry through its delivery commitments. He can reduce thereby the perceived transaction uncertainty of the buyer. This can be achieved by building up a buffer stock for the customer or by developing a joint transport and stock system. Tactics intended to increase the buyer's perceived transaction uncertainty toward the seller are not meaningful; this can, however, be the purpose of the information tactics of the competitors.

We conclude that the seller, by influencing the uncertainty perceptions of the buyer in these three dimensions, can cause certain desired behavioural reactions. The influence tactics of an industrial seller toward a certain customer describe how the seller simultaneously influences the buyer in all the three uncertainty dimensions. The influence tactics can be described in the matrix presented in Table 1. Three levels of change are distinguished. The seller can either try to keep the uncertainty perception of the purchaser constant or to increase or decrease it. The matrix makes it possible to distinguish a fairly large number (27) of influence tactics. Some of them are frequent, some are more or less exceptions.

Table 1. Descriptive matrix for influence tactics

| Direction of change | Increase | Constant | Reduce |
|---|---|---|---|
| Need uncertainty | | | |
| Transaction uncertainty | | | |
| Market uncertainty | | | |

## APPLICATIONS

So far we have discussed how the influence tactics of the industrial goods producer can be described. We shall now use this descriptive model as a norm in order to guide industrial marketing managers in their planning of information activities. Different influence tactics are of varying efficiency depending on the nature of the marketing situation. We can identify two basic marketing situations, which require opposite influence tactics. In one very common marketing situation the firm has well established relations with the customers and is primarily concerned with the development and the stabilization of those relations. In the other situation, which is also very common, there are strong relations between a competitor and potential customers and the important task is to break these relations in order to have the opportunity to establish new relations. In the first situation the influence tactics should attempt to reduce the customer's perceived uncertainty which is expected to lead to increased stability and closer cooperation between the two firms. In the other situation influence tactics which seek to increase perceived need uncertainty and market uncertainty are preferable. A situation is thereby created where the customer will be interested in more information about alternative sellers and will in some cases test new sources. In the first situation it was advantageous to stabilize the relation with the customer by reducing the uncertainty perception of the buyer. In the other it is appropriate to unsettle the situation by an increase in the uncertainty.

These two marketing situations are fairly clear-cut and the proposed influence tactics rather obvious. The cases in the next section partly illustrate these clear-cut situations and the influence tactics observed correspond to the results from the theoretical analysis. However, more detailed normative discussions of the effectiveness of different influence tactics in different marketing situations must derive from a much broader data base. Our descriptive model can then be used in order to generate hypotheses regarding the effectiveness of specific tactics in particular marketing situations.

In the following case studies we describe and classify actual influence tactics. In each case we have observations in the matrix described above.

Before presenting the cases it is necessary to outline the measurement of the tactics, i.e. the manner of locating the tactical behaviour of a firm in our matrix. On an unambitious level it is possible to let a marketing manager make intuitive judgements of the firm's activities. A more ambitious approach is to let the researcher pass judgement after exhaustive discussions with marketing people about the context of various marketing activities.

In the following cases we used the latter approach. Activities in real marketing situations are described in detail on the basis of interviews with marketing managers and supplementary written material. The descriptions are focused on the seller's marketing activities. The descriptions of the cases were written together with the actual firms whereas all comments and discussions of the influence tactics are our own. This is the reason why our concepts are used in the discussions and the comments on each case. The cases describe average influence tactics for each selling firm. In accordance with the discussions in this chapter there is a unique tactic in relation to each customer. However, it was impossible to obtain information about these individual tactics and an average tactic for a group of important customers was measured instead.

## THREE CASES

### Söderberg and Haak and Structural Alloy Steel

#### *The Case*

In September 1974 Söderberg and Haak (SH) started the marketing of structural alloy steel in Sweden.[5] The market was new to SH. The firm had, however, long enjoyed a strong position as a steel wholesaler. As the expansion opportunities in this market were considered unsatisfactory, SH was systematically searching for new steel products which could be expected to fit the firm's structure with regard to organization, marketing methods, handling equipment, and so on. Structural alloy steel was considered to have the desired synergy effects in relation to the other activities. The special steel is used in mechanical engineering works for products which are exposed to high quality demand such as cogwheels, shafts, etc. The total Swedish market is estimated as 50 000 tons per year. The biggest user is the car industry. As the firms in that industry and some other big engineering firms are major users of structural alloy steel they buy the steel direct from the producers. SH's potential customers were therefore the great number of firms which can be characterized as small and medium-sized engineering firms. This group can be estimated to include more than 10 000 firms. An investigation showed that fewer big customers of alloy steel than expected were already steel customers of SH. The available data did not allow a more precise estimate of the market.

Four Swedish steel works dominated the market. SKF was the biggest with 50% of the market. Bofors and Uddeholm, who had coordinated their marketing, could be considered as a unit with around 20% of the market. Fagersta was the smallest with a market share of less than 10%. The rest of the demand was covered through imports. To a great extent this took the form of direct buying by the car industry from continental steel works.

The market was regarded as "sleeping". Advertising and other kinds of mass communication were modest. The communication mainly contained quality arguments. It was emphasized that structural alloy steel was a technically rather complex product where it was essential that the supplier provide both technical advice and technical service. According to the common opinion among customers this could only be offered by a steel producer and not by a wholesaler such as SH.

SH entered this market with an aggressive and somewhat strident voice. Their behaviour was in stark contrast to the communication style of their four Swedish competitors. For their part SH wished to tell the market that something new was happening, that there was a new way of thinking. A new mode of distribution was in fact introduced to the market. In contrast to the steel works, SH emphasized the width of their product line and the speed of delivery as important decision variables from the customer's point of view. The price was in no way stressed. SH preferred rather to maintain the same price level as the Swedish steel works.

SH employed five salesmen who had specialized in structural alloy steel and possessed previous experience of the market. They were also trained to give the customers technical advice. During the first period their work was to visit and inform customers about the product line and emphasize "traditional" wholesale arguments, i.e. the width of the product line and the efficiency of distribution.

### *Classification of the Influence Tactics*

At the time of SH's entry the structural alloy steel market was stable with a number of established seller–buyer relations. Sellers on this market had always stressed their need solving ability, whereas SH, as a wholesaler, emphasized the transfer ability. Indirectly SH also implied that the level of need solving ability claimed by the steel producers was in most cases exaggerated.

The problem faced by SH was how to break these stable buyer–seller relations, so that SH could establish their own relations. The customer is assumed to have had a medium need uncertainty, a low market uncertainty and a low transaction uncertainty at the time of SH's entrance. The SH advertising campaign was an attempt to make the buyer perceive a higher market uncertainty by informing him about a new and different alternative. Of course, the hope was to initiate processes in the customers' organizations meaning that new supplier alternatives would be considered, and that the interest in changes toward these new alternatives would increase.

SH did not push the need uncertainty dimension too hard but tried to make a modest reduction of the potential customers' need uncertainty. They also sought to get technical competence regarded as necessary in relation to the customers' need uncertainty.

The buyer's perceived transaction uncertainty in relation to SH was intended to be reduced. The buyers had known their former suppliers for a long time and generally considered them safe from a delivery point of view. Compared to them SH were new, even if they were old in neighbouring product markets. SH invested in equipment for material handling and a wide initial stock which covered all important dimensions and sizes.

SH's influence tactics are summed up in Table 2.

Table 2. The influence tactics of Söderberg and Haak

| Direction of change | Increase | Constant | Reduce |
|---|---|---|---|
| Need uncertainty | | | × |
| Transaction uncertainty | | | × |
| Market uncertainty | × | | |

## ASEA Synchronous Motors

### *The Case*

Synchronous motors are generally produced to order at ASEA in Västerås. The size of the effects of the motors varies between 50 and 500 kW and the price between 15 000 and 2 million Sw. Cr. The total ASEA sales of synchronous motors are about 80 million Sw. Cr. per year.

The functional demands on the motors are very high and they have to be adapted to the specific demands of different users. To obtain a high load capacity the motors must have a mechanical strength and the coils must be well insulated so that they can endure vibrations for instance. The motors are generally a very important part of the customers' production system as a breakdown can stop the whole production process and cause very high costs. The rising demand concerning performance and reliability means that the motors are more and more differentiated, at the same time as the producers try to reduce the number of variants by increased standardization, e.g. with regard to size.

The supply of synchronous motors is characterized by a small number of big international firms and a great number of local producers. For instance Siemens, General Electric, General Electric Company, and Hitachi are important international competitors to ASEA. All four generally have bigger market shares than ASEA on most markets. Siemens, for instance, has a very high market cover and also excellent service.

Some other international firms, which, from a market share point of view are smaller than ASEA, are Brown Bovery Company, AEG, and Westinghouse. Their competitive profile is also somewhat different from the profile of the four biggest. They bid on separate occasions and offer shorter delivery time or lower price.

ASEA is regarded as a technically advanced firm with highly reliable products. Information from ASEA is also accepted as correct as regards functional characteristics, delivery times, etc. The price of ASEA's products is thus somewhat high and ASEA heavily emphasizes in their marketing the long term economic consequences of a motor rather than its price. In recent years ASEA has made heavy investments in order to raise the capacity and reduce the delivery times. The characteristics of customers are very different with regard to size, industry and knowledge. Some customer firms have a wide knowledge and experience base, while others are much less experienced. On the whole there are very stable relations between ASEA and its customers. The ten biggest customers within each product range are very loyal to ASEA and usually represent 50–90% of the sales.

As usual in industrial marketing most marketing resources are allocated to personal selling. The selling activities together with other competitive means such as pamphlets are controlled by the desire to give relevant technical information. The sales force informs about ASEA in general, about the product line, about its products in comparison with products of the competitors, and so on. An important part of the information, which is especially emphasized in contacts with new and inexperienced customers, consists in the discussion of difficulties and problems in connection with motors. The salesmen – who are generally technicians – thus raise problems which have occurred earlier and which ASEA has attempted to solve. In this way the salesmen try to make the customers realize problems which they have not met and note that more aspects than price and functional effect should be considered in the decision to buy.

In addition to ASEA's normal service division there are some service technicians who are experts on synchronous motors. At present they are primarily utilized as trouble-shooters, i.e. they are called in when problems arise at the customers.

### *Classification of Influence Tactics*

From the above description it is clear that ASEA emphasizes the functional characteristics of its products at the same time as attempts are made to raise the degree of standardization. This means that ASEA neither wants, nor is able to manufacture, motors which are adapted to the specific demand of each customer. The need-solving ability can be characterized as the means. ASEA has tried to increase the transfer ability during the last few years by making investments in new plants in order to reduce delivery times.

The influence tactics are the same for all customers with respect to market uncertainty and transaction uncertainty. Firstly ASEA makes no attempt to influence the perceived market uncertainty in any direction, i.e. the tactics are neutral in this dimension. Secondly, ASEA always tries to reduce the perceived transaction uncertainty by emphasizing the safety and reliability of its deliveries. However, in the third dimension – need uncertainty – there are different tactics for different customers. ASEA tries to increase the perceived need uncertainty of those customers who are inexperienced and or have low technical competence.

Experienced buyers on the other hand know all the possible problems and therefore already have a high need uncertainty. ASEA does not try to influence these customers in the need uncertainty dimension. The tactics to induce the customer to perceive a high need uncertainty are built on the principle that a high need uncertainty means that the customer will make heavy technical demands on the seller, which will favour ASEA which is assumed to have this technical competence.

ASEA's influence tactics are summed up in Table 3.

Table 3. The influence tactics of ASEA's synchronous motors in relation to some customers

| Direction of change | Increase | Constant | Reduce |
|---|---|---|---|
| Need uncertainty | × | | |
| Transaction uncertainty | | | × |
| Market uncertainty | | × | |

## ASEA Quintus Presses

*The Case*

The Quintus department of ASEA markets presses for hydrostatic extrusion, plate forming and isostatic pressing. An isostatic press consists of a pressure vessel in which the material to be pressed is enclosed and subjected to a high uniform pressure from a pressure medium. ASEA's Quintus isostatic press consists of a pre-stressed cylinder having straight inner walls and non-threaded enclosures which are kept in position by an outer frame. The cylinder consists of a steel core which has been wound with high strength wire, pre-stressed to such a degree that the steel core is always kept under compression even at maximum compaction pressure. Due to the combined effect of pre-stressing, the absence of axial forces in the mantle of the cylinder and the straight cylinder wall the stress configuration obtained is very favourable especially from the fatigue point of view.

Two types of isostatic presses are manufactured:

- Presses for cold isostatic pressing where the pressure medium is a fluid. Cold Quintus isostatic pressing equipment is available with pressure vessels for pressures up to 6300 bars, inside diameters up to 1400 mm and inside heights up to 3150 mm.

- Presses for hot isostatic pressing where gas, usually argon, is used as pressure medium. In a hot isostatic press, pressing is effected by a combination of high pressure and high temperature.

Quintus hot isostatic pressing equipment is available with pressure vessels for pressures up to 3200 bars and furnaces for temperatures up to 1750°C. The maximum diameter of the hot zone is 1290 mm and the maximum length 2550 mm.

The isostatic pressing process is used for producing billets, tungsten carbide parts such as tool bits, press tools and rolls for cold-strip mills, jet engine parts of special alloys, and so forth.

The prices of the presses vary between 0.5 and 10 million Sw. Cr. with a mean around 3 million. The total market for these types of press is 20–40 presses annually. ASEA delivers around half of them.

The two biggest competitors are National Forge and Autoclave, both in the USA. The state-owned Carbox is a small Swedish competitor. Autoclave is the strongest of the American firms in the smaller dimensions.

Swedish authorities were quick to formulate rigorous safety requirements for equipment in Sweden. To meet these demands without additional safety precautions in the form of concrete bunkers the ASEA presses are more technically advanced in this safety respect and as a consequence the prices on the ASEA presses are somewhat higher than those of their competitors.

National Forge has almost the same product programme as ASEA but the prices are usually somewhat lower. In the final stage of negotiation there is generally a difference of 10% to the advantage of National Forge. There is very hard competition for the big projects, while for the small projects ASEA is sometimes the only manufacturer approached.

ASEA is generally considered to have the best technical solutions but, as stated above, at a somewhat higher price.

The customers are normally private industrial firms working with powder technology where they are looking for material characteristics and/or production methods which cannot be attained by conventional techniques.

Those who handle the purchases are usually very advanced technically and always know their requirements with respect to temperature and pressure uniformity. They are often new customers as only a few have bought several presses. The explanation is that the technique of isostatic pressing is so new that there has not been any need for replacement purchases.

The most important means to influence the customers is the salesmen. The first contacts with a new customer are usually made by the field salesmen who belong to the organization of the sales companies and to some extent are specialized on the Quintus presses. These salesmen try to form an opinion about the need of the customer and usually obtain the information which ASEA needs to be able to submit a preliminary offer. These are usually within ± 10% of the final offer with respect to both technical performance and price. The customers generally ask for offers from several suppliers and on the basis of these offers the final specifications are made. During this process extensive discussions are held between the customer and the supplier. Besides the field salesmen, one or several of the specialists at the production unit in Västerås take part in these discussions. There are altogether 14 such specialists – all of them with technical education to university level. During these contacts ASEA emphasizes the technical solution and the safety of the equipment. The time from the first contact to the final order varies between eight months and three years. During this period several tests and technical investigations are often made.

ASEA has a high pressure laboratory where the pressure and test conditions desired by the customer can be tested. The tests are sometimes made free of charge, i.e. as a sales promotion activity, but usually the customer has to pay for them.

ASEA spends very limited amounts on the advertising of this product. They participate in exhibitions, in particular those with advanced technical character.

### *Classification of the Influence Tactics*

Information to customers is characterized by ASEA's emphasis on their need-solving ability. This emphasis is made in the information of the salesmen as well as in information pamphlets. The development of the ASEA high pressure laboratory emphasizes the need-solving ability too. ASEA designs the product direct according to the need of the customer and also helps in identifying and specifying this need. The transfer ability is not emphasized in the same way, only through ASEA's general reliability.

The influence tactics are characterized by the fact that ASEA does not try to influence need uncertainty and market uncertainty. It is probably difficult to increase the perceived need and market uncertainty of the customers for this type of product, as the buyers normally perceive a high need uncertainty and are well aware of the differences between the suppliers. As ASEA's long-term strategy aims at creating a high need-solving ability there is no reason to try to reduce the perceived uncertainty in these two dimensions. On the other hand ASEA always tries to reduce the perceived transaction uncertainty by emphasizing reliability.

The influence tactics are summarized in Table 4.

Table 4. The influence tactics of ASEA's Quintus presses

| Direction of change | Increase | Constant | Reduce |
|---|---|---|---|
| Need uncertainty | | × | |
| Transaction uncertainty | | | × |
| Market uncertainty | | × | |

## THE THREE CASES – SOME CONCLUSIONS

In all three cases the observed influence tactics had the expected effects from the selling firm's point of view. Söderberg and Haak actually succeeded in breaking stable buyer–seller relations and in building up new relations. ASEA (case 2) succeeded in stabilizing and developing already existing relations. These two cases are similar insofar as both illustrate industrial buying with a high degree of rebuy situations. The problem for the selling firm with the entry onto a new market is to be considered a serious source. In order to be considered an alternative, an efficient tactic is to increase the market uncertainty and thereby induce search processes for new alternatives (Söderberg and Haak). If you already are a working supplier you will have to develop existing relations by efficiently solving current problems (functional, delivery, etc.). If the firm is highly competent technically an appropriate tactic in situations where the need uncertainty is modest will be to try to increase the need uncertainty by identifying possible problems and thereby inducing the buyer to choose a technically advanced firm (ASEA case 2).

In case 3 there was a clear-cut picture. There was no doubt that purchasers perceived a high need uncertainty and that they also knew the existing differences between actual suppliers. In other words there are few opportunities to change this accepted picture. In a certain situation, however, it might be appropriate to emphasize technical problems in order to increase the need uncertainty. In buyer–seller relations ASEA always tries to show that it has the competence to handle the complex situation perceived by the buyer.

Söderberg and Haak were confronted with exactly the same situation but on a much lower technical level. They really had to show the customers that they as a wholesaler had the technical competence to solve the technical problems. Söderberg and Haak also tried to effect a modest reduction of the buyers' perceived need uncertainty.

The discussions in this chapter raise a number of questions which should be the focus for further research. An important one concerns the degree to which the organization design is a key variable in shaping adequate influence tactics. As mentioned before, organization design is probably an important variable in order to control the process of building up relationships with customers.

Another important research question is to discuss more explicitly the normative implications of the influence tactics model presented here. It will be necessary to develop more definite measurements of the fit between the influence tactics and the marketing situation.

## NOTES

1. See e.g. Boyd and Massey (1972), Howard (1973), Hill, Alexander and Cross (1975) and Kotler (1976).
2. The theoretical background for this interaction approach is presented in Håkansson and Östberg (1975). The present chapter is part of the research programme outlined there. The ideas from these two papers have formed the basis of a research project dealing with international industrial marketing which involved Jean-Paul Valla, University of Lyon; David Ford, University of Bath; Malcolm Cunningham and Peter Turnbull, University of Manchester, Institute of Science and Technology; and the Group for Industrial Marketing, University of Uppsala.
3. For a more detailed discussion of these questions, see Håkansson and Östberg (1975).
4. The social exchange concept is described in Håkansson and Östberg (1975).
5. This case is a summary of Wootz (1977).

## REFERENCES

Boyd, H. W. and Massey, W. F. *Marketing Management.* Harcourt Brace Jovanovich, New York (1972).

Håkansson, H. and Östberg, C. Industrial Marketing: An Organizational Problem? *Industrial Marketing Management* **4**, 113–123 (1975).

Håkansson, H. and Wootz, B. Supplier Selection in an International Environment – An Experimental Study. *Journal of Marketing Research,* **Vol. XII**, 46–51 (1975a).

Håkansson, H. and Wootz, B. *Changes in the Propensity to Import – An Interaction Model on the Firm Level.* Department of Business Administration. University of Uppsala (1975b).

Håkansson, H. and Wootz, B. Företags inköpsbeteende (English translation of the Swedish title: Organizational Buyer Behavior). Studentlitteratur, Lund (1975c).

Håkansson, H. Studies in Industrial Purchasing with special reference to Determinants of Communication Patterns. *Acta Universitatis Upsaliensis*: University of Uppsala (1975).

Hill, R. M., Alexander, R. S. and Cross, J. S. *Industrial Marketing.* Richard D. Irwin, Homewood, Illinois (1975).

Howard, J. A. *Marketing Management, Operating, Strategic and Administrative.* Richard D. Irwin, Homewood, Illinois (1973).

Kotler, P. *Marketing Management, Analysis, Planning and Control.* Prentice-Hall, Englewood Cliffs, New Jersey (1976).

Wootz, B. Studies in Industrial Purchasing with special reference to Variations in External Communication. *Acta Universitatis Upsaliensis*: University of Uppsala (1975).

Wootz, B. Söderberg and Haak. MTC case series, Stockholm School of Economics (1976).

# 3

# The Development of Buyer–Seller Relationships in Industrial Markets*

*D. Ford*

## INTRODUCTION

It has frequently been noted that buyer–seller interdependence is a crucial characteristic of industrial marketing,[1] i.e. that industrial firms establish buyer–seller relationships which are often close, complex and frequently long-term. Despite this, the nature of these relationships has, until recently, received scant attention in the literature.[2] Instead, marketing writers have been more concerned with analysis of the (albeit complex) process by which buying firms arrive at individual purchase decisions, and the ways in which the seller can influence this process in its favour.

This paper examines the nature of buyer–seller relationships in industrial markets by considering their development as a process through time. It is based on ideas generated from the IMP project[3] and is particularly concerned with the following factors:

- What is it that makes a buyer establish and develop relationships with one or a few suppliers, as an alternative to "playing the market"?
- How do the relationships between buying and selling firms change over time? What are the factors which aid or hinder the development of close relationships? Which of these are within the control of the two companies?
- What are the implications of close buyer–seller relationships for the two organizations involved? What problems can they lead to? How are the day-to-day dealings between the companies affected by, and how do they affect, the overall relationship?

---

*The author acknowledges the contribution of Anna Lawson who read earlier drafts of this article.

Reprinted with permission from *European Journal of Marketing*, Vol. 14, No. 5/6, pp. 339–354.

## THEORETICAL BASIS

Buyer–seller relations can be examined with reference to the interaction approach as developed by the IMP group[4] as well as concepts drawn from the "New Institutional lists" within economics.[5]

### The Interaction Approach

This sees buyer–seller relationships taking place between two *active* parties. This is in contrast to the more traditional view of marketing which analyses the *reaction* of an aggregate market to a seller's offering. The interaction approach considers that either buyer or seller may take the initiative in seeking a partner. Further, both companies are likely to be involved in adaptations to their own process or product technologies to accommodate each other. Neither party is likely to be able to make unilateral changes in its activities as buyer or seller without consultation, or at least consideration, of the possible reactions of their individual opposite numbers. Thus, industrial marketing and purchasing can properly be described as the "management of buyer–seller relationships".

### The Nature of Relationships

Not all of the dealings between industrial buying and selling firms take place within close relationships. There are clear differences between the supply of paper clips and automotive components, or lubricating oil and factory buildings. The product and process technologies of the two companies are important factors in determining the nature of buyer–seller relations. Also important are the buyer and seller market structures which exist and hence the availability of alternative buyers and sellers.

Companies will develop close relationships rather than play the market, where they can obtain benefits in the form of cost reduction or increased revenues. These benefits are achieved by tailoring their resources to dealing with a specific buyer or seller, i.e. by making "durable transaction specific investments".[6] These investments mark major *adaptations* by a company to the relationship. By definition, they are not marketable, or at least their value in other transactions is less than in the specialized use for which they were intended. Therefore these adaptations mark a *commitment* by the buyer or seller to the relationship. They can be seen most clearly in such things as a supplier's development of a special product for a customer, a buyer's modification of a production process to accommodate a supplier's product or the joint establishment of a stock facility in a neutral warehouse. On the other hand, companies can be involved in "human capital investments",[7] i.e. alterations in procedures, special training, or allocation of managerial resources. These human adaptations produce savings by the familiarity and trust which they generate between the parties.

## Overall Relationships and Individual Episodes

The complexity of buyer–seller relations and the importance of mutual adaptations means that the analysis of relationships must be separated between the overall relationship itself and the individual *episodes* which comprise it. Thus, each delivery of product, price negotiation or social meeting takes place within the context of the overall relationship. Each episode is affected by the norms and procedures of the relationship as well as the atmosphere of co-operation or conflict which may have been established. Additionally, each episode affects the overall relationship and a single episode can change it radically, e.g. a relationship can be broken off "because" of a single failure in delivery. In fact, this failure is more likely to be the culminating episode in a worsening relationship. Thus, only a partial analysis of buyer–seller relations is achieved by researching individual episodes, e.g. a particular buying decision. On the other hand, an incomplete picture is obtained by examining the overall atmosphere of a relationship, for example in terms of power and dependency. Thus it is important to analyse both individual episodes and the overall relationship, as well as to understand the interaction between the two.[8]

## The Development of Buyer–Seller Relationships

This article is less concerned with the reasons for the choice of buyer or seller partners (although this is acknowledged as a question of considerable importance!). Instead, it analyses the process of establishment and development of relationship over time by considering five stages in their evolution. We should also note that the process described here does not argue the inevitability of relationship development. Relationships can fail to develop or regress depending upon the actions of either party or of competing buyers or sellers. Throughout the examination, the bilateral nature of relationships will be stressed, particularly the similarity of the buyer's and seller's activities. The five stages are illustrated in Table 1. Throughout the analysis we consider the variables of Experience, Uncertainty, Distance, Commitment and Adaptations.

## Stage 1: The Pre-relationship Stage

Previous authors have stressed the *inertia* of buying companies, when it comes to seeking new sources of supply.[9] Buyers may continue with existing sources with relatively little knowledge or evaluation of the wider supply markets available to them. We will take as our starting point the case of a company which has grown to rely on a main supplier for a particular product purchased on a regular basis, as in the case of equipment, or continuously as with a component.

In these circumstances a decision to evaluate a potential new supplier can be the result of a particular episode in an existing relationship. For example, a UK producer of consumer durables started to evaluate alternative suppliers following a major price increase by a company, which had until then supplied all its requirements for a certain product.

Other reasons which may cause evaluation of new potential suppliers include: a regular vendor analysis in which the performance and potential of existing suppliers

Table 1. The development of buyer–seller relationships in industrial markets – summary

| 1<br>Pre-relationship stage | 2<br>Early stage | 3<br>Development stage | 4<br>Long-term stage | 5<br>Final stage |
|---|---|---|---|---|
| Evaluation of new potential supplier | Negotiation of sample delivery | Contract signed or delivery build-up | After several major purchases or large scale deliveries | In long-established stable markets |
| Evaluation initiated by: | Experience<br>Low | Increased | High | |
| Particular episode in existing relationship | | | | |
| General evaluation of existing supplier performance | Uncertainty<br>High | Reduced | Minimum<br>Development of institutionalization | Extensive institutionalization – Business based on Industry Codes of Practice |
| Efforts of non-supplier | | | | |
| Other information sources | Distance | | | |
| Overall policy decision | High | Reduced | Minimum | |
| Evaluation conditioned by: | | | | |
| Experience with previous supplier | Commitment<br>Actual: low<br>Perceived: low | Actual: increased<br>Perceived: demonstrated by informal adaptations | Actual: maximum<br>Perceived: reduced | |
| Uncertainty about potential relationship | | | | |
| "Distance" from potential supplier | Adaptation<br>High investment of management time.<br>Few cost-savings | Increasing formal and informal adaptations<br>Cost-savings increase | Extensive adaptations,<br>Cost-savings reduced by institutionalization | |
| Commitment | | | | |
| Zero | | | | |

is assessed; the efforts of a non-supplying company to obtain business, perhaps based on a major change in its offering, e.g. a new product introduction; some change in requirements or market conditions experienced by the buyer, e.g. a UK car manufacturer began evaluating overseas sources for windscreens following the move towards tempered glass for which there was a European capacity shortage.

Alternatively, the evaluation of potential suppliers can be the result of a general policy. For example, widespread industrial troubles in the UK in 1974 ("the three-day week") caused one manufacturer to adopt the policy of obtaining approximately 40% of its components from overseas. It then started a search to find and evaluate potential sources of supply to carry out this policy.

A company's evaluation of a potential new supplier will take place without any commitment to that supplier at this stage. The evaluation will be conditioned by three factors: experience, uncertainty and distance. Experience in existing and previous relationships provides the criteria by which the potential and performance of a new partner will be judged – a partner of which the company has no experience. The buyer will face uncertainty about the potential costs and benefits which are likely to be involved in dealing with a new supplier. The costs can be separated into those involved in making a change to a particular partner, e.g. in a buyer modifying its own product to suit that of a new seller. Additionally, there are the opportunity costs involved in the continuing relationship, when compared with alternative partners, e.g. in a buyer having to accept less frequent deliveries.

The distance which is perceived to exist between buyer and seller has several aspects:

- *Social distance:* the extent to which both the individuals and organizations in a relationship are unfamiliar with each others' ways of working
- *Cultural distance:* the degree to which the norms, values or working methods between two companies differ because of their separate national characteristics.
- *Technological distance:* the differences between the two companies' product and process technologies.
- *Time distance:* the time which must elapse between establishing contact or placing an order, and the actual transfer of the product or service involved.
- *Geographical distance:* the physical distance between the two companies' locations.

Technological distance is likely to be great in evaluations for the purchase of innovative products. Social distance will be considerable in all new relationships as the companies know little of each other. This is combined with large cultural and geographical distance when the companies are dealing across national boundaries.[10] Finally, the companies will be considering a purchase which is unlikely to take place for a considerable time, with consequent apprehension that it will not come to fruition as desired.

We can now see the effects of these variables of Experience, Uncertainty, Distance and Commitment in the early stages of dealings between the companies.

### Stage 2: The Early Stage

This is the time when *potential* suppliers are in contact with purchasers to negotiate or develop a specification for a capital goods purchase. This stage can also involve sample delivery for frequently purchased components or supplies. The stage can be characterized as follows.

*Experience*

At this early stage in their relationship, both buyer and seller are likely to have little experience of each other. They will only have a restricted view of what the other party requires of them, or even of what they hope to gain from the relationship themselves. No routine procedures will have been established to deal with issues as they arise, such as sample quality, design changes, etc. These issues can only be resolved by a considerable investment of management time at this stage. This investment of human resources is likely to precede any investment in physical plant.

*Uncertainty*

Human resource investment will be made at a time of considerable uncertainty, when the potential rewards from the relationships will be difficult to assess and the pattern of future costs is undetermined.

*Distance*

There will have been little opportunity to reduce the distance between the parties at this early stage in their dealings.

*Social distance.* There will be a lack of knowledge between buyer and seller companies as well as an absence of personal relationships between the individuals involved. This will mean that many of the judgements made of each company will be on their reputation, as a substitute for experience of their abilities.

*Geographical–cultural distance.* Geographical distance is, of course, beyond the control of the seller except in so far as it can be reduced by the establishment of a local sales office or by sending staff out to the customer on a residential basis. Cultural differences can only be reduced by employment of local nationals. The lack of social relationships means that there is nothing to reduce the effects of geographical and particularly cultural distance. This can result in a lack of trust between the companies. For example, a supplier may believe that he is simply being used as a source of information and that the customer has no intention of placing major orders or building a relationship. Further, the distrust of an individual supplier can cause a purchaser to place emphasis on cultural stereotypes – e.g. a customer may attach importance to the alleged "discipline" of German suppliers, as opposed to a lack of faith in "undisciplined" British suppliers.

*Technological distance.* Inexperience of a supplier's product will emphasize any differences which may exist between the product or process technologies of the two companies.

*Time distance.* In the early stage of a relationship, companies are likely to be negotiating about agreements or transactions which may only come to fruition at some considerable time in the future. This maximizes the buyer's concern about whether he will receive the product in the form specified and at the promised price and time. Similarly, the seller will be concerned as to whether orders being discussed will ever materialize in the way it expects.

*Commitment*

Both companies will be aware of the risks involved and will have little or no evidence on which to judge their partner's commitment to the relationship. In fact, it is likely that the actual commitment of both parties will be low at this time. Thus, perceptions of the likely commitment of the other company are strongly influenced by factors outside the relationship such as the number and importance of its other customers or suppliers.

The actions of seller and buyer in the future will be influenced by their initial assessment of the performance and potential of their partner. Their judgement of the place and importance of this relationship within the company's portfolio of suppliers or clients will also be important. Thus, a US engineering manufacturer clearly separates those "development suppliers" from others, very early in their dealings. It is these suppliers who receive the customer's investment of time, money and expertise to build the relationship. It may be that one of the partners may seek to develop the relationship, while the other remains passive. Also, efforts at development may founder, either because of the unwillingness of the partner or the incompetence of the initiator in overcoming the problems inherent in the early stages of a relationship.

We can now consider the development of a relationship beyond the early stage in terms of the tasks of building experience, increasing commitment and the associated reduction in uncertainty and distance.

**Stage 3: The Development Stage**

The development stage of a relationship occurs as deliveries of continuously purchased products increase. Alternatively, it is the time after contract signing for major capital purchases. Staged deliveries may be being made or the supplier may have started work on the item. Both buyer and seller will be dealing with such aspects as integration of the purchased product into the customer's operations of pre-delivery training, etc.

*Experience*

The development stage is marked by increasing experience between the companies of the operations of each other's organizations. Additionally, the individuals involved will have acquired some knowledge of each other's norms and values.

*Uncertainty*

The uncertainties which exist for both parties in the relationship will have been reduced by experience. In particular, the adaptations required to meet the wishes of the partner company will have become more apparent and the costs involved in these adaptations will also become clearer. Each company will be better able to judge the adaptations to meet its own requirements. These include those made by itself and those which it should require from its partner.

*Distance*

*Social distance.* This is reduced by the social exchange which takes place between the companies. As well as increasing their knowledge of each other, these personal relations establish trust between individuals. Nonetheless, this trust cannot be based upon social relationships alone. It also requires personal experience of the other company's satisfactory performance in exchange of product or services and finance.

*Geographical and cultural distance.* The reduction in social distance also contributes to a lessening of the effects of geographical and cultural distance. However, in a relationship between companies in different countries, it is possible that the seller company may reduce geographical and cultural distance through the establishment of a local office and employment of local nationals as business builds up.

*Technological distance.* The adaptations which companies make to suit each other reduce the technological distance between them. Thus, their respective products, production and administrative process become more closely matched with each other. This produces consequent savings for one or both parties.

*Time distance.* The experience of transactions means that the time distance between negotiation and delivery is eliminated in the case of continually delivered products. However, in the case of irregular purchases of, for example, capital goods then each cycle of order and delivery can be marked by similar time distances. Nevertheless, the importance of this distance decreases as the companies' mutual experience and trust of each other builds up.

*Commitment*

Much of a company's evaluation of a supplier or customer during the development of their relationship will depend on perceptions of their commitment to its development. Efforts to reduce social distance are one way for the supplier to demonstrate commitment. Commitment can also be shown in other ways:

It can be indicated by "adapting" to meet the needs of the other company, either by incurring costs or by management involvement. It is useful to separate these adaptations into *formal* adaptations which are contractually agreed between the companies and *informal* adaptations which may be arranged subsequently, to cope with particular issues which arise as the relationship develops. It is possible that the formal adaptations between companies may be dictated by the nature of the industry, e.g. that special products must always be developed for individual customers. On the other hand, a supplier's informal adaptations beyond the terms of a contract are often an important indicator of commitment.[11] For example, one large UK buying organization lists a major criterion in assessing the commitment of suppliers to be their "flexibility", for example in arranging a rapid increase in supply to cope with a sudden demand change.

In the international context, a company can demonstrate its commitment to a general market. This can be done by setting up a sales or buying office in that market. For example, a UK manufacturer and a French company had not progressed beyond the stage of exchanging "letters of intent" to buy. This was despite being in contact with each other for over two years. It was clear that the buyer doubted the supplier's commitment to it or the market, because of its unwillingness to establish a French office or assign specific personnel to the relationship during its development.

Finally, a company can emphasize commitment to a relationship by the way it organizes its contact with its partner. This includes both the status of personnel involved and the frequency of contact. For example, a British buyer of packaging machinery formed an unfavourable impression of the commitment of a Swedish supplier because of the lack of seniority of the people with which it had to deal and their slow speed of response in their contacts.

The process of development of an inter-company relationship is associated with an increasing level of business between the companies. Over time, many of the difficulties existing in the early stages of relationship are removed through the processes we have described in the development stage. However, development does not continue indefinitely. The relationship can be discontinued by either party on the basis of their assessment of its potential, the performance of the other party, or of the actions of outsiders. Even if this does not occur, the character of a relationship will change gradually. The changes which slowly develop are of vital significance to both buying and selling firms and we now turn to their description.

### Stage 4: The Long-term Stage

It is not possible to put a timetable on the process by which a relationship reaches the long-term stage. This stage is characterized by the companies' mutual importance to each other. It is reached after large-scale deliveries of continuously purchased products have occurred or after several purchases of major unit products.[12]

#### *Experience*

The considerable experience of the two companies in dealing with each other leads to the establishment of standard operating procedures, trust, and norms of conduct. For example, a UK supplier of components to a German truck producer has arrangements for deliveries against three-month "firm" and six-month "tentative" orders. Prices are negotiated on an annual basis with an effective date of 1 January . . . "although we often don't get round to firming them up until well in the spring, so we just apply them retrospectively". Similarly, a UK producer of marine diesel engines will start construction of an individual unit costing up to £100 000 on the basis of a verbal order from a main customer. Formal orders often follow much later.

*Uncertainty*

Uncertainty about the process of dealing with a particular partner is reduced to a minimum in the long-term stage. Paradoxically, this reduction in uncertainty can create problems. It is possible that routine ways of dealing with the partner will cease to be questioned by this stage. This can be even though these routines may no longer relate well to either parties' requirements. We refer to this phenomenon as *institutionalization.* For example, discount structures may have become unrelated to developing delivery patterns, product variety may involve increased production costs for the seller whilst the buyer may be able to use a much narrower range of product.

These institutionalized patterns of operation make it difficult for a company to assess its partner's real requirements and so it may appear less responsive or uncommitted to the relationship. Institutionalized practices may also allow a company to drift into overdependence on a partner or incur excessive costs in its dealings. One company may exploit the other's institutionalized practices and lack of awareness and hence reduce its own costs at the expense of the partner. Finally, institutionalized practices of one relationship can affect a company's whole organization and hence its development of other relationships. For example, a supplier of high-grade alloys had become very heavily involved with a large domestic customer. It then attempted to transfer its experience with this customer to others in different market segments overseas. So many aspects and operations within this relationship had become institutionalized, or taken for granted that the supplier was unable to modify its procedures to suit new customers.

*Distance*

*Social distance.* This is also minimized in the long-term stage. There are three particular features to the close relationship established by this stage.

Firstly, an extensive contact pattern will have developed between the companies. This may involve several functional areas and its aim will be to achieve an effective matching and adaptation of the systems and procedures of both supplier and customer. However, in the long-term stage the interactions by the different functions may become separated. For example, the technical problem solving between a supplier and its customers can become quite separate from the commercial transactions which take place. This can lead to problems of co-ordination and control if different departments are not to work in conflict with each other. For example, a German engineering company had 40 of its staff in constant contact with 12 people in a UK supplier. In view of this, the customer appointed a section head to "manage" the relationship. It was his responsibility to ensure that all of the separate interactions with the supplier were mutually compatible and in line with the overall policy of the buying company.

Secondly, strong personal relationships will have developed between individuals in the two companies. The strength of these can be seen by the extent of mutual problem solving and informal adaptations which occur. However, it may be difficult for an individual to separate these personal relationships from the business relation. Difficulties can arise when company interests are subordinated to those of the personal relationships. This has its most extreme form in the phenomenon of "side-changing" where individuals act in the interests of the other company and against their own, on the strength of their personal allegiances.

Thirdly, in the long-term stage, companies may become personified in an individual representative. Indeed, it may be the seller's policy to identify closely a relationship with the person of the local representative. This may be of value in establishing a presence in an overseas market. However, it inevitably involves problems if this individual has to be replaced or acts in his own interests rather than those of the company. For example, a UK exporter of machinery had to re-negotiate spares prices charged to its main French customer. These had previously been fixed by the supplier's local representative at a very low level. This had been done because the representative was greatly concerned about the effects of losing this business in his own position.

*Technological distance.* Successive contracts and agreements between the companies lead to extensive formal adaptations. These closely integrate many aspects of the operations of the two companies. This close integration is motivated by cost reduction for both companies as well as increased control over either their supply or buyer markets. De Monthoux has emphasized the barriers to the entry of other companies to which this close integration leads.[13]

### *Commitment*

By the long-term stage, both seller and buyer companies' commitment to the relationship will have been demonstrated by the extensive formal and informal adaptations which have occurred. Nevertheless, the seller company faces two difficulties over commitment at this stage.

Firstly, it is likely to be difficult for a company to balance the need to demonstrate commitment to a client against the danger of becoming overly dependent on that client. This was expressed by a UK supplier faced with a major customer as follows: "We want them to think they are still important to us. At the same time we also want them to believe that they must work for our attention in competition with other customers".

Secondly, a customer's perception of a supplier's commitment to a relationship may differ from the actual level. This is because the required investment of resources has largely been incurred before the long-term stage is reached. It is also possible that the level of business between the companies has stabilized. Thus, paradoxically, when a supplier is at his most committed to a long-term and important client, he may *appear* less committed than during the development stage.

We have now come "full circle" in the description of relationship development. We have reached that stable situation before evaluation of potential new suppliers which was our starting point. In this, a company may continue with existing sources of supply or customers with little knowledge or evaluation of the available supply or customer markets. However, before concluding, it is worthwhile to mention a final stage which buyer–seller relationships may enter.

### Stage 5: The Final Stage

This stage is reached in stable markets over long periods of time. It is marked by an extension of the institutionalization process to a point where the conduct of business is based on industry codes of practice. These may have relatively little to do with commercial considerations, but correspond more to a "right way to do business", e.g. the avoidance of price cutting and restrictions on changes in the respective roles of buyer and seller. It is often the case that attempts to break out of institutionalized patterns of trading in the final stage will be met by sanctions from other trading partners or the company's fellow buyers or sellers.[14]

## MARKETING IMPLICATIONS

We have described how the development of buyer–seller relationships can be seen as a process in terms of:

- The increasing experience of the two companies;
- The reduction in their uncertainty and the distance between them;
- The growth of both actual and perceived commitment;
- Their formal and informal adaptations to each other and the investments and savings involved.

We can now turn to some of the implications of this process for the marketing company. The most obvious implication is that a company cannot treat its market in some overall way. Not only must it segment that market according to the different requirements of companies, it must also see its potential market as a network of relationships. Each of these must be assessed according to the opportunity they represent and how the relationship can be developed. The company's marketing task then becomes the establishment, development and maintenance of these relationships, rather than the manipulation of a generalized marketing mix. Further, this management of relationships must take place with regard to the company's skills and the costs involved, as well as the allocation of its resources between different relationships according to the likely return.

### Establishing Relationships

The existing relationships between buying and selling companies in an industrial market are a powerful barrier to the entry of another company. The barrier consists of the inertia in existing relationships, the uncertainties for the customer in any change of supplier, the distance which exists between buyer and a potential seller, and the lack of awareness or information about possible alternative partners. These factors are particularly significant in the case of overseas purchases,[15] where buyers may form stereotypes of national characteristics.

The marketer should be involved in the following activities to overcome these problems:

### *Market Analysis*

An analysis is required, which goes beyond determining which markets or sectors to enter. This analysis must examine the relationships held by potential customers and existing competitors. Customers may be categorized into those with long-established supplier relationships for the product, or those in the development or early stages. It is difficult to generalize at which stage relationships are easiest to break into, although different approaches will be required depending on this stage. Thus, a potential customer in the early stages of a relationship with a supplier may be facing problems which require considerable management involvement. This may mean that the company is in a position to evaluate alternatives and is aware of the inadequacies of its existing relationship. In contrast, a company which has begun to adapt and become committed to a suppler may be unwilling to face further uncertainty by considering a change. Thus, in the case of a satisfactorily developing or long-term relationship, it is likely that a new supplier will only be considered if there is some failure or particular inadequacy in an existing supplier. For example, we have pointed out that a buyer's perception of a supplier's commitment can decrease in the long-term stage and that problems may arise through institutionalized practices.

The analysis we refer to will indicate the required approach to different potential customers. Breaking into existing, early-stage relationships may involve emphasis on a broad range of factors, e.g. product specification, prices and delivery. Also, the approach may be to the senior management which is likely to be involved at this stage. The approach to customers with more established relationships involves determining the *specific* problems they are facing. Also, the seller must examine whether an attempt to solve these problems is within its capabilities. The company must question whether the adaptations it must make will provide adequate returns. Finally, it must tailor its approach to the individuals within the customer who are in the areas of the relationship where problems have arisen.

### *Developing Relationships*

We have discussed the importance of commitment and distance reduction in the development of relationships. Those involve a supplier in human and capital costs – in an overall market. It is worth noting that commitment to a market normally involves investment, in the form of local offices, etc., *before* business has developed. This contrasts with the attitudes of many industrial exporters who seem only prepared to invest in a sales or service operation *after* sales have been achieved.

The development of relationships can also be considered as a problem of strategy and organization. We must distinguish between the "strategic management" of relationships and the "operational management" of a single relationship. Strategic management involves the assessment of any one relationship within the company's strategy in a particular market or markets. Further, strategic management covers a portfolio of relationships. It is concerned with the interplay between them, their respective importance and the consequent resource allocation between them. It is difficult for those people involved in detailed interaction with a customer to see the relationship in perspective or to see the possible effects of institutionalization on it. It is because of this that the strategic management function should be carried out by marketing staff who are not involved in the day-to-day operation of relationships.

A company's marketing structure should also follow from the nature of its relationships. A functional organization within marketing may be appropriate for a firm with a large number of small clients. However, the complexity of the interaction with major clients emphasizes the importance of co-ordination of all aspects of a company's dealings with a client. There is a clear role for a "relationship manager" as in the German buying company referred to earlier. This is someone of sufficient status to co-ordinate all aspects of the company's relationships with major clients at the operational level. This individual is the major "contact man" for the company. He takes overall responsibility for the successful development of a relationship. This is based on his assessment of appropriate resource allocation to that relationship and his orchestration of the interactions between *all* functions – product development, production, sales, quality, and finance, etc. This requires more than the kind of authority usually given to an industrial salesman or "key account executive". In fact, the relationship manager should be independent of those departments which he co-ordinates in managing his portfolio of important relationships. Relationship management is most likely to be seen in operational form in industrial export marketing. Paradoxically, the limited resources often allocated by the seller company to export business mean that one man is involved directly or indirectly in all contacts – hence providing effective co-ordination. The relationship manager has a vital function in the case of irregularly purchased products, e.g. capital equipment. In this case, there is a clear need to *maintain* the relationship between purchase opportunities, either using sales staff or by his own contact.

Our research indicates that industrial companies are more likely to invest marketing resources at the operational than at the strategic level, perhaps because of their more immediately apparent results. This means that many companies are better staffed in the sales areas than under such designations as market planning or market development managers. Thus, staff are often pulled between the separate tasks of day-to-day operations and longer-term strategic planning. Under these circumstances it is not surprising that strategic planning is inadequately covered in the company.

### *Maintaining Relationships*

We have noted that perhaps the most significant aspect of long-term relationships is the problem of institutionalization. This can make a seller unresponsive to the changing requirements of its customers. The separation of operational and strategic management within the company's marketing is the key to reducing these problems. Strategic management includes a company's market analysis and points to differences in market sector and customer characteristics. Hence, it reduces the danger of transferring inappropriate marketing practices from one market to another. Strategic management involves a re-examination of the company's existing operations to see if they continue to be relevant to particular client relationships and market conditions. Finally, strategic management determines the resource allocation between different relationships according to their potential and stage of development. The over-emphasis on operational marketing within many companies means that they do not have the staff or the time to re-examine those activities which have been taken for granted in the company's long-term relationships.

### Final Remarks

In conclusion, it is important to emphasize that companies should examine their existing relationships whether home or overseas to see which of the stages described here they fall into. This examination should be a preliminary to an assessment of each relationship, as follows:

1. What is the likely potential of this relationship?
2. What resources are required to fulfil this potential?
3. Where do the threats to this development come from?
4. Where does this relationship fit within the context of the company's overall operations and resource allocation in that market?
5. Are the current efforts devoted to the relationship appropriate to this overall strategy?
6. Are we over-committed to this customer?
7. Finally, are our ways of dealing with this customer appropriate both to its needs and our strategy or are they dealings based on habit or history?

## REFERENCES AND NOTES


1. For example: Webster, F. E. *Industrial Marketing Strategy*. Wiley, New York (1979).
2. Exceptions include: de Monthoux, P. B. L. G. Organizational mating and industrial marketing conservation – some reasons why industrial marketing managers resist marketing theory. *Industrial Marketing Management*, **4**, 25–36 (1975); Blois, K. J. Vertical quasi-integration. *Journal of Industrial Economics*, **XX**, July, 253–72 (1972): HåKansson, H. and Wootz, B. A framework for industrial buying and selling. *Industrial Marketing Management*, **3**, 28–39 (1979).
3. For details see: Cunningham, M. T. International marketing and purchasing of industrial goods: features of a European research project. *European Journal of Marketing*, **14**(5/6), 322–38 (1980).
4. *Ibid.*
5. See for example: Williamson, O. E. *Markets and Hierarchies: Analysis and Anti-Trust Implications*. Free Press, New York (1975).
6. Williamson, O. E. Transaction cost economics: the governance of contractual relations. *Journal of Law and Economics*, **22**(2), October, 232–62 (1979).
7. *Ibid.*
8. For a discussion of the methodological implications of analysis of episodes and

relationships see: Ford, I. D. A methodology for the study of inter-company relations in industrial market channels. *Journal of the Market Research Society*, **22**(1). 44–59 (1980).

9. See for example: Cunningham, M. T. and White, J. G. The determinants of choice of supply. *European Journal of Marketing*, **7**(3), 189–202 (1973).
10. For use of a similar concept of distance in international business see: Johanson, J. and Wiedersheim-Paul, F. The internationalization of the firm – four Swedish case studies. *Journal of Management Studies*, October, 305–22 (1975). For an attempt to analyse the effect of distance on purchase behaviour see: Håkansson, H. and Wootz, B. Supplier selection in an international environment – an experimental study. *Journal of Marketing Research*, **XII**, 46–51 (1975).
11. Suppliers' informal adaptations are often referred to in the purchasing literature as "Supplier Value Added".
12. This does not mean that a single supplier has been responsible for all of a customer's requirements of a continuously purchased product or every purchase of a major item.
13. de Monthoux, *op cit.*
14. For further discussion of institutionalized practices in long-established markets see: Ford, I. D. Stability factors in industrial marketing channels. *Industrial Marketing Management*, **7**, 410–27 (1978).
15. See: Håkansson, H. and Wootz, B. Supplier selection in an international environment. *Journal of Marketing Research*, **XII**, February, 46–51 (1975).

# 4

# How Do Companies Interact?*

*D. Ford, H. Håkansson and J. Johanson*

## INTRODUCTION

The past 10 to 15 years have seen a growth in the number of studies within what has become known as the "Interaction Approach", see for example Håkansson (1982) and Turnbull and Valla (1986). These studies have examined aspects of the interaction and relationships between companies in industrial and/or international markets and have had the objective of increasing understanding of the behaviour of buying and selling companies in those markets. This article is an attempt to go one step further than previous studies by exploring some ideas which have emerged over these years about the basic nature of interaction between companies. One of our purposes is to develop a model which identifies the strategic options available to companies in their interactions with others. This does not mean that we believe that there exist a number of clear-cut interaction strategies which a company can choose between. On the contrary we think that, for several reasons, inter-company interaction is basically ambiguous rather than clear cut. Furthermore, we believe that this ambiguity is an important element in an company's interaction.

### A Starting Point

Our starting point is that every working company exists within a complex network of interactions between companies as they exchange with each other information, expertise, goods and services, payments and loans, etc. A company can be viewed as a node in an ever-widening pattern of interactions, in some of which it is a direct participant, some of which affect it indirectly and some of which occur independently of it. This web of interactions is so complex and multifarious as to deny full description or analysis. Indeed, the interaction between a *single* buying and

---

*An earlier version of this article was presented at the second open IMP International Research Seminar, Uppsala, September 1985.

Reprinted with permission from *Industrial Marketing and Purchasing*, Vol. 1, No. 1, pp. 26–41.

selling company can be complex enough, as shown by the following illustration.

Salespeople and sales managers from a selling company seek contacts with personnel in a potential customer. Contact is likely to be with buyers but also may be with production or other technical personnel. The sellers try to demonstrate the qualities of their products and their company's capability to manufacture and deliver them and to support the customer with technical services, spare parts, etc. They may bring to the customer various technical specialists in order to discuss and analyse any particular problems of the customer which may require modification of products or production processes. They may also bring in logistical expertise in order to analyse delivery and scheduling questions. If a deal is reached then new and more practical problems are likely to be encountered during production. To solve them, still more personnel are involved. Even after delivery new problems may emerge and need to be handled, future requirements are anticipated and further negotiations may be started. In this example the producer was the most active partner and the influence of any third party was neglected. In contrast a customer company, for example a manufacturer of consumer goods, may approach a number of potential suppliers of producer goods, services or finance. Similar interactions will take place, where the buyer seeks to explain its requirements, assess the suppliers and show its own value as a customer for those suppliers.

Companies interact, react, re-react etc., with each other both in words and other forms of action such as purchases, deliveries, and payments. These interactions may be frequent or infrequent, regular or irregular, explicit or implicit, conscious or unconscious. Each interaction may be individually more or less important, but collectively they comprise a comprehensive picture both of the company and of the reasons for its existence. Thus there are good reasons to try to deepen our understanding of this interaction.

## THE NATURE OF COMPANIES' INTERACTIONS

Within companies a number of inter-related activities are performed. These activities are in turn interwoven with activities in a larger industrial system. All of these demand resources of various kinds; physical – plant, machinery and raw materials; human – skills, knowledge and experience of the organizational members; financial, etc. These resources are in themselves essentially *passive* and fragmented.

It is the company's interaction with others which leads to an *activation* and an integration of its resources. The company's control of these resources, its use of them in activities, its adding to and changing of its resource base is a response to interactions and anticipated interactions. The interaction with others is, in this way, the force that unifies the company and gives it the *capability* to perform its activities. The effects of this force are not the same in all situations. They depend on variations both in the interactions and in the company itself. The company can respond to interaction differently and it can influence the other parties in the interaction in different ways.

Thus, all companies are continuously involved in a wide range of interactions, for example in the acquisition of production inputs or finance, the sale of products or services, joint product development activities, systems selling or co-operation within a trade association. Because of this the company exists in an "interacted environment". This may be compared with Weick's (1979) concept of the "enacted environment". It is against this background that we view companies as sets of interrelated interactions, through which capabilities are developed and employed. Similarly, wider industrial systems are seen as networks of inter-related interactions. In such networks several interdependent companies interact in order to influence and adapt each other's future activities and resources. This implies that the companies have both common and conflicting interests. It may be in the interest of companies which are dependent on each other to develop matching activities and capabilities. To that extent they have common interests. On the other hand, which company is to bear the costs of the adaptations and developments necessary for interaction to take place successfully is not predetermined. Thus, all intercompany relations have elements of both mutual and conflicting interest and their relative importance depends on how the companies view each other.

Intercompany interactions are performed by human beings. They have intentions when interacting and they make interpretations of the interaction and the intentions of others (Giddens, 1975; Klint, 1985). Every interaction is based on intentions and is interpreted from at least two sides. Through these interpretations the interaction is given meaning by the parties. In the rest of this article we will concentrate on these meanings and more or less disregard the form of interaction, noting however that the form of interaction is often chosen in order to underline its meaning. This approach means that we shall view interaction as a process of giving and receiving information, rather like streams of questions and answers given to each other by the parties involved.

A fundamental characteristic of interaction is that it is at least bilateral and sometimes multilateral; there are at least two parties involved at each moment. The parties are aware of each other's existence and try to understand and influence each other. As we have stated, in all interactions there are intentions and interpretations from at least two sides. Furthermore, as the parties are aware of each other they are also aware of the importance of trying to give a favourable picture of their own intentions. The situation is made more complicated in some ways by the fact that the parties have memories and thus also interpret current interaction on the basis of previous experience. However, this previous experience can also simplify interaction as it increases predictability and leads to standard procedures, often based on trust.

As the interaction is often complex and between several persons from each party there will be numerous intentions and interpretations involved. This complexity requires that each company has the necessary capacity to turn its intentions into acts as well as to interpret what intentions lie behind the acts of its counterparts. Unfortunately, both sides usually have limited capacities to act and to interpret and this leads to an unclear situation. The parties do not usually have a clear, consistent and common view of where they stand with each other and what are each others' intentions. For these reasons each new interaction is seen as a test of the relationship between the parties and a way of learning about each other. The flow of "questions" and "answers" between the parties calibrates the relationships between them repeatedly and adjusts their activities and capabilities to this calibration. Furthermore, the meaning of an interaction is not given by the interaction itself but by its relations to previous interactions as well as to other interactions the parties are involved in with other actors. Thus, every interaction is unique at the same time as it is influenced by the whole network of interactions. Thus, interaction is both particular and universal (Belshaw, 1965, p. 114).

Against this background we suggest that analyses of company interaction should focus on four aspects of interaction which capture the general features described above. These aspects are interesting from the interaction parties' points of view because they are important to their own company's development. Additionally, the aspects can to some extent be used consciously by the parties and each has a measure of discretion in handling them. Each aspect can be discussed through a question and the answers to that question:

- What can you do for me?
- How do you see me?
- What are you prepared to do for me, compared to what you do for others?
- Which variations are there in these "whats" and "hows"?

The aspect of interaction which relates to the handling of the first question centres on the *capability* aspect of interaction. It describes the relationship between the parties in terms of what they can do for each other and concerns the functions which they fulfil. We are concerned with both the width and the importance of these functions. In examining capability we see both counterparts *together* forming a functional entity and are concerned with the functional interdependence between their capabilities.

The second aspect of interaction, dealing with the second question, focuses on the social relations between the parties. It is labelled *mutuality* and is based on the assumption that different parties, at least to some extent, share common goals or interests. Mutuality describes how the parties handle the relations between their respective and common interests. Interaction may be dominated by the self-interests of the parties, such as in one-off price negotiation. In contrast, it may be based on a view of mutual interest, such as in joint negotiations with a third party. We are also concerned with the ways in which the parties demonstrate their interest in each others' well-being. Thus mutuality involves a view of the interacting parties as a social entity and deals with the basic social interdependence between them.

The third aspect of interaction, which handles the third question, is an attempt to characterize the interaction in terms of direction and uniqueness: it relates the interaction between the parties to their interactions with other actors. This aspect is called *particularity*. In some extreme cases interaction between two parties is unique and directed solely towards each other – there is a high degree of particularity. This would be seen, for example, in a company's negotiations with the government body which controls its operations. At the other extreme there may be no interaction which is particular to a company and any one of its counterparts. All counterparts are dealt with as a group and interaction is of standard form, as in the case of a large supplier and its many small customers. Of course many parties will want to be seen as more or less particular. However, they are seldom likely to be prepared to pay for the higher costs which follow such special treatment.

*Inconsistency* refers to the ambiguity or lack of clarity in interaction. This ambiguity is in the "messages" passed to the counterpart concerning, for example, the company's wishes or intentions. Interaction can be inconsistent over time or there can be inconsistency between different interactions with the same partner undertaken by different personnel. In this way, the concept focuses on the possible coexistence of conflict and co-operation within the interaction. Thus, co-operation is possible between parties which have conflicting interests as well as conflicts which can occur between those with interests in common. Inconsistency also implies the opportunity for short-term expediency or changes in individual acts without changes to principal policies. In this way, inconsistency captures the dynamic nature of interaction. We can refer to inconsistency in both intentions and interpretations and the concept has important bearings on the other three aspects of interaction already discussed. Inconsistency is an important but neglected aspect of interaction. It is probably one of the most difficult aspects to handle managerially as it goes against most normal managerial advice which stresses "clear and consistent policies" (Porter, 1985). Inconsistency is, however, an important key to change and development in interaction and the management of inconsistency is central to inter-company interaction.

The four aspects of interaction are closely related to each other in various ways and will now be discussed in more detail. First we discuss the two aspects which are primarily concerned with the *effects* of interaction – capability and mutuality. Then we discuss the two other aspects, particularity and inconsistency, which are more concerned with the *implementation* of interaction.

## Capability

We noted earlier that it is through interaction with others that the resources of a company are integrated and activated. Interaction between companies takes place because each seeks to gain from the other and from their association with each other. For interaction to be worthwhile, the interacting parties must form together something that is meaningful and they must have a function for each other. In this way, interaction takes place in the form of continuous questioning: What can you do for me? Can you do this or that for me? What can I do for you? Through this process, the essentially passive resources of a company – financial, physical plant, technological or managerial – are translated into capabilities for a specific partner or partners. Clearly, a company must be able to analyse and describe itself in terms of the needs of counterparts which it has the capability to satisfy. Similarly, those resources which have no value to any counterpart remain passive and do not constitute worthwhile capabilities, nor are they likely to be of value to the company itself. Certain capabilities can be more or less unique to a single company – and hence counterparts may have greater or less difficulty in finding similar alternatives.

The resources of a company may be wide or narrow in range. Irrespective of this, a counterpart may seek interaction with that company because of a single capability which it recognizes as significant, for example the low price of its product or its speed of delivery. It may be quite uninterested in the company's resources for technical problem solving. Alternatively, interaction can take place because of a combination of capabilities which the company possesses or seeks to offer. These variations in resources are illustrated in Fig. 1 in a simple two-by-two matrix which also shows some of the implications of these factors for the nature of interaction. For example, cell 2 approximates to perfect competition in that interaction is based on a single capability, e.g. the ability to deliver a standard product, which is widely available for a standardized price. Perhaps the buyer may seek to move away from this position so that interaction involves more capabilities – product modification, improved delivery for a correspondingly higher price. This would move the interaction into cell 3 and would probably require both parties to enhance their capabilities for each other by "particularity". Cell 1 may approximate to the situation of a monopoly supplier or monopsonistic buyer. Interaction is based on a single capability by either party, but only one company has that capability, or companies each have significantly different capability from each other. Examples would include the superior product technology of a supplier or the great sales potential of a customer. Over time, it may be that further capabilities are required in the interaction, in which case it moves into cell 3. Conversely, if the significant single capability on which the interaction is based becomes more common then the interaction moves back into cell 2. Finally, cell 4 refers to the complex, widespread interaction that we might expect to find in much of industrial marketing and purchasing. Here the differences between companies' capabilities may be relatively small and dealings are based on a number of abilities. Management under these circumstances seek to improve its efficiency in providing the capabilities required or may try to move from this cell to cells 1 or 3 through capability development.

Thus, not only does interaction employ the capabilities of a company, it may also lead to their change or development over time. Interaction or anticipated interaction enables the organization to learn what is required by counterparts, as well as what it can expect in return. Through this the company will seek to add or to develop its resources in particular directions. In many cases, companies will seek to initiate contact with others, mainly as means of developing their capabilities. An example of this would be when a small supplier seeks work with a larger or higher technology

| Number of dimensions | Differences from alternative partners: Great | Differences from alternative partners: Small |
|---|---|---|
| One | 1<br>One dimensional interaction | 2<br>Easy to change partners |
| Several | 3<br>Extensive well developed interaction | 4<br>Common well developed interaction |

Fig. 1. Interaction variations.

company, so that the process of meeting the client's requirements will enhance its own skills or product quality. Over time, too, a company has choices in relation to its capabilities. If a particular type of interaction, or interaction with a specific counterpart is valuable to it then the company may choose to invest more of its resources in that interaction – hence enhancing its capabilities there, through developing new products, or applying more management time, etc. Alternatively, the company can minimize or reduce its investment. Thus it will *extract* its own resources from the interaction whilst at the same time seeking to maximize the capabilities of its counterpart which it uses. An example of this is the often discussed tactic of "milking" a declining product through higher prices and a lack of product improvement investment.

## Mutuality

The concept of mutuality rests on the importance of collective goals or common interests between more than one company. Mutuality is a measure of how much a company is prepared to give up its own individual goals or intentions in order to increase the positive outcomes of others and, through this, increase its own ultimate well-being. This inevitably involves trade-offs between short-term opportunism and longer-term gain. Mutuality can be seen both in bilateral interaction and between larger groups of companies. For example, many industrial customers will share technology with suppliers on the basis that both will benefit through enhancement of the suppliers' capabilities. Alternatively, manufacturers will sometimes supply goods on consignment to a distributor, if the distributor faces cash-flow problems. These examples can be contrasted with the view of buyer–supplier interactions which are seen by the participants as a zero sum game, typically concentrating on price negotiation. An example of strong mutuality between larger numbers of companies is provided by the members of trade associations who will sometimes agree to common marketing practices in their joint interests as "the industry". Sometimes, this activity goes beyond the law, in such arrangements as market sharing or price fixing.

Mutuality costs nothing to show at the spoken level – in for example the promises of a salesperson. However, mutuality can only really be demonstrated over time. Similarly, the extent of the mutuality demonstrated on specific occasions is often long remembered. For example there were customers within the European paper and pulp industry who in the late 1970s still remember and used in argument how different suppliers had acted towards them during the scarcity period of the Korean War, 25 years previously.

Mutuality is the mirror of the trust which exists between parties. One way in which this trust can be demonstrated is through the commitment shown to the counterpart by use of the company's various capabilities in interaction. This is often seen in the case of sellers who adapt product, price of delivery schedules, often on an informal basis. It is through these adaptations or "Transaction Specific Investments" (Williamson, 1979) that close relationships are developed over time (Ford, 1980). In well-established relationships, mutuality is more or less taken for granted and the relationship can withstand short-term problems which may arise. This is an analogous situation to that of a marriage. Here also, once the parties feel that mutuality has been lost then the relationship is in danger or, alternatively, it will take a long time for mutuality to be re-established.

Mutuality is not the opposite of conflict. In contrast, the existence of many conflicts requires a certain minimum level of mutuality. It is common for companies to have an overall idea of mutual interest whilst simultaneously being in conflict over what should be their respective contributions towards its achievement. Conflict can exist when one party to interaction is prepared to operate on the basis of a higher level of mutuality than is the other. Thus, conflict in this case often takes the form of argument over short-term as opposed to long-term gain, or is expressed in terms of accusations of "selfishness".

Finally, a company may wish to reduce the mutuality on which interaction is based. The adaptation and commitment involved may become burdensome when compared with the rewards. Thus, the company may seek to substitute immediate self-interest instead of joint and, by implication, longer-term interest.

### Particularity

The concept of particularity is based on the existence of the complex, interlocking network of interaction in which a company exists. Because of this, interaction with one counterpart may indirectly affect others. For example, the amount of product development capability employed by a manufacturer towards the requirements of a particular customer will directly affect the amount available for solution of other customers' problems. Interactions are always relative in the sense that they are compared to each other. If one customer is treated in some special way then others may request the same type of special treatment.

The extent of particularity in interaction is often strongly influenced by the specific situation or wider network in which it takes place. For example, a customer buying certain electronic products from a single supplier will inevitably have to develop production processes compatible with these and incompatible with the products of other suppliers. However, companies do have a certain discretion in particularity. An obvious example of this is the price structure which companies adopt and whether or not they are prepared to negotiate special prices for individual customers. Discounts are often seen by customers as illustrations of the selling company's priority structure and we have found companies which have developed very complicated price structures in order to make it more or less impossible for customers to calculate the price level for others – hence disguising their particularity. Network structure influences the importance of particularity. The more tight and well-structured a network, with close and well-established interaction between the companies, then the more likely that this interaction is based on strong particularity. Particularity often increases over time as adaptations are made to suit each other's requirements. In this way particularity becomes imposed on the company by the enacted environment and hence is a constraint.

However, the company can also choose to use particularity as a type of strategic variable. For example, it can decide to give certain counterparts special treatment depending on their perceived value, while others only get standard treatment. It can, in the same way, choose to differentiate between counterparts in certain dimensions while keeping others standardized – for example it may vary the delivery or services but not the products to certain customers. Furthermore, the company can choose to give special treatment in certain situations but not in others, such as dealing differently with orders of different sizes.

Particularity is often closely related to costs, when companies make specific investments dedicated to their interaction with a counterpart. The issue is therefore often formulated in terms of whether or not a special approach to interaction will pay off over time. Many companies, however, seek to find ways to give special treatment without increasing the costs, that is to find standardized methods to produce individual solutions. This has been referred to in the general context of marketing as the "industrialization of service" (Levitt, 1976).

## Inconsistency

It is self-evident that companies consist of individuals and subgroups, and it is these who are involved in the company's interactions. This provides a starting point for our examination of inconsistency because it means that a company can never present a wholly unified approach in its interactions. We refer to this as "interpersonal inconsistency". Each person involved in interaction between companies will have his or her own expectations of his or her counterpart. Some individuals will be more committed to interactions with a particular company than will others. For example, it is possible that a company's salesperson could devote great efforts to finding out the precise requirements of a customer and to tailoring his or her own offering to meet these. At the same time these requirements could appear self-indulgent to the company's production-planning department. Similarly, individuals may approach interaction on the basis of their own personal interests rather than those of the company. Thus, salespeople may feel a sense of commitment to serve the interests of a customer, based on personal ties, even though this may be against the instructions given by their own company. This phenomenon is often referred to as "sidechanging".

As well as interpersonal inconsistency, a company will also demonstrate "intertemporal inconsistency". We would expect that different considerations will be important to the company at various times in its interactions. Thus when it is first trying to establish contact with a new potential customer we would expect a supplier to be more solicitous in initial interactions than with a customer with whom it has been dealing for many years and which it has come to take for granted. Ford (1980) has discussed this phenomenon in terms of institutionalization in the development of relationships. There is a parallel between this inconsistency and what is referred to by Cyert and March (1963) in the intra-organizational context as "sequential attention to goals".

The discussion so far may have indicated that inconsistency is an unfortunate, but unconscious or unavoidable, factor associated with interaction. However, in our view, companies are intricate webs of inter-related activities and resources. Through interaction these are embedded in wider networks of similarly intricate, inter-related activities and resources. This is a complex, ever-changing world which is impossible to survey from outside, but possible to understand and influence, at least partially, from inside. In such a world inconsistency may make it possible to explore and test different developments. Inconsistencies in interaction may also help in rearranging relationships with other companies. Inconsistency may also be a way to handle both conflicting and common interests. Hence, inconsistency in interaction may be fruitful for the company. And even if it may be difficult to plan it may very well be supported consciously. A company in negotiation with another may use two people, one of whom plays the "hard man" and one who is more conciliatory. Similarly, the interactions between the respective research and development departments of two companies may be allowed to be based on greater mutuality than those between the corresponding salesperson and buyer. Further we would expect a company to change its interactions with a customer when its relative importance as a source of revenue increased or decreased.

Inconsistency is important to both sides in an interaction – both the company performing a particular activity and the corresponding party which is trying to interpret the action. The action will include elements of inconsistency and there will be inconsistencies in the counterpart's interpretation. An activity which is notionally based on mutuality will include elements of self-seeking. Any such action may be interpreted as friendly by some representatives of the counterpart, but by others as unfriendly.

Inconsistency is a powerful concept in interpreting inter-company interaction. We often speak of "companies interacting" and thus we reify the organization. We would argue that it is appropriate to describe the dealings of organizations at the level of the collectivity. Nevertheless, an adequate understanding of company behaviour can only be provided by also analysing the company as a collection of interactions by individuals and subgroups which are more or less inconsistent with each other and over time.

## THE INTER-RELATIONSHIP BETWEEN THE DIMENSIONS: THE DYNAMIC CHARACTER OF INTERACTION

The four dimensions are closely related to each other. Inconsistency is, for example, a dimension that can be used to characterize a company's activities in the three other dimensions (mutuality, particularity and capability). Mutuality and particularity can in the same way be seen as two dimensions of a company's capability. Furthermore, as already described, mutuality and particularity are related to each other in several ways. However, this interconnectedness is not at such a level that there are reasons to integrate the four dimensions into one total dimension. Instead it can be seen as an indication of the dynamic character of the interactions.

The four dimensions may be used to characterize interaction which in turn is very much time related. The dynamics of interaction are shown by the fact that it can be perceived as a learning process. The actors take part in mutual learning where they successfully get to know when and how they should utilize each other. Each participant will increase his or her knowledge and experience, not just of the interaction itself but of the characteristics and expectations of his or her counterpart. The similar development of trading relationships in traditional society has been described by Belshaw (1965):

> The exchanges are accompanied by forms of words and ceremonial acts, all of which reinforce the notions of honourable gift giving and mutual dependence between persons who in most instances would be strangers in other circumstances. But since the institution has been passed on from generation to generation so has been the interlinkage of partners in a relationship which is itself passed on and developed through generations.

Nevertheless, the development of a relationship is in no way deterministic. Williamson (1979) has discussed those circumstances where relationship development is likely to occur. For our purposes here, we can simply note that these relationships may be close, complex and long-term – as in the case of a components supplier to the automotive industry. Alternatively they may be intense, but only at irregular intervals as in the case of purchase of capital equipment, or distant and irregular as in the case of the contact and relationship between competitors in some industries. Therefore interaction over time provides the opportunity for both mutuality and conflict. Relationships may develop, stagnate or be close or distant depending upon variations in commitment and expectations. For a further discussion of relationship changes over time see Ford and Rosson (1982).

This means that a relationship is defined in terms of the existing and previous pattern of interaction. As well as interaction defining a relationship, it is the relationship itself and the participants' experience of it which provides the context for all subsequent interaction. This means that no single element or episode in the dealings between companies can be considered in isolation.

## SOME MANAGERIAL ISSUES

This article has suggested that the interaction between a company and its counterparts is a process of managing mutuality, particularity, and the company's capabilities, whilst at the same time coping with and positively using inconsistency in its dealings with others. It is through interaction that a company's capabilities are used and developed and from which it receives rewards. Crucial decisions for the company concern the extent of the capabilities it will apply to interaction with a particular counterpart and its willingness to invest in capability development for long-term reward. Decisions on the development of interaction have long-term implications. For example, the decision to devote resources to a particular project of a potential customer means that those resources cannot be applied elsewhere and, perhaps more importantly, that further resources or investment may be made necessary at later stages of this interaction.

Some of these issues can be addressed through Fig. 2. This matrix illustrates the inter-relationships between different aspects of interaction. Cell 1 raises central questions about the extent to which a company should tailor its capabilities towards interaction with a particular counterpart. This issue is of major concern to those sellers faced with a single customer responsible for a large part of its production. The particularity of a company's capabilities has long-term implications because of the non-transferability of many investments made in interactions, e.g. tailored product development or dedicated production facilities. Because of this, companies must be concerned about the extent to which mutuality is related to particularity (cell 2).

| | Particularity | Inconsistency |
|---|---|---|
| Capability | 1 | 3 |
| Mutuality | 2 | 4 |

Fig. 2. Inter-relationships between variables.

Considerations here involve the extent to which *both* parties have invested their capabilities with a common view of mutual benefit. If we return to our example of the selling company, then often such a company will closely watch the attitude and actions of a customer to measure its commitment to a continuing relationship, as well as the level of its own investment (cell 1).

Cells 3 and 4 concern inconsistency in capability and mutuality in interactions. Here we must again differentiate between inconsistency as an unfortunate consequence of differences in approach between different members of a company's staff, or over time *and* inconsistency as conscious strategy. In the former case, a company must analyse whether it is giving the right message to its partner through its interaction. For example, after a salesperson has secured an order on the basis of arguing his or her company's commitment to a customer, then production staff or service personnel may give the impression that the company is not committed to this client. Further, it is possible for a company to waste its capabilities by seeking to apply them to too many counterparts or by failing to be seen to maintain commitment over time to an important counterpart.

Conscious inconsistency is an important strategic choice. For example, a company may seek to withdraw some of the capabilities it offers to a counterpart in order to draw its attention to their importance. One specialized metal manufacturer faced with a single customer who accounted for much of its sales used this tactic to strike a balance between making the customer feel important, but not taking the supplier for granted. Similarly, a selling company must examine its charging basis as a tactic in mutuality. For example, it may sometimes be appropriate for a company to accept the development charges for a project on the basis that the success of the project is in both parties' interests. At other times, the company must emphasize the importance of its reward and insist on payment for its development costs.

These four aspects of interaction raise a host of issues for managerial decision making. We argue that a primary focus for analysis of these decisions is to view companies in the context of their network of interactions. This is instead of taking a narrower perspective which focuses on the company alone and views it as a (more or less) unilateral decision maker and controller of its resources. It is through interaction with other companies that resources are mobilized and strategy implemented and indeed through which the very nature of a company is defined.

## REFERENCES

Belshaw, C. S. *Traditional Exchange and Modern Markets.* Prentice Hall, Englewood Cliffs, NJ (1965).

Cyert, R. M. and March J. G. *A Behavioral Theory of the Firm.* Prentice Hall, Englewood Cliffs, NJ (1963).

Ford, D. The development of buyer–seller relationships in industrial markets. *European Journal of Marketing,* **14** (5/6), 339–53 (1980).

Ford, D. and Rosson, P. The relationship between export manufacturers and their overseas distributors. In *Export Management, An International Context.* pp. 257–75. Praeger, New York (1982).

Giddens, A. *New Rules of Sociological Method.* Anchor Press, Essex (1975).

Håkansson, H. (ed.) *International Marketing and Purchasing of Industrial Goods: An Interaction Approach.* Wiley, Chichester (1982).

Klint, M. B. *Mot en konjunturanpassad kundstrategi – om den sociala relationens roll vid marknadsforing av massa och papper.* [Towards a customer strategy allied to the business cycle: about the role of the social relationship in the marketing of pulp and paper]. Ph.D. thesis with an English summary, Department of Business Administration, University of Uppsala (1985).

Levitt, T. The industrialization of service. *Harvard Business Review,* September/October (1976).

Porter, M. E. *Competitive Advantage. Creating and Sustaining Superior Performance.* The Free Press, New York (1985).

Turnbull, P. W. and Valla, J. P. (eds). *Strategies for International Industrial Marketing.* Croom Helm, London (1986).

Weick, K. E. *The Social Psychology of Organizing,* 2nd edn. Addison-Wesley, Reading, Mass. (1979).

Williamson, O. E. Transaction-cost economics; the governance of contractual relations. *Journal of Law and Economics,* **22** (2), 232–62 (1979).

# 5

# The Relationships between Export Manufacturers and their Overseas Distributors

*David. Ford and Philip J. Rosson*

The use of overseas distributors* is an important way for many manufacturers to develop their foreign markets (Business International, 1970; Duguid and Jacques, 1971; Tookey, Lea, and McDougall, 1967). This is particularly the case with small- or medium-sized companies that may not have the necessary scale of operations, financial resources, or experience to operate more directly in foreign markets (Duguid and Jacques, 1971; Tookey, 1975). Two issues in the use of overseas distributors have received considerable attention in the literature. First, a number of writers have examined those circumstances where distributor use may be appropriate (Brady and Bearden, 1979; Daniels, Ogram, and Radebaugh, 1976; Tookey, 1975). A second issue that has been dealt with is that of the selection of the most suitable overseas distributor. Various authors (Bickers, 1971; Heck, 1972; McMillan and Paulden, 1974) provide guidance on how to approach the selection decision. Further, Ross (1972) attempted to relate selection factors and distributor attributes to varying situations that might confront the manufacturer in overseas markets.

A third issue concerns the nature of the association between manufacturer and overseas distributor once the relationship has been established. There is a lot of advice in the literature on how these relationships should be managed (Beeth, 1973; Bickers, 1971; Terpstra, 1972). However, this advice lacks a real empirical base, for few studies have investigated how manufacturers *do* manage their overseas distributor relationships, or whether performance *is* associated with certain practices (Mechanical Engineering EDC, 1968; ITI Research, 1975; Cunningham and Spigel, 1971; Business International, 1970; Rosson and Ford, 1980a, 1980b).

This chapter develops a model of exporter–overseas distributor relationships by drawing upon writings in the fields of interorganizational relations and buyer–seller

*The term "distributor" is used here in the sense defined by Miracle and Albaum (1970, p. 356). They distinguish between distributors and agents as follows: "a distributor is a merchant middleman and as such, he is the customer of the exporter. An agent, on the other hand, is a representative who acts on behalf of the exporter; he is not a customer."

relationships in industrial marketing. This model is then tested empirically through examining data on 21 pairs of companies, that is, 21 Canadian exporters of industrial goods and their UK distributors. Finally, the results are discussed and recommendations are made about the management of manufacturer–overseas distributor relations.

## THEORETICAL BACKGROUND

Two sources of useful writing on manufacturer–overseas distributor relationships were mentioned above. Marrett (1971), an organizational theorist, provides a good starting point for discussion of the question, "How do organizations relate to each other?" Based on her review of a number of field studies of health and welfare agencies, Marrett proposed four dimensions for the analysis of interorganizational relations. Each of these four dimensions are defined below, together with an indication of the relevance of the dimension in the manufacturer–overseas distributor context.

*Formalization.* This refers to the extent to which the relationship is agreed upon and made explicit. In the exporting context, distributor relationships come into being when two organizations agree to work with each other. Such an agreement, however, may vary with regard to its explicitness and importance. For example, some agreements involve verbal undertakings, whereas others may involve a legal contract.

*Intensity.* This is the level of contact and resource exchange between the parties. Resource exchange (for example, sales aids, stock held) is an important dimension of a distributor relationship, while the export literature places great emphasis on the level of interfirm contacts as contributors to the efficiency of these business relationships (ITI Research, 1975; Cunningham and Spigel, 1971).

*Reciprocity.* This is the extent to which the two parties are *both* involved in decision making, despite the traditional domains of each. The formation of a distributor relationship implies that a certain division of labour will occur. Thus, product design decisions would tend to be the prerogative of the manufacturer, while deployment of the sales force in the overseas market tends to be that of the distributor. However, certain decisions (for example, shipping and delivery scheduling) may require joint efforts. A similar joint involvement may be experienced when the party with major responsibility for a decision area accepts advice from the other. For example, the distributor may have a perspective on the market that allows him to make useful comments regarding the manufacturer's new product program. If both dyad members are involved in decision making and if the involvement is of a constructive and selfless kind, it can be termed reciprocal. In contrast, joint involvement may be less balanced than that implied above, for decision making provides an arena for the exercise of power. (For a discussion of manufacturer–distributor power relationships, see Wilkinson, 1973).

*Standardization.* This is the extent to which the established roles and routines of the relationship are adhered to, for example, on the basis of a manufacturer's standard procedure. Continuing transactions in these relationships require that the roles of each party are understood and that routines are established that permit effective operation. From time to time, roles and routines may need modification. This may be externally induced (for example, strikes at the port of entry leading to revised shipping routine) or internally induced (for example, poor distributor product servicing leading to the manufacturer taking over the servicing role).

Marrett's four dimensions – formalization, intensity, reciprocity, and standardization – have been tested empirically by Aldrich (1976) and Schmidt and Kochan (1977). In the latter case, further items were included "to capture dimensions of conflict processes, namely incompatible goals, tension, conflict and influence" (p. 225). The inclusion of conflict as a dimension for study in the manufacturer–overseas distributor setting has merit. Stern and Reve (1980, p. 58) have argued that relations in distribution channels are of a "mixed-motive" kind, and numerous studies have shown that conflict frequently exists between manufacturer and distributor (see, for example, Ford, 1978).

A second source of insight regarding manufacturer–overseas distributor relationships is provided by Ford (1980). Whereas Marrett's approach is static, that is, "What are the dimensions of interorganizational relations? Ford's is dynamic, that is, "How do intercompany relations change?" This growth model proposes five stages in such relationships: prerelationship, early, development, long-term, and final stages. It suggests that the nature of the relationship between buying and selling companies changes through these stages over time. The stages are described in terms of the experience, uncertainty, commitment, and mutual adaptation of the two parties as well as the distance that exists between them.

Experience here refers to each party's corporate and individual knowledge of the relationship and the other company. The uncertainty faced by the two companies concerns the possible costs and benefits of the relationship with the other party. This uncertainty is likely to be particularly great at the start of a relationship or when changes have been introduced, or where the relationship has deviated from the expectations of either company. Commitment is a measure of the importance of a relationship to a company in terms of the "durable transaction-specific investments" (Williamson, 1979) that it is prepared to make in it. These investments can be seen most clearly in such things as a supplier's development of a special product for a customer, or a buyer's modification of payment procedures to suit the financial requirements of a supplier. Additionally, companies may be involved in "human capital investments" (Williamson, 1979) in a relationship (for example, alterations and procedures, special training or allocation of managerial resources to the relationship).

The investments by companies mark major adaptations by them to the relationship. These adaptations can be formal as in the case of contractual agreements, or companies may make informal adaptations to cope with each other's requirements as circumstances arise. The use of the terms "commitment" and "adaptation" provide a useful link with the export literature, for this contains numerous references to the need for commitment and adaptability if manufacturers are to achieve overseas success (see, for example, Cunningham and Spigel, 1971; Keegan, 1969; Tookey, 1964). Finally, the distance between buyer and seller is defined as the sum of factors preventing flows of information between seller and buyer. It includes elements of geographic, cultural, and social distance (Hallen and Wiedersheim-Paul, 1979; Johanson and Wiedersheim-Paul, 1975).

In summary, in Ford's (1980) model the development of a buyer–seller relationship is seen as a process of increasing experience and commitment as transactions take place. This process is marked by a reduction in uncertainty as the two companies learn more of each other, the nature of the relationship, and its potentialities. Additionally, the process of social exchange between the companies is seen as a means of reducing the distance between them. The model stresses the importance of informal adaptation as a way of demonstrating commitment to the relationship. Additionally, it points out the potential dangers of the developed experience to the relationship. This danger is that companies may allow their dealings with each other to become overly standardized or based on routine or institutionalized practices. In this way the company may appear unresponsive or uncommitted in the eyes of its partner. This is one of the ways in which the model suggests that the relationship may fail to progress. Other factors are the inability of either of the parties to fulfil the requirements of the other, or to achieve suitable rewards for their investments in their relationship. However, this model does not explicitly diagram the failure of a relationship to grow, nor does it detail the characteristics of declining or static relationships.

## THE RESEARCH MODEL

The model presented in Fig. 1 shows how the views of Marrett (1971) regarding relationship dimensions and Ford (1980) regarding relationship development can be integrated and extended. The integration of these separate strands is made explicit in the discussion that follows. The model shown in Fig. 1 has three main parts: relationship dimensions, participant dimensions, and relationship development states.

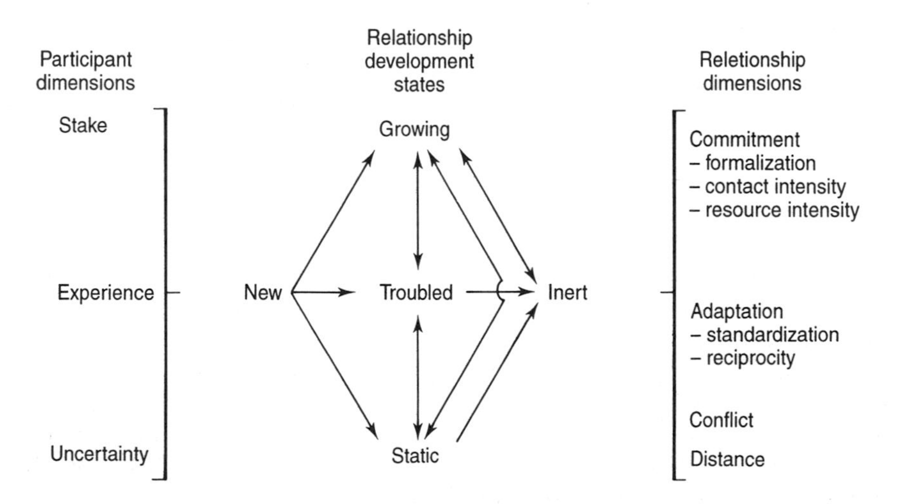


Fig. 1. A model of manufacturer–overseas distributor relationships.

## Relationship Dimensions

Marrett's (1971) four relational dimensions are adopted in this study and supplemented by the dimensions "conflict" and "distance". A connection is seen between Marrett's four dimensions and two mentioned by Ford (1980). Thus, the latter's dimension of commitment to the relationship clearly encompasses Marrett's dimensions of intensity of the relationship, and the formalization of the parties' responsibility to it. Similarly, the degree of standardization in intercompany dealings, and of reciprocity in decision making, can be held to be indicators of the adaptability of the two parties. In this manner, Marrett's four dimensions can be accommodated under two of Ford's.

Finally, the geographic and cultural separation between manufacturer and overseas distributor creates distance (Ford, 1980; Hallen and Wiedersheim-Paul, 1979; Johanson and Wiedersheim-Paul, 1975), and provides an opportunity for tension and disagreement, and, thus, contributes to the overt conflict that may exist between the companies (Schmidt and Kochan, 1977).

## Participant Dimensions

The model used three dimensions to describe the participants in the manufacturer–overseas distributor relationship: stake, experience, and uncertainty. Thus, the behaviour of companies in the relationship is to be likely shaped by the knowledge (or experience) that the firms have of each other (Van de Ven, 1976), as well as their uncertainty about the future of the relationship (Etgar, 1977; Goodnow and Hansz, 1972; Hirsch, 1972; Williamson, 1975).

Stake is defined as "what a party (or the parties) stands to lose if the relationship is terminated." A number of studies suggest the importance of this variable in buyer–seller relationships (ITI Research, 1975; Rosenberg, 1969; Terpstra, 1972). In particular, it has been asserted that the degree of importance of the exporter to the distributor (stake) determines the leverage of control the former has over the latter (Business International, 1970). In summary, the stake, experience, and uncertainty of both manufacturer and overseas distributor are regarded as connected to behaviour within such a relationship, and, indeed, the development of the relationship. This point is raised again below.

## Relationship Development States

The modelling approach here considers relationships as being in one of five possible "states" of development. Unlike earlier work, the only assumption made here regarding progression is that dyads move from being "new" toward being "inert". Between this beginning point and end point, three relationships states are possible, namely, growing, troubled, or static. In the middle relationship period, any sequence of states may be experienced. For example, the "growing" state might be followed by "troubled" to be followed by a "growing" state again. In this way, the model accommodates fluctuations in relationships.

New relationship states are those where an agreement to work together has been made, but where there is little experience of interaction or transactions. The growing state may describe relatively new or well established dyads, for it simply means that reasonable growth is being achieved. The troubled state may be one in which sales growth is being experienced, but where there is uncertainty for other reasons. Alternatively, the uncertainty may relate to sales inadequacy. Relationships may also be in the static state. Here sales might show little variation from year to year because of lack of potential and/or because of an unwillingness of the parties to increase their stake in it. Finally, the inert state characterizes those relationships that, while still in existence, can scarcely be justified. Termination may be considered, or the association may continue because there is no wish to end it.

The five relationship states have a heavy performance emphasis. This is natural since there are real benefits expected by both parties from their association, and any shortfall from expectations will normally be reviewed and remedial action considered. The dynamic of the relations will thus sharply reflect the extent to which the association currently meets the expectations of the dyad members.

The research model shows a potentially useful way in which previous work can be integrated and extended. The work of Marrett (1971) and others on interorganizational relations is meshed with Ford's (1980) ideas about relationship development to produce a framework for understanding manufacturer–overseas distributor relations in exporting. Next, attention turns to examining the following two propositions (P1 and P2), which flow from the discussion above:

P1: Five relationship development states are found in manufacturer–overseas distributor exporting arrangements: new, growing, troubled, static, and inert.

P2: Different relationship characteristics will be found in the three middle periods* – growing, troubled, static – development states.

## RESEARCH METHODOLOGY

The study data were collected through personal interviews in the spring and summer of 1978. Initially, interviews were conducted in 21 Canadian firms that exported industrial goods to the United Kingdom, using an overseas distributor in that market. The interviewee in each case was the person responsible for business with the UK firm. Once the Canadian fieldwork was completed, interviews were conducted with each Canadian firm's UK distributor. The respondent here was the person responsible for business with the Canadian manufacturer, that is, the Canadian respondent's UK contact.

As far as possible, interviews followed a standard format, guided by a questionnaire pretested in two companies. Interviews in Canada averaged 1.75 hours, while those in the United Kingdom averaged 1.5 hours. In each case, the interviewer completed the questionnaire and (in all but two cases) recorded the interview on cassette tapes. The

*Attention is focused on the three middle period relationship states, as these appear of most importance, that is, few relationships remain new or (hopefully) inert for long, but the period between these states may be very protracted and potentially profitable.

transcribed tapes provided very full information and were used for data coding purposes.

A large amount of information was collected, some of which is reported here. For the most part,† the data reported here are summed, that is, the response of manufacturer and overseas distributor is added. In this way, the response of both parties is reflected in the data.

The resulting sample of companies showed considerable variety as to products (sole leather to electronic equipment), exporting and importing experience (2 to 50 years and 1 to 30 years, respectively), level of UK sales ($6000 to $1.5 million per year), and size (manufacturers: 28 to 930 employees; distributors: 5 to 1509 employees).

## PROPOSITION TESTING

### Proposition 1

It has been argued that three participant dimensions largely determine the development state the manufacturer–overseas distributor occupies. Therefore, questionnaire data covering these dimensions were used to categorize the 21 dyads to a development state. The questionnaire items were as follows:

| *Dimension* | *Item* | *Scale or measure* |
|---|---|---|
| Stake | Sales trend over last 3 years | 5 point scale, range: (1) declining quickly, to (5) growing quickly |
| Experience | Length of manufacturer–overseas distributor relationship | Years of association |
| Uncertainty | Plans for the future of the relationship | 4 point scale, range: (1) end relationship, to (4) work together more closely |

Categorization proceeded as follows. All three items provided data but these were not equally weighted. For example, the "growing" and "static" state memberships were based on sales trend information. The "troubled" state members were categorized either because their sales were in decline, or because future plans were very uncertain (even though sales growth had been experienced). The two dyads in the "inert" category were so categorized after inspection of both sales trend and future plans. Finally, "new" state membership resulted from considering the length of association.

The categorization of dyads by development state is shown in diagr mmatic form

†In two cases that are indicated in Table 1, single responses were recorded.

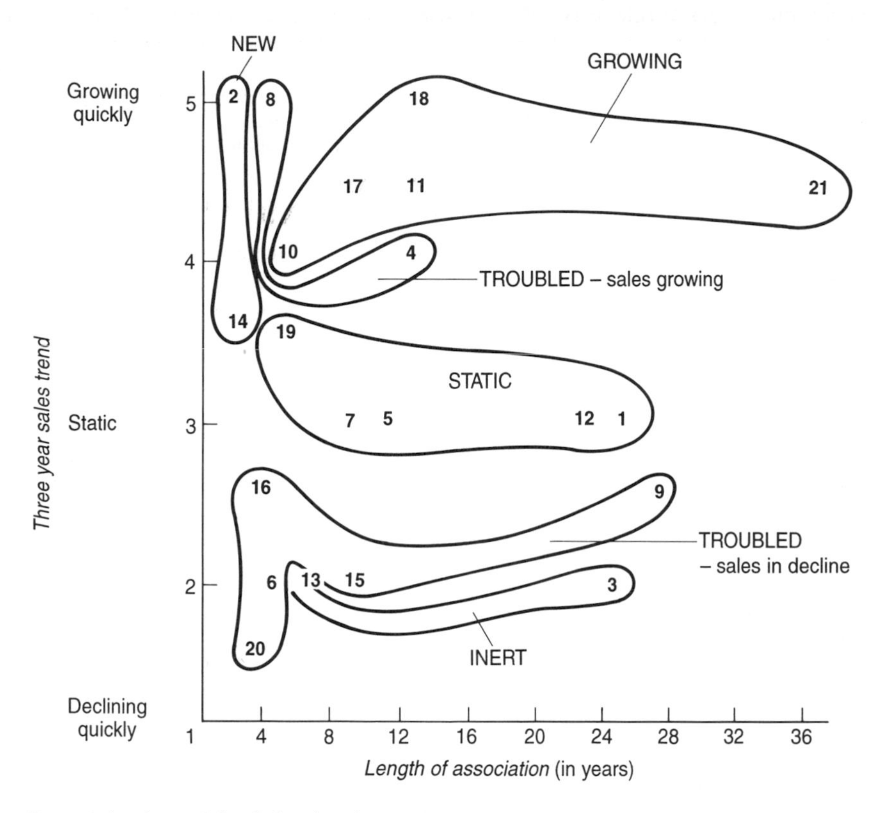


Fig. 2. Categorization of dyads by development state.
*Note:* Read as follows: Dyads 10, 11, 17, 18, and 21 are categorized as growing.

in Fig. 2. Since it was possible to realistically categorize the dyads in this way, the proposition is regarded as supported in this study.

**Proposition 2**

Seventeen dyads were categorized above as being in the growing, troubled, or static development states. Mean values were calculated for various measures of the relationship dimensions: formalization, standardization, reciprocity, intensity, and conflict,* on a development states basis. In view of the small number of dyads involved, these mean values are not subjected to tests of statistical significance. The differences between the mean values are summarized in Table 1 and are regarded as being suggestive only.

Contrasting manufacturer–overseas distributor relations are found for each of the three middle period development states. When *growing* state dyads are considered,

*Distance is not considered here since this can be considered relatively uniform, given that each dyad was involved in the same Canada–UK trading.

Table 1. Characteristics of relationships in growing, troubled, and static development states

<table>
<tr><th rowspan="2">Relationship dimensions</th><th colspan="3">Development states</th></tr>
<tr><th>Growing ($n = 5$ dyads)</th><th>Troubled ($n = 7$ dyads)</th><th>Static ($n = 5$ dyads)</th></tr>
<tr><td>*Commitment*</td><td></td><td></td><td></td></tr>
<tr><td>Formalization</td><td></td><td></td><td></td></tr>
<tr><td>Type of agreement</td><td>most formal</td><td>less formal</td><td>least formal</td></tr>
<tr><td>Contact intensity</td><td></td><td></td><td></td></tr>
<tr><td>Number of letters</td><td>most letters</td><td colspan="2">less letters</td></tr>
<tr><td>Number of visits</td><td colspan="2">less visits</td><td>most visits</td></tr>
<tr><td>Other contact frequency</td><td>most frequent</td><td colspan="2">less frequent</td></tr>
<tr><td>Resource intensity</td><td></td><td></td><td></td></tr>
<tr><td>Support materials[a]</td><td>less support</td><td>most support</td><td>less support</td></tr>
<tr><td>Stock carried[b]</td><td>most stock</td><td>least stock</td><td>less stock</td></tr>
<tr><td>Effort expended</td><td>most effort</td><td>less effort</td><td>least effort</td></tr>
<tr><td>*Adaptation*</td><td></td><td></td><td></td></tr>
<tr><td>Standardization</td><td></td><td></td><td></td></tr>
<tr><td>Stability of roles and routines</td><td>least stable</td><td>most stable</td><td>less stable</td></tr>
<tr><td>Reciprocity</td><td></td><td></td><td></td></tr>
<tr><td>Extent of joint decision making</td><td>most joint</td><td>least joint</td><td>most joint</td></tr>
<tr><td>*Conflict*</td><td></td><td></td><td></td></tr>
<tr><td>Conflict frequency</td><td>least frequent</td><td>most frequent</td><td>less frequent</td></tr>
</table>

[a]*Single* response measure, that is, support materials provided by manufacturer to overseas distributor.
[b]*Single* response measure, that is, stock of manufacturer's products carried by overseas distributor.

these are found to generally exhibit more commitment and adaptation, as well as less conflict between the two parties. *Troubled* state dyads present almost the opposite set of characteristics; generally less commitment and adaptation is suggested, together with more conflict. Dyads in the *static* development state present a less sharply contrasting set of characteristics. In many ways these dyads show characteristics that are consistent with "partial withdrawal" from the relationship. Thus, on most counts companies falling into this category are less committed to each other but at the same time quite adaptive and free of conflict. These points are discussed further in the next section. The findings shown summarized in Table 1 suggest some tentative support for P2.

## DISCUSSION

In this final section the results presented earlier are considered more fully and from a more managerial viewpoint.

## Proposition 1

Two sets of findings are worth noting in relation to P1, where dyads were categorized by development state. The first set of findings results from viewing the distribution of dyads across development states: new – 2, growing – 5, troubled – 7, static – 5, inert – 2. Only five dyads (or 23 per cent) were categorized as being in the development state labelled "growing". Why is this number so small? One explanation might be that manufacturer–overseas distributor relationships are intrinsically hard to manage and that, as a result, success is difficult to achieve. Another explanation relates to Robinson's (1973) thesis of stages of international business involvement. This states that exporting if often the method first used by most firms in international business. Good success in exporting, however, tends to be followed by more direct involvement overseas involving sales subsidiaries and sometimes overseas production. If this argument holds true, then it would seem unreasonable to expect to find a high proportion of *very* successful relationships in a sample such as this one.

The second set of findings concerns the distribution of dyads by development state and length of association and is shown in Table 2. This analysis brings a time dimension to the consideration of relationship development. Naturally, both new relationships in the sample fall into the under-two-years category, but it is in the two- to five-years category that an important finding is seen. Four of the six relationships in this category are troubled. This contrasts markedly with proportions in other length-of-relationship ranges. It seems that if relationships have a tendency for trouble, then the trouble will show up relatively early on in the association. This finding seems reasonable enough, for by the end of four years, enough time should have elapsed to permit evaluation of one dyad member by the other. Equally, it may be two years before companies are able to differentiate between what might be regarded as "teething" problems, and those that are more substantial. The seemingly high incidence of "trouble" in the two- to five-year association period is an interesting finding, but caution is urged here in view of the small sample size involved. The other point to make regarding the "troubled" state is that some dyads experience this state relatively late in their association. It seems that there is always the possibility of the dyad entering the "troubled" state, although there is a greater likelihood of the state in the first two to five years.

Turning to the growing and static states, it is evident that dyads may experience these states at almost any time. Sales may become static soon after the relationship is established. Then again, sales growth may begin or persist long into an established

Table 2. Development state groups and length of dyadic association

| Length of relationship | New | Growing | Troubled | Static | Inert |
|---|---|---|---|---|---|
| Less than 2 years | 2 | | | | |
| $\geqslant$ 2 years $<$ 5 years | | 1 | 4 | 1 | |
| $\geqslant$ 5 years $<$ 10 years | | 2 | 1 | 1 | 1 |
| $\geqslant$ 10 years $<$ 20 years | | 1 | 1 | 1 | |
| 20 years or more | | 1 | 1 | 2 | 1 |

association. Clearly time is not an important determinant of performance, for many other factors have a more potent effect on sales, for example, selling efforts by D (distributor), M's (manufacturer) prices, UK competition.

Finally, the inert state is merely a residual one, in that the useful purpose once served by the association is past. Thus, both relationships in this state are somewhat older in years than more dynamic state dyads.

These points make it clear that the relationship development process is not necessarily orderly or progressive over time. This, in turn, implies that relationship management is crucial under this kind of export arrangement. How these relationships *are* managed and how they *should* be managed are matters that can be addressed from the P2 results.

## Proposition 2

The facts that various development states are found to exist in the 21-dyad study sample and that quite contrasting relationship characteristics were found suggest that these relationships are managed quite differently. (This point was certainly marked when the transcriptions of individual interviews were analysed). Interesting information on the range of actual management and what management might be recommended is provided by a description of troubled and static dyads and contrasting these to growing dyads.

Static state relationships were described earlier as exhibiting "partial withdrawal" characteristics. Sometimes this situation resulted from a long trading history where sales were considered difficult to expand. In other cases the association between manufacturer and overseas distributor was newer, but manufacturers were not very committed to exporting. In some instances a large home market absorbed the exporter's attention. In one case sales to other divisions within the conglomerate cushioned the firm from more competitive market realities. Along with this reduced commitment to export markets, there was also found either a reluctance to, or failure at, product adaptation to overseas market requirements. The lack of product adaptation was often matched by a lack of procedural adaptation. Thus, the distributor claimed that these exporters were often remiss in terms of replies to inquiries, delivery delays, and in matters of documentation. In this situation, distributors tended not to be very enamoured of their relationship. Nevertheless, the exporters hoped for improved sales, however unrealistic this may have been. Overt conflict was not very frequent in these relationships, even though performance was not all that it might have been. This appeared to be due to the fact that the firms were not very intensely involved with each other.

Troubled state relationships involve two subcategories, that is, troubled–growing sales and troubled–sales in decline. As a result, somewhat differing situations prevail. For example, where sales are in decline, both parties seem ready to blame the other, whereas in the two cases where sales are growing, there appeared more agreement about the problems faced. Generally, distributors in these dyads regarded their export principals as being poor performers. This complaint was levelled at various facets of the manufacturer's operations, that is, product value-for-money, technical innovativeness, support offered to distributor. In some cases exporters were critical too. Sometimes the exporter's criticism was concerned with the scale and resource abilities of the distributor, and overall lack of sales aggression was cited in other instances. In these dyads, disagreements were more frequent and open conflict more apparent. Naturally, in these circumstances thought was more often being given to alternate trading arrangements.

Both static and troubled dyads show contrasting characteristics to those of growing state dyads. These differences were presented in Table 1 and are extended here. In simple terms, growing state dyads show more commitment to exporting/importing and to the arrangement they are currently involved in. Thus, these manufacturers display a commitment not only to the UK market but also to the distributor they have chosen to operate through in that market. As a result there is more likely to be a formal distributor agreement in these dyads than in others. In addition, contacts are more frequent between these firms, as are the resources exchanged, for example, stock, reports, promotional assistance. A willingness to modify products and routines is also found in these dyads. In this way (and often in response to distributor requests), the potential presented by the market can be tapped. This is not meant to imply that no problems are faced by these companies. Sometimes product modification is less than successful, and often parties disagree on pricing matters. However, bargaining behaviour on these and other points results in workable and mutually satisfactory solutions, whereas in other development states this is less often so. Naturally, conflict is less open or serious in these dyads.

The characteristics of growing, troubled, and static development state dyads have been pointed to above. While causal relations were not tested in this study, the contrasting relationships characteristics found suggest that a change in management may well lead to a change in development state. For example, it might be that the manufacturer that increases the frequency of contact with the distributor and/or takes a more adaptive view toward exporting would help his dyadic relationship out of the troubled category.

In general terms, the study findings reaffirm the view that manufacturer–overseas distributor relations are not always (or even often) harmonious or successful. The findings presented here are instructive in that they offer insight to the manufacturer and distributor that is considering becoming involved with an overseas trading partner. The extent to which the other party will make commitments and adaptations are important factors to explore at the establishment state in a relationship, for numerous factors make success a particularly difficult objective to attain when exporting through overseas distributors.

## REFERENCES

Aldrich, H. E. An interorganizational dependency perspective on relations between the employment service and its organization set. In Kilman, R. H., Pondy, L. R. and Slevin, D. P. (eds.) *The Management or Organization Design*, Vol. II. North-Holland, New York (1976) pp. 231–66.

Beeth, G. Distributors – finding and keeping the good ones. In Thorelli, H. B. (ed), *International Marketing Strategy*. Penguin, Harmondsworth, Middlesex (1973).

Bickers, R. L. T. *Export Marketing in Europe*. Gower Press, London (1971).

Brady, D. L. and Bearden, W. O. The effect of managerial attitudes on alternative exporting methods. *Journal of International Business Studies*, **10**, winter, 69–84 (1979).

Business International. *Improving Foreign Distributor Performance.* Management Monographs, No. 22. Business International, New York (1970).

Cunningham, M. T. and Spigel, R. I. A study in successful exporting. *British Journal of Marketing*, **5**, Spring, 2–12 (1971).

Daniels, J. D., Ogram, E. W. and Radebaugh, L. H. *International Business: Environments and Operations.* Addison-Wesley, Reading, Mass. (1976).

Duguid, A. and Jacques, E. *Case Studies in Export Organization.* Her Majesty's Stationery Office, London (1971).

Etgar, M. Channel environmental and channel leadership. *Journal of Marketing Research*, **14**, 69–76 (1977).

Ford, I. D. Stability factors in industrial marketing channels. *Industrial Marketing Management*, **7**, 410–27 (1978).

Ford, I. D. The development of buyer–seller relationships in industrial markets. *European Journal of Marketing*, **14** (5/6), 339–53 (1980).

Goodnow, J. D. and Hansz, J. E. Environmental determinants of overseas market entry strategies. *Journal of International Business Studies*, **3**, Spring, 33–51 (1972).

Hallen, L. and Wiedersheim-Paul, F. Psychic distance and buyer–seller interaction. *Organization Marknad och Samhälle*, **16** (5), 308–24 (1979).

Heck, M. J. *International Trade: A Management Guide.* American Management Association, New York (1972).

Hirsch, P. M. Processing fads and fashions: an organization-set analysis of cultural industry systems. *American Journal of Sociology*, **77**, 639–59. (1972).

ITI Research. *Concentration on Key Markets: A Development Plan for Exports*, Betro Trust Committee. Royal Society of Arts, London (1975).

Johanson, J. and Wiedersheim-Paul, F. The Internationalization of the Firm – Four Swedish Cases. *Journal of Management Studies*, **12**, 307–22 (1975).

Keegan, W. K. Multinational product planning: strategic alternatives. *Journal of Marketing*, **33**, 58–62 (1969).

Marrett, C. B. On the specification of interorganizational dimensions. *Sociology and Social Research*, **56**, 83–99 (1971).

McMillan, C. and Paulden, S. *Export Agents: A Complete Guide to Their Selection and Control.* Gower Press, Epping, Essex (1974).

Mechanical Engineering EDC. *Market – The World: A Study of Success in Exporting.* National Economic Development Organization, London (1968).

Miracle, G. E. and Albaum, G. S. *International Marketing Management.* Irwin, Homewood, Illinois (1970).

Robinson, R. D. *International Business Management.* Dryden Press, New York (1973).

Rosenberg, L. J. An empirical examination of the causes, level and consequences of conflict in a high-stake distribution channel. *Ph.D dissertation*, Ohio State University (1969).

Ross, R. E. Selection of the overseas distributor: an empirical framework. *International Journal of Physical Distribution*, **3**, Autumn, 83–90 (1972).

Rosson, P. J. and Ford, I. D. Some aspects of manufacturer–distributor relations in exporting. Paper presented at the 1980 Academy of International Business Conference, New Orleans (1980a).

Rosson, P. J. and Ford, I. D. Stake, conflict, and performance in export marketing channels. *Management International Review*, **20** (4), 31–37 (1980b).

Schmidt, S. M. and Kochan, T. A. Interorganizational relationships: patterns and motivations. *Administrative Science Quarterly*, **22**, 220–34 (1977).

Stern, L. W. and Reve, T. Distribution channels as political economies: a framework for comparative analysis. *Journal of Marketing*, **44**, Summer, 52–64 (1980).

Terpstra, V. *International Marketing.* Holt, Rinehart and Winston, New York (1972).

Tookey, D. A. Factors associated with success in exporting. *Journal of Management Studies*, **1**, 48–66 (1964).

Tookey, D. A. *Export Marketing Decisions.* Penguin, Harmondsworth, Middlesex (1975).

Tookey, D. A., Lea, E. and McDougall, C. M. H. *The Exporters: A Study of Organization, Staff and Training.* Ashridge Management College, Ashridge, Berkshire (1967).

Van de Ven, A. H. On the nature, formation and maintenance of relations among organizations. *Academy of Management Review,* **1**, 24–36. (1976).

Wilkinson, I. F. Power and influence structures in distribution channels. *European Journal of Marketing,* **7**, Summer, 125–30 (1973).

Williamson, O. E. *Markets and Hierarchies: Analysis and Antitrust Implications.* The Free Press, New York (1975).

Williamson, O. E. Transaction cost economics: the governance of contractual relations. *Journal of Law and Economics,* **22**, 232–62 (1979).

# 6

# Business Dancing – The Nature and Role of Interfirm Relations in Business Strategy*

*Ian F. Wilkinson and Louise C. Young*

## INTRODUCTION

The concept of "relationship marketing" represents part of a larger theme fast gaining centre stage in many business disciplines. This is the recognition that a firm's performance depends not only upon its own efforts, skills and resources but also on the efforts, skills and resources of other organizations which provide it with valued inputs. These other organizations include suppliers of materials and components, suppliers of machinery and specialists services, channel organizations that help link a firm to its customers and organizational customers themselves. The development and management of relations with these organizations thus becomes a key focus of strategic attention, for it is through these relations that key resources are accessed and value created and delivered to customers.

In this paper we consider the nature of the relationships that exist between firms and how they can be managed. In particular, relationships are examined in terms of their degree of cooperativeness and competitiveness. We draw on some of the results of a program of research carried out in Australia to study interfirm relations in order to illustrate various types of interfirm relations that exist. We then suggest an alternative to the oft used marriage metaphor for analysing and guiding relationship management. Instead we propose a dancing analogy. We argue that this offers a richer base for considering the variety of interfirm relations that exist and persist in business systems and avoids the often implicit notion that relations must necessarily develop towards a uniform type of mature state, the "successful marriage", which is usually characterized in terms of a long-term committed relationship. Finally, we consider the implications of our analysis for the management of interfirm relations.

---

*Presented at the First International Colloquium in Relationship Marketing, Monash University, Australia, August 1993.

Reprinted with permission of Department of Marketing, Monash University, 1996, from *Asia–Australia Marketing Journal*, Vol. 2, No. 1, pp. 67–79.

## THE CO-OPERATIVE AND COMPETITIVE NATURE OF BUSINESS RELATIONSHIPS

Business relationships and individual interactions are often conceptualized as either competitive or cooperative in nature (Argyle, 1991). In cooperative interactions both parties can gain from the interaction while in competitive interactions the relevant goals of both parties cannot be simultaneously satisfied (Deutsch, 1949; Stern, 1971). It is often argued that cooperation and competition are either mutually exclusive or inversely related. Thus high or low levels of cooperation and competition cannot exist simultaneously in relationships.

Life cycle models of relationship development such as those proposed by Ford (1980) and Dwyer, Schurr and Oh (1987) imply an inverse relationship between cooperation and competition. In early phases of relationships parties are "distant" from one another, compete for benefits and take advantage of opportunities which may present themselves. In later phases, relations are characterized by increasing commitment and cohesion stemming from the increasing scope and scale of cooperation and the diminished or absent competition. In the final stage relations may decline or their patterns of interaction become institutionalized. This development pattern is depicted in Fig. 1.

An alternative view is that within a relationship cooperative and competitive aspects are likely to coexist (Nisbet, 1972). As Deutsch (1962) observes, "people may be promotively interdependent with respect to particular goals and not others. Firms manufacturing the same product may be cooperative with regard to expanding the total market but competitive with regard to the share of it each attains" (p. 278). An example would be a relation where parties cooperate to achieve reliable quality, delivery, and acceptable price but compete for the most favourable payment terms. Each party may wish to hold the money involved in their transactions as long as possible with the seller wanting cash on delivery, the buyer wanting 90 days interest-

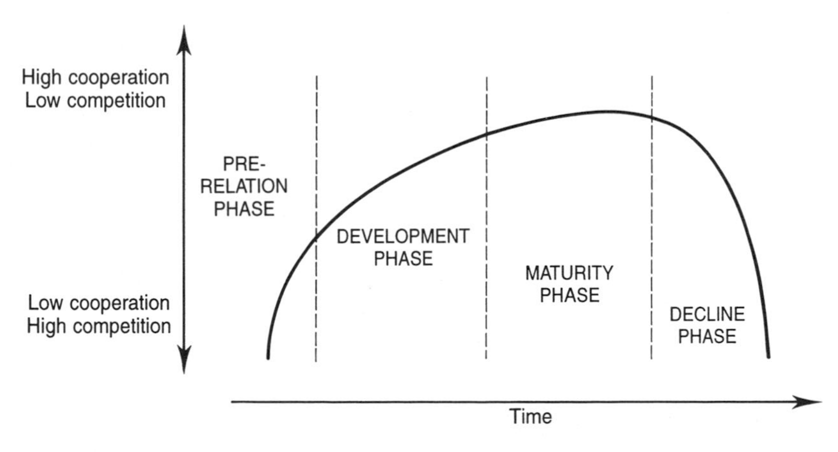


Fig. 1. A relationship life cycle model.

free credit. Parties may continue to compete for more advantageous financial terms within the context of an otherwise cooperative relationship.

Competition may be built into the legal and social norms and expectations which are themselves a type of cooperative structure. For example, the market may be structured in a way which precludes more than a certain amount of cooperation between trading parties (e.g. anti-collusion laws or price fixing legislation) and require the relation to be regulated by the market. Or, competition between suppliers may be structured as a tendering process based on lowest price, as exists in some government departments.

## FOUR TYPES OF INTERFIRM RELATIONSHIPS

In this section we describe four types of interfirm relations in terms of their cooperative and competitive characteristics. This analysis is based on some of the results of the Interfirm Relations Research Program (IRRP) which aims to develop a general methodology and questionnaire for studying all types of interfirm relations. The methodology and questionnaire have been refined through a number of studies and a large and diverse data base of interfirm relations has been created. To date over 1000 interviews concerning over 600 interfirm relations have been conducted. (More details about the IRRP research program are to be found in Young, 1992; Young and Wilkinson, 1989a, 1989b, 1992.)

As part of this research multiple item measures of various aspects of a firm's trust and cooperation in a relationship were developed. These in turn were used to identify two underlying dimensions of firms' behaviour that could be used to classify relationships. These have been labelled relationship cooperativeness and competitiveness.

Relationship cooperativeness is made up of three components. The first is a measure of the trust and cooperativeness of the respondent firm, including their concern for the interests and welfare of the trading partner and various indicators of their own cooperative behaviour. The second component is a measure of the trust and cooperativeness of the trading partner, including the level of trust in the trading partner and a belief that they act in a fair and honest way. The third component measures the positive motivation of the trading partner, including their perceived concern for the interests and welfare of the respondent's firm. Relationship competitiveness comprises measures of the extent to which the respondent firm and the trading partner try to gain advantage at the other firm's expense.

Relationships were classified into high and low cooperative and competitive groups based on whether they scored above or below average on each of these dimensions. This results in a four way classification of relations. In the following, case studies are used to illustrate some of the main characteristics of each type of relationship.

### Low Cooperation and Low Competition

Relations with low levels of cooperation and competition are likely to be those where there is a non-crucial relationship in place between the parties, i.e. there is limited or no interdependence between the trading parties. This lack of interdependence could stem from a relationship being in its infancy or near its end such that few ties have been established or remain. An example of a relationship with very low overall competition and cooperation scores is that of a large financial institution that has been providing a tyre retailer with a line of credit for twelve months. Two different respondents in the financial institution agreed that the retailer's incompetent management led the firm to trading losses. The relationship is unlikely to continue because the retailer's liquidity problems were so severe that he is perceived to be likely to go under.

Neither the financial institution nor the retailer behave particularly cooperatively or competitively. The retail firm's lack of competence and declining opportunities decrease both their cooperative and competitive options. They too may perceive themselves as likely to go under and may have already "given up". The respondent's lack of cooperation and competition seems to stem from the lack of importance of this customer to the financial institution. The retailer represents a minuscule percentage of the respondent's total business and their success or failure means little to the respondents. The respondents have obviously already written this relationship off and are, psychologically at least, in the "dissolution" stage of relationship development (as per the classification of Dwyer *et al.*, 1987).

But relations with less extreme but still below-average overall cooperation and competition scores may well be ongoing and of the mutually convenient, uninvolved, "transaction-based" type. These would include relations where firms are essentially unimportant to each other due to multi-sourcing, competitive bidding or only have intermittent need of one another.

An example of a relationship with moderately below-average cooperation scores and competition scores is that of a fast-food chain with a printer supplying promotional material. The printer in this instance is competent and has a history of successful interactions with the respondent firm. But purchaser policy precludes establishment of highly committed relationships. The printing firm is a member of a pool of similarly competent print suppliers, used always on a quote-for-job basis. Their best efforts will achieve them no more than "always-a-share" of the available business (Jackson, 1985). This situation is not unusual, as a buyer's policy is often to keep a small number of competent suppliers available (and thus in business). Such a policy would seem likely to lead to low but stable cooperation and competition in a relationship which can continue indefinitely.

### Low Cooperation and High Competition

A combination of low cooperation and high competition is often seen as the classic "poor" and/or eroding relationship. An example is a relationship between an Australian importer and a Fijian clothing manufacturer registering very high levels of competition and very low levels of cooperation. The three year relationship was described as difficult to coordinate with much negotiation needed; formal and informal rules and regulations from a variety of sources are used to organize the interactions between these two firms. There is much conflict in the relationship, in particular with respect to financial arrangements and delivery of goods. This appears to be exacerbated by very poor communication from both parties. The poor exchange of information occurs both deliberately as parties withhold information for advantage or to "get even", and due to geographic (and perhaps psychic) distance.

Both parties are very self-interested. They frequently let each other down in the pursuit of their own objectives. The respondent firm frequently coerces its trading partner to get its way. Yet threats are unlikely to be effective. The manufacturer is not dependent on the respondent and so threats lack "teeth". It is exasperation rather than their best interests which lead the respondents to threaten, as they are highly dependent on this manufacturer. They perceive that it is likely the relationship will end in the foreseeable future – primarily to their cost. There are no alternative suppliers for them.

Relationships of this type are under stress and there is consequently pressure to change. Sometimes the relationship can cease, as is occurring in the first example. In other instances relationships continue because of contractual agreements which require that they do so. Resignation characterizes a relationship with moderate to high competition and moderate to low cooperation scores. Two transportation companies operating in the leisure and tourism industry entered into a quasi joint venture which now exists solely because there is a ten year agreement tying the two firms together. The "wronged" respondent firm is merely biding their time until they can end the relationship with a partner they describe as incompetent and opportunistic. The respondent firm behaves neutrally, providing only the minimum cooperation specified in the contract and they take advantage of whatever opportunities present themselves with the aim of strengthening their future market position and weakening that of their trading partner, who will be a competitor at the end of the joint venture.

Rather than end, relationships may "improve" their character by increasing their cooperativeness, and/or decreasing their competitiveness, thus becoming a different relationship type. Some firms not now in the low cooperation–high competition group report past behaviour indicating that the relationship used to be low in cooperation and high in competitiveness but no longer is. For instance, this has been reported by firms who have introduced some sort of quality management into their relationships. A supplier to the automotive industry discussing a moderately good (and improving) relationship using a just-in-time supply system reported a relationship history of considerable competitiveness and minimal cooperation that had gradually and painfully evolved to being more cooperative and less competitive. This evolution from a "bad" past to a "better" present often is characterized by strong mutual dependence which leads to a strong motivation to make things work.

### High Cooperation and High Competition

High cooperation and high competition relationships are generally perceived by respondents to be effective. Sixty-six per cent of the relations in this group are described as good working relationships. Only 8% are perceived as not good or poor. This would indicate that the enhanced social and operational functioning often associated with high cooperation can outweigh or overcome many of the problems often thought to be associated with high competition.

Sometimes competitiveness is not perceived to be a problem but rather part of the normal practices of doing business. A firm distributing pipes prides themselves both on working well with their customers and on being loyal to their own interests, i.e. achieving everything they can for their company. They assume their trading partners do likewise and accordingly have set up systems and procedures which minimize the effect of other firms' opportunistic actions on themselves. However, this opportunism (their own and their partner's) is not perceived to be inappropriate or conflict-inducing but rather sound business practice. This is reflected in moderately high levels of cooperation and competition in the relationship discussed with a major customer.

Often above-average "competitiveness" scores are based on respondents reporting that their trading partner behaves in their own interests to the detriment of the relationship. But the score may reflect unacceptable behaviour or behaviour which has become part of the norms of a stable relationship. The manufacturing manager of a company producing consumer appliances describes a somewhat competitive and cooperative relationship with a supplier of their components in this way: "we have been doing business for so long we know each other inside out; there is tremendous involvement with each other now and (it) has been so for a long time."

Why is this relationship competitive as well as cooperative? The purchaser is now much larger, more powerful and more innovative than their relation partner. But the reverse was true 30 years ago when they commenced trading. Each firm has differing ways in which they wish to evolve and to respond to market conditions (as well as different overall conditions to respond to). They each attempt to incorporate their own approach into the relationship. The respondent firm recognizes that their supplier will either not benefit from or will not perceive the benefits of the management techniques and marketing initiatives the respondent firm continues to introduce. The supplier almost always has to be compelled into any change. But this seems to be accepted as just part of the process of their doing business, has been going for quite a while and is anticipated to continue. In other words, a combination of high competition and cooperation can be embedded in the relationship culture as long as it remains within acceptable bounds and occurs within a history of effective interactions.

The relationship between a distributor of video tapes and a retailer which has been in operation for six years is one with very high cooperation and competition scores. One informant in the distributor firm categorized the relationship as "good" and the other as "moderately good." The firms are highly interdependent and committed and both firms are reported as fairly satisfied with the relationship. The relationship has improved through time with mutual respect and trust increasing. It continues to improve slowly and is described as one of the best by a senior executive and above-average by a middle manager in the company.

This relationship is characterized by moderately high levels of conflict. There are frequent disagreements about payment and price and some disagreements about product nature and quality. It often requires considerable negotiation before they reach agreements. The firms behave opportunistically towards one another at least some of the time. The respondent firm occasionally increases prices and/or decreases product quality without advance warning to the retailer. Both firms mislead one another on occasion. However, the informants report that their conflicts with their trading partner are satisfactorily resolved.

Why do firms so interconnected, possessing ties of strong mutual trust and respect, continue to behave in these competitive ways? Or, how could norms of mutual trust and respect arise in this type of atmosphere? One possible reason is that the interdependence between these firms seems to be based on shared history rather than the unique contributions the respondents can and do make to one another. They have worked together well in the past and as a result think they will continue to do so. However, the trading partner's competitors are perceived as similar in quality to potential relation partners and there are no unique systems of procedures which tie these firms together. Therefore, the ties may not be as strong as might be the case when deeply entrenched systems and procedures and shared technology bind firms.

The second reason is that the relationship appears to exist in a "win–lose" culture. Some of the business opportunities available involve loss to the trading partner; and these opportunities are not passed by. There is no indication of the perception of mutual opportunities (i.e. win–win). This competitive culture and the behaviour associated with it are probable reasons for the high levels of conflict which characterize the relationship.

The underlying reason for this cooperation–competition mix and the nature of the dependence and culture associated with it may in part be the result of the degree of change and adapt both firms have had to deal with during the relationship's history. The video market has increased dramatically since the initiation of this relationship, as has the competition. Both firms have grown considerably in size, in particular the retailer who, during the life of the relationship, has started franchizing outlets. While both firms' prospects are seen as good, the environment is not now nor has it ever been stable.

The firms are tied together by their shared history of successful interaction and ability to overcome their conflicts. They do this in volatile industry conditions where good relationships are likely to be difficult to achieve and to maintain. This difficult environment most probably contributes to the high levels of competitiveness. The fact that the firms try hard and are able to successfully interact in such adverse conditions in turn probably contributes to the high levels of cooperativeness. Since the respondents perceive the relationship to be improving and very likely to continue in the foreseeable future (and because the market is becoming increasingly stable), one possible outcome for this relationship is that it will become increasingly cooperative and less competitive in the longer term.

### Low Competition and High Cooperation

The low competition and high cooperation relationship is often envisaged as the "ideal" relationship that firms will try to develop towards. These relationships appear to be similar to those depicted as mature relations in models of relationship development (Dwyer *et al.*, 1987; Ford, 1980) in that they are committed, usually long term and highly effective.

For example, high cooperation and low competition is found in the relationship between a manufacturer of industrial safety equipment and a supplier of its packaging material. This relationship has been in operation for 25 years with the informant being involved for the past twenty years. This is a highly committed relationship with very strong personal, though not social, links between the respective firms. Both firms are highly satisfied with the relationship.

This is a relationship between a small firm supplying a substantial amount of their output (35%) to a significantly larger customer. While there is a contract between the firms, this is relatively unimportant. The relationship is coordinated by understandings based on past interactions, although the rules and regulations of their market do play a role. Mostly however the transactions are largely routine with rates and delivery times being easily renegotiated periodically. The firms are highly interdependent and would find it difficult to replace one another. And there is no desire to do so. The respondent characterizes the success of the relationship as due to their trading partner being "a small firm extremely responsive to our (evolving) needs." This is a highly stable and mature relationship which will almost certainly continue far into the future.

The most predictable evolution and greatest stability seems to be associated with relationships which are low in competition and high in cooperation. Their life expectancy is uniformly good. Over 95% are expected to continue indefinitely. The nature and evolution of relationships of this type often resembles the descriptions of the development of cooperative relations set out in previously mentioned models of relationship development (Dwyer *et al.*, 1987; Ford, 1980). The nature of the relationship nurtures it and the ties that bind them together grow ever-stronger and more meaningful to the participants.

However, relationships may evolve to this state via a circuitous route. An example is that of a small advertising agency with its building company client. The relationship was described as being excellent for a number of years; then market conditions conspired to push the client company from a minor to major player in its industry. Their changed requirements and expectations were extremely difficult for the agency to adapt to. The relationship survived and again prospers, probably due to its strong past ties, but went through very high levels of competition for a number of years as the firms struggled to retain and adapt their relationship.

## RELATIONSHIP DEVELOPMENT PATHS

The preceding examples highlight both the range of cooperative and competitive combinations possible in relationships and the routes by which relationships may develop. A summary is provided in Fig. 2 which shows the position of the case studies described in the previous section according to their cooperativeness and competitiveness scores. Also shown are the direction(s) from which each relationship is reported to have come. This has been ascertained from a series of open-ended questions about the degree, nature and scope of change in the relationship.

Figure 1 shows that respondents' reports of the way in which their relationships have developed do not conform in any clear way to the patterns suggested in the models of relationship development. Most respondents report their relationships as moving from the low cooperation and low competition quadrant to either the high

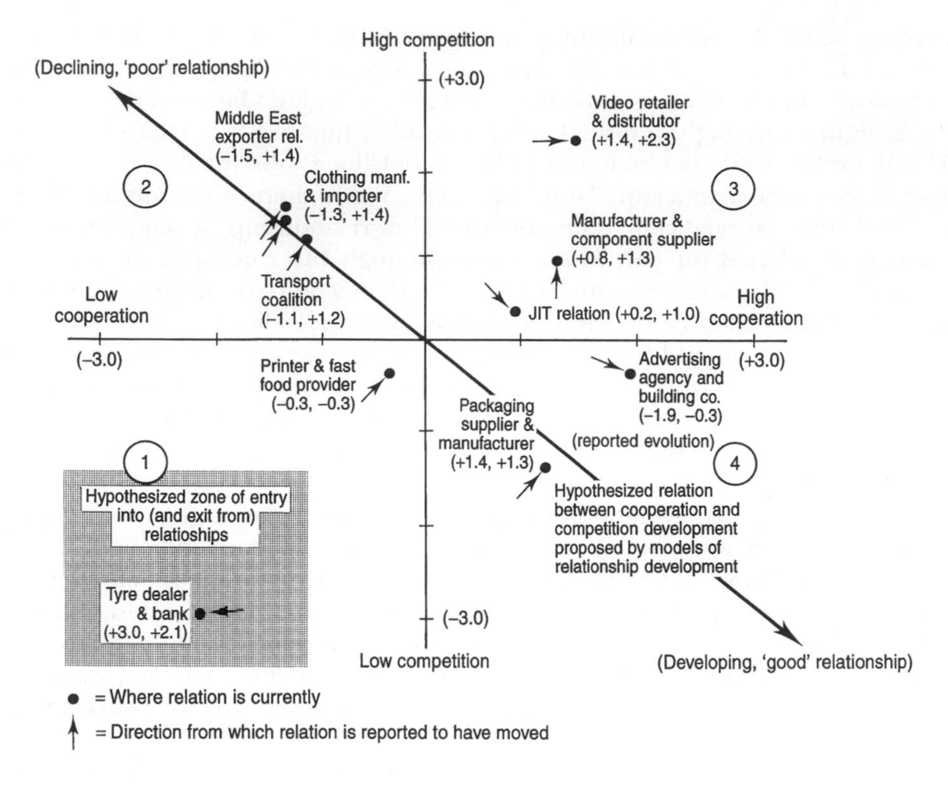


Fig. 2. The reported evolution of selected IRRP relationships.

cooperation–low competition or the low cooperation–high competition quadrant. The exception is the printer–fast food chain relationship, which reports the amounts of cooperation and competition increasing but remains in the low cooperation–low competition quadrant.

The high cooperation and high competition relationships appear to have developed from either highly cooperative and not competitive relations in the past on the one hand, or highly competitive and not cooperative patterns of past behaviour on the other. In the former cases the respondents report that high levels of competition developed subsequently as a result of difficult environmental circumstances. In the latter cases high levels of cooperation developed due to better management of interdependence, such as the development of effective conflict resolution mechanisms and/or the introduction of quality management techniques.

Only two respondents report relationships developing according to the life cycle models. The advertising agency relationship became both less cooperative and more competitive for a period of time before reversing itself and becoming more cooperative and less competitive. The relationship with just-in-time purchasing in place similarly reported both a decrease in competition and an increase in cooperation as they worked towards a more effective management of their interdependence.

## A CHOICE OF METAPHORS – DANCING VERSUS MARRIAGE

A commonly used metaphor to characterize interfirm relations is that of a marriage, e.g. Levitt (1986), Dwyer, Schurr and Oh (1987), Business International (1990). We contend that this metaphor is limited in its ability to capture the full range and diversity of interfirm relations described. The tendency is to portray relations unidimensionally in terms of a life cycle of development towards the "perfect marriage" which tends to be seen as a strong, cooperative, committed, trusting relation. The alternative to marriage usually proposed is that of "affairs" when one plays the field in terms of short term superficial encounters. Some have argued that a variety of different types of marriages can be successful. For example the "shotgun wedding" versus "the arranged marriage" versus the "career couple" can achieve success in strategic alliances (Business International, 1990). However these distinctions are more about the reasons for formation of the partnership or the character of the participants than about the nature of the alliance itself. The dance metaphor, we suggest, is more capable of capturing essential facets of relations as revealed in our studies.

First, the concept of business dancing captures the central notion of the role of cooperation. Value comes from firms working with other firms rather than from their separate actions. The issue becomes that of working with existing partners to jointly achieve more, instead of seeking permanent or transient partners which will maximize one's own rewards.

Second, the dancing metaphor leads to a process view of relationships rather than a structural view. Dancing involves an active cooperation, not a formal type of connection. A relationship is described in terms of the interaction between partners rather than the form of the link between them. In business, firms are held together through ongoing patterns of interaction that shape the nature of the attitudes and perceptions of the partners and can become institutionalized in various ways in the organizational structures or rules governing behaviour. These rules in turn shape further interaction.

Third, there are an infinite number of types of dances requiring various types and degrees of coordinated action varying from the close coordination of ballroom dancing to the looser disco dancing. Dances can be in dyads or involve larger numbers of partners as in formation and line type dancing. You cannot marry everyone but you can dance in many ways with many others. So it is with business. Many types of relations emerge in business reflecting the different types of coordinated action required, from the routine mechanical relations for standard items to strongly coordinated relations involving co-developed resources, technology, products and services.

Fourth, the different types of dances reflect the variety of coordination and cooperative tasks required in industry as a result of different technological and environmental conditions. The rules of the dance mimic the inherent logic of the processes that must be effected in a value chain. Further, the other dancers on the floor shape the problems confronted in much the way that a particular business relation is influenced by the other relations to which it is connected in both a cooperative and competitive way.

In Table 1, the dance metaphor is used to dramatize the various types of interfirm

Table 1. Contrasting the marriage and dance metaphors

| Relation type | Connection type | Type of dance | Character of dance | Quality of relationship |
|---|---|---|---|---|
| 1A Extreme Low Cooperation–Low Competition | Just met or getting divorced | Walking on or off the dance floor | Warm up or cool down exercise – not really dancing with your partner | Commencing or finishing |
| 1B Moderate Low Cooperation–Low Competition | Placid and occasional affair | Line dancing | Coordinated and in unison but not partnering | Arms length – fairly indifferent, neither good nor bad |
| 2A Extreme Low Cooperation–High Competition | Stormy affair – quarrels and throwing things or marriage by proxy (great distance between parties) | Salsa – lots of screaming and fire | Repeatedly (and perhaps deliberately) steps on foot, partners may deliberately send false signals when they lead | Likely to be poor and declining |
| 2B Moderate Low Cooperation–High Competition | Affair or unhappy marriage may be no possibility of divorce, may be in "counselling" to try to improve | Inept "New Vogue" | Going through the set motions (not very well) | Poor relation in process of change, could be for the better or the worse |
| 3A Extreme High Competition–High Cooperation | Tempestuous but devoted marriage | Latin medley, (including the tango) | Lots of unexpected tempo changes, maybe a crowded dance floor, requires an expert couple | Good relationship despite dynamic environment and probable self-interest |
| 3B Moderate High Competition–High Cooperation | Dual career marriage – joint and conflicting interests | Ballet as well as ballroom | At least as concerned about one's solo parts as the duo's | Good relationship which normalizes some opportunism |
| 4A Extreme Low Competition–High Cooperation | Marriage made in heaven | Waltz or rumba | Smooth and semi-spontaneous glide, cheek-to-cheek with someone you love | Highly committed and good quality relationship |
| 4B Moderate High Cooperation–Low Competition | Newly weds or semi-committed relationship[1] | Cha-cha-cha or new vogue | Beginners with talent or parties (re)establishing partnership, they undertake simple steps or those predetermined by rules | Relationship in process of developing higher levels of commitment |

[1]A number of different types of marriages (or affairs) could be considered as semi-committed, e.g. the "old married couple" who undertake separate but complementary tasks and interact indifferently and/or infrequently, the "arranged marriage" where partnerships have been formulated outside the dyad by third party (perhaps government or other network members), or "shotgun weddings" where parties have unwillingly contracted a relationship to ensure survival.

relations suggested in the above analysis. Of course this is only illustrative and speculative but it serves to capture some of the essence of relations in a novel way. Eight types of relationships are presented. The four types identified in our typology are further differentiated according to whether cooperation and competition levels are extreme or moderate. Each type is portrayed in terms of both the link involved using the marriage metaphor as well as in terms of a type of "dance" or coordinated action required.

The marriage metaphor captures to some extent the differences between the low cooperation–high competition relationships (which correspond to affairs) and low competition–high cooperation relationships (which correspond to marriages). In order to distinguish between other types of relations different types of marriages and affairs are suggested. Thus marriages are specified to be "tempestuous" (3A) or "made in heaven" (4A) and affairs as "stormy" (2A) or "placid" (1B).

The dance metaphor allows a large range of types of interaction to be easily envisaged. Dances are faster–slower (e.g. the salsa in 2A versus the waltz in 4A); are easier or more difficult (e.g. a new vogue dance of 1B requiring one lesson to learn the sequence of steps versus the ballet in 3B requiring years of concentrated training); require more or less physical and psychic contact (e.g. the tango in 3A versus the cha-cha in 4B); and, perhaps most importantly, are characterized by more or less interdependence (e.g. the line dance in 1B which requires rules to ensure everyone dances in unison but no partner, versus a ballet duet where a failure to catch your partner could result in a crippling injury). The quality of the dance varies depending on the specific skills of each partner (e.g. talent, fitness, and ability to lead/follow) and on their combined skills (e.g. compatible steps and styles).

In dancing, as well as in relationships, history matters. Partners develop partnership-specific skills within the course of relations. Long term partners such as the Olympic ice dancers Torville and Dean will retain only some of their abilities if they terminate their partnership and form new ones. Within a partnership many patterns of evolution are possible but these depend to some extent on past history. Parties can, through time, change the type of dancing they do together and/or add different types of dances to their repertoire. Partners move from one dance to another. But skill, based on past experience, largely influences the additional dances they may successfully attempt. Partners over time become more expert and are able to do more complicated dances together (and with other partners). But not all development paths are possible for partners. The relationship's history dictates the choices available.

## RELATIONSHIP MANAGEMENT IMPLICATIONS

Overall the foregoing results and discussion support and reinforce the "interaction approach" that has been developed by the European based Industrial Marketing and Purchasing Group (Håkansson, 1982; Ford, 1990; Axelsson and Easton, 1992). Several types of implications for relationship management emerge.

First, relationship management is not so much about one party developing and imposing a structure on the relationship to their advantage but about managing an ongoing process of action and interaction taking place on multiple levels between organizations. The traditional distinction between marketing and buying behaviour approaches to business markets is replaced by an integrated approach in which both aspects are closely interwoven. Further, interpersonal relations and social interaction play an important role in facilitating or inhibiting relations and should be seen as part of the overall management process.

This integrated relationship orientation is not encompassed by some extension of the marketing mix paradigm, such as adding another P for people or politics, or by a more sensitive application of existing elements of the mix. It calls for us to stop "P-ing" on the customer and to focus instead on interacting and cooperating with them.

Relationship management is not something that one firm does to another in a stimulus response manner, but a two-way process in which initiatives can be taken by either party with each responding to the problems and opportunities of the other. In terms of our dance metaphor we must recognize that following is as important a part of the skill of dancing as leading and the two styles must match to be mutually supportive. Similarly, relationship management is as much about "being manageable", including being responsive to the initiatives of others and facilitating their relating to you, as about managing others, i.e. being the initiator. An emphasis on being manageable is particularly relevant when the perspective of the less powerful actor in a relationship is taken. However, the perspective often taken in discussion is that of the powerful actor, initiating things and dictating terms and conditions. The less powerful actor situation requires equal attention as many firms are likely to find themselves in this situation. Moreover, research suggests that less powerful firms can play an important role in introducing change to networks of relations (Easton, 1992).

Relationship management is as much about creating value through relationships as it is about protecting and safeguarding the value of existing assets and resources. Value is created through jointly planning and mutually adapting products, processes, people and resources. These adaptations result in what are termed relationship specific investments or assets, which bond the parties together and make them mutually dependent. The focus of attention in much of the literature tends to be on the potential problems created by such investments and assets due to one firm being able to exploit the dependency of another. For example, the transaction cost literature is largely devoted to the problem of designing relationships between exchange partners (or governance structures in their terms), which protect against such risks. Obviously these risks cannot be ignored but here we stress that relationship specific investments are an important potential outcome of a relationship, rather than being something that pro-exists "outside" the relationship and determines the way the relationship should be designed. Relationship specific assets such as mutual trust and respect, mutual understanding, and personal relationships as well as more tangible adaptations of products and processes arise though a process of working together over time. They are an integral part of the relationship, not something protected by the relationship. They are not easily or quickly developed or replaced and yet they can have an important bearing on the strength and viability of a company.

Our results indicate that there is no one, ideal type of relationship. High performing relationships are to be found of all of the four types described. For example, as previously noted, relationships high in both cooperation and competition are often perceived as effective. The appropriate type of relationship obviously depends on the objectives of the parties involved, the tasks to be performed and the environment in which the relationship operates. This does not always dictate the development of strongly committed, long term cooperative relations (Low, 1994). Performance evaluation in a relationship is also relative rather than absolute. It depends on the expectations and comparisons available to those involved and these are provided by history and the environment. History matters in that the problems and issues confronted over time in a relationship and how they have been dealt with will influence both perceptions of benefit and expectations of benefit. The environment of relationships establishes more general norms and standards of behaviour expected. The case of video industry relation is an example of an environment creating limited expectations of non opportunistic behaviour.

Following on from the previous point, there is not one best way of managing and directing relationships as they are not all headed in the same direction and do not operate from similar starting places. Elsewhere we have suggested four broad types of strategies firms can adopt in dealing with situations in which the behaviour of another firm affects the outcomes of the firm's own behaviour (Wilkinson and Young, 1994). Each one results in quite different types of relations between the firms involved. a) A firm can spend resources to better predict the behaviour of the other firm and adjust its behaviour accordingly. In complex dynamic environments such predictions can become costly and unreliable. b) A firm can attempt to control the behaviour of the other firm through the exercise of power. This strategy is only available to the powerful and, depending on the way power is exercised, can have adverse effects on the future development of the relationship. c) A firm can attempt to reduce the dependence on another firm. This could be done by switching to standardized product or service inputs that are available from many firms and relying on arms length market dealing. Alternatively, vertical integration could be used to internalize the activities of the supplier, bringing it under direct control. Of course, technological and market constraints can limit the feasibility of either of these approaches. d) Lastly, a firm can seek to cooperate with the other firm to jointly plan and implement strategies for mutual advantage. It is this latter type of strategy that has been the subject of much recent attention in the business literature. Evidence of all four types of strategies and the relationships that result are to be found in the foregoing analysis.

Two further issues affecting the development of relationship management strategies are highlighted by our research and analysis. First, it should be noted that firms may not be able to choose their relationship partners freely and this will affect the nature and quality of the relationship management strategies available. Lack of choice can arise because of an absence of other firms capable of providing the necessary inputs or because firms may be locked in to particular relations as a result of past contracts or agreements. Second, our research indicates that cooperativeness and competitiveness should be regarded as separate dimensions of relations rather than opposites. This means that strategies to increase cooperation and reduce competition are not simple alternatives to each other. A balance of both is needed.

As a final point it should be noted that the focus here has been on the nature and management of relations between pairs of firms. But relationships do not occur in isolation from each other. Firms are connected to other firms both directly and indirectly through networks of relationships. These networks are the means by which resources are developed and accessed and products and services created and delivered to end customers. They both constrain firms' behaviour but also provide opportunities. Firms have to consider both their micro and macro positions in the network and how the two affect each other (Mattsson, 1984; Johansson and Mattsson, 1992). Micro positions concern the management of individual relations, whereas macro positions refer to a firm's position in the network as a whole. The macro position is not a simple aggregation of micro positions and changes in relations in one part of the network can have profound implications for relations in other parts. Hence, the management of individual relations must take into account the effects on other relations. One consequence of this is that evaluating relations becomes more problematic, because relations can act as conduits or bridges to other firms and relations. Hence the value of a particular relationship and its performance cannot be assessed without considering its network context. Similarly, effective decisions about commencing and terminating relations are made by considering the structure of the network and one's position within it. A focus on networks leads to new ways for understanding and developing business strategy, as well as several challenging research opportunities that are only now beginning to be explored.

## REFERENCES


Argyle, M. *Cooperation: The Basis of Sociability.* Routledge, London (1991).

Axelsson, B. and Easton, G. (eds) *Industrial Networks: A New View of Reality.* Routledge, London (1992).

Business International *Making Alliances Work.* Business International Ltd., Economist Group, London, March (1990).

Deutsch, M. A theory of cooperation and competition. *Human Relations,* **2**, 129–51 (1949).

Deutsch, M. Cooperation and trust: some theoretical notes. In Jones, M. R. (ed) *Nebraska Symposium on Motivation,* University of Nebraska Press, Lincoln (1962), pp. 275–319.

Dwyer, F. R., Schurr, P. H. and Oh, S. Developing buyer seller relations. *Journal of Marketing,* **51** (2), 11–28 (1987).

Easton, G. Industrial networks: a review. In Axelsson, B. and Easton, G. (eds) *Industrial Networks: A New View of Reality.* Routledge, London, (1992), pp. 1–27.

Ford, I. D. The development of buyer seller relations in industrial markets. *European Journal of Marketing,* **14**, 339–53 (1980).

Ford, I. D. *Understanding Business Markets: Interaction, Relationships and Networks.* Academic Press, London (1990).

Håkansson, H. (ed). *International Marketing and Purchasing of Industrial Goods by the IMP Group.* John Wiley, Chichester (1982).

Jackson, B. B. *Winning and Keeping Industrial Customers.* Lexington Books, Lexington, Massachusetts (1985).

Johansson, J. and Mattsson, L.-G. Network positions and strategic action – an analytical framework. In Axelsson, B. and Easton, G. (eds) *Industrial Networks: A New View of Reality.* Routledge, London (1992), pp. 205–217.

Levitt, T. *The Marketing Imagination.* The Free Press, New York (1986).

Low, B. Long-term relationships in industrial marketing: reality or rhetoric? Paper presented at 10th IMP Conference, Groningen September 29–October 1 (Department of Marketing Working Paper Series 94/2, University of Western Sydney, Nepean) (1994).

Mattsson, L.-G. An application of a network approach to marketing: defending and changing market positions. In Dholkia, N. and Arndt, J. (eds) *Changing the Course of Marketing: Alternative Paradigms for Widening Marketing Theory*. JAI Press, Greenwich, Connecticut (1984).

Nisbet, R. A. Cooperation. In *International Encyclopedia of Social Sciences*, Vol. 3. Collier–Macmillan, New York (1972), pp. 384–90.

Stern, L. W. Antitrust implications of a sociological interpretation of competition, conflict, and cooperation in the marketplace. *The Anti Trust Bulletin*, **16** (3), 509–30 (1971).

Wilkinson, I. F. and Young, L. C. The space between: the nature and role of interfirm relations in business. AMA Research Conference on Relationship Marketing, Emory University, Atlanta, Georgia (1994).

Young, L. C. The nature and role of trust and cooperation in marketing channels. *Ph.D. thesis*, School of Marketing, University of New South Wales (1992).

Young, L. C. and Wilkinson, I. F. The role of trust and cooperation in marketing channels: a preliminary study. *European Journal of Marketing*, **23** (2), 109–22 (1989a).

Young, L. C. and Wilkinson, I. F. 1989 Survey of interfirm relations –preliminary findings. Report 89/3, Interfirm Relations Research Program, School of Marketing, University of New South Wales (1989b).

Young, L. C. and Wilkinson, I. F. Towards a typology of interfirm relations in marketing systems. 8th I.M.P. Conference, Lyon, France (1992).

# Part II

## Business Markets as Networks

In the introduction to this book, I said that in order to understand what goes on inside a business company we need to know about its relationships. To understand what goes inside a company's relationships we need to try to understand the network of which they form part. Network analysis is not something that is separate and distinct from relationship analysis. Instead, networks can often best be seen as *sets* of connected relationships. But analysis at the network level also provides insights into the nature of business behaviour that cannot be gained by observation at the level of individual relationships. It is only at the network level that we can start to make sense of the dynamics of many business markets. These include such phenomena as complex joint ventures and consortia, the processes of technological evolution between companies and the increasingly fluid patterns of activity of many companies that are dependent on alliances to combine the technologies of other companies with their own increasingly concentrated skills.

In this section I have included a number of readings that provide a basis for trying to understand networks and I have tried to choose those that provide some sort of link between the relationship and the network level. Of course, once we move from the level of the single relationship, or even from the portfolio of a company's relationships, we introduce a further level of complexity. This complexity is apparent in a number of the readings here. However, the selection does provide both an overview of the characteristics of business networks and a number of concepts for their analysis.

We start with a reading by Easton, which provides a general review of the area. This reading relates some of the ideas on networks by the IMP group to other research traditions and also discusses a number of different views of business networks that will be useful to the reader of later articles in the book. The first view is the one mentioned above, which sees networks as sets of *relationships*. The second is of networks as some sort of *structure* for the activities that go on between firms. The third view sees networks as the aggregation of the separate *positions* of different firms. The idea of network position will recur a number of times in the book. Finally, Easton discusses the *processes* that occur in networks. The second reading also forms a building block for later pieces. In this one Håkansson and Johanson provide a simple model of what happens in business networks using three terms that are common in the network literature; *activities, actors* and *resources.*

Following from this general introduction to ideas on networks, the third reading by Håkansson and Snehota discusses what some of these ideas mean for companies. They draw the conclusion that looking at inter-company networks will lead to changes in many traditional assumptions about how we can manage in business markets and judge organizational effectiveness in them. More profoundly, a network perspective leads to changes in our understanding of the boundaries that surround companies, the processes of strategy and, indeed, the nature of companies themselves. The fourth reading is also by Håkansson and Snehota and is taken from a book that reports on the IMP2 project into business networks. It is included at this stage because it shows how ideas on the nature of a single business relationship are linked to the pattern of a number of relationships of each company, as well as to a wider network. The paper draws conclusions on what this means for the managerial task in business markets.

The following two readings are both by Johanson and Mattsson. The first develops ideas on network position further and the second takes a network approach to the issue of company internationalization. This reading is useful for its examination of different positions that a company might have in an international network and also because it contrasts the network approach to understanding the process of internationalization with other, more traditional, views. The next reading by Hallén, "Infrastructural networks in international business" provides an interesting contrast to the previous works in this section. The reading draws an important distinction between organization-centred networks, such as those discussed elsewhere in the section, and person-centred networks. Hallén uses the networks of chairpersons and chief executives to illustrate this distinction.

The final reading, by Anderson, Håkansson and Johanson, is also the most recent. The reading presents a strong conceptualization of the connectedness of individual business relationships within complex networks, and illustrates this conceptualization with two case examples.

## CONTENTS

# 1

# Industrial Networks: A Review

*G. Easton*

## INTRODUCTION

Research in the area which encompasses organisational marketing, business to business marketing and organisational buying behaviour has developed in two quite different traditions. The first, and original, approach has, to a large extent, taken its lead from consumer marketing, has by and large opted for study of either buyers or sellers and is generally associated with writers in the United States. The second tradition has its home in Europe, has been influenced by work outside the marketing area and focuses on the "space" between organisations. Neither exhibits monolithic paradigms; both traditions have had rrom for a variety of approaches. Within the European tradition, and a twenty-year history allows the use of the word, the industrial network approach has emerged as a separate and viable paradigm in its own right. It shares with other approaches a belief that the existence of relationships, many of them stable and durable, among firms engaged in economic exchange provides a compelling reason for using interorganisational relationships as a research perspective. It differs from other approaches mainly in terms of its scope. It is concerned to understand the totality of relationships among firms engaged in production, distribution and the use of goods and services in what might best be described as an industrial system. The boundaries of such a system are problematic and will probably vary depending upon the purposes for which the boundary is being drawn. The focus of research is, ultimately, the network and not the firm or the individual relationship, although firms and relationships must be studied if networks are to be understood.

Much of the work on industrial networks has been published but in far-flung places that are often difficult to access. What is surprising, and gratifying, is that it is available at all to an international audience since the bulk of the work has been done in Sweden by Swedes. The objective of this review it to provide a stepping off point for the remainder of the book. To do so it must be relatively comprehensive yet succinct. It has not been an easy task. For such a young paradigm there exist a

Reprinted by permission of International Thomson Industrial Networks: A Review by G. Easton from *Industrial Networks: A New View of Reality*, Edited by B. Axelsson and G. Easton, pp. 3–27.

remarkable number of alternative views and perspectives, sometimes espoused by the same author at different times. In addition since these are views of the same phenomena from different angles they are irreconcilable and cannot be integrated and I have not attempted to do so. However the paradigm is socially rather cohesive and there are many shared assumptions.

The problem of multiple perspectives is not an uncommon one especially in the social sciences. Morgan (1986) has championed the cause of a metaphorical mode of analysis. In *Images of Organisation* he apportions the literature on organisations among a series of metaphors. More recently Mintzberg (1988) has described five alternative metaphors for strategy. A similar approach will be taken here. Four metaphors for industrial networks are used to structure the chapter. They are: networks as relationships; structures; processes; and positions. However, first, to set the scene, the history and provenance of the industrial networks approach is described. The final section is concerned with the normative implications of network ideas and areas of application.

## PROVENANCE

The industrial network approach has a number of progenitors although the exact relationships to their offspring is not always clear. At an early stage, studies of distribution channels both in Europe and the United States were concerned with the relationships between channel members and dealt with issues of power and control which are also held to be important for industrial networks. The nature of the functions, retailing/distribution, meant that a relatively narrow approach to inter-organisational activities could be taken and the assumption of a homogeneous channel could be justified. This assumption is not made in the industrial network approach. In a parallel field of study, research into the process of internationalisation has dealt with similar issues, i.e. how do firms organise to export and manufacture abroad. The interaction approach, which was a product of the first, pan European, I.M.P. study used as the basic unit of analysis the dyadic relationship between buyers and sellers of manufactured products in different countries (Hakansson, 1982b). The I.M.P. group successfully demonstrated the existence of stable long-term buyer–seller relationships and were able to characterise their richness and diversity in a four element analytical framework. Industrial networks, by definition, comprise many such relationships and so any account of them not only has to sacrifice some of the descriptive richness of the interaction approach but also has to concentrate on those aspects which have particular implications for network operation.

The resource dependence model provides another perspective on inter-organisational relationships (Pfeffer and Salancik, 1978). Unlike the interaction approach it is concerned with a focal organisation but attempts to describe the multiplicity of relationships of any industrial or commercial organisation. The basic assumption is that organisations use these relationships in order to gain access to the resources which are vital to their continuing existence. Firms access resources not only through suppliers and customers but also through banks, shareholding institutions, government, distributors, consultants, associations, etc. The resource dependence model mainly focuses on the way in which firms handle individual relationships. It sees the behaviour of firms as the resultant of two opposing forces; the competing and often contradictory desires of stakeholders within organisations and the external requirements of the organisations to which and from which resources flow. The resource dependence model brings to the study of industrial systems a vision of the multiplicity of relationships and the dominant role of resources in determining behaviour. However it differs from the industrial network perspective by concentrating on the actions of a single firm. The network, or more accurately net, is viewed through the eyes of that firm and the working of the network is seen to be of secondary importance. In other words the units of analysis are very different.

The second I.M.P. study has, in some ways, a similar focus. It is concerned with individual relationships as in the first study but has moved on to examine each relationship in the context of the other relationships a particular firm may have. It therefore operates at a higher level of aggregation than the first programme of work and might be said to provide one form of link between studies of firms buying and selling and the full blown network level of analysis.

By contrast theories of social exchange are primarily interested in explaining the operation of network phenomena: "The primary focus of social exchange theory is the explanation of the emergence of various forms of social structure, including networks and corporate groups" (Cook and Emerson, 1984). The central construct of social exchange theory is that of connection. "Two exchange relationships are connected to the extent that exchange in one relationship is contingent, positively or negatively, upon exchange in the other relationship." This concept allows us to move beyond the dyad, sequentially, to invoke and model system-wide effects. It defines the idea of indirect relationships where A may affect C through B simply because there are connected exchange relationships between all three parties. Viewing an industry as a network of interconnected exchange relationships implies adopting a systemic focus and level of explanation. In practice the approach of social exchange theory has been to test simple analytical models of network behaviour using experimental methods. It is thus rather distant from the empirical and naturalistic approach adopted by workers in the industrial network tradition. Nevertheless the debt is a very real one. Social exchange theory argues that complex network behaviour can result from the interplay of relatively simply defined exchange relationships. It is an aggregative approach and one which has influenced at least one strand of network methodology as well as providing a building block for theoretical developments.

By contrast, research into communication and social networks has been largely inductive in character (Rogers and Kincaid, 1981). The unit of analysis is commonly the individual in a social context and the network is defined in terms of the patterns of communication and/or social interactions occurring regularly between and among those individuals. The problems have occurred not in data collection but in analysis. The large numbers of links which may exist in such a network make the discernment of patterns particularly difficult. In response a whole series of matrix manipulation techniques have been developed. While these are only just beginning to be used to characterise industrial networks, network studies have influenced the language and orientation of the industrial network approach. In particular they share the view that networks should be treated as a whole, that network boundaries are problematic and that network models must be dynamic in nature.

Defining a paradigm is often helped by making clear what it is not. The industrial network approach has used traditional, and not so traditional economics, as stalking horses. In particular the notions of pure competition with atomistic and unconnected firms striking individual and instant deals with one another, in the face of competitors doing the same thing, is rejected. If strong relationships exist among buyers and sellers then the facile switching among easily available alternatives which is assumed in economic analysis no longer applies. History becomes important. Inertia is introduced into the system and the rules of optimum resource allocation fail as relational constraints start to bite and motives other than short term profit maximisation begin to dominate.

The branch of economics described as industrial organisation theory may be said to address similar issues to those dealt with by the industrial networks approach. In particular it is concerned with the structure of industries and the relationships among firms in those industries. However, once again, the relationships between suppliers and customers are assumed to be atomistic and, in this model, marginal to the central issue of rivalry among the competitors that defines, somewhat narrowly, the boundaries of the industry. Indeed in Porter's articulation of industrial organisation theory customers are identified as "extended rivals" in that they constrain the focal organisation in direct relation to the power they are capable of drawing upon.

The development of institutional economics which gives transaction costs a major role in determining vertical market mechanisms, comes closest to addressing the same issues as the industrial network approach (Williamson, 1975). It assumes that transactions between suppliers are not without friction and that, as a result, costs arise which are dependent on the particular nature of the transactions. These costs, in turn, help determine which organisational form – free markets, vertical integration or bilateral governance – is most likely to emerge assuming firms seek to minimise costs. Johanson and Mattsson (1986), however, argue that the similarities are more superficial than profound. The transaction cost approach focuses on the single relationship not the network. It assumes equilibrium under cost minimisation and economic rationality (albeit bounded). Most fundamentally it has little to say about the most interesting case, at least from a network view, that of bilateral governance. This omission is somewhat rectified in Williamson's later work when it is admitted that bilateral governance may be a stable organisational form (Williamson, 1985).

Similarly the model of marketing which derives from microeconomic assumptions is also rejected for most organisational markets. It is no longer sensible to assume seller dominated markets where the firm, as the focal unit, sets the mix parameters and the faceless market responds. Instead the market is seen to have a face. Many individual customers may be distinguished and dealt with separately which, in turn, creates a new and different set of marketing (and buying) problems. While the industrial network approach acknowledges these issues it is important to recognise a major difference in orientation. The focus is upon the network and not the individual firm. The goal is primarily description and explanation not prescription. A network perspective has profound normative implications but they spring from the approach rather than drive it.

Having described the roots, real or imaginary, of the industrial network approach we will now examine it from four different angles in the expectation that by doing so we may come to an understanding of its nature and essence.

## NETWORKS AS RELATIONSHIPS

If there are no "relationships", using the word in a rather general sense, between buying and selling organisations in an industrial system then the free market models beloved of economists should reign. In other words relationships among firms are the *sine qua non* of an industrial network approach. One approach to industrial networks is therefore to regard them as aggregations of relationships. While modelling the network is the ultimate goal it could be argued that one line of attack is to start at the most basic level and build. However there is nowhere in evidence the naive belief that the process of aggregation is likely to be simple or additive. "Adding together" relationships provides massive opportunities for systemic structures to emerge which overlay the simple and apparent linkages. Nevertheless relationships are important in determining network properties and a knowledge of their behaviour has important implications for understanding networks. The interaction approach provides a rich model of relationships between firms buying from and selling to one another. Much of this richness has, of necessity, to be discarded when an aggregate approach to relationships is required. In this section only those characteristics of single relationships which are thought to have relevance for the structure and processes of networks are discussed.

One analysis of interfirm behaviour distinguishes between relationships and interactions (Johanson and Mattsson, 1987). The relationship elements of the behaviour are rather general and long-term in nature. Interactions, by contrast, represent the here and now of interfirm behaviour and "constitute the dynamic aspects of relationships" (Johanson and Mattsson, 1987). Thus there is an interplay between the two variables. Interactions, in their turn, are said to comprise exchange processes and adaptation processes. The former represent the day-to-day exchanges of a business, social or informational nature that occur between firms. The latter comprises the processes by means of which firms adjust products, production and routines.

Relationships, in their various manifestations, will be discussed first. They may be presented as comprising four elements: mutual orientation; the dependence that each has, or believes it has, upon the other; bonds of various kinds and strengths, and the investments each has made in the relationship. Clearly each of these elements is strongly interrelated with the others and is itself capable of being further decomposed and elucidated.

One of the preconditions for the existence of an interfirm relationship is what has been termed mutual orientation. "This implies that the firms are prepared to interact with each other and expect each other to do so" (Mattsson, 1988). Cooperation is required and this depends, at least in terms of one view of cooperation, on the relationships between the firms' objective. "Vigorous relationships presuppose the existence of a certain complementarity between the objectives of the parties" (Hagg and Johanson, 1983). The cooperation may be instrumental in that each firm seeks to gain different ends from the same means, e.g. access to a new process and a new market entry from the same development programme. Alternatively the objectives might be commonly held, e.g. advancing a new technology.

Complementarity of objectives is a rather abstract rationale for entering into a relationship. Why would a firm seek, consciously or unconsciously, to develop relationships? A number of instrumental reasons can be identified and these appear to fall into two main categories. The first exploits the complementarities of an individual partner. "[R]elationships allow of a more effective acquisition of resources and sale of product" (Hagg and Johanson, 1983). By knowing a partner firm better and appreciating what they can do and have to offer, it is possible both to reduce costs and increase sales. Needs can be matched more exactly. Adaptations may be made which both reduce costs of production or transfer and increase effectiveness of exchanges. Knowledge may be created between firms by combining the existing knowledge and skills they both possess. Relationships also provide continuity and stability with an increased ability to plan, reduce costs and increase effectiveness.

The second set of rationale for entering into a relationship concern a firm's ability to exploit network access. A relationship implies a measure of control over another organisation and, through that organisation, the environment. The consequent reduction in uncertainty and increase in stability may be very valuable objectives for many organisations. Similarly a relationship offers access to third parties who may have resources that are either valuable or essential to survival. One such resource is information and relationships can serve as data conduits and provide firms with a perspective on what is taking place in distant parts of the network. Alternatively, through relationships, partners may be mobilised against third parties, i.e. competitive suppliers.

Dependence is the second element which was used to describe relationships and in some senses may be regarded as the price a firm may have to pay for the benefits that a relationship bestows. Dependence is partly a matter of choice and partly a matter of circumstances. An extreme example is the case of dealing with a monopolist or a monopsonist. Since there are by definition no alternatives, circumstances dictate a strong degree of dependence. However in the long-term a firm may choose to make changes in its operations such that it is no longer dependent upon a single source. Alternatively, even where choice exists a firm may decide to trade off the benefits of flexibility for the benefits, described above, which can accrue from a strong relationship.

Dependence brings with it the problems of power and control. If firms are mutually dependent then they may have difficulty dealing with other relationships but should be able to manage the focal relationship reasonably well. However, if the power is asymmetrically distributed then the relationship will not only be difficult to manage but the benefits for the junior partner less easy to realise.

The third element of a relationship is the bond which may be said to exist between firms. A bond implies a measure of tying, albeit unspecified, between partner firms which is implicit in all that has already been discussed. Firms are bonded together and are not usually entirely free to dissolve those bonds at will. The strength of a bond is a difficult parameter to measure. One suggestion for an operational procedure is to define it as the capacity to withstand a disruptive force (Easton and

Araujo, 1986). They identified different disruptive situations corresponding to the application of different kinds of force to a bond. Some bonds might well be able to withstand some kinds of force better than others, e.g. responding to changing needs of a partner compared with responding to the arrival of an alternative partner. In network terms strong bonds provide a more stable and predictable structure and one which is more likely to be able to withstand change. Weakly bonded networks are likely to be rather volatile. Patterns of strong and weak bonding provide one measure of the structure of networks in a way analogous with communication networks.

A related characteristic of network relationships is longevity. The original I.M.P. study demonstrated the existence of long-term relationships but the sampling frame did not allow estimation of the overall longevity of different types of relationship (Hakansson, 1982b). Gadde and Mattsson (1987) carried out a more complex analysis of relationship duration within the context of other relationships. They concluded that while individual relationships might endure, the changes to the total system of supplier relationships were rather large. Gradual changes were made, rarely a simple one for one exchange, and these accumulated so that at the end of a relatively few years the whole supplier structure had radically altered. These results would no doubt be reflected in network dynamics. Thus we would expect network structures to be stable but not static; they would gradually change in response to changes external and internal to the network. Nor should it be assumed that the nature of relationships will remain constant even though measures of product flow are the same. What is being exchanged may have little relationship to how it is being exchanged. The relationship between longevity and strength is not a simple one. Even a strongly bonded network will change if the external forces are powerful enough. A weakly bonded network may continue to exist in the same form in benign and unchanging conditions.

Similarly it can be argued that relationships may spring into being fully fledged and rather quickly should the circumstances be appropriate (Easton and Smith, 1984). Thus the applicability of the network concept is not entirely dependent upon the existence of long-term relationships. Similarly the stronger the relationship the more closely will the relationship be expected to determine the behaviour of firms towards one another. But weak relationships are still a far cry from no relationships and while the structure and processes of "weak" networks will differ from those of "strong" they are still, it is argued, best treated as networks. In other words where any form of relationship may be held to exist among firms in an industrial system a network approach will be appropriate.

Bonds thus far have been treated as unitary phenomena and there are arguments for so doing. However it was also thought to be helpful in some of the earlier writing on industrial networks to decompose the elements of a bond, or to describe different types of bond (Mattsson, 1984). Bonds may be thought of as having, variously, economic, social, technical, logistical, administrative, informational, legal and time based dimensions.

The economic element of a relationship is largely self evident and, when discussing industrial systems, may be regarded as the *sine qua non* for the existence of a network. Other types of networks may not be fundamentally economic in nature. Clearly the portfolio of products and services offered and the price agreed to consummate the exchange, are important and highly visible evidences of a relationship. The economic rationale for strong bonding is clearly dependent upon the satisfaction with the terms of the current exchange and the presence or absence of alternatives. More formal economic bonds may also exist as where firms invest in one another or in joint ventures or provide extended credit facilities. However the very existence of noneconomic exchange aspects of a relationship serves to down play the contribution of price in determining the behaviour of the two parties. Indeed the stronger the bond the less importance economic factors, at least as conventionally defined, have in the processes of exchange (Hagg and Johanson, 1983). It should also be pointed out that there are a number of types of relationship in a network where direct economic exchange is absent though other forms of relationship (primarily informational) may exist, e.g. between competitors.

Social exchange has been identified as a significant factor in the overall strength of interfirm relationships. Mattsson (1988) cites Blau's description of the process. "Social exchange relations evolve in a slow process, starting with minor transactions in which little trust is required because little risk is involved and in which both partners can prove their trustworthiness, enabling them to expand their relation and engage in major transactions" (Blau, 1968). And familiarity breeds affection. Social relations between firms are the resultant of the relations of the individuals involved. There is no guarantee that relations will be uniform although social pressures within a firm may induce conformity. It is also possible that social bonds will transcend and even replace economic bonds as the *raison d'être* for the relationship to continue. Social relationships extend beyond individual firms. Networks will usually have a social dimension characterised by patterns of individual social contacts (Hamfelt and Lindberg, 1987). They may also have what might be described as a culture, i.e. commonly held beliefs about the basis of social activity within the network.

Technical bonds stem from the characteristics of the products and services exchanged. Firms adjust products and processes to their partner's requirements, subject to the constraints of technology and economics. They also acquire technical knowledge some of which may be rather specific to one relationship. Partners adjust logistically to each other in respect of the physical transfers of product or execution of services. Such adjustments may be rather permanent or relatively flexible in nature. Administrative systems vary from organisation to organisation. However they have to interface where there is a continuing relationship. Again procedures may have to be adapted or else sub-routines or heuristics developed to cope.

Information is the common currency of interfirm relations. All of the other dimensions described operate through the communication of information, from the formal transmission of orders and invoices to the tone of voice used in a telephone conversation. Stocks of information, i.e. knowledge, may also be regarded as an investment that a firm can make in respect of a particular partner. Information clearly forges its own networks (Rogers, 1984). The collection of information is one of the primary uncertainty reduction activities that firms adopt and networks provide a necessary vector. The relative ease of exchange and transmission means that it can flow around a network very quickly when the communication nodes are in place and connected. In this sense it differs from the slower responses that are characteristic of the social or technical dimensions.

Firms may be bound legally by contracts or by rather more general articles of involvement or ownership. Such bonds are highly visible but may be less binding than they appear. Indeed the need to invoke a legal framework suggests that other types of bonding may not be working particularly well. Firms must also learn to adjust to what might be called the rhythms of their partners. There are characteristic activities, e.g. new product developments, which have a particular time horizon and urgency for the organisation concerned. Partner organisations have to learn what the time patterns of various crucial activities are and how to adjust to them or have them adjusted.

It is clear that other dimensions and subdivisions of existing dimensions could be used to better characterise bonds. However the process is not without penalties. In particular such an analytical approach courts the danger of ignoring the necessarily holistic nature of bonds:

> The different types of bonds are not independent of each other. Thus social bonds of more than minimal strength and content might e.g. be necessary for the development of knowledge based bonds which in turn might be a prerequisite for strong technical bonds. (Mattsson, 1984).

This whole/part problem occurs throughout the network literature largely because of the scope of the phenomena it is expected to describe.

The fourth element of relationships identified by Johanson and Mattsson is investment. "Investments are processes in which resources are committed in order to create, build or acquire assets which can be used in the future" (Johanson and Mattsson, 1986). In this case the investment is in a specific relationship. The returns to such an investment might include "The rendering more effective of the current transactions, accumulation of knowledge, control possibilities *vis-à-vis* the other party" (Hagg and Johanson, 1983). Such an investment may have all the hallmarks of a traditional investment, i.e. the purchase of a new machine solely for the purpose of supplying a particular customer. This is often termed hard investment. More likely the resources are people and their time. Soft investment of this kind may include such things as acquiring knowledge of the technical, administrative or logistical characteristics of a partner. It may also be time spent in establishing good social relationships. In one sense any resource committed above and beyond that required to execute the current exchanges may be regarded as an investment. As a result it is difficult to distinguish between investments and recurrent costs (Hagg and Johanson, 1983).

The recurrent costs of exchange activities are close to what some institutional economists call transaction costs. They are the costs of doing business with someone else. In economists' terms they represent the friction in the system which impedes optimum resource allocation. For transaction costs economists, minimum costs determine the form of relationship that firms will adopt. However in the industrial network approach costs are simply one way of describing exchanges in the contexts of relationships.

Relationship specific investments are not the only kinds of investment firms make and therefore they will both affect and be affected by those other investments. Again distinguishing among kinds of investment will not be easy. Buying a new machine, for example, may represent an investment in a new technology, a specific market and in several customer relationships. Where the investment is highly relationship specific it may have a very low or zero alternative value, e.g. the time spent wining and dining a specific technical salesman. On the other hand few human activities are without some transfer or learning value. Given the mutuality of relationships it is evident that investment by one partner depends upon the existence of complementary assets in the other. It is pointless investing in knowledge of a particular technical application if the partner firm is simply not interested in using it.

One final aspect of relationships not discussed by Johanson and Mattsson is that of atmosphere. Inherent in any relationship is the tension between conflict and cooperation (Ford, Hakansson and Johanson, 1986). It is inherent because in any relationships the partners will be concerned that they are receiving an equitable share of the benefits which accrue from the existence of the relationship. Conflict may also arise from absence of mutuality because of changes in the objectives of either party or because the processes of exchange are not being managed to the satisfaction of one or both parties.

Relationships form the context in which transactions take place. Transactions, as described earlier, may be divided into exchanges and adaptation procedures. The latter are closely associated with the investment element of relationships. Adaptation is a continuous process which results in changes in products or services bought or sold, in processes of manufacture or in routines and administrative procedures and which implies resource commitment. The resulting adaptations are investments in specific relationships. The returns to adaptation investment are strengthening of bonds between firms, easier resolution of conflicts, confirmation that continuing adaptation is possible and development of mutual knowledge and orientation (Johanson and Mattsson, 1987).

Adaptation processes are, in turn, related to exchange processes. "The more intensive the exchange process among firms, the stronger will be the reasons to make adaptations. The type of adaptations is also related to the characteristics of the exchange, including frequency, complexity, and regularity" (Johanson and Mattsson, 1987). Similarly exchange processes are intimately connected to relationships. Relational elements strongly influence the processes of exchange, for example a firm will not order a product from a partner firm that it knows the firm finds difficult to produce. Conversely continuing exchanges provide the only medium firms have to change the form of their relationship. For example social exchanges may be strengthening social bonds at the same time as product exchanges are weakening technical bonds.

Implicit in this analysis is the notion that strongly bonded relationships define networks. While this may be true in general it is arguable that other kinds of relationships exist in networks which can have a significant effect on their operation. Easton and Araujo (1986) distinguished weak, potential and residual exchange relationships as well as pointing out the existence of potentially influential noneconomic exchange relationships, e.g. those between competitors. Weak relationships may, for example, have the power to affect network outcomes through their use as communication conduits (Granovetter, 1973). Potential and residual relationships change the context in which a focal relationship operates since they offer visible alternatives. It is not necessary to have economic exchanges between firms for there to be direct effects on their behaviour.

Indirect relationships are another very different form of relationship though a crucial one since they provide a very direct link between dyadic relationships and networks. An indirect relationship is most simply described as the relationship between two firms which are not directly related but which is mediated by a third firm with which they both have relationships. Two rather important kinds of indirect relationships are vertical, firm to customer's customer, and horizontal, firm to competitor through mutual customer.

Taking a focal firm viewpoint it is clear that a firm will have, except in the sparsest of networks, more indirect than direct relationships. This adds considerably to the problem of relationship management. However it is equally likely that some law of "distance" will apply such that the more distant and indirect the relationship the less impact it will have. Indirect relationships also specify the routes by means of which firms gain access to resources. One could, for example, imagine a situation where an indirectly connected secondary ring of firms might be capable of insulating the focal firm from the rest of the network. In a similar way indirect relationships provide the context for direct relationships and are capable of strongly influencing them (Mattsson, 1986).

An important element in indirect relationships is the nature and operation of the firm which connects two other firms indirectly. Certain types of intermediary, for example, customers as compared with suppliers, may influence the indirect relationships in rather different ways. Particular kinds of firm may perform the task of network node rather differently and thus strongly affect the operation of the net to which they belong. Whatever the influence, the process of transmission of information, resource, power, etc. will not be unaffected by the route taken.

Mattsson (1986) identifies seven dimensions which can be used to characterise indirect relationships. They include distance from a focal firm; vertical or horizontal nature; complementary or competitive; narrow or wide connection; the strength, kind and content of the direct bonds concerned; the interdependency of the direct relations concerned and the value added of a focal firm's direct relationship. Such a characterisation provides a link between descriptions of the operation of direct relationships and the operation of networks. For example the predominance of widely or narrowly connected indirect relationships will fundamentally affect the structure of a network. In a sense a focus on indirect relationships provides the microstructure and microprocesses of networks. It remains to be seen whether this intermediate form of analysis provides a useful route to descriptions of aggregate network phenomena.

## NETWORKS AS STRUCTURES

If the firms in an industrial system are interdependent rather than independent then networks will have structure. Interdependence introduces constraints on the actions of individual firms which create structure "in the large". Where there is no interdependence, as is assumed in some economic models, then an industrial system will be unstructured and stochastic in nature. The greater the interdependence the clearer the structure of the network becomes and the more important it is in determining the behaviour of individual firms. Structure in this context is based upon firms as the elements of structure. Structures using alternative elements are described in a later chapter in the book.

A basic assumption of the industrial network approach is that networks are essentially heterogeneous in nature (Hagg and Johanson, 1983). Again this contrasts with the homogeneity assumptions of much economic writing. The sources of heterogeneity are easy to describe, less easy to model. Industrial systems exist to match heterogeneous resources to heterogeneous demands. It is indisputable that resources available to create products and services are heterogeneous in nature. This is not just a recognition of variety among resources but also the fact that such resources are themselves multi-dimensional in character. One might also expect that individuals or individual firsm would have dissimilar needs or, failing that, would accept that such needs could be met in a variety of different ways (Alderson, 1965). The third element of heterogeneity lies in the firms involved in the network transforming resources to meet needs. Each firm is individual in its structure, employee preferences, history, resources, investments, skills, etc. The role it chooses, or may be forced, to play in the transformation process will be determined partly by factors such as these. In addition the relationships such firms have, will themselves create new possibilities which may in turn generate new forms of relationship and provide an additional source of heterogeneity as well as stabilising the structure so created. Uncertainty reduction is one motive for forming strong relationships though it has been argued that networks also create uncertainty albeit of a different kind. Specialisation, learning by doing, and the existence of transaction specific investments support heterogenisation. Thus interdependence is not only a source of heterogeneity, it is also a result of it. They are mutually reinforcing.

Such a view of networks has a number of implications. The first is that for a given set of resources and a given set of needs there are a large, possibly infinite, number of network structures which are capable of carrying out the transformation process. That is not to say that all are equally likely to occur in practice. Conversely, as will be argued later, it should not be assumed that there exists some objective function for the network, defined for example in terms of entropy, efficiency or effectiveness, which would predict which structure would be the optimum and therefore emerge as the most preferred. That is not to argue that networks do not change. What is clear is that in networks, as in organisations, structure and process are intimately related.

One way of characterising the structure of a network is by the division of work among the firms in the network. It a series of transformation activities have to be carried out in order to transform resources into products and services for final consumption by customers at whatever point in the network then individual firms will have responsibility for those activities. Clearly one could envisage a rather monolithic network where there are few firms carrying out the bulk of transformation. Alternatively the network might have a large number of firms each carrying out a small proportion of the required conversion activities with a concomitant increase in exchange activities. The balance between conversion and exchange activities may be regarded as another measure of network structure.

One structural issue in network analysis is that of boundaries. Mattsson (1988) comments "We can regard the global industrial system as one giant and extremely complex network since there exist always some path of relationships that connect any two firms." However he goes on to say "for obvious analytical reasons, this total network must be subdivided according to criteria such as interdependence between positions due to industrial activity chains, geographical proximities etc." In general such subdivisions have been called nets though the usage is by no means consistent. Perhaps there is a reluctance to accept the "universal" network. More likely it is a question of level of aggregation. Networks defined as equivalent in scope to industrial systems are as large as any analyst is likely to be able to comprehend let alone analyse. Nets provide a lower level of analysis. It should, however, be recognised that all boundaries are arbitrary.

Nets may be identified in terms of the strength of complementarity among the members of the net (Hagg and Johanson, 1983). They may be thought of as local concentrations in the network. They have natural boundaries in the sense that relationships among members are stronger than relationships between members and non members. Nets may be characterised along different dimensions: product, geography, process, technology, etc. From this definition it is clear that a firm may be a member of more than one net which adds another dimensionality problem to the analysis of networks. A net may also be defined by the activities of a single powerful organisation. In fact Mattsson (1984) suggests that the term net be used to describe only this situation. It corresponds to the organisation set concept used by Aldrich (1981). Clearly there are arguments for both definitions. However it is important that the terminology should be clarified. Researchers will wish to use different net definitions depending upon their research objectives. However it should also be recognised that networks, being in part social constructions, will also be perceived by their participants in different ways. Networks are socially constructed and there are likely to be disagreements among participants and multiple models of structure.

Social network analysis has developed a number of concepts, all of which have operational measures, which describe what are regarded as key structural characteristics. Mattsson (1986) has applied four of these concepts to industrial networks. Structuredness refers to the general level of interdependence in a network. In a tightly structured network firms have strong bonds and clearly demarcated activities. Individual firms are heavily constrained and exits and entries to the network are infrequent. Loosely structured networks have the opposite characteristics. Homogeneity describes the similarity of firms in terms of their bond types, relative importance of firms and the functions each firm may undertake. Where a small number of firms have a dominating influence on the network then it may be said to be hierarchical though the form of the resulting hierarchies may be many and various. Exclusiveness refers to the extent to which a network is insulated from other networks. There are many other measures of network structure which could be employed. However *ad hoc* measures bring with them the danger of atheoretical analysis. Perhaps their use should await a clearer articulation of one or more network theories which can make predictions about structure and its relationship to other network variables.

## NETWORKS AS POSITION

The network as position perspective is partial but powerful. In addition it has links to other areas of business analysis such as industrial economics and strategy. It represents a different level of analysis since the focus is at least partly upon single firms rather than the network. To provide some measure of comparability, a network in this perspective may be thought of as an aggregation of interlocking positions though it is likely that the proponents would not describe it in these terms. Mattsson (1984) defines a position as a role "that the organisation has for other organisations that it is related to, directly or indirectly". This statement has echoes of the definition of social role. "Thus this implies that the firm is expected by other firms to behave according to the norms associated with the position" (Mattsson, 1984). Other organisations, in effect, define the position of a focal organisation through the relationships that they have with it. Hakansson and Johanson (1984a) describe a related concept, strategic identity "which refers to the views about the firm's role and position in relation to other firms in the industrial network".

Position is inherently a dialectical concept. The net clearly constrains and circumscribes the behaviour of the focal firm. However it also offers opportunities in terms of access to the resources of the rest of the network. There is a balance between constraint and opportunity and a key normative issue is the way in which firms manage this balance. In addition the resource dependence model suggests that firms will make conflicting demands upon the focal firm. Such demands have to be reconciled or dealt with in some fashion if a tenable, i.e. balanced position is to be maintained. There are tensions in the relationships, which keep the firm in its position. Positions are also balanced as between the past and the future. History determines the current position but the future offers opportunities for change.

Mattsson (1984) outlines four characteristics of position. Function describes the function firms are held to perform, the activities they are expected to undertake, for example, a limited line wholesaler. The identity of the net of firms that the focal firm has relationships with is a second feature of position. If the net changes the expectations change and so does the position. A third aspect of position is the relative importance of the firm in its net, measured by size or other correlates of power. Positions may be defined at different levels of analysis. Mattsson distinguishes macro- and micropositions. The former refers to relationships between individual firms and is therefore largely a recasting of the bonding or interaction concepts to make them more compatible with network description. The latter describes the firm's relationship to the network as a whole. Strength of relationship was later added as a fifth variable (Mattsson, 1987a).

In later work Johanson and Mattsson (1986) used micro- and macropositions as superordinate variables and described them in the following terms:

> The micropositions are characterised by: a) The role of the firm in relation to the (other) firm(s) b) its importance to the other firm, and c) the strength of the relationship with the other firm. The macropositions are characterised by: a) the identity of the other firms with which the firm has direct relationships and indirect relationships in the network b) the role of the firm in the network and, c) the strength of the relationships with other firms.

The separation of the two concepts allows us to speculate about the way in which micropositions build to macropositions. Originally Mattsson suggested that macropositions might be thought of as "aggregates or weighted averages of micropositions". However in later work this simple model is discarded. "Thus the macroposition, while referring to the whole network, is not an aggregation of the micropositions in the network" (Johanson and Mattsson, 1986). This is almost self evident since macropositions are affected by the whole network interdependencies while micropositions are not. It is to be expected that there will be strong interrelationships between the two kinds of position. For example taking on a new type of customer (a new microposition) may change other firms' expectations about the functions a focal firm can perform and its importance in the network (a macroposition change). Mattson (1984) discusses a variety of ways in which micro- and macropositions may be related.

Positions in networks are primarily concerned with the nature of network connections. Thus they provide a language to talk about network changes. Fundamentally, a change in the position of one firm will change, to a greater or lesser extent, the position of other firms in the network. Such changes need not be confined to those firms in direct relationship with the initiating firm. Position changes can spread out from the initiating firm through the whole network by way of a cascade of position changes. However it should not be thought that position changes are easy to achieve or even always possible. Firms may be in preferred positions and defend those positions by any means at their disposal including making other microposition changes to nullify the initiated change. Firms also have desired positions to which they may be seeking to achieve and which may be threatened by the proposed changes.

Mattsson provides a link to strategy by identifying four strategic situations in relation to network position: entering and exiting an established network, defending and changing existing positions. He goes on to describe specific strategies that firms might adopt in the last two situations. The analyses are complex and contingent. For example position changes may be marginal or structural, firm or other initiated, acceptable or unacceptable. Mattsson (1987a) goes further and argues that all strategies involve network position change whether or not this particular focus provides the best way of understanding or implementing them. The approach provides real insights into what might be called the microprocesses of network change. It corresponds to the strategy as position perspective as characterised by Mintzberg (1988) but contrasts strongly with the alternative positional, competitive models used by Porter.

## NETWORKS AS PROCESS

Change is a central feature of much of that is written about industrial networks. Networks are concerned with relationships and these cannot be conceived of in anything by dynamic terms. It is hardly surprising that the processes by which networks function have been a major preoccupation of workers in this field. There is no clear focus but a number of issues can sensibly be discussed under this heading.

Coordination of firms in an industrial system may be conceived as being effected by three kinds of mechanisms. Economists have argued for the invisible hand of the market. In particular, price formation provides the signals which determine which firms produce what products. The processes which achieve this coordination are difficult to model since the markets are by no means perfect and simple assumptions will not suffice. Nevertheless market mechanisms do exist, because firms can make choices, and may be said to have a coordinative role. Firms are not, however, mechanistic in their response to external stimuli nor are they simple in structural or process terms. They provide a form of coordination which is internal, self directing and managerial. It has been called the visible hand. Those activities which are under the control of a single firm are coordinated by them to their own plans towards their own ends, sometimes in conflict with market mechanisms, at other times replacing them. In the latter case we call this a hierarchy, *vide* transaction cost theory.

Where strong inter-organisational relationships exist, a third form of coordination emerges: network processes. Coordination is not achieved by some grand master plan or quasi hierarchy since the firms concerned are too independent and the activities too numerous and diverse to control. But neither, in general, are firms so independent from one another that the market dictates and controls their actions. The reasons for the existence of strong relationships between firms and the constraints they place upon them, have already been described. Where such relationships exist they exert a coordinative influence on the system through the need for coordination at the level of the dyad. Significant structural changes cannot occur without the breaking of strong bonds and this introduces inertia into the system. More important, the direction of change is governed by the pattern of relationships that the participant firms judge, on a resultant rather than a collective basis, to be most favourable. This is a form of coordination which is neither market nor hierarchy not yet an intermediate form. It is an alternative mode which operates by different mechanisms.

Network processes are dominated by the distribution of power and interest structures. Some firms in the network have access to more and better resources than others. This may be a result of historical accident (location, invention, synergy, etc.) or may be due to far sighted management of the resource base. Whatever the cause, the effect is to render some firms more powerful than others, i.e. many relationships are asymmetrical with respect to power. In addition not all firms have the same interests especially since an interest vector will be the resultant of the interests of the actors within the firm. The power/interest distributions dictate the way in which the network both operates and develops. A single powerful firm may dominate a part of a network and part of its interest structure may be a desire to remain in control at the expense of other possible goals. Conversely a network where the power is rather evenly distributed offers many opportunities for development. This is especially true if the interest structures of participants coincide or, more usually, where feasible trade-offs, between the cooperation required to coordinate and the conflict over the distribution of surpluses, can be made.

Two dialectical processes in networks are competition and cooperation. The picture of relationships provided by the network approach emphasises cooperation, complementarity and coordination. Firms buying and selling from one another have to have a minimal level of cooperation in order to complete even a single exchange. In practice, the existence of strong bonding demonstrates a high level of cooperation. Even those firms judged as market competitors by traditional standards, being indirectly linked through customers, may find themselves cooperating in order, for example, to develop new products as a benefit for the network as a whole.

Firms therefore find themselves in the position of having to make fine judgements about their modes of operation. In single relationships, nets and networks they have to decide the trade-off between cooperation, necessary in order to create benefit, and competition over the control, ownership or share of the resources so created.

Hagg and Johanson (1983) argue that competition in the traditional sense is replaced by rivalry for the control of resources. Such rivalry may occur at any level of aggregation. For example the fiercest competition may occur between networks rather than within them. There is no sense in which such rivalry will necessarily lead to optimal allocation of economic resources. An alternative but complementary view is that competition in networks is a function of the overlap of organisational domains. Complete overlap implies competition; partial overlap implies networking (Thorelli, 1986).

Networks are stable but not static. The continuing processes of interaction between firms are stabilised since they take place within the context of existing relationships. However such relationships are also changing, partly in response to events external to the relationships and partly because of the transactions which help to define them. In addition new relationships are formed and old relationships disappear. Evolution is the main mode; revolution is possible but unusual. Network inertia and interdependencies slow and shape change (Johanson and Mattson, 1986). Thus networks do not have lifecycles. They transform over time, merge, shift in focus and membership. Stability also provides a platform for change. The continuous interaction between firms offers, on the one hand, the opportunity for innovation and, on the other, the existence of a known and predictable environment in which it can be realised.

Industrial systems exist to create products and services. Innovation is a major force in networks and much of the empirical work on industrial networks has been done on new product development (Hakansson, 1987). It is argued that invention and innovation occur in networks not within but between firms. Even when the "Newton syndrome" seems to be at work it is often the problems or opportunities presented by other organisations which provide the necessary inspiration. More often it is the working through of mutual problems between supplier and customer which creates the novel solution. Either supplier or customer may take the lead in this process. Each brings a complementary set of skills, knowledge and resources to the problem.

For the invention to become a reality, network mobilisation must occur. It is not enough that the technical knowledge is available. Novelty requires changes in network structures as well as changes within the firms involved, i.e. self mobilisation. Firms must adapt old relationships and internal activities and develop new relationships. Mobilisation requires resources and if such resources are not available or, more likely, will not be made available by network participants then the innovation will fail. It is also apparent that they must be the right resources in the right combinations. In a network where innovation dominates, limitation of resources forces firms into increasing technical specialisation. This means that they, in turn, become increasingly reliant upon other firms which have complementary resources with whom they are driven to coordinate their research activities. Thus innovation leads to strongly bonded networks. Hakansson (1987) identifies these three aspects of innovation in a network perspective as knowledge development, resource mobilisation and resource coordination.

At a more general level any change in a network requires resources to be mobilised. In particular existing actors not only need to have the necessary resources but also the will and interest to deploy them. On the other hand any firm, however apparently powerless, may initiate change if it can draw upon the resources of the whole network by virtue of the acceptability of the change. 'If the power for change is to suffice then both knowledge and demand must be mobilised in a particular direction' (Hakansson and Waluszewski, 1986).

One fundamental issue remains about which there is strong disagreement. What are the forces which drive network changes? Hakansson and Johanson (1984a) argue that "it is meaningless to speak about optimal activity systems or configurations." Changes to improve network efficiency do occur but there is no mechanism by which the optimal direction can be discerned. Networks do not tend to optimal efficiency configurations. Mattsson (1986) suggests that "lack of balance between resources is an important driving force for investment processes to be initiated in different firms". This suggests that resource distribution in networks may tend towards some sort of equilibrium. Thorelli (1986) sees entropy as the driving force leading to the disintegration of networks. Resources are consumed and structures created in an attempt to arrest the process.

## IMPLICATIONS AND APPLICATIONS

The industrial networks approach, form whichever perspective it is viewed, offers a totally different view from that of traditional marketing and buying behaviour approaches. To start with it integrates these two separate fields of endeavour. It eschews markets and adopts relationships. It is positive and does not smuggle normative principles into its models. There are, however, normative implications which might contribute to the management of exchange processes under the general heading of relational marketing (or purchasing). They are, in a sense, external to the industrial networks approach but provide an interpretation of it by taking a focal firm viewpoint.

From a functional marketing or purchasing stand-point the emphasis lies in the management of relationships. Such a relationship may be dominated or initiated by either partner. The key issues are choice of partners, resource allocation among them and the management of individual relationships. The first issue is largely a strategic one and will be discussed later. The second issue has been described as the limitation problem. A firm has only limited resources; it must choose how much, and in what fashion, it will devote to each relationship, potential or actual. A portfolio approach to this issue has been both suggested (Campbell and Cunningham, 1984) and criticised (Easton and Araujo, 1985). The interesting question is how firms actually make the trade-offs. The third issues concerns how an individual relationship is managed. What the industrial network approach adds to the interaction approach is the knowledge that the focal relationship (a) cannot be managed in isolation from the other relationships a firm has and (b) represents a conduit to other relationships through which resources may be accessed.

In terms of strategy the networks as positions perspective provide not only useful insights but also a contrast with the Porterian position. Porter recognises extended rivalry and describes strategy in terms of strategic positions in relationship to the rival forces. The network position characterises these forces in terms of the organisations with which the focal firm has relationships and, in addition, handles both conflict and cooperation among them. The strategic alternatives have already been described in the position section. The general picture is of a firm at the centre of a web of relationships which both constrain it and provide opportunities. By changing patterns of relationships, itself no easy task, a firm can change position, acquire more control over its own destiny and better achieve what the stakeholders require. The central concept is one of balance and positional sense; a tightrope walking act.

There are, in addition, industrial policy implications of a network approach. Hagg and Johanson (1983, ch. 5) provide a useful summary. Perhaps the most salient change suggested is a move away from treating the individual firm as the unit of analysis. Nets and networks provide a more powerful focus since they recognise the fact that a policy intervention must take into account the relationship among the target firms. Further, governments may only be able to achieve their policy objectives by seeking to strengthen, weaken or restructure relationships *per se*.

The industrial networks approach has been applied to a wide variety of the phenomena of industrial life and reference has been made throughout this chapter to a number of relevant studies. However particular emphasis has been laid on the twin processes of internationalisation and technological development. In the former case an industrial network approach offers an alternative to the traditional economic and more recent transaction cost approaches. It argues that internationalisation follows the existing patterns of relationships (Hakansson and Johanson, 1988). The importance of networks in invention and innovation has been demonstrated (Hakansson, 1987). It is argued that these processes occur between firms and not solely within them. For an innovation to succeed the network must be capable of being mobilised. The resources must be available in the network and under the control of, or accessible to, the actors with an interest in the success of the innovation.

## CONCLUSION

This review has been a process of gathering together relevant material, restructuring and explaining the industrial network approach. No attempt has been made to provide a critical analysis. It is, however, easy to predict what criticisms it would attract from outside the paradigm. Where is the systematic evidence for the cornerstone assumption, that strong relationships among firms in industrial systems, prevail? Is it not simply a rather general approach incapable of being operationalized and tested? Why is the language of industrial networks so diffuse, contradictory and hence difficult to learn? Each of these criticisms can be answered, at least partially, and in some detail. However they would reflect different aspects of a rather more general answer. The industrial network approach is both new and rich. The paradigm is less than a decade old. The infant is precocious. It needs time to mature. But already it challenges the orthodoxy of traditional perspectives in a number of disciplines. It provides an alternative and plausible view of the world it seeks to describe. It depicts a new reality.

## BIBLIOGRAPHY

Alchian, A. A. and Demsetz, H. (1972) 'Production, Information Costs and Economic Organisation', *American Economic Review,* 62, p. 783.

Aldrich, H. E. (1979) *Organisations and Environments,* Englewood Cliffs, NJ, Prentice Hall.

Aldrich, H. E. (1981) *The Origins and Persistence of Social Networks. Social Structure and Network Analyses,* Beverly Hills, Calif., Sage.

Aldrich, H. E. and Whetten, D. A. (1981) 'Organisation-sets, Action sets and Networks. Making the most of simplicity' in P. C. Nystrom and W. H. Starbuk (eds) *Handbook of Organisational Design,* Vol. 1, Oxford, Oxford University Press pp. 385–408.

Alderson, W. (1957) *Marketing Behaviour and Executive Action,* Homewood, Ill., Richard D. Irwin.

Alderson, W. (1965) *Dynamic Marketing Behaviour. A Functionalist Theory of Marketing,* Homewood Ill., Richard D. Irwin.

Alexander, R., Surface, S. and Alderson, W. (1940) *Marketing,* Boston, Mass., Ginn and Company.

Arndt, J. (1979) 'Overview: The Impact of Stakeholder Publics in Shaping the Future of Marketing' in G. Fisk, J. Arndt, and K. Gronhaug, (eds), *Future Directions for Marketing* Cambridge, Mass., Marketing Science Institute, pp. 76–7.

Arrow, K. (1974) *Limits of Organisation,* New York, W.W. Norton and Co.

Astley, W. G. (1984) 'Toward an Appreciation of Collective Strategy'. *Academy of Management Review,* 9, 3, pp. 526–35.

Astley, W. G. (1985) 'The Two Ecologies: Population and Community Perspectives on Organisational Evolution'. *Administrative Science Quarterly,* 30, pp. 224–41.

Astley, W. G. and Fombrun, C. (1983) 'Collective Strategy: Social Ecology of Organisational Environments', *Academy of Management Review,* 8, pp. 576–87.

Averitt, R. T. (1968) *The Dual Economy: The Dynamics of American Industry Structure,* New York, W. W. Norton and Co.

Axelrod, R. (1984) *The Evolution of Cooperation,* New York, Basic Books.

Axelsson, B. (1982) 'Wilmanshyttans uppgang och fall. En kommentar till angreppssattet i en foretagshistorisk studie' ('The Rise and Fall of Wilmanshyttan Steel Works. A Commentary on the Approach in a Company History Study'), *Acta Universitatis Upsaliensis,* 15, Liber.

Axelsson, B. (1987) 'Supplier Management and Technological Development' in H. Hakansson (ed.) *Industrial Technological Development: A Network Approach,* London, Croom Helm.

Axelsson, B. and Hakansson, H. (1979) 'Wikmanshyttans uppgang och fall. En analys av ett stalforetag och dess omgivning under 75 ar' ('The Rise and Fall of the Wikmanshyttan Steel Works. An Historical Analysis of a Steel Company during 75 years'), Studentlitteratur.

Axelsson, B. and Hakansson, H. (1984) *Inkap for Konkurrenshraft, (Purchasing for Competitive Power)*, Liber.

Barney, J. B. and Ouchi, W. G. (1986) *Organisational Economics* San Francisco, Calif., Jossey Bass.

Berg, P. O. (1985) 'Organisation Change as a Symbolic Transformation Process' in P.J. Frost *et al. Organization Culture,* New York, Sage.

Bjorklund, L. (1988) *International Projekforsaljning (International Systems Selling)*, Research Report, EFI., Stockholm School of Economics, Sweden.

Blau, P. M. (1964) *Exchange and Power in Social Life,* New York, John Wiley.

Blau, P. M. (1968) 'The Hierarchy of Authority in Organisations', *American Journal of Sociology,* 73, pp. 453–67.

Blois, K. J. (1972) 'Vertical Quasi-integration', *Journal of Industrial Economics,* 20, pp. 253–72.

Bonoma, T. (1976) 'Conflict, Cooperation and Trust in Three Power Systems', *Behavioural Science,* 21, pp. 499–514.

Bucklin, L. P. (1960) 'The Economic Structure of Channels of Distribution' in B. Mallen (1967) *The Marketing Channel: A Conceptual Viewpoint*, New York, John Wiley and Son, pp. 63–6.

Burt, R. S. (1980) 'Testing a Structural Theory of Corporate Cooptation: Interorganisational Directorate Ties as a Strategy for Avoiding Market Constraints on Profits', *American Sociological Review*, 45, pp. 821–41.

Campbell, N. C. G. (1984) 'The Structure and Stability of Industrial Networks. Developing a Research Methodology. Research Developments in International Marketing', 1st IMP International Research Seminar, UMIST, Manchester.

Campbell, N. C. G. (1985) 'Network Analysis of a Global Capital Equipment Industry', 2nd IMP International Research Seminar, University of Uppsala, Sweden.

Campbell, N. C. G. and Cunningham, M. T. (1984) 'Customer Analysis for Strategy Development in Industrial Markets', *Strategic Management Journal*, 4, pp. 369–80.

Caves, R. (1982) *Multinational Enterprise and Economic Analysis*, Cambridge, Cambridge University Press.

Cavusgil, S. T. and Nevin, J. P. (1981) 'The State-of-the-Art in International Marketing. An Assessment' in B. M. Enis and K. J. Roerring (eds) *Review of Marketing*, Greenwich, Conn., JAI Press.

Contractor, F. J. and Lorange, P. (1988) 'Why Should Firms Cooperate? The Strategy and Economics Basis for Cooperative Ventures' in F. J. Contractor and P. Lorange, *Cooperative Strategies in International Business*, Lexington, Mass., Lexington Books.

Cook, K. S. (1977) 'Exchange and Power in Networks of Interorganisational Relations', *Sociological Quarterly*, 18, pp. 62–82.

Cook, K. S. (1981) *Network Structure from Exchange Perspectives in Social Structure and Network Analyses*, Beverly Hills, Calif., Sage, pp. 177–200.

Cook, K. S. and Emerson, R. (1978) 'Power, Equity and Commitment in Exchange Networks', *American Sociological Review*, 43: pp. 712–39.

Cook, K. S. and Emerson, R. (1984) 'Exchange Networks and the Analysis of Complex Organisations', *Research in the Sociology of Organisations*, Vol. 3, Greenwich, Conn., JAP Press pp. 1–30.

Cox, R. and Goodman, C. (1956) 'Marketing of Housebuilding Materials', *Journal of Marketing*, 11, 1, pp. 36–61.

Cummings, T. G. (1984) 'Transorganisational Development', *Research in Organisational Behaviour*, Vol. 6, Greenwich, Conn., JAI Press, pp. 367–422.

Cunningham, M. T. (1987) 'Interaction, Networks and Competitiveness: A European Perspective of Business Marketing', European–American Symposium "World Wide Marketplace for Technology Based Products', University of Twente, Enschede, The Netherlands.

Cyert, R. M. and March, J. G. (1963) *A Behavioural Theory of the Firm*, Englewood Cliffs, NJ, Prentice Hall.

Dahl, R. A. (1957) 'The Concept of Power', *Behavioural Science*, 2, pp. 201–15.

Dahmen, E. (1988) 'Development Blocks in Industrial Economics', *Scandinavian Economic Review*, 1, pp. 3–14.

Di Maggio, P. (1986) 'Structural Analysis of Organisational Fields', *Research in Organisational Behaviour*, Vol. 8, Greenwich, Conn., JAI Press, pp. 335–70.

Easton, G. (1988) 'Marketing strategy and Competition', *European Journal of Marketing*, 22, 1, pp. 31–49.

Easton, G. (1990) 'Relationships Among Competitors', in G. Day, B. Weitz and R. Wensley (eds) *The Interface of Marketing and Strategy*, Greenwich, Conn., JAI Press.

Easton, G. and Araujo, L. (1985) 'The Network Approach: An Articulation', 2nd International IMP Research Seminar, University of Uppsala, Sweden.

Easton, G. and Araujo, L. (1986) 'Networks, Bonding and Relationships in Industrial Markets', *Industrial Marketing and Purchasing*, 1, 1, pp. 8–25.

Easton, G. and Smith, P. (1984) 'The Formation of Inter-Organisational Relationships in a Major Gasfield Development', Research Seminar on Industrial Marketing, Stockholm School of Economics, Sweden.

Emerson, R. M. (1962) 'Power Dependence Relations', *American Sociological Review*, 27, pp. 31–40.
Emerson, R. M. (1972) 'Exchange Theory, Part II: Exchange Relations in Networks', in J. Berger, M. Zedditch and B. Andersson (eds) *Sociological Theories in Progress*, Boston, Mass., Houghton Mifflin, pp. 58–87.
Engwall, L. (1985) 'Fran vag vision till komplex organisation. En studie av Varmlands Folkblads ekonomiska och organisatoriska utveckling' (from a Vague Vision to a Complex Organisation. A Study of the Economic and Organisational Development of the Varmlands Folkbald'), *Acta Universitatis Upsaliensis*, 22, University of Uppsala, Sweden.
Engwall, L. and Johanson, J. (1989) 'Banks in industrial networks', Working Paper, Department of Business Studies, University of Uppsala, Sweden.
Evan, W. M. (1966) 'The Organisation-Set" Toward a Theory of Interorganisational Relations', in J. Thompson (ed) *Approaches to Organisational Design*, Pittsburg, Pa. University of Pittsburg Press.
Fiocca, R. and Snehota, I. (1986) 'Marketing e alta tecnologia', *Sviluppo e Organizzazione*, 98, pp. 24–31.
Fombrun, C. J. and Astley, W. G. (1983) 'Beyond Corporate Strategy', *Journal of Business Strategy*, 3, pp. 47–54.
Ford, D., (1978) 'Stability Factors in Industrial Marketing Channels', *Industrial Marketing Management*, 7, pp. 410–22.
Ford, D., Hakansson, H. and Johanson, J. (1986) 'How do Companies Interact?', *Industrial Marketing and Purchasing*, 1, 1, pp. 26–41.
Forrester, J. (1961) *Industrial Dynamics* Boston, Mass., MIT Press.
Forsgren, M. (1985) 'The Foreign Acquisition Strategy – Internationalisation or Coping with Strategic Interdependencies in Networks?', Working Paper, Department of Business Administration, University of Uppsala, Sweden.
Forsgren, M. (1989) *Managing the Internationalisation Process. The Swedish Case*, London, Routledge.
Fullerton, R. (1986) 'Understanding Institutional Innovation and System Evolution in Distribution', *International Journal of Research in Marketing*, 3, pp. 273–82.
Gadde, L.-E. and Mattsson, L.-M. (1987) 'Stability and Change in Network Relationships', *International Journal of Research in Marketing*, 4, pp. 29–41.
Gadde, L.-E., Hakansson, H. and Oberg, M. (1988) 'Change and Stability in Swedish Automobile Distribution', Report prepared for the 2nd Annual Forum of the International Motor and Vehicle Program, Boston, Massachusetts Institute of Technology.
Gattorna, J. (1978) 'Channels of Distribution Conceptualisations: A State-of-the-Art Review', *European Journal of Marketing*, 12, 7, pp. 471–512.
Glaser, A. and Strauss, B. (1967) *The Discovery of Grounded Theory*, Chicago, Ill., Aldine.
Giete, J. (1984) 'High Technology and Industrial Networks', International Research Seminar on Industrial Marketing, Stockholm School of Economics, Sweden.
Granovetter, M. S. (1973) 'The Strength of Weak Ties', *American Journal of Sociology*, 78, 6, pp. 1360–80.
Granovetter, M. S. (1984) 'A theory of Embeddedness', Department of Sociology, State University of New York.
Granovetter, M. S. (1985) 'Economic Action and Social Structure: The Problem of Embeddedness', *American Journal of Sociology*, 91, 3, pp. 481–510.
Grinyer and Spender (1979) 'Recipes, Crises and Adaptation in Mature Business', *International Studies of Management and Organisation*, 9, pp. 113–33.
Hagg, I. and Johanson, J. (1983) 'Firms in Networks', Business and Social Research Institute, Stockholm, Sweden.
Hakansson, H. (1982a) 'Teknisk Utveckling och Marknadsforing' ('Technical Development and Marketing'), *MTC* 19, Stockholm, Stockholm School of Economics, Liber.
Hakansson, H. (ed.) (1982b) *International Marketing and Purchasing of Industrial Goods: An Interaction Approach*, Chichester, Wiley.
Hakansson, H. (ed.) (1987) *Industrial Technological Development: A Network Approach*, London, Croom Helm.

Hakansson, H. (1989) *Corporate Technological Behaviour: Cooperation and Networks*, London, Routledge.
Hakansson, H. and Johanson, J. (1984a) 'Heterogeneity in Industrial Markets and its Implications for Marketing' in I. Hagg and F. Wiedersheim-Paul (eds) 'Between Market and Hierarchy', Department of Business Administration, University of Uppsala, Sweden.
Hakansson, H. and Johanson, J. (1984b) 'A Model of Industrial Networks', Working Paper, Department of Business Administration, University of Uppsala, Sweden.
Hakansson, H. and Johanson, J. (1988) 'Formal and Informal Co-operation Strategies in International Industrial Networks' in F. J. Contractor and P. Lorange *Co-operative strategies in International Business*, Lexington, Mass., Lexington Books.
Hakansson, H. and Ostberg, C. (1975) 'Industrial Marketing – An Organisational Problem', *Industrial Marketing Management*, 4, pp. 113–23.
Hakansson, H. and Snehota, I. (1989) 'No Business is an Island. The Network Concept of Business Strategy', *Scandinavian Journal of Management Studies*, 4, 3, pp. 187–200.
Hakansson, H. and Waluszewski, A. (1986) 'Technical Development in a Dense Network', 3rd International IMP Research Seminar, IRE, Lyon.
Hall, R. (1977) *Organisations: Structure and Process*, 2nd edn., Englewood Cliffs, NJ, Prentice Hall.
Hallen, L. (1984) 'Market Approaches in European Perspective', in P. Turnbull and J. P. Valla *Strategies in International Industrial Marketing: A Comparative Analysis*, London, Croom Helm.
Hamfelt, C. and Lindberg, A.-K. (1987) 'Technological Development and the Individual's Contact Network' in H. Hakansson (ed.) *Industrial Technological Development: A Network Approach*, London, Croom Helm.
Hammarkvist, K.-O. (1983) 'Markets as Networks', Marketing Education Group Conference, Cranfield, UK.
Hammarkvist, K.-O., Hakansson, H. and Mattsson, L.-G. (1982) *Marknadsforing for konkurrenskraft (Marketing for Competitive Power)*, Malmo, Liber.
Hampdon, G. M. and Van Gent, A. P. (eds) *Marketing Aspects of International Business*, Boston, Mass., Kluwer-Nijhoff.
Hannan, M. T. and Freeman, J. H. (1977) 'The Population Ecology of Organisations', *American Journal of Sociology*, 82, pp. 929–64.
Harrigan, K. (1983) *Strategies for Vertical Integration*, Lexington, Mass., Lexington Books.
Harrigan, K. (1985) *Strategies for Joint Ventures*, Lexington, Mass., Lexington Books.
Hawley, A. (1968) 'Human Ecology' in D. L. Sills (ed.) *The International Encyclopedia of the Social Sciences*, Vol. 4, New York, Macmillan and Free Press, pp. 328–37.
Hegert, M. and Morris, D. (1988) 'Trends in International Collaborative Agreements' in F. J. Contractor and P. Lorange *Co-operative Strategies in International Business*, Lexington, Mass., Lexington Books.
Henderson, J. M. and Quandt, R. E. (1971) *Microeconomic Theory*, 2nd edn., New York, McGraw-Hill.
Hettne, B. and Tamm, G. (1974) *Mobilisation and Development in India. A Case Study of Mysore State*, SIDA.
Hughes, T. P. (1983) *Networks of Power, Electrification in Western Society, 1880–1930*, Baltimore, Md., Johns Hopkins University Press.
Hultbom, C. (1990) 'Internal Exchange Processes. Buyer–Seller Relationships within Big Companies', Unpublished Ph.D. dissertation, Department of Business Studies, University of Uppsala, Sweden.
Hulten, S. (1985) 'What Can Theories of Industrial Change Contribute to the Understanding Of International Markets as Networks?', 2nd International IMP Research Seminar, University of Uppsala, Sweden.
Imai, K. (1987) 'Network industrial organisation in Japan', Working paper prepared for the workshop on 'New Issues in Industrial Economics' at Case Western Reserve University, Cleveland, OH, on 7–10 June.
Jansson, H. (1985) 'Marketing to Projects in South East Asia. A Network.' Working Paper 1985/3, Department of Business Administration, University of Uppsala, Sweden.
Johanson, J. and Mattsson, L.-G. (1984) 'Marketing Investments and Market Investments in

Industrial Markets', International Research Seminar in Industrial Marketing, Stockholm School of Economics, Stockholm, Sweden.
Johanson, J. and Mattsson, L.-G. (1985) 'Marketing and Market Investments in industrial networks', *International Journal of Research in Marketing*, 2, 3, pp. 185–95.
Johanson, J. and Mattsson, L.-G. (1986) 'Interorganisational Relations in Industrial Systems: A Network Approach Compared with a Transaction Cost Approach', Working Paper, University of Uppsala, Sweden.
Johanson, J. and Mattsson, L.-G. (1987) 'Interorganisational Relations in Industrial Systems: A Network Approach Compared with a Transaction Cost Approach', *International Studies of Management Organisation*, 17, 1, pp. 34–48.
Johanson, J. and Mattsson, L.-G. (1988) 'Internationalisation in Industrial Systems – A Network Approach, in N. Hood and J.-E. Vahlne (eds) *Strategies in Global Competition*, London, Croom Helm.
Johanson, J. and Sharma, D. (1985) 'Swedish Technical Consultants; Tasks, Resources and Relationships – A Network Approach', International Research Seminar on Industrial Marketing, Stockholm School of Economics, Stockholm, Sweden.
Kaynak, E. and Savitt, R. (eds) (1984) *Comparative Marketing Systems*, New York, Praeger.
Killing, K. P. (1982) 'How to Make a Global Joint Venture Work', *Harvard Business Review*, 61, 3, pp. 120–7.
Killing, J. P. (1983) *Strategies for Joint Venture Success*, New York, Praeger.
Kinch, N. (1988) 'Emerging Strategies in a Network Context: The Volvo Case', *Scandinavian Journal of Management Studies*, October.
Kranzberg, M. (1986) 'Technology and History: "Kranzberg's Laws"', *Technology and Culture*, 7, pp. 185–95.
Kutachker, M. (1982) 'Power and Dependence in Industrial Marketing' in H. Hakansson (ed.) *International Marketing and Purchasing of Industrial Goods: An interaction approach*, Chichester, Wiley.
Kutschker, M. (1985) 'The Multi-Organizational interaction approach to Industrial Marketing', *Journal of Business Research*, 13, pp. 383–403.
Laage-Hellman, J. (1984) 'The Role of External Technical Exchange in R&D: An Empirical Study of the Swedish Special Steel Industry', M.T.C. Research No. 18, Marketing Technology Centre, Stockholm, Sweden.
Laage-Hellman, J. (1987) 'Process Innovation through Technical Cooperation', in H. Hakansson (ed.) *Industrial Technological Development; A Network Approach*, London, Croom Helm.
Laage-Hellman, J. (1988) 'Technological Development in Industrial Networks', Working paper, Department of Business Administration, University of Uppsala, Sweden.
Laage-Hellman, J. (1989) 'Technological Development in Industrial Networks', Unpublished Dissertation, Department of Business Administration, University of Uppsala, Sweden.
Laage-Hallman, J. and Axelsson, B. (1986) 'Bioteknisk Foll i Sverigeforskninasuolam, forskninasinriktning, samartetsmonster. En studie av det bioteknisk Follnatverket 1970–1985' (Biotechnological R&D in Sweden. Research Volume, Direction of Research, Patterns of Cooperation. A study of the Biotechnological R&D Network 1970–1985), STU Information 536, Styrelsen for Teknisk Utveckling, Stockholm, Sweden.
Larsen, J. K. and Rogers, E. M. (1984) *Silicon Valley Fever*, New York, Basic Books.
Levine, S. and White, P. E. (1961) 'Exchange as a Conceptual Framework for the Study of Interorganisational Relationships', *Administrative Science Quarterly*, 5, pp. 583–601.
Lorenzoni, G. and Ornati, O. A. (1988) 'Constellations of Firms and New Ventures', *Journal of Business Venturing*, 3, pp. 41–57.
Lundgren, A. (1985) 'Datoriserad Bildbehandling i Sverige', ('Computerized Image processing in Sweden'), Working Paper, EFI, Stockholm School of Economics, Stockholm, Sweden.
Lundgren, A. (1987) 'Bildbehandlingens framvaxt', Working Paper, Stockholm School of Economics, Stockholm, Sweden.
Mallen, B. (ed.) (1967) *The Marketing Channel: A Conceptual Viewpoint*, New York, John Wiley and Son.

March, J. M. (1966) 'The Power of Power' in D. Easton (ed.) *Varieties of Political Theory*, Englewood Cliffs, NJ, Prentice Hall.
Marret, C. (1971) 'On the Specification of Interorganisational Dimensions', *Sociology and Social Research*, 56, pp. 83–9.
Mattsson, L.-G. (1969) *Integration and Efficiency in Marketing Systems,* EFI, Stockholm, Nordstedt & Soner.
Mattsson, L.-G. (1975) 'System Interdependencies – A Key Concept in Industrial Marketing', 2nd Research Seminar in Marketing, FNEGE, Senanque, France.
Mattsson, L.-G. (1981) 'Interorganisational Structures in Industrial Markets: A Challenge to Marketing Theory and Practice', Working Paper 1980/1, Department of Business Administration, University of Uppsala, Sweden.
Mattsson, L.-G. (1984) 'An Application of a Network Approach to Marketing: Defending and Changing Market Positions' in N. Dholakia and J. Arndt (eds) *Changing the Course of Marketing. Alternative Paradigms for Widening Marketing Theory*, Greenwich, Conn., JAI Press.
Mattsson, L.-G. (1986) 'Indirect Relationships in industrial networks: A Conceptual Analysis of their Significance', 3rd IMP International Seminar, IRE, Lyon, France.
Mattsson, L.-M. (1987a) 'Management of Strategic Change in a "Markets-as-Networks" Perspective' in A. Pettigrew *The Management of Strategic Change,* Oxford, Blackwell.
Mattsson, L.-G. (1987b) 'Conceptual Building blocks of Network Theory', Working Paper, Stockholm School of Economics, Stockholm, Sweden.
Mattsson L.-G. (1988) 'Interaction Strategies: A Network Approach' AMA Marketing Educator's Conference, Summer, San Francisco, Calif.
McCammon, B. (1964) 'Alternative Explanations of Institutional Change and Channel Evolution' in B. Mallen (ed.) (1967) *The Marketing Channel: A Conceptual Viewpoint,* New York: John Wiley and Son, pp. 75–81.
McCammon, B. and Little, R. W. (1965) 'Marketing Channels: Analytical Systems and Approaches' in G. Schwartz (ed.) (1970) *Science in Marketing,* New York, John Wiley and Son, pp. 321–85.
McVey, P. (1960) 'Are Channels of Distribution What the Textbooks Say?', *Journal of Marketing,* XXIV, 3, pp. 61–5.
Mintzberg, H. (1988) 'Opening up the Definition of Strategy' in J. B. Quinn, H. Mintzberg and R. M. James (eds) *The Strategy Process,* Englewood Cliffs, NJ, Prentice Hall International.
Morgan, G. (1986) *Images of Organisation,* Beverly Hills, Calif., Sage.
Nelson, R. R. and Winter, S. G. (1982) *An Evolutionary Theory of Economic Change,* Cambridge, Mass., Harvard University Press.
Nieschlag, R. (1954) 'Die Dynamik der Betriebsformen im Handel', Rheinisch-Westfahalches Institut für Wirtschaftsforschung, Essen, Schriftenreihe, Neue Folge nr 7.
Nilsson, A. (1987) 'Distributionssystems for Finpapper', ('Distribution Systems for Fine Paper'), Working Paper, EFI Stockholm School of Economics, Stockholm, Sweden.
Pascale, R. T. (1984) 'Perspectives on Strategy: "The Real Story Behind Honda's Success"' *California Management Review,* 26, 3, pp. 47–72.
Pettigrew, A. (1985) *The Awakening Giant: Continuity and Change in Imperial Chemical Industries,* Oxford, Basil Blackwell.
Pfeffer, J. (1978) *Organisational Design,* Arlington Heights, Ill., AHM Publishing Co.
Pfeffer, J. (1987) 'Bringing the Environment Back' in The Social Context of Business Strategy' in D. Teece *The Competitive Challenge: Strategies for Industrial Innovation and Renewal,* Cambridge, Mass., Balinger Publishers.
Pfeffer, J. and Lebjebici (1973) 'Executive Recruitment and the Development of Interfirm Organisations', *Administrative Science Quarterly,* 18, pp. 449–61.
Pfeffer, J. and Salancik, G. (1978) *The External Control of Organisations,* New York, Harper and Row.
Piori, M. and Sabel, F. (1984) *The Second Industrial Divide: Possibilities for Prosperity,* New York, Basic Books.
Porter, M. J. (1980) *Competitive Strategy: Techniques for Analyzing Industries and Competitors,* New York, The Free Press.
Reich, L. S. (1985) *The Making of American Industrial Research; Science and Business at G. E. and*

*Bell, 1876–1926,* Cambridge, Cambridge University Press.
Rogers, E. M. (1982) *Interorganisational Coordination,* Ames, Ia., Iowa State University Press.
Rogers, E. M. (1984) 'Organisations and Networks; Illustrations from the Silicon Valley Microelectronics Industry', International Research Seminar on Industrial Marketing, Stockholm School of Economics, Stockholm.
Rogers, E. M. and Kincaid, D. L. (1981) *Communication Networks: Toward a New Paradigm for Research,* New York, The Free Press.
Root, F. (1978/82) *Foreign Market Entry Strategies,* New York, AMACON.
Rosenberg, D. L. (1982) *Inside the Black Box: Technology and Economics,* Cambridge, Cambridge University Press.
Scherer, F. M. (1980) *Industrial Market Structure and Economic Performance,* 2nd edn, Boston, Mass., Houghton Mifflin.
Schumpeter, J. A. (1955) *The Theory of Economic Development,* Cambridge, Mass., Harvard University Press.
Scott, R. W. (1987) *Organisation: Rational, Natural and Open Systems,* 2nd edn, Englewood Cliffs, NJ, Prentice Hall.
Silverman, D. (1970) *The Theory of Organisations,* London, Heinemann.
Smith, P. and Easton, G. (1986) 'Network Relationships: A Longitudinal Study' 3rd International IMP Research Seminar, IRE Lyon, France.
Thorelli, H. B. (1986) 'Networks: Between Markets and Hierarchies', *Strategic Management Journal,* 7, 1, pp. 37–51.
Thompson, J. D. (1967) *Organisations in Action,* New York, McGraw-Hill.
Tichy, N. and Fombrun, C. (1979) 'Network Analysis in Organisational Settings', *Human Relations,* 32, 11, pp. 923–65.
Turnbull, P. W. and Valla, J.-P. (1986) *Strategies in International Industrial Marketing,* London, Croom Helm.
Van de Ven, A. (1976) 'On the Formation and Maintenance of Relations among Organisations', *Academy of Management Review,* 4, 4, pp. 24–36.
Van de Ven, A. and Ferry, D. L. (1980) *Measuring and Assessing Organisations,* New York, John Wiley.
Van de Ven, A. and Walker, G. (1984) 'Dynamics of Interorganizational Coordination', *Administrative Science Quarterly,* Dec. pp. 598–621.
Venkataraman, N. and Camillius, J. L. (1984) 'Exploring the Concept of "Fit" in Strategic Management', *Academy of Management Review,* 9, 3, pp. 513–25.
von Hippel, E. (1978) 'Successful Industrial Products from Customer Ideas', *Journal of Marketing,* 42, pp. 39–49.
von Hippel, E. (1986) 'Cooperation between Competing Firms. Informal Know-how Trading', Working Paper no. 1959–86, Sloan School of Management, March.
Walker, G. (1988) 'Network Analysis for Cooperative Interfirm Relationships' in F. J. Contractor and P. Lorange *Co-operative Strategies in International Business,* Lexington, Mass., Lexington Books.
Waluszewski, A. (1987) 'CTMP-Processen. Fran vedkravande till vedsnala processor', Department of Business Studies, University of Uppsala, Sweden.
Waluszewski, A. (1989) 'Framvaxten av en ny mekanisk massateknik – en utrecklingshistoria' ('The Emergence of a New Mechanical Pulping Technique – A Development Story'), Unpublished dissertation, Department of Business Studies, University of Uppsala, Sweden.
Weick, K. E. (1969) *The Social Psychology of Organizing,* 1st edn, Reading, Mass., Addison-Wesley.
Weick, K. E. (1970) 'Educational Organisations as Loosely Coupled Systems', *Administrative Science Quarterly,* 21, 1, pp. 1–19.
Weick, K. E. (1979) *The Social Psychology of Organizing,* 2nd edn, Reading, Mass., Addison-Wesley.
Weick, K. E. (1984) 'Small Wins: Redefining the Scale of Social Problems', *American Psychologist,* 39, pp. 40–9.
Weitz, B. (1985) 'Introduction to Special Issue on Competition in Marketing', *Journal of Marketing Research,* 22, pp. 229–36.

Wibe, S. (1980) 'Change of Technology and Day to Day Improvements', Umea Economic Studies, Umea University, Sweden.
Williamson, O. E. (1975) *Markets and Hierarchies*, New York, The Free Press.
Williamson, O. E. (1985) *The Economic Institutions of Capitalism*, New York, The Free Press.
Wind, Y. (1979) 'The Journal of Marketing at a Cross Road', *Journal of Marketing*, 43, pp. 9–12.
Yamagashi, T., Gilmore, M. and Cook, K. (1988) 'Network Connections and the Distribution of Power in Exchange Networks', *American Journal of Sociology*, 93, 4, pp. 835–51.
Zaltman, G., Le Masters, K. and Heffring, M. (1982) *Theory Construction in Marketing*, New York, John Wiley.

# 2

# A Model of Industrial Networks

*H. Håkansson and J. Johanson*


## SUMMARY

1 Alderson proposed micro-functionalism as opposed to macro-functionalism in the analysis of the market system. Instead of starting from defining the macro-function of the larger system, the micro-functional approach is set to identify the functions performed by the elements of the system, without defining any overriding purpose for the broader system as a whole.
2 A similar approach has been advocated by Axelrod (1984:38 ff.) when analysing the outcome of interactive behaviour.
3 The importance of rules and routines as means of coping with complexity is a theme not new to behavioural theorists. It raises the broad issue of formation of effective rules of conduct and of the role they play in 'rational behaviour'. It is relatively recent in the management literature, traditionally building on a conception of rationality that calls for assessment of each choice situation strictly on its own merits.


## STARTING POINTS

This chapter outlines a model of industrial networks. The main aim of the model is to make possible an integrated analysis of stability and development in industry. While stability is generally seen as the opposite to change and development this model views stability as vital for industrial development. A second aim of the model is to provide a basis for studies of the roles of actors and sets of actors in industrial development processes, given the relation between industrial stability and development.

The model's basic classes of variables are actors, activities and resources. These variables are related to each other in the overall structure of networks. This overall structure is mainly a matter of definition. Actors are defined as those who perform

Reprinted by permission of International Thomson, A Model of Industrial Networks by H. Håkansson and J. Johanson from *Industrial Networks: A New View of Reality*, Edited by B. Axelsson and G. Easton, pp. 28–34.

activities and/or control resources. In activities actors use certain resources to change other resources in various ways. Resources are means used by actors when they perform activities. Through these circular definitions a network of actors, a network of activities and a network of resources are related to each other (see Fig. 1).

## ACTORS

Actors control activities and/or resources. Individuals, groups of individuals, parts of firms, firms, and groups of firms can be actors. Thus, in an industrial network, there are actors at several organisational levels. Actors at lower levels can be part of actors at higher levels, independent of level, actors have five characteristics. First, they perform and control activities. They determine, alone or jointly, which activities to perform, how these activities are to be performed, and which resources are to be utilised when performing the activities. Second, through exchange processes actors develop relationships with each other. Each actor is embedded in a network of more or less strong relationships, which gives the actor access to other actors' resources.

Third, actors base their activities on control over resources. Such control can be direct or indirect. Direct control is based on ownership. Indirect control is based on relationships with other actors and the associated dependence relations with those actors. Relationships with other actors give indirect control over resources directly controlled by those actors to the extent that those actors are dependent on the focal actor. Within the constraints formed by ownership, control is also a function of knowledge. The existence of actors at several levels means that it is usually unclear which actors control which resources. Different actors may have different views about the control over a certain resource. Likewise opinions may differ widely as to the extent of control by a certain actor. The degree and nature

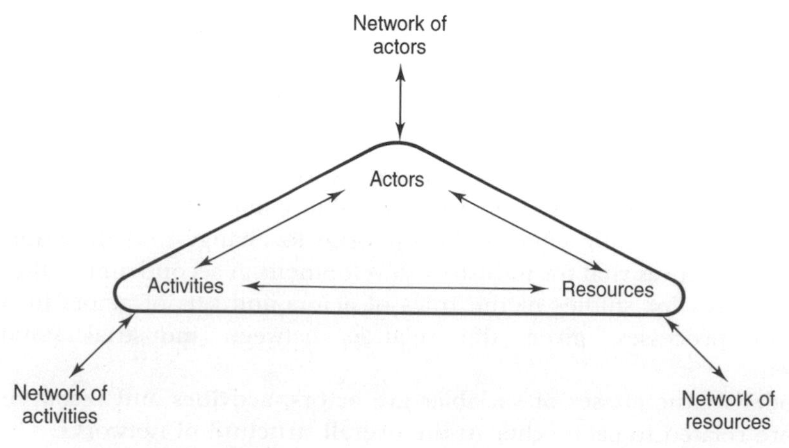


Fig. 1. Basic structure of the model.

of such differences in perceptions are important characteristics of industrial networks.

Fourth, actors are goal oriented. Irrespective of the goals of specific actors the general goal of actors is to increase their control over the network. The emphasis on the control goal follows from the assumption that control can be used to achieve other goals. Through their direct or indirect control, resources can be mobilised for other purposes. Network control is reached through control over resources and/or activities. Increased control over resources is a matter of increasing the control of resources directly, of increasing the indirect control over other resources via relationships, and of reducing indirect control by other actors through relationships, that is increasing autonomy. Control of activities is a matter of control over resources and of knowledge.

Fifth, actors have differential knowledge about activities, resources and other actors in the network. This knowledge is primarily developed through experience with activities in the network. Consequently, the knowledge of nearer parts of the network is greater than knowledge of more distant parts. The actors know different parts of the network, and even if they have experience of the same parts such experience may not be identical.

Network control is not evenly distributed over the actors in a network. The efforts of the actors to increase control affects the control of other actors. Increased control of one actor is always achieved at the expense of the control of at least one other actor. The actors have, to some extent, conflicting interests. On the other hand, increased control of one actor may, and generally will, lead to increased control of some other actors in the network. To some extent actors in a network also have common interests.

Thus, in a network, there are a number of conflicting and common interests as well as efforts to provide for those interests. In this struggle the actors use their knowledge of the network as well as their relationships with other actors in order to increase their control. Furthermore, as the actors are at different organisational levels this struggle takes place not only between actors but also within actors.

## ACTIVITIES

An activity occurs when one or several actors combine, develop, exchange, or create resources by utilising other resources. Because actors have different characteristics two main kinds of activities are distinguished, transformation activities and transfer activities. Through transformation activities resources are changed in some way. Transformation activities are always directly controlled by one actor. Transfer activities transfer direct control over a resource from one actor to another. Transfer activities link transformation activities of different actors to each other. They are never controlled by only one actor and they affect and are affected by the relationship between the actors involved.

Single activities are linked to each other in various ways. They constitute parts of more or less repetitive activity cycles where a number of interdependent activities are repeated. A complete activity cycle always contains both transformation and transfer activities. Either certain transfer activities are performed in order to make possible certain transformation activities or certain transformation activities are performed in order to make possible certain transfer activities. A complete activity cycle is never controlled by a single actor.

Some activity cycles are tightly coupled to each other while others are more loosely coupled. A sequence of tightly coupled activity cycles constituting a logical whole forms a transaction chain. Many activities are part of several activity cycles, and consequently, of several transaction chains. The different activity cycles of which an activity is part need not have the same regularity or periodicity; some of them may be more regular than others. And some are more frequently repeated than others. Actors performing single activities learn to perform those activities in a way which is to some extent dependent on the nature of the activity cycles and the transaction chains of which it is part. This experiential learning creates routines and informal rules which give the activities a certain institutionalised form. A basic stability is created.

Activities in the network are coupled to each other in various ways and to various degrees. Generally a certain activity is tightly linked to some other activities and loosely linked to others. Consequently there are a great number of relationships between activities. Direct relations exist between two activities which are directly coupled to each other, whereas indirect relations exist when activities are coupled to each other via intermediate activities. Specific relationships exist when two activities are linked to each other through specific actors whereas general relations between activities imply that the link between them is independent of specific actors.

From the perspective of the network, single activities by specific actors are almost never indispensable. They can always be dispensed with. This means that if a specific activity disappears the network can remain functionally intact because the surrounding activities are adjusted to that they take over the function of the absent activity. Furthermore, it is always possible to conceive of changes in the performance of single activities as well as in the couplings between them which would not affect the functioning of the network. Clearly, all such changes are associated with costs of adjustment which are not, however, necessarily born by those performing the activities.

The activity network is always imperfect in the sense that new activities, changes in old activities, or rearrangement of activities can make it more efficient. This is valid for whole networks as well as for any section of a network, even those controlled by single actors. Such changes are always occurring. Consequently, it is meaningless to speak about optimal activity systems or configurations.

## RESOURCES

Performing transformation and transfer activities requires resources. Resources are combined and thus combination requires resources. All resources are controlled by actors, either by single actors or jointly by several actors. Resources are heterogeneous. They have attributes in an unlimited number of dimensions. This means that the possibilities for the use of a specific resource can never be fully or finally specified. There are always further possibilities to use the resource in a different way or in a different setting. It is not possible to decide definitely how a certain resource can be combined with other resources. The result of combinations can always be elaborated.

Performing transformation activities requires transformation resources and performing transfer activities requires transfer resources (see Fig. 2). Transfer and transformation resources are mutually dependent on each other. The use and value of a specific resource is dependent on how it is combined with other resources. Those dimensions of a resource which are utilised and the value which is given a resource are dependent on the activity cycles in which it is utilised and on their functions in various transfer chains as well as their functions in the network.

Knowledge and experience of resources are important. First, when heterogeneous resources are combined their joint performance increases through experiential learning and adaptation. This is valid in the small scale when very specific resources are combined when performing specific activities. It is also valid in the large scale when bundles of resources controlled by one actor are combined with other bundles of resources. Second, when heterogeneous resources are combined new knowledge emerges which creates possibilities for new and improved combinations. New insights into the handling of resources can break existing activity cycles and transfer chains and contain the seeds for development and change in industrial networks. Thus, when resources are heterogeneous, change induces further change. This holds both for those resources which are used in the activities and those which perform and influence activities. It is also valid both for transformation resources and transfer resources.

Resources can be characterised, first, by the actors controlling the resource. They can be controlled directly by one actor or jointly by several actors. Indirectly the resources can be controlled by those actors who have relationships with the actor directly controlling the resource. The less available a resource the more important is

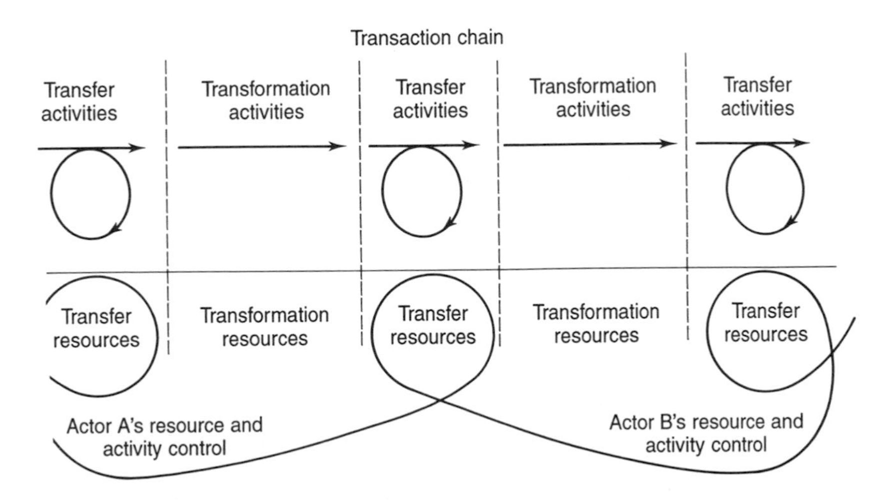


Fig. 2. Transaction chain.

the control over it and the more efforts will be spent on getting control over it. If there is a surplus of the resource, control is of no interest to the actors. A second characteristic is the utilisation of the resource in activities. How many dimensions of the resource are used and how standardised is the utilisation in each of the dimensions? We can conceive a scale with the resource used in one dimension in a standardised way as one extreme and in multiple dimensions in unique ways as the opposite extreme. Standardisation and uniqueness refer to how the resource is used by one actor as compared with the use of the resource by other actors. A third characteristic is the versatility of the resources. To what extent and at what cost can the resource be used in other activity cycles and in other transfer chains?

## THE NETWORK

For each of the three basic classes of variables, we have outlined relations between the elements. These elements form structures that can be described as networks. Actors develop and maintain relationships with each other and to understand the situation of an actor requires knowledge about the nature of the actor's relationships with other actors as well as an idea about the wider network of relationships around. In the same way the industrial activities are related to each other in patterns which can be seen as networks. Similarly resources are related to each other in networks and furthermore, the three networks are closely related to each other. They are interwoven in a total network. The three networks are bound together by forces, in terms of which the total network can be analysed. Important forces are as follows:

1 Functional interdependence: actors, activities and resources together form a system where heterogeneous demands are satisfied by heterogeneous resources. They are functionally related to each other.
2 Power structure: on the basis of control of activities and resources there are important power relations between the actors. The performance of the activities are to some extent organised on the basis of those power relations.
3 Knowledge structure: the design of the activities as well as the use of the resources is bound together by the knowledge and experience of present and earlier actors. And the knowledge of those actors is related one to another.
4 Intertemporal dependence: the network is a product of its history in terms of all memories, investments in relationships, knowledge, routines, etc. Changes of the network must be accepted by at least large parts of the network. Therefore all changes will be marginal and closely related to the past.

This last point suggests that stability and development within the network are closely related. Development in certain areas needs stability in others, and vice versa. Development of activities can be a means to secure stability in the power structure. Stable relationships can be important when one actor tries to develop the use of certain resources.

Actors in the network can act. Thus, the model is voluntaristic. On the other hand, the action possibilities are circumscribed by the relations between actors, activities and resources. But these relations are also the means for important changes in the network. Relationships make it possible to mobilise large parts of the network when great changes are required.

In summary, the network model described here suggests mechanisms whereby stability and change in industrial systems not only co-exist but are actually dependent one upon the other.

## BIBLIOGRAPHY

Alderson, W. (1957) *Marketing Behaviour and Executive Action*, Homewood, Ill., Richard D. Irwin.

Alderson, W. (1965) *Dynamic Marketing Behaviour. A Functionalist Theory of Marketing*, Homewood Ill., Richard D. Irwin.

# 3

# No Business is an Island: The Network Concept of Business Strategy

*H. Håkansson and I. Snehota*

## INTRODUCTION

Looking back over what has happened in the study of business organization over the last 20 years, we can see that two major trends emerge quite clearly. Firstly, there has been a growing interest in business strategy and how it is managed. Secondly, a shift can be noticed in the focus of organizational theory away from the internal processes of organizations and towards the organization–environment interface. Both trends have produced valuable new insights and have advanced our understanding of the behaviour of business organizations.

There is an interesting contraposition between the two fields of research. Organizational theory studies which focus on the interface between the organization and its environment have tended to conclude that the individual organization is often embedded in its environment and that its behaviour is thus greatly constrained if not predetermined, which means that it is not a free and independent unit. In contrast to this, research on strategy management has been concerned with the opportunities for directing and managing the behaviour of the individual organization, consequently assuming that the organization possesses a certain degree of freedom of choice. Cross-fertilization between the two fields of research has so far been limited, possibly because of this difference in perspective.

The purpose of this article is to explore the contribution that could be made to a conceptual frame of reference for business strategy management by one of the research programmes which focuses on the organizational–environment interface, and to which a network approach has been applied. We start by examining some of the assumptions underlying the current "strategy management doctrine". The network model of the organization–environment interface is then reviewed and three central issues of the strategy management doctrine are discussed from the viewpoint of the network model: (1) organizational boundaries, (2) determinants of organizational effectiveness, and (3) the process of managing business strategy.

Reprinted from *Scandinavian Journal of Management*, Vol 4, No 3, H. Håkansson and I. Snehota, No Business is an Island: The Network Concept of Business Strategy, pp. 187–200.

## THE CONCEPT OF BUSINESS STRATEGY

The conceptual frame of reference of business strategy management is not easy to grasp. It consists of a large and growing body of quite varied contributions from such groups as industrial economists (Chandler, 1962; Porter, 1980, 1985), organizational theorists (Hall and Saias, 1980; Miles and Snow, 1984; Mintzberg, 1987; Pfeffer, 1987) and management theorists and consultants (Ansoff, 1965; Hofer and Schendel, 1978; Henderson, 1979; Ohmae, 1982). These multifaceted contributions are pretty heterogeneous in their approach as well as in the areas covered. In their current forms they can only be loosely linked together in what will be referred to below as the doctrine of business strategy management.

The concept of strategy as applied to business studies has only been appearing with any great frequency since about 1960 (Chandler, 1962; Ansoff, 1965). Since that date, it has gained wide acceptance, although "strategy" remains an ambiguous and elusive concept. Its meaning in the military context, "the art of so moving and disposing troops as to impose upon the enemy the place and time and conditions for the fighting preferred by oneself" (*Oxford English Dictionary*) does not seem to lend itself easily to business organizations. In particular, it is argued, because resources of business organizations (i.e. their "troops") are largely fixed in place and time (Pennings, 1985, p. 2) it is difficult to dispose resources in time and space. In business organization contexts "strategy" has sometimes been defined with a certain degree of opportunism. Its definition often remains implicit, open to intuitive interpretation. (Among others Ansoff (1965) avoided any definition of strategy). Explicit definitions of strategy are nevertheless quite numerous. The content assigned to the concept varies from one author to another, but the essence of the many definitions converges in the concept of strategy as "the pattern in the stream of decisions and activities ... (Mintzberg and McHugh, 1985, p. 6) ... that characterizes the match an organization achieves with its environment ... and that is determinant for the attainment of its goals ..." (Hofer and Schendel, 1978, p. 25). The emphasis is on the pattern of activities which has an impact on the achievement of the organizational goals in relation to its environment.

Research on business strategy has been concerned primarily to understand what makes a business organization effective in its environment, and to explore the organizational processes required to enhance this effectiveness. It is usually assumed that the criterion of effectiveness in the case of business organizations is the accumulation of monetary wealth over time, achieved by way of exchange with other parties in the environment. The accumulation of resources is supposed to be the prerequisite for the survival of the organization. The dominant idea in the conceptual core of business strategy research has been partly derived from biology ("survival of the fittest"). The effectiveness of the organization, its potential for accumulating resources, is assumed to be a function of matching the characteristics of the environment with the capabilities of the organization. A positive balance in the exchange of resources with the environment is ensured by adapting to this environment. The idea of "fit" between the capabilities of the organization and the characteristics of the environment (in particular customers and competitors, referred to as the "market") is the central theme in the strategy management doctrine (Miles and Snow, 1984; Venkatraman and Camillus, 1984).

The fit with the environment is assumed to be good, if the organization out-performs other organizations in competing for the resources held by other entities in the environment. To out-perform others is usually equated with offering "superior value" to one's counterparts in the exchange process (Porter, 1985, p. 3; Levitt, 1980). It is assumed that this "superior value" is based on overall efficiency in transforming inputs into outputs. This efficiency permits a company to "dominate" parts of its environment (Rhenman, 1973; Norman, 1977, p. 26).

Strategy management is seen as a process of adapting the pattern of activities performed by the organization to the external environmental conditions in which the organization operates. Managing strategy thus means managing the process whereby the pattern of activities to be performed by the organization is conceived (i.e. strategy formulation), and then creating the conditions necessary to ensure that these activities are carried out (i.e. strategy implementation). It is often stressed that, because the environment is always changing, this has to be a continuous process.

Three assumptions are generally made explicitly or implicitly about the nature of the process of adapting to the environmental conditions in the current strategy management doctrine.

First, the environment of an organization is faceless, atomistic and beyond the influence or control of the organization. Whatever happens to the task environment of the organization stems from forces outside the organization itself. Even it it is sometimes admitted that "political networking" with competitors, for example, may provide a way of exerting influence over some part of the environment, the basic assumption is still that the environment cannot be controlled. Consequently opportunities do exist in the environment, and they are there to be identified and exploited. They cannot be created or enacted; rather, the organization can exploit them by adapting itself to its environment. It is implied that a dividing-line exists between the organization and its environment. The environment exists, even without the organization.

Secondly, the strategy, the pattern of critical activities, of a business organization results from the deployment of resources controlled hierarchically (contractually) by the organization. Controlled resources are allocated in certain combinations, providing products/services to be exchanged with the environment. Further resources can be obtained by means of exchange with the environment, across the boundaries of the organization. In the supposedly competitive and "non-controllable" environment, the effectiveness or exchange potential of an organization will depend on its relative efficiency in combining its internal resources. Internal resources can be reallocated in order to adapt to environmental conditions, thus enhancing effectiveness.

Thirdly, environmental conditions change continuously, so that frequent if not continuous adaptation is required of the organization. There is a group of individuals (management) in the organization which is concerned by definition with managing organizational effectiveness. It is assumed that this group can and does interpret environmental conditions, after which it formulates and implements a future strategy. It decides and crafts the pattern of activities to be executed by the organization.

All three assumptions have been challenged, directly or indirectly by several streams of research, particularly in organization theory. Hannan and Freeman (1977) with their concept of the collective dependence of organizations, Pfeffer and Salancik (1978) who talk about the resource dependence of organizations, Weick (1969) who discusses the expost rationality of organizations, and Hall and Saias (1980) and Mintzberg (1987) who examine the nature of the strategy formulation process, are but a few examples of those who advocate the adoption of different assumptions regarding a number of issues.

In this paper we will examine in particular the position adopted by the proponents of the network model of the organization–environment interface. This proposition draws on the work of the organizational theorists referred to above, but it also constitutes a somewhat more elaborate set of propositions, particularly about the market behaviour of business organizations.

## NETWORK MODEL OF ORGANIZATION–ENVIRONMENT INTERFACE

What is referred to below as the network model is the outcome of a fairly broad research programme dealing primarily with the functioning of business markets, which originated in the mid-1970s at the University of Uppsala. The research programme has spread to a few other research institutions, mainly in Europe. The programme can be described as a collection of studies with a largely common frame of reference (Hägg and Johanson, 1982; Hammarkvist *et al.*, 1982; Mattsson, 1985; Kutschker, 1985; Ford *et al.*, 1986; Turnbull and Valla, 1986; Thorelli, 1986; Håkansson, 1982, 1987, 1989).

The network model of the organization–environment interface stems originally from casual observations that business organizations often operate in environments which include only a limited number of identifiable organizational entities (actors). These entities are involved in continuous exchange relationships with the organization. In such cases each individual party exerts considerable influence on the organization. This situation is encountered most often by industrial companies operating in business markets which include a limited number of suppliers, competitors and customers. However, some more extensive empirical studies (Turnbull and Valla, 1986; Håkansson, 1989) suggest that this type of situation may be the rule rather than the exception for a wider population of business organizations in general. The propositions of the network model refer to situations and cases in which the environment of the organizations is of a concentrated and structured kind, i.e. it is constituted by a set of other active organizations.

When the entities constraining and impinging on the behaviour of the organization are few in number, they are usually treated as unique counterparts, i.e. each one is endowed with a distinct identity. As a result of an organization's interactions and exchange processes with any of these, relationships develop that link the resources and activities of one party with those of another. The relationships (linkages) are generally continuous over time, rather than being composed of discrete transactions. They are often complex, consisting of a web of interactive relations between individuals in both organizations.

Within the framework of such an interorganizational relationship, a complex set of interdependencies gradually evolves. Activities within one party are connected with activities carried out in the other. Activities are carried out by actors pursuing their own goals and possessing their own perceptions of the interacting party's activity pattern, among other things. Activities undertaken by the parties in a relationship cannot, therefore, be connected without the active and reciprocal involvement of both parties. The establishment and development of an interorganizational relationship requires a "mutual orientation" (Ford *et al.*, 1986).

Relating the activities of the two parties to one another entails adaptations and the establishment of routines on both sides. Given the distinctive nature of the parties, the interdependencies in the relationship become further strengthened. Through their relationship either party can gain access to the other's resources. To some degree actors can therefore mobilize and use resources controlled by other actors in the network. An organization's relationships with others represent the framework and form for the exchange process with other parties.

The interaction between the parties in a relationship entails more than just passive adaptation. While the two parties are interacting, their problems are confronted with solutions, their abilities with needs, etc. Reciprocal knowledge and capabilities are revealed and developed jointly and in mutual dependence by the two parties. Distinct capabilities are thus generated and have meaning in an organization only through the medium of other parties. They are unique to each party, since no two sets of related organizations are alike. In this sense the identity of an organization is created in interaction with its major counterparts.

When the environmental conditions of a business organization are of the kind described, when it is gravitating towards a set of other active organizations, then analogous environmental conditions can be assumed for the whole set of organizations with which the focal organization is interacting. The organization is then embedded in relationships with identifiable counterparts. This web of relationships can be called a network. One of the salient properties of such a network consists of the interdependencies between the different relationships (Cook and Emerson, 1978). These interdependencies exist as regards activities, resources and actors. The activities in two different relationships can complement each other, if they are part of the same activity chain. Or they may be in competition. Similarly resources used, accessed or exchanged in one relationship can complement or compete with those used, accessed or exchanged in another relationship in which the organization is involved. Actors can use the existence of complementarity or competitiveness in their relationships in different ways, as they interact with one another. This can create not only triangular relationships, but even "dramas" involving four, five, six, or more participating business organizations.

The performance and effectiveness of organizations operating in a network, by whatever criteria these are assessed, become dependent not only on how well the organization itself performs in interaction with its direct counterparts, but also on how these counterparts in turn manage their relationships with third parties. An organization's performance is therefore largely dependent on whom it interacts with.

Before we can summarize the propositions of the network model, we must mention the concept of the environment of the organization. What appears to give a business organization its identity and to define its field of operations in the network view, cannot be fruitfully covered by the concept of the "environment", or by the more circumscribed concept of the "relevant environment". The environment is not a meaningful concept in these situations; more meaningful is the set of related entities. Moreover, the (inter)dependence of an organization on other entities makes it difficult to disconnect the organization from its network, since a business organization without its interactive environment loses its identity. It therefore seems useful to adopt the concept of the "context" of an organization rather than its environment, when we want to refer to the entities that are related to the organization. The context is enacted, it is created by the organization itself, and in a sense it even constitutes the organization itself. The propositions of the network model can at this point be summarized as follows:

1. Business organizations often operate in a context in which their behaviour is conditioned by a limited number of counterparts, each of which is unique and engaged in pursuing its own goals.
2. In relation to these entities, an organization engages in continuous interactions that constitute a framework for exchange processes. Relationships make it possible to access and exploit the resources of other parties and to link the parties' activities together.
3. The distinctive capabilities of an organization are developed through its interactions in the relationships that it maintains with other parties. The identity of the organization is thus created through relations with others.
4. Since the other parties to the interaction also operate under similar conditions, an organization's performance is conditioned by the totality of the network as a context, i.e. even by interdependencies among third parties.

When and if organizations operate under the conditions described above, then acceptance of the propositions of the network model calls for a review of the assumptions underlying the business strategy management doctrine. We will undertake such a review in the following discussion. Our intention is to contribute to the development of a frame of reference for the strategy management doctrine, relevant to organizations operating under the kind of conditions for which the network model has proved its descriptive adequacy. We shall try to see how far the present frame of reference for business strategy can be enriched to become a more effective conceptual tool for intervention in the funtioning of an organization if and when the organization is operating under the circumstances assumed by the network model.

## ORGANIZATIONAL BOUNDARIES

The definition of a "boundary", when applied to any social system, is naturally quite arbitrary (Hall and Fagen, 1956) and depends on the intentions and aims of the observer. When the perspective of management is adopted, as in the strategy management doctrine, the intention is to embrace within the boundaries of the organization those resources and activities that can be controlled and influenced by the organization, and to leave outside those that cannot be influenced. This control is assumed to be necessary in order to adapt and relate effectively to the environment. An organization's boundaries should thus be set as coterminous with the limits to its activity control: "the organization ends where its discretion ends and another begins" (Pfeffer and Salancik, 1978, p. 32).

The conventional view is that the boundaries are given by the hierarchical (proprietary or contract) control of resources (including individual actors). This view implies what can be referred to as a "membership criterion" for the definition of the boundaries of an organization. Such a criterion gives an apparently clear dividing-line between the organization and its environment, in effect between internal and external factors. Apart from the problem of the type of contractual arrangement that permits "hierarchical" control and discretion in the exercise of deliberate choice behaviour (Cheung, 1983), the issue that remains to be dealt with is whether such a view permits us to capture, within the boundaries of the organization, all the resources and activities that have a significant impact on its effectiveness. In a network perspective, this is hardly the case.

Where the network view of the organizational context holds, some of the organization's relationships with other organizations in the network constitute in themselves one of the most – if not the most – valuable resources that it possesses. Through these relationships with other parties, resources and activities are made available and can be mobilized and exploited by the organization in order to enhance its own performance. Access to the other party's resources – resources that complement those of the focal organization – constitutes an important asset (Fiocca and Snehota, 1986). According to a somewhat more extreme view of the assets of a business organization, it is claimed that the "invisible" or "intangible" assets assume a central role in organizational effectiveness, since they are the differentiating factor in performance that gives an organization its distinctive identity (Itami, 1987; Vicari, 1988). The invisible assets, consisting largely of knowledge and abilities, fame and reputation, are mainly created in external relationships. Furthermore they cannot be separated from these relationships.

Quite apart from the resource argument, another aspect emphasized in the network view of the organizational context has considerable bearing on the problem of boundary-setting, namely the interrelatedness that prevails in networks and the possible impact on the focal organization of relationships among third parties. The concept of interrelatedness is inherent in the network view. The magnitude of these effects on the behaviour of the organization has been stressed, for example, in some studies of technology development processes. The importance of resources and activities "external" to the traditional boundaries of the organization, and the interrelatedness with relationships to third parties, has been documented in studies that focus on the process of technology diffusion and technology development (von Hippel, 1982; Håkansson, 1987; Waluszewski, 1988; Imai, 1987) and in some of the research on growth patterns in new-venture organizations (Aldrich *et al.*, 1987; Lorenzoni and Ornati, 1988).

In view of the role of "external" resources and interdependencies stressed in the network view of business organizations, it becomes meaningless and conceptually impossible to disconnect the organization from its context. The organization appears without boundaries in as much as it is to a certain degree constituted by resources and activities controlled by other parties forming the network, and exists only in the perceptions of other parties. It develops its distinctive capabilities in relationships with others. The organization is constrained in the exercise of its discretion, as much as it constrains the discretion of those with whom it interacts. The organization exists and performs in a context rather than in an environment, in as much as it has a meaning and a role only in relation to a number of interrelated actors. This makes it difficult to define "where the discretion of an organization, and thus the organization itself, ends and another begins".

In comparison with the conventional view of an organization's boundaries, this approach means on the one hand that some of the resources and activities traditionally considered "internal" can hardly be controlled and influenced by the organization, while a number of what have been considered "external" resources and activities do actually constitute an integral part of the organization itself and are subject to its influence and control. The "membership" criterion, while legally clear and important in determining the outcome of exchange, does not permit a focus on the variables determining an organization's effectiveness.

The purpose of setting the boundaries of an organization in the business strategy management doctrine is to focus on the variables which determine the effectiveness of the organization and which are also subject to the influence of the organization (that can be managed). In this management perspective it is essential to make the distinction between controllable and non-controllable variables. If this is to be done with a view to identifying the determinants of the organization's performance then the boundaries of an organization should be defined more broadly so as to include the critical connected activities and the resources that can be mobilized as a result of the ongoing network relaitonships – in other words, the context of the organization. How much of the context constitutes the organization depends of course on the degree of interdependence within the context. To assess the interdependencies we need to look a little more closely at the question of organizational effectiveness.

## ORGANIZATIONAL EFFECTIVENESS

The issue of organizational effectiveness is central to the whole business strategy management doctrine. The content of a strategy, the activity patterns that affect the achievement of goals, can only be defined by reference to the factors that determine the organization's effectiveness. Assuming that survival is the overriding goal of the organization, which in the case of a business organization is based on the accumulation of monetary wealth through exchange, the effectiveness of the business organization is determined by its "bargaining position". An organization's bargaining position is "the ability of the organization to exploit its environment in the acquisition of scarce and valuable resources" (Yuchtman and Seashore, 1967, p. 898). The effectiveness of a business organization is thus given by its capacity to acquire resources through exchange with other parties in its context.

After relating effectiveness to "bargaining position" we have to ask ourselves how a certain bargaining position is reached by an organization and what are the determinants of this position. In organizational theory, the bargaining position is often interpreted in terms of organizational power, in the sense of a capacity to influence the behaviour of related actors. Few issues have been discussed with as much heat and as little result as the issue of interorganizational power. Hoping to avoid entanglement in the intricacies of this concept that have little bearing on our subject, we will resort to a slightly different view of the bargaining position.

In order to elaborate the idea of the bargaining position, it seems necessary to examine the nature of exchange transactions. A few disciplines such as economics, social anthropology and marketing have been concerned with this topic. The common view of the nature of exchange transactions is that the object of any exchange between two parties is some form of activity or performance, e.g. products and goods, services, money. The purpose of exchange is the acquisition of "performance" regardless of the form in which it is represented. What is acquired by the exchange is not goods or services or money, but what these things can do for the party engaged in the exchange (Levitt, 1980; Belshaw, 1965). Even when the purpose appears to be the acquisition of resources, the underlying rationale is the acquisition of activities (utility or performance). The outcome of an exchange process is thus determined by what the objects of the exchange can accomplish for the exchanging parties; it is therefore individual and subjective. (It should be noted that this view contains some elements of the notion of "distinct counterparts" rather than generic environment or market.)

The traditional view of economists and organizational analysts is that an organization's capacity to reach a favourable bargaining position, a position that permits a positive balance in exchange with the environment, depends mainly on the organization's efficiency in transforming input resources into output. It is said to be so, since in a certain situation the expected value of the organization's output (product, service, etc.) is assumed to be the same for all kinds of different counterparties. What can be obtained through exchange is, therefore, largely outside the control of the individual organizational unit. The unit can only exercise a certain amount of control over the cost side of the transformation. The bargaining position is thus assumed to be dependent on the arrangement of resources and activities internal to the firm (within the narrow boundaries). The fit of the activities of the organization with the characteristics of the environment is achieved by rearranging the activities and resources internal to the organization. It is conceded, mainly by those who adopt the management perspective and in particular by marketing theorists, that to a certain degree organizations can choose their environments, especially their customers, thus improving their bargaining position (Abel and Hammond, 1979). But it is still assumed that the move is achieved autonomously and unilaterally by the organization by making adjustments in its internal resources. The bargaining position of the organization is therefore conceived as determined by the deployment of the organization's own assets.

Two concepts that appear in the network model – "network position" and "strategic identity" (Johanson and Mattsson, 1985; Håkansson and Johanson, 1988) – could be useful to anyone exploring the issue of the bargaining position and the effectiveness of the organization. Both concepts have been used to stress some of the characteristics of the exchange processes in the network setting. To a party engaged in a transaction relationship with an organization, the expected value of the exchange is given by the amount of resources that can be accessed and the activities which the organization can perform for the focal party within the relationship. To the individual party the value of the performance available through the relationship is a function of the position that the organization assumes in that party's network. This "microposition" (Johanson and Mattsson, 1985) is the bargaining position of the organization *vis-à-vis* one specific counterpart. It depends on the efficiency of the resource deployment of the organization, and also on the effectiveness of the organization in relating to other entities constituting the network. It reflects the perceived potential of the organization to constitute a link with parts of the network that the focal party cannot access or relate to, or at least not with reasonable efficiency.

The composite of the micropositions – the macroposition – is qualitatively different. It reflects the role of the organization in its own network. Again, it is dependent on the capacity of the organization to constitute a link with resources and activities among the parties making up the network. It is therefore given partly by what is done within the organization itself and partly by what the organization does in relationships with others.

The network position, on the other hand, is a relative concept. Since no two parties' positions are alike, the network position means different things to different parties related to the focal organization. Moreover, the performance of an organization in a relationship is perceived and evaluated by another party on the basis of previous experience and present expectations. It is thus enacted rather than given by the amount and type of resources directly controlled. It exists only if perceived and recognized by the parties in the context. Recognition is dependent on the outcome of the interaction processes in an organization's relationships. The concept of "strategic identity" (Håkansson and Johanson, 1988) is thus included in the network model. Such a view seems to provide a slightly different picture of the means for achieving fit with the context. It suggests that the fit is obtained largely by establishing and maintaining relationships with other parties. For a relationship to come into existence requires that some action at least is taken by the other party. The action, or reaction, of the other party can only be triggered by the perceived exchange potential of the focal actor. The perception of exchange potential between the actors is largely determined by social interaction, and is therefore enacted rather than predetermined and given.

This leads us to regard the effectiveness of the organization as given, not by the organization's "adapting" to the environment but by its "relating" to the context. These "relating" activities include the quasi-integration of activities; the connection of resources in order to branch out into several actor levels, both to gain influence over others and to become dependent on others; and the influencing of one's own and other parties' perceptions of important dimensions in the context. While "adapting" necessarily leads to a focus on the internal processes of the organization, "relating" induces a shift in focus to its context. It is through its relationships with others that the distinctive capabilities of an organization are acquired and developed. It is therefore the activities taking place between the organization and the other parties, rather than activities within the organization itself, which are the determinants of the bargaining position and of the overall effectiveness of the organization in achieving its goals.

The concept of strategy, the pattern of activities determining effectiveness, thus acquires a different content from the one assumed in the prevailing strategy doctrine. Activities connected with positioning in the network and performed within the framework of external relationships – i.e. the process of relating – assume the primary role. The concepts of fit and misfit, which refer to states only, thus lose a great deal of their analytical power.

Such a view of strategy content has a significant bearing on the issue of management strategy, or the management of organizational effectiveness. We will now explore this further below.

## MANAGING THE EFFECTIVENESS OF AN ORGANIZATION

The traditional view of how the effectiveness of an organization is managed seems to concentrate mainly on *what* is to be managed and *how* it is to be done, and to a lesser degree on *who* does it. What is to be managed in order to enhance the effectiveness is, of course, related to the concept of effectiveness itself. Consequently the allocation of the organization's resources and its efficiency in transforming inputs into outputs are traditionally considered key issues. Positioning *vis-à-vis* the environment is said to be achieved by the type of output generated. The adaptation of output and internal efficiency are therefore the means to achieving a fit with the environment.

How is this done? Treatment of this issue has often been vague, except for the normative recommendations of the strictly managerial approach. The prevailing interpretation of the process is that strategy is first conceived and formulated on a basis of an assessment of the current and projected state of the environment and of the organizational resources. The assessment permits the identification of the adaptations that will be required of the organization, and which will subsequently be implemented (see among others Hofer and Schendel, 1978; Galbraith and Nathanielson, 1978). This process is continuous, or at least frequently recurring. It can be more or less explicit and formal, depending on the complexity and culture of the organization and the rate of change in its environment.

This view of the process of managing effectiveness could be called "the planning approach". It implies that decisions are taken after the scanning of environmental conditions, changes and opportunities; a plan of action is then formulated and implemented. It assumes that the management of the pattern of activities involves drafting a master plan of the pattern, which is then followed. Getting the organization to follow the plan may cause problems, but these can be solved by clear target setting, incentives and control. This view of the strategy management process has been challenged from quite different standpoints (Weick, 1969; Peters and Waterman, 1982; Kagono *et al.*, 1985). Its critics have invoked the bounded rationality of complex organizations in a complex and dynamic environment as their main objection.

When it comes to the question of who manages organizational effectiveness, the various opinions are delivered in disguise, especially and somewhat surprisingly in organizational theory. A clearcut but less convincing position has been offered elsewhere. It is generally suggested, sometimes implicitly, that strategy formulation and implementation are the concern of a group of individuals in the organization, namely management, whose primary function is to interpret the environment, to formulate strategy, and to make the adaptations required of the organization in order to pursue this strategy.

The network model seems to generate another approach to the question of effectiveness management in organizations. It was claimed above that relating to the context is the central issue of the strategy. Relating to the context, that is to say creating a distinctive identity, is something that has to be managed. Given the relativity of the context concept, the context itself is conceived not as given beforehand or predetermined, but as enacted: it cannot be assessed. Strategic identity, the basis of effectiveness, is achieved by the interaction behaviour of individuals in relationships. Interaction is the stream of events that ultimately determines effectiveness and constitutes strategy. Thus the effectiveness of an organization – its strategy – is based on interactive behaviour. How can interactive behaviour be directed and managed?

Within a relationship interaction takes place between actors who are pursuing their own goals and acting purposefully. In such a setting, reacting to other actors' actions can be more important than acting itself. And the reactive behaviour in the process of interaction is something that can hardly be planned. Rather, the behaviour of actors in these circumstances can only be guided by norms and values based on past experience, possibly in the form of organizational routines (Nelson and Winter, 1982, p. 124). The pattern of activities that determines effectiveness can thus be directed and managed by values and norms of behaviour, not by prescriptions about the pattern.

This brings us back to the concept of context. The context of an organization is a social symbolic reality in which an organization chooses to exist, and does so by "framing" it (Berg, 1985). The framing of a context, i.e. assuming its structural and dynamic properties, is the basis of any attempt to create an identity for an organization and to position it in the context. The framing of a context can only be achieved by interpreting and rationalizing past experience. This ex-post rationalization constitutes the organization's learning which, when formulated into norms and routines, guides the behaviour of the different actors in the organization (March and Olsen, 1976; Weick, 1969; Mintzberg, 1987; Kinch, 1988). Organizational effectiveness is thus managed by framing the context rather than by designing (planning) a future pattern of activities.

The framing of a context at the organizational level is a social process. It is carried out by individuals but is coded and stored collectively. The individuals who implement the socialization of the context-framing are thus those who *de facto* manage the effectiveness and the strategy of the organization. They may not necessarily be identical with those who plan and design the pattern of activities, but it is the management of the organization which is accountable for the results achieved through exchange.

## CONCLUDING REMARKS

Throughout the above discussion we have been addressing one broad issue: what contribution can be made to the conceptual frame of reference of the business strategy doctrine on a basis of the insights gained by adopting a network view of business organization. A few areas in which the business strategy doctrine could be developed in the case of organizations operating under "network conditions" have been identified and discussed.

We have touched upon the problems of defining the boundaries of an organization, of assessing organizational effectiveness and finally of managing organizational effectiveness. We have claimed that when a network view is adopted some not inconsiderable changes are required in all the three areas with respect to the basic assumptions of the business strategy model. All our arguments stem from a basic proposition about the situations described by the network model: continuous interaction with other parties constituting the context with which the organization interacts, endows the organization with meaning and a role. When this proposition applies, any attempt to manage the behaviour of the organization will require a shift in focus away from the way the organization allocates and structures its internal resources and towards the way it relates its own activities and resources to those of the other parties that constitute its context. Such a shift in focus entails a somewhat different view of the meaning of organizational effectiveness: what does it depend on and how can it be managed?

By applying the network concept to the analysis of the behaviour of the business organization, we open up another broader issue that we have not addressed here, concerning the assumptions that are made about the very scope of the concept of the business organization. We have been referring throughout to the concept of the business organization as it is used in the literature of strategy management, with its roots in the microeconomic theory of the firm. The firm or organization is viewed primarily as a production function, which is thus concerned mainly with the control and allocation of internal resources according to the criterion of efficiency. This view has also been institutionalized in the legal system, for example, in terms of laws regarding ownership (i.e. the legal boundary of the company), accounting, tax regulations, and so on. It has led to a fairly narrow perspective on the basic issues addressed by the strategy management doctrine. There have been other attempts to broaden and adjust this perspective apart from our own, but hardly any attempts to change it radically.

When we look back over the implications of the network model we get the impression that if the network view is adopted, it will constitute a challenge to the prevailing view of the business organization as a production function. The network model leads to quite a different view of the range and role of the business organization. The emphasis on the linking of activities and resources within a network as a primary task of the business organization seems to suggest that enterprise should be conceived as a transaction function rather than a production function. Such a concept of enterprise could lead naturally to a shift in focus, away from the control of resources towards the integration of resources, and away from the management of acting towards the management of reacting. Although we feel that such a new concept of enterprise is called for, it still seems to be pretty far off.

## REFERENCES

Abel, D. F. and Hammond, J. S. *Strategic Market Planning*. Prentice Hall, Englewood Cliffs, NJ (1979).

Aldrich, H., Rosen, B. and Woodward, W. A social role perspective of entrepreneurship, Working paper. UNC School of Business Administration (1987).

Ansoff, I. H. *Corporate Strategy.* McGraw-Hill; New York (1965).

Belshaw, C. S. *Traditional Exchange and Modern Markets.* Prentice Hall, Englewood Cliffs, NJ (1965).

Berg, P. O. Organization change as a symbolic transformation process. In P. J. Frost *et al.* (eds), *Organization Culture.* Sage, New York (1985).

Buzzel, R. D. and Gale, B. T. *The PIMS Principles.* The Free Press, Macmillan, New York (1987).

Chandler, A. D., Jr. *Strategy and Structure.* MIT Press, Cambridge, MA (1962).

Cheung, S. N. C. The contractual nature of the firm. *Journal of Law and Economics,* April, 2–21 (1983).

Cook, K. S. and Emerson, R. M. Power, equity and commitment in exchange networks. *American Sociological Review,* 721–39 (1978).

Fiocca, R. and Snehota, I. Marketing e alta tecnologia. *Sviluppo e Organizzazione,* **98**, 24–31 (1986).

Ford, D. I., Håkansson, H. and Johanson, J. How do companies interact? *Industrial Marketing and Purchasing,* **1**, 26–41 (1986).

Galbraith, J. R. and Nathanielson, D. A. *Strategy Implementation, The Role of Structure and Process.* West Publishing, St. Paul, MN (1978).

Hägg, I. and Johanson, J. (eds), *Företag i nätverk – ny syn på konkurrenskraft* (Firms in Networks – A New Perspective of Competitive Power), SNS, Stockholm (1982).

Håkansson, H. (ed.) *International Marketing and Purchasing of Industrial Goods. An Interaction Approach.* John Wiley, Chichester (1982).

Håkansson, H. (ed.) *Industrial Technological Development. A Network Approach.* Croom Helm, London (1987).

Håkansson, H. *Corporate Technological Behaviour. Cooperation and Networks.* Routledge, London (1989).

Håkansson, H. and Johanson, J. Formal and informal cooperation strategies in international industrial networks. In F. J. Contractor and P. Lorange (eds), *Cooperative Strategies in International Business.* Lexington Books, MA (1988).

Hall, A. D. and Fagen, R. E. Definition of system. *General Systems: The Yearbook of the Society for the Advancement of General Systems Theory.* (1956), pp. 18–28.

Hall, D. J. and Saias, M. A. Strategy follows structure. *Strategic Management Journal,* 149–63 (1980).

Hammarkvist, K.-O. Håkansson, H. and Mattsson, L-G. *Marknadsföring för konkurrenskraft* (Marketing for Competitive Power). Liber, Malmö (1982).

Hannan, M. T. and Freeman, J. The population ecology of organizations. *American Journal of Sociology,* 929–65 (1977).

Henderson, B. D. *Hendersson on Corporate Strategy.* Boston Consulting Group Inc. Abt Books, Cambridge, MA (1979).

Hofer, C. W. and Schendel, D. *Strategy Formulation, Analytical Concepts.* West Publishing, St. Paul, MN (1978).

Imai, K. Network industrial organization in Japan. Working paper prepared for the workshop on "New Issues in Industrial Economics" at Case Western Reserve University, Cleveland. 7–10 June 1987.

Itami, H. *Mobilizing Invisible Assets.* Harvard University Press, Boston, MA (1987).

Johanson, J. and Mattsson, L.-G. Marketing investments and market investments in industrial networks. *International Journal of Research in Marketing,* 185–95 (1985).

Kagono, T., Nonaka, K., Sakakibara, K. and Okumura, A. *Strategic vs Evolutionary Management: A U.S.–Japan Comparison of Strategy and Organization.* North Holland, Amsterdam (1985).

Kinch, N. Strategic illusion as a management strategy. Working Paper. Dept of Business Administration, University of Uppsala (1988/2).

Kutschker, M. The multi-organizational interaction approach to industrial marketing. *Journal of Business Research,* 383–403 (1985).

Levitt, T. Marketing success through differentiation – of anything. *Harvard Business Review,* January/February (1980).

Lorenzoni, G. and Ornati, O. A. Constellations of firms and new ventures. *Journal of Business Venturing*, 41–57 (1988).

March, J. G. and Olsen, J. P. *Ambiguity and Choice in Organizations*. Universitetsforlaget, Bergen, Norway (1976).

Mattsson, L.-G. An application of a network approach to marketing. Defining and changing market positions. In J. Dholakia and J. Arndt (eds), *Alternative Paradigms for Widening Marketing Theory*. JAI Press, Greenwich, CT (1985).

Miles, R. E. and Snow, C. C. Fit, failure and the hall of fame. *California Management Review*, **3** (Spring), 10–28 (1984).

Mintzberg, H. Crafting strategy. *Harvard Business Review*, July/August, 66–75 (1987).

Mintzberg, H. and McHugh, A. Strategic formulation in an adhocracy. *Administrative Science Quarterly*, 160–97 (1985).

Nelson, R. R. and Winter, S. G. *Evolutionary Theory of Economic Change*. Harvard University Press, Cambridge, MA (1982).

Norman, R. *Management for Growth*. John Wiley, Chichester (1977).

Ohmae, K. *The Mind of the Strategist*. McGraw-Hill, New York (1982).

Pennings, J. M. (ed.) *Organizational Strategy and Change*. Jossey-Bass, San Francisco (1985).

Peters, T. J. and Waterman, R. H. *In Search of Excellence*. Harper and Row, New York (1982).

Pfeffer, J. Bringing the environment back in the social context of business strategy. In D. Teece (ed.), *The Competitive Challenge. Strategies for Industrial Innovation and Renewal*. Ballinger, Cambridge, MA (1987).

Pfeffer, J. and Salancik, G. R. *The External Control of Organizations. A Resource Dependence Perspective*. Harper Row, New York (1978).

Porter, M. E. *Competitive Strategy*. Free Press, Macmillan, New York (1980).

Porter, M. E. *Competitive Advantage*. Free Press, Macmillan, New York (1985).

Rhenman, E. *Organization Theory for Long Range Planning*. Wiley, London (1973).

Thorelli, H. B. Networks: between markets and hierarchies. *Strategic Management Journal*, 37–51 (1986).

Turnbull, P. and Valla, J. P. (eds), *Strategies for International Industrial Marketing*. Croom Helm, London (1986).

Venkatraman, N. and Camillus, J. C. Exploring the concept of "fit" in strategic management, *Academy of Management Review*, **3**, 513–25 (1984).

Vicari, S. Risorse immateriali e comportanto incrementale. Working Paper no. 1 88. SDA Bocconi, Milan (1988).

von Hippel, E. Appropriability of innovation benefit as a predictor of the source of innovation, *Research Policy*, **2**, 95–115 (1982).

Waluszewski, A. CTMP-fallet. Processutveckling inom skogsindustrin (The CTMP-case. Process Development within the Forest Industry). Working Paper. Dept of Business Administration, University of Uppsala (1988).

Weick, K. E. *The Social Psychology of Organizing*. Addison Wesley, Reading, MA (1969) (2nd edn, 1979).

Yuchtman, E. and Seashore, S. E. A system resource approach to organizational effectiveness, *American Sociological Review*, 891–903 (1967).

# 4

# Analysing Business Relationships

*H. Håkansson and I. Snehota*

Faced with the empirical evidence of long-lasting relationships in business, the scholars of management have reacted in rather different ways. At first the phenomenon was largely ignored. It is only during the last decade or so it has received some attention from researchers (e.g. Arndt, 1979; Håkansson, 1982; Astley, 1984). More recently we have witnessed an upsurge in interest for business relationships, especially among academics in the US (e.g. Webster, 1992; Miles and Snow, 1992; Nohria and Eccles, 1992; Alter and Hage, 1993; Achrol, 1991). Some have argued that what we labelled as business relationships is a relatively new phenomenon while earlier business was conducted much more on an arm's-length basis. Others, often practitioners and those studying the so-called business markets, have claimed that relationships have always been an important part of the business landscape and that today we are simply becoming more aware and are telling the practitioners to do what they have been trying to do for many years.

Indeed, business relationships do not easily find a convincing explanation in the traditional, transaction-focused framework of economics that inspires management studies. It requires redrawing the conceptual framework, which always is difficult and risky. The purpose of developing an analytical framework with respect to a phenomenon is to provide guidance for acting on it. In management studies an analytical framework is supposed to help identify the problems to be handled, to structure the situation assessment in order to identify the intervening variables, and to identify alternative courses of action. To make a step in that direction we need first to understand how relationships between companies develop and what forces they are subject to. Relationships are a complex phenomenon.

When we propose a conceptual framework we have to single out the variables that are critical in the explanation of the phenomenon. We have to focus on some aspects and to exclude many others. The value of a theory for the praxis lies in that it dismisses a number of possible explanatory variables. A broad descriptive framework of the substance and functions of business relationships will be outlined in this chapter. A few dimensions that can be used to assess and analyse business

Reprinted by permission of International Thomson, Analysing Business Relationships by H. Håkansson and I. Snehota from *Developing Relationships in Business Networks*, Edited by H. Håkansson and I. Snehota, pp 24–49.

relationships will be proposed. The choice of these is always a critical step as it determines what will be observed and put in focus in the further analysis.

## THE CONCEPT OF RELATIONSHIP

While intuitively appealing, the notion of "relationship" may be difficult to grasp. What makes dealings between two companies in a market become a relationship? It is not easy to define what a relationship is. Tentatively we can say that a relationship is mutually oriented interaction between two reciprocally committed parties. One reason why we choose the notion of relationship in analysis of intercompany interaction is that it evokes the concepts of mutual orientation and commitment over time. Mutual orientation and commitment are common in interactions between companies, if we judge from the empirical studies discussed earlier. Another reason is the high degree of interdependency between business organizations, as their very existence depends on exchange with other economic subjects. A relationship often arise between two parties because of the interdependence of outcomes, even if it can arises for other reasons. As it entails mutual commitment over time a relationship creates interdependence which is both positive and negative for the parties involved. A relationship develops over time as a chain of interaction episodes – a sequence of acts and counteracts. It has a history and a future. In this way a relationship creates interdependence as much as it is a way to handle interdependence.

We believe that exchange interaction between companies in industrial markets can be fruitfully described in terms of relationships essentially for two reasons: one is that actors themselves tend to see their interactions as relationships, another is that the interaction between companies over time creates the type of quasi-organization that can be labelled a relationship (Blois, 1972).

The research findings discussed in chapter 1 indicate that mutual orientation and commitment over time, as well as interdependence, are typical of the exchange interaction between companies in industrial markets. The interaction between, for example, suppliers and industrial customers appears as a series of acts and counteracts creating interdependencies and affecting their behaviours. Mutual commitment and interdependence of companies in the industrial market constrains their behaviour as much as it creates opportunities; relationships are mutually demanding besides being being mutually rewarding. Time has to be explicitly considered in order to identify the forces shaping the behaviour. The combination of a process over time and the interdependencies make the relationships produce something unique by interlocking activities and resources of the two companies. Relationships produce something that neither of the two can produce in isolation and something that cannot easily be duplicated. That is why we choose to conceive the interaction between businesses in industrial markets as relationships. This is what is at the core of the "relationship" view of business markets.

The empirical research on business relationship discussed earlier shows that, despite certain similarities, there is a large variation between different relationships. Relationships always have some unique features. We observed earlier that no two relationships are alike. Still, there is a certain pattern in the effects they produce.

There are two dimensions that appear to capture the effects and which can be used to categorize business relationships: one regards who is affected by the relationships, the other what is affected. We will call the former the function and the latter the substance of business relationships.

What makes the relationship concept slippery is that it cannot be conceived as "just a relationship". A relationship is a result of an interaction process where connections have been developed between two parties that produce a mutual orientation and commitment. A relationship is thus not a given, but a variable that can take on different values. That is why we have to go beyond the consideration that relationships exist between companies and are important. We need to look at the elements being connected in a relationship and the effects the connections produce. This is the reason for choosing to describe business relationships in the two dimensions of substance and function.

The first dimension regards what the relationship affects on the two sides – the "substance" of a business relationship. Three different layers of substance can be identified in a business relationship. First, there is an activity layer. A relationship is built up of activities that connect, more or less closely, various internal activities of the two parties. A relationship links activities. Clearly the activity links affect the outcomes of the relationship for the parties. Second, there is a resource layer. As a relationship develops, it can connect various resource elements needed and controlled by two companies. A relationship can tie together resources. Relationships consist then to various degree of resource ties. As a relationship makes various resource elements accessible for the parties it also constitutes a resource that can be used and exploited. Third, there is an actor layer. As a business relationship develops, actors become connected. Bonds between actors are established which affect how the actors perceive, evaluate and treat each other.

The three layers of substance can be taken as three different effect parameters that are determinants of the values involved in a relationship and thus of its outcome. They add up to a relationship. A relationship between two companies can be characterized by the relative importance of the three layers. The more effects there are in the three layers in a relationship, the "thicker" and the more complex it will be. Major relationships between companies tend to have complex substance. Still, there is a large variety in their substance, dependent on the existence, type and strength of the activity links, resource ties and actor bonds.

In sum, a relationship between two companies has a profile in terms of activity links, resource ties and actor bonds:

- *Activity links* regard technical, administrative, commercial and other activities of a company that can be connected in different ways to those of another company as a relationship develops.
- *Resource ties* connect various resource elements (technological, material, knowledge resources and other intangibles) of two companies. Resource ties result from how the relationship has developed and represents in itself a resource for a company.
- *Actor bonds* connect actors and influence how the two actors perceive each other and form their identities in relation to each other. Bonds become established in interaction and reflect the interaction process.

The existing activity links, resource ties and actor bonds can be used to characterize the nature of a relationship that has developed between two companies. If we are to assess, predict or explain the importance and role of a relationship, they need to be examined.

The second dimension regards the effects a relationship has for different actors – what we have chosen to call the "functions" of business relationship. A relationship between two companies has different functions because it affects and is affected by different parties and other relationships.

We believe three different functions can be distinguished. First, a relationship has effects for the dyad in itself, i.e. the conjunction of two actors. A relationship is a place where some kind of interaction takes place, and something is produced; where activity links, resource ties and actor bonds are established. This kind of effect can be more or less pronounced in a relationship between two companies. Second, a relationship has a function for each of the two companies; it is likely to affect them in different ways and is affected by them. A relationship is one of the resources the company can exploit and use in combination with other resources (other relationships) available to the company. What is produced in a relationship can be used for different purposes and with different effects by either of the two companies. Third, as relationships are connected, what is produced in a relationship can have effects on other relationships and thus on other companies than those directly involved. A certain relationship is also subject to effects from other relationships and actors as it is an element of the larger structure and has a function in it. All the three types of effect originate and are intervening in business relationships.

Thus, if we are to find out what effects a relationship has and is subject to we have to take into account three different functions:

- *Function for the dyad* This originates in the conjunction of the two companies; their activities, resources and actors. Activity links, resource ties and actor bonds in a relationship integrate various elements and thereby some unique outcomes and effects are produced.
- *Function for the individual company* A relationship has effects on each of the companies, on what it can do internally and in other relationships. These depend on how what is produced in the dyad can be connected to other internal elements of the company and its other relationships.
- *Function for third parties* Being a building element in the larger network structure, what is produced in a relationship can affect and is affected by other relationships that involve other parties. The effects on third parties and from third parties and their relationships on the relationship in any of the three layers of substance depend on how tight the connectedness of relationships is in the overall network.

The three functions are closely interwoven but they can be more to less pronounced in a certain relationship. However, whenever analysing a relationship between two companies and its development potential, all three functions concur and therefore deserve attention.

We have examined in this section the premise that intercompany interaction can be conceived in terms of relationships as they show the traits of mutual orientation and commitment. We believe it is fruitful to consider intercompany interaction as relationships, but have argued that in doing so we need to go beyond and look into the substance and functions of the relationships. The argument we used is that if we are to use "relationship" as an analytical concept we need to find the underlying generative structures of relationships. In order to capture the variety of business relationships we proposed two dimensions: the substance and function. We posited that the substance of a business relationship becomes manifest in activity links, resource ties and actor bonds that arise as two companies become connected. The functions of a relationship can be conceived in terms of the effects a relationship between two companies produces for the dyad, for each of the involved parties and for third parties.

## THE SUBSTANCE OF BUSINESS RELATIONSHIPS

We have observed that the substance of the relationships between companies in business markets can have facets and layers that vary with respect to the kind of effects they produce. In this section we will discuss more extensively the three earlier identified layers of activities, resources and actors. For the sake of simplicity we will start by treating the three separately, although in practice they are very closely related.

### Activity Links

A relationship between two companies may affect the way the two companies perform their activities, that is, their activity structure. Compared to individuals, companies are much more complex as to the variety and volume of activities performed. Thousands of different activities are performed and coordinated within a company. Every company thus takes the (often complex) form of a coordinated activity structure. When two companies build up a relationship, certain of their different technical, administrative or commercial activities can become linked to each other. A business relationship grows as a flow of exchange episodes in which some activities are undertaken by either of the companies. These activities in a relationship link a number of other activities in the two companies. The internal activity structures in either of the two companies may need to be adapted. Also in other directions the activity links are important; as the activity structures of the two companies change over time the interaction activities in a relationship may need to be modified and adjusted. The linking of activities reflects the need of coordination and will affect how and when the various activities are carried out. That, in turn, will have consequences for both the costs and effectiveness of the activities.

Activity links have to reflect not only sequential but also horizontal (parallel) interdependencies of activities. Parallel activities are linked, for example, when a buying company tries to influence suppliers delivering complementary products to adapt to each other. The needs of parallel coordination and thus parallel activity links are particularly strong in certain industries such as, for example, construction or investment equipment businesses, where unit or small batch technologies prevail. Sequential activity links seem critical in industries where process technology is dominant. Both types of links are common in many other industries with large-scale manufacturing.

Linking activities can be regarded as a way to create a unique performance. By linking the activities of a company with those of its counterparts the company's performance is affected because of the effects either on its own activity structure or on the activity structure of the counterpart. Activity links are a factor in the productivity of the companies involved. They also affect, however, the productivity in the whole network.

As both companies have other relationships in which activity links can be important, an activity link in a relationship "links other links" in the activity pattern. A business relationship is thus a link in what might be conceived as an activity chain in which activities of several companies in a sequence are linked to each other (as exemplified in Fig. 1). Activities of a sub-supplier can affect those of a supplier which will in turn have effects on those of a buying company which in turn is reflected in those of its customers. These activity chains are quite robust in many industries, as for example in the automotive industry where the buying departments can be involved down to the third-tier level in the supplier network. In these industries the effects of change in an activity link may be very large. In other industries the sequential interdependence of activities tends to be weaker.

As the activity structures of companies become linked and coordinated through and by activity links in relationships, a complex activity pattern emerges in which different companies carry out different parts. Developing new relationships and activity linkages changes the overall pattern. Conversely, changes elsewhere in the activity pattern affect the activity links between two companies. This effect is palpable when new technological paradigms are being accepted by at least a subset of the network of which the two companies are part.

The wider activity pattern of which the company with its relationships is a part is often difficult to map as the activity links are mostly known only to those directly involved. This may be a problem for an outsider or newcomer who, in order to be accepted, has to find out what this pattern looks like and what interdependencies exist between various activities.

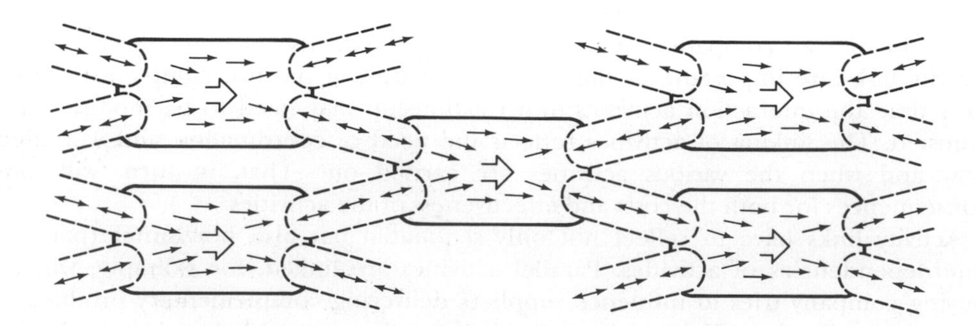

Fig. 1. Activity structures, links and pattern over five companies.

The activity aspect is present in all business relationships, but its importance can vary both with the ambitions that the two companies have in the relationship and with the complexity of their own activity structures. Companies are often involved in relationships with others where a substantial portion of the activities (in terms of volumes, frequencies, etc.) is performed and thus holds the key to the total costs and performance of the company. The flexibility of the pattern is very much dependent on the way the company has linked up with different counterparts. Even though the activity links are intangible, their effect on business relationships is often clearly manifest. If properly handled, they can be exploited by some companies for their own advantage.

In order to describe, explain or predict the effects of a relationship and how it is likely to develop, the assessment of activity links is an important starting point. The type and the strength of activity links are among the critical dimensions in our conceptual framework.

### Resource Ties

A relationship between two companies has effects on the way the companies are utilizing resources. Within a relationship different resource elements of the two actors can be tied together. A business enterprise consists of an assortment of different resources – manpower, equipment, plant, knowledge, image and financial means – that sustain its activities. Industrial companies in particular are as a rule large and complex resource units. In a relationship between two companies some of

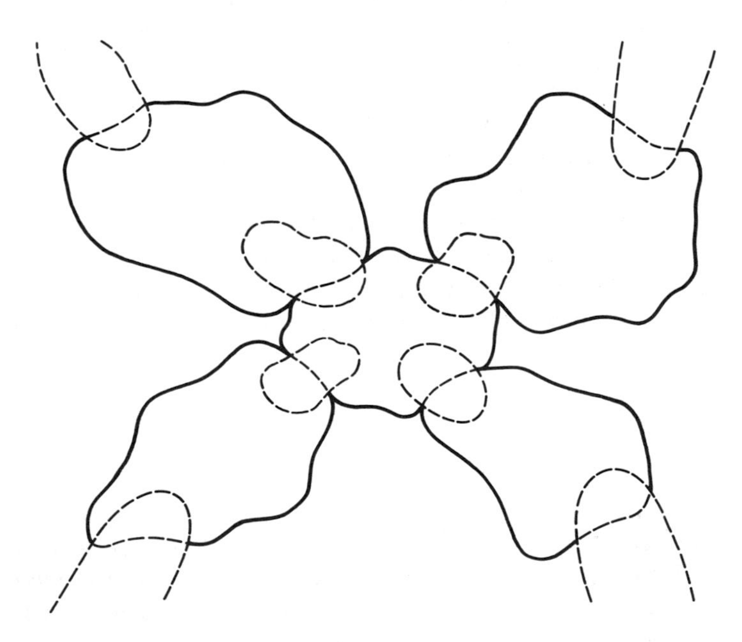

Fig. 2. Resource ties, resource collections and resource constellation over five companies.

the resources needed for their activities can be accessed and acquired. The resources sought by the parties respectively are of different types. Expectations, of either party, to get access to various types of resources are a common ingredient of a business relationship. Apart from the tangible resources in the form of products, various intangible, often vaguely defined, resources such as technical, commercial or administrative know-how can be of interest.

Relationships between companies are, however, not just a way to acquire and access resources. In a relationship some of the resources of the two companies are brought together, confronted and combined. The interface between the resources of the two companies, over time, can become both broad and deep; it can embrace different types of resources and activate these to various degrees. The effect on the resources will be that they become specifically oriented towards each other, that is, various resource ties will emerge. The resources of the two companies will be tied together. New resource combinations are thus likely to arise as a relationship develops. As different elements of the two companies, tangible as well as intangible, become integrated they constitute resources of new quality. As relationships are valuable bridges to access resources, they can also be regarded in themselves as resources. A relationship is a resource which ties together various resource elements. The process required to develop a business relationship has some characteristics that make it similar to an investment process. It usually is costly, and the costs precede the future benefits; when a relationship is developed it becomes an asset that must be taken care of and utilized in an efficient way.

On the whole the availability of resources provides opportunities and constraints on the activities that can be undertaken by a company. The relationships that a company develops to others are important for the collection of resources available, which affects what the individual company can do. They make it possible to mobilize and access the resources of others for a company's own purpose and advantage.

There are some resource ties among most of the interacting actors (resource providers), within a certain context. The result is a kind of aggregated resource structure – a resource constellation. In such a structure resource ties are but one of the structural elements – a piece of resource in a larger resource constellation. Resource ties in a relationship are an element of the aggregated structure. They can thus become both a valuable asset and a constraint for other third companies when different resources of the resource constellation can be connected. The extent and type of resource ties in a relationship can vary, and because of the economic consequences on productivity and innovation are the second central dimension in a relationship analysis.

### Actor Bonds

A relationship between two companies affects the two units in a way similar to that between two persons. Bonds between two actors may alter their way of seeing and interpreting situations, as well as their identities both in relation to each other and to others. Being seen as a "close friend" to a company known as advanced or powerful helps in other relationships. The perceived identity thus affects the possibilities to act. There are some specific problems with business relationships between collective

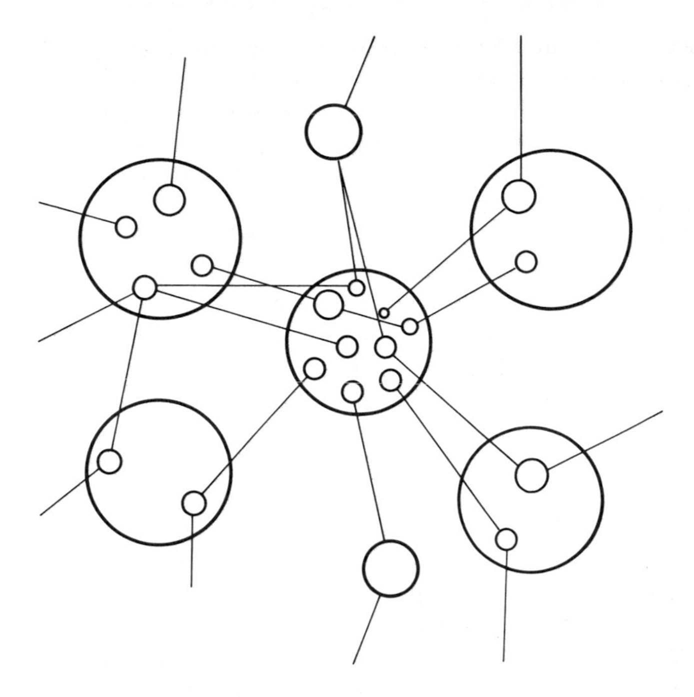

Fig. 3. Actor bonds, organizations and the web of actors.

actors as companies, as the interpersonal relationships in their organizations do not sum up in a simple linear way.

Bonds arise in a relationship between two companies as they direct a certain amount of attention and interest towards each other – they become mutually committed. To become mutually committed amounts to giving and being given some priority. Giving priority is closely interwoven with a building up of identity. Actor bonds have an effect on what the parties know about each other and what they can exchange. Identities in relation to each other but also to some third parties might change. Every act and counter-act in a relationship is based on an assumed identity by the counterpart. The assumed and created identities reflect actors' bonds, giving rise to or ending certain relationships, or meaning that they are never even attempted.

There are different clues to the assumed identity of a company; some stem from the direct past interaction experience, others from what is known, or believed to be known, about the counterparts. The process of shaping identifies in a relationship is close to that of learning. Learning (and "teaching") is central within relationships. The interdependencies of outcomes for the parties to a relationship in a specific situation are not always fully understood by those involved, and perhaps never can be. What and how a party learns about the interdependencies affects very much how it perceives the identity of the counterpart. In the relationship the two sides get to know each other's ambitions and perceptions, which increases the possibilities to utilize each other in some future situations.

Yet, neither mutual commitment nor identities are based on certainties; no amount of "learning" can ever fully dissipate the uncertainties. There is always a margin for beliefs and trust that in the end become essential for the commitment. The development of trust is a social process typical for relationship development. Neither the beliefs nor the trust are dependent solely on the direct interaction experience; other clues are also used. Perceived relationships of the counterpart to other third parties are one of those clues.

The interaction behaviour of either of the parties thus depends also on other relationships in which they are involved, that is, on the whole set of different roles, or identities, that a company assumes in its various relationships. The existence of a certain relationship will have effects on how others perceive the two companies involved in the relationship. Each of the two, in their relationships to other parties, will to some extent represent also its counterpart. The relationship between them will be perceived by some others as a fact, as something to which one should adapt. The relationship acquires and constructs some kind of joint, or collective, identity of which the parties are an integral part and that becomes a phenomenon with a life of its own – if not wholly independent of its components, at least with a distinct identity.

Commitment, identity and trust are processes that constrain and at the same time enable the behaviour of the actors in relation to each other. To be committed, to have a certain identity, to be trusted, means that an actor has to comply with some specific rules. We use the notion of "bonds" to indicate these restrictions.

As bonds are established between actors, an organized structure of actors emerges. Bonds in a relationship are but a portion of a wider web of actors. The bonds affect the actors' present and future interaction in the relationships. The peculiarity of the aggregated structure is its dependence on the processes of learning and perception and thus its continuing fluidity. The web of actors changes as the individual actors learn and adjust their bonds. At the same time, bonds affect the learning.

A particular property of the network form of organization is its indeterminateness. The set of actor bonds making up the structure is not given, as it is not related to some overriding purpose for the structure as a whole. Relationships arise for different and varying reasons; some evolve and others tend to decay. New relationships are created linking previously unconnected actors, others dissolve and cease to exist. Being a part in a larger structure, any relationship is both a source of change and a source of stability in the whole network structure.

When focusing on business relationships we have up to now abstracted organizations into a notion of a collective actor. This is not without problems. First, several individuals are usually involved in carrying out the activities that add up to a business relationship between two companies. Those involved pursue goals that are not identical and the interaction is subject to perceptual and other behavioural limits of the individuals involved. Individuals interact on the basis of their perceptions, they acquire their personal identity and position towards others as they learn and develop in conjunction. Second, all larger companies consist of several units. There are departments, business units, divisions, companies and groups of companies. As we will see later, relationships are influenced by who is defined as the "actor". In certain situations it is thus clear that a company must be seen as a multi-actor while in others it can be considered a single actor.

In summary, the bonds developed between companies in business relationships affect their behaviour and identities. The actor bonds are the third layer of substance of business relationships. In order to make any analysis of a certain relationship between two companies, the nature and strength of these bonds have to be taken into account.

## Interplay Between the Layers of Substance in Business Relationships

Every business relationship is an integrated entity and our ambition is not to decompose it into three different ones. When we propose to distinguish the three layers of substance it simply serves the purpose of identifying possible variations in the effects of intercompany relationships. Our ambition is to capture the differences in relationships important for the economic consequences.

There are relationships between companies which mainly consists of actor bonds. An example can be a customer who has a supplier of electronic components "just to keep in touch", to monitor what is happening, with a limited volume of exchange and coordination. In other relationships both actor bonds and resource ties have been developed but without many activity links. An example can be from the same electronic component industry when a supplier relationship becomes critical for the customer because of the need to access the test or development facilities, and resource ties develop. Another type can be relationships where the activity links are strong while bonds between actors and resource ties are weak. An example here can be the type of relationships that sub-suppliers of relatively simple products in the automotive industry have to their customers. The differences may reflect the type of

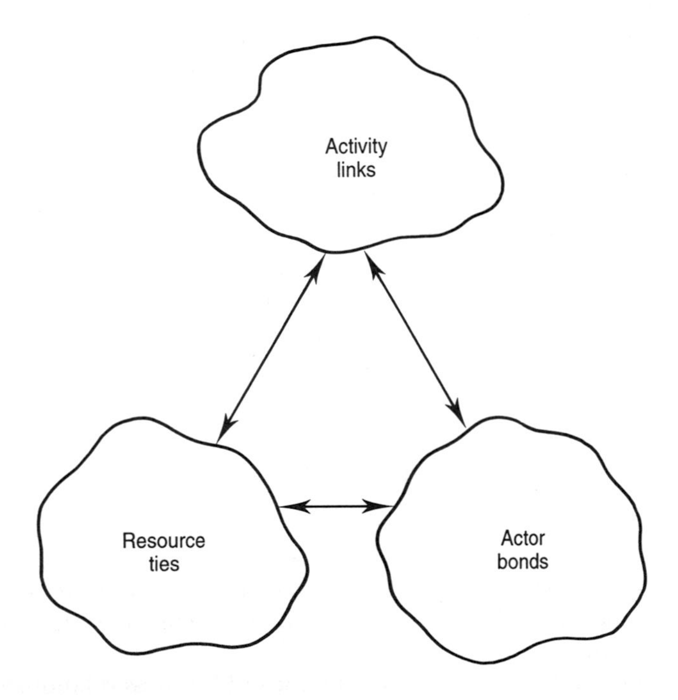


Fig. 4. Interplay of the three substance layers of business relationships.

industrial activity or company-specific circumstances. Most often, however, they reflect a more or less conscious choice on the part of the companies involved, or just neglect of the existing possibilities.

The possibilities of developing closer and economically more effective links, ties and bonds in existing relationships are often large. Thus, every relationship can be developed in one or several of the substance dimensions. Links, bonds and ties existing between two companies are, as a rule, but a few of the possible connections. There are always potential interconnections, that can be substantiated as they become perceived and enacted.

The three layers are not independent; there is an interplay between the actor bonds, activity links and resource ties (see Fig. 4). Actors carry out activities and activate resources. Activities are resource-consuming and evolve as the capabilities of actors develop. Resources limit the range of activities an actor can pursue. The existence of bonds between actors is a prerequisite for them to actively and consciously develop strong activity links and resource ties. Activity links make it likely that bonds can develop, and so on.

The interplay of bonds, ties and links is at the origin of change and development in relationships. Actor bonds evolve, resource ties and activity links change and the three become mutually adjusted. The interplay of the three dimensions is a driving force in the development of business relationships. Changes in connections account for much of the dynamics in business relationships.

Strong activity links direct the attention of actors to possible uses of resource elements that can be accessed at the other company or through it. Strong resource ties tend as a rule to lead to strengthening of activity links. There is a tendency towards some kind of balance in activity links, resource ties and actor bonds as the substance of a relationship develops in an incremental way and solutions are sought by the companies in the vicinity of the existing ones. The balance can, however, be on very different levels.

What connections will be acted upon and what level will be reached depends on different factors. First, it will depend on how the interaction evolves between the parties. Second, it will be influenced by the characteristics and ambitions of the actors that reflect their situation and circumstances. This will to large extent be an effect of the set of relationships these actors have developed. Third, there are the features of the aggregate structure – the network – and how the relationship is related to other exiting relationships to and between actors directly or indirectly connected. That brings us back to the issue of the functions of business relationships.

## FUNCTIONS OF BUSINESS RELATIONSHIPS

When discussing the substance of business relationships we concentrated on the various layers that can be used by different parties, for different purposes, under different circumstances. We thus came across what we will call different functions of business relationships.

A starting point for a discussion of the functions of business relationships is offered in the micro-functional perspective on market exchange proposed by Alderson

(1965). Adopting a micro-functional perspective on business relationships permits identification of at least three different functions of business relationships that were to some extent implied in our earlier discussion.

First, a relationship has a function as the junction of the two companies; it has a function for the dyad. Second, a relationship has a more or less clear function for each of the two parties involved, depending on how it connects to the other relationships they have. Third, a relationship between two companies can also have a function for some third parties either directly or indirectly connected to the two parties directly involved. We could use the notion of first-, second- and third-order functions of a business relationship in order to distinguish different levels of analysis. All the three levels are required to capture the factors affecting the development of the substance profile of a business relationship and the effects it has. They are thus needed in order to assess the economic consequences of a business relationship.

## The Function for the Dyad

A business relationship is developed as the two companies establish connections in the activity, resource and actor layer. If successful, the resources, activities and actors of the two companies are blended and melted together in a unique way. The substance of the dyad, the activity links, resource ties and actor bonds, will not be just the sum of what the two parties turn towards each other; it will become something qualitatively different. The relationship is a "quasi-organization" that amounts to more than simply the sum of its elements because of the existing links, ties and

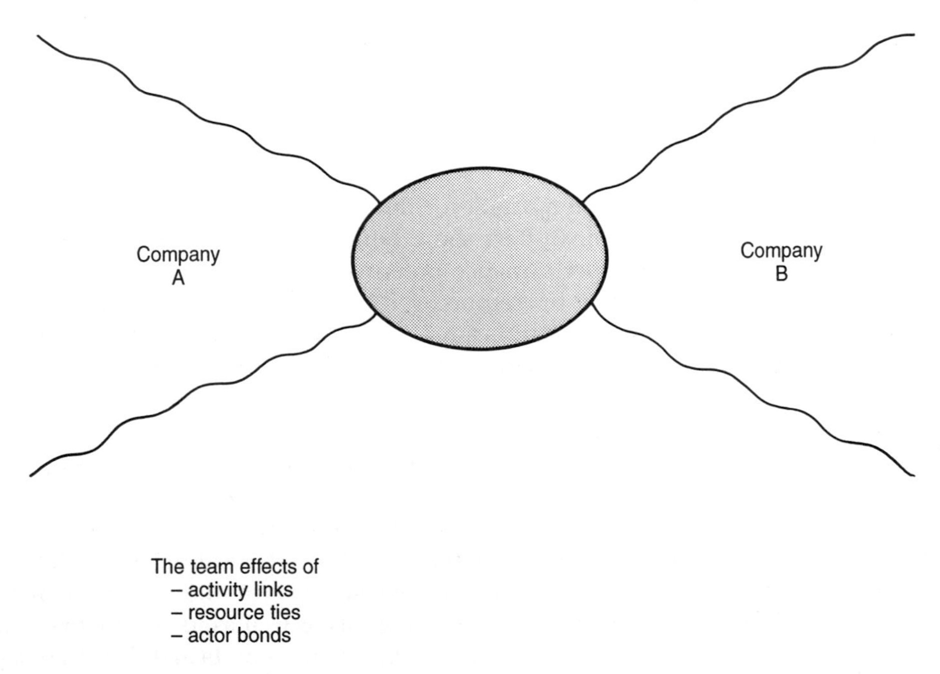


Fig. 5. Dyadic function of a business relationship.

bonds. There is a "team effect" (Alchian and Demsetz, 1972). Jointly, the two companies can perform activities and utilize resources which none of them could accomplish in isolation. What they can accomplish depends on how the relationship develops.

A relationship between two companies does not become automatically a perfect "team" (or quasi-organization), but the potential is always there. The team effects have to be tried out. They develop as the parties involved experiment with various connections and learn about their effects. The quality of the relationship is the extent to which this function will be exploited.

The degree to which team effects will come into being depends on the substance of the relationship in all three dimensions. In order to carry into effect the dyadic function at least some substance is needed. There has to be a significant development of activity links, resource ties or actor bonds if a relationship between two companies is to become a quasi-organization and the team effects are to materialize.

The function of a business relationship as a quasi-organization (i.e. for the dyad) acquires importance in proportion to how many new resources are created, novel combinations of activities emerge, knowledge is gained. Only the conjunction of the parties can produce these effects. As the activities, resources and actors become linked in a team it tends to provide a unique performance. The function of intercompany relationships for the dyad is its being the locus of the team effects.

From the above description it should be clear that the more the dyadic function of a relationship is understood and emphasized, the greater is the magnitude of the team effects that can be appropriated by the two companies. It provides either of the parties in the relationship with an opportunity to develop its capabilities, resources and/or activities. Exploiting these is a matter of tuning the marketing and purchasing function of the companies.

## The Single Actor Function

We argued that relationships are important for the performance of companies. Each of a company's main relationships offers some benefits but also entails substantial costs. A relationship affects the performance potential of a company by effects on its activity structure, the collection of resources it can use and its organizational structure. Given these effects relationships are an important factor in the development of capabilities of a company and thus for the economic outcomes of its operations.

For a business unit existing within a context where the counterparts are individually important, the impact of relationships is rather evident. Relationships affect the resource collection a company can use. They also affect the possibilities of carrying out certain production and development activities within the company, that is, its activity structure and its activity potential. Finally, each relationship affects the organization of the company. The total set of relationships to others a company has determines in this way the competence of the company as well as its productivity and innovativeness. Coping with relationships can be seen as a broad learning and attribute-developing process. Relationships offer the possibility of developing the

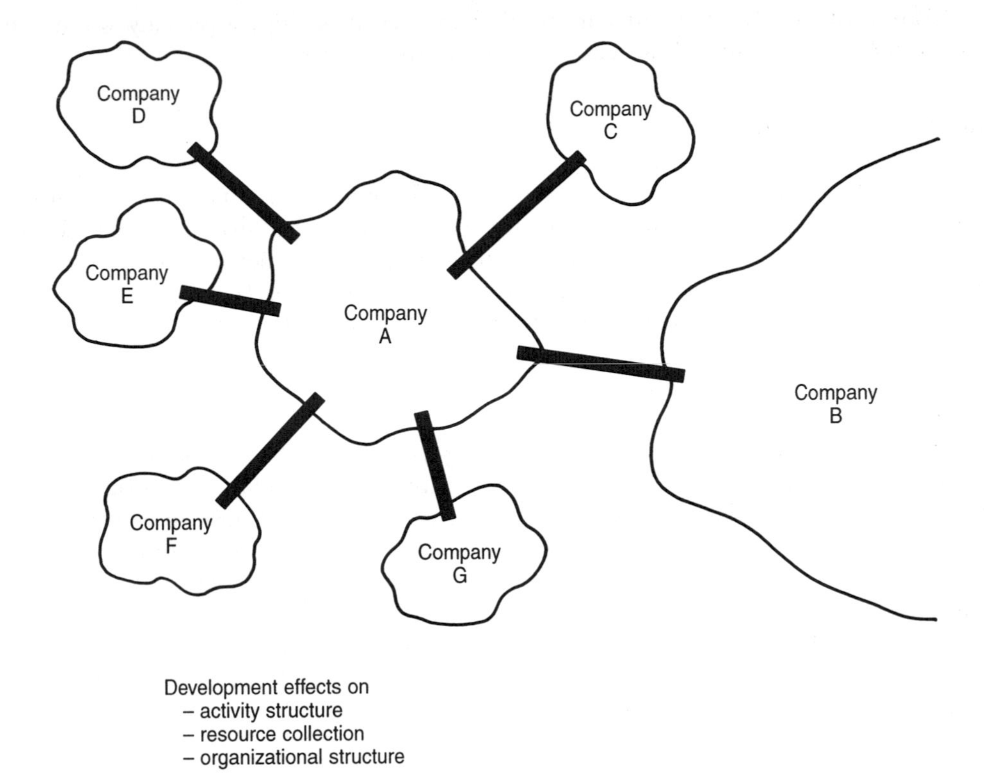


Fig. 6. Single actor function of a relationship.

competence, productivity and innovativeness of the company and are in this respect valuable assets.

The effects of a certain relationship stem from the combination (complementarity and relatedness) of the relationship with the activity structure, resource collection and organization of the company and with the set of other relationships it has. These effects are not simply cumulative of the dyadic effects of the single relationships. They originate in the quality and properties of the whole set of the relationships and their substance. That is, they depend on the type of activity links, resource ties and actor bonds that intersect the company. There are important synergies in some dimensions and contemporaneously important constraints in other dimensions.

Costs and benefits of engaging in a relationship are related to the consequences that a relationship has on the innovativeness, productivity and competence that stem from the impact it has on the activity structure, the set of resources that can be accessed, but also for the perceived goal structure of the actor.

The company develops by exploiting the potential offered by the dyadic function. How successful it will be will depend on its ability to perceive and handle the connectedness in the relationships in which it is directly involved.

A business relationship has different effects on the two companies in a relationship. While the potential of effects cannot be overrated it may be, and often is, a source of possible tension and conflict in a relationship, especially when the goals of the two differ greatly and are imposed in the interaction.

## The "Network Function"

As relationships are connected, change in the substance of a relationship may affect other relationships and thus companies other than the two involved. Every relationship has the network function; activity links are important in the activity pattern, resource ties in the resource constellation and actor bonds in the web of actors. At the same time, opposite effects are possible from the network structure on the single relationship.

A third party (like the companies C and D in Fig. 7) can react to the change in a relationship between two actors (companies A and B in Fig. 7) in different ways. They can try to exploit the development by adjusting their own activity links and resource ties in their own relationships in accordance with how the relationship between A and B looks like in these dimensions. Alternatively, they can choose to work against the connections created in the relationship (between A and B), attempting to adjust and develop their own relationships (bonds, links and ties) in such a way that the focal relationship will become less influential in the overall structure.

Any relationship is because of its substance a constituent element of the wider network in which relationships are interconnected. Activity links, resource ties and actor bonds in a relationship are connected, directly or indirectly, to some others.

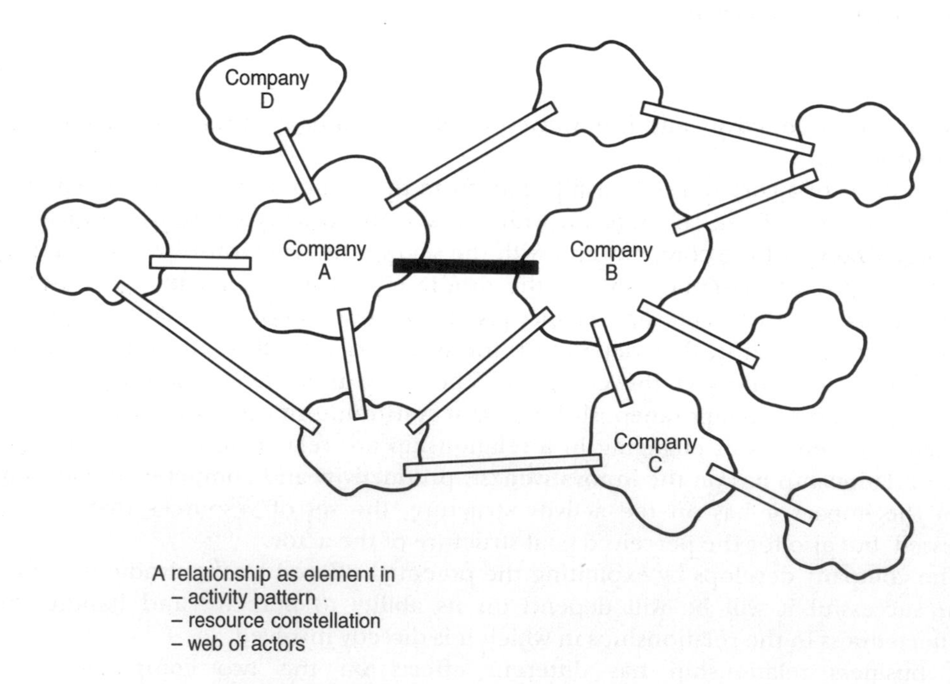


Fig. 7. Network function of a relationship.

The aggregated structure is an organized web of conscious and goal-seeking actors; it is also an organized pattern of activities as well as an organized constellation of resources.

We observed that the structure of business networks has certain peculiar organizational attributes. The actors (companies) have no common goal, but there exist some shared beliefs about the activity pattern as well as the resource constellation. A network has no clear boundaries, nor any centre or apex. It exists as an "organization" in terms of a certain logic affecting the ordering of activities, resources and actors. It can be seen as an "organization" as it affects how companies are reciprocally related and positioned. As a form of organization it will only be kept together as long as the network logic is accepted by enough actors.

Change in the substance of any of the relationships affects the overall structure. Since a change in any relationship affects the position of those involved, the whole set of interrelated relationships is subject to change and that has consequences for the outcome of a relationship for those involved. A dyad, a relationship, is a source as well as a recipient of change in the network.

The network is usually seen as a structure of actors. However, a challenging idea is to see it on a lower level. Then the position of all elements (actors, activities, resources and their bonds, links and ties) is given by the existing relations. The structure takes shape as relations between its elements evolve. It is thus a product of past connections between its elements and the emergent structure elicits developing connections. It impinges, directly and indirectly, on the possibilities to establish new and disrupt existing relations. It affects all layers of substance in a relationship. All relations get modified as structural constraints and possibilities are perceived (learned) by the actors.

The essence of the network function of business relationships is that as they arise they form a structure of actor bonds, activity links and resource ties where third parties are integrated. How the relationships develop and unfold is important for the features of the actors' organization, activity pattern and resource constellation and thus on the properties of the network structure such as its stability. The emergent structure has in any given moment a limiting effect on its actors at the same time as it provides the base for future development.

## The Balance of Functions of Business Relationships

The different functions of business relationships reflect the various effects of the substance of a given relationship. What is implied is that the outcomes of a relationship for a company over time will not depend simply on its own acts in specific interaction episodes but also on how the counterpart acts and will react and on how others, third parties connected to the two parties, have been, are and will be acting. The effects of a business relationship originate in activity links, resource ties and actor bonds and affect the dyad, the individual company and the network.

The magnitude of the effects will vary, for the specific relationship, with the circumstances and be dependent on the substance of the relationship, on how central the relationship is for the two involved companies and on how tightly the network is structured. The dyadic function of business relationships is value-creating and is a condition for the positive effects for the single actor. The network functions reflect the interdependence of individual and collective action.

There is a problem of balance with regard to the functions of business relationships. Too much emphasis on the functions for the single actor may become counterproductive, as it may destroy the dyadic team function. Too much emphasis on the dyadic function could also turn out counterproductive; being overly altruistic may be harmful for the self-interest. Disregard for the network functions can produce disastrous effects or mean that a company does not recognize certain development opportunities being offered or constraints which arise. It is up to management in each company to handle and take care of the various business relationships in a way that is favourable not just for itself but for important counterparts and third parties. Thus, coping with the relationships requires some concern and control of who is benefiting from them.

## DEVELOPMENT OF BUSINESS RELATIONSHIPS

The core of our argument is that business relationships are developed by the companies and thus voluntarily created, but when they come into existence they become a constraining element for the same companies. The development of relationships between companies in industrial markets cannot thus escape a pattern created by their own development. There is a path dependence in the development of business relationships and networks. Every actor within the network structure will have some discretion in certain areas and at the same time be entirely locked into others. The network of business relationships is both a prison and a tool.

Our discussion of the substance and functions of intercompany relationships exposed the complexity of effects that a relationship can produce and be subject to as it develops. All these have a bearing on the possibilities of a company to develop a relationship and may explain why certain relationships are weakened or interrupted. The complexity of effects and underlying factors of relationship development is difficult to reduce to manageable proportions. Yet it has to be done. It is needed in order to cope with relationship development. We will therefore outline an analytical scheme that sums up our earlier discussion and use it to identify the critical factors in the development of business relationships and the critical issues in coping with relationships. We will start by putting together the two dimensions of substance and function of business relationships.

### Development and Role of Business Relationships

A relationship develops between two companies as some activity links, resource ties or actor bonds are formed between two companies. These links, ties and bonds make up a relationship that can be conceived as a "quasi-organization". These connections are productive on their own merit; they are a source of value. How valuable they are depends on how each of the layers is taken care of and on their interplay. This can be schematically illustrated as shown in Fig. 8.

The development of a relationship (of activity links, resource ties and actor bonds)

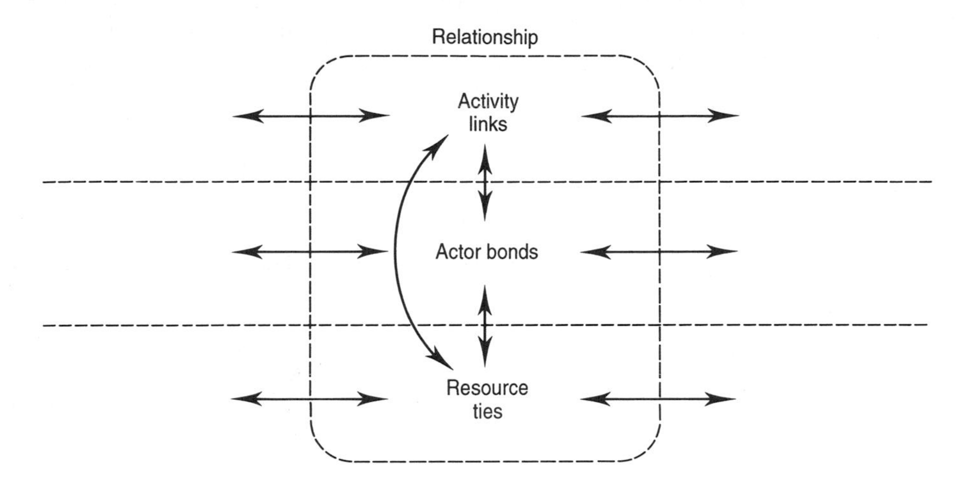


Fig. 8. Relationship as a dyad.

between two companies cannot be unilateral, it requires co-alignment of two parties. How it will develop depends on how each of the parties act and react in the relationship. Once established, a relationship has a life of its own, it gets its own substance as a dyad. It is improved or deteriorates as a result of actions taken by the parties.

Every business relationship is developed by two companies with certain requirements and capabilities. Both the requirements and capabilities result from existing relationships of each of the companies. The activity links, resource ties and actor bonds in a relationship between two companies affect the activity structures, the collections of resources and the organizational structures of the companies involved. At the same time the activity structures, resource collections and organizational structures of the companies will influence what kinds of links, ties and bonds can develop in a relationship. This kind of reciprocal conditioning is schematically illustrated in Fig. 9.

The effect of a relationship on the company will depend on its internal features, but also on the other relationships the company has. The economic consequences of a relationship will depend on how the productivity, innovativeness and competence of the company and thus its overall capabilities are affected by the activity links, resource ties and actor bonds that arise in a relationship. The development of a relationship has an effect on and at the same time is dependent on the capabilities of the company, that is, on its development potential.

The effects of a relationship between two companies are not limited to the two companies directly involved and their relationships. Other parties and relationships may be affected. An activity link is but a link in a broader activity pattern spanning several companies, a resource tie is but an element of a broader resource constellation that companies can mobilize, and an actor bond is but a part of a web of actors. Again there is a two-way conditioning between the relationship and the network structure, illustrated in Fig. 10. Development of a relationship between two

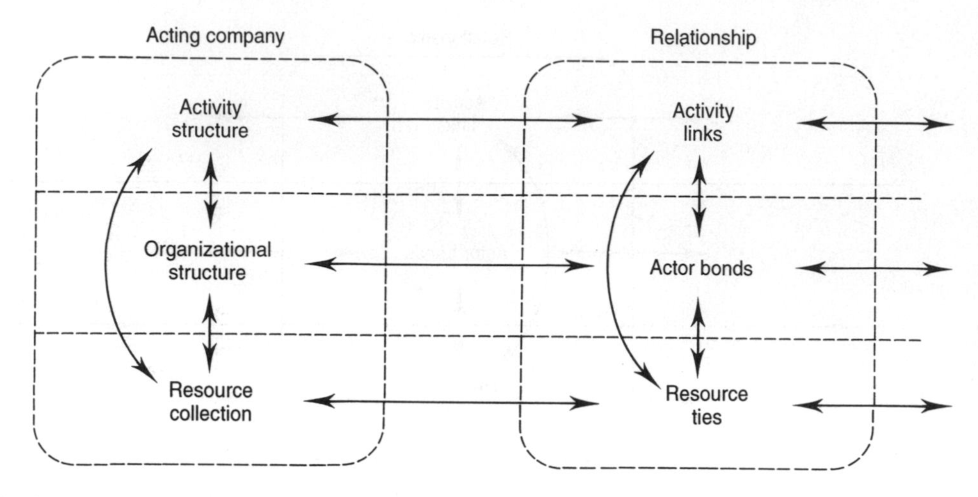


Fig. 9. Relationships and the company.

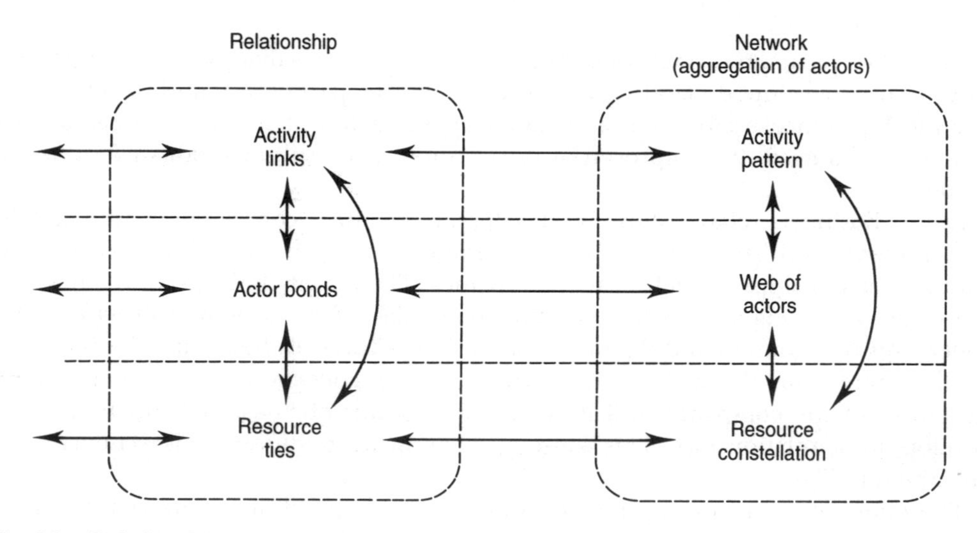


Fig. 10. Relationships in a network.

companies thus has an organizing effect on the overall network structure and every relationship has a role in it.

## The Scheme of Analysis

Putting together the two dimensions we can outline a broad analytical scheme to identify where and what effects are likely to occur as a relationship evolves, is established, develops or is interrupted. We believe the scheme outlined in Fig. 11 can be used in two ways: first, it can be used as a conceptual framework to analyse the

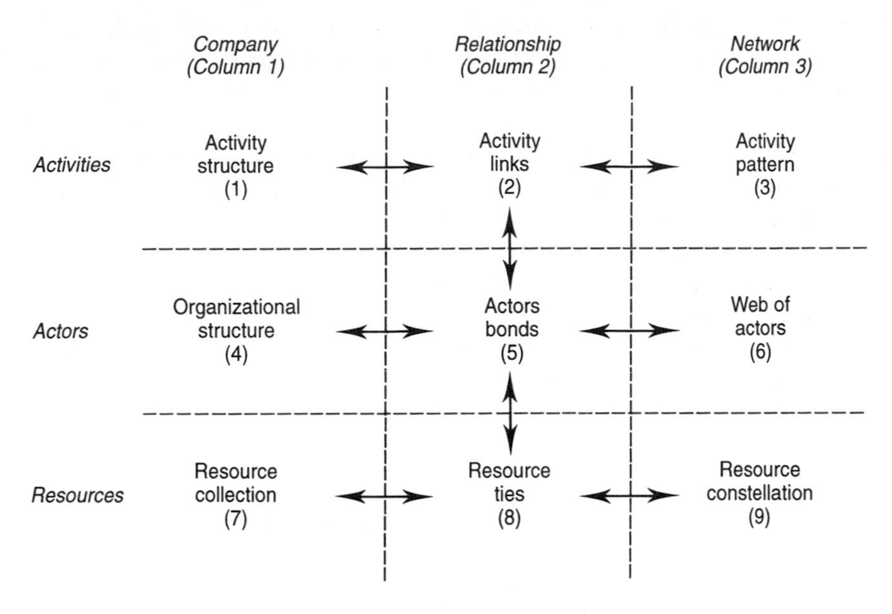


Fig. 11. Scheme of analysis of development effects of business relationships.

effects of change in a relationship and/or to identify the factors that affect the possibilities of development of a relationship. Second, it can be used as a heuristic device in coping with relationships in business. It can be used to single out the critical issues in coping with relationships, to assess the state of a relationship and its development potential. It can thus be used to identify where and how to intervene in relationships in order to get some desired effects. The scheme can be used to identify the dynamic effects in the development of a business relationship. It summarizes the main variables of relationship development discussed in this chapter.

It can be used in order to distinguish possible effects of change, for whatever reason, in a relationship. Any change in a relationship can have three types of effects. One is the direct effect changing the potential of the relationship. This will depend on how it affects the interplay of the different layers of the relationship (column 2). Another type of effect is on the companies involved and their cost–revenue parameters (column 1). A third more indirect effect takes place as the change might lead to different reactions, causing more or less of an "explosion" in the overall network (column 3). The scheme can be used for analysing all three types of effect.

The scheme can also be used to identify the impact of change on the development of a relationship. Any change (in any of the cells of the matrix) can affect the development of a certain relationship. If, for example, one or both of the companies are changing some activities this might have effects in both the horizontal and vertical dimensions of the scheme. It might have a direct effect in terms of increased or decreased efficiency in the performance of the internal activities of the company (cell 1). It might also have some direct effects for some third parties who have to adapt to the new link with accompanying positive or negative effects on its outcome (cell 3). The change might also have an indirect effect. It can give cause to make further changes within the relationship in terms of new ties (cell 8) or bonds (cell 5). It can also give cause to make adjustments in relationships to third parties (cell 3). One change can in this way cause a number of reactions which might be both expected (wanted) and unexpected (surprises) for the party initiating the change.

The value of the scheme in Fig. 11 is limited from an explanatory point of view, as it only identifies where effects might occur. It does not say anything about which changes shall produce certain effects. It provides just the frame that indicates the main direction of effects and their type. The scheme does not provide guidance in order to assess the likelihood or the magnitude of impact of changes in a relationship or elsewhere in the network. These require a further analysis that permits to assess the strength of connections in the various layers of substance of the relationships and the economic consequences of these. However, it provides the guidance in directing such an analysis.

## COPING WITH RELATIONSHIPS

Coping with relationships, exploiting them economically, requires an awareness of their effects and insight to the interdependence that accounts for their dynamics. The conceptual framework developed in this chapter can, we believe, be of some help for this purpose. It can be used to formulate some broad normative implications for management.

Compared with the more traditional view of determinants of a company's performance, the relationship perspectives yield rather different implications. The main points in our argument so far are as follows:

- In numerous companies, relationships have an overwhelming impact on their economic performance. When that is the case, i.e. when single specific relationships matter, they have to be managed.
- Companies cannot unilaterally control and decide the development of relationships; they are but part of relationships and of a larger whole that affects both their outcomes and their development potential. Awareness of this interdependence is needed in order to cope with relationships successfully.
- The time dimension becomes more important as conduct and its outcomes are rooted in the past and its effects become manifest in time. Interdependence and awareness of interdependence in the company and its counterparts will be decisive to the outcome of joint action. Insight into the dynamics of business networks is required in order to cope with relationships effectively.

The scheme of analysis developed from our discussion of the substance and functions of business relationships (see Fig. 11) can be used to identify the critical issues in coping with relationships in business.

There are three areas where effects of relationship are important and need to be coped with: marketing and purchasing; capability development; and strategy development. These can be illustrated schematically, as in Fig. 12. Marketing and purchasing is about relationship development. Capability development is about

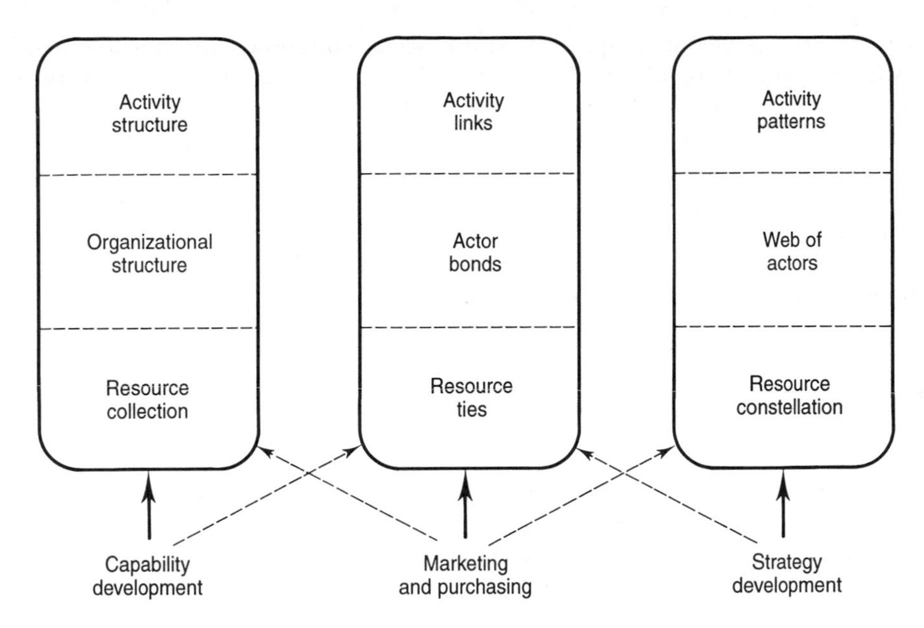


Fig. 12. Critical issues in coping with business relationships.

coping with the effect of relationships on the development potential of a company. Strategy development is about positioning the company in the overall network through the development of its relationships.

*Marketing and Purchasing*

Critical relationships to customers, suppliers and eventually other third parties have to be maintained and possibly developed. The issue here is how "team" effects can be produced or, in other words, the functioning of the quasi-organization that the major relationships constitute.

The main management task is to keep the customer and supplier relationships "productive". In terms of our scheme of analysis it is matter of coping with the interplay of the various substance layers in relationships and the mutuality of the interaction process. To intervene in a relationship is to develop (or to interrupt) activity links, resource ties and actor bonds in interaction with the counterpart. That requires an understanding of connections and assessment of their effects, as well as monitoring of changes and their likely impact on the relationship.

The primary task of marketing and purchasing function is thus close to what we called development of the function of relationships as a dyad.

*Capability Development*

This area is about exploiting the possible positive effects of business relationships on the activity structure, resource collection and organization of the company and on other relationships of the company. It also is about containing the possible negative effects in the same dimensions. The effects of relationships will depend on possible connections of links, ties and bond to those of other relationships.

Business relationships have, among other things, important effects on the development of the technical competence and capacity of the company. On the whole they seem to affect the productivity, innovativeness and competence – that is, all the components of a company's capability and thus its performance.
potential. The capabilities of a company reflect how successful it has been in combining relationships and its internal features.

*Strategy Development*

This area is about manoeuvring for a favourable position for the company in the business network. The position affects the economic outcome of a company's relationships over time and the possibilities of developing and maintaining relationships to various other parties. The position of a company with respect to others (its relationships) reflects its capacity to provide values to others (productiveness, innovativeness, competence). It is also a determinant of the possibilities of developing its capability by drawing on the capacity of others.

The critical issue for management here is monitoring the changes in the network structure that affect the position and thus the capability and capacity of the company. Changes must be assessed in terms of their likely impact on the position of the company with respect to the wider activity pattern, resource constellation and web of actors. Strategies need to be devised to meet the changes or to produce changes in the network. The overall position of a company is a composite of position with respect to the relevant resource constellation, activity pattern and structure of actor bonds.

Handling the single relationships, that is, managing the dyadic function, is a condition for exploiting the potential of relationships and for taking economic advantage of business relationships. It is a condition for developing capabilities and for the strategy development in a company. Conversely, to pursue a change in the strategy of the company requires that the development effects on the relationships are monitored and adjusted.

Handling relationships, their development, their impact on the company and on its strategy affects the economic performance of companies, as we have stated several times. The problem is that the effects may offset one another and that they can become manifest at different times. The economic consequences of actions taken in a relationship can thus hardly be quantified precisely. What is evident, however, is that they are significant both in terms of impact on the short-term economic efficiency and in terms of the longer-term effectiveness. That calls for a final consideration on the use of the scheme. We have observed several times that the effects of relationships are complex and can hardly be mapped in detail. Dynamics of business relationships would make such a map, possible in principle, obsolete the moment it is produced.

An accurate assessment in every specific case and situation is beyond the capacity of any company. No company is likely to be able to assess all the effects of the interdependencies in a specific situation, even if aware of their nature. So much more so because the effect will depend on how others will choose to behave, and the effects that will become evident over time are highly uncertain. Yet, if the outcome of the relationships is somehow to be managed, that is, controlled and influenced in favour of the individual company, awareness of the effects and insight into the interdependence is needed. The problem we face is how to cope with complexity of factors affecting the outcomes when an *a priori* assessment of relevant effects is ruled out. In general terms it has been argued that purpose-directed behaviour under such circumstances calls for the adoption of behavioural rules that do not necessarily derive from a cognitive elaboration of the specific situation as it is met, but rather from an individual elaboration of past experience (e.g. Weick, 1969; Starbuck, 1985, March 1988) or from the generalized collective experience somehow transmitted to the subject (Hayek, 1967; Kelley and Thibaut, 1978).

Awareness of the effects of and insight into the interdependencies can contribute to the formation of the behavioural rules that guide effective behaviour. The identification of the main variables of relationship development can serve to elaborate the experience and thus the adoption in a company of an effective "relationship strategy".

## BIBLIOGRAPHY


Achrol, R. S., 1991, 'Evolution of the Marketing Organization: New Forms for Turbulent Environments', *Journal of Marketing*, Vol. 55 (Oct.), pp. 77–93.

Alchian, A. A. and Demsetz, H., 1972, 'Production, Information Costs, and Economic Organization', *The American Economic Review*, Vol. 62, pp. 777–795.

Alderson, W., 1965, *Dynamic Marketing Behavior*. Homewood, Ill.: Richard D. Irwin Inc.

Alter, C. and Hage, J., 1993, *Organizations Working Together*. Newbury Park, Cal.: Sage.

Arndt, J., 1979, 'Toward a Concept of Domesticated Markets', *Journal of Marketing*, Vol. 43 (Fall), pp. 69–75.

Astley, G. W., 1984, 'Toward an Appreciation of Collective Strategy', *Academy of Management Review*, Vol. 9, No. 3, pp. 526–535.

Blois, K. J., 1972, 'Vertical Quasi-integration', *Journal of Industrial Economics*, Vol. 20, No. 3, pp. 253–272.

Håkansson, H., (ed.), 1982, *Internal Marketing and Purchasing of Industrial Goods – An Interaction Approach*. New York: Wiley.

Hayek, F. A., 1967, *Studies in Philosophy, Politics and Economics*. London: Routledge and Kegan Paul.

Kelley, H. H. and Thibaut, J. W., 1978, *Interpersonal Relations: A Theory of Interdependence*. New York: Wiley.

March, J. G., 1988, *Decisions and Organizations*. Oxford: Basil Blackwell.

Miles, R., and Snow, C., 1986, 'Organizations: New Concepts for New Forms', *California Management Review*, Vol. 28, pp. 62–73.

Nohria, N. and Eccles, R. G. (eds), 1992, *Networks and Organizations: Structure, Form, and Action*. Boston, Mass.: Harvard Business School Press.

Starbuck, W. H., 1985, 'Acting First and Thinking Later: Theory Versus Reality in Strategic Change', in Pennings, J. M. (ed.), *Organizational Strategy and Change*. San Francisco, Cal.: Jossey-Bass.

Webster, F. E., 1992, 'The Changing Role of Marketing in the Corporation', *Journal of Marketing*, Vol. 56, Oct. pp. 1–17.

Weick, K. E., 1969, *The Social Psychology of Organizing*. Reading, Mass.: Addison-Wesley.

# 5

# Network Positions and Strategic Action – An Analytical Framework

*J. Johanson and L.-G. Mattsson*

## INTRODUCTION

The basic idea in the industrial network model is that firms are engaged in networks of business relationships. The network structure, that is the ways in which the firms are linked to each other, develops as a consequence of the firms transacting business with each other. At the same time, the network structure constitutes the framework within which business is carried out. This chapter develops and discusses a notion of strategic action in industrial networks. Strategic action is interesting not only in its consequences for firms, but also because of its implications for the dynamics of industrial systems.

There are three specific attributes of the network model which are central to the argument developed in this chapter. First, it views networks as sets of connected relationships between actors. Further, a distinction is made between two levels in the industrial system; the network of exchange relationships between industrial actors and the production system where resources are employed and developed in production. Resources and activities form the production system. The network of exchange relationships is viewed as a structure governing the production system. Second, the concept of network position is used to describe how the individual actors in the network are related to each other in a network structure. Third, both the means and ends of strategic action are closely linked to the position concept.

The choice of these three characteristics may be justified on the following grounds.

1. The separation of the actors in the network from the resources and activities in the production system is analytically helpful first of all because the concept of strategic action presupposes actors. Actors have intentions, they make interpretations of conditions in the industrial system and they act. It is also useful because there is not necessarily a one-to-one correspondence between a production system and a network of relationships. For example an actor in a

Reprinted by permission of International Thomson, Network Positions and Strategic Action – An Analytical Framework from *Industrial Networks: A New View of Reality*, Edited by B. Axelsson and G. Easton, pp 205–217.

network may be engaged in exchange relationships covering several production systems or control different, widely separated clusters of resources in one production system. Correspondingly a production system may involve several actors who have no business relationships with each other.

2. The use of the position concept is not only a way to move from a dyadic to a network analysis, but it also provides a conceptual understanding of how the individual actor is related to, or rather embedded in, the environment.
3. The use of the position concept as both means and ends of strategic action makes it possible to give such action meaning in relation to the conditions for structural change in industrial networks. This is another way of saying that the individual actor's opportunities and constraints depend on the network and on the results of earlier strategic action. Thus, the notions of embeddedness and of investments in networks are given strategic meaning (cf. Pfeffer (1987) and Johanson and Mattsson (1985)).

The chapter proceeds as follows. First, the industrial system model is described. Since some of the conceptual building blocks are quite similar to what should already be common ground, and are referred to in Part I of the book, we concentrate on the specifics. Second, we make a somewhat deeper analysis of the position concept before, in the third and final section, discussing strategic action as efforts to change or preserve network positions.

## THE INDUSTRIAL SYSTEM

In production systems, resources are employed, combined and transformed in industrial production. Coordination and direction of activities in the production systems takes place through governance structures. The production system together with the governance structure constitutes the industrial system. The term production is taken in a wide sense to include all the different kinds of activities needed to create and use products and services (R&D, manufacturing, marketing, distribution, purchasing, etc.). The resources are dependent on each other in the sense that the outcome of the use of one resource is dependent on how another is used. The resources are more or less heterogeneous and specialised. The more they are specialised the stronger are the dependencies between actors. In the extreme case when two resources are completely specialised in a use where they are combined, they are completely complementary and there is a very high positive dependence between them. At the opposite extreme two specialised resources may be complete substitutes, in which case there is a high negative interdependence. On the whole, an operating production system can be characterised in terms of dependence between resources according to an industrial logic where resources are more or less complementary and/or substitutable inputs into, and outputs from, production.

Resource specialisation and interdependencies are, however, not solely determined by some technical imperative. In any specific situation they are a consequence of earlier use of the resources and of the structure of the production system. Resources are more or less heterogeneous, implying that they have properties in a number of different dimensions, so that over time, they can be used in different ways, combined in different ways, and transformed in different ways. Thus two heterogeneous resources which are combined can usually, through experience in use, become more specialised in their combined use leading to higher joint productivity, higher degrees of complementarity and increased interdependence between them.

In such production systems, where there are innumerable, different, and changing resource interdependencies, there is a strong need for some kind of coordination between resources not only to economise their use, but also to create changes of an innovative nature. Traditionally two different governance modes are assumed to bring about this coordination: the hierarchy and the market (Williamson, 1985). In the hierarchy, one supreme actor controls all the resources and brings about coordination. In the market model coordination takes place through price signals which inform the autonomous actors about the availability of, and need for, resources. In the present model it is assumed that the production system is governed through a network of exchange relationships between semi-autonomous actors. The actors are engaged in and develop exchange relationships with each other and can in this way handle the interdependencies between the resources they control (see Fig. 1).

We assume a circular causal relation between the network level and the production level. Through the exchange relationships the actors learn about each other and develop some trust in each other. On that basis they adapt and develop their resource use to increase the productivity which also leads to increased resource interdependence between them. At the same time, as a result of interdependence, the actors develop their relationships, thus linking them closer to each other. Consequently, unless no other factors intervene, through current activities the specific dependencies and relationships will become gradually stronger and closer. However, as the specific relationship is embedded in a network of such relationships and since this focal dependence is only one in an intricate fabric of such dependencies there are always such intervening factors affecting the causal circle.

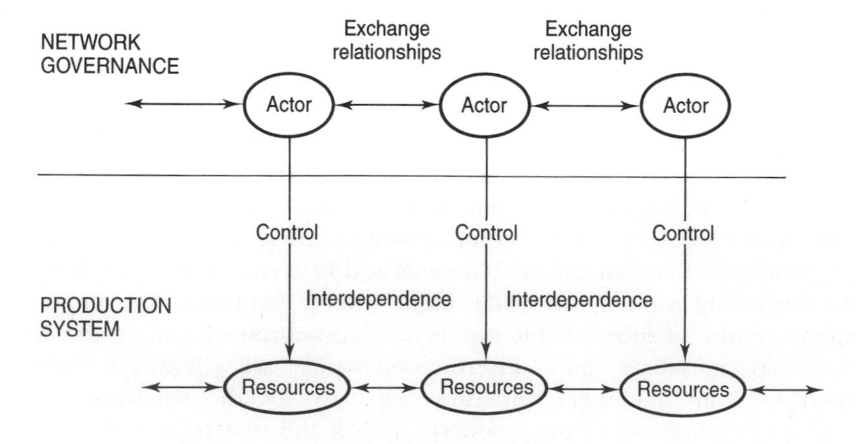


Fig. 1 Network governance in the industrial system.

Sometimes such forces are channelled via the network, sometimes they operate through the dependencies in the production system (see Fig. 2).

The exchange relationship is a mutual orientation of two actors towards each other. They are prepared to interact with each other in order to coordinate and develop interdependent resources that each actor controls. They interact to get access to some of the resources controlled by the other actor. These exchange relationships develop over time and resources are used to establish, maintain and develop them. Exchange relationships in networks may become lasting, especially if the heterogeneous resources controlled by the actors become adapted to each other and become highly specialised.

Exchange relationships also link actors indirectly to other actors with whom they do not have any such relationships. Evidently, actors in the industrial system also use resources which are interdependent without the actors having exchange relationships with each other. This is typically the case with competing actors. Similarly there may be interdependencies between actors with complementary resources, e.g. complementary suppliers who have no exchange relationship with each other. If actors consider such interdependencies important they may start interaction with each other, thus developing an exchange relationship. Correspondingly, actors may have more or less "sleeping" relationships with each other, for historical or other reasons without any resource dependencies between the resources they control. Such a relationship may be used to combine resources, thus creating new productive resource interdependence.

A basic characteristic of networks is that relationships are connected, i.e. exchange in one relationship is conditioned by exchange in others (Cook and Emerson, 1978). The connections may be positive or negative. A positive connection between two relationships implies that exchange in one relationship has a positive effect on exchange in the other. This is, for instance, the case with relationships handling a sequence of interdependencies along a production chain. Correspondingly, two competing suppliers to a customer are usually negatively connected via that customer. The two cases are examples of simple connections via the resource interdependencies in the production system. It is apparent that connections in a network may be much more indirect and complex so that two distant relationships in a network are connected with each other in multiple ways, some of which are positive and some negative.

However, the connections between relationships may also take place exclusively via the actors at the network level. In this case they are of a subjective nature and are a

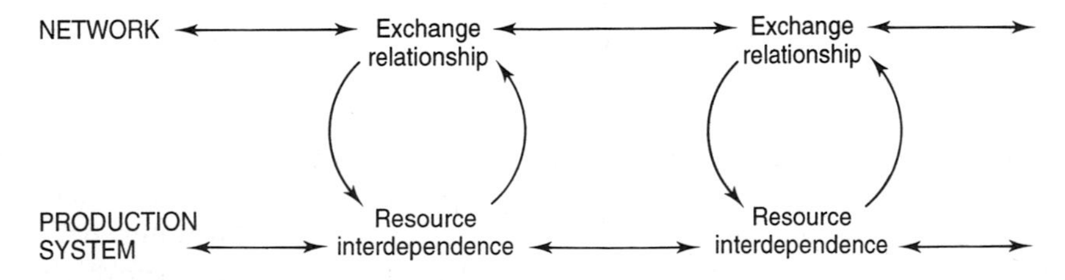


Fig. 2 Interlinked causal relationship/interdependence circles.

matter of intentions, strategies, views, and the "network theories" of the actors (Weick, 1979). Thus, an actor may, taking a long-term view of a market, consider two relationships as complementary in some sense, for instance in terms of technical development. Similarly the actor may see two relationships as substitutes for each other in a foreign market entry. Thus, although there are no interdependencies on the production level the two relationships may be negatively connected. Obviously, actor-mediated connections are much more ambiguous, fluid and invisible than those which are resource interdependence mediated. Nevertheless, they exist and have important implications for network development.

Since there are no objective criteria by which to decide which exchange relationships to include in networks and which to exclude, the boundaries of a specific network are necessarily fuzzy. However certain interdependence criteria may be used. A production system can be delimited on the basis of resource interdependencies in relation to some focal products, technology, country, region, etc. The inclusion of relationships is then a matter of determining who are the actors who control relevant resources. The excluded relationships can then be regarded as belonging to other networks and as a means of providing links between networks. If, for example, the focal production system exists in a certain geographic area, relationships with actors outside that area should reasonably be considered as links to other networks. On the other hand, if there are strong interdependencies between resources in that area and resources in other areas, the focal production system should not be delimited on an area basis. One test of such delimitations is whether there are important exchange relationships with actors in other networks. Thus, if the exchange relationships included coordinated resources which according to a specific industrial logic belong to a specified focal production system, a test of the suitability of such a definition is if any excluded exchange relationships coordinate resources that have important influences on the included relationships.

Since we are interested in industrial development and structural change, influences from actors outside the focal network, that is the network governing the focal production system, could be important. As an example it is sufficient to mention internationalisation of competition. Even if it is apparent that the whole world is connected we need, for analytical reasons, to consider production system boundaries. Thus, analytically there exist many networks and a specific actor may be engaged in several networks. To take another example, if we define a focal production system to exclude some of the resource interdependencies which one actor coordinates through exchange relationships, then this actor is defined as being involved in more than one network. This actor's resource interdependencies among several production systems might suggest that the delimitation of the production system as well as network should be "multi-industrial".

The actors in a network may view the network, its extensivity and the nature of its exchange relationships in quite different ways and also differently from the description that might be provided by an outside analyst who is not an actor. First, the network is extensive and includes exchange relationships in which the actor is not directly involved. Second, even in those relationships where the actor is involved, the counterparts may view the relationships in different ways. Third, network analysis deals not only with the present but also with the past and the future which means that the interpretations are influenced by different memories and different beliefs about the future. Since the actors form cognitive structures through experience and interpretations linked to theories about "reality", perceptions will be influenced by which conceptual framework the actors use (Zaltman *et al.*, 1982). Whether the actor's "theory" is that the industrial system is governed by a network or by a market mechanism will obviously be of importance. This means that there is a potential normative value in the idea that a network has less clear boundaries than a "market structure" based on a traditional industrial organisation model. The actor with a network perspective will focus some attention on influences from "outside" actors and might therefore extend the network boundaries and thereby perhaps increase the possibilities for effective strategic action.

## POSITIONS IN NETWORKS

Each actor is engaged in a number of exchange relationships with other actors. These relationships define the position of the actor in the network. Since positions can be defined for all the actors in the network, the concept can be used to characterise network structure and network distance between actors. A basic attribute of exchange relationships is that they are established and developed over time and so this process can be viewed as an investment process (Hakansson, 1982b). Thus, network positions are the result of investments in exchange relationships (Johanson and Mattsson, 1985). Positions are a consequence of the cumulative nature of the use of resources to establish, maintain and develop exchange relationships. The position of an actor also connects the separate, individual relationships with each other. The position characterises the actor's links to the environment and is therefore of strategic significance. The positions of all the actors in the network are also a major characteristic of the environment in which the actor is embedded. Furthermore, the position strongly influences the basis for an actor's development of exchange relationships in the future, i.e. forms the base for the actor's strategic actions (Mattsson, 1984).

A distinction can be made between a limited and an extended definition of positions. The limited definition refers purely to the network level. According to the limited definition, the position of an actor is a matter of the exchange relationships of the actor and the identities of the counterparts in those relationships. The identities of the counterparts are, in consequence, a matter of their relationships to others. This corresponds to the way in which positions are used in sociometric network analyses and makes it possible for us to use all the usual measures for characterising network positions: interconnectedness, distance, etc. (Di Maggio, 1986). When operationalising the limited definition it is possible to view relationships as integer variables that only take the values zero and one. It is, however, also possible to view relationships as continuous metric variables, defined on the same scale, with values between zero and one depending on the strength of the relationship. Further, relationships may be conceived of as vectors with values depending on the strength of a number of bond dimensions – legal, social, etc.

The extended definition, however, refers, in addition, to the role the actors have in the production system. Thus, according to the extended definition, the position of an actor includes also the productive processes – in a broad sense – in which it is involved and its direct and indirect network interdependencies. The production role has two dimensions, one qualitative and one quantitative. The qualitative dimension describes which function the actor has in the production system. In a sequential chain linking the separate resources, the individual actor has one or more specific functions, for which the resources it controls are specialised. The quantitative dimension characterises the relative importance that the resources of the actor have in relation to the resources of other actors, i.e. how much of the total quantity of substitutable resource are controlled by the actor. A network position gives an actor some power over resources controlled by other actors. This power is in no way absolute since exchange relationships by definition depend on voluntary mutual orientation and not on coercion.

Clearly, the positions of different actors in a network are money or less interreleated. This is the direct result of the basic assumption that networks are sets of connected exchange relationships. Connectedness means that exchange in one relationship is conditioned – facilitated or hindered – by exchange in another. Connectedness can occur on the production level. Through direct and indirect resource interdependencies the positions of two actors are interrelated. This type of position interrelation may be described as objective. It is a matter of the industrial logic. The stronger the resource interdependencies, the stronger are the position interrelations. This means that the closer two actors are in a production chain, the stronger are their position interrelations. This means also that the more specialised the production of the actors is in relation to each other in a network, the stronger are their position interrelations. It means also that the more closed the production system is in relation to other production systems, the stronger are position interrelations in the system. Furthermore, positions of different actors may be positively or negatively connected to each other in the sense that when the position of one is strengthened the position of the other is strengthened or weakened. This can also be seen as a matter of the industrial logic.

However, interrelations between positions can also occur at the network level, which means that they are a matter of intentions and interpretations of the actors. They are of a subjective nature. It seems reasonable to assume that the longer the time perspective the less important are the objective interdependencies driven by an industrial logic and the more important are the intentions and interpretations of the actors. Thus, in a long-term perspective, position interrelations become more of a subjective matter. The knowledge and the values of the actors are therefore important factors. Likewise it seems reasonable to assume that the smaller the investments in the production systems, the more important are the subjective views of the actors of the interrelations between positions. This does not mean that there are fewer position interrelations in soft industrial systems such as R&D or service industry systems than in manufacturing industry systems or that there are fewer position interrelations in the long term, only that they are more ambiguous. Generally, however, it can be assumed that the position interrelations are stronger the closer the actors are connected at the network level, as they will tend to have more analogous "network theories".

To sum up, the position of an actor is described by the characteristics of its exchange relationships. A limited, basic definition is that the position is a matter of with which actors the focal actor has exchange relationships. An extended definition of a position also involves the role of the actors in the production system. The role comprises the function accorded by the industrial logic and the relative importance of the actors.

The position of an actor changes all the time, not only because new exchange relationships are developed, old ones interrupted and others change in character, but also because the counterparts' positions are changing and, furthermore, the positions of third parties, with whom the focal actor has no direct relationships, are also changing. This follows from the definition of positions as being a matter of the identities of counterparts. But the ways in which position change may differ depending on whether the changes take place on the actor (network) or on the resource (production system) level.

## STRATEGIC ACTION

In the general strategy literature, strategic actions are usually characterised as efforts by actors to influence their relationship with their environment. In the network approach this general notion is translated to mean that strategic actions are efforts by actors to influence (change or preserve) their position(s) in network(s). The following discussion is about such strategic action by one focal actor. Strategic objectives are defined in terms of network positions. Obviously, almost all actions in networks have some effect on network positions. This is, for instance, the case with action in an exchange relationship concerning current production. When two actors carry out exchange they develop their exchange relationships thus modifying their positions as well as those of other actors in the network. In this chapter, however, only action which aims primarily at the positions is considered strategic. Plainly, it is difficult to make a distinction between such position-directed action and more production-directed action.

This view of strategic action means that strategic action by a focal actor aims not only at increasing that post-action network effectiveness. It is also a matter of developing the base from which future action can proceed. Within the framework of the limited definition of network positions, strategic action aims at influencing actors, relationships and network structures. It can be directed at the relationships of the focal actor, it can be directed at relationships between other actors in the network, or it can be directed at relationships with other networks. These goals may be achieved by breaking old relationships, establishing new, changing the character of existing, or preserving relationships endangered by adverse actions by other actors. The strategic action may also aim to influence actor perceived mediated connections between relationships, such as whether and to what extent actors view relationships as complementary or competing. This is a matter of influencing their "network theories". Such action may aim at influencing the "network theories" of a specific actor or a specific set of actors in a network. It may also aim at influencing or creating a dominant "network theory" in a network. This may imply attempts to make the "network theories" of different actors in the network more consistent. It may, however, also represent efforts to disconnect the network into two or more separate nets, where, for instance, the focal actor is the only link between the nets or where the focal actor has a strong position in one of the nets. Alternatively it may aim at connecting different sections more closely or at connecting different networks with each other.

Working within the framework of the extended definition of network positions, strategic action may also aim at restructuring the web of dependencies in the production system. An overall objective of such restructuring may be to develop the focal actor's role in the production system in a particular direction. Such action may, for instance, include weakening the dependence of the focal actor or reducing the dependence of a focal net on resources in certain other networks. This may include transforming specific dependencies between actors into more general dependencies which are not related to specific actors. The strategic action can also be designed to strengthen interdependencies in a production system in order, for instance, to create a specific dominant sequential chain of interdependencies. Correspondingly, it may aim at creating a set of dependencies around a certain resource controlled by the focal actor. Such actions may mean that general market dependencies are transformed into specific actor dependencies.

Using the limited definition of positions the base for strategic action by a focal actor are its (1) network positions, (2) resources, and (3) "network theory". The three bases of strategic action are not unrelated. Thus the quantity and quality of the resources influence the resource interdependencies which are closely related to the exchange relationships and consequently the network positions. The network position influences the network theory since that theory is to a large extent based on information channelled through the exchange relationships. Of the three types of strategic base the network position has a special status, since the strategic objectives are also defined in terms of network positions.

Let us finally illustrate the framework by discussing briefly strategic action in relation to the internationalisation of a focal firm. Such a strategic development involves, to an increasing degree, relationships cutting across national network boundaries. The focal firm beings internationalisation by establishing relationships with firms in other national networks. The first step may or may not involve control of production resources inside the new national network. Further internationalisation moves may include development of exchange relationships and positions in still more national networks and increased interdependency between the firm's positions in the different networks. The internationalisation of the firm can be seen as a consequence of strategic action by the firm to the extent that the moves are not the result of continuous development of current production activities or of actions taken by other actors.

The bases for internationalisation are, first, the firm's position, which can be used in various ways. Some of the exchange relationships in the old domestic network may be connected to existing or potential exchange relationships in the new network, depending to what extent these other firms have positions in those networks. Alternatively, the position of the actor in the old network can be communicated to actors in the new network thereby influencing their network theories so as to make them interested in becoming positively connected to the focal firm. A special case is that of actors who mutually exchange access to each other's positions in their respective networks. Observe, however, that the position in the old network can be a constraint on movement into new networks to the extent that commitments made in the old exchange relationships cannot be kept if new exchange relationships are added.

A second way that a firm may internationalise is that the firm's own resources can be made interdependent with resources controlled by actors in the other network. Quantitative and qualitative adjustments may or may not have to be made in order to establish and develop exchange relationships. Adjustments involve investments in new resources by the firm and purchase of already existing resources controlled by other actors. Another way to achieve the changes in resource structure is through explicit coordination with another firm.

Third, the firm's network theory not only directs the strategic action towards specific efforts to influence resources and positions, but can also be communicated to other actors in the network and thereby influence their action. For example, if the firm's network theory assumes expectations of network structure changes implying increasing interdependence between positions in different networks, i.e. internationalisation, this view can influence other actors with whom joint strategic action is desired or it can be used to affect dominant network theories in the new networks.

So far the discussion concerns the situation when a focal firm starts moving into new networks. Let us now look at a situation when both the focal firm and many other actors have positions in many national networks. The interrelated nature of network positions in different networks makes it even more important to consider the network theories of actors in the further internationalisation moves. Strategic actions, involving explicit linkages between a focal firm's and one or more other actors' network positions, are to a large extent based on communication of network theories and may result in changes from negative to positive or from positive to negative connections between positions. So called strategic alliances are a good example of this process in operation. They may create or handle interdependencies between production resources, but they also limit the number of potential alliances in the networks since some actors become appropriated. The survival of strategic alliances depends less on the extent to which resource coordination in the production system succeeds than on how network theories of both the involved and third actors develop.

Buying another firm is frequently referred to as a strategic action. An important issue in such a purchase is whether the buying firm can get control of the other firm's exchange relationships. In other words can the focal firm take over the position as well as the resources. Depending on the network theory in the focal firm, the major aim of the acquisition may be to get control of the exchange relationships, to change their character, or to change the connections between exchange relationships. Control of exchange relationships through acquisitions is, however, never certain, since there are always two actors involved.

As national networks become increasingly interdependent an obvious change in the actors' network theories is to regard the network boundaries as obsolete and to consider other boundaries as more relevant. Such changes in network theories might, for example, imply that the actors regard their positions as even more interdependent since they belong to the same network. Measures of network positions such as quantitative and qualitative aspects of resource interdependencies will become different when network boundaries change.

## BIBLIOGRAPHY


Alchian, A. A. and Demsetz, H. (1972) 'Production, Information Costs and Economic Organisation', *American Economic Review*, 62, p. 783.

Aldrich, H. E. (1979) *Organisations and Environments*, Englewood Cliffs, NJ, Prentice Hall.

Aldrich, H. E. (1981) *The Origins and Persistence of Social Networks. Social Structure and Network Analyses*, Beverly Hills, Calif., Sage.

Aldrich, H. E. and Whetten, D. A. (1981) 'Organisation-sets, Action sets and Networks. Making the most of simplicity' in P. C. Nystrom and W. H. Starbuk (eds) *Handbook of Organisational Design*, Vol. 1, Oxford, Oxford University Press pp. 385–408.

Alderson, W. (1957) *Marketing Behaviour and Executive Action*, Homewood, Ill., Richard D. Irwin.

Alderson, W. (1965) *Dynamic Marketing Behaviour. A Functionalist Theory of Marketing*, Homewood Ill., Richard D. Irwin.

Alexander, R., Surface, S. and Alderson, W. (1940) *Marketing*, Boston, Mass., Ginn and Company.

Arndt, J. (1979) 'Overview: The Impact of Stakeholder Publics in Shaping the Future of Marketing' in G. Fisk, J. Arndt, and K. Gronhaug, (eds), *Future Directions for Marketing* Cambridge, Mass., Marketing Science Institute, pp. 76–7.

Arrow, K. (1974) *Limits of Organisation*, New York, W.W. Norton and Co.

Astley, W. G. (1984) 'Toward an Appreciation of Collective Strategy'. *Academy of Management Review*, 9, 3, pp. 526–35.

Astley, W. G. (1985) 'The Two Ecologies: Population and Community Perspectives on Organisational Evolution'. *Administrative Science Quarterly*, 30, pp. 224–41.

Astley, W. G. and Fombrun, C. (1983) 'Collective Strategy: Social Ecology of Organisational Environments', *Academy of Management Review*, 8, pp. 576–87.

Averitt, R. T. (1968) *The Dual Economy: The Dynamics of American Industry Structure*, New York, W. W. Norton and Co.

Axelrod, R. (1984) *The Evolution of Cooperation*, New York, Basic Books.

Axelsson, B. (1982) 'Wilmanshyttans uppgang och fall. En kommentar till angreppssattet i en foretagshistorisk studie' (The Rise and Fall of Wilmanshyttan Steel Works. A Commentary on the Approach in a Company History Study'), *Acta Universitatis Upsaliensis*, 15, Liber.

Axelsson, B. (1987) 'Supplier Management and Technological Development' in H. Hakansson (ed.) *Industrial Technological Development: A Network Approach*, London, Croom Helm.

Axelsson, B. and Hakansson, H. (1979) 'Wikmanshyttans uppgang och fall. En analys av ett stalforetag och dess omgivning under 75 ar' ('The Rise and Fall of the Wikmanshyttan Steel Works. An Historical Analysis of a Steel Company during 75 years'), Studentlitteratur.

Axelsson, B. and Hakansson, H. (1984) *Inkap for Konkurrenshraft, (Purchasing for Competitive Power)*, Liber.

Barney, J. B. and Ouchi, W. G. (1986) *Organisational Economics* San Francisco, Calif., Jossey Bass.

Berg, P. O. (1985) 'Organisation Change as a Symbolic Transformation Process' in P. J. Frost *et al. Organization Culture*, New York, Sage.

Bjorklund, L. (1988) *International Projekforsaljning (International Systems Selling)*, Research Report, EFI., Stockholm School of Economics, Sweden.

Blau, P. M. (1964) *Exchange and Power in Social Life*, New York, John Wiley.

Blau, P. M. (1968) 'The Hierarchy of Authority in Organisations', *American Journal of Sociology*, 73, pp. 453–67.

Blois, K. J. (1972) 'Vertical Quasi-integration', *Journal of Industrial Economics*, 20, pp. 253–72.

Bonoma, T. (1976) 'Conflict, Cooperation and Trust in Three Power Systems', *Behavioural Science*, 21, pp. 499–514.

Bucklin, L. P. (1960) 'The Economic Structure of Channels of Distribution' in B. Mallen (1967) *The Marketing Channel: A Conceptual Viewpoint,* New York, John Wiley and Son, pp. 63–6.

Burt, R. S. (1980) 'Testing a Structural Theory of Corporate Cooptation: Interorganisational Directorate Ties as a Strategy for Avoiding Market Constraints on Profits', *American Sociological Review,* 45, pp. 821–41.

Campbell, N. C. G. (1984) 'The Structure and Stability of Industrial Networks. Developing a Research Methodology. Research Developments in International Marketing', 1st IMP International Research Seminar, UMIST, Manchester.

Campbell, N. C. G. (1985) 'Network Analysis of a Global Capital Equipment Industry', 2nd IMP International Research Seminar, University of Uppsala, Sweden.

Campbell, N. C. G. and Cunningham, M. T. (1984) 'Customer Analysis for Strategy Development in Industrial Markets', *Strategic Management Journal,* 4, pp. 369–80.

Caves, R. (1982) *Multinational Enterprise and Economic Analysis,* Cambridge, Cambridge University Press.

Cavusgil, S. T. and Nevin, J. P. (1981) 'The State-of-the-Art in International Marketing. An Assessment' in B. M. Enis and K. J. Roerring (eds) *Review of Marketing,* Greenwich, Conn., JAI Press.

Contractor, F. J. and Lorange, P. (1988) 'Why Should Firms Cooperate? The Strategy and Economics Basis for Cooperative Ventures' in F. J. Contractor and P. Lorange, *Cooperative Strategies in International Business,* Lexington, Mass., Lexington Books.

Cook, K. S. (1977) 'Exchange and Power in Networks of Interorganisational Relations', *Sociological Quarterly,* 18, pp. 62–82.

Cook, K. S. (1981) *Network Structure from Exchange Perspectives in Social Structure and Network Analyses,* Beverly Hills, Calif., Sage, pp. 177–200.

Cook, K. S. and Emerson, R. (1978) 'Power, Equity and Commitment in Exchange Networks', *American Sociological Review,* 43: pp. 712–39.

Cook, K. S. and Emerson, R. (1984) 'Exchange Networks and the Analysis of Complex Organisations', *Research in the Sociology of Organisations,* Vol. 3, Greenwich, Conn., JAI Press pp. 1–30.

Cox, R. and Goodman, C. (1956) 'Marketing of Housebuilding Materials', *Journal of Marketing,* 11, 1, pp. 36–61.

Cummings, T. G. (1984) 'Transorganisational Development', *Research in Organisational Behaviour,* Vol. 6, Greenwich, Conn., JAI Press, pp. 367–422.

Cunningham, M. T. (1987) 'Interaction, Networks and Competitiveness: A European Perspective of Business Marketing', European–American Symposium "World Wide Marketplace for Technology Based Products', University of Twente, Enschede, The Netherlands.

Cyert, R. M. and March, J. G. (1963) *A Behavioural Theory of the Firm,* Englewood Cliffs, NJ, Prentice Hall.

Dahl, R. A. (1957) 'The Concept of Power', *Behavioural Science,* 2, pp. 201–15.

Dahmen, E. (1988) 'Development Blocks in Industrial Economics', *Scandinavian Economic Review,* 1, pp. 3–14.

Di Maggio, P. (1986) 'Structural Analysis of Organisational Fields', *Research in Organisational Behaviour,* Vol. 8, Greenwich, Conn., JAI Press, pp. 335–70.

Easton, G. (1988) 'Marketing strategy and Competition', *European Journal of Marketing,* 22, 1, pp. 31–49.

Easton, G. (1990) 'Relationships Among Competitors', in G. Day, B. Weitz and R. Wensley (eds) *The Interface of Marketing and Strategy,* Greenwich, Conn., JAI Press.

Easton, G. and Araujo, L. (1985) 'The Network Approach: An Articulation', 2nd International IMP Research Seminar, University of Uppsala, Sweden.

Easton, G. and Araujo, L. (1986) 'Networks, Bonding and Relationships in Industrial Markets', *Industrial Marketing and Purchasing,* 1, 1, pp. 8–25.

Easton, G. and Smith, P. (1984) 'The Formation of Inter-Organisational Relationships in a Major Gasfield Development', Research Seminar on Industrial Marketing, Stockholm School of Economics, Sweden.

Emerson, R. M. (1962) 'Power Dependence Relations', *American Sociological Review*, 27, pp. 31–40.
Emerson, R. M. (1972) 'Exchange Theory, Part II: Exchange Relations in Networks', in J. Berger, M. Zedditch and B. Andersson (eds) *Sociological Theories in Progress*, Boston, Mass., Houghton Mifflin, pp. 58–87.
Engwall, L. (1985) 'Fran vag vision till komplex organisation. En studie av Varmlands Folkblads ekonomiska och organisatoriska utveckling' (from a Vague Vision to a Complex Organisation. A Study of the Economic and Organisational Development of the Varmlands Folkbald'), *Acta Universitatis Upsaliensis*, 22, University of Uppsala, Sweden.
Engwall, L. and Johanson, J. (1989) 'Banks in industrial networks', Working Paper, Department of Business Studies, University of Uppsala, Sweden.
Evan, W. M. (1966) 'The Organisation-Set" Toward a Theory of Interorganisational Relations', in J. Thompson (ed.) *Approaches to Organisational Design*, Pittsburg, Pa. University of Pittsburg Press.
Fiocca, R. and Snehota, I. (1986) 'Marketing e alta tecnologia', *Svihippo e Organizzazione*, 98, pp. 24–31.
Fombrun, C. J. and Astley, W. G. (1983) 'Beyond Corporate Strategy', *Journal of Business Strategy*, 3, pp. 47–54.
Ford, D. (1978) 'Stability Factors in Industrial Marketing Channels', *Industrial Marketing Management*, 7, pp. 410–22.
Ford, D., Hakansson, H. and Johanson, J. (1986) 'How do Companies Interact?', *Industrial Marketing and Purchasing*, 1, 1, pp. 26–41.
Forrester, J. (1961) *Industrial Dynamics*, Boston, Mass., MIT Press.
Forsgren, M. (1985) 'The Foreign Acquisition Strategy – Internationalisation or Coping with Strategic Interdependencies in Networks?', Working Paper, Department of Business Administration, University of Uppsala, Sweden.
Forsgren, M. (1989) *Managing the Internationalisation Process. The Swedish Case*, London, Routledge.
Fullerton, R. (1986) 'Understanding Institutional Innovation and System Evolution in Distribution', *International Journal of Research in Marketing*, 3, pp. 273–82.
Gadde, L.-E. and Mattsson, L.-M. (1987) 'Stability and Change in Network Relationships', *International Journal of Research in Marketing*, 4, pp. 29–41.
Gadde, L.-E., Hakansson, H. and Oberg, M. (1988) 'Change and Stability in Swedish Automobile Distribution', Report prepared for the 2nd Annual Forum of the International Motor and Vehicle Program, Boston, Massachusetts Institute of Technology.
Gattorna, J. (1978) 'Channels of Distribution Conceptualisations: A State-of-the-Art Review', *European Journal of Marketing*, 12, 7, pp. 471–512.
Glaser, A. and Strauss, B. (1967) *The Discovery of Grounded Theory*, Chicago, Ill., Aldine.
Giete, J. (1984) 'High Technology and Industrial Networks', International Research Seminar on Industrial Marketing, Stockholm School of Economics, Sweden.
Granovetter, M. S. (1973) 'The Strength of Weak Ties', *American Journal of Sociology*, 78, 6, pp. 1360–80.
Granovetter, M. S. (1984) 'A theory of Embeddedness', Department of Sociology, State University of New York.
Granovetter, M. S. (1985) 'Economic Action and Social Structure: The Problem of Embeddedness', *American Journal of Sociology*, 91, 3, pp. 481–510.
Grinyer and Spender (1979) 'Recipes, Crises and Adaptation in Mature Business', *International Studies of Management and Organisation*, 9, pp. 113–33.
Hagg, I. and Johanson, J. (1983) 'Firms in Networks', Business and Social Research Institute, Stockholm, Sweden.
Hakansson, H. (1982a) 'Teknisk Utveckling och Marknadsforing' ('Technical Development and Marketing'), *MTC* 19, Stockholm, Stockholm School of Economics, Liber.
Hakansson, H. (ed.) (1982b) *International Marketing and Purchasing of Industrial Goods: An Interaction Approach*, Chichester, Wiley.
Hakansson, H. (ed.) (1987) *Industrial Technological Development: A Network Approach*, London, Croom Helm.

Hakansson, H. (1989) *Corporate Technological Behaviour: Cooperation and Networks*, London, Routledge.
Hakansson, H. and Johanson, J. (1948a) 'Heterogeneity in Industrial Markets and its Implications for Marketing' in I. Hagg and F. Wiedersheim-Paul (eds) 'Between Market and Hierarchy', Department of Business Administration, University of Uppsala, Sweden.
Hakansson, H. and Johanson, J. (1984b) 'A Model of Industrial Networks', Working Paper, Department of Business Administration, University of Uppsala, Sweden.
Hakansson, H. and Johanson, J. (1988) 'Formal and Informal Co-operation Strategies in International Industrial Networks' in F. J. Contractor and P. Lorange *Co-operative strategies in International Business*, Lexington, Mass., Lexington Books.
Hakansson, H. and Ostberg, C. (1975) 'Industrial Marketing – An Organisational Problem', *Industrial Marketing Management*, 4, pp. 113–23.
Hakansson, H. and Snehota, I. (1989) 'No Business is an Island. The Network Concept of Business Strategy', *Scandinavian Journal of Management Studies*, 4, 3, pp. 187–200.
Hakansson, H. and Waluszewski, A. (1986) 'Technical Development in a Dense Network', 3rd International IMP Research Seminar, IRE, Lyon.
Hall, R. (1977) *Organisations: Structure and Process*, 2nd edn., Englewood Cliffs, NJ, Prentice Hall.
Hallen, L. (1984) 'Market Approaches in European Perspective', in P. Turnbull and J. P. Valla *Strategies in International Industrial Marketing: A Comparative Analysis*, London, Croom Helm.
Hamfelt, C. and Lindberg, A.-K. (1987) 'Technological Development and the Individual's Contact Network' in H. Hakansson (ed.) *Industrial Technological Development: A Network Approach*, London, Croom Helm.
Hammarkvist, K.-O. (1983) 'Markets as Networks', Marketing Education Group Conference, Cranfield, UK.
Hammarkvist, K.-O., Hakansson, H. and Mattsson, L.-G. (1982) *Marknadsforing for konkurrenskraft (Marketing for Competitive Power)*, Malmo, Liber.
Hampdon, G. M. and Van Gent, A. P. (eds) *Marketing Aspects of International Business*, Boston, Mass., Kluwer-Nijhoff.
Hannan, M. T. and Freeman, J. H. (1977) 'The Population Ecology of Organisations', *American Journal of Sociology*, 82, pp. 929–64.
Harrigan, K. (1983) *Strategies for Vertical Integration*, Lexington, Mass., Lexington Books.
Harrigan, K. (1985) *Strategies for Joint Ventures*, Lexington, Mass., Lexington Books.
Hawley, A. (1968) 'Human Ecology' in D. L. Sills (ed.) *The International Encyclopedia of the Social Sciences*, Vol. 4, New York, Macmillan and Free Press, pp. 328–37.
Hegert, M. and Morris, D. (1988) 'Trends in International Collaborative Agreements' in F. J. Contractor and P. Lorange *Co-operative Strategies in International Business*, Lexington, Mass., Lexington Books.
Henderson, J. M. and Quandt, R. E. (1971) *Microeconomic Theory*, 2nd edn., New York, McGraw-Hill.
Hettne, B. and Tamm, G. (1974) *Mobilisation and Development in India. A Case Study of Mysore State*, SIDA.
Hughes, T. P. (1983) *Networks of Power, Electrification in Western Society, 1880–1930*, Baltimore, Md., Johns Hopkins University Press.
Hultbom, C. (1990) 'Internal Exchange Processes. Buyer–Seller Relationships within Big Companies', Unpublished Ph.D. dissertation, Department of Business Studies, University of Uppsala, Sweden.
Hulten, S. (1985) 'What Can Theories of Industrial Change Contribute to the Understanding Of International Markets as Networks?', 2nd International IMP Research Seminar, University of Uppsala, Sweden.
Imai, K. (1987) 'Network industrial organisation in Japan', Working paper prepared for the workshop on 'New Issues in Industrial Economics' at Case Western Reserve University, Cleveland, OH, on 7–10 June.
Jansson, H. (1985) 'Marketing to Projects in South East Asia. A Network.' Working Paper 1985/3, Department of Business Administration, University of Uppsala, Sweden.
Johanson, J. and Mattsson, L.-G. (1984) 'Marketing Investments and Market Investments in

Industrial Markets', International Research Seminar in Industrial Marketing, Stockholm School of Economics, Stockholm, Sweden.
Johanson, J. and Mattsson, L.-G. (1985) 'Marketing and Market Investments in industrial networks', *International Journal of Research in Marketing*, 2, 3, pp. 185–95.
Johanson, J. and Mattsson, L.-G. (1986) 'Interorganisational Relations in Industrial Systems: A Network Approach Compared with a Transaction Cost Approach', Working Paper, University of Uppsala, Sweden.
Johanson, J. and Mattsson, L.-G. (1987) 'Interorganisational Relations in Industrial Systems: A Network Approach Compared with a Transaction Cost Approach', *International Studies of Management Organisation*, 17, 1, pp. 34–48.
Johanson, J. and Mattsson, L.-G. (1988) 'Internationalisation in Industrial Systems – A Network Approach', in N. Hood and J.-E. Vahlne (eds) *Strategies in Global Competition*, London, Croom Helm.
Johanson, J. and Sharma, D. (1985) 'Swedish Technical Consultants; Tasks, Resources and Relationships – A Network Approach', International Research Seminar on Industrial Marketing, Stockholm School of Economics, Stockholm, Sweden.
Kaynak, E. and Savitt, R. (eds) (1984) *Comparative Marketing Systems*, New York, Praeger.
Killing, K. P. (1982) 'How to Make a Global Joint Venture Work', *Harvard Business Review*, 61, 3, pp. 120–7.
Killing, J. P. (1983) *Strategies for Joint Venture Success*, New York, Praeger.
Kinch, N. (1988) 'Emerging Strategies in a Network Context: The Volvo Case', *Scandinavian Journal of Management Studies*, October.
Kranzberg, M. (1986) 'Technology and History: 'Kranzberg's Laws', *Technology and Culture*, 7, pp. 185–95.
Kutschker, M. (1982) 'Power and Dependence in Industrial Marketing' in H. Hakansson (ed.) *International Marketing and Purchasing of Industrial Goods: An interaction approach*, Chichester, Wiley.
Kutschker, M. (1985) 'The Multi-Organizational interaction approach to Industrial Marketing', *Journal of Business Research*, 13, pp. 383–403.
Laage-Hellman, J. (1984) 'The Role of External Technical Exchange in R&D: An Empirical Study of the Swedish Special Steel Industry', M.T.C. Research No. 18, Marketing Technology Centre, Stockholm, Sweden.
Laage-Hellman, J. (1987) 'Process Innovation through Technical Cooperation', in H. Hakansson (ed.) *Industrial Technological Development; A Network Approach*, London, Croom Helm.
Laage-Hellman, J. (1988) 'Technological Development in Industrial Networks', Working Paper, Department of Business Administration, University of Uppsala, Sweden.
Laage-Hellman, J. (1989) 'Technological Developments in Industrial Networks', Unpublished Dissertation, Department of Business Administration, University of Uppsala, Sweden.
Laage-Hallman, J. and Axelsson, B. (1986) 'Bioteknisk Foll i Sverigeforskninasuolam, forskninasinriktning, samartetsmonster. En studie av det bioteknisk Follnatverket 1970–1985' (Biotechnological R&D in Sweden. Research Volume, Direction of Research, Patterns of Cooperation. A study of the Biotechnological R&D Network 1970–1985), STU Information 536, Styrelsen for Teknisk Utveckling, Stockholm, Sweden.
Larsen, J. K. and Rogers, E. M. (1984) *Silicon Valley Fever*, New York, Basic Books.
Levine, S. and White, P. E. (1961) 'Exchange as a Conceptual Framework for the Study of Interorganisational Relationships', *Administrative Science Quarterly*, 5, pp. 583–601.
Lorenzoni, G. and Ornati, O. A. (1988) 'Constellations of Firms and New Ventures', *Journal of Business Venturing*, 3, pp. 41–57.
Lundgren, A. (1985) 'Datoriserad Bildbehandling i Sverige', ('Computerized Image processing in Sweden'), Working Paper, EFI, Stockholm School of Economics, Stockholm, Sweden.
Lundgren, A. (1987) 'Bildbehandlingens framvaxt', Working Paper, Stockholm School of Economics, Stockholm, Sweden.
Mallen, B. (ed.) (1967) *The Marketing Channel: A Conceptual Viewpoint*, New York, John Wiley and Son.

March, J. M. (1966) 'The Power of Power' in D. Easton (ed.) *Varieties of Political Theory*, Englewood Cliffs, NJ, Prentice Hall.
Marret, C. (1971) 'On the Specification of Interorganisational Dimensions', *Sociology and Social Research*, 56, pp. 83–9.
Mattsson, L.-G. (1969) *Integration and Efficiency in Marketing Systems*, EFI, Stockholm, Nordstedt & Soner.
Mattsson, L.-G. (1975) 'System Interdependencies – A Key Concept in Industrial Marketing', 2nd Research Seminar in Marketing, FNEGE, Senanque, France.
Mattsson, L.-G. (1981) 'Interorganisational Structures in Industrial Markets: A Challenge to Marketing Theory and Practice', Working Paper 1980/1, Department of Business Administration, University of Uppsala, Sweden.
Mattsson, L.-G. (1984) 'An Application of a Network Approach to Marketing: Defending and Changing Market Positions' in N. Dholakia and J. Arndt (eds) *Changing the Course of Marketing. Alternative Paradigms for Widening Marketing Theory*, Greenwich, Conn, JAI Press.
Mattsson, L.-G. (1986) 'Indirect Relationships in industrial networks: A Conceptual Analysis of their Significance', 3rd IMP International Seminar, IRE, Lyon, France.
Mattsson, L.-M. (1987a) 'Management of Strategic Change in a "Markets-as-Networks" Perspective' in A. Pettigrew *The Management of Strategic Change*, Oxford, Blackwell.
Mattsson, L.-G. (1987b) 'Conceptual Building blocks of Network Theory', Working Paper, Stockholm School of Economics, Stockholm, Sweden.
Mattsson L.-G. (1988) 'Interaction Strategies: A Network Approach' AMA Marketing Educator's Conference, Summer, San Francisco, Calif.
McCammon, B. (1964) 'Alternative Explanations of Institutional Change and Channel Evolution' in B. Mallen (ed.) (1967) *The Marketing Channel: A Conceptual Viewpoint*, New York: John Wiley and Son, pp. 75–81.
McCammon, B. and Little, R. W. (1965) 'Marketing Channels: Analytical Systems and Approaches' in G. Schwartz (ed.) (1970) *Science in Marketing*, New York, John Wiley and Son, pp. 321–85.
McVey, P. (1960) 'Are Channels of Distribution What the Textbooks Say?', *Journal of Marketing*, XXIV, 3, pp. 61–5.
Mintzberg, H. (1988) 'Opening up the Definition of Strategy' in J.B. Quinn, H. Mintzberg and R. M. James (eds) *The Strategy Process*, Englewood Cliffs, NJ, Prentice Hall International.
Morgan, G. (1986) *Images of Organisation*, Beverly Hills, Calif., Sage.
Nelson, R. R. and Winter, S. G. (1982) *An Evolutionary Theory of Economic Change*, Cambridge, Mass., Harvard University Press.
Nieschlag, R. (1954) 'Die Dynamik der Betriebsformen im Handel', Rheinisch-Westfahalches Institut für Wirtschaftsforschung, Essen, Schriftenreihe, Neue Folge nr 7.
Nilsson, A. (1987) 'Distributionssystems for Finpapper', ('Distribution Systems for Fine Paper'), Working Paper, EFI Stockholm School of Economics, Stockholm, Sweden.
Pascale, R. T. (1984) 'Perspectives on Strategy: "The Real Story Behind Honda's Success"' *California Management Review*, 26, 3, pp. 47–72.
Pettigrew, A. (1985) *The Awakening Giant: Continuity and Change in Imperial Chemical Industries*, Oxford, Basil Blackwell.
Pfeffer, J. (1978) *Organisational Design*, Arlington Heights, Ill., AHM Publishing Co.
Pfeffer, J. (1987) 'Bringing the Environment Back' in The Social Context of Business Strategy' in D. Teece *The Competitive Challenge: Strategies for Industrial Innovation and Renewal*, Cambridge, Mass., Balinger Publishers.
Pfeffer, J. and Lebjebici (1973) 'Executive Recruitment and the Development of Interfirm Organisations', *Administrative Science Quarterly*, 18, pp. 449–61.
Pfeffer, J. and Salancik, G. (1978) *The External Control of Organisations*, New York, Harper and Row.
Piori, M. and Sabel, F. (1984) *The Second Industrial Divide: Possibilities for Prosperity*, New York, Basic Books.
Porter, M. J. (1980) *Competitive Strategy: Techniques for Analyzing Industries and Competitors*, New York, The Free Press.
Reich, L. S. (1985) *The Making of American Industrial Research; Science and Business at G. E. and*

*Bell, 1876–1926,* Cambridge, Cambridge University Press.
Rogers, E. M. (1982) *Interorganisational Coordination,* Ames, Ia., Iowa State University Press.
Rogers, E. M. (1984) 'Organisations and Networks; Illustrations from the Silicon Valley Microelectronics Industry', International Research Seminar on Industrial Marketing, Stockholm School of Economics, Stockholm.
Rogers, E. M. and Kincaid, D. L. (1981) *Communication Networks: Toward a New Paradigm for Research,* New York, The Free Press.
Root, F. (1978/82) *Foreign Market Entry Strategies,* New York, AMACON.
Rosenberg, D. L. (1982) *Inside the Black Box: Technology and Economics,* Cambridge, Cambridge University Press.
Scherer, F. M. (1980) *Industrial Market Structure and Economic Performance,* 2nd edn, Boston, Mass., Houghton Mifflin.
Schumpeter, J. A. (1955) *The Theory of Economic Development,* Cambridge, Mass., Harvard University Press.
Scott, R. W. (1987) *Organisation: Rational, Natural and Open Systems,* 2nd edn, Englewood Cliffs, NJ, Prentice Hall.
Silverman, D. (1970) *The Theory of Organisations,* London, Heinemann.
Smith, P. and Easton, G. (1986) 'Network Relationships: A Longitudinal Study' 3rd International IMP Research Seminar, IRE Lyon, France.
Thorelli, H. B. (1986) 'Networks: Between Markets and Hierarchies', *Strategic Management Journal,* 7, 1, pp. 37–51.
Thompson, J. D. (1967) *Organisations in Action,* New York, McGraw-Hill.
Tichy, N. and Fombrun, C. (1979) 'Network Analysis in Organisational Settings', *Human Relations,* 32, 11, pp. 923–65.
Turnbull, P. W. and Valla, J.-P. (1986) *Strategies in International Industrial Marketing,* London, Croom Helm.
Van de Ven, A. (1976) 'On the Formation and Maintenance of Relations among Organisations', *Academy of Management Review,* 4, 4, pp. 24–36.
Van de Ven, A. and Ferry, D. L. (1980) *Measuring and Assessing Organisations,* New York, John Wiley.
Van de Ven, A. and Walker, G. (1984) 'Dynamics of Interorganizational Coordination', *Administrative Science Quarterly,* Dec. pp. 598–621.
Venkataraman, N. and Camillius, J.L. (1984) 'Exploring the Concept of "Fit" in Strategic Management', *Academy of Management Review,* 9, 3, pp. 513–25.
von Hippel, E. (1978) 'Successful Industrial Products from Customer Ideas', *Journal of Marketing,* 42, pp. 39–49.
von Hippel, E. (1986) 'Cooperation between Competing Firms. Informal Know-how Trading', Working Paper no. 1959–86, Sloan School of Management, March.
Walker, G. (1988) 'Network Analysis for Cooperative Interfirm Relationships' in F. J. Contractor and P. Lorange *Co-operative Strategies in International Business,* Lexington, Mass., Lexington Books.
Waluszewski, A. (1987) 'CTMP-Processen. Fran vedkravande till vedsnala processor', Department of Business Studies, University of Uppsala, Sweden.
Waluszewski, A. (1989) 'Framvaxten av en ny mekanisk massateknik – en utrecklingshistoria' ('The Emergence of a New Mechanical Pulping Technique – A Development Story'), Unpublished dissertation, Department of Business Studies, University of Uppsala, Sweden.
Weick, K. E. (1969) *The Social Psychology of Organizing,* 1st edn, Reading, Mass., Addison-Wesley.
Weick, K. E. (1970) 'Educational Organisations as Loosely Coupled Systems', *Administrative Science Quarterly,* 21, 1, pp. 1–19.
Weick, K. E. (1979) *The Social Psychology of Organizing,* 2nd edn, Reading, Mass., Addison-Wesley.
Weick, K. E. (1984) 'Small Wins: Redefining the Scale of Social Problems', *American Psychologist,* 39, pp. 40–9.
Weitz, B. (1985) 'Introduction to Special Issue on Competition in Marketing', *Journal of Marketing Research,* 22, pp. 229–36.

Wibe, S. (1980) 'Change of Technology and Day to Day Improvements', Umea Economic Studies, Umea University, Sweden.

Williamson, O. E. (1975) *Markets and Hierarchies*, New York, The Free Press.

Williamson, O. E. (1985) *The Economic Institutions of Capitalism*, New York, The Free Press.

Wind, Y. (1979) 'The Journal of Marketing at a Cross Road', *Journal of Marketing*, 43, pp. 9–12.

Yamagashi, T., Gilmore, M. and Cook, K. (1988) 'Network Connections and the Distribution of Power in Exchange Networks', *American Journal of Sociology*, 93, 4, pp. 835–51.

Zaltman, G., Le Masters, K. and Heffring, M. (1982) *Theory Construction in Marketing*, New York, John Wiley.

# 6

# Internationalisation in Industrial Systems – A Network Approach

*Jan Johanson and Lars -Gunnar Mattsson*

## INTRODUCTION

International interdependence between firms and within industries is of great and increasing importance. Analyses of international trade, international investments, industrial organisation and international business behaviour attempt to describe, explain and give advice about these interdependencies. The theoretical bases and the level of aggregation of such analyses are naturally quite varied.

In this chapter we discuss explanations of internationalisation of industrial firms with the aid of a model that describes industrial markets as networks of relationships between firms. The reason for this exercise is a belief that the network model, being superior to some other models of "markets", makes it possible to consider some important interdependencies and development processes on international markets. The models that we have selected for some comparative analyses are the transaction cost based "theory of internalisation" for multinational enterprise and the "Uppsala Internationalization Process Model" emphasising experiential learning and gradual commitments. While the former is a dominating theoretical explanation of multinational enterprise (Buckley and Casson, 1976), the latter seems to be the most cited explanation of a firm's foreign market selection and mode of international resource transfer over time (Bilkey, 1978; Johanson and Vahlne, 1977).

We will first present some empirical data in support of some basic assumptions of the network model. We will then describe this model, commenting especially on the investment nature of marketing activities. Internationalisation of the firm and of the network is also given a conceptual interpretation. We are then in a position to analyse four cases concerning internationalisation of the firm and of the network: The Early Starter, The Lonely International, The Late Starter, and The International Among Others. Finally, we will comment on some research issues raised by our analysis.

Reprinted by permission of International Thomson, Internationalisation in Industrial Systems – A Network Approach by J. Johanson and L.-G. Mattsson from *Strategies in Global Competition*, Edited by N. Hood and J. E. Vahlne, pp 287–314.

## CUSTOMER–SUPPLIER RELATIONSHIPS IN INDUSTRIAL MARKETS: SOME EMPIRICAL FINDINGS

A number of studies in industrial marketing and purchasing have demonstrated the existence of long-term relationships between suppliers and customers in industrial markets (e.g. Blois, 1972; Ford, 1978; Guillet de Monthoux, 1975; Håkansson and Ötberg, 1975; Levitt, 1983; Wind, 1970). It has also been emphasised by a leading marketing scholar that "for strategic purposes, the central focus of industrial marketing should not be on products or on markets, broadly defined, but on buyer–seller relationships" (Webster, 1979; 50). Such relationships have also been noted in studies in contractual relations (Macneil, 1978; Williamson, 1979) and in studies of technical development (von Hippel, 1978).

In an extensive international research project, industrial customer–supplier relationships were investigated. Interviews were made with industrial suppliers in Germany, France, Britain, and Sweden about the relations to their most important customers in the four countries and in Italy. Interviews were conducted with managers who had personal experience of the customers (Håkansson, 1982). Business transactions with important customers generally took place within well-established relationships. The average age of the 300 relations investigated was around 13 years (Hallén, 1986). The relationships were important to the two parties involved. In export relationships the suppliers were "main supplier" – in the sense that they provided at least half of the customer's needs for the products concerned – in about half of the cases. In the domestic relationships the suppliers were more often main suppliers – in around 80 per cent of the relationships.

The customers were also important to the suppliers. In the German sub-sample in which data about the customer's share of the supplier's sales are available, the average share of the customers investigated was 5.5 per cent. If we (somewhat arbitrarily) define a relationship as important to the customer if the supplier provides at least half of the need, and important to the supplier if the customer purchases at least 1 per cent of the supplier's sales, then 35 per cent of the relationships are classified as mutually important, 25 per cent as important to the supplier only, 18 per cent as important to the customer only, and 22 per cent as not important.

One of the reasons for the existence of long-term relationships is that suppliers and customers need extensive knowledge about each other if they are to carry on important business with each other. They need knowledge not only about price and quality, which may be very complex and difficult to determine; they also need knowledge about deliveries and a number of services before, during and after delivery. Much of that knowledge can in fact only be gained after transactions have taken place. Besides, they need knowledge about each other's resources, organisation and development possibilities. Knowledge about all these issues is seldom concentrated in one person in the firms. Not only marketers and purchasers, but also specialists in manufacturing, design, development, quality control, service, finance, and so on may take part in the information exchange between the companies. Contacts on several levels in the organisational hierarchies may be required. Such contacts may include personnel on the shop floor, top management and, of course, middle and lower management. The average total number of interacting persons in the relationships is between seven and eight from each party. Such contacts take time to establish: it takes time to learn which persons in a company possess certain types of knowledge, and which have the potentiality to influence certain conditions. On many occasions direct experience is the only possible way to learn so much about each other that the information exchange between the parties works efficiently. Such experiences certainly take time to acquire, and the parties invest in knowledge about each other.

Around 40 per cent of the relationships include contacts on the general management level. Specialists from manufacturing are involved on the customer side in 60–70 per cent of the relationships. Specialists on design and development take part in about 50 per cent of the relationships, and in both cases the supplier side is most involved. On the whole there are quite complex contact and interaction patterns in the relationships between the firms. Another aspect of the relationships is that significant business transactions require that the parties have confidence in each other's ability and willingness to fulfil their commitments. It takes time and effort to build such levels of confidence. The perceived social distance to the customers indicates the investments in confidence in the relationships. In 60–70 per cent of the relationships the respondent considered the relation as involving "close personal relations" or "friendly business relations" rather than more "formal business relations". Evidently these important relationships are also usually rather close, implying that they result from investments in the relationships.

Suppliers and customers are also often linked to each other through various types of technical and administrative arrangements. They may adapt products, processes, scheduling, delivery routines and logistical systems to the needs and capabilities of the specific counterpart. In the German sub-sample some data are available about this type of investment in customer–supplier relationships. In the eight German customer relationships investigated, on average 2.5 inter-firm production system adaptations were made. In almost every relationship some adaptation of this kind was made. The adaptations were somewhat more common in domestic than they were in export relationships.

Against the background of this type of evidence, we assume that firms in industrial markets are linked to each other through long-lasting relationships. The parties in the relationships are important to each other; they establish and develop complex, inter-firm information channels, and they also develop social and technical bonds with each other. Generally, domestic relationships seem to be more developed and stronger than export relationships. However, many export relationships are also important and long-lasting. We assume that the relationships are important for the functioning of industrial markets and for the market strategies of industrial firms.

## MARKETS AS NETWORKS – A GENERAL DESCRIPTION

The network approach in the form described in this section has been developed by a group of Swedish researchers whose background is research on distribution *systems*, internationalisation *processes* of industrial firms, and industrial purchasing and marketing behaviour as *interaction* between firms (Mattson (1985) describes this background). The approach is developed in a general way in Hägg and Johanson (1982) and Hammarkvist, Håkansson and Mattsson (1982). This section builds on those publications, and on Johanson and Mattsson (1985, 1986).

The industrial system is composed of firms engaged in production, distribution and use of goods and services. We describe this sytem as a network of relationships between the firms. There is a division of work in the network which means that the firms are dependent on each other, and their activities therefore need to be co-ordinated. Co-ordination is not brought about through a central plan or an organisational hierarchy, nor does it take place through the price mechanism as in the traditional market model. Instead, co-ordination occurs through interaction between firms in the network, where price is just one of several influencing conditions (cf. Lindblom, 1977). The firms are free to choose counterparts and thus "market forces" are at play. To gain access to external resources and make it possible to sell products, however, exchange *relationships* have to be established with other firms. Such relationships take time and effort to establish and develop, processes which constrain the firms' possibilities to change counterparts. The need for adjustments between the interdependent firms in terms of the quantity and quality of goods and services exchanged, and the timing of such exchange, call for more or less explicit co-ordination through joint planning, or through power exercised by one party over the other. Each firm in the network has relationships with customers, distributors, suppliers, and so on (and sometimes also directly with competitors), as well as indirect relations via those firms with suppliers' suppliers, customers' customers, competitors, and so on.

The networks are stable *and* changing. Individual business transactions between firms usually take place within the framework of established relationships. Evidently, some new relationships are occasionally established and some old relationships are disrupted for some reason (e.g. competitive activities), but most exchanges take place within earlier existing relationships. However, those existing relationships are continually changing through activities in connection with transactions made within the relationship. Efforts are made to maintain, develop, change and sometimes disrupt the relationships. As an aspect of those relationships, *bonds* of various kinds are developed between the firms. We distinguish here between technical, planning, knowledge, social, economic, and legal bonds. These bonds can be exemplified by, respectively, product and process adjustments, logistical co-ordination, knowledge about the counterpart, personal confidence and liking, special credit agreements, and long-term contracts.

We stress complementarity in the network. Of course, there are also important competitive relations. Other firms want to obtain access to specific exchange possibilities either as sellers or as buyers, and co-operating firms also have partially conflicting objectives. The relationships imply that there are *specifc inter-firm dependence relations* which are of a different character compared with the general dependence relations to the market in the traditional market model. A firm has direct and specific dependence relations to those firms with which it has exchange relationships. It has indirect and specific dependence relations with those firms with which its direct counterparts have exchange relationships – that is, the other firms operating in the network in which it is engaged. Because of the network of relationships the firms operate in a complex system of specific dependence relations which is difficult to survey.

To become established in a new market – that is, a network which is new to the firm – it has to build relationships which are new both to itself and its counterparts. This is sometimes done by breaking old, existing relationships, and sometimes by adding a relationship to already-existing ones. Initiatives can be taken both by the seller and by the buyer. A supplier can become established in a network which is new to the firm, because a buying firm takes the initiative.

This model of industrial markets implies that the firm's activities in industrial markets are *cumulative processes* in which relationships are continually established, maintained, developed, and broken in order to give satisfactory, short-term economic return, and to create positions in the network, securing the long-term survival and development of the firm. Through the activities in the network, the firm develops relationships which secure its access to important resources and the sale of its products and services.

Because of the cumulative nature of the market activities, the market *position* is an important concept. At each point in time the firm has certain positions in the network which characterise its relations to other firms. These positions are a result of earlier activities in the network both by the firm and by other firms, and constitute the base which defines the development possibilities and constraints of the firm in the network. (See Mattsson (1985) for an analysis of the position concept and its use in a discussion of market strategies.) We distinguish here between *micro-positions* and *macro-positions.* A micro-position refers to the relationships with a specific individual counterpart; a macro-position refers to the relations to a network as a whole or to a specific section of it. A micro-position is characterised by:

1. the role the firm has for the other firm;
2. its importance to the other firm; and
3. the strength of the relationship with the other firm.

A macro-position is characterised by:

(1) the identity of the other firms with which the firm has direct relationships and indirect relations in the network;
(2) the role of the firm in the network;
(3) the importance of the firm in the network; and
(4) the strength of the relationships with the other firms.

The macro-positions are also affected by the interdependencies in the whole network as well as by the complementarity of the micro-positions in the network. Thus, in the context of the whole network, the macro-position is not an aggregation of micro-positions.

*Example: Firm A's micro-position in relation to firm B.* (1) It is a secondary supplier of fine paper and of knowhow about printing purposes. (2) The sales volume is 100, A's share of B's purchases of fine paper is 30 per cent and A is an important source of technical information. (3) The knowledge bonds are strong, but social bonds are rather weak due to recent changes in personnel in both A and B.

*Example: Firm A's macro-position.* (1) Lists exist of suppliers, customers, competitors and other firms in the network to whom the firm is directly or indirectly related. (2) It has the role as a full line distributor of fine paper in southern Sweden. (3) Its market share is 50 per cent, making it the market leader. (4) It enjoys strong knowledge, planning and social bonds to its major customers, and strong economic and legal bonds to its suppliers.

The positions describe the firm's relations to its industrial environment and thereby some important strategic possibilities and restrictions. All the other firms in the network have their own positions and likewise have future objectives regarding those positions. Desired changes or defence of positions thus describe important aspects of the firm's strategy. The strategies of firms can be complementary to each other, or competitive, or both. Important dimensions of the network structure are related to the set of positions of the organisations that are established there. The *degree of structuring* of the network is the extent to which positions of the organisations are interdependent. In tightly structured networks, the interdependence is high, the bonds are strong, and the positions of the firms are well defined. In loosely structured networks, the bonds are weak and the positions are less well defined.

The global industrial network can be partitioned in various ways. Delimitations can be made concerning geographical areas, products, techniques, and so on. We use the term "net" for specifically defined sections of the total network. When the grouping is made according to national borders we distinguish between different "national nets". Correspondingly we refer to "production nets" when the grouping is made on the basis of product areas. A production net contains relationships between those firms whose activities are linked to a specific product area. Thus, it is possible to distinguish a "heavy truck net" including firms manufacturing, distributing, repairing and using heavy trucks. This heavy truck net differs from the corresponding "industrial branch" as it also comprises firms with complementary activities, whereas the individual branch comprises firms with similar, mostly competing, activities. The firms in the net are linked to each other and have specific dependence relations to each other.

Within the framework of a product area with its production nets, different national production nets can be distinguished. Thus, in the heavy truck field we can speak of a Swedish, a Danish, a West German, an Italian, etc. heavy truck net, comprising the firms or operations in each country engaged in manufacture, distribution service and use of heavy trucks.

To sum up: we have described markets as networks of relationships between firms. The networks are stable *and* changing. Change and development processes in the networks are cumulative and take time. Individual firms have positions in the networks, and those positions are developed through activities in the network and define important possibilities and constraints for present and future activities. Marketing activities in networks serve to establish, maintain, develop and sometimes break relationships, to determine exchange conditions and to handle the actual exchange. Thus, important aspects of market analyses have to do with the present characteristics of the positions, the relations and their development patterns, in relevant networks for the firm. Important marketing problems for both management and for researchers are related to *investments*, since activites are cumulative; to *timing* of activities, because of interdependencies in the network; to *internal coordination* of activities, since "all" the firm's resources are involved in the exchange and since the micro-positions are interdependent; and to *co-operation* with counterparts, since activities are complementary.

## INVESTMENTS IN NETWORKS

Investments are processes in which resources are committed to create, build or acquire assets which can be used in the future, assets which can be tangible or intangible. Examples of the former are plants and machinery, while examples of the latter are production and marketing knowledge, and proprietary rights to brand names. We call these assets *internal assets*: they are controlled by the firm and are used to carry out production, marketing, development and other activities.

A basic assumption in the network model is that the individual firm is dependent on resources controlled by other firms. The firm gets access to these external resources through its network positions. Since the development of positions takes time and effort, and since the present positions define opportunities and restrictions for the future strategic development of the firm, we look at the firm's positions in the network as partially controlled, intangible "*market assets*". Market assets generate revenues for the firm and serve to give the firm access to other firms' internal assets. Because of the interdependencies between firms, the use of the asset in one firm is dependent on the use of other firms' assets. Thus, in addition, the investment processes, including their consequences, are interdependent in the network. (The reasoning in this section is developed at greater length in Johanson and Mattson (1985).)

## INTERNATIONALISATION ACCORDING TO THE NETWORK APPROACH

According to the network model, the internationalisation of the firm means that the firm establishes and develops positions in relation to counterparts in foreign networks. This can be achieved (1) through establishment of positions in relation to counterparts in national nets that are new to the firm, i.e.*international extension*; (2) by developing the positions and increasing resource commitments in those nets abroad in which the firm already has positions, i.e. *penetration*; and (3) by increasing co-ordination between positions in different national nets, i.e. *international integration.* The firm's degree of internationalisation informs about the extent to which the firm occupies certain positions in different national nets, and how important and integrated are those positions. International integration is an aspect of internationalisation which it seems motivated to add to the traditional extension and penetration concepts, against the background of the specific dependence relations of the network model. Since position changes mean, by definition, that relationships with other firms are changed, internationalisation will according to the network model direct attention analytically to the investments in internal assets and market assets used for exchange activities. Furthermore, the firm's positions before the internationalisation process begins are of great interest, since they indicate market assets that might influence the process.

The network model also has consequences for the meaning of internationalisation of the market (network). A production net can be more or less internationalised. A high degree of internationalisation of a production net implies that there are many and strong relationships between the different national sections of the global production net. A low degree of internationalisation, on the other hand, means that the national nets have few relationships with each other. Internationalisation means that the number and strength of the relationships between the different parts of the global production network increase.

It can also be fruitful to distinguish between the internationalisation of production nets, implying more and stronger links between the national sections of the global production net; and the internationalisation of national nets, implying that they are becoming increasingly interconnected with other national nets. The difference is a matter of perspective: in the former case, attention is focused on a production net, in the latter on a national net. The distinction is interesting, because there may be important differences between the degree of internationalisation of different national nets. In one country the production net may be highly internationalised, whereas the corresponding net may not be very internationalised in another country. The distinction is also interesting, because in some situations internationalisation of the global production net affects all the national sections of the global production net. In other situations only some specific national nets with their production nets are internationalised. This may be the case when two or more national economies are integrated.

## AN APPLICATION OF THE NETWORK MODEL TO ANALYSES OF THE INTERNATIONALISATION OF INDUSTRIAL FIRMS

What are the reasons explaining why firms internationalise their activities? Let us assume that the driving forces for increased internationalisation are that the firm wants to utilise and develop its resources in such a way that its long-run economic objectives are served. Firms then internationalise if that strategy increases the probability of reaching the general objectives. According to the network model, the firm's development is to an important extent dependent on its positions: it can use its market assets in its further development. Thus, the internationalisation characteristics of both the firm and of the market influence the process. The firm's market assets have a different structure if the firm is highly internationalised than they do if it is not. Furthermore, the market assets of the other firms in the network have a different structure if the market has a high or low degree of internationalisation. We will therefore make a comparative analysis of four different situations, as set out in Fig. 1.

The analysis of the four situations thus concerns internationalisation processes in the three dimensions, extension, penetration and integration; and how these processes can at least partially be explained by reference to the network model. After this exercise we will make a comparison with what the internalisation model and the internationalisation model offer in the same types of situations.

| | | Degree of internationalisation of the market (the production net) | |
|---|---|---|---|
| | | Low | High |
| Degree of internationalisation of the firm | Low | The Early Starter | The Later Starter |
| | High | The Lonely International | The International Among Others |

Fig. 1. Internationalisation and the network model: the situations to be analysed.

**The Early Starter**

The firm has few and rather unimportant relationships with firms abroad. The same holds for other firms in the production net. Competitors, suppliers and other firms in the domestic market, as well as in foreign markets, have few important international relationships. In this situation the firm has little knowledge about foreign markets and it cannot count upon utilising relationships in the domestic market to gain such knowledge. As ventures abroad demand resources for knowledge development and for quantitative and qualitative adjustments to counterparts in the foreign markets, the size and resourcefulness of the firm can be assumed to play an important role. The strategy, often found in empirical studies, that internationalisation begins in nearby markets using agents rather than subsidiaries can be interpreted as (1) minimisation of the need for knowledge development; (2) minimisation of the demands for adjustments; and (3) utilisation of the positions in the market occupied by already-established firms. The firm can utilise the market investments that the agent in the foreign market has made earlier, thereby reducing the need for its own investment and risk taking. As the volume sold in the foreign market increases, the increase in the market assets may justify investment in production facilities in the foreign market.

The alternative strategy, to start with an acquisition or greenfield investment, would require a greater investment in the short run, but might perhaps enhance the long-term possibilities for knowledge development and penetration in the market. This is a strategy which is possible mainly for firms which have already become large and resourceful in the home market before internationalisation.

The importance of agents and other middle men is reinforced by the presumptive buyers' lack of experience of international operations. If those buyers happened to be at all conscious of foreign supply alternatives, they would probably be somewhat reluctant. This means that the supplier must let some third party – an agent – guarantee the firm's delivery capability, or itself invest in confidence-creating activities – for example, getting "reference customers", keeping local stocks, building a service organisation or even a manufacturing plant in the foreign market. This means further market investments.

Initiative in the early internationalisation of the firm are often taken by counterparts – that is, distributors or users in the foreign market. Thus, the foreign counterpart uses its own market assets to establish a new firm within its own network.

Whether the firm, with this introdcution as base, can develop its position in the market is very uncertain, and may depend on the degree of structuring of the network and on the positions of the "introducer". If the "introducer" is a leading distributor in a tightly structured network, the conditions are favourable for rapid penetration by the firm, given that the adjustments to the network are made. An obstacle may be that the demands for quantities become so high that the production capacity of the firm is too small. This may require increased engagement in the market through the establishment of production units. To reduce the risk of overcapacity, the parties may have to enter into long-term supply contracts, a process which is quite consistent with a tightly structured network.

As already discussed, the need for resource adjustment may become quite heavy in connection with a first step abroad. Such adjustments can be assumed to imply investments and it must be important to minimise the resource adjustment requirement in connection with early steps abroad. This holds for quantitative resource adjustments in connection with the capacity increases which the added market may demand, and it also holds for qualitative resource adjustments which may be required because of the possibility of new market needs deviating from earlier ones. Obviously, it may be possible to complement the resources through external sources. To the extent that such resource completions are made in the domestic market, they probably imply the same type of problems. They mean commitments which may be difficult to fulfil if the foreign engagement is a failure. On the other hand, they are probably risk reductions if they can be made in the actual foreign market. It is, however, not likely that a firm which has no experience of foreign operations would have qualifications for organising resource completions in the foreign market – that is, to establish positions in relation to local suppliers.

Another problem is that some resource adjustments can be made possible by giving up control over the operations in exchange for the flexibility needed to reduce risk taking in connection with foreign ventures. Such ventures may be carried out if the old owner transfers control of the firm to someone who is able to complement the firm's resources. In the absence of internationalisation of the environment, the extension to additional foreign markets will also be determined in general by the need for knowledge development and the need to create, or use already-existing, market assets. If conditions in markets which are new to the firm are similar to the conditions in the home market (and/or in the foreign markets in which the firm began its internationalisation), then there is a greater likelihood that these markets will be the next ones. If, however, the network is tightly structured, or if there is a lack of effective "introducers" on the foreign market that is "next in line", from a knowledge and adjustment point of view we expect to find extension patterns with other characteristics.

As the firm becomes more internationalised, it changes from an Early Starter situation to becoming a Lonely International.

## The Lonely International

How is the situation changed if the firm is highly internationalised while its market environment is not? To start with, in this situation the firm has experience of relationships with and in foreign countries. It has acquired knowledge and means to handle environments which differ with respect to culture, institutions, and so on, and failures are therefore less likely. The knowledge situation is more favourable when establishing the firm in a new national net.

The second advantage is that the international firm probably has a wider repertoire of resource adjustments. The need for resource adjustments is likely to be more marginal and less difficult to handle. This holds for both quantitative and qualitative adjustments even if the former are perhaps more strongly affected by the greater size which attends internationalisation than they are by the internationalisation *per se.* In particular it is easier for the international firm to make various types of resource completions in the foreign markets. This is a special case of the general advantage of international firms, because of much greater resource combination possibilities. Note that resource combinations also include those external resources to which the positions give access. The firm which is highly internationalised may also use its market investments to get a rapid diffusion of its new products. It may use its positions partially to control the internationalisation moves of competitors, but may also involuntarily stimulate such moves (see below).

With regard to the structuring of the national nets, it can be assumed that the international firm will experience less difficulties than others in entering tightly structured nets. It already possesses good knowledge about many kinds of national markets. Further extension is not so dependent on similarities between markets as it is for the Early Starter. Experience and resources give the firm a repertoire which allows it to make the heavy market investments which are required to enter a tightly structured production net. It also has better possibilities for taking over firms with positions in the structured net or establishing relationships with such firms. It can also give its counterparts access to other national nets: for example, the international firm has greater possibilities than others to engage in barter trade.

Initiatives for furthering internationalisation do not come from other parties in the production nets, since the firm's suppliers, customers and competitors are not internationalised. On the contrary, the Lonely International has the qualifications to promote internationalisation of its production net, and consequently of the firms engaged in it. The firm's relationships both with and in other national nets may function as bridges to those nets for that firm's suppliers and customers. Perhaps they have a similar effect on competitors (cf. Knickerbocker, 1973). Firms which are internationalised before their competitors are forerunners in the internationalisation process and may enjoy advantages for that reason, in particular in tightly structured nets, because they have developed network positions before the competitors.

To exploit the advantages of being a Lonely International, the firm has to co-ordinate activities in the different national nets. International integration is therefore an important feature in the development of the highly internationalised firm. However, the need to co-ordinate is probably less than for the International Among Others.

### The Late Starter

If the suppliers, customers and competitors of the firm are international, even the purely domestic firm has a number of indirect relations with foreign networks.

Relationships in the domestic market may be driving forces to enter foreign markets. The firm can be "pulled out" by customers or suppliers, and in particular by complementary suppliers, e.g. in "big projects". Thus, market investments in the domestic market are assets which can be utilised when going abroad. In that case it is not necessary to go from the nearby market to more distant markets and the step abroad can already be rather large in the beginning. In addition, nearby markets may be tightly structured and already "occupied" by competitors. Thus, the extension pattern will be partly explained by the international character of indirect relations and the existence of entry opportunities.

Is the market penetration process of the firm affected by the degree of internationalisation of the production network where it is operating? The need for co-ordination is greater in a highly internationalised production net, which implies that establishment of sales subsidiaries should be made earlier if the firm is a Late Starter than if it is an Early Starter. The size of the firm is probably important: for example, a small firm going abroad in an internationalised world probably has to be highly specialised and adjusted to problem solutions in specific sections of the production nets. Starting production abroad probably is a matter of what bonds to the customers are important. If joint planning with customers is essential it may be necessary to start local production early. Similarly, if technical development requires close contacts with the customers, it may be advantageous to manufacture locally. On the other hand, it may be better to use relationships with customers in the domestic market for development purposes, especially if these customers are internationalised (as they to some extent are, by definition, in the Late Starter case). However, such customers also have access to alternative, internationally based counterparts for their own development processes which might reduce the importance of their domestic suppliers.

The situation is different for large firms. As firms which have become large in the domestic market often are less specialised than small firms, their situation is often more complex than in the case of the small firm. One possibility is that of becoming established in a foreign production net through acquisition or joint venture. Of course, this is associated with great risks to a firm without experience of foreign acquisitions or joint ventures, particularly if other firms in the production net are internationalised. In general, it is probably more difficult for a firm which has become large at home to find a niche in highly internationalised nets. Unlike the small firm, it cannot adjust in a way which is necessary in such a net, nor has it the same ability as the small firm to react on the initiatives of other firms – which is probably the main road to internationalisation in a net in which other firms are already international.

The Late Starter has a comparative disadvantage in terms of its lesser market knowledge as compared with its competitors. Furthermore, as suggested above, it is often difficult to establish new positions in a tightly structured net. The best distributors are, for example, already linked to competitors. More or less legally, competitors can make the late newcomer unprofitable, by means of predatory pricing. In addition in comparison with the Early Starter the Late Starter probably has a less difficult task with regard to trust. Firms in the foreign markets already have experience of suppliers from abroad.

In a highly internationalised world the firms are probably more specialised.

Consequently, a firm which is a Late Starter has to have a greater customer adaptation ability or a greater ability to influence the need specifications of the customers. However, the influence ability of a Late Starter is probably rather limited. The comparison between the Early Starter and the Late Starter illustrates the importance of timing as a basic issue in the analysis of strategies in networks.

### The International Among Others

In this case both the firm and its environment are highly internationalised. A further internationalisation of the firm only means marginal changes in extension and penetration, which, on the whole, do not imply any qualitative changes in the firm. It is probable, however, that international integration of the firm can lead to radical internationalisation changes.

Both with regard to extension and penetration the firm has possibilities to use positions in one net for bridging over to other nets. A necessary condition for such bridging is that the lateral relations within the firm are quite strong. Some kind of international integration is required, not only in the "vertical", hierarchical sense, but also in the lateral, decentralised sense (Galbraith, 1973). As extension takes place in a globally interdependent network, the driving forces and the obstacles to this extension are closely related to this interdependence. Models of global oligopolies fit the argument here. Entries are made in those sections of the global production net which the competitors consider their main markets in order to discourage the competitor from making threatening competitive moves in other markets. In such a situation the entry may meet some resistance, but it is difficult for the competitors to use predatory pricing.

For the Early Starter, penetration through production in a foreign market was mainly a result of a need to bring about a balance between internal resources and external demands and possibilities in the specific market. For the International Among Others, the situation is different. The operations in one market may make it possible to utilise production capacity for sales in other markets. This may lead to production co-ordination by specialisation and increased volumes of intra-firm international trade. When the markets are expanding, it is possible in that case to put off capacity increases in one market, while capacity increases are made in another market before the positions in that market motivated such expansion. The surplus capacity could be linked to the wider international network, and this requires strong international integration of the firm.

Establishment of sales subsidiaries is probably speeded up by high internationalisation, as the international knowledge level is higher and there is a stronger need to co-ordinate activities in different markets. The need for co-ordination places heavy demand on the organisation. The competitors can utilise weaknesses in one market if they are not likely to meet counter-attacks in markets in which the firm is strong. Co-ordination gains in procurement, production and R&D are more likely than if the internationalisation of the firm and of the network is low. National differences are smaller, innovations are diffused more rapidly, and indirect business relations via the "third country" become more important to utilise. The market investments in one country will probably be more important as the external resources to which the relationships give access are more dispersed internationally.

The many positions which the International Among Others occupies in internationally linked networks give it access to, and some influence over, external resources. This means that the possibility for "externalisation" increases. The international manufacturing firm may thus increasingly tend to purchase components, sub-assemblies, etc. rather than do the manufacturing itself. Such subcontracting is sometimes required by host governments, but may also be a way to make the multinational enterprise more effective. Since important customers or joint-venture partners in one country are also by definition international, the International Among Others is faced with opportunities for further extension or penetration in "third countries". Thus, a Swedish firm might increase its penetration in a South American market because of its relationship in Japan with an internationalising Japanese firm. Other examples of such international interdependence are "big projects" in which design, equipment supply, construction, ownership and operation can all be allocated to firms of different national origin, but with internationally more or less dispersed activities. In such production nets, further internationalisation is probably predominantly dependent on the firm's configuration of network positions and on its ability not only to co-ordinate its own resources in different parts of the world, but also to influence, through its market assets, the use of resources owned by other firms.

The advantage of being able to co-ordinate operations in international networks is still more evident when changes take place in the environment. Assume that such changes spread from country to country: the international firm is then likely to have better possibilities to discover such changes as well as better opportunities to take advantage of them. A third advantage may be that the international firm can dominate and influence the international diffusion process and thus affect the development – but this probably requires size as well. Changes also occur in the localisation of economic activity. The internationally co-ordinated firm has better opportunities to detect and adjust to such changes. It can, for example, use its earlier established positions in an expanding national market to increase its penetration in that market and perhaps also its extension to other national markets within an expanding region of such markets. A driving force for further internationalisation by the International Among Others is to increase its ability to adjust to (or perhaps to influence) the geographical reallocation of activities in the production net.

The International Among Others predominantly faces counterparts and competitors who are themselves internationally active and markets that are rather tightly structured. This means that major positions changes in this situation will increasingly take place through joint ventures, acquisitions and mergers, in contrast with the other three cases that we have analysed. If, finally, we compare with the Early Starter situation, internationalisation for the International Among Others will be much less explicable by reference to the need for knowledge development and the similarities between the foreign markets and the home market. Instead, the driving forces and the restrictions are related to the strategic use of network positions.

## THE NETWORK APPROACH COMPARED WITH TWO OTHER MODELS

### The Theory of Internalisation

The theory of internalisation (Buckley and Casson, 1976; Rugman, 1982) currently seems to be generally accepted as an explanation of multinational enterprise. The theory assumes that a multinational enterprise has somehow developed a firm-specific advantage in its home market. This is usually in the form of internally developed, intangible assets giving the firm some superior production, product, marketing and/or management knowledge. If this asset cannot be exploited and safeguarded effectively through market (or contractual) transactions, an "internal market" has to be created. Expansions outside the firm's domestic market, given that local production is advantageous, will then take place through horizontal and/or vertical integration. The firm either establishes or buys manufacturing plants outside its home market. Thus, the multinational enterprise exists because of "market failures" or high "contracting costs". The firm wants to protect its intangible assets and to be able to control the price others pay for the use of these assets. There are, however, also costs of internalising in the form of internal administrative systems and risk-taking. These costs of internalisation will be lower, the less different the foreign market is from the home market. Thus, the internalisation model will predict that internalisation starts in "nearby" markets (Caves, 1982, chapter 1). It should be noted that the internalisation model is not intended to explain processes: rather, it tries to explain a specific economic institution, the multinational enterprise. It does say something, however, about the driving forces for internationalisation and the modes of international resource transfer.

We believe that the explanatory power of the internalisation model is greater in the situations in which the environment is not internationalised. The application of the model to the Early Starter situation is somewhat less than straightforward, though, since in the beginning the Early Starter is not a multinational enterprise and it exports products rather than manufacturing them abroad. However, we might extend the reasoning underlying the internationalisation model to include not only manufacturing, but also marketing activities. Given such an interpretation, if the advantages of local manufacturing are small, then it seems reasonable to expect the firm to export its intangible assets "embedded in products", and that the marketing activities in the foreign market are carried out by a sales subsidiary rather than by an independent agent (unless the contracting costs are less than the cost of internalising). The internationalisation model could be used to explain why firms enter a market using a sales subsidiary and not an independent agent, while the internationalisation model discussed below could be used to explain why agents precede sales subsidiaries. While the first model emphasises the need for exploiting and protecting internally created intangible assets, the second model emphasises the need for gradual development of market knowledge and the need to learn from interaction with other firms during the process.

In addition, the further expansion into the Lonely International case seems to fit with basic assumptions in the internalisation approach. The intangible assets constitute a firm-specific advantage that can be exploited in many markets through the operations of a multinational enterprise. However, it if takes a long time from the beginning of the internationalisation process to the status of Lonely International, the question arises as to how the firm can further develop its firm-specific advantage and not merely preserve and exploit it. It seems to be an implicit assumption in the internalisation approach that the firm's development activities are "internal". In the network approach, development activities are to an important extent dependent on the relationships with other firms, and thus on the network positions of the firm. Since internationalisation is a process by which network positions are established and changed, internationalisation as such influences the further development of the products, production processes, marketing behaviour, etc.

We said earlier that firms in networks invest in relationships with other firms. The positions thus created are in this chapter regarded as market investments, or in other words, as a form of intangible assets. These assets give partial access to external resources. Thus, the multinational enterprise increasingly enjoys direct relationships with customers and users in foreign markets rather than the indirect relations through agents or licensee's enjoyed by the less internationalised firm, operating only in its home market. This leads to a further observation linked to the network model. The highly internationalised firm may use its network positions effectively to "*externalise*" some of its activities, without losing control of its crucial intangible assets. The manufacturing value added by multinational industrial firms might decrease because of increased "subcontracting". We believe that this is especially true in the International Among Others case.

If both the firm and its environment are highly internationalised, it seems that a model which aims to explain multinational enterprise loses some of its relevance for analysis of further internationalisation. We might, of course, still be helped by the transaction cost approach in our attempts to understand just what institutional form penetration, expansion and integration actually take. However, the approach does not consider the cumulative nature of activities, the use of external assets, the development potential of network relationships, or the interdependence between national markets.

## The (Uppsala) Internationalisation Model

The internationalisation process described as a gradual step-by-step commitment to sell and to manufacture internationally as part of a growth and experimental learning process is a model that is associated with the research on the internationalisation of Swedish manufacturing industry that has been carried out at the University of Uppsala (see, for example, Hörnell *et al.*, 1973; Johanson and Wiedersheim-Paul, 1974; and Johanson and Valine, 1977). Focusing especially on export behaviour Bilkey (1978) conceptualised, and found evidence for, the exporting process as a sequential learning process by which the firm goes through stages of increasing commitment to foreign markets. This "stage model" has lately come under some criticism, even if its general acceptance in the research community as a valid description seems to be high. Reid (1983) argues that the model is too deterministic and general: according to him, the firm's choice of entry and expansion modes are more selective and context-specific, and can be explained by heterogeneous resource patterns and market opportunities. Firms will therefore use multiple modes of international transfers. Reid suggests that a transaction cost approach is superior to the experiential learning model. Hedlund and Kverneland (1984, p. 77) also criticise the model, concluding that the "experiences of Swedish firms in Japan suggest that establishment and growth strategies on foreign markets are changing towards more direct and rapid entry modes than those implied by theories of gradual and slow internationalisation processes".

We believe that the internationalisation model is less valid in situations in which both the market and the firm are highly internationalised. The firms which started their internationalisation during the early twentieth century were usually in the Early Starter situation. The studies of Swedish industrial firms, on which the Uppsala model is based, describe and explain this situation and its transition to the Lonely International stage. There is no explicit consideration in the model of the internationalisation of the firm's environment. We would therefore expect the internationalisation model to be most valid in the Early Starter case and least valid in the International Among Others stage. Both the network approach and the internationalisation model stress the cumulative nature of the firm's activities. The latter, however, is a model focusing on the internal development of the firm's knowledge and other resources, while the network approach also offers a model of the market and the firm's relations to that market.

In the Late Starter situation, we therefore expect the internationalisation model to be less valid than the network model because of the importance of indirect international relations in the home market and because of the probably quite heterogeneous pattern of entry opportunities when foreign markets are compared. In the International Among Others case, the internationalisation model seems to lose much of its relevance. Reid's, and Hedlund and Kverneland's arguments seem to be valid. Since by definition the firm and its counterparts and competitors have positions in a large number of markets, penetration and integration aspects of internationalisation seem to be more important strategic moves than further extension. In such a global perspective, specific national market differences will likely have less explanatory power.

To sum up: we believe that both the internalisation and the internationalisation models leave out characteristics of the firm and the market which seem especially important in the case of "global competition" and co-operation in industrial systems.

## SOME CONCLUDING REMARKS CONCERNING RESEARCH ISSUES

Against the background of the above discussion, we believe that more research in two, closely related, fields will serve to increase knowledge about the internationalisation of business: firstly, network internationalisation processes; and secondly, use of market assets in international competition.

### Network Internationalisation

Studies of network internationalisation may focus on internationalisation of national nets or of production nets. Such studies should describe and analyse the roles of different types of industrial actors in the process. They should also investigate the implications of the cumulative nature of network processes. More specifically, we advocate research into foreign market entry strategies in different situations with regard to network internationalisation. According to the network we can distinguish entry strategies which differ with regard to the character and number of relationships the entry firm seeks to establish with other firms in the network. We can also study which of the actors in the network take initiative in different entry processes and in networks which are more or less internationalised. Furthermore, the entry strategies may differ with regard to the ambitions of the entry firm in adopting or influencing the network structure in the entry market.

The network approach also implies that the strategic discretion is constrained by the character of the network in which the firm is operating or into which it intends to enter. This indicates that during the internationalisation of a network, the timing of the operations of a firm is important. It can also be expected that, because of the cumulative nature of network processes, the sequential order of activities in international markets is important and should be given more attention in research. Perhaps, however, the problem of timing is next to impossible to solve. From a strategic point of view the most interesting research issue, then, is that of analysing how to build preparedness for action when the time is ripe. Presumably, preparedness is largely a matter of having relationships with other parties.

This view on industrial markets implies that there are strong interdependencies between different sections, i.e. national nets, of the global networks: hence, integration of operations is important. At the same time, the view implies that action has to be taken close to other actors in the market, often in response to their actions. Strategies can probably not be planned and designed by remote headquarters, and their implementation requires some kind of lateral relation between organisational units operating in different national nets. Research about the organisation problem of integrating operations in international networks is required.

## Use of Market Assets in International Competition

We have emphasised the strategic importance of market assets and suggest research about their use in international competition. In particular, there is scope for work on the use of the market assets of one country as they affect competition with other countries. We think it would be interesting to study how market assets in one country are used when entering other country markets. Such studies should concern not only the use of domestic market assets in the first step abroad, but also the use of foreign market assets when entering third-country markets. They could focus on different types of market assets, or the country of the assets utilised – in terms of networks – or the target markets.

Another interesting research issue is the use of market assets in global competition. Such research could focus on the use of relationships with more or less multinational companies in global competition. Relationships with suppliers, customers, distributors or consultants are of different importance when competing in various types of production nets and national nets.

Finally, the strategic importance of market assets implies that fruitful research can be made about control of foreign market assets. Whereas internal assets are usually controlled hierarchically with ownership as the base, control of market assets must have other bases. Research has demonstrated that such factors as access to critical resources, information or legitimacy are often important as bases of control. The significance of those factors may differ considerably in different contexts. Both conceptual and empirical research is required.

## REFERENCES

Bilkey, W. J. An attempted integration of literature on the export behavior of firms. *Journal of International Business Studies,* Spring, 93–8 (1978).

Blois, K. J. Vertical quasi-integration. *Journal of Industrial Economics,* **20** (3), 253–72 (1972).

Buckley, R. J. and Casson, M. C. *The Future of Multinational Enterprise.* Macmillan, London (1976).

Caves, R. E. *Multinational Enterprise and Economic Analysis.* Cambridge University Press, Cambridge (1982).

Ford, J. D. Stability factors in industrial marketing channels. *Industrial Marketing Management,* **7** (6), 410–22 (1978).

Galbraith, J. *Designing Complex Organizations.* Addison-Wesley, Reading, Mass (1973).

Guillet de Monthoux, P. Organizational mating and industrial marketing conservatism – some reasons why industrial marketing managers resist marketing theory. *Industrial Marketing Management,* **4** (1), 25–36 (1975).

Hägg, I. and Johanson, J. (eds) *Företag i Nätverk.* SNS, Stockholm (1982).

Håkansson, H. (ed.) *International Marketing and Purchasing of Industrial Goods: An Interaction Approach.* Wiley, Chichester (1982).

Håkansson, H. and Östberg, C. Industrial marketing – an organizational problem? *Industrial Marketing Management,* **4**, 113–23 (1975).

Hallén, L. A comparison of strategic marketing approach. In P. W. Turnbull, and J. P. Valla (eds), *Strategies for International Industrial Marketing: A Comparative Analysis.* Croom Helm, London (1986).

Hammarkvist, K.-O., Håkansson, H. and Mattsson, L.-G. *Marknadsföring för Konkurenskraft.* Liber, Malmö (1982).

Hedlund, G. and Kverneland, Å. *Investing in Japan – The Experience of Swedish Firms.* Institute of International Business, Stockholm School of Economics, Stockholm (1984).

Hörnell, E., Vahlne, J.-E. and Wiedersheim-Paul, F. *Export och utlandsestableringar.* Almqvist and Wiksell, Uppsala (1973).

Johanson, J. and Mattsson, L.-G. Marketing investments and market investments in industrial networks. *Industrial Journal of Research in Marketing* **2** (3), 185–95.

Johanson, J. and Mattsson, L.-G. International marketing and internationalization processes – A network approach. In S. Paliwoda and P. N. Turnbull (eds), *Research in International Marketing.* Croom Helm, London (1986).

Johanson, J. and Vahlne, J.-E. The internationalization process of the firm – a model of knowledge development and increasing foreign market commitments. *Journal of International Business,* **8** (Spring–Summer), 23–32 (1977).

Johanson, J. and Wiedersheim-Paul, F. The internationalization of the firm – four Swedish case studies. *Journal of Management Studies,* **3** (October), 305–22 (1974).

Knickerbocker, F. T. *Oligopolistic Reaction and Multinational Enterprise.* Division of Research, Harvard Graduate School of Business Administration, Cambridge, Mass. (1973).

Levitt, T. *The Marketing Imagination.* The Free Press, New York (1983).

Lindblom, C.-E. *Politics and Markets.* Basic Books, New York (1977).

Macneil, I. R. Contracts: adjustment of long-term economic relations under classical, neoclassical, and relational contract law. *Northwestern University Lay Review,* **72** (6), 854–905 (1978).

Mattsson, L.-G. An application of a network approach to marketing: defending and changing market positions. In N. Dholakia and J. Arndt (eds), *Alternative Paradigms for Widening Marketing Theory.* JAI Press, Greenwich, CT (1985).
Reid, S. Firm internationalization, transaction costs and strategic choice. *International Marketing Review,* Winter, 44–56 (1983).
Rugman, A. M. (ed.) *New Theories of the Multinational Enterprise.* Croom Helm, London (1982).
Von Hippel, E. Successful industrial products from customer ideas. *Journal of Marketing,* **42**, 39–49 (1978).
Webster, F. E., Jr. *Industrial Marketing Strategy.* Wiley, New York (1979).
Williamson, O. E. Transaction cost economics: the governance of contractual relations. *Journal of Law and Economics,* 233–61 (1979).
Wind, Y. Industrial source loyalty. *Journal of Marketing Research,* **8**, 433–6 (1970).

# 7

# Infrastructural Networks in International Business

*Lars Hallén*

## INFRASTRUCTURAL NETWORKS

> The major function of international personal contacts is not to make business. What is most important is to use them to explain and soothe agitated feelings caused by statements from politicians. There is a need for people who placate negative feelings and assist in opinion formation, i.e. who act as good-will ambassadors and meet with opinion creators. Another important task is to inform about the actual stability and solidity of Swedish firms, as the foreigners, e.g. the Wall Street Journal, cannot read the financial reports from Swedish companies. Some companies employ former ambassadors for international tasks. However, their function is different. They can be used to open doors at a pre-business stage, particularly in developing countries. But neither here is it a matter actually of making business.
>
> The networks get superimposed on each other, and you never know when they may get activated. And you cannot claim that certain contacts or networks are used for certain purposes, as any network can be used for any purpose. You might want to find a person with a specific competence or certain connections, and thus you ask someone whom you might meet or pretend to call for another purpose: "By the way, do you know anyone who could help us with a certain matter – it is quite secret – do not mention it to anyone else . . .". Whether or not this produces results in a specific case is a matter of serendipity, but with many contacts you get many chances. (Chairman, Financial Group)

Contact nets, such as those described in the above quotation from one of the grand old men of the Swedish business world, are associated with high status and a considerable amount of mystique. They are an integral part of the industrial networks, which link business firms to each other, and can be seen as infrastructural to the business networks in about the same sense as telecommunications, railways, road transport systems etc., i.e. they provide underlying preconditions and support for industrial and business activities. For instance, a railway network is not built to link specific individuals or organizations with regard to pre-specified tasks but to provide a possibility of communication. Similarly, the infrastructural contact networks are not designed for specific business deals. Instead, they are used to acquire advance

Reprinted by permission from the publisher, Infrastructural Networks in International Business by L. Hallén from *Managing Networks in International Business*, Edited by M. Forsgren and J. Johanson, Gordon and Breach, Philadelphia, pp 77–92.

information, to influence the framework within which business is conducted, or to give communication possibilities where regular paths are not so well-trodden.

The influence of factors beyond the direct business issues has been discussed in many contexts, e.g. as non-task factors influencing purchasing (Webster and Wind, 1972) or as non-market relationships, i.e. relationships and environment which do not involve the firm's buying and selling relationships (Boddewyn, 1988). The distinction between task and non-task refers to the degree of orientation towards the actual business deals, i.e. the distinctiveness of the business purpose of the activity, whereas the market/non-market dichotomy indicates whether the counterpart is inside or outside of the business world.

The present paper focuses on non-task relationships. These non-task relationships, which include business actors as well as non-business (non-market) actors, are seen to constitute networks which are infrastructural to the business networks.

On the basis of the task orientation, at least three different levels of the business networks can be defined. Level 1 includes the inter-firm relationships which directly concern the business deals. These include not only links between actual customers and suppliers but also relations to many third parties connected to the business relationships, e.g. other suppliers or customers of the business parties in question, other companies which assist in bringing about business deals (such as banks, law firms, marketing or technical consultants). However, all these contacts are task-oriented. Thus, there is an impact on the business relationships by task-oriented parties which are not directly in contact with the customer and supplier involved in a specific business transaction: important task-oriented relationships might very well be unknown to the central parties, e.g. suppliers or customers further upstream or downstream the manufacturing chain. These indirect relationships as well as those task-oriented relationships which are directly connected to the customer-supplier relationship create a business network structure, which forms a major part of the industrial network of connected interfirm exchange relationships (cf. Johanson and Hallén, 1989).

The relationships with non-business actors such as government and local authorities, trade unions, industrial federations, and private-interest associations may be as important as the business relationships, and represent important assets to the firm. They can be connected to the business relationships, and if so constitute part of the business network. However, they can also form an important part of a secondary structure, with the properties of an infrastructure, which has emerged as an effect of the primary functions. This emergence can either be spontaneous or brought about more or less by plan. Basically, the infrastructure is assumed to be generated by the processes in the primary structure. These infrastructural networks can grow either around the company's business activities (organization-centred infrastructural networks – level 2) or around specific individuals in their capacity both as professional businessmen and as private persons (person-centred infrastructural networks – level 3). The distinction between the last two levels depends on whether the network connections are basically created by and related to the company of the person disposing of the contacts, or if they are related to him personally: created by him at various stages of his career and retained – although perhaps as dormant contacts – over the years. The infrastructural networks as defined on level 2 can mostly be expected to be transferable to other individuals, whereas this normally would not be the case with regard to those on level 3. The company is the focal actor on level 2; the individual plays the corresponding role on level 3. This is summarized in Table 1.

The definition of the business and the infrastructural networks on the basis of the task-orientation of the relationships results in corollaries regarding their strength and function.

The strength of the ties, defined in Granovetter's terms (1973) as the amount of time, the emotional intensity, the intimacy (mutual confidence), and the reciprocal services which characterize the tie, can be assumed to decrease as the degree of task orientation decreases. Thus, a larger number of links – be they bridges or not – can be kept alive if they can be maintained with weak rather than strong interaction. For certain periods, they may even be dormant but still be capable of resuscitation when required.

The function of the ties can also be expected to be related to the network levels. Business relationships can be considered to connect the resources, the activities, and the actors of the different parties (cf. Håkansson (ed.), 1986), whereas the non-market relationships only link the activities and the actors of the parties. In the case of lobbying, for instance, there are obvious actor connections as well as connections between activities, i.e. the activities of the lobbyist influence – or at least are intended to influence – those of the agency which is the object of the lobbyist's efforts. The reverse activity connection is also clear, as there would be no need for the lobbyist to try to influence the agency if the latter's activities would not have any impact. No resources are, however, jointly mobilized to obtain results in production, development, marketing or other business areas.

Finally, infrastructural relationships are defined as only involving connections between actors. The absence of a common task to be performed is seen as the denominator, and this disinterestedness gives these relationships their particular usefulness.

Table 2 summarizes the argument concerning the function of relationships on the different network levels.

The infrastructural networks are important in handling links to parties with whom the company has no direct or indirect business relationships, i.e. in cases where no

Table 1. Business networks and infrastructural networks

| | | NETWORK ACTORS | | | |
|---|---|---|---|---|---|
| | | Business | Non-business | | Level |
| | High | Business networks | Business relations | Non-market relations | 1 |
| TASK ORIENTATION | | Infrastructural networks | Organization-centred infrastructural networks | | 2 |
| | Low | | Person-centred infrastructural networks | | 3 |

Table 2. Network level and relationship function

| RELATIONSHIP FUNCTION | NETWORK LEVEL Business relationships | Non-market relationships | Infrastructural relationships |
|---|---|---|---|
| Resource connection | X | | |
| Activity connection | X | X | |
| Actor connection | X | X | X |

products are bought or sold or paid for. Without having any business transactions with e.g. competitors, government agencies, potential customers, or opinion leaders, firms are dependent on their actions (or failure to act). With some of these actors business transactions are impossible by definition, and the dependence on them takes the form of adaptations to the rules of the game and the framework for action. With other such parties business exchange may just be non-existent for the time being, although potentially possible.

In order to handle dependence in situations where commercial transactions are excluded as a possibility, information is required – preferably advance information. Involvement in political or social activities, which have a bearing on opinions, is another, more direct way of handling such dependence. In situations where firms are dependent on parties with whom business is possible but at present non-existent, e.g. potential customers, it is also useful to be able to influence opinions, although in such cases within a narrower circle. A common approach in such situations is to use well-placed contacts as "door-openers".

The role of public agencies for the handling of such dependence seems to be important and apparently increasing. But also private companies and their organizations are involved in such influencing activities, e.g. by employing former ambassadors, activities within industrial federations, and participation in the public debate both in articles and in advertising campaigns.

The handling of dependence can be specified further with regard to the target of the influencing activities. A basic difference exists between influence through mass communication (e.g. public relations) on the one hand and individual contacts on the other. Additionally, a distinction can be made between influence activities for different purposes: marketing purposes or long-term influence on the framework for company action. In all these cases, however, the infrastructural networks provide avenues for action.

The purpose of this chapter is to discuss infrastructural networks which are not directly designed for business purposes, using the distinction between person-centred and organization-centred networks made above. This is illustrated with empirical data derived from interviews with senior officials on the boards or in the executive offices of six major Swedish industrial groups and in two private-interest organizations. Furthermore, the managing directors of two foreign subsidiaries of Swedish companies (one German, one Australian) were interviewed. One of these managers was Swedish, the other one was a native. Finally, interviews were held with four officials of international organizations. These officials – all of them Swedes – did not represent Sweden within these organizations, but as they were of Swedish nationality it was assumed that by virtue of their positions they might nevertheless influence the attitude or behaviour of their environment in a manner relevant to the circumstances of Swedish business abroad.

In all, seventeen interviews were held in 1983 and 1984, dealing with individual international contacts well placed to influence the general conditions for Sweden's international business by creating understanding of Sweden's position, and to "open doors" for Swedish firms in various contexts. It was stressed that it was not a matter of finding out how specific business deals had been handled.

## ORGANIZATION-CENTRED AND PERSON-CENTRED NETWORKS

The infrastructural networks are described with regard to the nodes to which the focal actors are connected via one or two links. These nodes, around which the networks are built up, often derive from the network actors' previous assignments or tasks. Individual contacts may thereby have been obtained that have either survived or else hibernated in such a manner that they can be revived when required. Furthermore, the nodes may be organizations of which the actor is or was a member in non-task contexts. The nodes may also be related to the company in which he now works, and in such a case the nets are often organizational rather than individual. Thus, the central descriptive aspects are the characteristics of the focal actor (individual or organization), and the nodes that relate the focal actor to the connected networks.

A major function of the network is to provide contacts to be used when required. The capability of the network to fulfil such functions is dependent on the extent of actual connections, i.e. how many relevant contacts are connected to the node, and their character in terms of their further connections as a second or third link as seen from the node, as well as the relative position or strength of influence of different actors in the network. A major purpose of the networks which are not directly related to business, i.e. networks on levels 2 and 3 (organization- and person-centred networks), is to handle information flows to and from the company regarding matters that are extraneous in some sense, be they unforeseen, outside of normal areas, environment-related in general, etc. The function of the networks to provide contacts for such unforeseen purposes imposes special requirements on them. Firstly, they should be diverse, i.e. incorporate many different types of contacts, again to provide for the unforeseeable. Secondly, they should include many loosely joined contacts. Weak ties can be expected to have a cohesive power in connecting different subnetworks to each other (Granovetter, 1973). Bridges between networks are in the form of weak ties, and new data and valuable haphazard information is likely to flow via such weak links.

Business relationships in industrial markets often have the character of strong ties. Customers and suppliers invest in their relationship in the form of adaptations in the technical, commercial, or social spheres, which strengthens the relationship between them and involves high switching costs due to the cost sunk in the relationship. Such strong relationships have many advantages, e.g. by providing the security required for technical collaboration or efficient handling of the product exchange. However, there might also be risks involved: for instance, the parties may thereby become insulated from new ideas and impressions. Using a sociological analogy, the set of strong customer–supplier ties can be likened to a Gemeinschaft, whereas the set of weak ties involves the firm in a Gesellschaft. Thus, persons "enmeshed in a Gemeinschaft may never become aware of the fact that their lives do not actually depend on what happens within the group but on forces far beyond their perception and hence beyond their control. The Gemeinschaft may prevent individuals from articulating their roles in relation to the complexities of the outside world. Indeed, there may be a distinct weakness in strong ties" (Coser, 1975). The cloistered features of social structures of this kind not only insulate the actors from new information but may also generate inflexibility and a sense of infallibility.

However, not all weak ties are of this special value by connecting the individuals to the Gesellschaft: "only bridging weak ties have this function; the significance of weak ties is that they are far more likely to be bridges than are strong ties" (Granovetter, 1982). Thus, by providing bridges to other networks, the infrastructural relationships can be crucial for securing long-term survival for companies otherwise mostly involved in tightly knit day-to-day business relationships.

Furthermore, Granovetter (1982) concludes "that occupational groups that make the heaviest use of weak ties will be those whose weak ties do connect to social circles different from one's own. In Langlois's Canadian study, the most frequent users are managers and professionals, just the persons who, to use Robert Merton's terms, are most likely in an organization to be 'cosmopolitans' rather than 'locals – most likely to deal with acquaintances in other organizations or other branches of the same organization". One would thus expect infrastructural networks which provide many bridges to be centred on persons with a diverse career background rather than on those whose networks originate with their present employment.

## NETWORK EXAMPLES

Person-centred and organization-centre infrastructural networks are exemplified in Figs 1 and 2. The networks are characterized by the orientation of the connections, e.g. towards journalists, bankers, politicians, industrialists, etc. The interviewed manager is in the centre of the diagram, and surrounding him are the "nodes" from which the infrastructural networks are built up. These networks are summarily described in the diagram in terms of type of organization, connections, and in one of the examples their geographical extension, i.e. whether it provides contacts particularly in the US, Western Europe, the Scandinavian countries, etc.

The example in Fig. 1 summarizes the infrastructural network of a former bank chairman with previous professional experience from abroad and several subsequent memberships of boards and committees in private, public, and international entities. The connections are private in character, i.e. they are mostly his own and not his company's. It is possible to specify geographic dimensions of the networks, as the connections of the other individuals involved are mostly to be found in specific regions of the world.

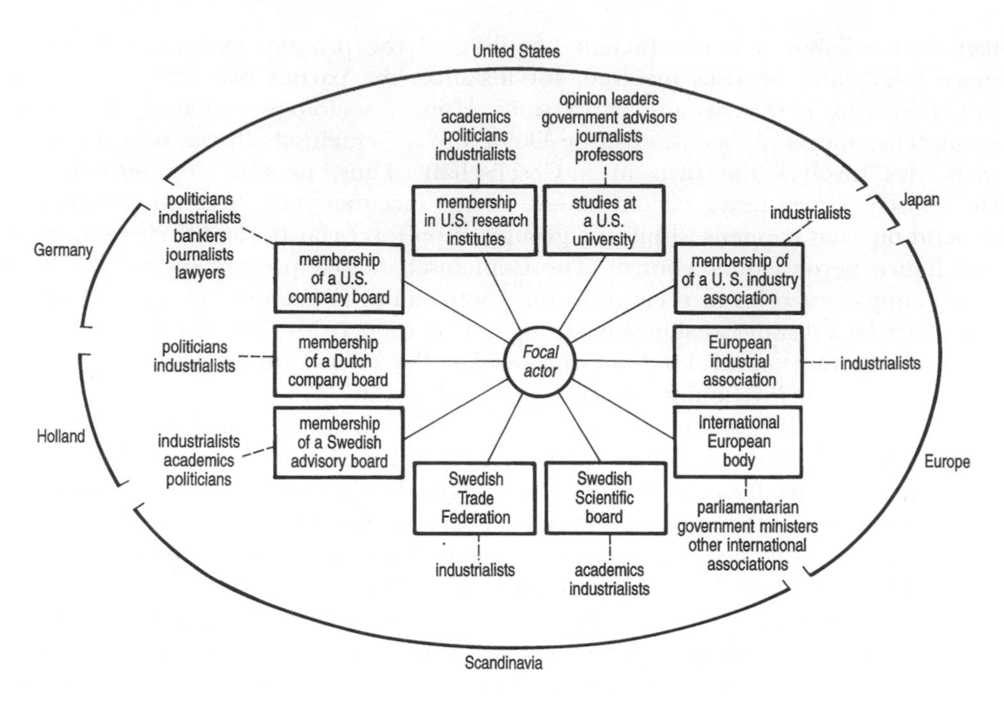


Fig. 1. A person-centred network.

The example in Fig. 2 is different. The focal actor is the deputy managing director of a rather large company in a high technology industry. The contacts are established and mediated through the focal company, and it is likely that most of them could easily be transferred to other persons in the firm if and when this is necessary. Here it is not meaningful to specify a geographical dimension. Either the contacts are truly world-wide, as in the case of the professional conferences, or else they are similar in most countries. The nodes in Fig. 2 are types of organizations, not specific organizations as in the person-centred network in Fig. 1. This to some extent explains why the number of units depicted in the organization-centred network is smaller than in the person-centred one, but there is certainly a real difference as well. There is a larger number of individual ties in the person-centred network, and these ties are undoubtedly closer. However, the institutional ties in the organization-centred network have proved very efficient, e.g. in the introduction of new products and techniques. The network is of higher density than shown in the diagram.

Person-centred networks may be planned on an individual level, but many of the contacts of course result from chance. These chances, however, seem to have been well utilized in the case illustrated here. In contrast, the organization-centred network is to a large extent planned, e.g. regarding the organization of subsidiaries, contacts with user associations. In this case, too, contact development through gradual involvement in various activities is very important. Thus, the spontaneity versus planning difference should not be exaggerated when comparing the two network types.

The two types of infrastructural networks are unevenly distributed between the respondents. In Table 3 the respondents, divided into the functional groups of

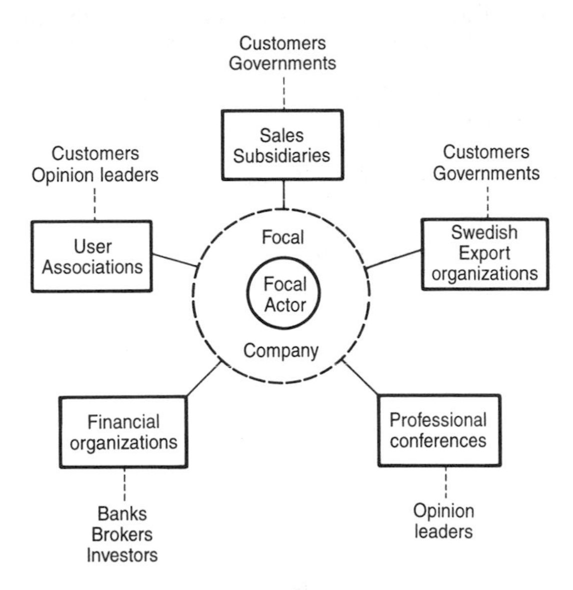


Fig. 2. An organization-centred network.

Table 3. Person- and organization-centred networks

| | Person-centred nets | Organization-centred nets | Total |
|---|---|---|---|
| Chairman or ex-chairman | 3 | 2 | 5 |
| Managing director or deputy | 1 | 5 | 6 |
| Functional director | 0 | 6 | 6 |
| Total | 4 | 13 | 17 |

chairman, managing director, and functional director, are classified with regard to the distinction between person-centred and organization-centred networks. The organizaton-centred networks are more common. Moreover, the two types are unevenly distributed between the functional groups.

Thus, a striking observation from Table 3 is the impact of the traditional division of labour between chairmen of the board on the one hand and executives on the other (cf. Stewart, 1987). The person-centred networks in the sample are controlled either by the chairman (3 cases) or by the managing director of a subsidiary abroad (1 case). These contacts were acquired during long careers in several jobs and in several countries, and the persons in question consider it to be their duty more or less specifically to provide this kind of general contact to their companies. This attitude is illustrated by the chairman of the board of one of the foreign subsidiaries. He specifies his function as follows:

> The role of chairman of the board includes the normal function, i.e. chairing the board, as well as other functions between meetings. This means acting as a second opinion for

> the chief executive, to act as a sounding board regarding both internal and external relations. The company would expect its chief executive to understand the business scene, the organization, the products, pricing etc. Certainly he would be able to deal with all the internal factors. Therefore he is kept up to date regarding policies, practices, and organization. He will obviously also build up external relations. The chief executive does, however, not necessarily know all about external relations. In the case of the two Swedish firms in my country, where I am chairman, these Swedish firms have let their chief executive stay with their firms here longer than e.g. U.S. firms normally do. There is thus no immediate need for me to intervene. Still I assist in business introductions and introductions to business negotiations, and I have a wider knowledge of the business environment in this country regarding economic conditions as these affect markets. I provide my assessments of what may happen in the future regarding such matters as inflation, exchange rates, interest rates, and regulation. I can give a feeling of what may happen. I can also help with remunerations and fringe benefits, as the foreign firm is probably not quite familiar with the practices that go with business in my country. This may concern a company car, regular company loans to executives, or expenses that are reimbursable. I have a long experience of when and how these practices apply. (Managing Director, Foreign Subsidiary)

This example not only points to the role of the chairman in using his personal contacts for the company, but also to the role of nationals on the boards of subsidiaries abroad. The infrastructural network of such national members of the boards of subsidiaries is illustrated by this statement of the managing director of a Swedish firm in a Latin country:

> You should start building your contact net in the country where you are operating by means of a contact of rather high status. It does not matter whether he is a politician, a businessman or a professional of some other kind. Such contacts can be established e.g. at lunches organised by the Chamber of Commerce, but it is of course always a lottery with whom you may happen to be seated. It is also useful to have a social position of one's own, e.g. a membership of the board of the Chamber of Commerce. In this way you get a possibility to approach highly placed officials. In the country where I have been working it is necessary to approach such a person through an intermediary, thus organising for instance a lunch for three. Such an intermediary is called an "enchufe", literally a "plug for a wall-socket". This system is typical for Latin countries. (Managing Director, Foreign Subsidiary)

Thus, national culture, business habits and traditions impinge on the role of infrastructural networks. For instance, contacts of the kind described above are often crucial not only in Latin countries but also elsewhere, e.g. in South-East Asia (cf. Jansson, 1988).

## PLANNED OR SPONTANEOUS GROWTH OF INFRASTRUCTURAL NETWORKS

It is a difficult task to establish and manage infrastructural networks in a planned and systematic manner, and an inherent feature is that they cannot easily be built up systematically in detail. They are specifically to be used for purposes which cannot be determined clearly in advance. However, it is conceivable to handle both person-centred and organization-centred networks either as planned or as emerging systems.

Table 4. Planning of infrastructural networks

| | Planned | Spontaneous |
|---|---|---|
| Organization-centred | 1 | 2 |
| Person-centred | 3 | 4 |

Combining these two dimensions gives the matrix shown in Table 4. There is no clear dividing line between planned and spontaneously emerging networks, as some combination of intention and chance is probably present in all situations. However, the basic approach could be intentional or laissez-faire. Furthermore, in the case of a planned approach, there is also the issue of whether the network is planned by the organization or by the concerned individual himself.

The last quotation in Section 4 above is an example of a planned person-centred network, and indeed planned by the individual himself. There are several such examples, but all are likewise planned by the individuals themselves. But as a totality these networks have emerged more or less spontaneously, as any curriculum vitae is beyond complete planning. Organizational planning of person-centred networks, on the other hand, is considered dubious by many of the interviewed managers:

> Every dynamic person in business has contact nets of his own. The best known and most extensive were probably those of Marcus Wallenberg, not least through the International Chamber of Commerce. Today for instance P. G. Gyllenhammar is systematically building up such nets. Many have tried to make business on providing nets, e.g. via conferences, institutes or informal movements. However, this type of nets often emerges spontaneously, and they are closely tied to the individuals. (Chairman, Industrial Group)

> It is difficult to understand how business were to get organised to produce people with the kind of contacts that Wallenberg had. But such people are certainly needed. It is necessary for the business world to be seen and heard internationally. Thus, people should be given opportunities to widen their horizons. For instance, a future trade secretary should first be trained at the Foreign Office, or at least work for some time at a subsidiary abroad. But it is difficult to recruit people for such purposes. When private companies are approached with the purpose of temporary recruitment of candidates for service abroad, the good candidates are often only available for service for at most a year, whereas the candidates that are offered for this broadening of their networks are people that the companies really do not want to have back after the assignment. (Managing Director, International Agency)

Thus, is it possible to organize this kind of network and transfer them to other members of the organization when necessary? The chairman of a large industrial firm with a previous career as an ambassador has this to say:

> This kind of network is created through spontaneous processes. Of course you want your network to include a certain mixture of people, but you cannot contact e.g. an American banker for the sole purpose to include him when you find that such a person is missing in your network. A precondition for this kind of network is voluntarity. If a certain type of person is missing, that box may stand open for many years. But on the whole, the networks are probably bigger than required, because it is fun to meet people.

> The contacts are personal, not the company's. I can of course introduce people in my company to my contacts, but they can only be kept viable if the personalities are compatible. But the need to transfer contacts may not be so great. As you get older, your contacts do so as well. Wallenberg's network decreased in importance during the last 10–15 years of his life, as many of his important contacts were already dead. But one must keep in mind that personal contact nets do not only serve the company but also the individual himself – they may be a tool for the development of his own trajectory. This personal ambition – rather than the establishment of potentially valuable contact nets for the company – may explain many non-business activities, such as for instance the sponsoring of symphony orchestras. (Chairman, Industrial Group)

## CONCLUDING REMARKS

A typical feature of the infrastructural networks is their impermanence. Individual contacts grow and strengthen as those involved interact with each other, and their potential value also increases as the position of contact persons within their own networks is strengthened. The number of contacts is also likely to multiply over time. Paradoxically, the value to the companies of the contact nets seems to decrease as the actors reach senior positions and when the nets are widespread and include many well-known names. At this stage the counterparts partially or completely retire from active service and thus lose touch with the current issues. To use an apt image, the networks which previously formed inner circles instead form outer circles without their previous access to information and influence but still having much prestige.

This impermanence has the advantage of making the difficult task of transferring individual contact nets less important. Transfer of infrastructural networks implies a linking between network levels 2 and 3 as defined above, i.e. transferring person-centred to organization-centred networks, as the person who takes over the contacts would not do so in his individual capacity but as a member of a certain company. It also means changing from spontaneous growth to planned network management, or in terms of Table 4, going from cell 4 to cell 1, i.e. from one extreme to another.

If one of the aims is to maintain infrastructural networks which originated as networks of the type represented by cell 4, it may be simpler to allow them to grow as indicated by cells 2 or 3. The planning of person-centred networks as represented by cell 3 would involve enabling individuals to establish networks of their own by sending them on various international assignments. The difficulties of such practices are however evidenced by many: either the wrong persons are sent out, or else the company loses people in the process, e.g. as they are naturalized abroad (cf. Borg, 1988). Allowing spontaneous growth of organization-centred infrastructural networks (i.e. cell 2) may be easier, but involves both motivational and control problems: how should non-business related contact creation and maintenance within the framework of ordinary business operations be stimulated?

Furthermore, the notion of managing infrastructural networks is in a sense inherently contradictory. The strength of these networks often consists in that they are neither planned nor managed. To be effective, they must not appear opportunistic. In other words, they may be effective for the very reason that they do not seem to be organized for those practical purposes – information-gathering, influencing, etc. – for which they are actually used. Organizing may deprive the network connections of their usefulness.

Can the usefulness of the infrastructural networks be assessed? In a general sense, this is hardly possible, but still some observations can be made. As mentioned above, the usefulness of the infrastructural networks built up around individuals probably declines when they reach their widest extent and highest prestige. At the same time as this seems advantageous, since it reduces the need to transfer networks, it also creates problems for the companies. At this stage, it may be unclear whether the networks are used by the individuals concerned in the companies' best interest, or whether the net effect is instead that the companies are used by the individuals. The core question concerns whether the company is able to mobilize the infrastructural networks of the senior officials when required, or if they only have the company as a basis for their personal network. Still, there are obviously many highly competent senior officials, and it is essential to use their qualifications.

The usefulness of the networks can be illustrated by the somewhat surprising observation that the re-emergence of the European Communities after the adoption of the Single European Act in 1985 was not at all foreseen by the respondents in the empirical investigation reported here. For instance, one of the functional directors interviewed stated in 1984 that

> . . . the EEC contacts are no longer so important. The EEC is an old and powerless organization which cannot any more achieve any results. (Functional Director, Industrial Group)

Another respondent, a company chairman, claimed that

> EFTA and EEC are of no importance nowadays. (Chairman, Industrial Group)

This attitude supports Hamilton's observation (1989, p. 40) that the EEC issue was virtually absent from public discussion in Sweden between 1973, when the Free Trade Agreement between EEC and EFTA was concluded, and 1987, when the process leading up to the internal market of 1992 was launched. Thus, the infrastructural networks do not seem to have provided any other information in this case to the persons involved than that of the prevalent general opinion in Sweden of the time.

Infrastructural networks are difficult to manage. However, this is not as problematic as it may appear at first. These networks should anyhow not be too rigidly managed, because this may destroy their effectiveness. Their usefulness is difficult to assess as regards actual gathering of advance information or "pulling strings". However, they are connected with much prestige, which can benefit both the companies and the individuals involved. When the infrastructural networks are treated as if they were important, they indeed become so inside and outside the company. They have a high symbolic value, which provides a motivational force for daily business life.

## REFERENCES

Boddewyn, J. J. (1988). Political Aspects of MNE Theory. *Journal of International Business Studies*, Fall, 341–363.

Borg, M. (1988). *International Transfers of Managers in Multinational Corporations.* Acta Universitatis Upsaliensis, Studia Oeconomiae Negotiorum 27, Almqvist & Wiksell International, Stockholm.

Coser, R. (1975). The Complexity of Roles as Seedbed of Individual Autonomy. In L. Coser (ed.), *The Idea of Social Structure: Essays in Honor of Robert Merton.*, New York: Harcourt Brace Jovanovich, 237–263.

Granovetter, M. S. (1973). The Strength of Weak Ties. *American Journal of Sociology*, **6**: 1360–1380.

Granovetter, M. S. (1982). The Strength of Weak Ties: A Network Theory Revisited. In P. V. Marsden and N. Lin, *Social Structure and Network Analysis.* Sage Publications, Beverly Hills, 105–130.

Håkansson, H. (ed.), (1986). *Industrial Technological Development, A Network Approach*, London: Croom Helm.

Hallén, L. and J. Johanson (1989). Introduction: International Business Relationships and Industrial Networks. In L. Hallén and J. Johanson (eds.), *Advances in International Marketing*, **3**. Greenwich, Conn.: JAI Press Inc.

Hamilton, C. B. (ed), (1989). *Europa och Sverige* (Europe and Sweden), Stockholm: SNS Förlag.

Jansson, H. (1988). *Strategier och organisation på avlägsna marknader: Svenska industriföretag i Sydöstasien* (Strategies and Organization in Distant Markets), Lund: Studentlitteratur.

Stewart, R. (1987). Chairmen and General Managers: a Comparative Study of Different Role Relationships. Paper presented at the British Academy of Management, University of Warwick, September.

Webster, F. and Y. Wind (1972). A General Model of Organizational Buying Behaviour. *Journal of Marketing*, **36**: 12–19.

# 8

# Dyadic Business Relationships Within a Business Network Context

*James C. Anderson, Håkan Håkansson and Jan Johanson*

In recent years, several models and frameworks have contributed significantly to our understanding of working relationships between firms in business markets (e.g. Anderson and Narus, 1990; Anderson and Weitz, 1989; Dwyer, Schurr, and Oh, 1987; Frazier, 1983; Hallén, Johanson, and Seyed-Mohamed, 1991). Each approach focuses on the dyadic relation between two firms. Some recent developments in business practice, however, strongly suggest that the connections between a firm's dyadic relations are of growing interest.

"Deconstructed" firms are emerging, in which firms focus on a subset of the value-adding functions traditionally performed within a firm (e.g. research and development, design, manufacturing) and rely on coordinated relationships with other firms to provide the remainder of the value-chain activities needed for a market offering (Verity, 1992). Another development is the "value-adding partnership" (Johnston and Lawrence, 1988, p. 94), which is "a set of independent companies that work closely together to manage the flow of goods and services along the value-added chain," enabling groupings of smaller firms to compete favorably against larger, integrated firms. A final development to note is the "virtual corporation," a transitory network of firms organized around a specific market opportunity, lasting only for the length of that opportunity (Byrne, Brandt, and Port, 1993).

A crucial question is how these developments in business practice should be regarded conceptually as well as managerially. A ready answer, drawing on recent work by organizational theorists (e.g. Miles and Snow, 1992; Snow, Miles, and Coleman, 1992) and European marketing scholars largely associated with the International Marketing and Purchasing group (e.g. Ford, 1990; Håkansson, 1987; Mattsson, 1987), is to move from dyadic business relationships to business networks. Yet this answer is deceptively simple – no particular conceptualization is implied. For example, business networks can be regarded as sets of connected firms (e.g. Astley and Fombrun, 1983; Miles and Snow, 1992) or alternatively, as sets of connected

Reprinted with permission from *Journal of Marketing* Vol 58, pp 1–15.

relationships between firms (e.g. Cook and Emerson, 1978; Håkansson and Johanson, 1993). And, even when this latter view is held, consideration of the individual relationships and what occurs within them often is scant, with the relationships themselves rapidly diminished to links within a network that is of focal interest. This is surprising because if business networks are to possess advantages beyond the sum of the involved dyadic relations, this must be due to considerations that take place within dyadic business relationships about their connectedness with other relationships. Therefore, we intend to provide further conceptual development of dyadic business relationships that captures the embedded context within which those relationships occur. As an integral part of this, we formulate business network constructs from the perspective of a focal firm and its partner in a focal relation that is connected with other relationships. In doing so, we also advance the conceptualization of business networks as sets of connected relationships.[1]

We first examine the environment of the firm. We then discuss dyadic business relationships and networks and follow this with two recent case studies of business networks that, taken together with business network concepts, provide inductive grist for further conceptual development. We next conceptualize some network constructs that can be incorporated within dyadic business relationship models. Our intent is to provide a means of representing the connectedness of dyadic business relationships within these kinds of models. To furnish some empirical support that these proposed constructs are sufficiently well delineated and generate some suggested measures for them, we conduct a substantive validity assessment. We conclude with a prospectus for research on business relationships within business networks.

## THE ENVIRONMENT OF THE FIRM

One critical specification in all approaches developed to analyze managerial problems involves the interface between the firm and its environment. Classically, there has been an assumption of a clear boundary between the two, in which *environment* has been defined as "anything not part of the organization itself" (Miles, 1980, p. 195). Firms have been viewed as "solitary units confronted by faceless environments" (Astley, 1984, p. 526). A firm's relationship with its environment is one of adapting to constraints imposed by an intractable externality (Astley and Fombrun, 1983).

This conceptualization of the environment of the firm has been questioned in both economics and organizational theory.[2] Resource dependence theory and related perspectives (Astley, 1984; Pfeffer, 1987; Pfeffer and Salancik, 1978) have argued that because firms' environments "are primarily socially constructed environments... the boundary between organizations and their environments begins to dissolve" (Astley,

[1]Let us further clarify our intent by stating what we are *not* pursuing. Our interest is not in explicating networks and their structural properties (e.g. cliques, actor equivalence), as, for example, has been done recently by Iacobucci and Hopkins (1992) in their presentation of a set of related statistical models for network analysis. Rather, our interest is in managers' perceptions and imputed meanings of the connectedness of a focal relationship to other relationships, as they act as key informants on its effects on their firms' decisions and activities.

1984, p. 533). Thus, the perspective changes to one of a firm interacting with its perceived environment (Pfeffer, 1987; Pfeffer and Salancik, 1978).

Drawing on this and related work (e.g. Thibaut and Kelley, 1959), a stream of research in marketing has stressed the importance of dyadic busines relationships (e.g. Anderson and Narus, 1990; Anderson and Weitz, 1989; Dwyer, Schurr, and Oh, 1987; Frazier, 1983; Hallén, Johanson, and Seyed-Mohammed, 1991). Yet the existence of relationships themselves questions the very meaning of the boundary between a firm and its environment. A relationship gives each firm a certain influence over the other (Anderson and Narus, 1990), which means that each firm is gaining control of at least one part of its environment while giving away some of its internal control. Relationships also indicate that firms do not treat the environment in a generalized or standardized way but interact with specific "faces" (Håkansson and Snehota, 1989; Thorelli, 1986).

The existence of relationships gives some specific faces to the environment of a firm, but this raises another question: How should the environment of these relationships be regarded? Should this environment be looked on as some faceless forces, or should it instead be regarded as having some specific, organized character? Although past work in marketing has largely and implicitly regarded the studied relationships as existing within some faceless environment, we argue for the latter. In the next section, we elucidate the perspective of a firm within a focal relationship that is itself connected to other relationships and the nature of the environment as it relates to this.

## BUSINESS NETWORKS AND DYADIC BUSINESS RELATIONSHIPS

Business networks recently have been of interest to a group of marketing academics in Europe (e.g. Ford, 1990; Gaddé and Mattsson, 1987; Håkansson and Johanson, 1993): Seeking a compatible framework, these researchers generalized the social exchange perspective on dyadic relations and social exchange networks (e.g. Cook and Emerson, 1978; Emerson, 1972) to dyadic business relationships and networks. Here, we examine the nature of business networks and firms within business networks and, in doing so, present the principal concepts for each.

### Business Networks

The developments in business practice mentioned at the outset are examples of what can be called *business networks.* A business network can be defined as a set of two or

---

[2]In recent development of transaction cost economics, Williamson (1991a, 1991b) discusses the existence of hybrid forms of economic organizations between (faceless) markets and hierarchies, in which cooperative adaptation is required between two organizations. Nonetheless, questions remain about the applicability of transaction cost economics to embedded contexts (cf. Granovetter, 1985) and contexts of recurrent and relational contracts, in which reliance on trust among the organizations is high (cf. Ring and Van de Ven, 1992). Thus, for our purposes, approaches based in social exchange theory (Homans, 1958; Thibaut and Kelley, 1959), such as resource dependence theory (Pfeffer and Salancik, 1978), appear to be more useful.

more connected business relationships, in which each exchange relation is between business firms that are conceptualized as collective actors (Emerson, 1981). Connected means the extent to which "exchange in one relation is contingent upon exchange (or non-exchange) in the other relation" (Cook and Emerson, 1978, p. 725). Moreover, two connected relationships of interest themselves can be both directly and indirectly connected with other relationships that have some bearing on them, as part of a larger business network. As illustrated in Fig. 1, a focal relationship is connected to several different relationships that either the supplier or the customer has, some of which are with the same third parties.[3]

What functions do the relationships fulfil it we look on them from a network point of view? To answer this question, we can take as a starting point the concept of the firm as an actor performing activities and employing resources (cf. Demsetz, 1992; Henderson and Quandt, 1971). According to this view, the function of business relationships can be characterized with respect to three essential components: *activities, actors,* and *resources.* We can also draw a distinction between primary and secondary functions. By *primary functions,* we mean the positive and negative effects on the two partner firms of their interaction in a focal dyadic relationship. The *secondary functions,* also called *network functions,* caputre the indirect positive and negative effects of a relationship because it is directly or indirectly connected to other relationships. However, in a given relationship, secondary functions can be as important as the primary ones, or even more so.

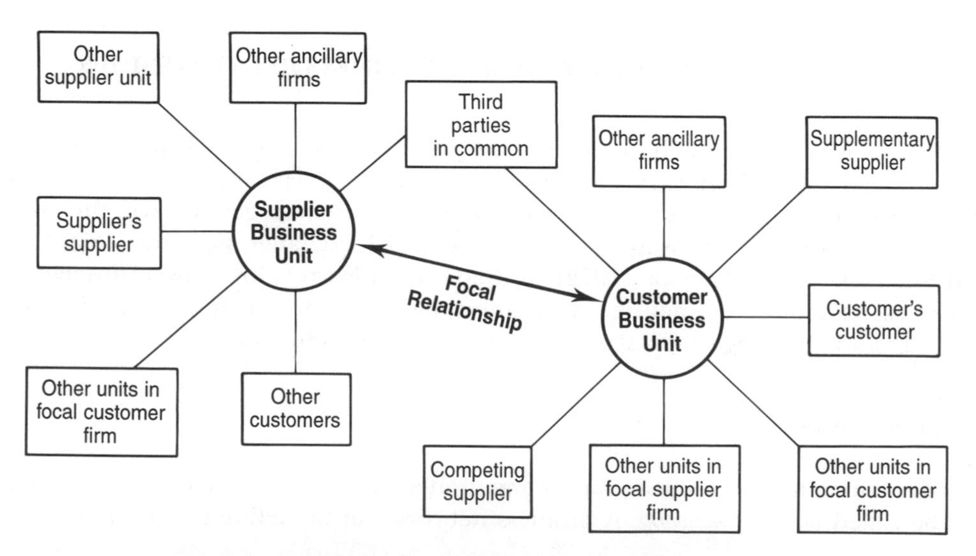


Fig. 1. Connected relations for firms in a dyadic relationship.

[3]Our perspective can be usefully compared and contrasted with Aldrich and Whetten's (1981, p. 386) concept of an *organization-set,* which they define as "those organizations with which a focal organization has direct links." Although our perspective might be viewed as the sum total of the organization-sets for each of the two firms engaged in the focal dyadic relationship, we believe that this misses our emphasis on the *dyadic relationship* as the unit of primary interest within business networks, rather than the individual firms themselves.

The primary functions of the relationships corresponding to activities, resources, and actors are efficiency through interlinking of activities, creative leveraging of resource heterogeneity, and mutuality based on self-interest of actors. Activities performed by two actors, through their relationship, can be adapted to each other so that their combined efficiency is improved, such as in just-in-time exchange (Frazier, Spekman, and O'Neal, 1988). The two parties also can learn about each other's resources and find new and better ways to combine them; that is, the relationship can have an innovative effect (Lundvall, 1985). Finally, in working together, two actors can learn that by cooperating, they can raise the benefits that each receives (Axelrod, 1984; Kelley and Thibaut, 1978).

Secondary or network functions are caused by the existence of connections between relationships. With regard to the three components, the secondary functions concern *chains of activities* involving more than two firms, *constellations of resources* controlled by more than two firms, and *shared network perceptions* by more than two firms. By adapting activities in several relationships to each other, thus raising the complementarity of sequences or other interdependent activities, activity chains stretching over several firms are created. Similarly, resources developed in a relationship not only are important to those engaged in that relationship, but also may have implications for resources of parties engaged in connected relationships. Thus, innovations developed as a result of interaction in several relationships may support each other. Finally, by getting close to its partners, a focal firm may have its views shaped by, and shape the views of, its partners' partners.

Relationships are dyads, but the existence of the secondary functions means that they also are parts of networks. A business network is built up by business relationships, but the latter are also caused by the secondary functions, reflecting the business network. However, a critical point is that there is no simple one-to-one relation between the relationship and the network, which can be seen by considering their dynamic features (cf. Aldrich and Whetten, 1981; Van de Ven, 1976). Developing relationships can have stabilizing and/or destabilizing consequences. If the development builds further on the earlier principles of the network, it will strengthen it. If, on the other hand, the development is a contradiction to the earlier structure, then it can be a first step toward network extension or consolidation (Cook, 1982; Emerson, 1972) – that is, a new network.

## Firms Within Business Networks

*Network context and strategic network identity.* Evidently, actors have bounded knowledge about the networks in which they are engaged (Emerson, 1981; Håkansson and Johanson, 1993). This is due to not only the network extending farther and farther away from the actor but also the basic invisibility of network relationships and connections. The network setting extends without limits through connected relationships, making any business network boundary arbitrary. For the purpose of analysis, however, it is possible to define *network horizons*, which denote how extended an actor's view of the network is. The network horizon can be expected to be dependent on the experience of the actor as well as on structural network features. This implies that the network horizon of an actor changes over time as a consequence of doing business. At the same time, it clearly demonstrates that any business network boundary is arbitrary and depends on perspective.[4]

The part of the network within the horizon that the actor considers relevant is the actor's *network context* (Håkansson and Snehota, 1989). The network context of an actor is structured, we posit, in the three dimensions identified in the discussion of primary and secondary functions of relationships: the *actors*, who they are and how they are related to each other; the *activities* performed in the network and the ways in which they are linked to each other; and the *resources* used in the network and the patterns of adaptation between them. The contexts are partially shared by the network actors, at least by actors that are close to each other.

In this ambiguous, complex, and fluid configuration of firms that constitute a network, in which the relations between firms have such importance, the firms develop *network identities* (Håkansson and Johanson, 1988). Network identity is meant to capture the perceived attractiveness (or repulsiveness) of a firm as an exchange partner due to its unique set of connected relations with other firms, links to their activities, and ties with their resources. It refers to how firms see themselves in the network and how they are seen by other network actors.

Because network identity is represented as a perception, it is crucial to specify the vantage point of the perceiver. A firm's network context provides the vantage point for its perceptions of the network identities of other firms within the network. And, significantly, even though network contexts of different firms may be partially shared, they are always unique in at least some respects. Thus, because network identity depends at least partly on the network context of the viewer, a focal firm has a distinct, though perhaps congruent, identity to each other firm in the network.[5] Similarly, a firm's perception of its own network identity is based on its own network context. We call this the firm's *strategic network identity*. This captures the overall perception of its own attractiveness (or repulsiveness) as an exchange partner to other firms within its network context. It is a reference point against which the firm perceives and judges its own and other firms' actions (Ring and Van de Ven, 1994).

Because identities are context related, they are described in the same dimensions. Each identity communicates a certain orientation toward other actors; it conveys a certain competence, because it is based on each actor's perceived capability to perform certain activities (Albert and Whetten, 1985); and it has a certain power content, because it is based on the particular resources each actor possesses (Cook *et al.*, 1983; Yamagishi, Gillmore, and Cook, 1988).

These actor orientations, activity competencies, and resources possessed are largely actualized and made apparent through exchange interaction in a firm's set of connected relations (cf. Goffman, 1959). At the same time, these connected relations impart additional meaning about a focal firm's actor orientations, activity competencies, and resources. For example, a firm will be viewed as strong in resource terms if it is seen as being able to mobilize and leverage the substantial resources of a connected partner. In summary, an actor is seen as "belonging" together with some

---

[4]Because of this, the social network concept of *centrality* (Cook *et al.*, 1983; Emerson, 1981), whose definition depends on some objective delimiting of a network, appears problematic for a business network setting (cf. Aldrich and Whetten, 1981).

[5]Although network identities are distinct, two firms must establish a congruent understanding of each other's network identity for a relation between them to prosper (Ring and Van de Ven, 1994).

others, having a certain competence in relation to those others, and being more or less strong in resource terms. This network identity, which can be more or less clear, conscious, and uniform, is itself a reference point against which all of a focal firm's acts are perceived and judged (Ring and Van de Ven, 1994).

*Network context and environment.* In what ways can we usefully distinguish between the concept of a network context and the previous, related concept of environment? Recently, for example, in presenting alternative forms of the marketing organization that are responsive to turbulent environments, Achrol (1991) appears to use the terms *environment* and *network* interchangeably. In contrast, our view is that the firm is embedded within a business network context that is itself enveloped by an environment.[6] Under this view, at least two useful distinctions between environment and network emerge: the different ways in which boundaries of the firm are regarded and different conceptual clarities in characterizing disparate impacts on a focal firm (or focal business relation).

In contrast with the classical specification, a network perspective better captures the notion that the boundary between the firm and its environment is much more diffuse. The environment is not completely given by external forces but can be influenced and manipulated by the firm, and there will also exist external, known actors that are influencing some of the firm's internal functions. Importantly, the network approach does not suggest merely that it is not meaningful to draw a clear boundary between the firm and its environment, but that much of the uniqueness of a firm lies in how and with whom it is connected (Håkansson and Snehota, 1989).

A difficulty in understanding what is meant by environment, let alone how it differs from a network, is that it has been discussed in numerous ways (cf. Miles, 1980). Moreover, in a given discussion, to capture *disparate impacts* on the firm, *levels* of environment are often assumed or posited (Miles, 1980). As a particularly germane example, in their analysis of the marketing environment of channel dyads, Achrol, Reve, and Stern (1983) distinguish between primary task environment, secondary task environment, and macro environment. The primary task environment is composed of a focal dyad's immediate suppliers and customers, in which any impact can be traced back to specific firms – to the "direct exchange network," as it is referred to at one point (Achrol, Reve, and Stern, 1983, p. 59). The primary task environment, in turn, is assumed to be affected by the secondary task environment, which comprises actors that are indirectly connected to the focal dyad (through exchange relations with actors in the primary task environment). Achrol, Reve, and Stern (1983) contend that the secondary task environment falls beyond the scope of their political economy framework and that its impact on the dyad can be best characterized in terms of abstract qualitative dimensions. The relatively amorphous effects of the macro environment are manifested only

[6]Shortell and Zajac (1990, p. 168) recently have observed, "We prefer to demystify the discussion of organizational environments by viewing the environment of a health care organization as simply the collection of other specific organizations that are interconnected to or interdependent with it. . . In other words, when a health care organization 'looks out' with concern at its turbulent environment, what it sees are other organizations 'looking out' at it!" Consistent with our own position, they then recognize the existence of environmental forces that are nonorganizational in nature, which are viewed as less germane to the focal organization.

through their impact on the qualitative dimensions of the secondary task environment.

We conjecture, as Achrol, Reve, and Stern (1983) seem to do, that the primary task environment is structured as a network. We differ, however, in the way we deal analytically with the parts of the environment that are outside this "direct exchange network." Given our basic social exchange framework, it is logical to consider those parts or aspects of the environment that the actor perceives as relevant (Håkansson and Snehota, 1989). Thus, the concept of network context, which may encompass indirectly connected exchange relations in addition to the direct exchange network, appears to offer a natural delimiter of network from environment. Finally, similar in spirit to Achrol, Reve, and Stern (1983), we posit that the impacts of the relatively amorphous or imperceptible parts of the secondary task and macro environments, which we refer to simply as the environment, are mediated through the network context.[7]

## TWO BUSINESS NETWORK CASES

A basic conclusion from the previous discussion is that every relationship should be viewed as being part of a network. The identity of the firm is embedded in the network through its relationships, which are connected to each other. This naturally leads to consideration of how network embeddedness contributes to the understanding of dyadic business relationships. As grist for inductive theory development (Deshpandé, 1983; Leonard-Barton, 1990), we present two European case studies of business networks.

*Development of new saw equipment.* A network – labeled the *wood saw network* – was studied in Håkansson (1987). The focal relationship was between a saw equipment producer and a sawmill but, as depicted in Fig. 2, several other relationships were connected. Cooperation was required to develop band saw equipment that could be used for cutting frozen timber, a necessity for the equipment to be used in Sweden. By working together with its components supplier, the equipment supplier managed to provide an initial solution technically.

In the next phase, this solution was tried out together with two customer firms – one small sawmill located nearby with which the supplier had worked on other projects and a large sawmill that was viewed as an opinion leader. The latter was interested because it had several large investment projects coming up. The first prototype, a small band saw, was developed successfully and tested with the small customer. But when this solution was transferred to the larger customer, cracks developed in a

[7]Although Emerson (1972) and Cook (1982) discuss network extension and network consolidation as mechanisms for balancing network dependence, these concepts also can be employed to capture the dynamic character of the network and its environment. Network extension occurs when relatively amorphous forces (which alternatively might be viewed as latent actors) become manifest actors with which the firm has a direct or connected relation, either because of their impact on the network or because of proactive search by network actors for the resources and activities these new actors can contribute within the network. Conversely, network contraction occurs when relations with actors whose resources and activities no longer contribute to the network are ended, with the terminated actor receding to a relatively imperceptible force in the environment.

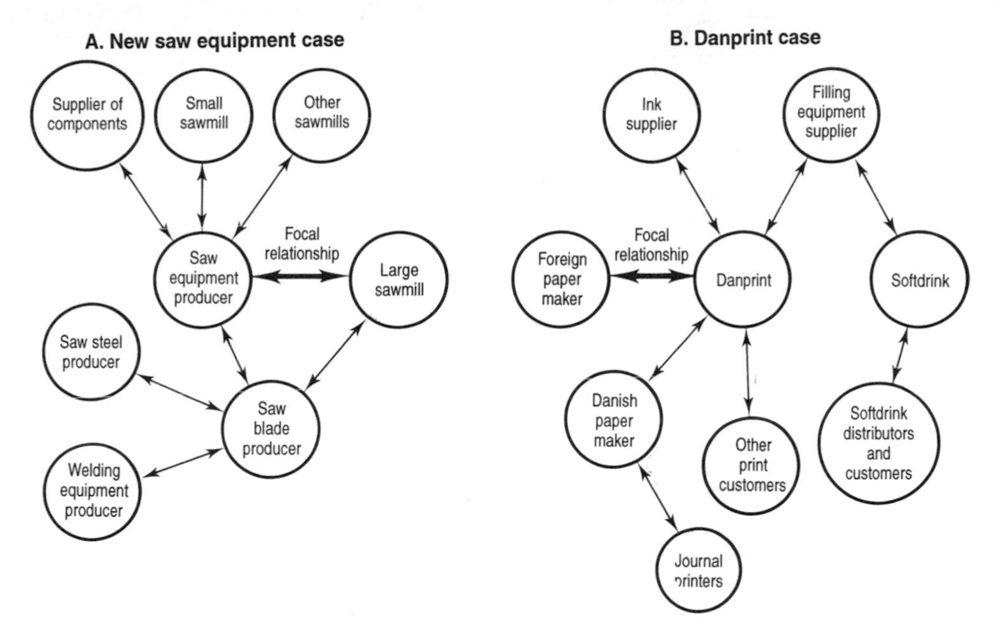


Fig. 2. Two business network cases.

bigger prototype, and there were even some serious breakdowns in which the whole band saw broke off. Weaknesses in the steel and especially in the welding seams in the band saws were regarded as the problems. So the large sawmill initiated technical cooperation with a saw blade producer in the belief that it would be possible to eliminate these problems by making changes in the saw blade producer's production process. However, it was found that it was necessary for the saw blade producer to get adaptations in the steel it bought from a saw steel company as well as acquiring new equipment for the welding operation. These efforts were not wholly successful, so the saw equipment producer had to make further adaptations to its equipment. The total process took several years to accomplish but was, in the end, very successful.

*Danprint.* Danprint is a small Danish printer that has supplied labels to a big Danish soft drink producer, Softdrink, for many years (Sjöberg, 1991). The labels were printed on a simple paper produced by one of the mills of a Danish paper maker, which also supplied other papers from its other mills to Danprint. Although simple, the paper was quite special in that it had a certain yellow shade that was strongly associated with Softdrink's image among its distributors and customers. Due to its wood content, the paper also was well-adapted to Softdrink's equipment for cleaning and filling return bottles. These relations appear in Fig. 3.

Danprint, however, was only a marginal buyer of this product in comparison with journal printers. When they changed to another, more "elegant" paper, the paper maker had to close the mill where Danprint's paper was made. Worse still, the paper maker could not produce a paper with Softdrink's specifications in any of its other mills. After some search, Danprint found a foreign paper mill that, after some

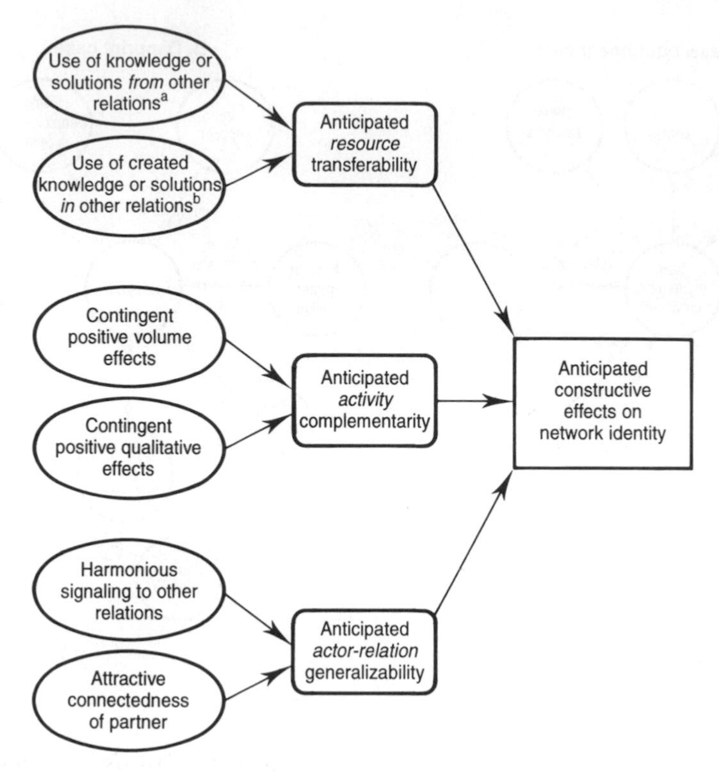


Fig. 3. The constituent facets of the construct: anticipated constructive effects on network identity.

cooperation, could produce a paper with almost the same yellow color as the original paper. This new paper was more expensive than the old, but rather than taking the risk of relaunching the drink with a new label, Softdrink accepted the higher price.

But the guarantee of Softdrink's filling equipment supplier concerning the speed and functioning of its equipment was not valid unless they, too, found the paper acceptable. Consequently, some cooperative activities between Danprint and the equipment supplier were required to gain this acceptance. In parallel, Danprint also engaged in cooperation with its ink supplier to be able to print on the new paper to the satisfaction of Softdrink and its connected distributors and customers. Moreover, Danprint learned from the cooperation with the foreign mill the exact prescription of and procedure for testing this yellow paper. On the basis of this new know-how, Danprint returned to their old Danish paper maker in a stronger position and induced this supplier to produce and supply the new paper in competition with the foreign mill.

Consider now Danprint's situation when it engaged in cooperation with the foreign paper maker (this is the focal relationship in Fig. 3). Several network effects can be discerned. First, Danprint had to take their relationship with Softdrink into consideration. The primary anticipated effect was development of a paper that could be used in Softdrink's filling equipment to the satisfaction of Softdrink and its connected equipment supplier, distributors, and customers. Second, Danprint wanted to demonstrate to Softdrink that it was dependable even when considerable efforts were required. The relationship with Softdrink was important not only because of the sales volume involved; Softdrink was prestigious, and the relationship with it showed other Danprint customers that it was a capable print supplier.

Danprint also had to consider their relationship with the Danish paper maker, which still was its main supplier of other papers. Switching to the foreign supplier might harm other activities in their relationship. Yet cooperation with the foreign supplier could lead to a new product solution that could be transferred to the Danish relation, thus strengthening their long-run relationship.

Moreover, when engaging in cooperation with the foreign paper maker, Danprint had reason to consider the possibilities to coordinate these activities with those in relationships with the filling equipment and ink suppliers and to develop complementary solutions.

*Some observations.* Taken together, these cases provide a worthwhile, practical basis for considering and developing constructs that capture the embedded context within which dyadic business relationships occur. They also show some points of departure from the social network literature. Before developing some network constructs, we note some aspects of these cases.

The cases show both interesting similarities and differences. In both, the focal relationship is affected by the broader context of connected relationships. Activities or resources of other actors in this way are partly determining what is achieved in the focal relationships. Because of this, consideration of secondary or network functions will be especially critical in developing constructs. One important difference between the cases is that in the new saw equipment case, the connected relations provide positive, complementary development sources. In the Danprint case, several of the connected relations function as restricting connections.

The cases also show that these connections cannot be seen simply as positive or negative, as suggested in Cook and Emerson's (1978) analysis of social exchange networks. Rather, a relationship, in different ways, can be both positively and negatively connected with another relationship at the same time. Danprint's relationship with the foreign paper mill was, to some extent, negatively and positively connected to its relation with the Danish paper maker. And, apart from this, though some connections are rather easy to estimate quantitatively, others are entirely a matter of perceptual judgment or interpretations. Finally, the cases also stress the importance of time dependence in the analysis of business networks and the connections between dyadic relationships. Two firms might be positively connected in one time period but negatively connected in another. The dyadic relationships develop over time within a network context, which is also evolving as time goes by.

## CONSTRUCTS THAT CAPTURE THE EMBEDDED CONTEXT OF DYADIC BUSINESS RELATIONSHIPS

An essential commonality of a dyadic business relationship perspective and a business network perspective is a consideration of the interdependencies that exist between firms doing business with one another and the resultant need for cooperation.

Unquestionably, cooperation emerges as the pivotal construct from the two cases. Our intent here is to conceptualize, in a fundamental way, some network constructs that contribute to or have an effect on cooperation in dyadic business relations. Then, to illustrate how these constructs might be incorporated in dyadic relationship models, we sketch out some construct relationships with cooperation and what we view as its critical consequence: commitment. We conclude this section with a substantive validity assessment of our proposed constructs.

In positing constructs that capture network properties, a critical difference between perspectives that must be resolved is the focus on relationship *states* (e.g. the state of cooperation in the relationship) in the dyadic relationship perspective versus the focus on *activities* in the network perspective. How are activities and resources translated into perceptions of relationship states? Our reconciliation of this difference in perspectives is that activities requiring resources are undertaken in pursuit of outcomes, which, when evaluated by actors, provide judgments of relationship states. Viewed in this way, network properties underlie the network constructs that we conceptualize.

## Constructs that Capture the Focal Relationship's Connectedness

Most often, models of dyadic business relationships have the implicit assumption of ceteris paribus in all other relations. The cases reveal that this is likely not a realistic assumption. As one instance of connectedness, the guarantee of Softdrink's filling equipment supplier was invalidated without its acceptance of label changes. Thus, antecedent constructs in dyadic perspective models can provide only a partial understanding of consequent constructs of interest (e.g. cooperation, relationship commitment) in that no constructs have been put forth that reflect the influence of this connectedness on the decisions and activities of a focal firm in a dyadic relationship of interest.

We offer two constructs that capture the connectedness of the focal relationship, as perceived by each partner firm. The first is *anticipated constructive effects on network identity*, which can be defined as the extent to which a focal firm perceives that engaging in an exchange relation episode with its partner firm has, in addition to effects on outcomes within the relation, a strengthening, supportive, or otherwise advantageous effect on its network identity. Given the conceptualization of network effects and network identity, three constituent facets can be distinguished: anticipated resource transferability, anticipated activity complementarity, and anticipated actor-relationship generalizability. These constituent facets, along with their principal aspects, appear in Fig. 3.

*Anticipated resource transferability* refers to the extent to which knowledge or solutions are transportable. As its principal aspect use of knowledge or solutions from other relations indicates, resources needed for developing the focal relationship may exist already in some other relationship. A solution, or at least its basic principles (Hallén, Johanson, and Seyed-Mohamed, 1991), can be taken from this other relationship and employed in the focal relationship. Furthermore, cooperation in the focal relationship may develop resources that can be combined with resources from other relationships. Alternatively, the other principal aspect, use of created knowledge or solutions in other relationships, indicates that resources developed through exchange in a focal relationship can strengthen network identity when they can be utilized in one or more other relationships. The relationship between the saw equipment producer and the small mill can be seen as an instance of anticipated resource transferability.

*Anticipated activity complementarity* captures the notion that the value of the outcomes from activities undertaken in connected exchange relationships may be contingent on activities performed in the focal relationship; thus, these focal relationship activities have a strengthening effect on the firm's network identity. As its principal aspects indicate, these positive effects can be volume based or qualitative in nature. An increase in volume may have positive scale effects in other relationships, such that the costs of performing the same types of activities in all other relationships are lowered. In a similar way, qualitative changes in activities performed in a focal relationship may have qualitative effects in other relationships. The cooperative activities between Danprint and the equipment supplier to uphold the fill-rate guarantee for Softdrink illustrate activity complementarity of contingent positive volume effects, whereas Danprint and the ink supplier working together on printing quality can be seen as an example of contingent positive qualitative effects.

*Anticipated actor-relationship generalizability* refers to the possibility that cooperation with a certain actor may have broader implications for other actors. As its principal aspect harmonious signaling to other relations indicates, when a focal firm cooperates with another firm in such a way that it is visible to other actors, it sends a message that it is willing and capable of having cooperative relations (Hill, 1990). Therefore, this harmonious signaling can alter or reinforce other firms' network perceptions of the focal firm in an advantageous way. Consider, for example, the signals from Danprint to its other print customers that it is prepared to make strong cooperative efforts to solve technical problems. Its other principal aspect, attractive connectedness of partner, captures the notion that by getting closer to a certain partner firm, the focal firm also gets closer to its partner's other partners. Thus, the relationship with the well-known and prestigious Softdrink was a central element in Danprint's network identity.

In summary, anticipated constructive effects on network identity, with its constituent facets, aims at capturing the effects of positive connections between the focal relationship and all other relationships from the focal firm's point of view. These connections are not of marginal import. On the century, a firm's uniqueness can be found in its way of interrelating its set of relationships.

Participation in the focal relationship also can be expected to have harmful consequences on the focal firm's relations with other firms. Accordingly, our second construct is *anticipated deleterious effects on network identity*, which can be defined as the extent to which a firm perceives that engaging in an exchange interaction episode with the partner firm has, in some way, negative, damaging, or otherwise harmful effects on its network identity. Given the conceptualization of network effects and network identity, three constituent facets of this construct can be distinguished: anticipated resource particularity, anticipated activity irreconcilability, and anticipated actor-relationship incompatibility. These constituent facets, along with their principal aspects, appear in Fig. 4.

*Anticipated resource particularity*, with its principal aspects of tying up resources from

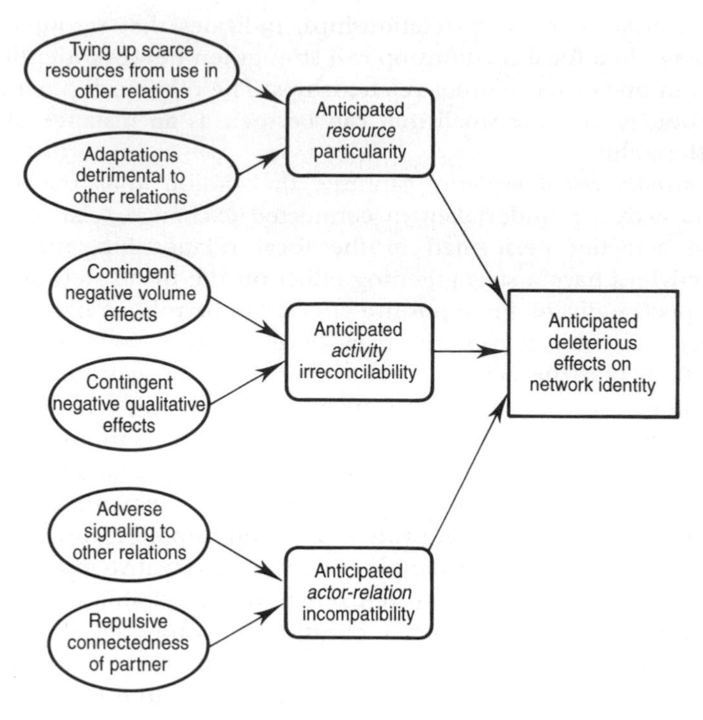


Fig. 4. The constituent facets of the construct: anticipated deleterious effects on network identity.

use in other relationships and adaptations detrimental to other relationships, captures the potentially problematic nature of using resources in more than one relation (cf. the related but more narrow concept of asset specificity (Williamson, 1985)). A focal firm simply may have limited resources for exchange.[8] Thus, the involvement of those scarce managerial resources may require reallocating resources from other relationships, which get less attention, with a subsequent harmful effect on the focal firm's network identity. Other customers of the saw equipment producer – sawmills having other production problems – may have seen the whole project as a waste of time and efforts.

*Anticipated activity irreconcilability* refers to the difficulty or impossibility of integrating activities in different relations with each other. As its principal aspects indicate, these negative effects can be volume based or qualitative in nature. Activity

[8]Support for negative effects due to limited resources for exchange can be found in the recent experimental studies of Molm (1991). Subjects in negatively connected exchange relations, in which exchange with one partner meant nonexchange with another, had a tendency to follow nonexchange by a partner with punishment for that partner in the next exchange opportunity. Great caution must be taken, though, in generalizing the findings from experimental studies of social exchange networks to business networks because several of the conditions and assumptions in such studies (e.g. that resources have fixed values, are constant across longitudinal exchange sequences, have the same value to each actor) make them less relevant, or even problematic, for business networks (cf. Aldrich and Whetten, 1981). For a noteworthy exception, in which the value of resources was not held constant for actors in a network, see Yamagishi, Gillmore, and Cook (1988).

patterns often must be tailored to the requirements of the focal relationships (Hallén, Johanson, and Seyed-Mohamed, 1991), yet these activity patterns may be harmful and disturbing to other relationships. For example, Danprint could not change to a new paper if this was not accepted by Softdrink's filling equipment supplier.

Finally, *anticipated actor-relationship incompatibility* represents the unwanted "baggage" that may come from engaging in a focal relationship, in which relations with specific actors can be perceived as a threat by other actors or regarded by them as noxious in some way. Other affected firms may even take sanctions against the focal firm. Its principal aspect, adverse signaling to other relations, refers to the possibility that cooperation with a certain actor may convey to other firms that the focal firm is moving in a strategic direction that is inimical to their own best interests. Danprint's working together with the foreign supplier may have been construed as an adverse signal by the Danish paper maker. Its other principal aspect, repulsive connectedness of partner, represents the potential problems for the firm with negative connectedness of its partner. For example, it has recently been reported that Mitsubishi has been reluctant to engage in cooperative relations with Daimler–Benz because Mitsubishi has a strong supplier relationship with Boeing whereas Daimler–Benz is part of the Airbus consortium, an ardent competitor of Boeing (Brull and Mitchener, 1993).

In summary, a focal business relationship, in addition to desired effects on outcomes within that relationship, inevitably may have some downsides as well with respect to a focal firm's network identity. Moreover, anticipated constructive effects on network identity and anticipated constructive effects on network identity likely each will be present to a varying extent in each business relationship. The saw equipment producer working together with the two saw mills and Danprint working together with the foreign paper maker each had, to some extent, both constructive and deleterious effects. Much like influence over and influence by the partner firm (Anderson and Narus, 1990), they represent separate constructs, not opposite ends of a single continuum.

### Outcomes Given Comparison Level and Comparison Level for Alternatives as Network Constructs

How do firms evaluate the outcomes they obtain from working together? Under a dyadic relationship perspective, Anderson and Narus (1984) suggest that the outcomes (economic and social) that each firm obtains within an exchange relation are judged relative to the firm's own *comparison level* (CL) and *comparison level for alternatives* ($CL_{alt}$), which are standards that represent, respectively, expectations of benefits from a given kind of relationship based on experience with similar relations, and the benefits available in the best alternative exchange relation (Thibaut and Kelley, 1959). How would the meaning of these change in moving to a network perspective?

We can reconceptualize CL as a standard representing the synthesis of all perceived *connected* relationships for a firm in its network context. In contrast, $CL_{alt}$ can be reconceptualized as a standard representing the synthesis of all directly or nearly substitutable relations for a firm in its network context. In most business-to-business settings, relations are only nearly substitutable in that some adaptation will be needed, even though it may be rather minor (Hallén, Johanson, and Seyed-Mohamed, 1991). Thus, the concept of network context defines the pertinent network structure, which, significantly, provides the firm's judgment frame (Tversky and Kahneman, 1981) for evaluating its outcomes from each dyadic relationship and making decisions about allocating resources in the next period.[9] Put simply, network context provides the evoked set for judgments about a firm's dyadic relationships, and CL and $CL_{alt}$ capture this in their respective, integrative ways.

The constructs of interest, though, are *outcomes* given CL and *outcomes* given $CL_{alt}$. Even as we move to a network context for the focal relationship, outcomes still refer to the economic and social rewards obtained minus costs incurred by each firm in what it does in the focal relationship and thus are akin to the primary functions of relationships discussed previously (and the potentially enhanced results produced by them). That is, outcomes that occur within the focal relationship are judged against CL and $CL_{alt}$. Although what a firm does in a focal relationship also may affect outcomes in other connected relationships, as in the Danprint case, these outcomes are *not* reflected in outcomes given CL and $CL_{alt}$. Instead, these connectedness effects on outcomes that occur in a firm's other relations are captured by the constructs of anticipated constructive and deleterious effects on network identity and thus are akin to the secondary functions of relationships discussed previously.[10]

This link of social exchange concepts to network concepts provides an underpinning for them that has been, by and large, implicit in social exchange theory writings (cf. Thibaut and Kelley, 1959, chapters 6 and 7). And although the concepts of outcomes given CL and $CL_{alt}$ have not been discussed in marketing as business network concepts, clearly their meaning is dependent on the presence of

---

[9]Because time dependence is an important feature of relationships and network content and the analysis focuses on ongoing exchange processes, CL, and to a lesser extent $CL_{alt}$, are based on the firms' past, present, and perhaps even expected future outcomes from the relevant relationships.

[10]Some readers may wonder why we have not simply defined overall outcomes given CL and $CL_{alt}$ for a focal firm at a network context level; that is, omnibus constructs that capture both the outcomes in the focal relationship *and* the outcomes in all other relations in its network context. This, in some ways, would subsume the constructs of anticipated constructive and deleterious effects on network identity and appear to be in keeping with Thibaut and Kelley's (1959; Kelley and Thibaut, 1978) consideration of larger groups, such as triads. Out conceptualization for a business context departs from Thibaut and Kelley's (1959) social context for at least two reasons. First, Thibaut and Kelley consider only groups, so that, by definition, the actors are completely interconnected. By contrast, within a business network context, some actors germane to each member of a focal dyad will not be directly connected to the other member. Thus, CL and $CL_{alt}$ for the group have more cohesive meanings than for a business network context. Second, in the Thibaut and Kelley analysis, which largely focuses on triads of friends, an actor simply changes groups when exercising $CL_{alt}$ for the group. It would be much more difficult, if not impossible, for a focal firm to move to a new network context, which has a completely different set of connected business relationships.

Apart from these conceptualization differences, omnibus constructs would blur a critical conceptual and managerial distinction between outcomes that occurred in a focal relationship and those related outcomes that occurred outside it in the connected relationships. Thibaut and Kelley (1959, chapter 4; Kelley and Thibaut 1978, chapter 11) appear to support this distinction in their discussion of facilitation and interference in interaction in the focal dyad due to other relationships. Finally, even when considering triads, Thibaut and Kelley (1959, chapter 11) recognize the existence of CL and $CL_{alt}$ for each of the three constituent dyads of the triad and, interestingly, discuss outcomes given $CL_{alt}$ for the individual's best dyad as the limiting condition for that individual remaining in the triad ($CL_{alt}$ triad), much as being alone might be the best alternative to being in a given dyad.

other business relationships that are in some way connected with the focal business relationship. Network context thus provides an explicit conceptual mechanism for a more complete understanding of what other relations constitute the defining sets for CL and $CL_{alt}$.

## Posited Construct Relationships with Cooperation and Commitment

Although a comprehensive model of dyadic business relationships is beyond our scope here, we present some posited construct relations simply to illustrate how the constructs we have proposed might be incorporated in such models. To understand them better, we first provide brief conceptualizations of the constructs of cooperation and commitment.

*Cooperation* can be defined as similar or complementary coordinated activities performed by firms in a business relationship to produce superior mutual outcomes or singular outcomes with expected reciprocity over time (Anderson and Narus, 1990). Surprisingly, cooperation seldom has been studied explicitly as a construct (see Anderson and Narus (1990) for a recent exception). Yet in recent work in interorganizational theory and marketing, several processes and studied constructs can be construed as compatible with our conception of cooperation. In their interorganizational process model for transactional value analysis, which is offered as a preferred alternative to transaction cost analysis, Zajac and Olsen (1993) discuss a "processing" stage in which value-creating exchanges occur. Ring and Van de Ven (1994) view cooperation more broadly as characterizing a particular kind of interorganizational relationship. However, the "execution" stage in their process framework, in which the actors engage in mutually preagreed activities requiring resources, appears to capture what we mean as cooperation.

In marketing, several recently studied constructs can be viewed as cooperation. Heide and John (1990) studied the construct of joint action, in which two firms in a close relationship carry out "focal activities in a cooperative or coordinated way" (p. 25). Cooperation can be viewed broadly as occurring within the relationship maintenance process outlined by Heide (1994) and is more specifically reflected in the flexible adjustment process construct studied. In the relationship development framework of Dwyer, Schurr, and Oh (1987), cooperation is a part of the initiation and expansion phases. Finally, in work that embraces a transaction cost perspective, the constructs of specific investments (Heide and John, 1990) and idiosyncratic investments (Anderson and Weitz, 1992) can be interpreted as dedicated activities and resources employed in cooperation between firms.

*Relationship commitment* captures the perceived continuity or growth in the relationship between two firms (Achrol, 1991; Anderson and Weitz, 1992). A closely related construct is relationship continuity (Anderson and Weitz, 1989; Heide and John, 1990), which reflects each firm's "perception of the likelihood that the relationship will continue" (Anderson and Weitz, 1989, p. 311). Growth in the relationship refers to a broadening and deepening of the exchange relation. The relationship can broaden through the extent of joint value created between firms (Zajac and Olsen, 1993). It deepens through having established role behavior be increasingly supplemented with "qua persona behavior... as personal relationships build and psychological contracts deepen" (Ring and Van de Ven, 1994), p. 103). Ring and Van de Ven (1994) and Dwyer, Schurr, and Oh (1987) each argue that relationship commitment, through its increasingly unique economic and social psychological benefits to each partner, forecloses comparable exchange alternatives for each firm.

Considering construct relationships, we posit positive causal paths from anticipated constructive effects on network identity to cooperation and relationship commitment. The cases provide ample support for these hypothesized effects. Of course, whether the constructive effects on relationship commitment are direct and indirect or are solely mediated through cooperation remains an empirical question.

Contemplating the construct of anticipated deleterious effects on network identity, a negative, causal path is hypothesized from it to cooperation. By its nature, this construct would appear to hamper cooperation in the focal relationship. But, on further thought, this negative effect might not be as predictable as the positive effect of anticipated constructive effects on network identity on cooperation. This is because adverse effects on network identity might be compensated by the focal firm changing cooperation in other relations. Instead of decreased cooperation in the focal relationship, deleterious effects might be compensated by increased cooperation in those other relationships. Danprint's cooperating with the filling equipment supplier is an instance of such cooperation.

A negative causal path also is hypothesized from anticipated deleterious effects on network identity to relationship commitment. In support of this, Kogut, Shan, and Walker (1992) found that new biotechnology firms become increasingly unwilling to make commitments to relations that are counter to their established set of relations. Similar to our previous prediction, whether the deleterious effects are direct and indirect or are solely mediated through cooperation remains an empirical question. A final consideration in our posited relationships for anticipated constructive and deleterious effects on network identity is that changes in significant relationships will have both strong positive and negative network effects. This coexistence of strong reasons both for and against cooperation suggests the need to have separate constructs that capture anticipated constructive effects and anticipated deleterious effects on network identity.

Considering outcomes given CL and $CL_{alt}$, we hypothesize positive, causal paths from them to cooperation. To the extent that past outcomes exceed expectations and/or alternatives, the focal firm is motivated to sustain the relationship with its partner. Cooperative activities represent a primary means for each firm to maintain, or improve on, its outcomes (Zajac and Olsen, 1993).

Finally, as implied, we posit a positive causal path from cooperation to relationship commitment. Interestingly, however, although process frameworks typically have cooperation and commitment leading to one another over time, specification of their causal ordering in a given exchange episode has varied (cf. Anderson and Weitz, 1992; Heide and John, 1990). The work of Axelrod (1984) supports the position that for a given exchange episode, cooperation causes commitment. In studying trench warfare in World War I, Axelrod (1984, p. 85) concludes, "The cooperative exchanges of mutual restraint actually changed the nature of the interaction. They tended to make the two sides care about each other's welfare."

### Substantive Validity Assessment

To provide some initial empirical support that the constructs that we have proposed are sufficiently well delineated and to generate some suggested measures for them, we conducted a substantive validity assessment (cf. Anderson and Gerbing, 1991). As Anderson and Gerbing (1991) discuss, their pretest method for substantive validity assessment provides not only predictions on the performance of measures in a subsequent confirmatory factor analysis, but also feedback "*on the adequacy of the construct definitions as well*" (p. 739, emphasis in original). So, our primary intent in employing this substantive validity pretest method was to gain this feedback.

The seven constructs studied were network identity, anticipated constructive effects on network identity, anticipated deleterious effects on network identity, outcomes given comparison level, outcomes given comparison level for alternatives, cooperation, and relationship commitment. We followed the Anderson and Gerbing (1991) methodology precisely. Single-sentence definitions were written for each construct that captured their theoretical meaning using everyday language (Angleitner, John, and Lohr, 1986). As an example, consider network identity:[11]

> *Network identity* captures the perceived attractiveness (or repulsiveness) of a firm as an exchange partner due to its unique set of connected relations with other firms, its links to their activities, and its ties with their resources.

Because our primary interest was in anticipated constructive and deleterious effects on network identity, 16 measures were written for each of them, and 4 measures were written for each of the other 5 constructs for a total of 52 measures. Twenty-four Swedish managers participating in a management development program served as research participants and assigned each item to the concept that they decided it best indicated. Substantive validity coefficients ($c_{sv}$) were calculated for each item and tests of their statistical significance were conducted.

In our context, statistically significant values of $c_{sv}$ would indicate that a construct was sufficiently well defined; research participants were able to assign intended measures of a construct to it meaningfully. Overall, 36 of the 52 items (.692) have significant ($p < .05$) $c_{sv}$ values. Of greater interest, 7 of 16 items for anticipated constructive effects and 15 of 16 items for deleterious effects on network identity have significant $c_{sv}$ values. The difference in number of significant items suggests either that writing negative or harmful effects measures is easier to do or that research participants are more sensitive to these effects in relationship practice (perhaps because of painful past experience) and thus are able to make item assignments more accurately. Moreover, these results provide strong initial support for our proposed constructs and their definitions.

Considering the remaining constructs, the number of items having significant $c_{sv}$ values were as follows: network identity, 3 of 4; outcomes given comparison level, 3 of 4; outcomes given comparison level for alternatives, 1 of 4; cooperation, 4 of 4; and relationship commitment, 3 of 4. In Table 1, we provide some suggested measures for

---

[11]The complete set of construct definitions employed are available from the first author.

Table 1. Suggested measures for proposed business network constructs

**Anticipated Constructive Effects on Network Identity**

What we gain from working with this customer will be useful in other relations. ($c_{sv}$ = .70, $p <$ .001)[a]

By working closely with this customer, our firm becomes more attractive to our suppliers. ($c_{sv}$ = .67, $p <$ .001)

Our way of doing business with this customer has positive consequences on our activities with other customers. ($c_{sv}$ = .50, $p <$ .05)

Because this customer is a demanding one, competence developed in working with it can be used to enhance the productivity in all our firm's relations. ($c_{sv}$ = .50, $p <$ .05)

**Anticipated Deleterious Effects on Network Identity**

Institutionalizing quality programs with this one customer may make it difficult to work together with other firms. ($c_{sv}$ = .92, $p <$ .001)

Too close a relationship with this particular customer may destroy the balance among our firm's exchange partners. ($c_{sv}$ = .79, $p <$ .001)

Collaborating with this specific customer may be rewarding in some ways, but harmful to our reputation with certain other firms. ($c_{sv}$ = .75, $p <$ .001)

Although working close together with this customer will likely provide some benefits, important other customers and suppliers may not be happy about this. ($c_{sv}$ = .71, $p <$ .001)

**Network Identity**

Our firm can attract the most competent suppliers. ($c_{sv}$ = .71, $p <$ .001)

Due to our supplier relations, our firm is regarded as one of the most attractive suppliers to our present and potential customers. ($c_{sv}$ = .54, $p <$ .05)

Our firm has the capability to influence the development in our field. ($c_{sv}$ = .42, $p <$ .05)

**Outcomes Given Comparison Level**

What we have achieved in our relationship with this customer has been beyond our predictions. ($c_{sv}$ = .63, $p <$ .01)

The financial returns our firm obtains from this customer are greatly above what we envisioned. ($c_{sv}$ = .50, $p <$ .05)

The results of our firm's working relationship with this customer have greatly exceeded our expectations. ($c_{sv}$ = .46, $p <$ .05)

**Outcomes Given Comparison Level for Alternatives**

Working together with this particular customer puts less strain on our organization than does working with other potential partners. ($c_{sv}$ = .50, $p <$ .05)

[a]The measure's substantive validity coefficient value and its associated probability level are given in parentheses.

our proposed constructs generated from this assessment. Because of our discussion of them within a business network context, we also include suggested measures for network identity, outcomes given CL, and outcomes given $CL_{alt}$.

## A PROSPECTUS FOR RESEARCH

We provide some conceptual development of dyadic business relationships embedded within business networks. The perspective we have taken differs from others. We are interested in managers' perceptions and imputed meanings of the connectedness of a focal relationship to other relationships and its effects on their firm's decisions and activities. To further study what we discuss, we propose a prospectus for research that encompasses both theory development and testing and management practice.

### Theory Development and Testing Research

Two complementary research approaches are outlined to provide empirical support for the proposed constructs and their posited effects: directed case studies to guide and refine theory development, and survey research using key informants and structural equation modeling.

*Directed case studies.* Qualitative field research such as field-depth interviews and case studies play an essential part in refining the construct definitions we have given and elaborating the content domains of each construct. Directed case-study research may suggest the need for additional constructs or alteration in the structures of the constructs we have proposed.

To develop our knowledge, detailed case studies of development processes within different types of networks are needed. These case studies should cover substantial time periods and be based on material from several of the firms as well as from different functions within the firms. Leonard-Barton (1990) recently has described a dual methodology for field case study of these kinds of complex phenomena. With her approach, a single real-time longitudinal case study is combined synergistically with multiple retrospective case studies to enhance the internal and external validity of the research findings.

*Key informant and structural equation modeling research.* Field survey research employing key informant reports and structural equation modeling is well accepted by marketing academics in the channels and business marketing areas. The issue of single versus multiple informants (Phillips, 1981) is especially critical in studying networks, given that individual actors appear to have bounded knowledge about their firms' networks (Emerson, 1981). Thus, a multiple informant approach would appear to be necessary – but this has been problematic in practice (cf. Anderson and Narus, 1990). However, the firm hybrid-consensual methodology recently described by Kumar, Stern, and Anderson (1993) appears to offer a means of gaining perceptual agreement among the multiple informants for each firm with respect to phenomena of interest.

Another issue to consider is the inherent trade-off between the breadth of structural equation model that a researcher might desire to capture the complexity of network phenomena and practicality (cf. Bentler and Chou, 1987). Being mindful of this, our conceptualization has focused on four constructs, and for two of these – outcomes given CL and outcomes given $CL_{alt}$ – we simply have provided business network underpinnings to constructs that have already appeared in models of business relationships (Anderson and Narus, 1984, 1990). Thus, researchers wanting to understand the effects of connectedness would need to add only two new constructs to their models: anticipated constructive effects on network identity and anticipated deleterious effects on network identity. Although we have articulated the constituent facets and principal aspects for each of these constructs, only the constructs themselves and their indicators (e.g. the generated measures appearing in Table 1) should be incorporated in structural equation models of dyadic business relationships.[12]

## Management Practice Research

The inherently ambiguous, complex, and fluid nature of business networks place unfamiliar and often perplexing demands on managers. In our experience, two areas greatly in need of management practice research are analyzing and building business networks.

*Analyzing business networks.* To understand what business networks mean for their firms, managers first must be able to define germane networks and then analyze them in some consistent way. Networks can be defined meaningfully at different levels of granularity, depending on the analytical purpose. The concepts of network horizon, network context, and network identity can be applied at each level with correspondingly different substantive meanings. Whatever network context is selected, definition of the network should focus on the set of significant relationships. For example, Håkansson (1989) has found that the ten largest suppliers and the ten largest customers account for an average of 72% and 70% of the total volume bought and sold, respectively, by a business unit. Finally, because we regard business networks as sets of connected business relationships rather than as sets of connected firms, secondary functions of relationships should be of predominant interest for analysis and study by managers.

*Building business networks.* Managers who understand the potential of business networks for their firms naturally would like to know how to build one in practice. Snow, Miles, and Coleman (1992) argue that, in constructing business networks, certain managers operate as brokers, creatively marshaling resources controlled by other actors. They sketch out three broker roles that significantly contribute to the success of business networks: the *architect*, who facilitates the building of specific networks yet seldom has a complete grasp or understanding of the network that ultimately emerges; the *lead operator*, who formally connects specific firms together into an ongoing network; and the *caretaker*, who focuses on activities that enhance network performance and needs to have a broader network horizon. Research is needed to understand how performance of these roles and what other factors (e.g. resources and activities) contribute to successful business networks.

---

[12]Note that we have given a formative specification in Figs 3 and 4 for the relationships of the constituent facets and principal aspects to the constructs, such that these facets and aspects might be viewed as causal indicators (cf. MacCallum and Browne, 1993). So, in empirical research on these structures, we concur with MacCallum and Browne's (1993) recommendation to incorporate effects indicators for each construct, which overcomes identification problems. Importantly, from our perspective, they then are represented as endogenous constructs rather than composites.

## CONCLUSION

In business-to-business settings, dyadic relationships between firms are of paramount interest. Emerging practice strongly suggests that to understand these business relationships, greater attention must be directed to the business network context within which dyadic business relationships take place. Drawing on business network research and social exchange theory, we have provided a fundamental conceptualization to capture network properties and relationship connectedness within dyadic business relationship models. Granovetter (1992) cautions that it is easy to slip into "dyadic atomization," a type of reductionism in which an analyzed pair of firms is abstracted out of their embedded context. By building out from focal dyadic relationships to consider effects of their embedded network contexts, we attempt to enrich the study of exchange relationships in marketing, which largely has had a dyadic atomization character.

Because of the extraordinarily complex nature of network phenomena, without doubt, refinement and elaboration are needed. As means for accomplishing this, we have proposed some directions for research that embrace the complementary strengths of two methodological approaches. Although research on business networks is challenging, it has the potential to make significant contributions to not only business marketing theory, but evolving business practice as well.

## REFERENCES

Achrol, R. S. Evolution of the marketing organization: new forms for turbulent environments. *Journal of Marketing*, **55** (October), 77–93 (1991).

Achrol, R. S., Reve, T. and Stern, L. W. The environment of marketing channel dyads: a framework for comparative analysis. *Journal of Marketing*, **47** (Fall), 55–67 (1983).

Albert, S. and Whetten, D. A. Organizational identity. In Cummings, L. L. and Staw, B. M. (eds), *Research in Organizational Behavior*, JAI Press, Greenwich, CT (1985), pp. 263–95.

Aldrich, H. and Whetten, D. A. Organization-sets, action-sets, and networks: making the most of simplicity. In Nystrom, P. C. and Starbuck, W. H. (eds), Oxford University Press, New York (1981), pp. 385–408.

Anderson, E. and Weitz, B. Determinants of continuity in conventional industrial channel dyads. *Marketing Science*, **8** (Fall), 310–23 (1989).

Anderson, E. and Weitz, B. The use of pledges to build and sustain commitment in distribution channels. *Journal of Marketing Research*, **29** (February), 18–34 (1992).

Anderson, J. C. and Gerbing, D. W. Predicting the performance of measures in a confirmatory factor analysis with a pretest assessment of their substantive validities. *Journal of Applied Psychology*, **76** (October), 732–40 (1991).

Anderson, J. C. and Narus, J. A. A model of the distributor's perspective of distributor–manufacturer working relationships. *Journal of Marketing*, **48** (Fall), 62–74 (1989).

Anderson, J. C. and Narus, J. A. A model of distributor firm and manufacturer firm working partnerships. *Journal of Marketing*, **54** (January), 42–58 (1990).

Angleitner, A., John, O. P. and Lohr, F. It's *what* you ask and *how* you ask it: an itemmetric analysis of personality questionnaires. In Angleitner, A. and Wiggins, J. S. (eds), *Personality Assessment Via Questionnaires*. Springer, Berlin (1986), pp. 61–108.

Astley, W. G. Toward an appreciation of collective strategy. *Academy of Management Review*, **9** (3), 526–35 (1984).

Astley, W. G. and Fombrun, C. J. Collective strategy: social ecology of organizational environments. *Academy of Management Review*, **8** (4), 576–87 (1983).

Axelrod, R. *The Evolution of Cooperation*. Basic Books, New York (1984).

Bentler, P. M. and Chou, C. Practical issues in structural modeling. *Sociological Methods and Research*, **16** (August), 78–117 (1987).

Brull, S. and Mitchener, B. The alliance demands patience: five years on, Daimler and Mitsubishi are still talking. *International Herald Tribune*, (December 15), 11 and 15 (1993).

Byrne, J. A., Brandt, R. and Port, O. The virtual corporation. *Business Week*, (February 8), 98–103 (1993).

Cook, K. S. Network structures from an exchange perspective. In Marsden, P. V. and Lin, N. (eds), *Social Structure and Network Analysis*, Sage Publications, Beverly Hills (1982), pp. 177–99.

Cook, K. S. and Emerson, R. M. Power, equity, commitment in exchange networks. *American Sociological Review*, **43** (October), 721–38 (1978).

Cook, K. S., Emerson, R. M., Gillmore, M. R. and Yamagishi, T. The distribution of power in exchange networks: theory and experimental results. *American Journal of Sociology*, **89** (2), 275–305 (1983).

Demsetz, H. *The Emerging Theory of the Firm*. Acta Universitatas Uppsaliensis, Uppsala, Sweden (1992).

Deshpandé, R. "Paradigms lost": on theory and method in research in marketing. *Journal of Marketing*, **47** (Fall), 101–10 (1983).

Dwyer, F. R., Schurr, P. H. and Oh, S. Developing buyer–seller relationships. *Journal of Marketing*, **51** (April), 11–27 (1987).

Emerson, R. M. Exchange theory, Part I: Exchange relations and network structures. In Zelditch, M. and Anderson, B. (eds), *Sociological Theories in Progress*, 2. Houghton Mifflin, Boston (1972), pp. 58–87.

Emerson, R. M. Social exchange theory. In Rosenberg, M. and Turner, R. (eds), *Social Psychology: Sociological Perspectives*. Basic Books, New York (1981), pp. 30–65.

Ford, D. (ed.) *Understanding Business Markets: Interaction, Relationships and Networks*. Academic Press, San Diego (1990).

Frazier, G. L., Interorganizational exchange behavior in marketing channels: a broadened perspective. *Journal of Marketing*, **47** (Fall), 68–78 (1983).

Frazier, G. L., Spekman, R. E. and O'Neal, C. R. Just-in-time exchange relationships in industrial markets. *Journal of Marketing*, **52** (October), 52–67 (1988).

Gaddé, L.-E. and Mattsson, L. -G. Stability and change in network relationships. *International Journal of Research in Marketing*, **4**, 29–41 (1987).

Goffman, E. *The Presentation of Self in Everyday Life*. Doubleday, New York (1959).

Granovetter, M. Economic action and social structure: the problem of embeddedness. *American Journal of Sociology*, **91** (November), 481–510 (1985).

Granovetter, M. Problems of explanation in economic sociology. In Nitin, N. and Eccles, R. G. (eds), *Networks and Organizations: Structure, Form, and Action*. Harvard Business School Press, Boston (1992), pp. 25–56.

Håkansson, H. (ed.) *Industrial Technological Development*. Routledge, London (1987).

Håkansson, H. *Corporate Technological Behavior: Co-operation and Networks*. Routledge, London (1989).

Håkansson, H. and Johanson, J. Formal and informal cooperation strategies in international industrial networks. In Contractor, F. J. and Lorange, P. (eds), *Cooperative Strategies in International Business*. Lexington Books, Lexington, MA (1988), pp. 369–79.

Håkansson, H. and Johanson, J. Industrial functions of business relationships. In Deo Sharma, D. (ed.), *Advances in International Marketing*, Vol. 5. JAI Press, Greenwich, CT (1993), pp. 15–31.

Håkansson, H. and Snehota, I. No business is an island: the network concept of business strategy. *Scandinavian Journal of Management*, **5** (3), 187–200 (1989).

Hallén, L., Johanson, J. and Seyed-Mohamed, N. Interfirm adaption in business relationships. *Journal of Marketing*, **55** (April), 29–37 (1991).

Heide, J. B. Interorganizational governance in marketing channels. *Journal of Marketing*, **58** (January), 71–85 (1994).

Heide, J. B. and John, G. Alliances in industrial purchasing: the determinants of joint action in buyer–supplier relationships. *Journal of Marketing Research*, **27** (February), 24–36 (1990).

Henderson, J. M. and Quandt, R. E. *Microeconomic Theory*, 2nd ed. McGraw-Hill, New York (1971).

Hill, C. W. L. Cooperation, opportunism, and the invisible hand: implications for transaction cost theory. *Academy of Management Review*, **15** (3), 500–13 (1990).

Homans, G. C. Social behavior as exchange. *American Journal of Sociology*, **63** (May), 597–606 (1988).

Iacobucci, D. and Hopkins, N. Modeling dyadic interactions and networks in marketing. *Journal of Marketing Research*, **29** (February), 5–17 (1992).

Johnston, R. and Lawrence, P. R. Beyond vertical integration – the rise of the value-adding partnership. *Harvard Business Review*, **88** (July/August), 94–101 (1988).

Kelley, H. H. and Thibaut, J. W. *Interpersonal Relations: A Theory of Interdependence*. John Wiley & Sons, Inc., New York (1978).

Kogut, B., Shan, W. and Walker, G. The make-or-cooperate decision in the context of an industry-network. In Nitin, N. and Eccles, R. G. (eds), *Networks and Organizations: Structure, Form, and Action*. Harvard Business School Press, Boston (1992), pp. 348–65.

Kumar, N., Stern, L. W. and Anderson, J. C. Conducting interorganization research using key informants. *Academy of Management Journal*, **36** (December), 1633–51 (1993).

Leonard-Barton, D. A dual methodology for case studies: synergistic use of a longitudinal single site with replicated multiple sites. *Organization Science*, **1** (August), 248–66 (1990).

Lundvall, B. Å. *Product Innovation and User–Producer Interaction*. Aalborg University Press, Aalborg, Denmark (1985).

MacCallum, R. C. and Browne, M. W. The use of causal indicators in covariance structure models: some practical issues. *Psychological Bulletin*, **114** (November), 533–41 (1993).

Mattsson, L.-G. Management of strategic change in a "markets-as-networks" perspective. In Pettigrew, A. (ed.), *The Management of Strategic Change*. Basil Blackwell, London (1987), pp. 234–56.

Miles, R. E. and Snow, C. C. Causes of failure in network organizations. *California Management Review*, **34** (Summer), 53–72 (1992).

Miles, R. H. *Macro Organizational Behavior*. Scott, Foresman and Company, Glenview, IL (1980).

Molm, L. D. Affect and social exchange: satisfaction in power–dependence relations. *American Sociological Review*, **56** (August), 475–93 (1991).

Pfeffer, J. Bringing the environment back in: the social context of business strategy. In Teece, D. J. (ed.), *The Competitive Challenge: Strategies for Industrial Innovation and Renewal*. Ballinger Publishing, Cambridge, MA (1987), pp. 119–35.

Pfeffer, J. and Salancik, G. R. *The External Control of Organizations: A Resource Dependence Perspective*. Harper & Row, New York (1978).

Phillips, L. W. Assessing measurement error in key informant reports: A methodological note on organizational analysis in marketing. *Journal of Marketing Research*, **18** (November), 395–415 (1981).

Ring, P. S. and Van De Ven, A. H. Structuring cooperative relationships between organizations. *Strategic Management Journal*, **13**, 483–98 (1992).

Ring, P. S. and Van De Ven, A. H. Developmental processes of cooperative interorganizational relationships. *Academy of Management Review*, **19** (January), 90–118 (1994).

Shortell, S. M. and Zajac, E. J. Health care organizations and the development of the strategic management perspective. In Mick, S. S. *et al.* (eds) *Innovations in Health Care Delivery: Insights for Organizational Theory*. Jossey-Bass Publishers, San Francisco (1990), pp. 144–80.

Sjöberg, U. Produktförandringar i nätverk. Ett fall från pappersindustrin. (Product changes in networks: a case from the paper industry): Working paper, Uppsala University, Department of Business Studies (1991).

Snow, C. C., Miles, R. E. and Coleman, H. J. Jr. Managing 21st century network organizations. *Organizational Dynamics*, **20** (Winter), 5–19 (1992).

Thibaut, J. W. and Kelley, H. *The Social Psychology of Groups*. John Wiley & Sons, Inc., New York (1959).

Thorelli, H. B. Networks: between markets and hierarchies. *Strategic Management Journal*, **7** (January/February), 37–51 (1986).

Tversky, A. and Kahneman, D. The framing of decisions and the psychology of choice. *Science*, **211** (January), 453–58 (1981).

Van de Ven, A. H. On the nature, formation, and maintenance of relations among organizations. *The Academy of Management Review*, **1** (October), 24–36 (1976).

Verity, J. W. Deconstructing the computer industry. *Business Week* (November 23), 90–100 (1992).

Williamson, O. E. *The Economic Institutions of Capitalism*. The Free Press, New York (1985).

Williamson, O. E. Comparative economic organization: the analysis of discrete structural alternatives. *Administrative Science Quarterly*, **36** (June), 269–96 (1991a).

Williamson, O. E. Strategizing, economizing, and economic organization. *Strategic Management Journal*, **12**, 75–94 (1991b).

Yamagishi, T., Gillmore, M. R. and Cook, K. S. Network connections and the distribution of power in exchange networks. *American Journal of Sociology*, **93** (January), 833–51 (1988).

Zajac, E. J. and Olsen, C. P. From transaction cost to transaction value-analysis: implications for the study of interorganizational strategies. *Journal of Management Studies*, **30** (January), 131–45 (1993).

# Part III

## Developing Marketing Strategy

The first two parts of this book try to build a conceptual basis for analysing business relationships and inter-company networks. The remaining three concentrate on how the conceptual basis can be used to understand three aspects of business markets: marketing strategy, purchasing strategy and the issue of technology.

The readings in Part 3 are chosen to illustrate a number of different aspects of business marketing strategy. The first two readings, by Cunningham with Homse and Campbell respectively, set the scene by examining the vital issues in business marketing of effectively analysing a portfolio of customers, allocating the company's resources between them and managing the patterns of its contacts with them. The following two readings by Wilson and Jantrania and by Turnbull and Zolkiewski are also linked and build on the first two. They show that it is important for the marketer to have a clear understanding of the *value* to the company of each significant customer (or group of customers). This relationship value can be considered only in terms of the contribution of each relationship *as part of* an overall portfolio. Wilson and Jantrania point out that value in relationships can take many forms. The Turnbull and Zolkiewski reading concentrates on the financial value (costs and profit) of relationships and reports on one of a series of studies into the real costs and profitability of relationships, when the actual costs of managing those relationships are factored in.

The remaining three readings in this section have been chosen because they offer an international perspective. The reading by Hallén and Johanson examines how international strategy varies between countries in terms of emphasis on quality and adaptation. These strategies are related to the different industrial environments in the supplier countries and the cultural "distance" between supplier and buyer. The reading by Håkansson is not included simply as a detailed analysis of the ways in which exporters from Sweden have organized their international operations in Europe. More importantly, it provides a fascinating picture of the difference in requirements of relationship partners and the choices open to international marketers when dealing with them. The final reading by Salmi is very recent and uses a network perspective to provide interesting insights into behaviour in business markets in Russia.

## CONTENTS

# 1

# Controlling the Marketing–Purchasing Interface: Resource Development and Organisational Implications

*M. T. Cunningham and E. Homse*

## INTRODUCTION

Supplier–customers interdependence is a feature of many concentrated industrial markets. Marketing and purchasing in such circumstances can be construed as an exchange process leading to the adaptive behaviour of both parties over time. This is achieved through the mechanisms of organizational interaction. At the core of these exchange processes between suppliers and customers is the person-to-person dyadic relationship involving a salesman and a buyer. Supporting this narrowly based dyad is a complex network of inter- and intra-organizational personal contacts.

In this article we consider the organizational and resource allocation issues arising from the patterns of personal contacts between suppliers and their customers. The ideas and empirical data have evolved from the "interaction approach" of the IMP (International Marketing and Purchasing) research group's five-country study of supplier–customer relationships in European industrial markets (Håkansson, 1982).

First, we examine these personal contacts within the context of interaction theory. This leads on to a discussion of the roles which personal contacts play in developing and maintaining supplier–customer relationships. Third, we investigate some of the factors determining the resource allocation to different customers. Fourth, we analyse the networks of supplier–customer contacts, focusing upon their frequency, breadth and the managerial levels involved. Finally, we develop a taxonomy of patterns of contacts between suppliers and customers and consider the management issues involved.

Interorganizational personal contacts represent a scarce human resource in which is vested much of the expertise, credibility and authority of the participating companies. This raises several managerial questions for a supplier company:

Reprinted with permission from *Industrial Marketing and Purchasing*, Vol. 1, No. 2, pp. 3–27.

How should human resources be allocated among different markets and customers? What is the correct balance between technical, marketing and senior managerial staff required to have personal contact with customers?
How frequently, and at what venue (customer or supplier) should personal contacts occur to achieve the objectives?
What factors should determine the amount of resources which must be deployed to handle various supplier–customer relationships?

No simple answers to such questions have so far emerged from previous research. Here we present some evidence of current practice and offer explanation for these resource allocation decisions.

## THE INTERACTION CONTEXT OF PERSONAL CONTACTS

The interaction model of buyer–seller relationships proposed by the IMP research group (Håkansson, 1982) focuses attention upon the different categories of variables affecting the processes of interaction between individuals and also between formally and informally constituted organization groups in the supplier and customer companies.

Four major groups of variables provide the framework for describing and analysing supplier–customer relationships. First, the interaction processes involved in exchanging goods, services, information, etc.; second, the parties to the exchange, comprising individuals, groups and formal organizations; third, the economic and market environment surrounding the exchange; and, fourth, the atmosphere

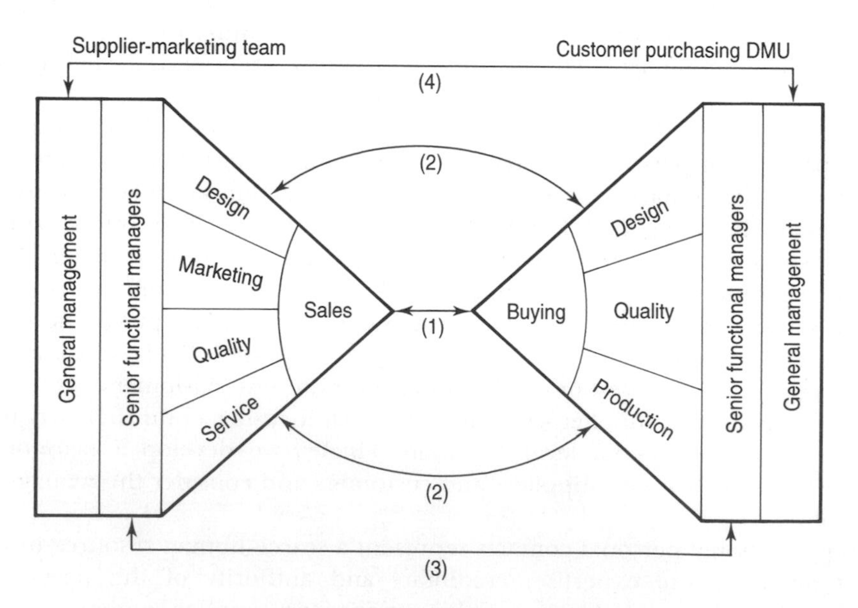


Fig. 1. Interface between parties in supplier–customer relationships.

characterizing the relationship between the supplier and the customer. The interaction model recognizes that personal contacts between the two companies are a frequently used mechanism for initiating, developing and maintaining such relationships.

A major task of the industrial marketer is to manage the interface between the business and its customers in a competitive environment. On one side of the supplier–customer interface is the customer's purchasing decision-making unit (DMU) of which the buyer is but one part (Webster and Wind, 1972). The mirror image of this DMU is the supplier's sales-service-design team who are frequently in personal contact with customers (see Fig. 1).

Figure 1 illustrates four types of interorganizational contacts. First, a single dyadic relationship existing between salesman and buyer; second, a series of interfunctional contacts between personnel in different supplier and customer functional departments; third, the contacts between the senior managers of functional departments and, fourth, contacts between the general management in the two companies.

## THE ROLES OF PERSONAL CONTACTS IN SUPPLIER–CUSTOMER RELATIONSHIPS

Interpersonal contacts between supplier and customer companies are identified in the IMP interaction model as performing vital roles in problem solving, in exchanging social values and information and in demonstrating commitment to, and credibility with, the other party. Ford (1984) pointed out the strong association which exists between buyers' assessments of the professional and commercial skills of their suppliers and the extent of the perceived commitment, adaptability and capability of suppliers to reduce the "distance" that can exist between them and their customers. This followed his earlier ideas (Ford, 1981), developed from the interaction model which took the form of a multi-stage paradigm demonstrating how such characteristics as commitment, uncertainty, distance reduction and adaptations change as the buyer–seller relationship proceeds through developmental stages over time. Clearly, personal contacts are one means of accomplishing this "distance reduction".

Based upon Ford's ideas, the stepwise evolution of the patterns of inter-organizational contacts between a supplier and customer can be represented as in Fig. 2. The emphasis in this diagrammatic portrayal is on how the perceived distance between the two parties (social distance, technological distance, cultural distance and geographical distance) is reduced in stages as the personal contacts change from a simple salesman–buyer relationship to a multi-functional network of contacts. This stage is characterized by limited experience, high uncertainty, low commitment and limited information exchange (Fig. 2a). The next stage is characterized by increasing experience, increasing confidence, perceived high commitment and moderate information exchange (Fig. 2b). The long-term relationship stage is characterized by interdependence, extensive experience, high resource commitment, extensive adaptations and reciprocal information exchange. The functional departments

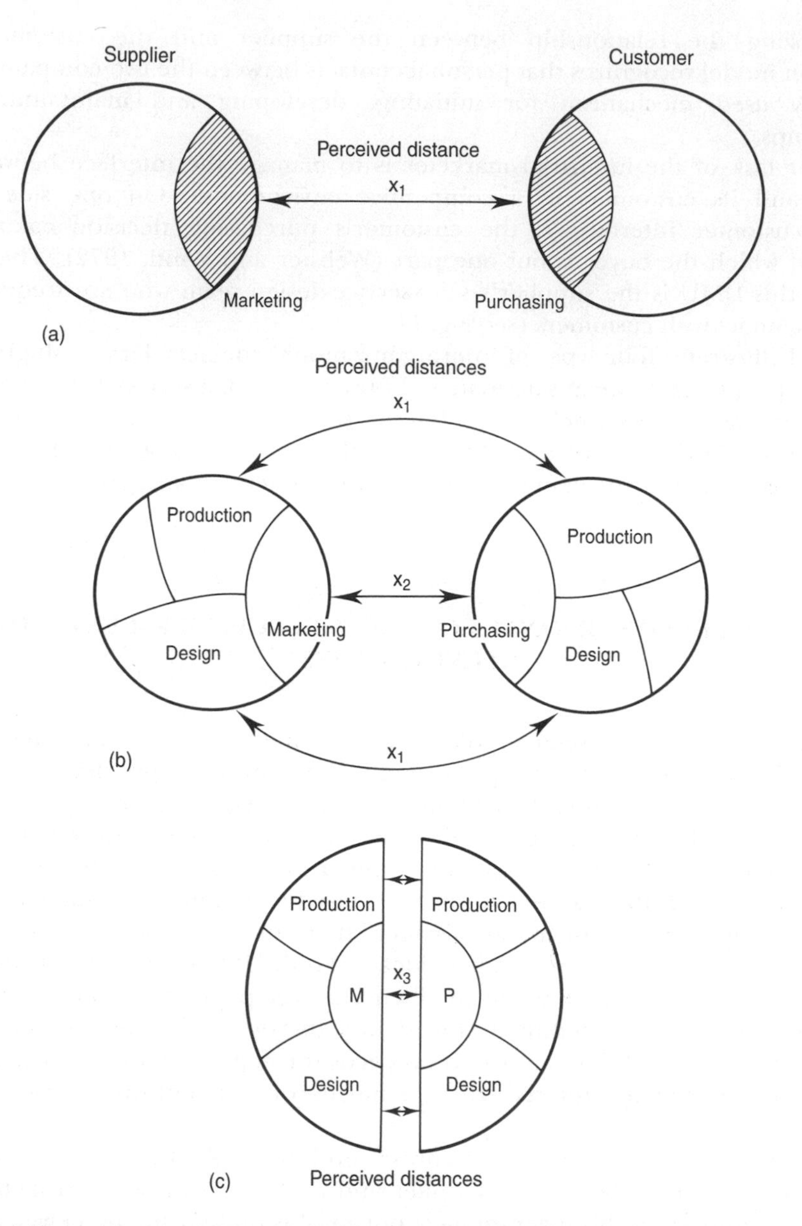


Fig. 2. (a) The early stage of the relationship. (b) The development stage. (c) The long-term relationship stage.

develop bonds which are of comparable strength to those between salesman and buyer.

Personal contacts as a mechanism for the reduction of "psychic" or cultural distance between exporters and importers have been researched by others (Hallen and Wiedersheim-Paul, 1982). They focus upon the acquisition of market knowledge, the development of close business connections and the transmission/reception of information between buyers and sellers.

However, based on their analysis of over 100 supplier–customer relationships in international markets, interorganizational personal contacts were found to serve other roles than those of distance reduction (Cunningham and Turnbull, 1982). These roles were identified as:

Information exchange;
Assessment;
Negotiation and adaptation;
Crisis insurance;
Social bonding;
Ego enhancement.

These widely varying roles may be achieved by different forms, structures and patterns of personal contacts. For example, reducing distance and demonstrating commitment may be fulfilled either by a small number of very senior staff in infrequent interaction, or by a large number of junior personnel in frequent contact.

Adopting an alternative perspective (that of the buyer) the roles of personal contacts can be considered according to their contribution to gaining and retaining business from customers in a highly competitive environment. An analysis of the attitudes and experiences of over 400 buyers of industrial goods in Europe revealed that there are eight major groups of factors which characterize relationships between suppliers and customers (Turnbull and Cunningham, 1981). Buyers can compare the relative capabilities of competing suppliers on these factors. These eight factors are closely related to the key marketing tasks which the supplier must perform in order to be an acceptable supplier and on which they will be evaluated by members of the customer's purchasing DMU. These eight factors and the marketing tasks characterizing successful supplier–customer relationships are summarized in Table 1.

It is in performing the tasks described in Table 1 and particularly in communicating them effectively and convincingly to customers that the role of personal contacts can best be appreciated.

These tasks represent the core requirements which are most likely to meet customers' needs. However, the particular strategy being pursued by suppliers in different markets in different competitive environments and with selected target customers are clearly going to impinge on the way in which the scarce human resources of the supplier are going to be deployed. Competitive marketing strategies based on superior technical innovations call for a different mix of resources from those required to implement strategies of being the lowest price supplier or strategies which are dependent upon offering guaranteed delivery reliability.

## RESEARCH METHODOLOGY

The research reported here is based on an analysis of the intercompany personal contacts between 49 British suppliers of industrial goods and their customers in

Table 1. Characteristics of supplier–customer relationships

| | |
|---|---|
| 1. *Customer orientation* | Suppliers must analyse customer needs, be international in outlook, show interest in the customer's problems and be sensitive to the way foreign firms operate |
| 2. *Technological expertise* | The technical competence of marketing staff must be complemented by the willingness of suppliers to offer new technology and innovative products to the customer in order to solve any technical problems |
| 3. *Commercial competence* | The supplier organization should be able to provide adequate and speedy responses to requests for information and be able to handle complaints |
| 4. *Flexibility and adaptability* | A willingness to adapt products, manufacturing processes, payment systems, delivery dates and administrative procedures |
| 5. *Supply performance capability* | The supplier must demonstrate an ability to provide a reliable delivery, quality assurance, after-sales service and information |
| 6. *Price competitiveness* | A price representing good value for money; accompanied by a willingness to negotiate on price and to recognize the other cost consequences of purchase in addition to an initial price |
| 7. *Organizational effectiveness* | The organization structure and co-ordination of the supplier's marketing, technical and manufacturing expertise has to be compatible with the customer's needs. This has important implications for the interorganizational personal contacts between the two companies in order to facilitate communications and negotiations |
| 8. *Social integration* | An atmosphere of co-operation, trust, commitment, closeness and legitimate exercise of power is a key feature of relationships with suppliers |

France, Germany, Italy, Sweden and the UK. It is part of a larger data base generated from 876 personal interviews with marketing and purchasing executives in five European countries. A full description of the research methodology is to be found in Håkansson (1982). The data relating to personal contacts between supplier and customer companies were obtained by focusing upon a small number of identifiable and important specific customers. No claim for representativeness of all its customer relationships for each company is made. Rather, the research is exploratory to gain a deeper understanding of relationships in industrial markets, especially across national boundaries as in export marketing and international purchasing.

Nature and frequency of intercompany contact pattern

Nature purpose of contact (N)
1 = Commercial negotiations
2 = Technical negotiations
3 = General commercial information exchange
4 = General technical information exchange
5 = Commercial problem solving
6 = Technical problem solving
7 = Technical training and advice
8 = Progressing (delivery and technical)
9 = Other (appendix var 365)

Frequency of contact (F)
1 = Very frequent (weekly or more)
2 = Frequent (once every 3 months or more but less than weekly)
3 = Infrequent (less than every 3 months but more than once a year)
4 = Very infrequent (once a year or less)

Customer functions

| | | 1 | | 2 | | 3 | | 4 | | 5 | | 6 | | 7 | | 8 | | 9 | |
|---|---|---|---|---|---|---|---|---|---|---|---|---|---|---|---|---|---|---|---|
| | | General mgt | | Prodn | | Quality | | R&D eng | | Finance | | Mkting | | Prchsing | | Other | | Other | |
| | Supplier functions | N | F | N | F | N | F | N | F | N | F | N | F | N | F | N | F | N | F |
| 1 | Gen. mgt | 34 | 4 | | | | | | | | | | | | | | | | |
| 2 | Prodn | | | | | | | | | | | | | | | | | | |
| 3 | Quality | | | | | 6 | 3 | | | | | | | | | | | | |
| 4 | R&D eng | | | | | 46 | 2 | 46 | 2 | | | | | 46 | 3 | | | | |
| 5 | Finance | | | | | | | | | | | | | | | | | | |
| 6 | Jun mkt. | 34 | 4 | | | 6 | 3 | 246 | 2 | | | 3 | 4 | 135 | 2 | 8 | 4 | | |
| 7 | Sen mkt. | | | | | | | 4 | 3 | | | | | 3 | 3 | | | | |
| 8 | Sal. abr. | | | | | | | | | | | | | | | | | | |
| 9 | Other*** | | | | | | | | | | | | | | | 8 | 3 | | |

*Note:* Supplier personnel and functions are listed on the vertical axis and the customer equivalent on the horizontal axis. Where data are recorded in a cell of this matrix then the respective supplier and customer personnel are in face-to-face contact. The data record the many purposes of their meetings and the frequency with which these occur. For example, in this illustration general managers from both companies meet once a year for a general exchange of commercial and technical information (N = 3.4; F = 4).

Fig. 3. Interorganizational personal contact pattern.

The form in which the data were summarized and coded for computer analysis is as shown in Fig. 3. The supplier company personnel were identified by consultation with the marketing/sales executive primarily responsible for handling the customer relationship. By a similar process of enquiry the customer personnel were identified. Subsequently, the matrix or network of intercompany contacts was mapped out. Finally, the frequency of contact, site location and topics dealt with through these personal contacts were elicited. Figure 3 illustrates one such supplier–customer relationship.

From these data the subsequent analysis of personal contacts covering the three dimensions of frequency, breadth and organizational level was made.

## FACTORS INFLUENCING THE ALLOCATION OF RESOURCES TO CUSTOMERS

In the introduction to this article, we posed several important questions to be faced by managers in supplier companies when handling customer relationships. It is possible to investigate current practice in individual markets to shed light on these issues. In doing so we draw on concepts arising from the interaction model. It has already been argued that the stage of a supplier–customer relationship is likely to be a major determinant of the resources involved. In the following section we focus on three major factors: market structure (a feature of the environment of relationships), customer importance (derived from the value of product exchanges involved in the interaction process) and product complexity (arising from technology of the supplier/customer parties).

### Market Structure

Although other researchers have argued that interaction between suppliers and customers is affected by the recognition of their mutual interdependence and interest in gaining access to each other's resources (Melin, 1977), no effective measure of interdependence was proposed. Interdependence is clearly influenced by market structure which determines the available choice and power of prospective partners in a market. We can easily speculate that market structure will have a major impact upon the amount of interaction and, therefore, on the human resources committed to develop or defend special relationships in industrial markets. For example, we see from Fig. 4 that in concentrated markets, where few suppliers and few customers exist (such as in cell 1), there is likely to be a "pairing off" between some customers and their preferred suppliers. Less equally balanced supplier–customer relationships, as in cells 2 and 3 of the matrix, are characterized by one party exercising power over the other. Finally in cell 4 the mutual commitment between suppliers and customers may be low and there is greater freedom for both parties to change partners, with the consequential lower switching costs.

### Customer Importance

Clearly the economic importance of the customer is one vital factor in resource allocation. Yet the resource investment in personal contacts between suppliers and

| *Number of customers* | *Number of suppliers*: Few | *Number of suppliers*: Many |
|---|---|---|
| Few | Mutual interdependence<br>Cell 1 | Customer dominated<br>Cell 2 |
| Many | Supplier dominated<br>Cell 3 | Relative independence<br>Cell 4 |

Fig. 4. Market structure and supplier–customer relationships.

customers cannot be simply correlated with the amount of business being transacted with a customer. For instance, information and social exchange often precedes financial and product exchange and there is a significant time lapse between resources (investment) and business (financial return).

### Product and Transaction Complexity

Exchanges between suppliers and customers are not all of equal complexity and so the amount of resources allocated to a customer is likely to be affected by the technological complexity of the product and of the commercial complexities of the contract being negotiated. Perceived risk occurs in buying and this risk is significantly affected by the transaction complexity. It is in highly complex exchanges that interpersonal contacts are a much valued mechanism used by supplies and customers alike to reduce the perceived risk. Such contacts clearly serve as a vital part of the continuous information gathering (inputs) of buyers and of the long-term communications mix (outputs) of suppliers.

*How do British Suppliers to European Markets Allocate their Human Resources between Customers?*

Our research findings allow us to look at the influence of markets, customers and product technology on this resource allocation question.

Some interesting insights are to be found by analysing some of the data in such a way as to compare domestic with foreign customers. We also choose two product categories from the large number in our sample and use two alternative measures of customer importance (sales value and proportion of total sales revenue of the supplier). The data are presented in Table 2.

In Table 2 an index of resources allocated to each customer relationship is shown for the relatively complex Product A and the technologically simpler Product B. The index was compiled to take into account only human resources involved in personal contact with customers. The index incorporates the number of staff, the number of functional areas, their frequency of contact and the management level in the

Table 2. Resource allocation to different customers and product markets.

| | Product A customers | | Product B customers | |
|---|---|---|---|---|
| | Domestic customers | Foreign customers | Domestic customers | Foreign customers |
| Average value of sales to each customer | £9m | £0.5m | £1.4m | £0.3m |
| Customer purchases as a percentage of supplier's total sales | 29% | 1.5% | 5% | 0.9% |
| Index of resources allocation to each customer | 15.5 | 5.3 | 5.2 | 1.7 |

organizational hierarchy of personnel involved in the supplier–customer relations.

As might be expected, domestic customers for both categories of products represent the more important customers and receive a higher allocation of resources than do foreign customers. However, foreign customers receive a proportionately higher resource than their current financial importance would suggest. It will also be seen that domestic customers for Product A receive *three* times more resources than their equivalents for the less technically complex Product B. But each Product A domestic customer is approximately six times more important than each Product B domestic customer.

Therefore product complexity appears to be a less important factor than the importance of the customer (either in terms of financial volume or export potential) in allocating personal contact resources.

## NETWORKS OF SUPPLIER–CUSTOMER CONTACTS

So far, it has been argued that the personal contacts allocated to customers and markets are determined by such factors as the value of the order, the stage which the supplier–customer relationship has reached, the complexity of the product or contract, and the tasks to be performed to meet customers' requirements or to gain differentiated advantage in the eyes of the customers. They are also idiosyncratic in so far as they depend upon the specific strategy being pursued by suppliers. These interorganizational contacts span many functions, involve varying frequency of visits and take place at many levels in the hierarchy of the supplier and customer firms. Figs 1 and 3 portray the network of contacts involved.

The measurement or evaluation of the human resources which suppliers allocate to handle customer relations can be considered under three headings or dimensions:

The frequency of interpersonal contacts.
Their breadth across different functions.
The level in the organization at which they occur.

### The Frequency of Interpersonal Contact

Very frequent personal contact may be needed for a number of reasons such as performance monitoring, demonstrating commitment, information gathering and social bonding. The frequency with which the partners meet is one important indicator of the amount of resources being committed to the relationship by the parties. It is also an important measure of the quantity (but not necessarily the quality) of actual exchanges that take place between companies.

It would seem natural to refer to the frequency of contacts in terms of the number of meetings between suppliers and customer personnel. However this is an inadequate measure of the resource commitment because research evidence suggests that there is probably an inverse relationship between the frequency of visits and the time spent on each visit.

It was found that a high correlation exists between the distance or cost of travel and the time spent with the customer on each visit, particularly as far as foreign customer visits are concerned in comparison with domestic ones. The concentration or dispersion of customers in different markets determines the supplier's approach to cost effective planning of customers' visits.

A summary of the frequency with which interpersonal contacts occur between British suppliers and their customers is shown in Table 3. For the 59 relationships analysed, meetings occur 10 times per annum though the vast majority of these take place at the customer's premises. As one would expect, the frequency of meetings with domestic customers is much greater (approximately 20 times per annum) than with foreign customers (six times per annum). It is of interest to note that the foreign customers pay visits to their British suppliers almost once each year.

## The Breadth of Contact

We use the term breadth of contact to indicate the number of areas or subjects covered by the pattern of personal relationships. A narrow relationship may be concerned only with the minimum commercial contacts needed for the exchange of product and payment to be effected.

A broad relationship brings together supplier and customer staff to discuss commercial and technical matters, special arrangements for the storage and movement of goods, quality control procedures, market situation, product and process departments, future plans and strategies and so forth. Relationships can be considered as developing through different levels of integration. A broad personal contact pattern can perhaps best be described as reflecting a "highly integrated" relationship.

We have defined the breadth of the contact pattern in terms of the diversity of content of personal exchanges rather than any "physical" characteristics of the pattern. As defined, this dimension is complex to observe and analyse. However, there are several "proxy" measures which are much more readily observable. The best measures are probably the number of functional departments, people and organization levels involved in the relationship.

In Table 4 we present a summary of the breadth of personal contacts in 59

Table 3. Frequency of interpersonal contacts in supplier–customer relationships

| | All relationships ($n = 59$) | In domestic markets ($n = 18$) | In export markets ($n = 41$) |
|---|---|---|---|
| Average number of meetings per annum at suppliers' premises | 1.5 | 2.6 | 0.9 |
| Average number of meetings per annum at customers' premises | 8.7 | 16.6 | 5.2 |
| Average frequency of meetings in total (per annum) | 10.2 | 19.2 | 6.1 |

Table 4. Breadth of personal contact in supplier–customer relationships

| | All relationships ($n = 59$) | In domestic markets ($n = 18$) | In export markets ($n = 41$) |
|---|---|---|---|
| Average number of supplier staff involved | 8 | 14 | 5 |
| Average number of customer staff involved | 9 | 13 | 6 |
| Average number of supplier functions involved | 3.2 | 4.2 | 2.8 |
| Average number of customer functions involved | 3.3 | 3.7 | 3.2 |

relationships between British suppliers and their customers. Overall, across all markets, on average eight supplier staff are interacting with nine customer staff. At least three different departments are involved in both the supplier and customer organizations.

The breadth of contact varies widely depending upon whether the relationship is between a British supplier and its British customer or whether relationships are in export markets. For domestic markets 14 supplier staff from more than four functional departments interact with 13 customer staff in almost four departments on average. In marked contrast, relationships in foreign markets involve five supplier staff and six customer staff representing approximately three functional departments in their respective companies.

## The Level of Contact

The level of contact refers to the position in the organization hierarchy of those involved.

It is evident in a number of the relationships studied that a matching of levels took place. If customer contact was made by a supplier representative of a particular status, customer staff on a similar level would be available for him to see. In order to establish a point of direct contact with a customer at director or general management level, the involvement of similar high level staff in the supplier company was also needed.

In some of the more involved relationships, a matching of status at a number of levels takes place. The research also produced evidence of different forms of interpersonal contacts between staff at various levels in the supplier and customer companies. First, the simple chief executive to chief executive dyadic contact. Second, the matched status, multi-level contacts as shown in Fig. 5a. Third, the multi-status contacts as shown in Fig. 5b. Fourth, the multi-status, multi-functional, multi-level contacts as shown in Fig. 5c.

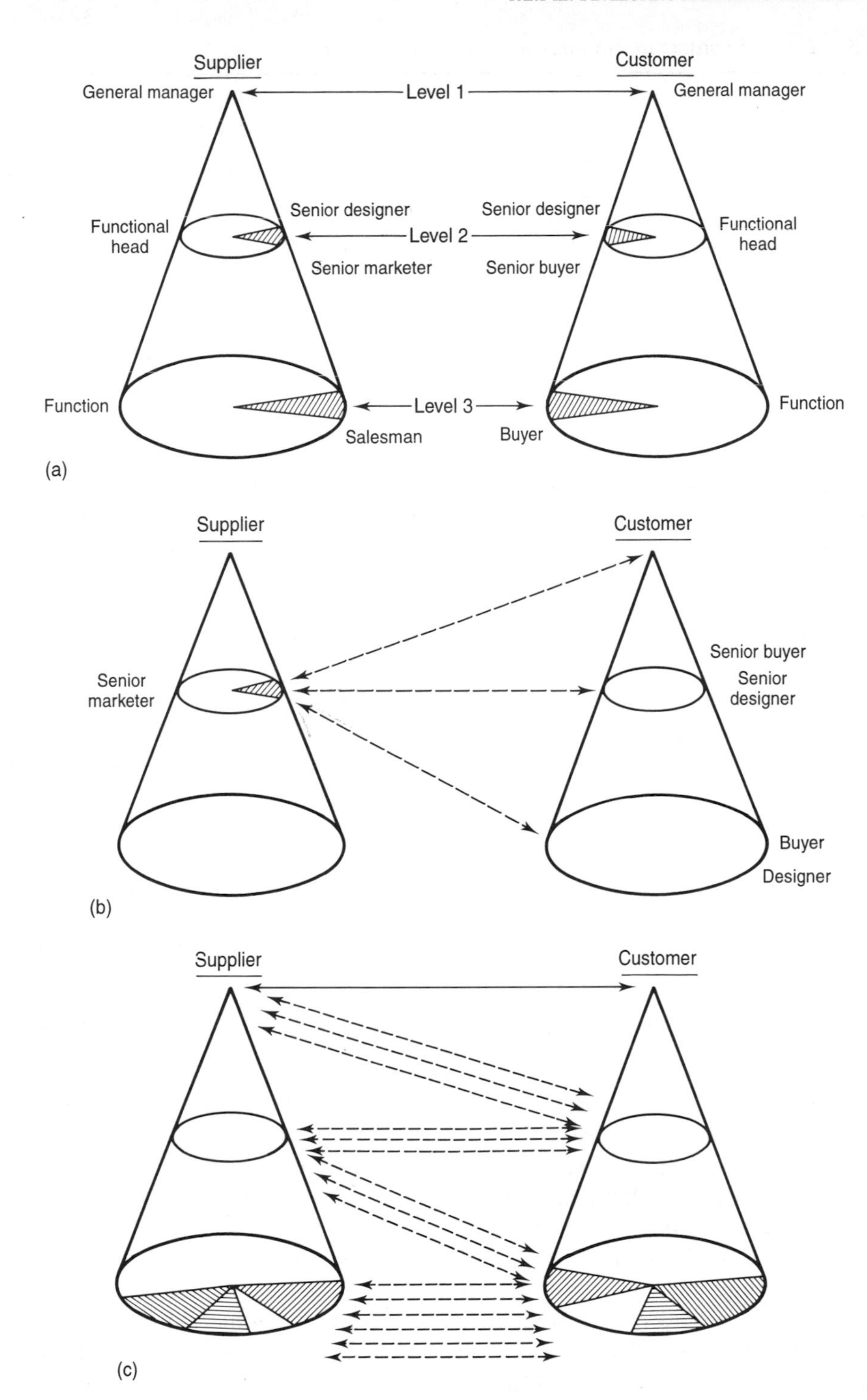


Fig. 5. (a) Matched status, multi-level contact. (b) Multi-status contacts (c) Multi-status, multi-functional, multi-level contacts.

Table 5. Level of contact in supplier–customer relationships

| | All relationships ($n = 59$) | In domestic markets ($n = 18$) | In export markets ($n = 41$) |
|---|---|---|---|
| Relationships involving suppliers' senior general management and directors | 50% | 77% | 32% |
| Relationships involving customers' senior general management and directors | 39% | 50% | 34% |

In this instance the supplier–customer relationship involved 16 interpersonal contacts between six major supplier functions (marketing, finance, quality control, design, manufacturing and service) at the middle and lower hierarchical levels, reinforced by general management contacts with senior and middle management personnel in the customer company.

In our research we analysed the levels of interpersonal contacts in 59 relationships involving British suppliers and customers. Due to disparities between organization structures in companies it was only feasible to standardize the data to represent three hierarchical levels. These are categorized as senior, middle and junior levels. The senior level includes functional directors, such as Purchasing or Engineering Director and also general management or managing director positions. In Table 5 we present abbreviated data which show that at some time during the year 50% of all the relationships involved personal contacts by senior management in the supplier companies and 39% of relationships involved senior customer staff. Domestic relationships made greater demands on senior management, 77% for suppliers and 50% for customers than did the foreign relationships (32 and 34% respectively).

## A TAXONOMY OF PATTERNS OF INTERORGANIZATIONAL CONTACTS

Important issues of control and co-ordination of personal contacts between suppliers and customers arise from our research. In this final section we present some evidence of the various organizational mechanisms in use in supplier–customer relationships. Here we are more speculative than definitive and further research is needed into these organizational forms observed.

The contacts established between supplier and customer companies usually centre on the marketing and purchasing departments respectively. Often a particular customer is the special responsibility of a Customer Account Manager, or a sales representative who handles all customers in a certain industry or geographical territory. In the purchasing organization, sectional managers often have responsibility for the relationship with suppliers of certain categories of products. Here we examine certain categories of control and co-ordination.

## Marketing and Purchasing Controlled Contact Patterns

The concepts of boundary spanning units and boundary spanning activities are commonly used in organizational theory. In some companies all direct contact with supplier or customer staff is made by the marketing or purchasing departments. They are the only functions which "break through" the boundary that surrounds the organization and separates it from the supply or customer environment, and they conduct all boundary spanning activities in relation to these parts of the environment.

Relationships with customers where all direct contact is channelled through the marketing department we shall refer to as "marketing controlled". Similarly, where only purchasing staff interact directly with a supplier, the relationship is "purchasing controlled". Figures 6a, b and c show a marketing controlled, a purchasing controlled, and a marketing and purchasing controlled pattern of personal contacts, respectively. The concept of "breaking through" the organization boundary is reflected in the graphical presentation of these relationships.

Several "pure" marketing controlled contact patterns were found in the present study in interviews with unit or small batch manufacturers of capital plant. Such companies often had separate contracts departments specializing in developing tailor-made product offerings to suit a particular customer's needs. In the companies studied, the contracts department staff were rarely involved in direct personal contact with the potential customer. In a similar manner, it was evident in many of the large automotive components suppliers that a considerable amount of "behind the scene" engineering work was carried out for specific customers, but with little or no direct personal contact between the supplier engineers doing this work and their opposite numbers in the customer companies.

## Marketing and Purchasing Co-ordinated Contact Patterns

The marketing and purchasing functions may co-ordinate rather than control completely the personal interactions that take place between supplier and customer. In a marketing co-ordinated relationship there may be direct personal contact between other supplier functions and various customer departments, but in all such contacts, marketing staff are also involved.

Typically, such relationships are when the sales representative "brings along" a member of the engineering department, for example, and together they visit the customer's engineering personnel. Figures 7a, b and c illustrate a marketing co-ordinated, a purchasing co-ordinated and a both marketing and purchasing co-ordinated relationship, respectively.

## Stratified Contact Patterns

When the pattern of personal contacts between supplier and customer staff is neither controlled nor co-ordinated by either marketing or purchasing staff, we have a stratified contact pattern. This term was chosen because, when depicted diagrammatically, the impression is one of different "layers" or "strata" of contacts. This is shown in Fig. 8.

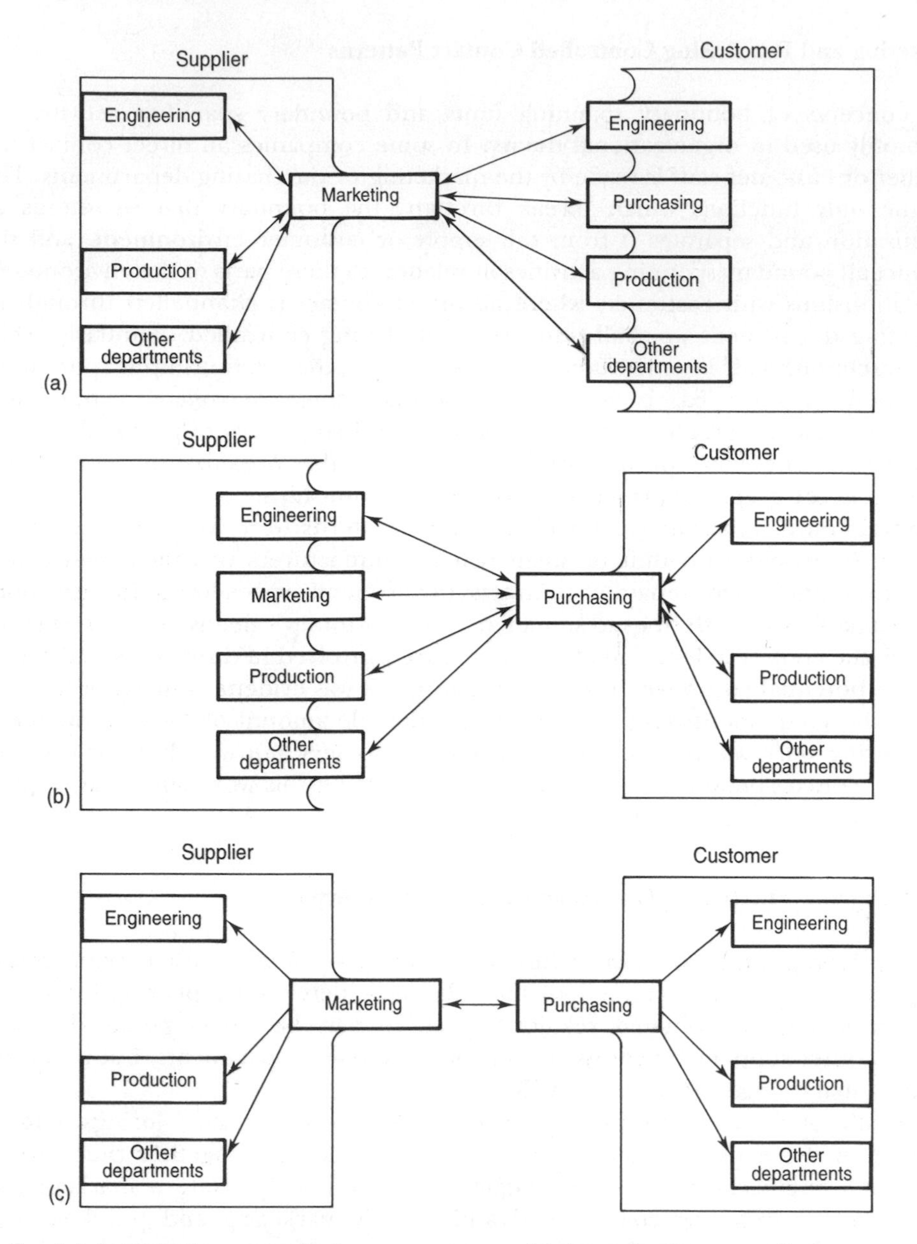


Fig. 6. (a) A marketing controlled contact pattern. (b) A purchasing controlled contact pattern. (c) A marketing and purchasing controlled contact pattern.

For a stratified contact pattern to occur, both the supplier and the customer organization have to be highly specialized in terms of functional departments. In addition, it would appear that one of the following three conditions has to be present – good internal communications, an explicit strategy for dealing with the counterpart company or an open relationship based on trust, integrity and loyalty.

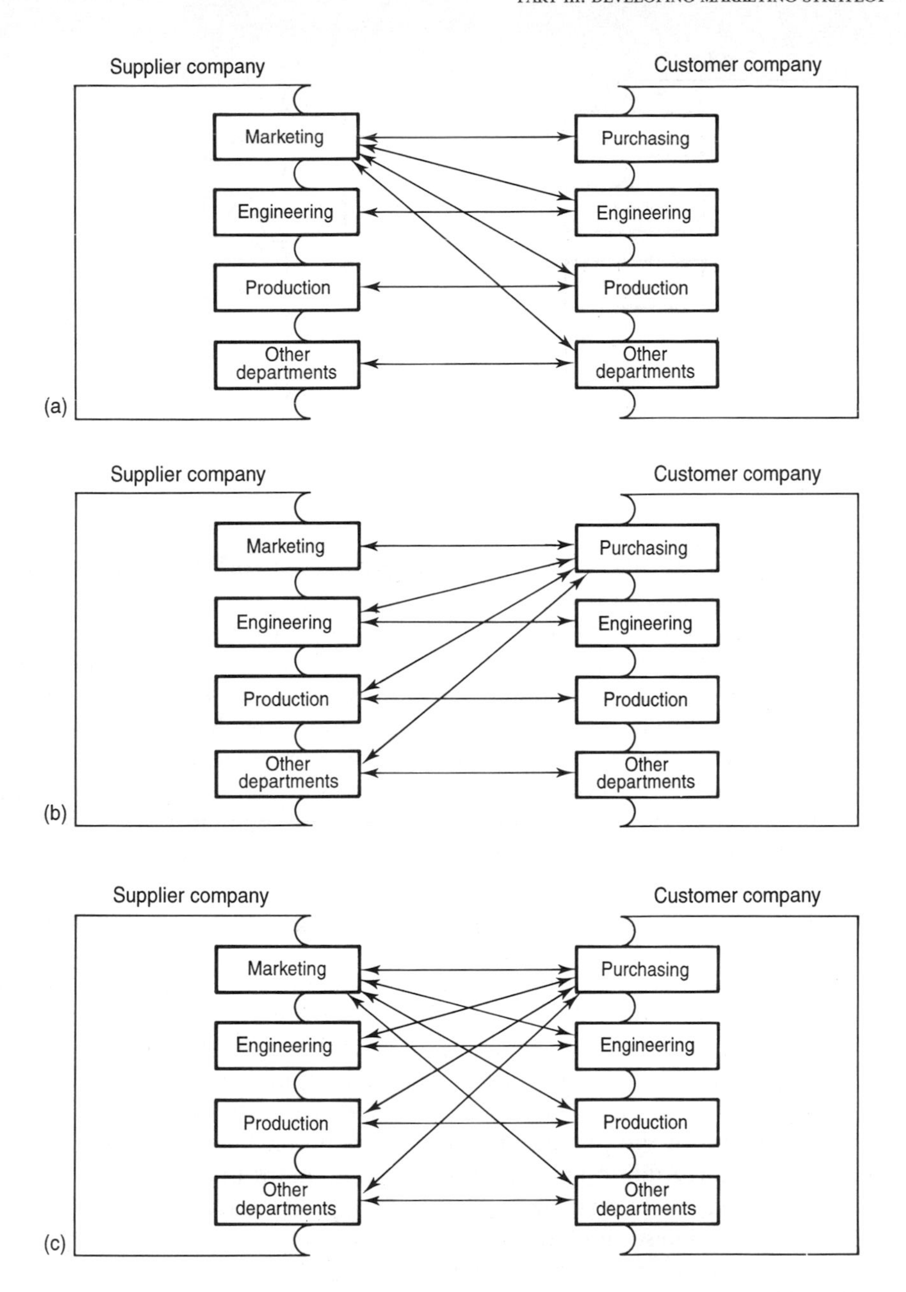


Fig. 7. (a) A marketing co-ordinated contact pattern. (b) A purchasing co-ordinated contact pattern. (c) A marketing and purchasing co-ordinated contact pattern.

## SUMMARY AND DISCUSSION

The relationships which we have analysed are not intended to be representative of what occurs generally in British home and export markets. They were deliberately

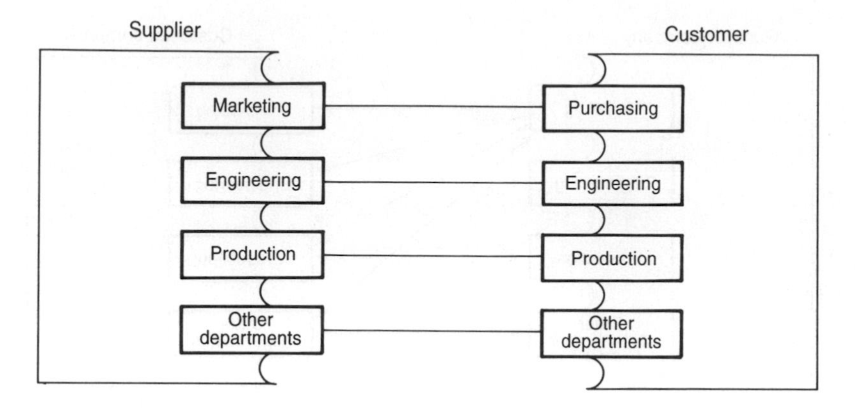


Fig. 8. A stratified contact pattern.

selected to allow a further and better understanding of the more important supplier–customer relationships in medium/high technology industrial markets. They are most likely to be "representative" of key accounts with major customers in concentrated and highly competitive international markets. Overall, marketing and purchasing executives in 49 companies were interviewed and illustrations are given from these organizations. A more detailed study of 59 supplier–customer relationships was carried out and the results have been presented in summary form.

Interface contacts in industrial markets between suppliers and customers rarely take the form of simple dyadic relationships between salesman and buyer or, indeed, of salesmen's face-to-face meetings with different members of the customer's DMU. Several personnel in different functional departments in supplier companies are involved in a network of contacts with their counterparts in the customer firm and this embraces multiple levels in the organizational hierarchy. These contacts develop into a variety of extremely complex patterns as the stages of a supplier–customer relationship evolve over time. Many different roles formed by these contacts were identified through interviews and case study analysis in specific relationships. From a supplier's perspective they account for a substantial deployment of scarce and costly human resources but from a customer's perspective they are instrumental in achieving a reduction of the perceived "distance" between his organization and that of a potential supplier. Additionally, the research data point to eight major groups of factors or criteria which buyers take into account in evaluating their current and potential suppliers. These include Customer Orientation, Technical Expertise, Commercial Capability, Adaptability, Supply Reliability, Price Competitiveness, Organizational Effectiveness and Social Integration. The personal contacts between the two organizations are a vital means for the supplier to demonstrate his company's competitive ability on these criteria.

Three measures of resource implications of the network of interpersonal contacts between supplier and customer staff have been used to portray the essential features of organizational relationships in industrial markets. These are the frequency, breadth and hierarchical level.

First, the *frequency of contact*. On average, face-to-face meetings between supplier and customer staff occur almost weekly in domestic markets and once every two months with foreign customers. The meetings take place both at the customer's and at the supplier's premises, though the vast majority (over 85%) are when supplier staff call on customers.

Second, the *breadth of contact* represents the range of issues dealt with in the relationship. In a broad relationship, exchanges between representatives cover commercial matters as well as issues relating to technical development, production, quality, logistics, administration, long-term plans and strategies, etc. Although the breadth of contact refers essentially to the content of exchanges, both the number of people and the number of functions involved in the relationship are good "proxy" measures of the resources involved.

The complexity and resource implications of supplier–customer relationships is in evidence from the results showing that, for each customer, an average of eight supplier staff and nine customer staff are involved in the network of interpersonal contacts. In domestic markets 14 suppliers and 13 customer staff, on average, are involved. Contacts by such supplier functions as sales, design, quality control, manufacturing and finance take place and, in general, four functions from both supplier and customer companies are brought into domestic market relationships and three functions from each organization in export market relations.

Third, the *level of contact* refers to the position of the organizational hierarchy of those involved. A matching level in the two companies often occurs.

At least three levels of management in supplier and customer companies are committed to many key account customer relationships. Each higher level represents an increasingly scarce and costly resource. In 77% of major domestic relationships the senior general managers or directors are occasionally called upon to make personal contacts with customers but only 32% of foreign relationships get the allocation of senior management time in face-to-face meetings. Customers likewise commit senior management to be involved in relationships with suppliers though not to the same extent. Customer senior management are more involved in domestic than foreign supplier relationships.

Finally, a taxonomy of patterns of supplier–customer contacts was derived from the empirical evidence; these patterns reflect various mechanisms used for the *control and co-ordination of contacts.* There is a certain similarity between the extent of formalization and the degree of control. However, the former refers more to the "atmosphere" and the content of exchanges, whereas the latter deals more with the "physical" pattern of personal contacts.

A *controlled* contact pattern is where all contacts are physically channelled through a single department or individual, typically through the marketing or purchasing department which has personal contacts with the other company. In a *co-ordinated* contact pattern, many different departments have direct personal contacts with the other company, but there is one department or person, usually a buyer or sales representative, who is involved personally in all other contacts that take place.

In a *stratified* contact pattern there are no persons or functions either controlling or co-ordinating personal contacts.

Pure examples of these patterns are relatively rare. It is therefore more meaningful to refer to the degree of control, co-ordination or stratification.

The *resources deployed* and the pattern of intercompany personal contacts reflect the importance of the specific relationship within the overall strategy of each of the two parties. Each partner will be involved in many other relationships in the market. The major factor determining the resources allocated to individual customer relationships is the economic importance of the customer, as perceived by the supplier. The structure of the market, the mutual interdependence of supplier and customer and the complexity of the transaction in different stages of the relationship are important determinants of the deployment of resources by suppliers. The actual pattern of personal contacts at the interface will reflect elements of opportunism and resource constraints.

The complexity, resource implications and organizational problems of managing interpersonal contacts between supplier and customer are clear from the foregoing discussion and results. Most companies develop procedures and controls for ensuring that different categories of customers are called upon at specified intervals by marketing and sales staff. Rarely is it appreciated that other scarce human resources in technical, manufacturing and quality control functions as well as in senior general management levels in the supply company can become committed in an *ad hoc* manner to a company's array of customers and prospects in both domestic and foreign markets. Some of the factors affecting the allocation of a supplier's human resources are under the company's direct control, others occur because of environmental and competitive forces in the market. There is a clear requirement for management to identify these key factors and ensure that their resources are being directed at appropriate markets and customers in order to establish and defend vital relationships.

## REFERENCES

Cunningham, M. T. and Turnbull, P. W. Interorganizational personal contact patterns. In Håkansson, H. (ed.), *International Marketing and Purchasing of Industrial Goods: An Interaction Approach.* Wiley (1982) pp. 304–16.

Ford, D. The development of buyer–seller relationships in industrial markets. *European Journal of Marketing,* **14**, (5/6) (1981).

Ford, D. Buyer–seller relationships in international industrial markets. *Industrial Marketing Management,* **13**, (101–12) (1984).

Håkansson, H. (ed.). *International Marketing and Purchasing of Industrial Goods: An Interaction Approach,* Wiley (1982), Ch. 2, pp. 10–27.

Hallen, L. and Wiedersheim-Paul, F. Psychic distance and buyer–seller interaction. *Organization Marked og Samfunn.* **16**, (5) 305–24 (1982).

Melin, L. *Strategisk Inkopsverkamhet–Organization och Interaktion* (Strategic Purchasing Actions–Organization and Interaction) (with summary in English). University of Linkoping, Linkoping, Sweden (1977).

Turnbull, P. W. and Cunningham, M. T. *International Marketing and Purchasing: A Survey of Attitudes of Marketing and Purchasing Executives in Five European Countries.* Macmillan (1981).

Webster, F. E. Jr. and Wind, Y. A general model of organizational buying behaviour. *Journal of Marketing,* **36**, (2), 12–19 (1972).

# 2

# Customer Analysis for Strategy Development in Industrial Markets

*N. C. G. Campbell and M. T. Cunningham*

## INTRODUCTION

Assessment of a company's strategic position must include an analysis of the company's situation in the markets which it serves. Normally, this analysis focuses on the company's products relative to competitors with questions such as: what are the sales trends, profits and market shares of different products in different market segments?

To do this analysis business planners have available an array of tools such as the well-known product portfolio matrix (Henderson, 1970), the product-positioning matrix (Hofer and Schendel, 1978) and the product/performance matrix (Wind, 1982). Such tools neglect trends in purchases by individual customers, and profits and market shares by customer. This may be a weakness, particularly in concentrated industrial markets which have a small number of key customers.

This paper suggests that, in many industrial markets, a company should develop its strategy from an analysis of existing customers. The analysis should highlight the current allocation of resources to different customers and customer groups and identify the company's position with key customers relative to competition in different market segments. The purpose of the analysis is to improve the allocation of scarce technical and marketing resources between different customers to achieve the supplier's strategic objectives. It leads to a reappraisal of a supplier's competitive strength with different customers, and it also ensures that relationships with key customers are managed more effectively.

In contrast to Porter (1980) who lays stress on the need to counteract buyers' bargaining power, this paper emphasizes the scope for developing relationships of mutual interdependence and shared objectives. This approach has its origin in a major research study which is briefly described in the next section.

Reprinted by permission of John Wiley and Sons Limited, Customer Analysis for Strategy Development in Industrial Markets by N. C. G. Campbell and M. T. Cunningham in *Strategic Management Journal*, Vol. 1, pp 360 – 380.

## METHODOLOGY

The new approach to industrial marketing and purchasing which underpins this paper is based on a continuing effort by the IMP research group (Håkansson, 1982) to understand the nature of buyer/seller relationships in industrial marketing. The major part of the IMP project was an international cross-sectional study with companies selected to represent different types of products and different production technologies in a 3 × 3 matrix as below:

| | | Buyer's production technology | | |
|---|---|---|---|---|
| | | Unit production | Batch or mass production | Process manufacture |
| Seller's product technology | Raw materials | | | |
| | Components and parts | | | |
| | Capital equipment | | | |

This matrix enabled the research group to investigate the influence on supplier/customer relationships of the nature of the supplier's product and the nature of the customer's production process. Product complexity, product essentiality, frequency of purchase, consequences of product failure, and extent of adaptations by each partner, were among the factors investigated.

Some 300 companies drawn from 15 different industries in five countries were involved in the research. Interviews were conducted with marketing and purchasing managers, who were directly involved in, or knew about, particular relationships.

The ideas presented here came from further research carried out to complement the previous IMP project. An intensive study over a two year period was conducted in the packaging industry in one European country. The research, using a "direct" approach (Mintzberg, 1978), focused on the marketing strategy of a leading company through a detailed analysis of its relationships with 63 customers. Information about customer relationships was obtained from company records (sales and profit histories, age of relationships, resource allocation) and from semi-structured interviews with the 27 senior managers who had contact with customers. Several managers were interviewed more than once. Wherever possible each relationship was considered in the context of trading relations between other suppliers and customers in the same market segment. Altogether data were collected from the supplier for 167 trading relationships in 10 market segments. In addition, a cross-section of customers and non-customers was interviewed which generated additional information about their supplier relationships. In several cases, interviews were conducted with the buyer and seller on both sides of the same relationship.

The "interaction" approach to marketing and purchasing strategy which emerged from this research emphasizes the active role of both buyer and seller. Their interaction can lead to co-operation or conflict, and the implications of this approach for marketing and purchasing strategy are reported by different members of the IMP group in Håkansson (1982).

## THE NEED FOR CUSTOMER ANALYSIS

That there is a need for customer analysis may seem self-evident. In fact there are a number of particular reasons why a customer analysis, in addition to a market and product analysis, is particularly relevant to industrial markets.

In industrial markets, a company's customers are often its greatest assets. Corey (1976, p. 5) says that "the development of strong, multidimensional and constructive working relationships with one's customers is the key to industrial marketing success". In addition, researchers beginning with Wind (1982) and including Cunningham and Kettlewood (1976) and Håkansson (1982) have testified to the importance of source loyalty and long term relationships. One consequence is that, particularly in mature markets, it is difficult to break into new customers. This means that the supplier should avoid any erosion of loyalty by his existing customers. He must maintain his competitive strength with key customers on a regular basis.

Industrial concentration is high and probably increasing. Sawyer (1981) reports figures for the five firm concentration ratios derived from the British Census of Production for 1975. For 118 industries, at the three digit SIC level, the largest five firms produced, on average, 50.6% of the net output. A similar high concentration is found in American industry (Mueller and Hamm, 1974) and in the European Community (Locksley and Ward, 1979) and, although slight, there seems to be a continuing upward trend. With the largest four or five firms accounting for such a high proportion of activity in many industries, an emphasis on customer analysis seems greatly overdue.

Empirical evidence shows that suppliers tend to follow the growth and development of customers often by adding new products, and even new technologies, to continue to serve the needs of that customer. Indeed, Parkinson (1980) states that close co-operation between suppliers and customers enhances technical innovation, and Achiadelis *et al.* (1971) have proposed that a thorough knowledge of customers' needs increases the probability of successful marketing of new products.

Although the argument above has concentrated on industrial markets, it also applies to many consumer markets, where manufacturers develop or sell "retailer branded" or "own label" products to a few large retailers and distributors. Indeed, Arndt (1979) has suggested that the 1980s will be an era of "domesticated" marketing. With the need for a customer analysis established, the next section describes the three steps proposed.

## THE THREE STEPS PROPOSED

### Step 1: Life Cycle Classification of Customer Relationships

Despite its limitations the product life cycle is a useful concept. Why not apply the same idea to customers? Porter (1980) points out that, as an industry matures, customers tend to become more price sensitive. Their own margins are squeezed and they become more expert purchasers. To counteract this tendency the supplier must either develop new substitute products, or find ways to lower his production costs. He must allocate his resources appropriately to different customer groups. Table 1 suggests a simple classification of customers to each category.

Management should have all the information available except possibly customer profitability and the use of strategic resources. The concept of strategic resources is the same as that used by Hofer and Schendel (1978). It includes the financial, technical, marketing and production resources, which are devoted to developing future business, rather than maintaining existing business. The classification of customer relationships is derived from the work of Cunningham and Homse (1982) and it owes a debt to Drucker (1963), who proposed a similar analysis for products. Before describing each customer category it is necessary to emphasize that only customers for one product or one relatively homogeneous product group should be included in the same table. Where a company manufactures several different products, separate tables are needed. Thus, a company which is a regular customer for product A may appear as tomorrow's customer for a new product B.

*Tomorrow's Customers*

These are the customers that the company is trying to gain, or regain, at home or abroad. They may be customers in a new market area, opened up as a result of

Table 1. Life cycle classification of customer relationships

| Criteria for classification of customers | Customer categories | | | |
|---|---|---|---|---|
| | Tomorrow's customers | Today's special customers | Today's regular customers | Yesterday's customers |
| Sales volume | Low | High | Average | Low |
| Use of strategic resources[a] | High | High | Average | Low |
| Age of relationship | New | Old | Average | Old |
| Supplier's share of customer's purchases | Low | High | Average | Low |
| Profitability of customer to supplier | Low | High | Average | Low |

[a]The technical, marketing and production resources devoted to developing future business rather than maintaining existing business.

technical developments, or they may be vital "reference point" customers in an export market. Sales to these customers are low, but strategic resources are allocated to improve the current sales position and to develop the relationship.

*Today's Special Customers*

These customers usually purchase large quantities: they are old-established and the company is continually engaged in development work with them. Frequently a supplier and its special customers have adapted to each other in various ways, mutual trust and commitment are at a high level and many people from each side are in regular contact. For example, such relationships exist between British Leyland and Lucas, between British Steel and Davy Engineering; Black and Decker and Marks and Spencer have policies of developing such special relationships with suppliers, and reports from Japan suggest that the structure is favoured there (Campbell, 1982).

*Today's Regular Customers*

These customers also purchase large quantities and the relationships are old-established, but the exchanges are less intimate, the customers are less loyal and more price sensitive; development work tends to be intermittent.

*Yesterday's Customers*

These customers are often numerous, but, although the relationships are old-established, each contributes only small sales volume and they receive little or no technical development work. Customers in this category are those in market segments now abandoned, or those whose requirements are now more like "commodities". The company continues to serve them, but without any great enthusiasm. However, they provide useful additional volume for little effort.

The number of customers and the proportion of sales in each category will differ from company to company. In the packaging company studied the proportions were as in Table 2. This company pursues an innovation strategy so that considerable resources are devoted to developing tomorrow's customers. The company also has two

Table 2. A packaging company's customer analysis

| Category of customer | Number of customers | Percentage of sales | Percentage of technical development expenditure |
|---|---|---|---|
| Tomorrow's customers | 7 | 1 | 39 |
| Today's special customers | 2 | 43 | 38 |
| Today's customers | 38 | 44 | 23 |
| Yesterday's customers | 175 | 12 | – |
| Total: | 222 | 100 | 100 |

very special and important customers with whom relationships are especially close.

In any one year the number of customer companies and the proportion of sales in each category is not, by itself, very significant. The value comes from carrying out the exercise regularly and from monitoring the progress of tomorrow's customers. To justify the development expenses committed to them they must move to become either special or regular customers. The length of time before such a move takes place will vary depending on the industry. The time also varies depending on the circumstances under which the customer took on the new supplier. Contrast the following two situations. In the first, the customer's demand for the product is expanding; he is seeking additional sources of supply, and so he approaches the supplier. If the supplier is familiar with what is required, he will be able to meet the specification quickly, and the time from the start of the relationship to regular supplies may last only a matter of months. By contrast, assume that the second situation involves a proposal from the customer for the development of a substitute product which will save him money. If the application is outside the supplier's current knowledge, he must learn the requirements, and devote research and development time to establishing whether his technology will provide a solution. This process may take years.

To summarize, this classification provides management with a useful overview of its customers. It shows how the strategic resources, which will ensure the future health of the business, are allocated among customers. Management can ask whether the resources devoted are sufficient and, by following their progress, verify that prospects yield a reasonable return. The existence of special relationships with some customers is highlighted as well as the customer's dependence on them. Is the loyalty of such customers in danger of being eroded? What can be done to strengthen the relationships? Or, are market conditions such that management should try to disengage from such customers, whose position in their own markets is weakening?

### Step 2: Customer/Competitor Analysis by Market Segment

The life cycle classification of customers provides a general overview. The allocation of critical resources is highlighted and management can take decisions to retain or modify the amount. The next stage is to introduce competition and this is done by the use of a customer/competitor chart for each market segment. A typical chart is presented in Fig. 1 for one of the food markets in which the packaging company operates.

The horizontal axis simply measures the customer's share in his market. Thus in Fig. 1 customer A has about 50% of the market, customer B has 25%, and there are two smaller companies. The vertical axis is a measure of the growth rate in the customer's demand for the product. This is not the same as the customer's sales growth, as it also reflects changes that may occur in usage of the product, owing to design changes at the customer or, because of penetration of the market by substitutes.

The size of each circle is a measure of the volume of the supplier's product purchased by each customer and the size of the "pie slice" represents the share of each competitor. Detailed market share information of this kind is not easy to obtain.

Fig. 1. Customer/competitor analysis: primary packaging for a range of packaged foods.

Buyers are often reluctant to divulge the split of their business between suppliers. To get round this reluctance, the supplier needs to seek information from several sources—from technical and production staff of the customer, from other non-competitive suppliers, from other more open customers, and so on. In this way, suppliers can build up a reasonably accurate picture. In Fig. 1, customer B purchases about half as much as customer A; supplier 1 has a dominant position with customers A and C, but does not sell to B; supplier 2, on the other hand, has a strong position with customer B, but a weaker one with A and C. The explanation for this pattern is bound up with the historical development of the trading relationship of each company.

To be useful, management should procure a customer/competitor chart for one product or one homogeneous product group. The product should serve the same customer function and be manufactured by the same basic technology for all customers on the chart. Thus, in Fig. 1 the function is the primary packaging of a food product and the competitors all use the same technology. In other words, the chart does not mix different types of packaging (glass, plastic bags, cartons, etc.). Although Fig. 1 is for a homogeneous product range it still masks differences between individual members of the range. Management can prepare separate charts where the additional analyses would yield greater insights.

The customer/competitor chart must also have a geographical boundary. Should it include only domestic customers and competitors, leaving out overseas companies?

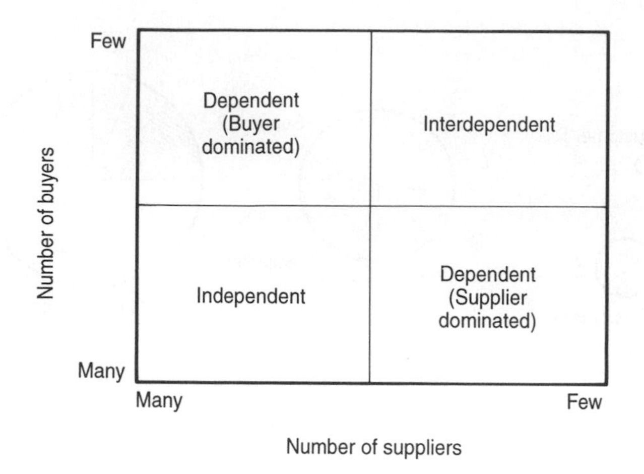


Fig. 2. Power balance in buyer/seller relationships.

The choice depends on what is relevant and what is practically available in the way of data. It is best to make the geographical spread as wide as possible.

The value of the customer/competitor chart is to assess opportunities and threats. In Fig. 1 supplier 1 has no sales to customer B. Should supplier 1 attack this customer? If it did, would supplier 2 retaliate and attack its large market share with customer A? Such questions are highlighted by the customer/competitor chart, as it enables management to see the strength of its position compared to competitors. Charts prepared over a number of years will indicate whether competitors are increasing their penetration.

In carrying out the customer/competitor analysis management may find it helpful to think broadly about the type of buyer/seller relationships which operate in their market segments. Buyer/seller relationships can take a wide variety of forms, but three general categories can be distinguished, as shown in Fig. 2 and Table 3 (Campbell and Cunningham, 1983).

Relationships are characterized by dependence when either the buyer or the supplier dominates. Relationships are buyer dominated when there are many suppliers and few buyers; when the share the buyer takes of the supplier output is high; and when the buyer has a low need for the supplier's skills, but the buyer's requirements are specialized, so that suppliers must make an investment (in special facilities or knowledge). There are many examples of such buyer dominated relationships between the automotive companies and their smaller suppliers. Independent relationships arise when there are few suppliers and few customers; when each party is dependent on the other; and when the buyer needs the supplier's skills, because the purchase is customized in some way. The supplier dominated and independent categories have opposite characteristics to those identified above for buyer dominated and interdependent relationships.

This type of analysis can also help management in the third and final step of the analysis.

Table 3. Power balance in buyer/seller relationships

| Criteria for classifying buyer/seller relationships | Categories of buyer/seller relationships | | | |
|---|---|---|---|---|
| | Dependent | | | |
| | (Buyer) dominated) | (Supplier dominated) | Interdependent | Independent |
| Number of suppliers | Many | Few | Few | Many |
| Number of customers | Few | Many | Few | Many |
| Share of supplier's output taken by the buyer | High | Low | High | Low |
| Share of buyer's requirements purchased from the supplier | Low | High | High | Low |
| Buyer's need for supplier's skills | Low | High | High | Low |
| Buyer's need for customized product | High | Low | High | Low |

## Step 3: Portfolio Analysis of Key Customers

This final step involves the analysis of key customers. Management can choose which customers to include. Key customers are likely to be existing large customers plus those on which strategic resources are expended. First, the key customers are analysed together, and then the most important ones analysed individually. The customer portfolio in Fig. 3 is an analysis of the key customers of the packaging supplier using a variation of the familiar growth share matrix. The co-ordinates are the competitive position of the company with the customer on the horizontal axis, and the growth rate of the customer's market on the vertical axis. Competitive position is measured by the share the supplier holds of the customer's purchases relative to the share held by the largest competitor. The positions are plotted on a log scale to accommodate the wide variations. Within the matrix the size of the circles represents the sales volumes of each customer. Thus, Fig. 3 shows that the company has one key customer in cell 4 whose business is growing steadily and where the company's share of purchases is very high. The company also holds a very high share of the purchases of customers on the borderline between cells 7 and 10. However, the markets in which these companies operate are not growing. On the right hand side of Fig. 3, the company has a weak competitive position because of its low share of the customer's purchases.

The main purpose of Fig. 3 is to show the position of the largest customers, but it can also be used to indicate the position of tomorrow's future prospects. These are represented by dots rather than circles as sales are negligible at present. There are three dots in cell 9, one in cell 8 and only one in cell 1. Thus, the supplier is devoting some of its strategic resources to developing sites with customers whose markets are not growing. The supplier justified this because its objective was to develop a substitute, which, if successful, would lead to substantial business. Nevertheless, the company would have preferred more prospects in the top left hand corner of the

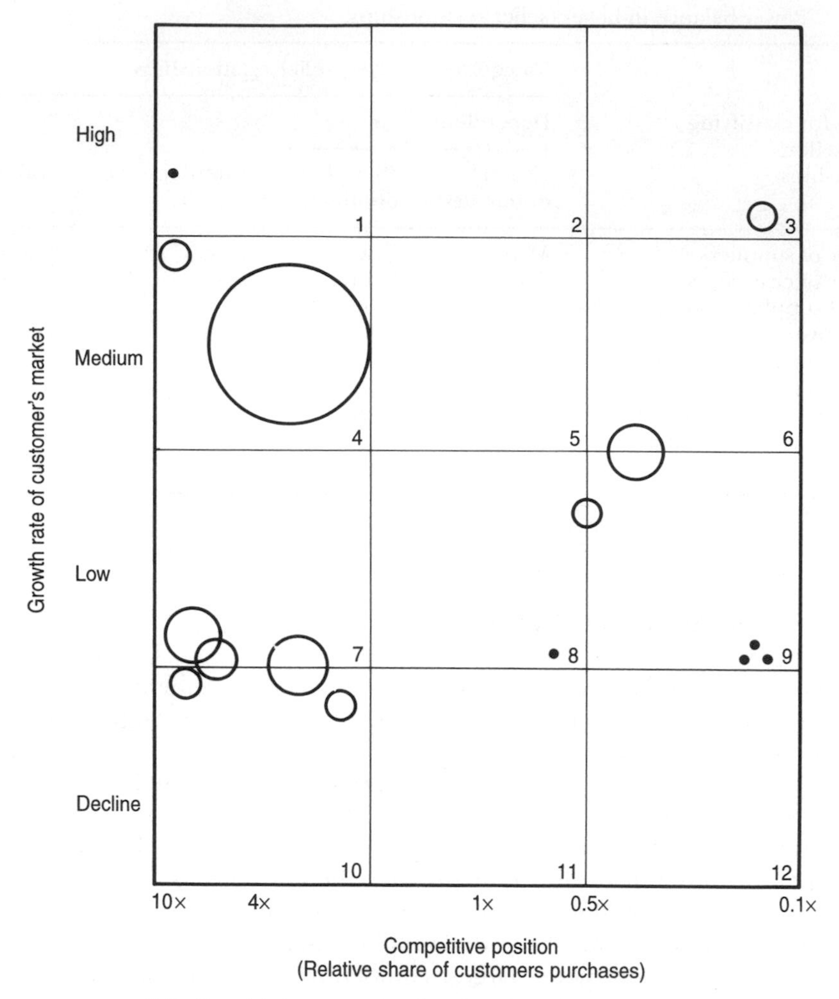


Fig. 3. Portfolio of key customers.

portfolio. The management implications of Fig. 2 are discussed in the conclusions.

Although Fig. 3 gives useful information about key customers, clearly, this is not sufficient where the largest customer itself represents 45% of sales, as in the case of the packaging company studied. A more detailed breakdown is needed as shown in Fig. 4 where the customer is split up into a series of subcustomers. This part of the analysis is similar to that proposed by Fiocca (1982). Figure 4 shows that the largest customer really consists of four separate businesses which have been classified on the horizontal axis using the life cycle categories. The vertical scale shows, as before, the real growth in the customer's purchases. The size of the circle is drawn to represent the size of the customer's purchases. A "pie slice" can be added to represent the share held by the supplier company.

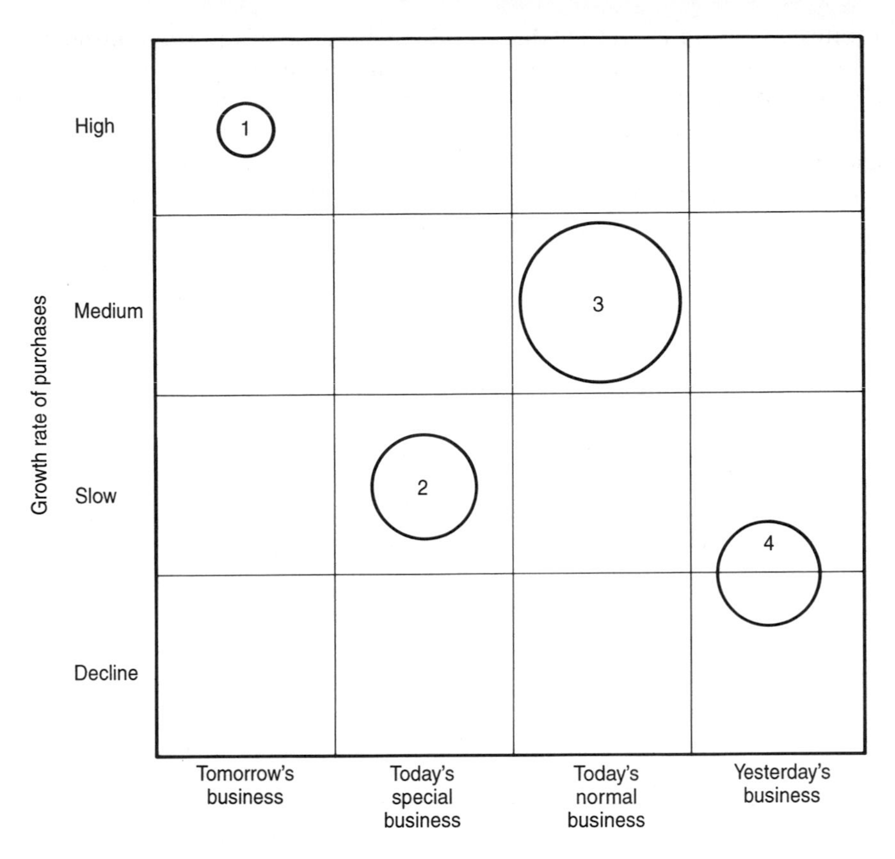


Fig. 4. Analysis of a key customer.

For the life cycle classification and for the customer/competitor chart only customers who bought products with similar usages manufactured by the same technology were included together; for the analysis of key customers the reverse is true. The chart should display all the different products sold to that customer. Figure 4 shows that there is a small but developing business for product 1; a slow growing, but specialized business for product 2; a large and steadily growing, standard business for product 3; and an average, slightly declining, business for product 4.

With the aid of these two analyses management can obtain a clear picture of its strategic position with key customers.

## CONCLUSIONS

This paper has put forward proposals to help managers in industrial companies analyse their customers in a way which will highlight critical issues. The analysis concentrates on customers rather than products because of the small number of key customers in so many markets. The emphasis on customers is compatible with the way forward thinking management intuitively carry out their activities, but not in the way in which company planning is undertaken. The presentation here makes explicit and logical what is latent and unco-ordinated practice in many firms.

The analysis comprises three stages which start with a life cycle classification of customer relationships designed to give prominence to those to whom the company is allocating strategic funds in the hope of developing future business, and to emphasize those on whom the company is very dependent. An analysis of the allocation of strategic resources leads to a number of useful questions. Are sufficient resources being devoted to developments with customers? Is the allocation right? Is the company obtaining the expected co-operation from customers? What sales are forecast to flow from the development underway during the planning period? What has been the record of success with previous development projects? Management may want to probe these questions in the light of their initial investigations. In addition, management can look at the number and importance of special customers and discuss whether the company is too dependent on them. To throw further light on such questions the next stage in the analysis allows management to take a closer look at its competitive position with different customers, in particular end-use markets.

The customer/competitor chart allows management to evaluate its competitive position in each market segment and assess threats and opportunities. A review of charts prepared in previous years enables a company to observe the impact of competition, and of changes in the relative importance of different buyers.

The final stage of the analysis takes the key customers, who have appeared in different market segments, and groups them into a customer portfolio along the lines of the growth/share matrix. Management can assess the strengths and weaknesses of the company's position with its key customers and question the choice of key development customers. The most important and largest customers are then subjected to a further analysis of their component parts to ensure that the overall relationship with the customer is being managed satisfactorily.

The overall emphasis in this paper is on the need for segmentation and market share calculation down to the level of the individual customer. This is all the more necessary given the inertia in buyer/seller relationships and the discretion which the buyer has in dealing with a supply market. Suppliers can waste much time and money in attempting to gain business from a customer who has no intention of switching from his preferred supplier. Management may have to accept a small share of the business and concentrate on producing, for this customer, an acceptable product with the minimum of service at as low a cost as possible (Campbell, 1982). Special developments, with higher margins, may have to seek more friendly opportunities elsewhere.

The emphasis on customer analysis has its origin in the IMP Group's approach to industrial marketing and purchasing. Many leading firms operating in concentrated and highly competitive markets recognize the crucial importance of the effective management of supplier–customer relationships, and the need to provide guidelines for the allocation of scarce resources to different customers.

The analysis proposed here was developed as a result of the experience of working with one company. The company concerned is a market leader in a mature market with a diversity of end user segments. It is to be hoped that other research will take up the challenge of developing and improving these proposals.

## REFERENCES


Achiadelis, B., Jarvis, P. and Robertson, B. Project Sappho: a study of success and failure in industrial innovations. *Report to the Science Policy Research Council.* Science Policy Research Unit, University of Sussex, Brighton (1971).

Arndt, J. Toward a concept of domesticated markets. *Journal of Marketing,* **43**, 69–75 (1979).

Campbell, N. C. G. Organizational buying behaviour: an interaction approach. *Organizational Buying Behaviour Workshop,* EIASM, Brussels, December 1982.

Campbell, N. C. G. and Cunningham M. T. Interaction strategies for the management and buyer/seller relationships. *Journal of Marketing,* in review (1983).

Corey, E. R. *Industrial Marketing: Cases and Concepts,* 2nd edn. Prentice Hall, Englewood Cliffs (1976).

Cunningham, M. T. and Homse, E. An interaction approach to marketing and purchasing strategy. In Håkansson, H. (ed.), *International Marketing and Purchasing of Industrial Goods: An Interaction Approach.* Wiley, Chichester (1982).

Cunningham, M. T. and Kettlewood, K. Source loyalty in the freight transport market. *European Journal of Marketing,* **10**, 60–79 (1976).

Drucker, P. K. Managing for business effectiveness. *Harvard Business Review,* **41**, May–June (1963).

Fiocca, R. Account portfolio analysis for strategy development. *Industrial Marketing Management,* February, 53–62 (1982).

Håkansson, H. (ed.) *International Marketing and Purchasing of Industrial Goods: An Interaction Approach,* Wiley, Chichester (1982).

Henderson, B. D. *The Product Portfolio,* Perspective Series, Boston Consulting Group, Boston (1970).

Hofer, C. W. and Schendel, D. *Strategy Formulation: Analytical Concepts.* West Publishing, St Paul (1978).

Locksley, G. and Ward, T. Concentration in manufacturing in the EEC. *Cambridge Journal of Economics,* **3**, 91–7 (1979).

Mintzberg, H. An emerging strategy of direct research. *Administrative Science Quarterly,* **24**, 582–9. (1979).

Mueller, W. F. and Hamm, L. G. Trends in Industrial market concentration 1947–1970. *Review of Economics and Statistics,* **56**, 511–20 (1974).

Parkinson, S. T. User–supplier interaction in new product development, Ph.D. Dissertation, University of Strathclyde, Glasgow (1980).

Porter, M. E. *Competitive Strategy.* The Free Press, New York (1980).

Sawyer, H. C. *The Economics of Industries and Firms.* Croom Helm, London (1981).

Wind, Y. *Product Policy: Concepts, Methods and Strategy.* Addison-Wesley, Reading, Mass. (1982).

# 3

# Understanding the Value of a Relationship

*David T. Wilson and Swati Jantrania*

TQM, global markets, the emerging Pacific-Rim economies, free trade, are examples of the forces propelling business to seek some form of alliance to protect and enhance their competitive position. Buyers seeking to lower costs through JIT and quality programs found that they could not manage these programs with their current supplier base, so they reduced the size of the base by creating single source relationships. Effectively managing the costs of these transactions is best accomplished through a close relationship between the firms.

Alliances are formed to develop new products or enter new markets. Joint ventures are developed to enter markets or to vertically integrate resources. New distribution patterns are emerging as firms seek low cost ways to reach competitors and to create competitive advantage.

Close business relationships are not new, but the purposeful development of relationships to achieve strategic goals is a recent development. Traditional relationships developed organically as the key individuals in each firm built close personal or business friendships. Their mutual trust allowed their firms to make specialized non retrievable investments that created structural bonds which served to hold the relationship together (Williamson, 1975, 1979; Wilson and Mummalaneni, 1986; Han, 1992; Han and Wilson, 1993). The slow naturalistic development of these traditional relationships permitted governance structures and a relationship culture to develop that supported the continuance of the relationship. Both partners (firms and individuals) found value in the relationships and strove to enhance and protect the relationship.

The IMP Group (Håkansson, 1982; Ford, 1990) model reflects their research on firms where relationships had developed in a naturalistic way over time. Today, however, strategic relationships are forced growth relationships and the failure rate as reported by scholars and the popular press is high (Harrigan, 1988).

How to develop relationships is our subject. We offer a conceptual framework that can be applied by both researchers and business people to guide their understanding and development of relationships. The goals of relationship development are in a broad sense to create a satisfactory and successful relationship. We draw upon current research to specify these goals in terms of the factors that seem to lead to

Reprinted with permission of Department of Marketing, Monash University, 1996, from *Asia – Australia Marketing Journal*, Vol. 2, No. 1, pp 55 – 66.

successful relationships. Then we use the concepts of a hybrid relationship as the process element for goal attainment. Within the hybrid development process we explore in depth the construct of value in a relationship and seek not only to specify the concept but to begin to explore ways of measuring value. We conclude with suggestions for research.

We draw upon the work of Wilson and Moller (1992) to specify the factors that lead to committed relationships and for the hybrid model development.

## THE KEY CONSTRUCTS

A strategic alliance or partnership may be defined as a relationship where a synergistic combination of individual and mutual goals encourages the partners to invest time, effort and resources to create a long term collaborative effort that achieves individual and partnership strategic advantage. This definition may be the motivator of a relationship but the glue that holds it together and allows it to develop are the constructs outlined in Table 1.

The constructs will now be discussed in some detail.

Table 1. Factors affecting relationship success

- Goal Compatibility
- Trust
- Satisfaction
- Investments
- Structural bonds
- Social bonds
- Comparison level of the Alternatives

### Goal Compatibility

Some significant portion of each partner's goal must be seen as being met only by collaborating in a relationship. The synergistic aspect comes from the merging of quality and price where buyers are concerned about "the lowest all-in-cost, the lowest cost when all is said and done, not the lowest initial price per unit" (Burt, 1989). Under these circumstances both parties may receive financial rewards and the supplier may become a better business and increase its operating profits from other customers. Becoming a single source supplier may have significant value. Having goal compatibility is important for the long run survival of the relationship because as long as both partners see their goals being met by joint action they are motivated to maintain the relationship.

### Trust

Trust or distrust has always been a part of business relationships. It is a construct in most models of long term relationships. Yet, it is a difficult construct to define as its definition seems to depend upon the research paradigm being used. Parsons (1977) suggests that trust is more basic to the formation of solidarity in groups than are moral, economic or power factors. Deutsch (1958), an experimental psychologist using Prisoner Dilemma situations, assumes the presence of trust to be groundwork supporting all acts of cooperation. Rotter (1967), a social psychologist, sees trust as a personality trait. Sociologists Lewis and Weigart (1985a) believe that, "Trust functions as a deep assumption underwriting social order and is not reducible to individual characteristics". This focus is what Dwyer and Lagace (1986) refer to as the "relational" conceptualization of trust.

The sociological view suggests that trust is a socially constructed reality that exists at the relational level and is characterized by reciprocity ("Trust is Trust"). "Sociologically, trust is conceptualized as a reciprocal orientation and interpretive assumption that is shared, has the social relationship as the object and is symbolized through intentional action" (Lewis and Weigert, 1985b).

Given this position, trust is critically related to the perceptions held by one party of another party's abilities, expertise and knowledge, as well as to the individual's perceptions of the other party's motives and intentions.

In the business exchange relationships, trust in the IMP Group model is seen in a social exchange context between individuals and between organizations. Young and Wilkinson (1989) investigating relationships among Australian firms support the grounding of trust on relationship history. However they found that trust is positively related to relative power among the trading partners. They state, "more powerful firms were very trusting... less powerful firms were less confident of the trustworthiness of partners even when the relationship was progressing smoothly" (1989). It is clear that trust is a construct that needs to be defined and measured. Nevertheless, it is the gateway to a successful relationship.

### Satisfaction

Satisfaction relates to performance of the key elements of the exchange process. A relationship will not endure if the supplier is unable to meet the buyers expectations. However, many sophisticated buyers are now willing to work with selected suppliers to raise their performance and make the suitable partners. Buyers must be satisfied with their side of the exchange or they will seek alternative partners.

### Investments

Both partners make investments in the relationship. These investments range from physical facilities to knowledge and training investments that may not be recovered if the relationship ends. In transaction cost theory these are transaction specific investments while Wilson and Mummalaneni and Han would call them irretrievable investments which bond the partners together. In both instances they affirm the partners' trust in each other and create a barrier to exit from the relationship.

### Social Bonding

Mummalaneni (1987), Mummalaneni and Wilson (1991) and Han (1992) examine the social bonding relationship between the salesperson or relationship contact person and the buyer contact person in a relationship setting. They found that social bonding leads to higher levels of commitment to the relationship. However, commitment is also influenced by the level of the investment in the relationship and the quality of available alternatives. Mummalaneni and Wilson conclude that, "Close personal relationships between the principals thus seem to have some, if not an absolute effect in enhancing their commitment to the future continuance of their role relationships". It should be noted that their study used a range of relationships which had more likely developed in an organic way whereas in many of the accelerated relationships that are occurring today the partners are being pushed into personal working relationships. It is clear that the individuals who must interact with each other within the context of the relationship need to have some positive level of social bonding for the relationship to reach its full potential.

### Structural Bonding

Organizations become tied together in relationships when the cost of existing becomes high. Investments dedicated to the relationship that cannot be used again tend to hold partners together. Intertwined technologies make it difficult to end relationships. Structural bonds may include social pressures one group in the firm places on another group to maintain the relationship because the former group is enjoying great benefits from the relationship. Structural bonds are a richer version of the transaction cost analysis (TCA) framework.

### Comparison Level of the Alternatives

Thibaut and Kelley (1959) have suggested that outcomes from a relationship can be evaluated at two levels: the comparison level (CL) and the comparison level of alternatives ($CL_{alt}$). The comparison level is the expected level of performance based on one's past and present experience with similar relationship situations. The comparison level of the alternative represent the level of performance that can be obtained by changing relationships. It becomes a minimum level of performance that is acceptable from the incumbent. However, structural bonding may offset the acceptable level of incumbent performance as the cost of obtaining the alternative level of performance may be too high to be offset by the gain in performance. Anderson and Narus (1984, 1990) have used these constructs in their models of distributor working relationships and found both CL and $CL_{alt}$ contributing to the understanding of the model. There is face validity for including these constructs in the model. Han (1992) found that $CL_{alt}$ had a negative effect on structural bonding meaning that the better the alternative relationship the weaker the structural bond. In a business situation a very attractive alternative relationship is worth giving some level of transaction specific investment or irretrievable investment.

## HYBRID ORGANIZATIONS

Thorelli (1986), Williamson (1991) and Borys and Jemison (1989) describe relationships using the term "hybrid". Williamson describes hybrids in relationship to the polar models of markets and hierarchies with hybrids being in the middle between the two forms of governance structures. Although transaction cost analysis (TCA) has been a major conceptual framework in the conceptualization of channel relationships it has not had the same impact on buyer–seller models. The concept of transaction specific assets does have a major role in the more behavioral driven model of buyer–seller relationships. Thorelli describes hybrids as organizational networks that straddle markets and hierarchies. Hybrids use networks of relationships of power and trust to exchange either influence or resources. His is a more behavioral view than the TCA framework.

Borys and Jemison (1989) define hybrids as "organizational arrangements that use resources and/or governance structures from more than one existing organization" (p. 235). This broad definition covers a wide range of organizational forms which makes it difficult to precisely define and analyze hybrids. They suggest that a theory of hybrids should, "address the multiplicity of issues raised by hybrids, and it should integrate previous research in these areas into a theoretical whole. Existing theory fails on these counts" (Borys and Jemison, 1989, p. 235). They identify four key elements that provide a useful framework to define the process of creating a hybrid relationship.

The four key elements are:

1. Purpose
2. Boundary definition
3. Value creation
4. Hybrid stability.

Borys and Jemison developed their view of hybrid organizations mainly to deal with problems between organizations such as mergers, acquisitions and joint ventures. They add supplier arrangements mainly as an after thought and as such in their paper, do not spend much time discussing supplier relationships. Their view that a new hybrid structure emerges when two organizations join together in an intimate relationship is a powerful and compelling concept. We extend the concept by merging the work done on modelling relationships with the four key elements of hybrid creation. We treat the first three elements of the hybrid relationship as stages in the development of the relationship. Hybrid stability is achieved by continuance of performance of the processes and outcomes of the other stages in the model. Within each stage there are processes that will take the potential partners to a set of end points that will allow the relationship to go forward, to recycle or to terminate.

Fig. 1 depicts the model and describes some of the issues to be resolved at each stage. When a relationship enters the stability stage the probability of long run success increases dramatically. Since we are focusing on the value creation stage we will not discuss the earlier stages in the process or the relationship maintenance stage.

PURPOSE
- Goal Definition
  - Your Goals
  - Mutual Goals
- Assess Corporate Culture Compatibility
- Openness of Communication
- Define Mutual Purpose of Relationship

BOUNDARY DEFINITION
- Resource Commitment
  - You
  - Partner
- Limits to Resources
- Trust
  - Corporate Reputation
  - Individuals
- People Commitment
  - You
  - Partner

VALUE CREATION
- Value Created by the Relationship
- Value Measurement
- Sharing Value
- Changes in Value

HYBRID STABILITY
- Hybrid Culture Maintenance
- Reward Systems to Support the Relationship
- Relationship Expansion

Fig. 1. Stages and issues at each stage in creating a hybrid relationship

## VALUE CREATION IN BUYER–SUPPLIER RELATIONSHIPS

Hybrid arrangements such as long term buyer–supplier relationships are created with an expectation of synergy, i.e. an expectation that the hybrid will create value in a way that each of the partners alone could not (Borys and Jemison, 1989). Sharing of knowledge, technology, and other resources between buyers and suppliers takes place in order to improve the competitive advantage of the hybrid and/or the partner(s). The process by which this happens is called value creation by Borys and Jemison; it is the joint effort that occurs once the relationship is formed. As the relationship develops, both partners need to assess the value created by their partnership versus alternative choices. Knowledge of where value lies for the buyer is critical for the supplier firms. In a recent state-of-the-practice study of customer value assessment, Anderson *et al.* (1993) found a number of business decision areas such as new product development or product modification, marketing communication, and pricing, where the knowledge of value was very useful to the suppliers.

In order to be able to understand how value is created in a strategic alliance, we need to look into the basic question: What is value? This section deals with these issues.

## What is Value?

Lawrence Miles, who popularized the use of value analysis in the U.S. industries in the 1940s and 50s said, "value means a great many things to great many people because the term VALUE is used in a variety of ways. It is often confused with cost and with price. In most cases, value to the producer means something different from value to the user. Furthermore, the same item may have differing value to the customer depending upon the time, place, and the use" (1961, p. 3). The situation is not much different today. Even when "value marketing" is the buzzword of the day (*Business Week*, November 1991), the questions still remain the same: What is value? What are its components? It is difficult to find answers to these questions because value has to be "closely defined to be meaningful, yet a close definition can be established only when we build a framework for reference" (Helfert, 1966, p. 1). Here we have presented such a framework and discussed the issues that need further research. Any discussion on value has to be in relation to the social, economic, political, and religious systems and environments surrounding the individual(s) concerned. However, in order to avoid further complications in this already murky area, we have focused on the general realm of economic value, rather than ethical or philosophical values.

In order to develop the construct of relationship value, we first need to examine the concept of value itself. It is a concept widely used in different disciplines in different contexts. Hence we start with reviewing the ways in which value is being used across disciplines; for example, finance and accounting, purchasing, microeconomics and marketing.

## Accounting, Finance, and Real Estate

Valuation of an asset is one of the key functions of these three areas. In finance, maximizing the value of the firm's stock is the primary goal of management (Brigham and Gapenski, 1990). Helfert's book on valuation (1966) is the main source for the different aspects of value presented below:

*Recorded value*: This is based on the accounting principle that the values of physical and intangible goods should be stated in terms of the original cost of the items. Hence recorded value is the amount a customer pays for a good in the transaction.

*Market value*: In this concept, the value is viewed from the stand point of the buyer and seller. Market value is a fair approximation of the place of a good or service on the value scale of the business community or society in general. It is dependent upon the nature of exchange mechanisms and the conditions under which buyer and seller meet. Market value as an indicator of economic value is most reliable when good in question has a broad market, i.e. when demand is frequent and supply adequate and stable. For example, New York Stock Exchange or the distribution systems for consumer goods. Market value is a current concept whereas recorded value loses its immediacy with the passage of time.

In real estate, the market value approach is based on a comparison of a property in question with other similar properties that have been sold recently, plus current asking price and offers, which helps measure the market reaction to the subject property (Tosh, 1990).

*Replacement value*: This represents an attempt to determine, for a particular asset, the current market value of an asset that could take its place, in order to establish a fairer value for the old asset than its original cost less any accumulated depreciation.

*Assessed value*: Assessments of value are made of real property for purposes of taxation. The current market value may be a starting point from which the assessor proceeds to make adjustments according to governmental policy guidelines.

*Appraised value*: This form of value is different from the assessed value in that appraisals of value are made in order to determine a "fair value" of the good in question usually to establish a selling price where no ready-made market value of the tangible asset exists. The appraiser normally specializes in making judgements of this sort and is familiar with supply and demand of the goods s/he is asked to appraise. Thus, appraised value can often be an approximation of market value.

*Earning potential*: Value, according to this concept, is measured by the total expected earnings (economic benefits) that will accrue to a long-lived asset over its useful life. Its elements are contained in the market value of an asset, because the demand for a good or service and the price a buyer is willing to pay will depend on the economic usefulness of the good or service. Its elements are also contained in appraised value, since the skilled appraiser will arrive at his/her judgement by taking into account the earning potential. Expected earning power is considered a key source of value for both tangibles and intangibles (Hendriksen, 1970). For a real estate property, the stream of net income that it is likely to produce for an investor, or its equivalent to the user, during the property's economic life is estimated (Tosh, 1990).

The value of most financial assets such as stocks and bonds lie in the streams of expected cash flows, therefore, all such assets are valued in similar ways: (i) Estimate the cash flow stream, i.e. find both the expected cash flow for each period and the riskiness of each cash flow, (ii) Establish the required rate of return for each cash flow based on its riskiness and the returns available on their investments, (iii) Discount each cash flow by its required rate of return, and (iv) Compute the present values to arrive at the value of the asset (Brigham and Gapenski, 1990).

*Liquidation value:* This value arises when an enterprise is in financial trouble or is on the brink of termination. Due to the unusual circumstances and urgency related to the selling of assets under such situations, their value upon liquidation will be a fraction of what they "were worth" to the going concern. Thus, liquidation value is related to market value, the difference being largely one of the circumstances under which the exchange takes place.

**Economics**

As Carver said in his article on value in the Encyclopedia Americana, "Value is the most important word in the whole science of economics" (cf. Falcon, 1964). All economic systems are concerned with production and distribution of goods that are of value to individuals, groups or society as a whole (Helfert, 1966). Given below is the summary of different aspects of value based on economics. Miles (1961), Falcon (1964), and French (1970) have been the key sources of these definitions:

*Use value or value in use*: It is the properties of a product or service that accomplish or contribute towards accomplishing a task or work. It is the utility of some particular object (Adam Smith, 1776).

*Exchange value or value in exchange*: This is the power of purchasing other goods with the goods possessed by us. Adam Smith (1776) contradicts value in use and exchange value by saying that the things that have the greatest value in use may not have high exchange value, whereas the things with the highest exchange value may have little value in use.

*Cost value*: From this perspective, value is the sum total of labor, material, and overhead costs required to produce a good. Marx (1912), for example, viewed value as an absolute magnitude – its cost of labor. Ricardo (1963) spoke of value as computed by the cost of production.

### Purchasing/Materials Management

In this field, value is examined mainly from its functional utility and cost perspectives. Miles (1961) views value as a measure of the appropriateness of the costs involved. He defines value as "the minimum dollars which must be expended in purchasing or manufacturing a product to create the appropriate use and esteem factors" (p. 3). Miles further defines use and esteem value as follows:

*Use value*: It is the lowest cost of providing for the reliable performance of a function.

This is similar to the functional aspects of value described by Dobler *et al.* (1990).

*Esteem value*: It is the lowest cost of providing the appearance, attractiveness, and features which the customer wants.

The key to assessing value of a product or component in purchasing management is value analysis. Value analysis is an organized sequence of investigation aimed at challenging existing product specifications, design, and production method (Fallon, 1971). Depending on the nature of the product, typical value analysis involves an inquiry such as: (1) What the material or part under consideration contributes to the end product? (2) What is the minimal function it must perform to give the end product the desired performance capabilities? (3) How much this minimal or contribution is worth? (4) Does the part or material used need all its features? (5) What else would perform the same function? (6) Can it be made at lower cost? (7) Can it be obtained from another dependable supplier for less? (Hill *et al.*, 1986).

### Marketing

Finally, let us look at the concept of value as described in marketing literature. Researchers in marketing have extensively examined the concept of value in the context of consumer products; the focus of which has been the relationship among price, brand name, quality, and perceived value (e.g. Zeithaml, 1988; Monroe and Chapman, 1987; Dodd *et al.*, 1991; Monroe and Krishnan, 1985).

Holbrook and Corfman (1985) define the value as "an interactive relativistic preference experience – or, more formally, as a relativistic (comparative, personal, situational) preference characterizing a subject's experience of interacting with some object. The object may be any thing or event" (p. 40). They present a typology of value with these three dimensions: extrinsic/intrinsic, self-oriented/other-oriented, and active/passive value. Mattson (1990) advocates the use of Hartman Value Profile which classifies value in another set of three dimensions: emotional, practical, and logical.

In business marketing, the work on value is in terms of value-based strategies (Forbis and Mehta, 1981; Wind, 1989; Wilson *et al.*, 1990), and in terms of assessment of product value using different value analysis techniques (Anderson *et al.*, 1993; Keeney and Lilien, 1987). Forbis and Mehta (1981) recommend the use of Economic Value to Customer which they define as follows: "The economic value to the customer (EVC) of a given product X is calculated by subtracting its start-up costs and its post-purchase costs from the life-cycle costs of a reference product Y, then adding the amount of incremental value it offers relative to the reference product" (p. 34).

Value-in-use (VIU) has been a popular concept in marketing. Lee's (1978) idea of VIU is essentially similar to EVC, it is "the calculated worth of an alternative (or "candidate") product when substituted for the product now in use (the "incumbent")" (p. 60). Lee (1978) and Uradnisheck (1978) have outlined the way to use VIU. Some of the other techniques of assessing product value as identified by Anderson *et al.* (1993) have been given in Table 2. Anderson *et al.* define value in business markets as "the perceived worth in monetary units of the set of economic, technical, service and social benefits received by a customer firm in exchange for the price paid for a product offering, taking into consideration the available alternative suppliers' offerings and prices" (p. 5). As mentioned earlier, they found that businesses and market research organizations use the value concepts in a wide range of strategies. Wind (1989) and Wilson *et al.* (1990) demonstrated the use of value-based pricing. Keeney and Lilien (1987) successfully used multiattribute value analysis for designing and evaluating a high tech industrial product.

Reddy's (1991) classification of product value components is a useful approach to understanding overall value. In Fig. 2, we present a part of his model, a 2 × 2 matrix. The two dimensions of value are economic–non-economic and intrinsic–extrinsic. Components listed in each quadrant are potential sources of value.

## RELATIONSHIP VALUE

We have discussed how value is measured in a number of disciplines and now will examine how we might begin to measure the value created in a relationship. In Fig. 3, we conceptualize relationship value along three dimensions: economic, psychological or behavioral, and strategic. The economic dimension moves from a simple cost reduction that is achieved through the relationship partnership to a complex concurrent engineering relationship that creates values through cost savings in design, in assembly and field service and also has the benefit of reducing the time

Table 2. Value analysis techniques (Anderson *et al.*, 1993)

1. Internal Engineering Assessment: An estimate of the value for a product offering is obtained by laboratory tests conducted by engineers within the supplier's own firm.
2. Field value-in-use assessments: Interviews are conducted at customer firm(s) to determine a comprehensive listing of cost elements associated with the usage of a product offering compared with the incumbent product offering (e.g. life cycle cost). Making explicit assumptions, values are assigned to these cost elements to estimate the overall value-in-use of the product offering in that application in cents per pound or dollars per unit.
3. Indirect survey questions: In a field research study, respondents are asked what the effects of one or more changes in the present product offering would be on certain aspects of their firm's operations. From these answers, typically combined in some way with other known information, estimates of the value or worth of each product offering change can be obtained.
4. Focus group value assessment: Within a focus group setting, participants are exposed to potential product offerings or product concepts, and are then asked what the value or worth of them would be to their firms: "What would your boss be willing to pay for this?"
5. Direct survey questions: In a field research survey, respondents are given a description of a potential product offering or concept, and are then asked what the value or worth of it would be to their firms: "What would your firm be willing to pay for this?"
6. Conjoint or Tradeoff analysis: In a field research survey, respondents are asked to evaluate a set of potential product offerings in terms of their firm's purchase preference for each of the offerings. Each offering consists of an array of attributes or features, and the levels of these attributes are systematically varied within the set of offerings. Respondent provide a purchase preference rating (or ranking) for the offerings. Statistical analysis is then used to "decompose" these ratings into value ("part-worth") that the respondent placed on each level of each attribute. The range of these values for the levels of each attribute determines the relative value of attributes themselves.
7. Benchmarks: In a field research survey, respondents are given a description of a product offering, typically representing the present industry standard, that serves as a "benchmark" offering. They are then asked how much more their firm would be willing to pay for the selected additions in product attributes or features to this "benchmark" offering. Likewise, they might be asked how much less their firm would expect to pay for selected reductions in attributes or features from the "benchmark" offering.
8. Compositional approach: In a field research survey, respondents are asked to directly give the value of selected levels of attributes or features to their firm. For example, respondents might be asked to give the value in cents per pound or dollars per unit for each of the alternate levels of a given attribute, where all other attributes of the product offering were the same. The values given for the attribute levels can then be added to give estimates of the overall value of various offerings to the firm.

to market. It may be possible to develop some estimates for initial cost savings of the design but costs reductions in assembly and field repair may be more difficult to estimate *a priori*.

Relationships should be driven by strategic goals. We use relationships to gain competitive advantage, to strengthen our core competencies and to create market position. Assessing the value of adding to a core competency is a difficult task. We may be able to make short term estimates of the benefits but it is difficult to forecast the future. IBM turned over the operating system of the PC to Microsoft not

| | ECONOMIC | NON-ECONOMIC |
|---|---|---|
| INTRINSIC (PRODUCT) | Performance<br>Reliability<br>Technology<br>Price | Brand name<br>Styling<br>Packaging<br>Appearance |
| EXTRINSIC (VENDOR) | Operator training<br>Maintenance training<br>Warranty<br>Parts<br>Identifiable post-purchase costs | Reputation<br>Reliability<br>Responsiveness<br>Diad relations<br>Service |

Fig. 2. Components of product value (adapted from Reddy, 1991)

believing it was a core element of this new product. Similarly chip development was placed in the hands of Intel. These technologies became the key to the future of computing.

It is difficult to assess the value of reducing the time to market on a firm's ability to compete. We know there are first-mover advantages but what value is created and how should the partners share it? The strategic elements of relationships are reason for creating relationships and yet they are the most difficult part to measure because of the need to project the future.

The behavioral dimension of relationships ensures the long term growth of the relationship assuming the basic product performs. People make a relationship work or fail. Social bonding of key individuals helps develop trust in the relationship. The establishment of shared goals is important as we may be able to estimate the economic value of reaching these goals. With time a hybrid culture develops that will help bond the relationship. This culture is likely to carry values from both organizations and may develop values not present in either organization. The closer the partners' culture at the beginning the easier it will be for the hybrid culture to emerge. Dissimilar national or organizational cultures make it difficult to find the common values upon which to build a hybrid culture to support the relationship. The value of the culture to support and promote the relationship is very difficult to measure.

In assessing the value of a relationship we may best begin with economic value. Then we may attempt to evaluate the strategic value created and finally estimate some qualitative estimate of the behavioral elements of the relationship.

The estimation of a value-in-use price of a product can be done most easily in business-to-business relationships.

Table 3 gives an example calculation of the value-in-use of a biocide chemical. The value-in-use price is about $40 for a 30 day treatment while the market price of a relatively ineffective competing product is approximately $5.00 for a 30 day treatment. The small machine shop owner may have a perceived value price of $10 based upon her/his estimate of the relative value between the products. A machine

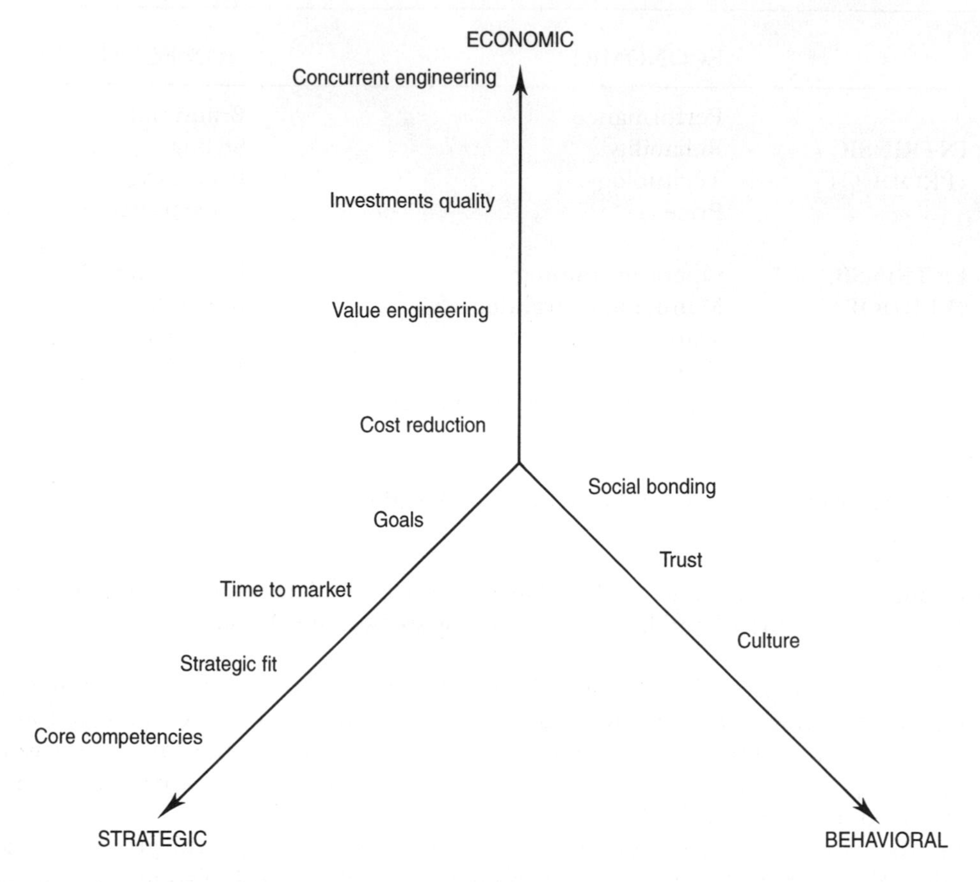


Fig. 3. The expanding dimensions of relationship value

shop owner spends approximately $950 per machine per year to maintain the fluid and assuming 20 machines the cost of fluid is $19000 per year. Any price up to $40 will save the machine shop owner money but the economics become blurred with the comparison to the current product. Although not very effective, the competing product may be seen by the machine shop owner as providing more value than its chemistry actually provides. The perception of value even in a relatively straight forward economic example illustrates the difficulty in estimating value in a more complex relationship. The economic dimensions of a relationship are going to be much easier to measure than the strategic and the behavioral dimensions in the relationship.

## CONCLUSIONS

Any relationship or strategic alliance creates some value to both partners. How this value is shared is likely to be a major issue in the life of the relationship. The greater

Table 3: Example calculation of value-in-use

Metal working fluids are used to cool and lubricate the work piece and the machine and to clear debris from the work surface. Being 90% to 95% water, the fluids become host to microorganisms such as bacteria, fungi and yeast which cause staining of the metal, clog filters, flow lines and drains and are foul smelling. Treatment of the metal working fluid for small machines with 50 gallon reservoirs ranges from using household bleach to using a sump chemical in pill form that lasts three days. Treating a single machine costs about $5.00 per 4 weeks.

Disposal of the used fluid costs $1.36 per gallon. The fluid is changed every 4 weeks. Two gallons of replacement concentrate ($5.68/gallon) is mixed with 48 gallons of water to make the 50 gallons of fluid needed.

A new product has been developed that treats 50 gallons of diluted metal working fluid for 4 weeks and can be used for 8 weeks before changing. The value-in-use is:

**No biocide treatment.**

a) 50 gallons × 12 × $1.36
= $816/annum

b) Every 4 wks add MWF (2 gallons)
= 5.68/gallon × 12 × 2
= $136.32/annum
Total Cost = 816 + 136.32
= $952.32 (1)

**If New Product (NP) used every 4 weeks but Metal Working Fluid taken away every 8 weeks.**

a) 50 gallons × 6 × $1.36
= $4.08

b) Every 8 weeks 2 gallons NP used 6 × 2 ×5.68
= 68.16

c) 2 packets of NP
2 × 5 × Pv
Pv is Price of New Product
Total Cost = 476.16 + 10 Pv. (2)

**Value Price**

| | | |
|---|---|---|
| (1) | = | (2) |
| 952.32 | = | 476.16 + 10 Pv |
| Pv | = | 47.62 |

the value created, the greater the issues in sharing the value. Understanding the value created makes it easier to negotiate a position within the relationship.

Short term value is easier to estimate than the longer term value that may be created during the life of a relationship. It is this future value that may be created that makes both parties concerned about dependence and opportunity costs. Han, Wilson and Dant (1993) found that two major fears about forming a relationship for both buyers and sellers was becoming dependent upon their partner and missing the opportunity because they were committed to a partner.

It is the uncertainty of the value of the relationship in the future that fuels these fears. If one knew which relationship was going to create high value in the future it would be an easy task to commit to the high value producing relationship.

Value is a problematic concept which cannot be ignored. We have attempted to raise some of the issues in understanding value and how to measure value in relationships.

## REFERENCES

Anderson, J. C. and Narus, J. A. A model of the distributor's perspective of distribution–manufacturer working relationships. *Journal of Marketing*, **48** (Fall), 62–74 (1984).

Anderson, J. C. and Narus, J. A. A model of distributor firm and manufacturer firm working partnerships. *Journal of Marketing*, **54** (January), 42–58 (1990).

Anderson, J. C., Jain, C. and Chintagunta P. K. Customer value assessment in business markets: a state-of-practice study. *Journal of Business-to-Business Marketing*, **1** (1), 3–29 (1993).

Borys, B. and Jemison D. B. Hybrid arrangements as strategic alliances: theoretical issues in organizational combinations. *Academy of Management Review*, **14** (February), 234–49 (1989).

Brigham, E. F. and Gapenski L. C. *Intermediate Financial Management*. The Dryden Press (1990), pp. 95–96.

Burt, D. N. Managing suppliers up to speed. *Harvard Business Review*, July–August, 127–35 (1989). *Business Week*, November 11, 132–40 (1991).

Deutsch, M. Trust and suspicion. *Journal of Conflict Resolution*, **2:** (4), 265–79 (1958).

Dobler, D. W., Burt, D. N. and Lee, L. Jr. *Purchasing and Materials Management: Text and Cases*. McGraw-Hill Publishing Company (1990), pp. 560–98.

Dodds, W. B., Monroe, K. B. and Grewal, D. Effects of price, brand and store information on buyers' product evaluations. *Journal of Marketing Research*, **XXVIII** (August), 307–19 (1991).

Dwyer, F. R. and Lagace, R. On the nature and role of buyer–seller trust. In Shimp, T. *et al.* (eds.) *AMA Summer Educator's Conference Proceedings*, Series 52. American Marketing Association, Chicago (1986).

Dwyer, F. R., Schurr, P. H. and Oh, S. Developing buyer–seller relationships. *Journal of Marketing*, **51** (April) 11–27 (1987).

Fallon, C. The all-important definitions. In Falcon, W. D. (ed.), *Value Analysis Value Engineering*. American Management Association, New York (1964).

Fallon, C. *Value Analysis to Improve Productivity*. Wiley-Interscience (1971).

Forbis and Mehta. Value-based strategies for industrial products. *Business Horizons*, **24** (May–June), 32–42 (1981).

Ford, D. (ed.) *Understanding Business Markets: Interaction Relationships Network*. The IMP Group, Academic Press (1990).

French, W. A. *An Analysis of the Brand Name–Product Quality Relationship within a Value Format*. Dissertation, Penn State University (1970).

Håkansson, H. (ed.) *International Marketing and Purchasing of Industrial Goods: An Interaction Approach*. Wiley, New York (1982).

Han, S. L. *Antecedents of Buyer–Seller Long-Term Relationships: An Exploratory Model of Structural Bonding and Social Bonding*. Working Paper, Institute for the Study of Business Markets, Penn State University (1992).

Han, S. L. and Wilson, D. T. *Antecedents of Buyer Commitment to the Supplier: A Model of Structural Bonding and Social Bonding*. Working Paper, Institute for the Study of Business Markets, Penn State University (1993).

Han, S. L., Wilson, D. T. and Dant, S. P. Buyer–supplier relationships today. *Industrial Marketing Management*, **22** (4), 331–38 (1993).

Harrigan, K. R. Strategic alliances and partner asymmetries. In Contractor F. J. and Lorange, P. (ed.) *Cooperative Strategies in International Business*. Lexington Press, Lexington, MA (1988), pp. 205–26.

Helfert, E. *Valuation: Concepts and Practice*. Wadsworth Publishing Company, Inc., Belmont. CA (1966).

Hendriksen, E. *Accounting Theory*. Richard D. Irwin, Inc. (1970), pp. 251–84.

Hill, R. M., Alexander, R. S. and Cross J. S. *Industrial Marketing*. Richard D. Irwin, Inc., Homewood, IL (1986).

Holbrook, M. B. and Corfman, K. P. Quality and value in the consumption experience: Phaedrus rides again: In Jacoby and Olson (eds) *Perceived Quality*. Lexington Books (1985).
Keeney, R. L. and Lilien, G. L. New industrial product design and evaluation using multiattribute value analysis. *Journal of Product Innovation Management*, **4**, 185–98 (1987).
Lee, D. *Industrial Marketing Research*. The Chemical Marketing Research Association (1978).
Lewis, J. D. and Weigert, A. Social atomism, holism and trust. *The Sociological Quarterly*, **26** (4), 455–71 (1985b).
Lewis, S. D. and Weigert, A. Trust as a social reality. *Social Forces*, **63** (14) June, 967–85 (1985a).
Marshall, A. *Principle of Economics*, (ed. Guillabaud), 9th edn. Macmillan, London (1901).
Marx, K. *Capital: A Critique of Political Economy* (ed. Engles), vol. 1. Charles H. Kerr & Co., Chicago (1912).
Mattson, J. Measuring inherent product value. *European Journal of Marketing*, **24** (9) (1990).
May, A. *The Valuation of Residential Real Estate*. Prentice-Hall, Inc. (1942).
Miles, L. D. *Techniques of Value Analysis and Engineering*. McGraw-Hill Book Company (1961).
Mill, J. S. *Principles of Political Economy*, 5th edn, vol. 1, Appleton & Co., Book III, Ch. VI (1865).
Monroe, K. B. and Krishnan, R. The effect of price on subjective product evaluations. In Jacoby and Olson (eds) *Perceived Quality*. Lexington Books (1985).
Monroe, K. B. and Chapman, J. D. Framing effects on buyers' subjective product evaluation. In Anderson and Wallendorf (eds), *Advances in Consumer Research*, **14**, Association for Consumer Research, Provo, UT (1987).
Mummalaneni, V. *The Influence of Close Personal Relationship Between the Buyer and the Seller on the Continued Stability of Their Role Relationship*. Doctoral dissertation. The Pennsylvania State University (1987).
Mummalaneni, V. and Wilson, D. T. *The Influence of a Close Personal Relationship Between a Buyer and a Seller on the Continued Stability of Their Role Relationship*. Working Paper, The Institute for the Study of Business Markets. The Pennsylvania State University, University Park: Pennsylvania (1991).
Parsons, T. *Social Systems and the Evolution of Action Theory*. The Press, New York (1977).
Recaro, D. *The Principles of Political Economy and Taxation*. Ch. 1. Irwin, Homewood, IL (1963).
Reddy, M. N. Defining product value in industrial markets. *Management Decisions*, **29** (1), 14–19 (1991).
Rotter, J. B. A new scale for the measurement of interpersonal trust. *Journal of Personality*, **35**, 651–65 (1967).
Smith, A. *The Wealth of Nations* (1776).
Thibault, J. W. and Kelley, H. H. *The Social Psychology of Groups*. New York, Wiley (1959).
Thorelli, H. B. Networks: between markets and hierarchies. *Strategic Management Journal*, **7**, 37–51 (1986).
Tosh, D. S. *Handbook of Real Estate Terms*. Prentice Hall, Englewood Cliffs, NJ (1990).
Uradnisheck, J. Estimating when fiber optics will offer greater value-in-use. *Electronics*, Du Pont, November 9 (1978).
Williamson, O. E. *Markets and Hierarchies: Analysis and Antitrust Implications*. Free Press, New York.
Williamson, O. E. Transaction cost economics: the governance of contractual relations. *Journal of Law and Economics*, **22** (October), 223–61 (1979).
Williamson, O. E. Comparative economics organization: the analysis of discrete structural alternatives. *Administrative Science Quarterly*, **36**, 269–96 (1991).
Wilson, D. T. and Moller, K. K. *Relationship Development as a Hybrid Model*, Working Paper no. 19-1992. The Institute for the Study of Business Markets, The Pennsylvania State University, University Park: Pennsylvania (1992).
Wilson, D. T. and Mummalaneni, V. Bonding and commitment in supplier relationships: a preliminary conceptualization. *Industrial Marketing and Purchasing*, **1** (3), 66–58 (1986).
Wilson, D. T., Corey, R. J. and Ghingold, M. Beyond cost-plus: a checklist for pricing under pressure. *Journal of Pricing Management*, **1** (Winter), 41–9 (1990).
Wind, Y. Getting a read on market-defined "value". *Journal of Pricing Management*, **1** (Winter), 5–14 (1990).

Young, L. C. and Wilkinson, I. F. Characteristics of good and poor interfirm relations: Australian experience. *European Journal of Marketing* **23** (2) 109–22 (1989).
Zeithaml, V. A. Consumer perceptions of price, quality, and value: a means–end model and synthesis of evidence. *Journal of Marketing,* **52** (July), 2–22 (1988).

# 4

# Profitability in Customer Portfolio Planning*

*P. Turnbull and J. Zolkiewski*

## INTRODUCTION

The importance of supplier–customer relationship management is increasingly recognized as a central theme of strategic marketing management. As a supplier develops relationships and its position in the market, a complex network of relationships will evolve, which will need to be formalised and planned. Central to the management of sets of relationships must be an integrated information system which includes both internal and external analysis of the marketing environment. A particularly important, yet often neglected, issue is the need for a real understanding of customer costs and profitability as a key input to strategic marketing.

This chapter investigates the managerial issues arising from the theories related to relationship and customer management. Much of this theory has developed from the work of the International Marketing and Purchasing (IMP) and Nordic School researchers (such as Håkansson, 1982; Turnbull and Valla, 1986; Gronroos, 1980; Turnbull and Cunningham, 1980; Ford, 1982). In particular the theories developed by Shapiro *et al.* (1987) relating to the management of customers for profit not just for sales, and of Krapfel and co-workers (1991) relating to assessment of a firm's supplier relationship portfolio, were tested.

A brief review of some of the pertinent literature is provided, followed by the results of an extensive and detailed case study which was undertaken in order to test recent theories of customer and supplier portfolio management. The analysis of the data from the case study, together with a synthesis of recent theories, leads the authors to suggest a new method for the classification of customer–supplier relationships. A three-dimensional classification matrix is proposed which takes into account selling price, costs and the value of the relationship. This classification matrix can provide useful information for strategic marketing decisions.

---

*An earlier version of this paper was presented at the 11th Annual IMP International Conference, UMIST, September 1995.

## RELATIONSHIPS MANAGEMENT

The importance of supplier–customer relationships has long been recognized as being at the heart of effective marketing management. The Interactive Approach postulated by the IMP group (Håkansson, 1982; Turnbull and Cunningham, 1981) proposes that both suppliers and buying firms are often involved in close, long lasting relationships within which episodes of exchange determine the nature of the relationships through adaptation. The relationship is itself a dynamic process which is partially determined by the environment in which the parties operate and also by the atmosphere of the relationship itself.

Turnbull and Valla (1986) observe that the management of this relationship atmosphere is an important marketing challenge at the micro level (see Fig. 1) in terms of developing a single relationship. They propose a revised marketing strategy framework and note the importance of management from both macro and micro market perspectives. In recognizing the contribution of the interaction approach postulated by the IMP group (Håkansson, 1982), they point out that effective marketing challenges such as market segmentation, industrial channel positioning

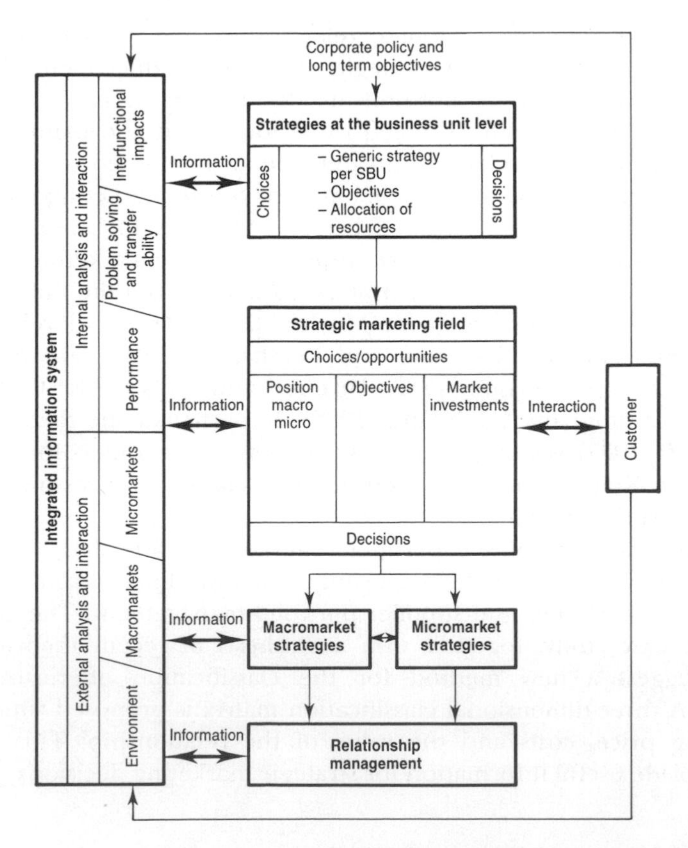


Fig. 1. Framework for interactive strategic market planning. From Turnbull, P. W. and Valla, J. P. (1986), p. 286.

and competitive position. Equally challenging is the management of the whole array of complex relationships that a supplier has. Cunningham and Homse (1984), recognized this issue when they introduced the concept of a portfolio of customer relationships. Cunningham (1986) also stresses the strategic importance of the successful development of various, different customer relationships that a firm has, especially with respect to their conflicting requirements in terms of scarce marketing resources.

Another important theme which management of relationships implies is that of relationship stages or life cycles, as introduced by Ford (1982) and Grönroos (1980) respectively. These two theories have a number of similarities:

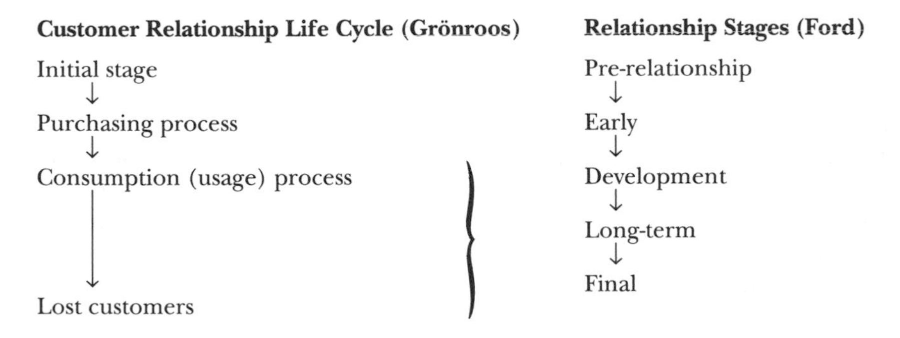


In his model Grönroos does not put much emphasis on the long-term and final (institutionalized) stages of a relationship, preferring to see the relationship as one of continuous movement round the same cycle without the introduction of specific adaptations.

Another important aspect of the management of relationships is that it is valid for both buying and selling. Axelsson and Håkansson (1986) investigated the role of the purchasing function within industrial firms and noted, amongst other findings, the importance that the purchasing firm attaches to the handling of the various relationships that it has with the suppliers and how the purchasing function can have an important role to play in balancing the roles of internal and external resources when adaptations/joint developments are being made. Turnbull and Valla (1987) in proposing an interactive strategic marketing planning framework argue that such planning "should integrate the adaptation aspect of interaction and recognize that the output of transactions is often the result of reciprocal adaptations by both supplier and customer" (p. 99). It is also important to recognize that as a result of this the supplier does not always have total control over relationships and strategy.

Ford (1990) also comments on the importance of relationship management but notes that it is most often seen only in the context of industrial export management rather than in the role of maintaining the whole portfolio of relationships which a company has. Developing Turnbull and Cunningham's (1981) argument he stresses the importance of a team approach to industrial marketing (rather than letting personnel operate in isolation). When a team approach to customer relationship management is adopted, all the appropriate departments in both the selling and buying firms (e.g. sales, production, technical, administration, etc.) are involved. This invariably results in better understanding of both the seller's and buyer's needs and successful adaptations are more readily made and managed by both parties.

Yorke and Droussiotis (1994) also recognized the importance of customer portfolio management in a firm's strategic marketing management. In an empirical study, they investigated the development of a customer portfolio by using the following variables: strategic importance of the account and the difficulty of managing that account. Following this approach they were able to make suggestions regarding future marketing strategy and resource allocation for specific accounts.

Shapiro *et al.* (1987) investigated the management of customers for profit rather than just for sales. They looked at the managerial implications of profit dispersion by examining three factors: costs to suppliers, customer behaviour and management of customers. When looking at costs to suppliers they found that a single supplier will often be selling goods with a wide range of gross margin even though the supplier may believe that they are aware that costs and prices are correlated. This factor is illustrated graphically (see Fig. 2). Shapiro *et al.* identify four main variable areas of cost: presale, production, distribution and postsale service.

Shapiro *et al.* further develop this concept when investigating customer behaviour and produce a matrix to classify customer types, as illustrated in Fig. 3. They describe the characteristics of each type of customer; for example, the "carriage trade" costs a great deal to serve but will pay high prices, while "aggressive" customers demand top quality while paying the minimum possible. They also suggest that while many suppliers believe that if they analyse the breakdown of their accounts most will fall into the "carriage trade" and "bargain basement" quadrants, actual analysis will usually show that over half a supplier's accounts fall into the "passive" and "aggressive" quadrants. Shapiro *et al.* (1987) comment that "Four aspects of the customer's nature and position affect profitability: customer economics, power, the nature of the decision-making unit, and the institutional relationship between the buyer and the seller" (p. 104).

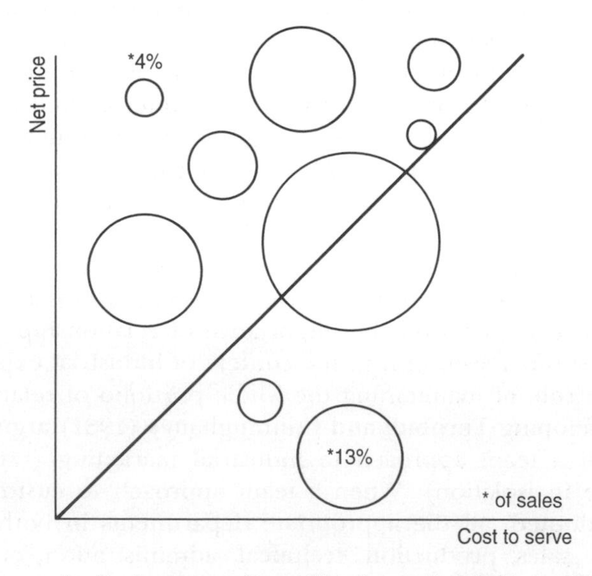


Fig. 2. Wide gross margin displacement. From Shapiro *et al.* (1987), p. 103.

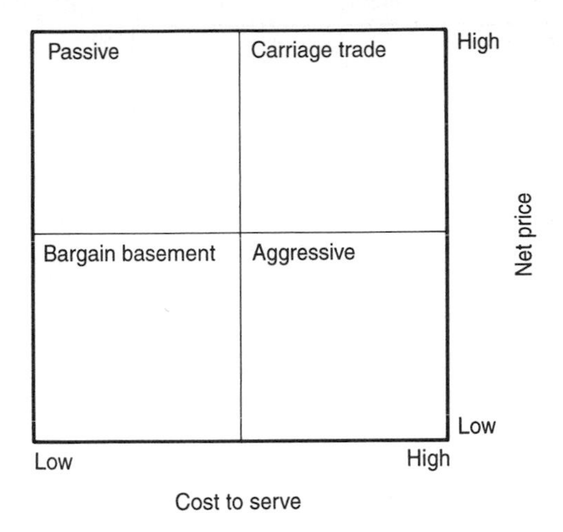


Fig. 3. Customer classification matrix. From Shapiro *et al.* (1987), p. 104.

They also observe that the position of any one account is likely to migrate over time, often starting in the "carriage trade" segment and migrating towards another segment. The direction of migration is likely to vary according to the customer's perception of the product and associated services. For example, customers who perceive the product as trivial will migrate towards the "passive" and "bargain basement" segments while customers who value the product will migrate towards the "aggressive" segment. Shapiro *et al.* believe that this dispersion of customer profitability can be managed by following an action plan, which involves: repeated analysis, pinpointing costs, preparing profitability, dispersions, focusing strategy and providing support systems.

Krapfell and colleagues (1991) also use a portfolio approach to analyse customer–supplier relationships and propose a relationship classification matrix based upon the concepts of "relationship value" and "interest commonality". This matrix is illustrated in Fig. 4. They also define four types of relationship – partner, rival, friend and acquaintance – and suggest that this analysis provides the basis for supplier relationship management which recognizes the importance of "internal political dimensions" in this process. They suggest that relationship management style should be varied according to the perception of power and interest commonality, giving six management modes: Accommodation, Submission, Collaboration, Negotiation, Administration and Domination.

The preceding review of the literature has shown how the theories of relationship management and marketing have developed from a wide range of areas. There have been inputs from both industrial and service marketing theories and from both European and American researchers. Clearly, the IMP researchers have made a significant contribution to the foundations of relationship management and marketing in explicitly recognizing the importance of relationships in an industrial marketing situation. Additionally, their recording of the various stages in a relationship along with investigations in the management and development of

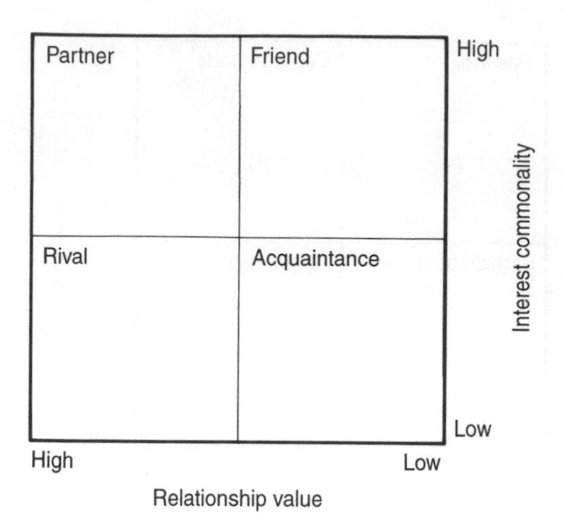


Fig. 4. Krapfel, Salmond and Spekman supplier classification matrix. From Krapfel, R. E., Jr., Salmond, D. and Spekman, R. (1991), p. 27.

relationships form much of the core research into this field. Similarly researchers from the Nordic School, particularly Grönroos and Gummesson, have also made important contributions to research. Grönroos (1980) proposed theories of customer life cycle and interactive marketing, while Gummesson (1985) concentrates on marketing as a series of customer influencing activities.

The management and development of relationships has also attracted a number of other significant contributions, such as those from Berry (1985), Jackson (1985), Dwyer *et al.* (1987), Shapiro *et al.* (1987) and Frazier *et al.* (1988) and more recent contributions from Krapfel *et al.* (1991), For *et al.* (1992), and Morgan and Chadha (1993). The authors would suggest that it is these managerial issues that are of great interest to working industrial marketers and, as such, the application of some of these theories form the basis for the research reported here.

## RESEARCH PROCESS AND METHODOLOGY

### Introduction

The brief review of the theories relating to customer relationship management, profitability and portfolio management suggest that this is an area which needs further investigation. Hence, it was decided to test Shapiro *et al.'s* (1987) theories relating to gross margin dispersion and to the behavioural types of a customer (carriage trade, aggressive, etc.) and Krapfel *et al.*'s (1991) theory of relationship classification and management, with respect to a number of "projects" performed by an operations group within a Computer Systems house.

Shapiro *et al.* consider the management of profit dispersion to be one of the key factors that managers should consider and suggest that managers have a tendency to manage their operations according to sales rather than considering the individual profitability of customers. They identified the three key areas of profit dispersion: Costs to Suppliers, Customer Behaviour (Customer Classification) and Management of Customers. These areas provide a number of avenues for further investigation, as discussed below.

While most organizations, if questioned, would believe that they were aiming for consistent gross profit margins, Shapiro *et al.* and Turnbull and Turku (1994) have noted a consistent lack of correlation between the net price charged and the actual costs to serve a customer, with some orders and customers generating losses and others very large profits (see Fig. 2). Shapiro *et al.* have also noted trends over time in which customers migrate from one quadrant to another; for example, customers who start in the carriage trade position are believed to migrate towards the aggressive quadrant as they become familiar with the product and become less dependent on the support of the supplier.

Shapiro *et al.* suggest that the dispersion of customer profitability can be managed and believe that provision of support systems and repeated analysis of the available data is central to this, while Krapfel and colleagues believe that management should be based on perceptions of power and the interest commonality of the relationship. They also see the process being driven from a supplier management point of view, compared with Shapiro *et al.* who see the process being driven by the seller.

## Research Objectives

Given the central importance of customer profitability management this study attempts to apply the above theories to an actual case. The objectives of the research were:

1. To identify whether wide variations in profit dispersion exist.
2. To examine the key aspects of profit dispersion identified by Shapiro *et al.*:
   (a) *Costs of suppliers*: To identify the actual costs and profits of the chosen projects (using the Shapiro *et al.* definition of costs) and to compare them with the costs recorded by the company.
   (b) *Customer classification*:
   (i) To identify where the various projects appear on the Shapiro *et al.* customer classification matrix.
   (ii) To compare (i) with the Krapfel *et al.* relationship grid classification matrix position.

## Research Approach

It was decided to use a case study approach for this research because, as Chisnall (1992) notes: "Some companies deal with a very restricted number of customers and, sometimes, two or three of these take almost the entire production. In cases like these, it would obviously be incorrect to use a random sampling technique..." (p. 277).

A considerable amount of secondary internal data was available for the chosen company, both in the form of internal accounting information and in the availability of staff for in-depth interviewing. The decision to use internal sales data as a primary source is supported by Crisp (1961): "analysis of your own sales records is a *basic first step* in any program of marketing management based on facts" (p. 42).

### The Case Company and its Markets

The Systems House chosen for the case study addresses a wide range of industrial markets, including: utilities, electricity generation, oil and gas production and distribution, and process industries. The company provides real-time control and monitoring systems to these industries and has an annual turnover of £20 million. The systems, both the hardware and the software aspects, are designed and developed within the group. Hardware is bought in from another division and other computer manufacturers such as Hewlett-Packard and DEC. Applications software is developed in-house and incorporated into software provided by others.

The relative importance of the different market areas addressed by the group changes over time. For instance, the process industries market has been depressed for a number of years and was relatively stagnant over the period being studied. On the other hand, the oil and gas sector has historically been one of the most important market sectors addressed by the company and this was the case over the time period being studied. For instance, in 1991 the oil and gas market sector was providing approximately 25% of the group's input. At the same time the utilities distribution market was beginning to reactivate, while power generation had moved into decline. The recent "dash for gas" is currently impacting on the scenario as is a considerable investment programme by the privatized utilities.

### Research Sample

Customers from one particular operations group were investigated, the Oil, Gas and Process Industries group, as they formed a convenient data sample. Ten projects, all of which had been completed within a 3-year period, for four different customers were used in this study. These were chosen because:

1. They comprised the majority of the work undertaken by one office during the period being studied.
2. They included a wide range of project values, from around £50 000 to £2 000 000, which is generally representative of the business undertaken by the company.
3. The clients were considered to be important, long-term customers by the company.

For reasons of confidentiality, these projects are identified as projects A to J in the following calculations. Projects A to E and I were for customer 1; the relationship with the parent group of customer 1 was established in the mid 1970s, while the relationship with this group had been in place since the late 1980s. The relationship with the group was complicated by interfaces with different operational groups and third party contractors.

Project F was for customer 2; the relationship with the company had been in place for the order of 15 years (since the early 1980s).

Projects G and J were for customer 3; this relationship was established approximately 6 years before (1988/89, making it the "newest" relationship in the study).

Project H was for customer 4; another long-standing customer who had been doing business with this company for over 10 years (since 1982/3).

The methodology used was based on cost and profit analysis on a project-by-project basis. The calculation methods used are outlined below. It should be noted that it is not possible to describe in detail here the complexities of the research analysis and how certain measures were determined and the underlying assumptions for some of these. This methodology is, however, fully enumerated by Zolkiewski (1994).

## Cost and Relationship Value Measurement

Shapiro *et al.* identify four areas of costs to suppliers which were examined: presale costs, production costs, distribution costs and postsale service costs. In the study these costs were determined from the management accounts, sales force records, etc., and, when costs had not been individually recorded, detailed interviews were carried out with the personnel involved. The management accounting system produced very accurate information for "direct" costs and very general information for "indirect" costs; in this case "indirect" costs covered many of the presale and postsale costs which meant that much care had to be taken in estimating these results.

The following were identified as presale costs and included in the calculations:

1. Sales time and expenses
2. Costs of bidding
3. Use of new technology/contribution to R&D
4. Contracts time and expenses
5. Management time and expenses.

Because of the complex technical nature of the systems provided by the group and the demands for detailed sales proposals made by customers, it was necessary to take into account these costs, which can be anywhere in the range from £2 000 to £50 000. Again, the control systems market is one in which technology is rapidly changing, and as such the group has to make considerable investments in R&D to maintain its position in the market and ensure that its customers' investments in technology are protected. Since 1991 spend on R&D has been monitored in the same way as the spend on customer projects. This provided data that were used to estimate the costs of the developments used in the systems supplied. However, such estimates are fraught with difficulties, especially if investment in R&D is considered in the long term and can be regarded as only arbitrary. (Discussion of how to apportion the cost of R&D in an environment such as this is beyond the scope of this discussion).

The production costs for the projects being studied included both time and materials and were taken directly from the management accounts, where they were recorded in great detail because they were considered to be direct costs by the company.

Distribution costs are negligible in this type of business and are included as a direct cost in all offers made to customers. Hence they were not considered as a separate cost in these calculations.

The following postsale costs were identified and included in the calculations:

1. Management time and expenses
2. Contracts time and expenses
3. Support time and expenses
4. Sales time and expenses
5. User conference

The user conference is held once a year for existing customers to provide a forum for customers to describe the systems they have introduced and the company to give details of its future plans and developments.

Relationship value was calculated (in the manner defined by Krapfel *et al.* as "a function of four factors: criticality, quantity, replaceability and slack...

$$RV_i = f(C_j, Q_j, R_j, S_j)$$

$RV_i$ is the value of the relationship to the seller
$C_j$ is the criticality of the goods purchased by the buyer
$Q_j$ is the quantity of the seller's output consumed by this buyer
$R_j$ is the replaceability of this buyer (i.e. the switching cost of assessing other buyers)
$S_j$ is the cost savings resulting from the buyer's practices and procedures" (p. 26).

## RESULTS AND DISCUSSION

### Costs to Suppliers

Table 1 summarizes the cost to serve for the ten projects analysed. The calculated costs for these projects have a number of estimates of costs and effort expended included. Hence, to allow for an appropriate margin of error, plus and minus 10% figures are also included with the results. These figures comprise amended values for presale and postsale costs while the production costs remain unchanged.

The results of the cost to serve calculations for the projects being studied are very interesting. The managing accounts recorded only the production and direct costs for individual projects and the managers at the company in question do not make any efforts to calculate the presale and postsale costs for individual projects or customers. This finding supports Shapiro *et al.*'s postulation that managers do not know the real cost to serve individual customers. The figures show that presale and postsale costs can form a significant percentage of the costs, as shown in Table 1.

The high value of pre and postsale costs is something which managers cannot afford to neglect, especially as in one case these costs are more than 20% of the total cost to serve. These results indicate very strongly that managers do not really understand the full implication of the cost to serve for individual customers and that, in this company, the management accounts system is not set up to record them.

Table 1. Cost to serve of projects A to J to September 1993

| Project | Cost to serve | | | | Total | + 10% | − 10% | Pre and postsale costs as a percentage of cost to serve |
|---|---|---|---|---|---|---|---|---|
| | Presale costs | Production costs | Distribution costs | Postsale costs | | | | |
| A | 57 180 | 615 154 | 0 | 3062 | 675 396 | 682 090 | 670 018 | 8.9 |
| B | 14 165 | 107 860 | 0 | 4415 | 126 440 | 128 504 | 125 514 | 14.7 |
| C | 13 299 | 133 039 | 0 | 1910 | 148 248 | 149 938 | 146 727 | 10.3 |
| D | 36 327 | 545 486 | 0 | 5316 | 587 129 | 591 756 | 582 965 | 7.1 |
| E | 16 462 | 102 958 | 0 | 1229 | 120 649 | 122 615 | 118 880 | 14.7 |
| F | 26 059 | 363 936 | 0 | 2159 | 392 154 | 395 289 | 389 332 | 7.2 |
| G | 14 025 | 226 840 | 0 | 573 | 241 438 | 243 060 | 239 978 | 6.1 |
| H | 9 812 | 64 029 | 0 | 9227 | 83 068 | 85 183 | 81 164 | 22.9 |
| I | 71 080 | 1 734 506 | 0 | 8657 | 1 814 243 | 1 823 103 | 1 806 269 | 4.4 |
| J | 34 485 | 663 652 | 0 | 9216 | 707 353 | 712 209 | 702 983 | 6.2 |

Indeed with pre and postsale costs, in the above sample, forming an average of 10% of the cost to serve (ranging from a low of 4% to a high of 23%) it is clear that they should be given serious attention.

However, the manner in which pre and postsale costs are recorded can prove to be extremely difficult to implement in a technically complex product context. The amount of time spent by R&D staff, sales engineers, managers, etc. on the various projects can be difficult to determine exactly, especially as the relationships are long term and involve a range of projects. In reality one can only expect records to be kept on a customer-by-customer basis, not a project-by-project one.

Also, the manner in which costs such as R&D are apportioned would be subject to great debate, as, very often, R&D expenditure is directed towards the needs of both existing and potential customers. Another problem area is the manner in which the costs of bidding are apportioned; in the examples above the costs of bidding have only covered bids to existing customers. How the costs of bidding unsuccessfully to potential customers are accounted for is not easy to determine – writing off these costs in a separate area could be disastrous especially if these costs were larger than the total profit from existing customers.

Whatever the difficulties associated with calculating cost to serve, it surely must be important for the cost to serve values to be given due consideration by management, as they can give very important indications as to the true profitability of either individual projects or the overall profitability of different customers. Another aspect of the cost to serve figures that can be analysed is whether individual projects within the overall customer relationships have low or high costs to serve. In addition to these data being needed to prepare the customer classification matrix, it also gives a summary of the effort needed to support different projects and/or customers.

## Customer Classification – Positioning on the Shapiro *et al.* Matrix

Table 2 summarizes the net price and cost to serve values for the projects studied and Fig. 5 gives the Shapiro *et al.* matrix for these projects. Shapiro *et al.* do not define what values represent low and high costs to serve; hence for this research it was decided, somewhat arbitrarily, to define projects sold for less than £250 000 as having a low net price and a low cost to serve as being one that was less than 75% of selling price. This results in projects B, E and G being defined as having a low cost to serve. In the first instance it could be assumed that low cost to serve would ensure that the project was extremely profitable and in the examples chosen this is indeed the case. It would, therefore, seem to be a logical management aim to achieve a low cost to

Table 2. Net Price, cost to serve and profit dispersion for projects

| Project | Customer | Cost to serve (£) | Selling Price (£) | Cost to serve as a percentage of selling price | Profit margin: Gross contribution (£) | Profit margin: % |
|---|---|---|---|---|---|---|
| A | 1 | 675 396 | 733 230 | 92.1 | 57 834 | 7.9 |
| B | 1 | 126 440 | 188 600 | 67.0 | 62 160 | 33.0 |
| C | 1 | 148 248 | 191 732 | 77.3 | 43 484 | 22.7 |
| D | 1 | 587 129 | 674 257 | 87.1 | 87 128 | 12.9 |
| E | 1 | 120 649 | 164 163 | 73.5 | 43 514 | 26.5 |
| F | 2 | 392 154 | 353 111 | 111.1 | −39 043 | −11.1 |
| G | 3 | 241 438 | 332 894 | 73.5 | 91 456 | 27.5 |
| H | 4 | 83 068 | 54 765 | 151.7 | −28 303 | −51.7 |
| I | 1 | 1 814 243 | 1 701 534 | 106.6 | −112 709 | −6.6 |
| J | 3 | 707 353 | 795 000 | 89.0 | 87 647 | 11.0 |

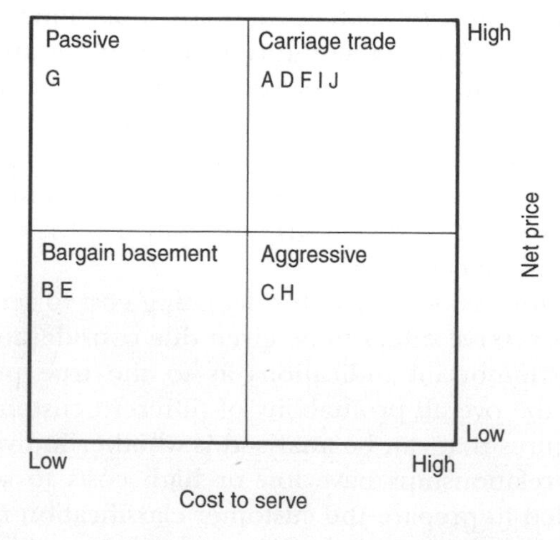


Fig. 5. Project positioning on the Shapiro *et al.* customer classification matrix.

serve and consequently highly profitable projects. However, such an aim must be treated with extreme caution as it may not always be good to have a low cost to serve; indeed the effort required to establish long-term relationships may often require a high initial investment, as suggested by Turnbull and Wilson (1989), i.e. a high cost to serve in the first instance. Indeed B, E and G were all follow-on purchases and the initial projects in the sequence, I and J, both have a high cost to serve.

Because of the nature of the business and the fact that only long-term relationships have been studied, it is not surprising to find that the majority of projects can be classified as being "carriage trade". However, the positioning of some projects in each of the three remaining quadrants shows that customer behaviour does change within a relationship and also varies from customer to customer. Hence, it is important for both managers and sales and marketing personnel to realize that a customer's reaction should not be taken for granted.

Another interesting observation on the positioning of the various projects on the grid is that the positions of some of the projects are not where the management in the company concerned predicted. For example, the group managers indicated that customer 2 (project F) was one of the most "aggressive" customers that he dealt with; this leads to the prediction that projects for the customer would have a low net price and a high cost to serve and therefore be classified as aggressive on the Shapiro *et al.* matrix. However, project F has been classified by the researchers as "carriage trade". This leads to the question of whether the arbitrary definition of low and high net price has caused the mispositioning on the matrix or even whether the nomenclature used by Shapiro *et al.* (i.e. aggressive) would lead to general confusion by non-specialist managers trying to use the classification matrix as a marketing tool. Another example, which has more interest as a research topic, is that discussions with the group's manager revealed that project G was considered (by him) to have both a high cost to serve and a high net price. Hence, it would be expected to be classified as carriage trade. However, the researchers calculated the cost to serve for the project as being low. Again this could be as a result of the arbitrary definition of low cost to serve or it could illustrate that the cost to serve a particular customer declines as a relationship matures (project G was the second major project for that customer).

Grid positioning can have much wider implications. For instance, should management aim to have as many customers as possible in the passive sector or simply aim not to have "aggressive" customers? It is also interesting to contemplate whether one customer can be positioned in more than one position on the grid when examining a particular time period even though this is not directly displayed in the examples studied. When considering industrial relationships where the links between buyer and seller are many and complex, it can only be expected that, if different operational groups are responsible for buying services, if the buyers change, of if the relationship has time to develop (perhaps even to a new stage), different behaviour is quite likely to be exhibited. For example, in the case of customer 1 above, the development group had close involvement with project A, which is in the carriage trade quadrant and has a high cost to serve, while the operations group awarded contracts B and E, which classify as bargain basement and have low costs to serve. Interestingly, if the environment of this customer was examined it was apparent to the researchers that the operations group were under much tighter financial constraints than the development groups. The operations group also tended to be responsible for "follow-on" work which by its very nature was much smaller than the development projects. This organizational arrangement can be seen to reflect the cost to serve positions observed above and that long-term relationships often have high set-up costs.

Studying these grid positions can have important consequences for marketing and this customer classification matrix can be a very useful tool for industrial marketing managers when they are formulating their strategies.

## Customer Classification – Positioning on the Krapfel *et al.* Matrix

In an attempt to test the Shapiro-based analysis and our conclusions, we also utilized the Krapfel *et al.* (1991) Supplier Classification Matrix (SCM). This is conceptually very similar to Shapiro *et al.*'s framework. Table 3 gives the relationship value functions for the projects studied. Clearly, this information is "softer" or more judgmental than the more specific cost data and requires certain assumptions to be made as described by Zolkiewski (1994). Not surprisingly, given the choice criteria of the sample, all projects studied have been classified as having interest commonality because they are all either repeat or follow-on purchases.

Table 3. Relationship values

| Customer | $C_j$ | $Q_j$ | $R_j$ | $S_j$ | $RV_i$ |
|---|---|---|---|---|---|
| 1 | High | High | High | Low | High |
| 2 | High | Low | High | Low | Low |
| 3 | High | High | High | Low | High |
| 4 | High | Low | High | Low | Low |

Figure 6 shows the customer positions on the SCM. Although the customers studied can be placed on the grid, they are positioned in only two of the quadrants (partner and friend). Hence, the rival and acquaintance quadrants do not appear to have any function; this may well be because the grid was designed to be used to categorize suppliers rather than customers. Also the positioning on the grid is not surprising as a "random" sample has not been used, i.e. because all the relationships are long term, the findings support the profile of the chosen group.

Having realized that the group studied is one in which long-term relationships are the norm, it calls into question whether the axes on the grid are pertinent for this situation. On first examination, it would seem that the interest commonality dimension does not provide any useful classification data. This may be because the interpretation used for interest commonality in this research is inaccurate or, indeed, because the dimension is inappropriate when considering purchasers rather than suppliers. Investigating this concept further requires another look at Krapfel *et al's* definition: "Interest commonality reflects an actor's economic goals and their perception of the trading partner's economic goals. When buyer and seller economic

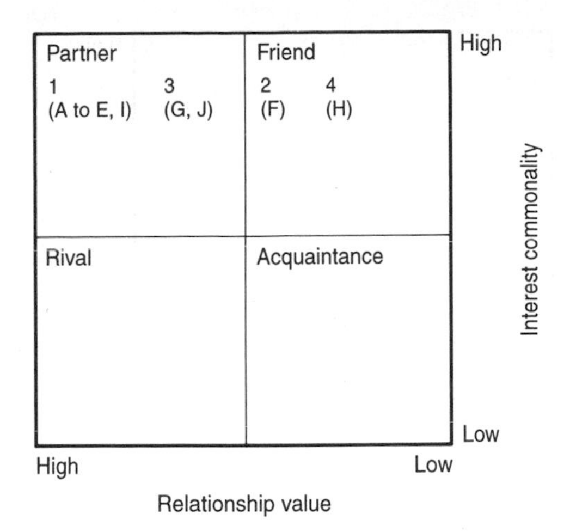


Fig. 6. Project positioning on the Krapfel, Salmond and Spekman supplier classification matrix.

goals are compatible, interest commonality is high, and vice versa" (p. 26). This suggests that the interpretation used in the research is reasonable. Hence, in a more holistic analysis of a total business environment where there was a mixture of new and long-term relationships, this grid could still provide some useful information. Even though this may be the case, it still seems apparent that the Krapfel grid is much more pertinent when analysing relationships with suppliers (as it was intended to do).

## Comparison of the Two Matrices

Studying Fig. 5 and 6 shows that there does not appear to be an easy correlation between the Krapfel *et al.* and the Shapiro *et al.* matrices. This is not surprising because of the differences in the axes, with the Shapiro axes being relatively easy to measure while the Krapfel axes are much more subjective. However, this observation does not mean that the concepts put forward by these two groups are completely separate. For instance using the Krapfel relationship value dimension to replace the Shapiro net price dimension can produce quite an interesting effect, as illustrated in Fig. 7.

This matrix provides an interesting comparison to the Shapiro matrix given in Fig. 5, and may well merit further investigation. However, as a straightforward management aid, the use of the net price cannot be ignored, and therefore it may not be more appropriate to develop a three-dimensional grid with cost to serve, net price and relationship value as the axes. Such a grid is illustrated in Fig. 8. This grid would certainly help when segmenting the customers of any firm, by providing a more detailed breakdown than could be gained from simply using a two-dimensional breakdown. For example, if the projects studied above are considered and positioned on this grid, six of the eight segments would be occupied, as given in Table 4.

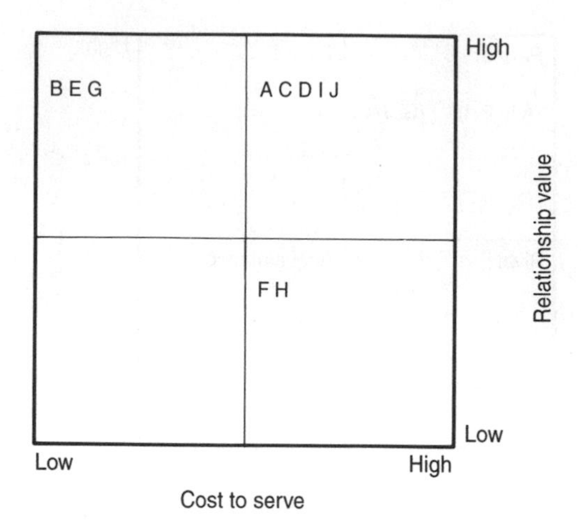


Fig. 7. Revised customer classification matrix.

## Profit Dispersion

*(1) Project Profitability*

Table 2 gives the individual project profitabilities using the profit margins calculated via the Shapiro *et al.* cost to serve method.

This matrix provides an interesting comparison to the Shapiro matrix given in Fig. 5, and may well merit further investigation. However, as a straightforward management aid, the use of net price cannot be ignored, and therefore it may be more appropriate to develop a three-dimensional grid with cost to serve, net price and relationship value as the axes. Such a grid is illustrated in Fig. 8. This grid would

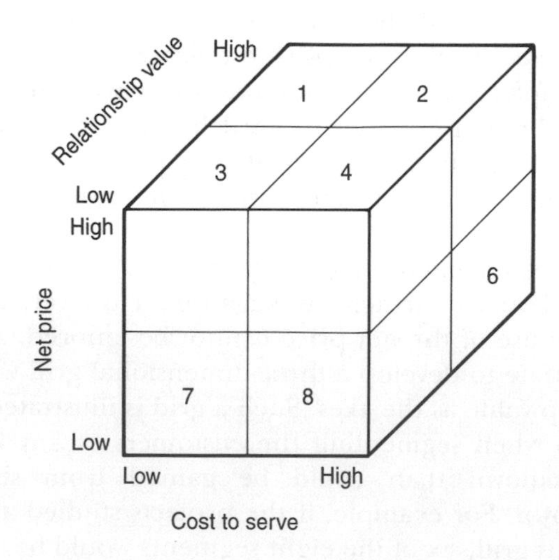


Fig. 8. Proposed three-dimensional customer classification matrix.

Table 4. Positioning on the three-dimensional customer classification matrix

| Project | Cost to serve | Relationship value | Net price | Grid position (cell 1 to 8) |
|---|---|---|---|---|
| A | High | High | High | 2 |
| B | Low | High | Low | 5 |
| C | High | High | Low | 6 |
| D | High | High | High | 2 |
| E | Low | High | Low | 5 |
| F | High | Low | High | 4 |
| G | Low | High | High | 1 |
| H | High | Low | Low | 8 |
| I | High | High | High | 2 |
| J | High | High | High | 2 |

certainly help when segmenting the customers of any firm, by providing a more detailed breakdown than could be gained from simply using a two-dimensional breakdown. For example, if the projects studied above are considered and positioned on this grid, six of the eight segments would be occupied, as given in Table 4.

## Profit Dispersion

*(1) Project Profitability*

Table 2 gives the individual project profitabilities using the profit margins calculated via the Shapiro *et al.* cost to serve method. Graphical representation of net price

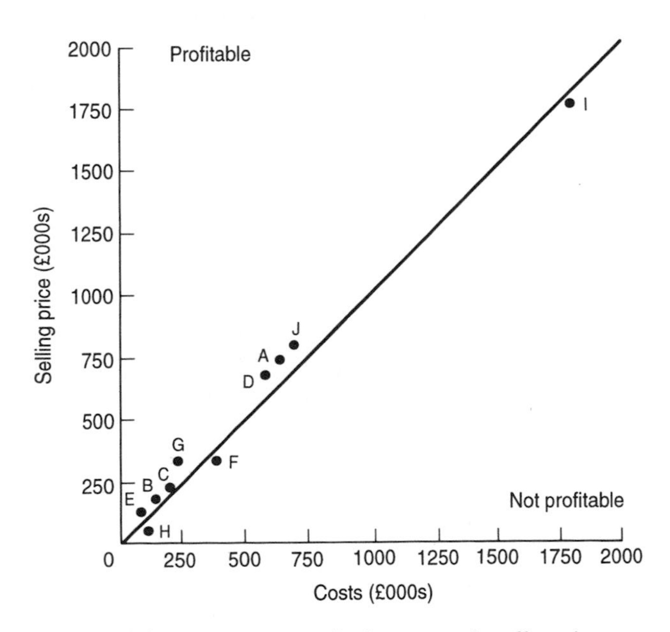


Fig. 9. Overall summary of the gross margin displacement for all projects.

against cost to serve is shown in Fig. 9. It is interesting to note that a wide range in project profit margin (from – 52% to 33%) is observed across the whole range of projects and that there is some indication that customers could also be classified as having a wide range of profitability. This observation confirms Shapiro *et al.*'s supposition about the variability of profitability and is also interesting from a management point of view, as the managers stated aim is to make about 5% net profit on all projects and this is clearly not the case.

*(2) Customer Profitability*

The average profitability of each customer has been calculated:

| | |
|---|---|
| customer 1 | 16.1% |
| customer 2 | −11.1% |
| customer 3 | 19.3% |
| customer 4 | −51.7% |

which illustrates that a wide range of customer profitability has been observed in this study.

The results give a customer profitability ranking of 3, 1, 2 and 4. This ranking suggests that the relationships with customer 2 and (especially) 4 should be reviewed. However, the data sample used is only part of the overall picture; for example, it does not cover all the work done for the customers being studied and does not, therefore, give a good overview of the real situation.

It is also interesting to note the change in profitability over time by customer. For customer 3 it increases from 11.02% to 27.47% while for customer 1 the fluctuations are not quite so straightforward and are illustrated in Fig. 10. This also seems to reflect the situation noted by Shapiro *et al.* in one capital equipment company where "the big national accounts were generating losses that were large enough to offset the rise in volume and the profitability of smaller, allegedly less attractive accounts"

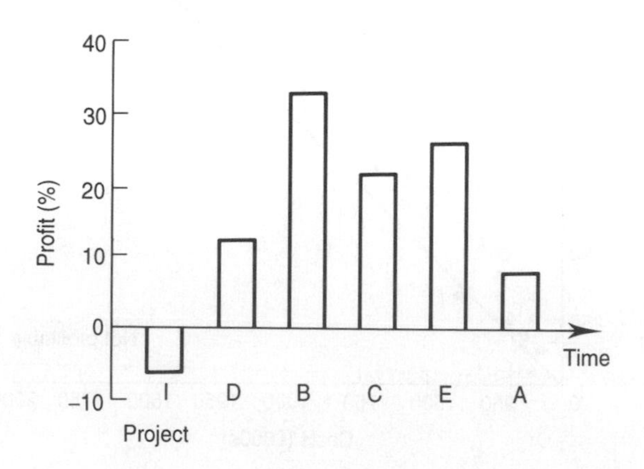


Fig. 10. Changes in profitability of customer 1's projects over time.

(p. 101). This finding gives an indication of the complex nature of the customer–supplier relationship and shows that it would be simplistic to expect a constantly upward increase in the profits made from a single customer (see Turnbull and Turku, 1994).

### Management of Customer Relationships/Portfolio Management

The results of the study support the suggestion made by Shapiro *et al.* that the dispersion of customer profitability can be managed and shows that the need for the provision of support systems and repeated analysis of the available data is extremely pertinent for effective relationship management. It seems to be especially important in an environment such as that in the firm being studied, where long-term customer–supplier relationships are crucial and need a considerable amount of investment. Managers need to consider the cost to serve of each project/customer and how this is changing over time, rather than simply writing off management and sales/marketing time as an overhead.

Also of interest is the variation in customer classification positioning on the Shapiro *et al.* grid, over the short time-span of the study. This clearly supports the concept of considering the individual projects (or buying episodes) for a customer as a portfolio of projects and suggests that a portfolio management approach may be a useful tool. For example, customer 1 has projects that appear in three different quadrants: carriage trade (projects A, D and I), bargain basement (projects B and E) and aggressive (project C). The single project for customer 2 (F) is classified as carriage trade. Customer 3 has two projects, each of which is in a different quadrant: carriage trade (project J) and passive (project G). Customer 4's project is classified as aggressive (project H).

## SUMMARY AND CONCLUSION

The costs of the projects being studied have been identified and calculated and have been used to categorize those projects in terms of both the Shapiro *et al.* and Krapfel *et al.* matrices. However, it is interesting to note that, apart from calculations of the profitability of the various projects and customers, quantitative measures of customer/portfolio management have not been easy to identify.

This research has supported Shapiro *et al.*'s suggestion that the real costs of supporting various customers should not be considered in isolation by managers. It also shows a high variation in these costs, indicating that such figures should be considered by management, but with the caveat that high costs to serve are not necessarily an indication of inefficiency and may well be essential in a business that revolves around high capital investment and long-term relationships.

The Shapiro *et al.* customer classification matrix has been shown to have some value when considering a firm's current market position, while it seems that the Krapfel *et al.* supplier classification matrix is less appropriate, although it may be more useful for management of a firm's supplier portfolio. There may be, however, an argument for combining concepts from both schools of thought and producing a two-dimensional grid with cost to serve and relationship value as the axes and/or a three-dimensional grid with cost to serve, net price and relationship value as the axes to act as marketing analysis tools.

A wide range of profit dispersion has been observed, as predicted by Shapiro *et al.* but because of the small sample of data used and the relatively short time-period of the study (cf. the average length of customer–supplier relationships in this company) it should be regarded only as providing general evidence of their suppositions. Wide variations in the profitability of the work associated with a particular customer have been noted and these observations have important implications for the way in which customers should be managed. Limitations of the research study preclude any real consideration of the whole customer portfolio of the firm but do suggest that it may well be important to consider portfolios of projects on a customer-to-customer basis, i.e. portfolio within the overall portfolio.

These results suggest a number of implications for management, as follows:

1. Calculating the cost-to-serve for both individual projects and on a customer-by-customer basis would prove to be a very powerful management aid when undertaking strategic planning.
2. Monitoring "migration" patterns of customers (with respect to grid positioning) is extremely important and should be a central theme to strategic marketing planning.
3. Using different styles of management according to where a customer/project falls on the grid could also prove to be very beneficial.

There are also a number of implications for marketing theory:

1. The research seems to validate Shapiro *et al.*'s findings on the wide range of profit dispersion and the applicability of their customer classification matrix in an industrial market environment. However, where long-term relationships are the norm there could be an argument for developing the matrix in three dimensions or amending the matrix dimensions.
2. The observations suggest that the migration of customers over time is more complex than has been suggested by Shapiro *et al.* (for example, the movement from carriage trade to passive), and this area needs further investigation and explanation.
3. The concept of a portfolio of projects per customer, i.e. a portfolio within a portfolio, needs to be considered as an area within portfolio management.

## REFERENCES

Axelsson, B. and Håkansson, H. The development role of purchasing in an internationally oriented company. In *Research in International Marketing*. Turnbull, P. W. and Paliwoda, J. (eds), Croom Helm, London (1986).

Berry, L. L. Relationship marketing. In Berry, L. L., Shostack, G. L. and Upah, G. D. (eds), *Emerging Perspectives on Service Marketing*. American Marketing Association, Chicago (1985).

Chisnall, P. M. *Marketing Research*. McGraw-Hill, London (1992).

Crisp, R. D. *Sales Planning and Control*. McGraw-Hill, New York (1961).

Cunningham, M. T. The British approach to Europe. In Turnbull, P. W. and Valla, J. P. (eds), *Strategies for International Industrial Marketing*. Croom Helm, London (1986).

Cunningham, M. T. and Homse, E. *Controlling the Marketing–Purchasing Interface: An Analysis of Personal Contacts in Industrial Markets*, Occasional Paper No. 8401, Department of Management Sciences, UMIST (1984).

Dwyer, F. R., Schurr, P. H. and Oh, S. Developing buyer–seller relationships. *Journal of Marketing*, **51**, 11–27 (1987).

Ford, D. (ed.) *Understanding Business Markets*. Academic Press (1990).

Ford, D., Lamming, R. and Thomas, R. Relationship strategy, development and purchasing practice. In Salle, R., Spencer, R. and Valla, J. P. (eds), *Business Networks in an International Context: Recent Research Developments, Proceedings of the 8th IMP Conference*. Group ESC, Lyon (1992).

Frazier, G. L., Spekman, R. E. and O'Neal, C. R. Just-In-Time Exchange Relationships in Industrial Markets. *Journal of Marketing*, **52**, 52–67 (1988).

Grönroos, C. Designing a long range marketing strategy for services. *Long Range Planning*, **13**, 36–42.

Grönroos, C. *Service Management and Marketing*. Lexington Books, USA (1990).

Grönroos, C. and Gummesson, E. (eds). *Service Marketing – Nordic School Perspectives*. University of Stockholm, Stockholm (1985).

Gummesson, E. Applying service concepts in the industrial sector – towards a new concept of marketing. In Grönroos, C. and Gummesson, E. (eds), *Service Marketing – Nordic School Perspectives*. University of Stockholm, Stockholm (1985).

Gummesson, E. The new marketing – developing long-term interactive relationships. *Long Range Planning*, **20** (4), 10–20 (1987).

Håkansson, H. (ed.) *International Marketing and Purchasing of Industrial Goods*. John Wiley & Sons, New York (1982).

Jackson, B. B. Build Customer Relationships that Last. *Harvard Business Review, November-December 1985*, 120–128 (1985).

Krapfel, R. E. Jr., Salmond, D. and Spekman, R. A Strategic Approach to Managing Buyer-Seller Relationships. *European Journal of Marketing*, **25** (9) 22–37 (1991).

Morgan, R. E. and Chadha, S. Relationship Marketing at the Service Encounter: the Case of Life Insurance. *The Service Industries Journal*, **13** (1), 112–125 (1993).

Salle, R., Spencer, R. and Valla, J. P. (eds). *Business Networks in an International Context: Recent Research Developments, Proceedings of the 8th IMP Conference*, Lyon, Group ESC (1992).

Shapiro, B. P., Rangan, V. K, Moriarty, R. T. and Ross, E. B. Manage Customers for Profits (not Just Sales). *Harvard Business Review*, September-October 1987, 101–108 (1987).

Turnbull, P. W. Interaction and International Marketing: An Investment Process. *International Marketing Review*, **6**, 7–19 (1987).

Turnbull, P. and Cunningham, M. T. (eds). *International Marketing and Purchasing*. London: The Macmillan Press Ltd (1981).

Turnbull, P. W. and Paliwoda, S. J. (eds). *Research in International Marketing*. London: Croom Helm (1986).

Turnbull, P. W. and Paliwoda, S. J. (eds). *Proceedings of the 4th IMP Conference: September 1988, Research Developments in International Marketing*, Manchester: UMIST (1988).

Turnbull, W. and Turku. Customers' Profitability in Relationship Life Cycles. *Proceedings of the 10th IMP Conference*. Groningen, Netherlands (1994).

Turnbull, P. W. and Valla, J.-P. (eds). *Strategies for International Industrial Marketing*. London: Croom Helm (1986).

Turnbull, P. W. and Valla, J.-P. Strategic Planning in Industrial Marketing: An Interaction Approach. In *Understanding Business Markets*, David Ford, Academic Press (1990).

Turnbull, P. W. and Wilson, D. T. Developing and Protecting Profitable Customer Relationships. *Industrial Marketing Management*. **18** (1) 1–6 (1989).

Yorke, D. A. and Droussiotis, G. The Use of Customer Portfolio Theory: An Empirical Survey. *Journal of Business and Industrial Marketing*. **9** (3) 6–18 (1994).

Zolkiewski, M. Marketing of Large Contracts: Selling Costs and Profitability. MSc Dissertation, UMIST, UK (1994).

# 5

# Industrial Marketing Strategies and Different National Environments

*L. Hallén and J. Johanson*

This article analyses the marketing strategies of industrial suppliers in five Western European countries. The strategies are characterized in a quality dimension and a customer adaptation dimension. In the quality dimension the strategies are found to be related to characteristics of the industrial environment of the supplier country. In the adaptation dimension they are related to the cultural affinity with the customer country as perceived by industrial purchasers in these countries.

## THE PROBLEM

In international industrial markets, national environments can be expected to affect supplier performance in such a way that there are systematic differences among suppliers from different countries. Evidently, considerations of such differences are important when international marketing strategies of industrial suppliers are developed. This article analyses the effects of some environmental determinants on the industrial purchasers' evaluations of the suppliers' performances.

Comparative marketing studies have demonstrated that different marketing environments are associated with differences in marketing.[3,6] This is a basis of the issue of international standardization versus local adaptation in international marketing.[8,21] This article expands on the comparative marketing perspective as it deals with two sets of environments – the environment within the supplying country as well as the consuming country's environment and both their influences on the international marketing strategies.

Studies of country-of-origin effects on supplier and product evaluations have demonstrated that the country of origin has various effects on the evaluations.[4] The studies show that national stereotypes exist,[2] but the studies typically make no conclusions as to whether or not these stereotypes reflect actual differences between suppliers. The studies generally deal with consumer goods and are typically based on

Reprinted by permission of the publisher from Industrial Marketing Strategies and Different National Environments by L. Hallén and J. Johanson in *Journal of Business Research*, Vol. 13, pp 495–509.

opinions expressed by such respondents as students. It is clear that inferences to actual supplier performance cannot be drawn, in particular not to industrial supplier performance. However, three articles deal explicitly with industrial purchasing. One of these asserts that national stereotypes also exist in industrial markets,[28] another that the stereotypes deal with such factors as quality, marketing characteristics, and price,[29] and the third that this can be interpreted against the background of distance factors.[15] Furthermore, these studies are mostly based only on data collected in a single country. Only a few of the studies in the industrial field are cross-cultural in the sense that they use data from two countries (US and France,[9] and US and Japan[23]).

The determinants of the country-of-origin effects are treated in some studies.[4] The determinants mentioned include such factors as the economic development of the source country, its culture, political climate, and the similarity of belief systems between supplier and buyer country. A tendency also exists for consumers to evaluate their own country's products more favorably than they do foreign ones.[9] This is understandable against the background of the culturally related determinants. However, the combined effects of these suggested determinants are unclear, especially when applied to unidimensional evaluations of products or supplier performance. For instance, in many cases the economic development factor would make foreign suppliers more highly regarded than domestic ones.

In order to analyse industrial supplier performance, this article distinguishes between and evaluates two separate dimensions of supplier performance: (1) the extent of adaptations to individual customer needs and (2) the level of general quality of the offer. The performance evaluations, which are made by industrial purchasers, are interpreted as reflections of the suppliers' realized marketing strategies. Differences in evaluation – or strategies – are related to environmental characteristics in the supplier's and customer's countries. The model is tested on empirical data from five Western European countries.

## CONCEPTS AND HYPOTHESES

### Starting Points of Industrial Marketing Strategy

It is almost universally accepted that marketing should have the needs of the customer as a starting point.[22] In industrial marketing these needs originate in the production and marketing situations of the users. Against this background it has been suggested that the "product is what it does".[11] It is the total package of benefits offered to the customers that is of interest. Not only the physical product but also such intangibles as assurance of supply, technical assistance, maintenance, stockholding, and so forth should be included in this package. This total package can be considered as a solution offered to the customer by the supplier. If individual customers account for large shares of the supplier's output, or for other reasons are important to the supplier, then it may be profitable to adapt various aspects of the solutions to the industrial customer's need.

The capability of the firm is a second starting point of industrial marketing strategy. The literature on business strategy emphasizes the importance of assessing the firm's weaknesses and strengths when planning its strategy.[1,24] One underlying assumption is that the capability of the firm is based on a specific combination of resources and organization, which cannot easily be changed in the short run. Thus, different strategies are assumed to require different resources and organization. In organization studies, stress is laid on the consistency between the firm's strategy and its organization.[10,13] Long-term competitiveness requires the firm to follow a strategy that effects a match between the capability of the firm and the needs of the customers. This can be achieved either implicitly or explicitly through planning.

A third starting point of industrial marketing strategy is the observation that buyers and sellers in industrial markets often establish and develop long-lasting relationships with each other.[5,12,30] In such relationships the match between supplier capability and customer need is accomplished through interaction between the two parties and adaptation by one or both of them.[16] The supplier's adaptations may refer to various aspects of the solution offered to the customer. Time and resources are needed to establish relationships and, once established, they are important assets, which give both constraints and possibilities in marketing. Webster[26] has suggested that "for strategic purposes, the central focus of industrial marketing" should be on such relationships. The supplier's adaptation in each customer relationship is an important dimension of industrial marketing strategy.

## Industrial Marketing Strategies

Against this background, a classification of industrial marketing strategies can be derived from the characteristics of the total solution offered to the customer. In this solution we can distinguish between a general (or absolute) quality dimension and an adaptation dimension.[16] Thus it is assumed that high problem-solving capability can be attained in two ways. The general quality dimension refers to how "good", "difficult", or "advanced" the standard solution of the supplier is. The adaptation dimension defines how far the supplier is prepared to go in adapting the solution to the needs of the specific customer. Four basically different strategies concerning general quality and customer adaptation can be distinguished (Fig. 1). They differ with regard to required capabilities and customer interaction.

A *price strategy*, in which the solution is of standard quality not adapted to the specific customer's need, must be balanced by a low price and therefore requires

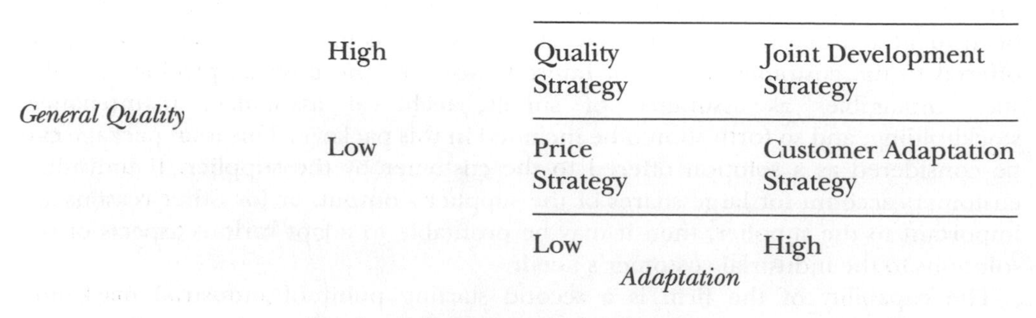


Fig. 1. Industrial marketing strategies.

access to low-cost resources or a comparatively efficient organization, e.g. due to large scale. The interaction need is low, because the offer is standardized and simple. Thus, the interaction is mainly concerned with commercial matters.

A viable *quality strategy* requires access to advanced equipment, resources for product development and technical assistance, and an organization that can transfer advanced products and services efficiently to the customers. Knowledge about the customer's future needs is essential. It is a resource-demanding strategy for which, as in the case of the price strategy, large scale and market share are imperative. It is a costly strategy and suitable only if a sufficient number of customers are prepared to pay for this high, yet standardized, quality. The need for customer interaction is minor, because the problem solutions are standardized. The transfer of knowledge, however, requires interaction, in which the supplier is active.

The *customer-adaptation strategy* is based on the assumption that the needs of all industrial users in a specific market are not identical. Differences in production systems, market situations, resources, and other factors interest the users in various types of adaptations of the solutions to their specific needs. Such adaptations may concern the design of the product, but may equally bear upon, for example, delivery, stockholding and technical advice. The ability to offer adapted solutions obviously imposes special demands on the resources and organization of the supplying firm. It should have a flexible manufacturing organization, capacity to adapt product designs, and a market organization that enables it to understand and interpret the individual customer's specific problems. Consequently, the need for customer–supplier interaction is comparatively strong. Like quality, adaptation has its costs, and the high-adaptation strategies are only feasible if customers are willing to pay these costs.

The *joint development strategy*, which is based on the assumption that the customer is prepared to pay both for customization and advanced quality, is difficult to apply. It is difficult because it combines the demands on resources and organization of both the high-quality strategy (efficiency) and the customer-adaptation strategy (flexibility), a combination that is difficult to attain.[7] It is perhaps only worthwhile in high-technology cases and calls for close customer interaction, because the advanced solutions are developed and adapted in interaction between the parties.

See Table 1 for a summary of the four strategies described above.

These concepts can serve as a basis for analysing industrial marketing strategies. In particular they should be used for the analysis of the long-term match between the capability of the supplier and the needs of the customer.

Which strategy befits the resources and the organization commanded by a particular firm? What changes in resources and organization are necessary for the strategy that seems appropriate to the needs of the customers? With what types of customer should the firm try to develop relationships in order to utilize the current structure most profitably? These questions indicate that the firm has a choice with regard to strategy. Nevertheless, different strategies can be expected to suit different situations. Thus, different strategies will be most fitting depending on the type of product or the production technology of the customers. However, a firm can make a strategic choice for a given product and *per se* any strategy could be applied to it in a competitive manner. Consider, for instance, the diesel engine market(s) in which suppliers pursuing price strategies, quality strategies, and customer-adaptation strategies may very well exist and be competitive side by side as they cater for

Table 1. Required interaction and capabilities in industrial marketing strategies

| Strategies | Interaction required | Capability required |
|---|---|---|
| Low price | Low interaction needed | Low cost resources<br>Efficient organization<br>Large scale |
| High quality | Not very high interaction<br>Only supplier is active | Resources for product development and technical assistance<br>Knowledge of future needs<br>Large market share |
| High adaptation | Active customers<br>High interaction need | Flexible design and manufacturing organization<br>Ability to understand customer needs |
| Joint development | Both parties active<br>Very high interaction | Resources for technical development<br>Flexible organization<br>Ability to understand future customer needs |

customers with different need structures and utilize different resource structures.

Environmental characteristics support the strategies differently; on average, the typical strategy realized by firms in one set of environments can be expected to differ from the strategies used in other environments. In the following section the effects of national environments will be in focus.

## International Industrial Marketing

Each country harbors an industrial environment characterized by certain levels of availability, quality, and prices of resources. This environment constrains the firms' possibilities of realizing different marketing strategies. Because of the requirements of the quality strategies it can be expected – in accordance with the theory of comparative advantage but on the firm level to which the theory does not usually refer – that firms from a particular industry in a country with a highly developed industrial environment will be more likely to follow a quality strategy than will a firm in the same industry from a country with an industrial environment that is less favorable in this respect.

Somewhat different adaptation–strategy patterns can be expected. According to the product life-cycle model, adaptations to specific customers' needs are probably more frequent during the introductory stage, when the product and the manufacturing process have not yet been standardized.[22] During the mature stage, when there is a big market, firms can be expected to adopt low-adaptation strategies. In the international version of the product-cycle model, new products are assumed to be developed in the domestic market in response to the needs there – the reason being the necessity for closer supplier–customer interaction during the early stage. The firms are assumed to go abroad when the market is no longer expanding and products and processes are standardized.[27] Thus, high adaptation strategies should be expected to be more frequent in the domestic than in foreign markets.

Operating in foreign markets means that a number of obstacles must be overcome. Tariffs and transport costs are not the only barriers to international marketing. The differences in cultural environments between countries and the lack of knowledge about the foreign environment are perhaps more important. Negotiations must be carried on in a different setting, according to different rules, and in a different language[14] from those with which the supplier is familiar. The degree to which those rules, customs, and communications resemble the usual way of doing business constitutes for the manufacturer a cultural affinity with the foreign market. It has been shown that low affinity in this respect forms a major obstacle to the internationalization of firms.[20] Similarly, it seems reasonable to expect such lack of affinity to represent an obstacle to the suppliers in industrial markets in their understanding of and adaptation to the individual foreign customer's needs.[15,18] Intimate relationships are easier to establish and develop with customers in culturally close countries. Consequently, high-adaptation strategies are expected to be more frequently realized the higher the cultural affinity with the customer.

As mentioned initially, the issue of the determinants of the country-of-origin biases is raised in several of the studies of consumer's attitudes to foreign products.[4] The reviewers group these determinants in two major categories:

1. Source country considerations (the degree of economic development or the political climate).
2. Consuming country considerations (import experiences, nationalism, or cultural affinity with the source country).

Factors that can be referred to these two major categories are assumed to influence different aspects of the marketing strategies in systematic ways. To summarize, industrial suppliers from different countries can be expected to be differentially clustered with regard to the general quality of their solution. High quality will be more frequently adopted by suppliers from industrially advanced countries (a supplier-country determinant). The degree of adaptation of the solution should be

| *General Quality* | | | |
|---|---|---|---|
| | High | High Industrial Development and Low Cultural Affinity | High Industrial Development and High Cultural Affinity |
| | Low | Low Industrial Development and Low Cultural Affinity | Low Industrial Development and High Cultural Affinity |
| | | Low | High |
| | | *Adaptation* | |

Fig. 2. Expected relations between marketing strategies and environments of suppliers and customers. Industrial Development refers to the industry of the supplier country and Cultural Affinity to the affinity with the customer country.

positively correlated with the cultural affinity between customers and suppliers (a customer–country determinant) (see Fig. 2).

## METHOD

### Data Base

The analysis is based on data from interviews with purchasers in industrial firms in five countries which were collected within a project involving researchers from five countries.[16] In all, 416 interviews were conducted with industrial purchasers almost equally divided among France, Great Britain, Italy, West Germany, and Sweden. In every participating country interviews were held concerning suppliers from all five countries. Given the complexity and extent of the data collection, a quota sampling method was used.[25] The quota sample was based on a four-dimensional sample matrix, specifying customer country, supplier country, product type, and user technology. Thus, about one-third of the interviews concerned each type of supplier: suppliers of raw materials, components, and equipment. Furthermore, about one-third of the interviews were held with each kind of purchaser: purchasers in small-batch industries, large-batch industries, and process industries.

The respondents were asked to agree or disagree (on a five-point scale) with a number of statements such as "German suppliers usually make punctual deliveries." The statements were first formulated in English and then translated into French, German, Italian, and Swedish. In order to avoid translation errors they were retranslated independently.

Each interview gives the generalized opinion on a number of aspects of the performance of suppliers from one of the five countries. The respondents are professional purchasers with experience of buying from the country in question. Assuming that their opinions are formed through their experiences as professional purchasers, it seems reasonable to interpret such opinions as indicators of the suppliers' realized strategies rather than just purchaser biases or stereotypes.

If the opinion is formed through professional experience, a purchaser of some types of components will express opinions about a certain country's suppliers, which are implicitly related to other suppliers of such components. Consequently, the opinions about the supplier's realized strategies can be expected to be standardized with regard to technology factors, which means that the relations investigated will not be affected by such technology factors.

### Operationalization

The two strategy variables – quality and adaptation – and the two environmental variables – industrial environment and cultural affinity – are operationalized by means of the opinions of the industrial purchasers. These are transformed to index variables with hypothetical variations from 0 to 100.

The operationalization of the quality dimension of the marketing strategy is achieved by the use of seven statements. The quality dimension is assumed to include an aspect directly related to the problem-solving ability of the supplier and an aspect related to the ability to transfer the problem solution to the customer. These two aspects account for half the weight of the index value. The items constituting the quality dimension of marketing strategies are listed in Part A of Table 2.

The adaptation dimension of marketing strategy is operationalized in the same way as is the quality dimension: on the basis of one aspect directly related to the problem-solving ability and one aspect related to the transfer of the solutions to the customer. Each aspect accounts for half the weight of the index variable. The items are listed in Part B of Table 2.

Table 2. Items defining the strategy and environmental indices

A. Quality Strategy Index[a]
- Suppliers of country *X* generally stress the product appearance aspect of their goods (P)
- The products of suppliers of country *X* are characterized by consistent quality (P)
- Suppliers of country *X* often want to offer us new technical solutions (P)
- Suppliers of country *X* usually make punctual deliveries (T)
- Suppliers of country *X* generally offer detailed technical information (T)
- Suppliers of country *X* do not usually take a long time to answer our request for a quotation (T)
- The commercial information supplied by suppliers of country *X* is seldom inadequate (T)

B. Adaptation Strategy Index[a]
- Suppliers of country *X* are often interested in joint product development activities (P)
- Suppliers of country *X* are generally willing to make the product adaptations that we require (P)
- Suppliers of country *X* are often willing to adapt their products to international standards (P)
- The ability to make deliveries is typical for suppliers of country *X* (T)
- Suppliers of country *X* mostly want to have face-to-face meetings before we reach agreements (T)
- Suppliers of country *X* are interested in following up on how their products are used (T)
- Suppliers of country *X* quickly respond to our request for one of their salesmen to call (T)
- We usually have close personal contacts with people in companies from country *X* when buying from country *X* (T)
- Suppliers of country *X* often suggest that we jointly coordinate our production plans (T)
- Suppliers of country *X* readily accept that deliveries are based on our production plans rather than theirs.

C. Industrial Environment Index
- Wage costs in country *X* give firms from this country a competitive advantage
- Disputes in the labour market of country *X* make it difficult to cooperate with suppliers from country *X*

D. Cultural Affinity Index
- Cultural differences seldom make it difficult for us to have close social relationships with suppliers from country *X*
- Language does not make it difficult to have social relationships with suppliers from country *X*
- Suppliers from country *X* generally have a good understanding of the ways in which foreign companies operate
- Buyers from our country are highly appreciated by suppliers from country *X*

[a]In the quality and adaptation strategy indices, P refers to items associated with the problem-solving aspect and T to the transfer aspect.

The index variable describing the industrial environment of the firms in the supplier country is composed of the respondents' opinions regarding two items (see Part C of Table 2). This index variable only partly reflects important factors of the industrial climate of a country. Nevertheless, we maintain that the two items indicate how the industrial resources in the country are utilized. This is evident with regard to the labour-market item. The reasoning behind the wage-cost item is that in the long term a high wage level can only be sustained if the economy is competitive enough. The main advantage of using an index based on purchasers' opinions rather than on official statistics is that the former are directed toward the relevant areas of the economy, e.g. certain industries or regions.

Cultural affinity is characterized by the customers' opinions regarding four items. The degree of cultural affinity between the countries of the selling and buying companies was computed from the purchasers' agreement or disagreement with the four statements listed in Table 2, Part D. These factors refer to aspects on a national level that are assumed to reflect ease of communication and the absence of alienation between individuals from the supplier and customer countries.

The cultural-affinity variable is based on supplier evaluations by foreign purchasers, whereas the other three variables derive from evaluations by both foreign and domestic purchasers.

## RESULTS

### The Quality Dimension and the Industrial Environment

There are differences between the five countries with regard to both the industrial environment index and the quality dimension of industrial marketing strategy. Figure 3 shows the country averages of the two variables. Two supplier countries (Germany and Sweden) have fairly high and two others (Britain and Italy) comparatively low averages in both variables. France has a medium value in both

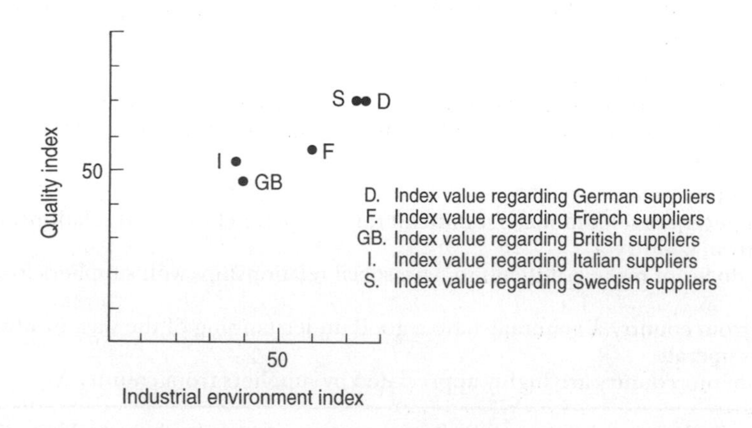


Fig. 3. National averages of quality strategy and industrial environment indices.

variables. The figure indicates a clear relation between the two variables at the country level. These values are also rather independent of customer country. In particular, it should be noted that in no case do the domestic purchasers on average give a higher quality rating than do the foreign purchasers.

To some extent these rankings are consistent with those in the study by Cattin *et al.*,[9] in which the two categories of respondents (US and French businessmen) preferred local products and selected West German products as their second choice. British and Japanese products were ranked lower. The difference here as compared with those findings is the ranking of the domestic producers. Their position in the present study is a strong indication that the opinions reflect actual supplier performance, because a pure influence of stereotypes probably would have given them a higher ranking.

On the customer company level a similar picture emerges. Table 3 describes the relationship between the two variables by means of the correlation and regression coefficients and the standard error of the regression coefficient as seen by all purchasers as well as by purchasers from each of the five countries.

This picture is very homogeneous. For the total and for each customer country – with Italy deviating slightly – the correlation coefficients are close to 0.45. All the regression coefficients are close to that of the total, i.e. 0.27; the rather small standard error of the regression coefficient indicates that this is a basic relationship that is independent of source. The Italian purchasers seem to be less consistent in their evaluations as well as less sensitive to quality differences.

The picture becomes still more distinct when the regression equations of raw material purchasers, component purchasers, and equipment purchasers are compared. The coefficients of the three equations are almost equal to the coefficients of the total. The same applies when regressions are made separately for purchasers in small-batch industries, large-batch industries, and process industries. There is evidently a basic relationship between the characteristics of the industrial environment and the quality strategy of industrial firms. It is strikingly independent of technological factors, as was expected above from the way in which the opinions were collected.

Table 3. Relation between quality strategy and industrial environment indices at the company level

| | $R^a$ | $B^b$ | Standard error $B$ |
|---|---|---|---|
| As seen by customers from: | | | |
| France | 0.45 | 0.29 | 0.06 |
| Germany | 0.51 | 0.21 | 0.05 |
| Italy | 0.31 | 0.17 | 0.08 |
| Sweden | 0.52 | 0.25 | 0.06 |
| Britain | 0.48 | 0.29 | 0.07 |
| Total | 0.46 | 0.27 | 0.03 |

[a]Correlation coefficient of General Quality Index with Industrial Environment Index.
[b]Slope of regression line.

### The Adaptation Dimension and Cultural Affinity

Cultural affinity refers to and characterizes relations between countries. Comparing the average affinity between each pair of countries (see Table 4) we find, firstly, a clear division into two groups: Latin countries and Northern countries. The average affinity between France and Italy is 75 (i.e. 78 + 73/2; see Table 4), between Germany, Sweden, and Britain 70 (i.e. 73 + 65 + 71 + 65 + 72 + 76/6), and between the two groups 58. It is interesting that the average cultural affinity between France and Germany is very low (54). These two countries are not only geographically close, but the economic integration in Western Europe – the European Coal and Steel Community and later the European Economic Community – has for decades often dealt primarily with German and French industry. Still, the traditional differences between the two are clearly perceived by industrial purchasers from these countries as far as their actual supplier relations are concerned. The obvious conclusion is that cultural affinity is a stable phenomenon.

Table 4 also shows some other characteristics of cultural affinity. The inter-country affinity is not necessarily symmetrical. Purchasers in Britain consider their affinity with German suppliers fairly high (72), whereas the German purchasers find their affinity with British suppliers much lower (65), indicating that the Germans are most active in bridging the gap between the two. It is not surprising that the others consider the affinity with suppliers from the small country of Sweden very high (71); perhaps unbalanced language ability is an important explanation.

The statements used to build up the cultural-affinity variable were formulated to measure opinions about foreign suppliers. Consequently, they were not answered by purchasers assessing the performance of domestic suppliers, and the variable can only be used in relation to foreign suppliers. Nevertheless, assuming high cultural affinity between domestic customers and their domestic suppliers, high-adaptation strategies are expected to be pursued more frequently with domestic than with foreign customers.

As indicated by the five diagrams in Fig. 4,[17] the purchasers in every country find that the suppliers from culturally close countries are generally more inclined than those from culturally distant countries to pursue high-adaptation strategies.

At the purchaser level there is a clear correlation between adaptation strategies of

Table 4. National averages of cultural affinity

| | Customer country | | | | | |
|---|---|---|---|---|---|---|
| Supplier country | France | Italy | Germany | Sweden | Britain | Total |
| France | – | 73 | 55 | 51 | 69 | 62 |
| Italy | 78 | – | 60 | 63 | 60 | 65 |
| Germany | 53 | 57 | – | 71 | 72 | 63 |
| Sweden | 66 | 67 | 73 | – | 76 | 71 |
| Britain | 45 | 53 | 65 | 65 | – | 57 |
| Total | 60 | 63 | 63 | 63 | 69 | 64 |

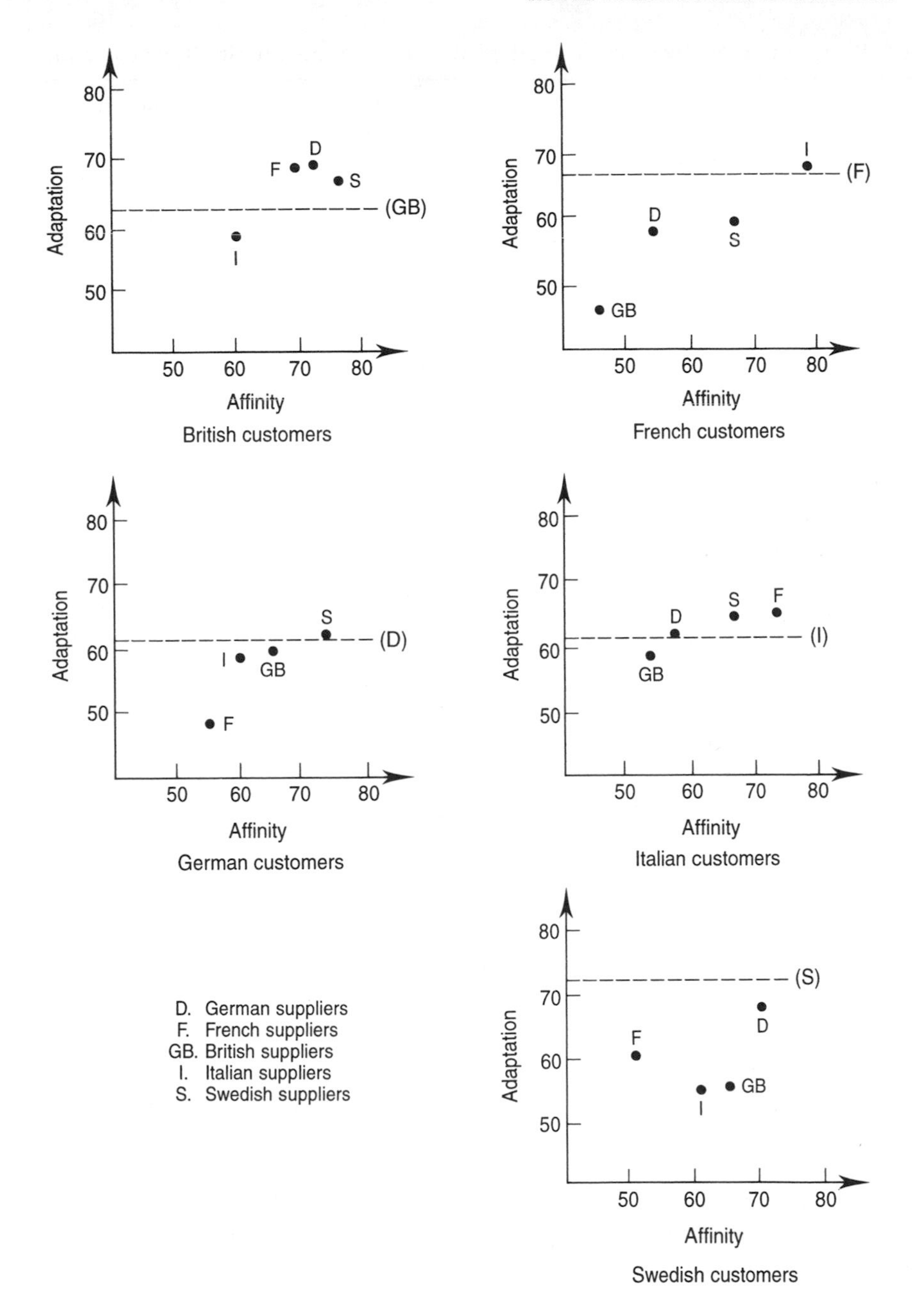


Fig. 4. National averages of cultural affinity and adaptation.

suppliers and cultural affinity with the customers. In the total material the regression coefficient 0.43 differs distinctly from zero (see Table 5). The relation is, however, not independent of the purchasers making the judgement. Thus, French purchasers are more consistent in their evaluations and more sensitive to differences in cultural

Table 5. Relationship between customer adaptation and cultural affinity at the company level

| | $R^a$ | $B^b$ | Standard error $B$ |
|---|---|---|---|
| As seen by customers from: | | | |
| France | 0.65 | 0.50 | 0.08 |
| Germany | 0.35 | 0.36 | 0.08 |
| Italy | 0.21 | 0.24 | 0.12 |
| Sweden | 0.30 | 0.25 | 0.10 |
| Britain | 0.40 | 0.29 | 0.10 |
| Total | 0.43 | 0.34 | 0.04 |

[a] Correlation coefficient of Adaptation Index with Cultural Affinity Index.
[b] Slope of regression line.

affinity than all purchasers or than purchasers from each of the other four countries whose judgements are rather close to the total.

It can be concluded that a correlation exists between cultural affinity and the adaptation dimension of marketing strategy, implying that the higher the cultural affinity between supplier and customer, the more the suppliers tend to adapt their offers to the customer. There are some differences between customers from different countries, but on the whole the picture is rather consistent.

The technology factor does not seem to influence this relationship either. The same regressions were made separately for each of the three product categories as well as for each of the three types of user technologies. All the coefficients are very close to those of the total, indicating that the relationship between affinity and adaptation is independent of technology. This does not show that technology is unimportant but rather that opinions are standardized with regard to the technology factor.

## CONCLUDING REMARKS

As seen by industrial purchasers from five European countries, supplier firms from these five different countries tend to pursue different industrial marketing strategies, defined in quality and adaptation dimensions. Furthermore, differences in the quality dimension can be explained to some extent by differences in the general industrial environment in the five supplier countries. Likewise, differences in the adaptation dimensions can in some measure be attributed to the inter-country cultural affinity.

The results are the same whether the analysis is made at the country level or at the purchaser level. This indicates direct relationships between the quality of industrial marketing strategy of suppliers and the characteristics of the industrial environment of the supplier, and between the adaptation to the customer's needs and the cultural affinity with the customers. At the same time there is a typical average level of every country with regard to industrial environment characteristics and quality of industrial suppliers and of every intercountry relation with regard to cultural affinity and adaptation of suppliers to the customers' needs.

The cross-country consistency of the quality evaluations supports the conclusion that the performance evaluations are valid indicators of the actual supplier performance.

The results have some implications for international industrial-marketing strategy. First, they support very generally the model of industrial-marketing strategy presented, including the requirements of these strategies.

Second, it was stated initially that the strategy of the firm requires a certain type of customer interaction and that it must be matched by its resources and organization. Because the need for customer interaction is rather low in the nonadaptive strategies, it can now be concluded that such a strategy – whether a quality or a price strategy – that is successfully pursued in the domestic market can usually be applied also in the export markets to the extent that this quality level corresponds to the needs of the industrial users in the export markets. The same structure with regard to resources and organization can be used in the export marketing.

Third, a successful domestic-customer adaptation strategy can, however, not so easily be pursued as such in foreign markets. A high-adaptation strategy with its strong demand for customers' interaction requires a marketing organization that can bridge the cultural distance to the export market so that close relationships can be established with the customer there. A strong marketing organization is required in the foreign markets so that the needs of the foreign customers really reach and influence design and manufacturing units of the firm. This requires a heavy investment in international marketing, an investment that increases with decreasing cultural affinity. In particular, this seems to hold for the French market, in which the purchasers on average perceive less affinity with foreign suppliers at the same time as they are consistently more sensitive to lack of affinity.

Fourth, product development usually requires profound knowledge of customer demands. Such knowledge can often be obtained only in close interaction between customers and suppliers.[19] Therefore, an important aspect of the industrial environment is the existence of demanding domestic customers, in relation to which joint development strategies can emerge more easily than in foreign markets. Such adaptation at home may mature into quality in exports.

Fifth, there is no reason to believe that single firms would not be able to pursue strategies that differ from national averages. Indeed, the gradual build-up of trust and experience between buyers and sellers within the framework of established relationships often leads to a reduction of the perceived distance between the parties involves. Cultural affinity may be seen as just one set of factors reducing this distance, i.e. the similarity in perceptions by sellers and buyers. Trust and experience are important factors reducing perceived distance and may offset low cultural affinity between firms from different countries. As the relationship develops, adaptations may be realized, although the cultural affinity between the countries remains low.

## REFERENCES

1. Abell, D. F. and Hammond, J. S. *Strategic Market Planning.* Prentice-Hall, Englewood Cliffs, NJ (1979).
2. Anderson, W. T. and Cunningham, W. H. Gauging foreign product promotion. *Journal of Advertising Research,* February, 29–34 (1972).

3. Bartels, R. Are domestic and international marketing dissimilar? *Journal of Marketing*, **32**, 56–61 (1968).
4. Bilkey, W. J. and Nes, E. Country-of-origin effects on product evaluations. *Journal of International Business Studies*, **13**, 89–99 (1982).
5. Blois, K. Vertical quasi-integration. *Journal of Industrial Economics*, **20**, 253–72 (1972).
6. Boddewyn, J. J. Comparative marketing: the first 25 years. *Journal of International Business Studies*, **12**, 61–79 (1981).
7. Burns, T. and Stalker, G. M. *The Management of Innovations*. Tavistock Publications, London (1961).
8. Buzzel, R. D. Can you standardize multinational marketing? *Harvard Business Review*, **46**, 102–13 (1968).
9. Cattin, P., Jolibert, A. and Lohnes, C. A cross-cultural study of "made in" concepts. *Journal of International Business Studies*, **13**, 131–41 (1982).
10. Chandler, A. D. *Strategy and Structure: Chapters in the History of the Industrial Enterprise*. MIT Press, Cambridge, Mass (1962).
11. Corey, E. R. *Industrial Marketing: Cases and Concepts*, 2nd edn. Prentice-Hall, Englewood Cliffs, NJ (1976), p. 40.
12. Ford, I. D. Stability factors in industrial marketing channels. *Industrial Marketing Management*, **7**, 410–22 (1978).
13. Galbraith, J. R. and Nathanson, D. A. *Strategy Implementation: The Role of Structure and Process*. West Publishing, St. Paul, Minn (1978).
14. Graham, J. L. *Cross-cultural Sales Negotiations: A Multilevel Analysis*. Ph.D. dissertation (mimeo), University of California, Berkeley (1980).
15. Håkansson, H. and Wootz, B. Supplier selection in an international environment – an experimental study. *Journal of Marketing Research*, **12**, 46–51 (1975).
16. Håkansson, H. (ed.). *International Marketing and Purchasing of Industrial Goods – An Interaction Approach*. John Wiley, Chichester (1982).
17. Hallén, L. *International Industrial Purchasing – Channels, Interaction and Governance Structures*. Almqvist and Wiksell International, Stockholm (1982), p. 55.
18. Hallén, L. and Wiedersheim-Paul, F. Psychic distance and buyer–seller interaction. *Organisasjon, Marked og Samfunn*, **16**, 308–24 (1979).
19. von Hippel, E. Successful industrial products from customer ideas. *Journal of Marketing*, **42**, 39–49 (1978).
20. Johanson, J. and Wiedersheim-Paul, F. The internationalization of the firm – four Swedish case studies. *Journal of Management Studies*, **2**, 305–22 (1975).
21. Keegan, W. J. Multinational product planning: strategic alternatives. *Journal of Marketing*, **33**, 58–62 (1969).
22. Kotler, P. *Marketing Management*, 4th edn. Prentice-Hall, Englewood Cliffs, NJ (1980).
23. Nagashima, A. A comparison of Japanese and US attitudes toward foreign products. *Journal of Marketing*, **34**, 68–74 (1970).
24. Porter, M. E. *Competitive Strategy. Techniques for Analyzing Industries and Competitors*. The Free Press, New York (1980).
25. Selltiz, C., Wrightsman, L. W. and Cook, S. W. *Research Methods in Social Relations*, 3rd edn. Holt, Rinehart and Winston, New York (1976).
26. Webster, F. E., Jr. *Industrial Marketing Strategy*. Wiley, New York (1979).
27. Wells, L. T., Jr. (ed). *The Product Life Cycle and International Trade*. Harvard Business School, Division of Research, Boston (1972).
28. White, P. D. and Cundiff, E. W. Assessing the quality of industrial products. *Journal of Marketing*, **42**, 80–6 (1978).
29. White, P. D. Attitudes of US purchasing managers toward industrial products manufactured in selected European nations. *Journal of International Business Studies*, **10**, 81–90 (1979).
30. Wind, Y. Industrial source loyalty. *Journal of Marketing Research*, **7**, 450–7 (1970).

# 6

# The Swedish Approach to Europe

*H. Håkansson*

## INTRODUCTION – INTERNATIONAL MARKETING STRATEGIES

The policy of a company in relation to its international operations can be designed in at least two different ways. Firstly, the policy can be designed once and for all through an extensive decision process where different alternative policies are analysed and evaluated. Secondly, the policy can be designed in a stepwise manner where only a limited number of alternatives are analysed in each step and where the experience and the results of earlier activities more or less continuously affect the policy. In this case different parts of the individual company can have different policies at the same time.

The first of these two alternatives is often seen as more rational and is therefore recommended in many textbooks. The second one is seen as more empirical and pragmatic. It is based on an assumption about the difficulties in being rational in decision-making. Lindblom (1959) has named these two alternative processes the Rational-Comprehensive and Successive Limited Comparisons methods.

Empirical studies of decision-making seem, in general, to support the second alternative. Earlier empirical studies, for example, of the international operations of Swedish companies have shown characteristics close to the Successive Limited Comparisons method. The findings (for a summary see Johanson and Vahlne, 1977) have been conceptualised in a model where the companies become international in a stepwise manner. The steps are taken in two directions by each company. Successively the company increases the geographical spread of its operations and increase its commitments in individual markets.

The successive limited comparisons method will be used in this chapter as an instrument to analyse the way Swedish manufacturing companies approach the European market. Using this method means that it is not sufficient merely to investigate the plans or formal strategies of companies, as it would be using the rational-comprehensive method. Instead, several aspects have to be considered in order to obtain a fuller understanding of the companies' way of approaching

Reprinted by permission of International Thomson, The Swedish Approach to Europe by H. Håkansson from *Strategies for International Industrial Marketing*, Edited by P. Turnbull and J.-P. Valla.

different markets. Another effect of using this method is that the word "approach" is more appropriate than the word "policy".

## CHARACTERISTICS OF THE PROCESS OF INTERNATIONAL DEVELOPMENT

It is our view, then, that the international approach of the company is developed in a stepwise manner and is based on earlier experience. Furthermore, in each step there are only a limited number of alternatives perceived as possible. Accordingly, a specific relationship between a company and a market can be seen as an exchange process where the company gets into different problem situations, carries through certain activities, gets reactions in several ways from customers, distributors and competitors, adapts its activities, gets new reactions and so on. During this "muddling through" process the company's approach towards the market is developed. In the early stages, for example, this approach can be characterised by being unclear and unstructured and the process makes it clearer and more structured. The opposite can also appear. A company can go into a market with a very clear and structured approach but end with a much more unclear and unstructured one. It all depends on what happens during the process, which in turn depends on the activities of the company as well as the reactions from the other units in the market.

Within this global development process of the international approach several, more limited, parallel processes can be identified. These are important as they can be seen both as indicators of the global process and as means to influence it. Here the discussion will be limited to four of these processes. These four have been identified using Thompson's (1967. p. 101) basic contention that:

> human action merges from the interaction of 1. the individual who brings *aspirations, standards* and *knowledge or beliefs about causation*; and, 2. the situation, which presents *opportunities* and *constraints*. Interaction of the individual and the situation is mediated by his perception or cognitions.

Here two processes are used to indicate each of Thompson's two groupings of variables. The "market perception process" includes not only the "passive" mediating interaction, as Thompson uses the term, but also the aspirations of the individuals. The "market knowledge and experience process" includes both the standards and the knowledge or beliefs of individuals about causation. The "customer interaction process" and the "channel organising process" are used to describe and characterize the series of situations that present opportunities and constraints.

Thus, four subprocesses within the global international approach process of the company have been identified. They are all interrelated as shown by Fig. 1. Each of them will now be described in more detail.

*Market perception process.* This process successively changes the way the company perceives a certain market.[1] It gives a generalised picture of the market and acts as a filter, letting through only certain stimuli. A company perceives, as an example, different markets to be of varying importance. If a certain stimulus comes from a

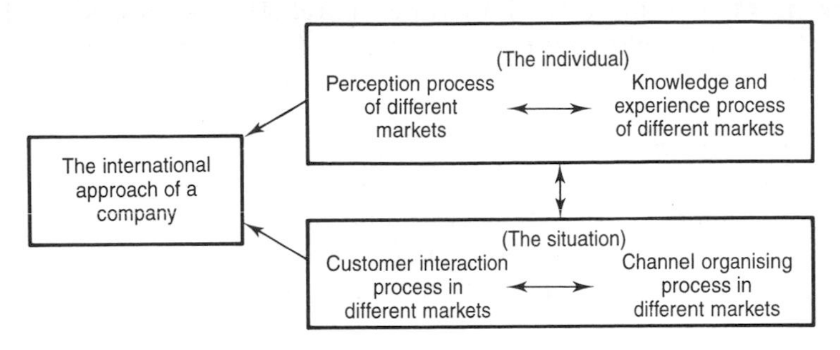


Fig. 1 Subprocesses within the international approach of a company

market that is ranked as Number one this will get much greater attention than if it had come from a low ranked market. The company can also perceive the markets to be working in different ways in terms of requirements of the customers and the policies of the competitors. Some markets can be seen to be more problematic than others, in that they are more demanding, less loyal, and so on.

The perception of a market is influenced by a large number of factors, some of which are related to the general social environment. Any company works within a certain social environment and the attitudes of its personnel are a mirror of the general attitudes in the environment, which are themselves dynamic and developed over time.

Some other factors are related to the specific experience and knowledge of the company. Thus, the perceptions are affected by the activities and the reactions during the global development process. Some other factors are of a more conscious character. Within the company there can exist or develop aspirations regarding different markets. These can in some situations be traced back to certain individuals or to certain policy decisions. This means that the perceptions also can be affected by training courses, recruitment and internal campaigns.

*Market knowledge and experience process.* Knowledge and experience can develop in many different ways within the global process. As a company gains more experience and knowledge its ability to interpret and analyse stimuli let through by the perception filter increases. However, experience and knowledge will themselves influence the perception filter and therefore the two processes are interwoven.

The more knowledge the company has of a certain market the more it can be expected to differentiate its way of reacting. It will observe and adapt to even small differences in the stimuli. The more experience the company has of a certain market the more it can be expected to have a routinized way of reaction since it has learnt how to deal with different situations. Thus, knowledge and experience are not presumed to be interchangeable but are believed to influence different aspects of the behaviour.

The knowledge and experience process is, in the same way as the perception process, influenced by many factors. Some are related to the environment, such as the education system and the general social interaction between the two countries (tourism, etc.). Others are related to other parallel processes, such as type of activities performed, whilst some are concerned with the company, such as recruitment, courses, and so on.

*Supplier–customer interaction process* The first two processes are related to the individuals within the company. The next two processes determine the nature of situations within which individuals operate and which present opportunities and constraints for those individuals. Both these processes include external units of different kinds. The first one is the "interaction process" with customers in the market. The relationships between sellers and customers develop in a stepwise manner through an interaction process, where both parties are active.[2] Due to the abilities and the ambitions of the two parties, the relationship can develop to a greater or lesser extent. Some develop to extensive and close relationships while others remain limited and at "arm's length".

The types of relationship the company takes part in or tries to establish determine the kinds of situations the company will encounter in at least two different ways. First, by the fact that different kinds of relationships create different kinds of problems. There is a significant difference between establishing a close relationship with an intensive technical exchange compared with a limited and impersonal relationship. Secondly, different types of relationships create different kinds of expectations and actions from the counterparts. These latter will act differently if they perceive the company to be able and willing to take part in extensive relationships compared with the reverse. Therefore, depending on how a supplier company is perceived by potential customers, it will receive different requests and propositions.

Thus, our third subprocess, supplier–customer interaction, is influenced both by the abilities and ambitions of the seller and by the needs and the ambitions of the customers.

*Channel organising process.* The fourth process, and the second that includes external units, is the "channel organisation process". This is closely connected with the supplier customer interaction processes, as its objective is to try to shorten the distance between the company and the customers.

The channel organising process is influenced both by internal and external factors. An important external one is that of the access to suitable units to cooperate with. Important internal factors include the number and characteristics of customer relationships that exist or are planned and the structure of the marketing organisation. Depending on the development of this process the company will face different situations regarding, for example, resource allocation, organisational problems, and so on. Thus, this process can involve external units such as agents or distributors but it can also create new internal units such as sales subsidiaries.

## The International Approach Process

The four different kinds of subprocesses described above are all interwoven in the larger process of the development of the international approach of the company. Furthermore, they are all interrelated. Changes in one of them will create changes in the others. All four, therefore, can be used as means to influence the others and thereby the whole process.

There is, of course, no one-to-one relationship between the processes. The more they do not harmonize the more likely will be inefficiencies in the behaviour of the company and there will be no consistency in its operations.

The company can modify and manipulate the four processes as they can be influenced by other means. The perception and the knowledge and experience processes can be influenced by courses, by recruiting certain personnel, by special campaigns, etc. The interaction process can be changed by approaching other customers or by internal changes of different kinds. Lastly, the channel organising process can be changed through internal organisational changes, through changes in the international processes, through cooperation with new external units, etc.

In the discussion so far we have identified one global and four minor processes. If we look at a company at a certain time the results of the processes can be seen in how the personnel of the company perceive different markets, in their knowledge and experience of these markets, in the relationships with the customers and in the organizational design. Fig. 2 illustrates this.

The total approach of one company in relation to a certain market is different from that of all other companies. In other words, there is always a unique feature in each company's approach. However, it is reasonable to expect that there will be similarities among companies with similar backgrounds. It seems likely that the behaviour and perception of a company situated in one country will show similarities with other companies from the same country due to the facts that the companies have developed under the same historical conditions and with the same geographical location towards different markets. There are also cultural similarities.[4]

Together these similarities ought to make it possible to identify certain common features in this approach of companies to different markets. We attempt to do this in this chapter using data at an aggregated level. The aim is to describe how Swedish manufacturing companies approach four markets in Western Europe compared with how they deal with the domestic market. By describing and analysing this in the different aspects identified earlier the opportunity is given for an increased understanding of how companies act internationally.

The chapter consists of six sections. In the first one the sample and the empirical investigation are described. The second states the analysis by presenting the

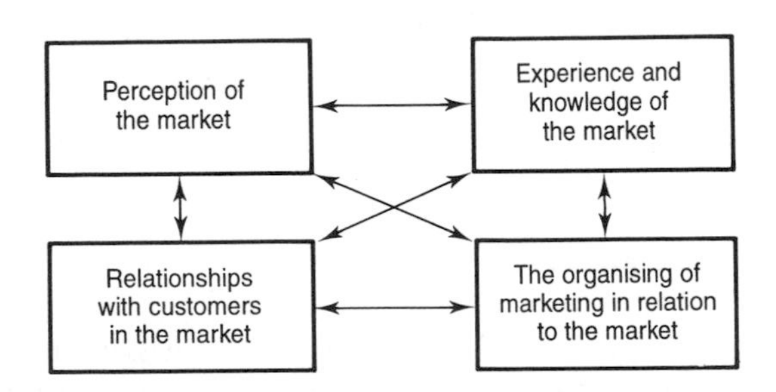


Fig. 2 A company's total approach towards a market at a certain point of time.

perceptions of the five markets by the investigated companies. Thereafter the relationship with the customers on the five markets are described and analysed followed by a section about the organisation of the marketing resources of the companies. The fifth section presents a profile of the knowledge and experience that the companies have of the five markets. The last section is devoted to a general discussion of the results and some managerial implications are drawn both from the theoretical model as well as from the empirical results.

## SAMPLE CHARACTERISTICS

The data that are analysed with the associated theoretical framework have been collected with the IMP study. Therefore the discussion here will be limited to an overview of the Swedish sample and its representativeness.

Ninety-four customer relationships were investigated in 20 business units. The relationships were relatively evenly distributed over the five markets. The lowest number was for Italy with 15 customer relationships and the highest number was for Sweden (i.e. the domestic market) with 22 customer relationships. For some of the customer relationships we were not able to obtain complete information for various reasons. Therefore in the following account, the data material varies between 77 relationships at the lowest and 94 at the highest.

Almost 50% of Swedish exports consists of products from the mechanical engineering industry (including electrical engineering). The next largest group is paper and pulp (about 15%) and the third group is iron and steel – mostly special steel – (about 8%). These three branches dominate the 20 business units which were investigated. Nine units are from mechanical engineering, seven from special steel, three from paper and pulp and one from the chemical industry. The majority of the investigated business units are relatively independent divisions or production units within large company groups. Thus the investigated group is comparable with the total Swedish export activity since 50 large international Swedish companies account for approximately two-thirds of the total Swedish export.

## THE EXPORT MARKETS AND SWEDISH COMPANIES

With the above description as background of how the investigated firms and customer relationships are spread over different branches and countries, the results which are presented later should give, at least from the sample point of view, a good picture of how Swedish firms approach the European markets.

### The Perception of the Five Markets

The analysis begins by looking at the way the five markets are perceived by the companies. This perception, as said earlier, is based, at least partly, on earlier experience and on the social environment. A discussion of the perception of different markets, therefore, can be begun from the standpoint of the average Swedish trading pattern during the last century.

Large Swedish companies are often highly international and their export share can reach 80–90% of their turnover. Europe is, and has been for a long time, a very important area for Swedish exports. In recent years Europe took almost 80% of Swedish exports by value.

The ninth largest export markets in 1979 are rated in relation to the exported volume in Table 1. Norway takes first place, followed by the United Kingdom and West Germany. France takes seventh place and Italy the ninth. If we look at the order of magnitude we find that the United Kingdom and West Germany account for more than double the volume of France and Italy.

## Customers' Requirements

The counterparts – the customers – can be perceived in different ways as exemplified in the presentation of the theoretical approach. The interviews included a section of standardized statements about the characteristics of the market in question. The respondents were asked to give a judgement on a five-point scale as to how true they found the statement to be for the actual market. Some of these statements focused on the kind of requirements the customers in the market had. The main results have been presented elsewhere and we will here only use some of the statements to illustrate the perception of the Swedish companies of their customers.[6]

The requirements of the customers will be described in terms of the kind of relationships they want to establish. Two two-dimensional concepts will be used to give a picture of how the Swedish companies perceive the requirements. The concepts are *problem solving* and *transfer* ability and the dimensions are *general* and *adaptive* (Håkansson, 1980, 1982).

Using these concepts the buying company's need can be characterized in terms of the problem it requires to be solved and how the problem solution can be transferred to it. A problem can be more or less difficult to solve (general dimension). It can also be more or less unique (adaptive dimension). In the same way, the buying company's demands on the transfer can be more or less extensive

Table 1. International profile of Swedish exports

| | % of total export value |
|---|---|
| 1. Norway | 12.8 |
| 2. United Kingdom | 11.1 |
| 3. West Germany | 10.3 |
| 4. Denmark | 9.5 |
| 5. Finland | 6.0 |
| 6. USA | 5.3 |
| 7. France | 5.0 |
| 8. Netherlands | 4.4 |
| 9. Italy | 3.0 |

(general dimension) and more or less unique (adaptive dimension). Correspondingly, the selling company can be characterized in terms of its problem solving ability and its transfer ability. This describes the seller's ability to meet the buyer's need for problem solving and transfer in the two dimensions respectively.

These four dimensions will now be used to describe the way the Swedish companies perceive the five markets. In order to measure each dimension indices based on several statements have been constructed. For each dimension four or five statements have been weighted together.[7] The results are given in Table 2.

The results show that the markets are perceived to be quite different on all the four dimensions. The customers in West Germany and Sweden are perceived to be much more demanding than in the other three countries. France takes a middle position in all the four dimensions. Italian and UK customers are perceived to have the lowest requirements. The difference is larger in the general dimensions than in the adaptive ones. Comparing the four dimensions with each other, one marked difference is that France is perceived to be more demanding in transfer than in problem solving.

The results are on one hand as expected, with Italy at the bottom and West Germany at the top, which is in line with common Swedish prejudices but, on the other hand, surprising in respect of the rankings of the other three countries. The perceived high requirements of the domestic market compared with France and the United Kingdom are surprising, as also are the perceived low requirements in the United Kingdom. These results cannot be explained by the general situation but we might find explanations when we now analyse the other processes.

## Supplier–Customer Relationships

The interaction between sellers and customers in industrial markets develop over time into relationships. One can characterize the relationship in a quantitative and a qualitative dimension. The quantitative dimension applies to the dependence on volume between the two sides, while the qualitative dimension concerns the function of each party for the other in other respects, such as on the dimensions of problem solving and transfer presented in the preceding section.

Table 2. Perceived requirements in the five markets

| | Product solving need[a] | | Transfer need[b] | |
|---|---|---|---|---|
| | General | Adaptive | General | Adaptive |
| Italy | 101 | 100 | 104 | 100 |
| United Kingdom | 100 | 110 | 100 | 107 |
| France | 106 | 111 | 131[b] | 114 |
| Sweden | 131[b] | 120[b] | 134[b] | 117[b] |
| West Germany | 135[b] | 126[b] | 149[b] | 120 |

[a]The lowest value in each dimension has been given the index 100.
[b]The differences between these values and the lowest value (100) are all significant at the 5% level.

*Quantitative Aspects*

The importance of a given relationship may vary significantly in relation to its quantitative dimension. For example, a customer may use a certain supplier as its main source and some customers will develop to be the seller's main customers. A relationship can be more or less balanced in these terms. It is balanced if the parties are of the same importance to each other. It is unbalanced if the relationship is more important to one side than to the other.

The analysis starts from the selling companies' point of view by determining the importance of individual customers in different markets. For our sample we have determined the relative importance of customer relationships by calculating what share of the sales, to the market in question, the buying companies account for. These figures are given in Table 3.

Table 3 shows that the largest customers in the United Kingdom, France and Italy, on average, take a larger share of the sellers' sales to respective markets than the customers in Sweden and West Germany do. With regard to France and Italy, the explanation is probably that these markets are smaller for the selling companies and therefore the marketing activities are concentrated on a smaller number of customers. The averages for the United Kingdom, West Germany and Sweden are more difficult to understand in relation to each other. The high value for the United Kingdom depends, to a great extent, on four relationships with very large shares. Hence, this value can eventually be explained by a chance variation. On the other hand, the low average for West Germany is very interesting. One explanation may be that the West German market is much larger or is approached by the Swedish companies in a much broader way than the other. Another explanation may be a difference in the behaviour of the German buying companies. We shall return to this point later.

The relationship will now have been looked at from the other side's point of view, i.e. by calculating the volume which the buying firms take from the Swedish producers. This can be seen in Table 4.

In Sweden the producers are usually the main suppliers and on average account for 76% of the purchased volume. In the foreign markets the situation is clearly

Table 3. Customer's relative importance by sales value

| | Percentage share of supplier's turnover in each country (number of relationships) | | | | |
|---|---|---|---|---|---|
| Customer location | 0 – 20 | 21 – 60 | 61 – 100 | Total | Average share (%) |
| France | 8 | 6 | 2 | 16 | 35 |
| Italy | 3 | 5 | 2 | 10 | 39 |
| Sweden | 11 | 5 | 2 | 18 | 25 |
| United Kingdom | 6 | 6 | 4 | 16 | 36 |
| West Germany | 13 | 5 | 1 | 19 | 19 |
| Total | 41 | 27 | 11 | 79[a] | 28 |

[a]15 missing value

Table 4. Swedish suppliers' relative importance by purchase value

| Customer location | Percentage share of customers' total purchase in each country (number of relationships) | | | | |
|---|---|---|---|---|---|
| | 0–29 | 30–69 | 70–100 | Total | Average share (%) |
| France | 6 | 3 | 7 | 16 | 55 |
| Italy | 3 | 4 | 3 | 10 | 55 |
| Sweden | 0 | 5 | 13 | 18 | 76 |
| United Kingdom | 3 | 6 | 7 | 16 | 60 |
| West Germany | 7 | 7 | 5 | 19 | 48 |
| Total | 19 | 25 | 35 | 79[a] | 59 |

[a]15 missing values.

different. In West Germany there are many examples where the Swedish company is a marginal supplier, or at best a minor supplier. The Swedish producer is combined with other suppliers, usually with the German supplier who is the main supplier. But there are also examples of the Swedish company as the main supplier. In the other markets the situation is similar to the German, although less pronounced. Tables 3 and 4 show that the Swedish companies' situation is rather different in the domestic market compared to the most important export markets. At home, the Swedish suppliers are largest and most important whilst in Europe they are marginal. By combining the two last tables it is possible to get a more comprehensive picture of the relationships as shown in Table 5.

The four cases identified in the matrix are interesting because they reflect different power-dependence situations between buyer and supplier. In the "independent" and the "mutually dependent" cases, the relationships are balanced from a quantitative perspective because in the first case the parties are both marginal to each other and in

Table 5. Types of relationships

| The importance of the buyer (share of selling firm's turnover) | Importance of the supplier (share of buying firm's purchases) | |
|---|---|---|
| | Marginal supplier (0 – 49%)[a] | Main supplier (50–100%)[b] |
| Marginal buyer (0–20%)[b] | (Independent) 18% | (Seller-dominated) 32% |
| Main buyer (21–100%)[b] | (buyer-dominated) 22% | (Mutually-dependent) 27% |

[a]In percentage of total number of relationships, $n = 77$, 17 missing values.
[b]The class grouping is based on the following reasoning. When the supplier accounts for more than 50% it is always the main supplier and therefore so much larger than the nearest supplier that the buyer would have major problems in replacing it quickly. When the customer, on the other hand, accounts for more than 20% of the seller's turnover this means that it will be a clear disadvantage to the seller (e.g. capacity utilization) if the customer turns to another supplier.

the second case both are important to each other. In the "seller-dominated" case the relationships are more important for the customer than for the seller and the latter, thus, will be in a powerful position. The opposite situation appears in the "buyer-dominant" case where the seller is more dependent on the relationship than the buyer is, which in turn will give the buyer a favourable position. More relationships are classified as favourable to one side or the other than as balanced.

Almost half of the relationships in the independent group are with German customers and none with Swedish. This situation seems to arise mainly with export and particularly when large markets are covered. The reason for this is, partly, that there is a large competitor (which is common in a large market) and a not very concentrated demand, in combination with a certain breadth (in terms of number of approach customers) in the selling company's marketing approach. The existence of the large competitor explains the supplier's marginal position and the dispersed demand, in combination with the number of customers approached by the supplier, explains the buyer's marginal position.

Almost half of the relationships classified in the seller-dominated groups are with Swedish customers, but German and French customer relationships are also somewhat over-represented. The conditions for this type of relationship are partly that the seller has a good position, and partly that the market is covered in a relatively intensive way. This is most common in the domestic market but these conditions can also apply to some companies who have established strong positions in export markets.

Among the relationships in the buyer-dominated groups there is an equal spread of customers in different countries. The characteristics for this situation is that the buyer has a very large need, in relation to the supplier's capacity, as it takes a very large part of the supplier's sales, yet still purchases its main volume somewhere else. As can be seen from the above described distribution, these conditions appear in all the markets that are included here.

In the groups with the mutually important relationships, Italian customer relationships are common with half of them classified into this group. English customer relationships are also frequently of this type. Relationships which are found here clearly contain a feature of exclusiveness. Both parties have given priority to the other – given each other exclusiveness. Such a situation can arise for a selling company when it sells to smaller markets. Then the selling company concentrates its marketing on one or a few key customers, as it usually does not have the resources to cover all customers. On the buyer side certain companies can choose to invest in foreign suppliers if, for example, there are no domestic producers, or the domestic producers have too close contacts with a large domestic competitor. This type of structural reasoning can lead to this kind of relationship, but there are also other reasons. These are associated with the qualitative aspect of the relationship.

In summing up this section it is possible to postulate a hypothesis that individual relationships, from a quantitative point of view, become less important to both sides when the market is large both in total terms and for the companies concerned (e.g. West Germany for Swedish companies), but that the opposite applies to markets at a greater distance (France and Italy for Swedish companies). We shall return to the quantitative aspects of the relationships later, but first we will deal with the qualitative aspects.

*Qualitative Aspects.* The qualitative dimension in the relationships relates to the role or function the partners play for each other. Earlier, we have used the concepts of *problem solving and transfer* to characterize the perceived requirements of the customers. The same concepts will be used here to characterize the qualitative dimensions of relationships investigated.

The analysis will be done in two steps. In the first one the customers' way of using supplier companies will be analysed. Within this section we begin by looking at the variation in how different suppliers are used. After that the differences between customers in the five countries are analysed.

In the second step the suppliers' way of using the customers in technical development is described and analysed in relation to different customers' groups.

*I. Customers' ways of using the Swedish suppliers.* First the problem solving and transfer concepts will be used to illustrate how different suppliers are used by their customers. This will be done by positioning some Swedish special steel and paper and pulp suppliers in diagrams concerning problem solving and transfer ability (Fig. 3). The two dimensions in the diagrams represent the general and the adaptive aspects respectively. In the diagrams the extreme positions have been named in order to give an idea of their content.

The positions have been estimated from the actual relationships, i.e. they are averages for the relationships which have been investigated for the respective business units. In other words, they reflect the largest customers' way of using the suppliers' ability. As can be seen from Fig. 3a and b there is a large variation in how different suppliers are used by their customers. There is a large variation with each group of companies but there is also an interesting difference between the two industries as they have different types of distribution. The positions of the special-steel companies vary primarily in the general dimension (vertical axis) while the paper and pulp companies vary in the adaptation dimension (horizontal axis).

Both the inter- and intra-industry variation are interesting as it indicates firstly that different suppliers have chosen different strategies in how to approach customers and secondly that there seems to be a systematic difference in terms of the direction of the variation between the two industries. Thus, the competition is in different dimensions in the two industries.

The position of a supplier in the two figures is important from a strategic point of view as it has implications both technically and organisationally. In order to be competitive the supplier having a "product development" position must have other features than if it has a "price cutter" or a "customer adaptor" position (see Håkansson, 1980).

The same type of diagram will now be used to describe how the Swedish companies relate to different foreign markets. This is done in Fig. 4a and b. Here the average for all the companies' relationships in a certain market have been calculated. The figures show that the largest variations between the different groups of customer relationships are in the adaptation dimension in both diagrams. In general, adaptations are much larger in relation to Swedish customers than to the other customers. This is interesting as the need for adaptations in relation to the Swedish customers compared to the foreign could be expected to be the other way around.

We would expect the greatest need for adaptations in the most "distant" market.

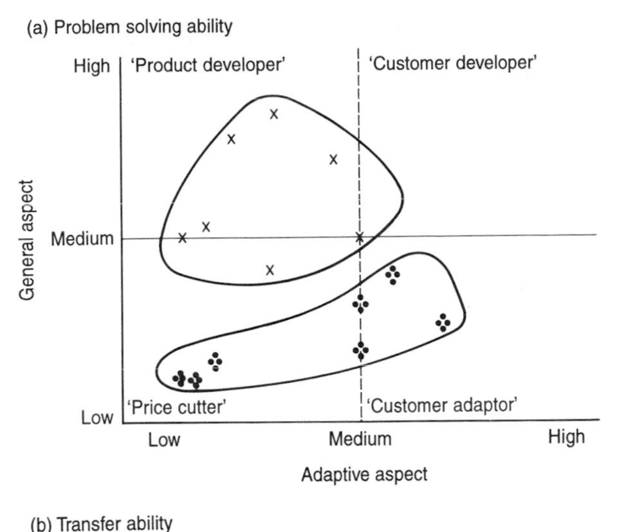


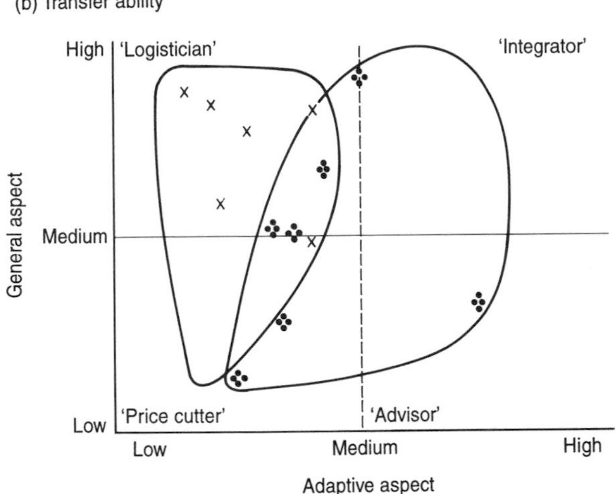


*Notes:* x = special steel units, • = paper and pulp units. Results from a separate study of four paper and pulp firms have been included.

Fig. 3 The market positions of Swedish company units.

Yet Italy has the lowest value on the adaptation dimension in both diagrams. Another interesting fact is that the relationships with buying companies in West Germany are classified as rather low in both the general and the adaptation dimensions for the problem solving ability, but are rated second on both these dimensions in the transfer ability. In other words, the interest of the German customers in questions of delivery is very apparent. Customers in England, however, are most interested in the selling company's ability to adapt solutions to their needs.

The variations in the general dimensions are rather small in both diagrams, compared to the variations in the adaptation dimension. The variations are almost twice as large in the adaptation dimension for problem solving ability as for the

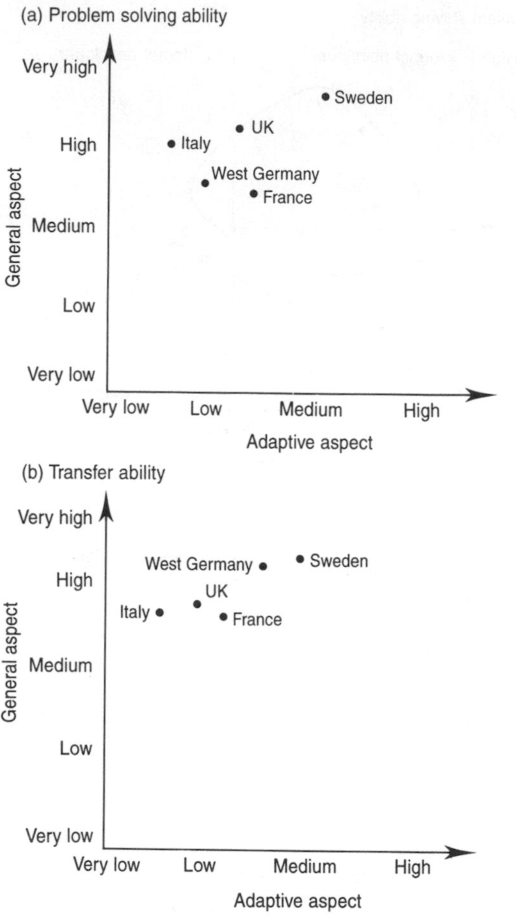


*Notes:* An average for each country has been calculated based on all investigated relationships between Swedish suppliers and customers in that country.

Fig. 4 Customer relationships of Swedish suppliers.

general dimension, and almost three times for the adaptation dimension in the transfer ability compared to the general dimension.

If the results are considered from the "selling companies" point of view there are two possible explanations for the differences. Firstly, the result can be a direct consequence of conscious marketing strategies. Secondly, the strategies may be the same, but because of the greater geographical and psychic distance, the effects are different. We know from the interviews with the companies that the first explanation is not very probable. The differences in this respect with regard to the companies' marketing strategies were not mentioned. Instead several managers claimed that their company treated customers in all the five markets in the same way.

The second explanation is therefore more reasonable. This means that it is more difficult for the selling companies to establish more intensive and individual relationships when the distance is greater, even if they have their own organizational unit in the market. The results therefore indicate a managerial dilemma. If the company wants to establish the same type of customer relationships in all markets it probably has to make larger investments in the marketing organization when the distance increases. Otherwise it has to reduce its ambitions in at least the adaptation dimension of the customer relationships. The results also give cause for a closer study of the connection between "company interaction processes" and the design of the selling company's marketing organization at home and abroad. The results are also interesting compared with the perceptions described earlier. We will return to this point in the conclusion.

*II. Swedish suppliers' way of using their customers.* A selling company can "utilize" relationships with its customer companies in different ways. For example, the selling companies can use the customers' development ability or their ability to give information. We shall look more closely at the development aspect. We can get a picture of this by looking at the type of person who is involved in the interaction. If research personnel are involved on the buying side, at least an indication is given that a certain part of the buying company's development capacity has been activated.[8] The data given in Table 6 illustrate this.

Two different groups can be identified in Table 7. One contains Sweden, the United Kingdom and West Germany, and the other contains Italy and France. In relation to the first group the Swedish suppliers utilize the customer's development ability in a much more extensive way than companies in the other group. In the first

Table 6. Customers' research and development involvement in the relationships

| Customer location | Share of relationships (%) |
|---|---|
| Sweden | 58 |
| United Kingdom | 53 |
| West Germany | 62 |
| France | 35 |
| Italy | 31 |
| Total | 49 |

Table 7. Suppliers' production staff involvement in the relationship

| Customer location | Share of relationships (%) |
|---|---|
| Sweden | 53 |
| United Kingdom | 35 |
| West Germany | 29 |
| France | 24 |
| Italy | 8 |
| Total | 31 |

group the figures are over 50%, while in the second group they are around 30%. This therefore means that the supplier utilizes the closest geographically located customers more extensively in research and development issues than the more distant customers.

The contribution of the research personnel on the buying side is an indication that there are discussions of the product's design and use. In the same way, it can be said that if the production personnel from the selling side are involved in the relationship this is an indication that there are discussions of how the product should be produced and/or delivered. This could be an indication that the selling company tries to utilize the buying company to get ideas to improve their own production or distribution (consciously or unconsciously). The degree of involvement of supplier production staff in relationships is shown in Table 7.

Three groups can be identified here. Sweden is in the first, the United Kingdom, West Germany and France are in the second and Italy is in the third. This indicator gives the same results as the earlier, i.e. the degree to which the selling firms use the customers' improvement potential is closely related to the distance to the different markets.

We can now sum up the qualitative aspects in the relationships. The situation seems to be clear. Both the selling and the buying companies utilize their counterparts in a much more limited way when the distance increases. This can hardly be caused by strategic reasons. A much more likely cause is the difficulty of establishing close relationships when the distance between the parties increases.

### *Total Relationships*

Having examined the quantitative and the qualitative dimensions of relationships, we notice an interesting difference. Both dimensions are related to the distance to the markets but only one – the quantitative dimension – is directly related to the size of the market. This is particularly evident for Swedish suppliers dealing with the West German market. The importance of the relationships from the quantitative point of view was there dependent on both the size of the market and on the distance. The qualitative dimension is first of all connected to the distance to the market. Taken together, this means that the marketing strategy of a selling company must be related to both the size dimension and to the distance dimension. This section can thus be summarized in Fig. 5.

As can be seen from Fig. 5 the selling firm is in a rather different situation in the four cases. Quantitatively, it has a certain relationship to the customers, and qualitatively another. As we have mentioned earlier, the results can be interpreted in various ways. Firstly, the difference we have identified can be viewed as a result of conscious planning by the selling companies. Secondly, the aims of the selling companies may be the same but owing to special circumstances in each case the different results have ensued. From our interviews everything points to the latter. If this is the case, it is clear that suppliers must adopt a more planned approach to both the qualitative and the quantitative aspects of relationships.

The quantitative and qualitative dimensions of the relationships can also be combined in a more direct way. This is done in Fig. 6.

| | Nearby Markets | Distant Markets |
|---|---|---|
| **Large Markets** | *Quantitative.* Either mutually independent or seller-dominated.<br>*Qualitative.* Both sides seek to utilise the other to the greatest possible extent. | *Quantitative.* Often mutually independent.<br>*Qualitative.* There are few examples of more extensive relationships. |
| **Small Markets** | *Quantitative.* Mutually important.<br>*Qualitative.* Both sides seek to utilise the other to the greatest possible extent. | *Quantitative.* Often mutually important but can also be buyer or seller dominated.<br>*Qualitative.* There are few examples of more extensive relationships. |

Fig. 5 Typical customer relationships in different types of markets.

The results indicate that the two variable groups have a clear connection. The group of relationships that we have characterized as "mutually independent" has the lowest values. The variation in the general dimension is much less (between 100 and 127) than in the adaptive dimension (between 100 and 283). The adaptive dimension is, thus, more affected by a variation in the quantity dimensions. The general and the adaptive dimensions have also somewhat different patterns in their variation. The general dimension varies primarily in the horizontal direction, that means in relation to differences in the supplier's position *vis-à-vis* the customer. The adaptive dimension varies both in the horizontal and in the vertical direction. These

| | Importance of supplier | | | |
|---|---|---|---|---|
| | Marginal supplier (0–49%) | | Main supplier (50–100%) | |
| **Importance of buyer** | (independent) | | (seller-dominated) | |
| | General dimension | Adaptive dimension | General dimension | Adaptive dimension |
| Marginal buyer (0–20%) | 100 | 100 | 112 | 213 |
| | (buyer-dominated) | | (mutually dependent) | |
| | General dimension | Adaptive dimension | General dimension | Adaptive dimension |
| Main buyer (21–100%) | 102 | 283 | 127 | 262 |

Fig. 6 Characteristics of customer relationships. (The quantitative dimensions – importance of supplier and buyer respectively – are the same as in Table 6. The qualitative dimensions – general and adaptive – have been calculated by adding general problem solving and general transfer to, respectively, adaptive problem solving and adaptive transfer. Then, the values in the independent cell have been used as the basis of an index in order to better show the relative positions of the four cells).

results indicate that in order to become a main supplier the company has to be better in the general dimension. The adaptive dimension, however, becomes important as soon as the relationship becomes important for at least one of the parties.

In summary, this section has shown that the characteristics of relationships both in quantitative and qualitative terms are affected by the distance to the market. Further, the quantitative dimensions are affected by the significance of the market to the companies. The quantitative and qualitative dimensions are also clearly related to each other.

### Organizing Channels for the Five Markets

A parallel process to the interaction processes with customers in a certain country relates to "channel organizing". The company, alone or together with some external unit, normally indicates activities in order to facilitate the interaction processes in several ways. Often these organizing activities include different forms of establishment.

Earlier studies have shown that most Swedish companies have followed a certain pattern in their establishment in foreign markets. Initially, the market is handled by the parent company directly. In the next phase the company use an agent and later on this agent is brought or replaced by a direct subsidiary. Sometimes this is followed by a manufacturing subsidiary (Hörnell *et al.*, 1973; Johanson and Wiedersheim-Paul, 1975; Johanson and Vahlne, 1977). The larger Swedish companies became international in the late nineteenth or in the early twentieth centuries (Carlsson, 1979, pp. 12–23). The European markets have been very important as was described earlier. Thus, the larger Swedish companies have normally been established in the larger European markets for a long time and are generally represented by their own subsidiaries (see Table 8). Many of the companies are highly internationalized and have found it functionally necessary to separate the sales in the domestic market from the parent company by establishing a special sales company in order to ensure an equal treatment of different markets.

The only export market of those investigated where there is a market variation in the companies' organizations is Italy. This market is considered by many to be unsafe and therefore companies do not wish to commit resources to setting up their own sales organizations.

Table 8. The organization in the five markets

| | Sales and manufacturing subsidiaries | Agents | Unrepresented or direct sales | Total |
|---|---|---|---|---|
| France | 18 | 4 | 1 | 23 |
| Italy | 10 | 7 | 3 | 20 |
| Sweden | 7 | 1 | 13 | 21 |
| West Germany | 18 | 3 | 1 | 22 |
| United Kingdom | 19 | 1 | 2 | 22 |

The data presented in Table 8 are based on 20 business units. The totals column in Table 8 shows that in some countries companies have both agents and their own subsidiaries. In these cases the agents may be particularly strong in a certain region or have an extensive distribution network covering certain customers. The size of the subsidiaries varies greatly, partly because some also have their own production. Therefore, there are companies that employ thousands, at the same time as there are others that consist of only a few people. The subsidiary is normally responsible for all day-to-day activities. The domestic organization backs up the field organization. How much depends clearly on, among other things, the type of product. With project deliveries, where the technical solution is adapted to the customer, the domestic organization must be involved in a completely different way than is the case with more standardized products.

The above description of the companies' international organization can be said to correspond to the companies' formal way of organizing its operations. This can be compared with its informal way of organizing its international customer relationships. This can be examined by means of sociograms. We shall use the contact network between Swedish companies and the different customer groups. The data used relate to the contacts between the Swedish head office and the customer and do not indicate contacts between the sales subsidiaries and customers. According to the earlier section, all the markets are treated more or less equally in terms of nominal organization, with each market served by its own sales subsidiary. The question now is, whether or not the informal organization gives the same picture.

Figure 7 gives the first picture of the contact network in terms of width and closeness. The width and closeness appear to follow a scale according to the following: Sweden, United Kingdom, West Germany, France and Italy. This scale probably corresponds well with how great the distances of the different markets are from Sweden. With increasing distance (geographical combined with psychic distance) the contact surface is diminished. This is regardless of the formal organization. One measurement in Fig. 7 that deviates somewhat from the general pattern is the number of persons in the Swedish selling companies who have contact with the German customers. The low value can partly be explained by the fact that the respondents pointed out that one must guard against sending too many people when visiting German customers as this is considered a sign of inefficiency there. Similarly the seller may not come too often – which can be seen in the closeness measurement.

Summing up, the companies' informal way of organizing their activities shows some interesting differences compared to their formal way of doing it. The differences are mainly related to the distance to the market. In this context the role of the sales subsidiary seems to vary in relation to the distance of the market. In the nearby markets the sales subsidiary can easily use the home office as a back-up while a more distant subsidiary has to take care of the whole customer relationship itself. Probably, this will make the subsidiary feel itself to be more independent and free to take its own actions but decrease its opportunities to design customer adapted solutions in dimensions where the home office must be involved. This can be an explanation of the low degree of adaptations towards distant customers noted earlier in this chapter.

Having examined the quantitative dimensions of the contacts let us go further and

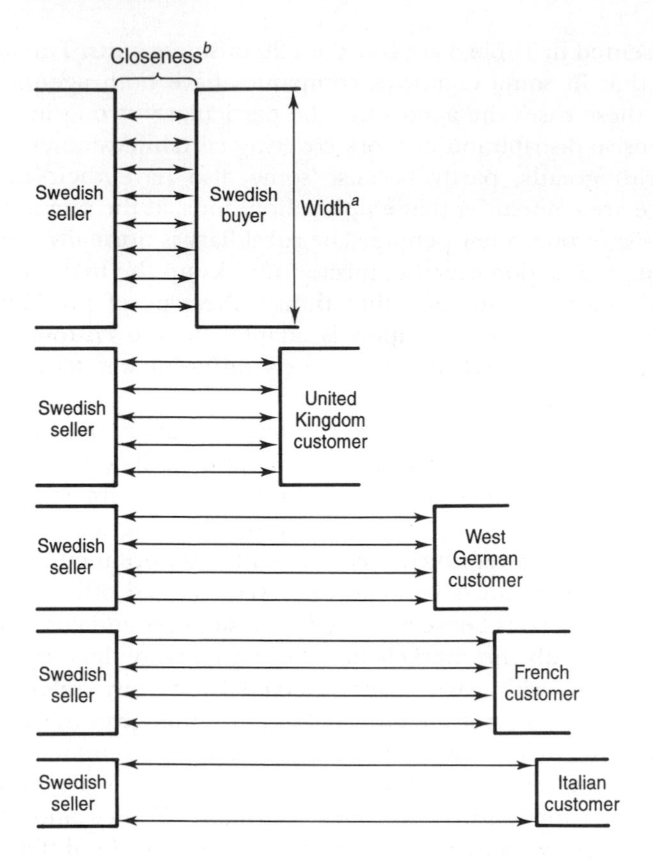


Fig. 7 Width and closeness between the Swedish suppliers and their customers in different countries. ([a]Width is measured by the number of persons from the respective sides who take an active part in the interaction. [b]Closeness is measured by the frequency of personal meetings.)

analyse the qualitative aspects by looking at which persons take part in the relationships. Since salesmen and purchaser always take part we disregard them here and focus on the production and the research and development personnel. The participation of these categories in the contact network is given in Table 9.

As can be seen from Table 9, research and development personnel in both supplying and buying companies play an active role in the relationships. On the supplier side, the research and development personnel are active in more than 60% of the relationships. The corresponding figure on the buying side is a little under 50%.

In respect of the different countries, this pattern does not however completely follows the pattern earlier found in Fig. 7. On the supplier side research and development staff are more active with Swedish and German customers. The same applies to the buying side. On the latter side, the British customers have also a relatively high figure, while the French and Italian are clearly on a lower level. On the supplier side the picture is diffuse. Here it is primarily in relation to the French customers that the figure is clearly lower than average.

Table 9. Research and development and production personnel's participation in the contact network–percentages

| | Research and development | | Production | |
|---|---|---|---|---|
| | Supplier side | Buying side | Supplier side | Buying side |
| Sweden | 68 | 58 | 53 | 84 |
| United Kingdom | 59 | 53 | 35 | 59 |
| West Germany | 71 | 62 | 29 | 81 |
| France | 53 | 35 | 24 | 76 |
| Italy | 62 | 31 | 81 | 85 |
| Averages | 63 | 49 | 31 | 77 |

Earlier, in Fig. 7, we noted some limitation in the width of the contacts with the German customers. Still, as Table 9 shows, this does not seem to affect the technical content of the relationships. Thus the fact that few people participate need not necessarily mean that the interpersonal contacts only relate to commercial matters, but they clearly put greater demands on the persons involved.

The production personnel often take part in the relationships, particularly on the buyer side. It is only the British companies that are somewhat below the others. The figures on the sales side show the earlier pattern of a successive diminution of the relationships where the distance is greater.

Figure 7 and Table 9 together indicate that the Swedish companies' informal way of organizing is quite different from their formal way of doing so. In the latter the markets were all treated in the same way but informally there is another picture. The three nearest markets – the domestic, the United Kingdom and West Germany – are more integrated with the present company's activities through a wider and closer contact network including more development and production personnel. The difference in this respect most certainly must be an important attribute in the companies' approach to the five markets.

## The Swedish Companies' Experience and Knowledge of the Five Markets

The experience and knowledge of a certain market increases gradually during the time the company deals with the market. This learning process is more rapid the more extensive the relationships are with the customers in the market or the larger the number of customers is. A company's behaviour in relating to a market in terms of perception, interaction processes with customers and channel organizing is probably highly dependent upon the total knowledge and experience it has of the market. The domestic market almost always takes a special place because the company's personnel have confidence in this in a completely different way than they have in the various export markets. Therefore, in relation to the latter we can speak of gaps of varying sizes. These can be overcome in different ways, one of which is to establish organizational units in the various markets. In these units, nationals of the foreign country are often employed, which should further decrease the gap, although there is a danger of a gap between the organizational unit and the parent company developing.

Regardless of whether a company has a unit – an agent or an office – in the foreign market or not, it is important that the parent company has knowledge and experience of the market in order to act properly. It is clear from Table 10 that Swedish companies have extensive experience of all the four export markets in question.

The domestic relationships are the oldest – on average 24 years. The relationships to the German and Italian customers have also reached a respectable age (on average 20 years). This shows that the companies that invested in Italy did so at an early stage and also that they succeeded in establishing long-term relationships. Therefore the distance does not necessarily make the relationships short term. It is only in relation to the French market that there is a significant number of younger customer relationships – seven are younger than three years. But even here there are many old relationships. One reason for the younger relationships is that the Swedish companies have recently come to regard the French market as vital with a large future potential and therefore a number of special campaigns have been carried out during the latter years. At the same time the French market is seen as very difficult for Swedish companies (Hallén, 1980).

As previously noted, measured in terms of the age of the relationships the Swedish suppliers have a substantial experience and knowledge of the four foreign markets. Earlier in this chapter, however, we have seen that the extent of contacts and the qualitative aspects of the relationships vary in relation to the four markets. The total knowledge and experience is therefore probably less for the more distant markets. Let us now see if this can be detected in some way at the individual level.

It is individuals who have responsibility for handling different markets from the head office. The experience and knowledge of these people is probably of decisive importance as to how the company is appraised by the foreign customer. It is also important in relation to the parent company's ability to manage its sales agents and subsidiaries.

Table 10. Age of relationships

| | No. of relationships by country | | | | | |
|---|---|---|---|---|---|---|
| No. of years | Swedish customers | United Kingdom customers | West German customers | French customers | Italian customers | Total |
| 1–3 | 0 | 3 | 2 | 7 | 1 | 13 |
| 3–9 | 1 | 4 | 2 | 1 | 1 | 9 |
| 10–19 | 5 | 5 | 7 | 8 | 5 | 30 |
| 20 | 12 | 4 | 9 | 1 | 5 | 31 |
| | | | | | | 81[a] |
| Average (years) | 24 | 14 | 20 | 10 | 20 | 19 |

[a]eleven missing values

If we first look at how much experience these persons have of marketing to the four markets, it can be seen in Table 11 that the total experience is substantial. In three of the markets more than 50% of the individuals have more than three years of marketing experience. It is only Italy where the experience is a little less. Still, 25% have more than six years experience of that market. This experience variable shows the same picture as the experience variable on the company level. It has also the same weakness in that it does not measure the quality of the experience.

An experience variables that may indicate the quality is the number of years the person has been living in the actual markets. By living in a country the experience and knowledge of that country reach quite another level than that gained only by visiting it. The results are shown in Table 12. Here there is a clear difference between Italy and the three other countries. The total number of years varies just a little for the other three, while it is much smaller for Italy. Of interest also is that the experience of other countries is rather substantial.

A knowledge variable that is of special interest in this international context is the persons' abilities to use foreign languages. Table 13 shows that the Swedish marketers are very good in using at least two foreign languages – English and German. Almost 50% are also good or rather good in using French. Very few have some knowledge of Italian and there are also few who can use other languages.

The problems caused by the low ability in Italian are not so great since Italian companies are used to using other languages (see Hallén, 1980). This is not the case

Table 11. General experience of marketing staff

| | Percentage of respondents with experience of | | | | | | | |
|---|---|---|---|---|---|---|---|---|
| No. of years | France | | Italy | | United Kingdom | | West Germany | |
| 0–2 | 46 | | 60 | | 49 | | 46 | |
| 3–5 | 28 | | 15 | | 17 | | 19 | |
| 6–10 | 13 | 54 | 13 | 40 | 16 | 51 | 19 | 54 |
| 11–20 | 12 | | 9 | | 17 | | 12 | |
| > 20 | 1 | | 3 | | 1 | | 4 | |
| | 100 | | 100 | | 100 | | 100 | |

Table 12. Marketers' experience of working abroad

| | No. of respondents | | | | |
|---|---|---|---|---|---|
| No. of years | United Kingdom | West Germany | France | Italy | Other countries |
| 1–2 | 5 | 3 | 6 | 0 | 8 |
| 3–5 | 2 | 3 | 1 | 1 | 6 |
| 6–10 | 0 | 0 | 1 | 0 | 2 |

Number of persons who have never lived abroad: 45

Table 13. Marketers' language abilities

| | Percentage of respondents | | | |
|---|---|---|---|---|
| | None | Some | Good | Very good |
| English | 0 | 0 | 5 | 95 |
| German | 8 | 1 | 27 | 64 |
| French | 28 | 25 | 16 | 31 |
| Italian | 89 | 7 | 3 | 1 |
| Other languages | 97 | 0 | 0 | 3 |

for the French companies and this may cause problems in French customer relationships.

In summary then, the experience and knowledge process seems to have developed in a more extensive way in relation to the United Kingdom, West Germany and France compared with Italy. But there are differences even among these three. This is most pronounced regarding the language ability. There are no or very few problems in the relationships with United Kingdom customers from this point of view but communication problems can be expected in relationships with French customers.

## CONCLUSIONS AND IMPLICATIONS

An important starting point for the analysis made in this chapter is the view that it is impossible for a company to allow rational and comprehensive decision processes when designing its international strategy. Instead we have, in accordance with Lindblom (1959), characterised the decision process as a process of muddling through where the company's international approach successively develops. The word "approach" is used instead of "strategy" in order to indicate the different characters of the decision processes. Furthermore, there is not just one single process behind the international approach of a company but several subprocesses each of which influence different aspects of it. These subprocesses involve different persons within and outside the company and they can develop in different ways.

Four such subprocesses have been dealt with here when analysing the Swedish companies' way of approaching some European markets. Two of these are related to the situation of the company and two to the development of the characteristics of the individuals within the company. The customer interaction process and the channel organizing process are the two characterizing the situation of the company. Of these, the interaction process is a main feature of the whole project. The relationships between selling and buying companies are believed to develop over time in different ways depending on the intentions and abilities of the two counterparts. The channel organizing process includes all the activities that are carried out in order to handle problems and resources in relation to different markets.

The two processes related to the individuals are the market perception process and the market knowledge and experience process.

Together these four processes have been used in this chapter to characterize the development of the Swedish companies' international approach. In this last section two integrating issues will be treated. First, the Swedish companies' approach towards each market will be summarized and compared with the approaches to the other markets. In this way we try to give a more complete picture of the approach towards individual markets. Secondly, we will discuss how a company can change its approach towards a market.

### General Approach of Swedish Companies Towards European Markets

The analysis of the four subprocesses towards the five country markets reveals a clear pattern which we attempt to summarize in Table 14. There are clear differences in respect to how the five countries are perceived and approached but mainly they seem to form three groups. In the first we have the domestic market. In the second we find the United Kingdom and West Germany and in the third France and Italy.[10]

Not unexpectedly the approach towards the domestic market is characterized by close contacts and by being perceived to be of a high general importance. More unexpected was the finding that the Swedish customers are highly demanding of the Swedish sellers in the relationships. These high requirements were found both in the perceptions and in the actual relationships. These relationships can be of major importance to the seller from a development point of view. Thus the importance of the domestic market is more significant for these highly international companies – exporting over 80% of their turnover – than we expected.

The United Kingdom and West Germany are two important and close markets of Swedish companies. The differences in the approaches to them are quite interesting. West Germany is perceived to be more important and demanding than the United Kingdom while at the same time the interaction and experience with the United Kingdom is more extensive. The differences in how the markets are perceived are a result of the difference in economic performance in the countries during the last 10

Table 14. How Swedish companies view and approach the five markets

| | Sweden | United Kingdom | West Germany | France | Italy |
|---|---|---|---|---|---|
| Perceived importance of the market[a] | 1 | 3 | 2 | 4 | 5 |
| Customer needs and requirements[b] | 2 | 4 | 1 | 3 | 5 |
| Knowledge and experience of the market[c] | 1 | 2 | 3 | 4 | 5 |
| Extent of interaction[d] | 1 | 2 | 3 | 4 | 5 |
| Extent of informal organization[e] | 1 | 2 | 3 | 4 | 5 |

Rankings are based on the various measures discussed in this chapter:
[a]1 = most important;
[b]1 = most demanding;
[c]1 = most knowledge and experience;
[d]1 = highest volume and extent of informal interaction;
[e]1 = largest network of informal contacts.

years. This has been observed by the companies and they try to adapt it in different ways but it takes time. The earlier contacts and knowledge "lock" the company into the old structure and any significant change can be likened to turning a large tanker.

France and Italy are also important markets but at a greater distance. Italy is especially seen to be a much more marginal market than the other four. A better description is that it is not perceived as a market but much more as a country where there is a limited number of companies that are worth dealing with. France is somewhat larger for the Swedish companies and more important and is given more attention. Still the French market is difficult to establish close contact with for Swedish companies. The distance effect – particularly in the psychic dimension – can be seen in the relationships in the way that both parties lower their requirements on each other in terms of adaptations. Thus, the parties do business with each other in a more standardized way than in the relationships in the three closer markets. It is too risky or troublesome to try for more extensive relationships.

### *Implications for Management*

The implications for management can be summarized under three headings. These are investments, organization and change.

#### *Investments*

To enter and develop a new market usually requires substantial investments. First, in order to establish relationships with new customers, resources are required during a certain time period – often over several years. Secondly, at the same time, resources are needed for organizing the activities in the market. Thirdly, the personnel at headquarters have to invest time and effort in developing their knowledge and experience as well as their perception. All the four processes require resources in order to develop.

From a managerial point this means:

1. There is a need to be aware of the total requirement of resources and the time involved when considering approaching a new market.
2. It is important to establish a long-term way of handling acute problems in each country where the company is.
3. The company must continually reassess the need or potential for further investments in relation to a market where the four processes have stagnated.
4. Investments may have to be made at the headquarters as well as in the actual market.

#### *Organization*

The investments in the four types of processes must be considered in order to be effective. This is to a large degree an organizational problem in terms of both structure and processes. There are several important issues:

1. The organizational unit in the market. This must be designed in such a way that it suits the type of interaction process the company wants to establish in the market.
2. The relationship between the home office and the market unit, which must reflect both the types of customer relationships and the aspirations of the headquarters.
3. The interface between the export/marketing department and other internal departments/functions such as production, development, etc.

All these three issues are interrelated and the degree to which the company has succeeded in integrating them will determine its ability to coordinate the different investments discussed earlier, which in turn is close to its local effectiveness in exporting to a certain market.

### Changing an Approach

An approach develops successively over time and is diffused through the whole company or at least a part of it. It includes, as we have seen above, investments and the total organization. To change such an approach takes time and substantial resources. But at the same time there are always changes, always developments. The problem is, of course, that the change can go too slowly or in the wrong direction from the management point of view. In order to speed up the change or alter the direction, it is not sufficient for the management just to make a decision and then require that it should be followed. Additionally, agreement and commitment are crucial aspects. For example, there must be an agreement between the people working in the market (in the sales subsidiary, etc.) and the people at the headquarters about the change. Even then it will take time. In the results presented earlier we saw that West Germany was perceived to be more important and demanding than the United Kingdom. This perception had not, however, yet influenced the behaviour throughout all the companies examined, although it probably will in due course.

A lot of companies try to accomplish changes by more limited activities. For example, some try to increase their knowledge or experience by recruiting staff who have previous experience of a certain market. Others encourage their personnel to follow language courses. Other types of activities are reorganizations of sales subsidiaries or replacement of agents by sales subsidiaries. But if these attempts do not follow a more long-term pattern they often fail to achieve the desired results, since other aspects of the approach are unchanged.

Thus in order to change an established approach towards a certain market there is a need both for a large initial effort and for a constant pressure over a period of five years. The initial activities as well as the longer term activities must be directed towards several of the aspects discussed earlier in this chapter. Some of the possible means that can be used will now be discussed in relation to each of the four variable groups.

*(a) Perception and experience.* The two variables relating to individuals can be treated together. There are basically two different ways these variables can be changed,

either by influencing the personnel or by changing the personnel. The second can be achieved in the long run by changing recruitment practices. For example the company can require that new personnel should have a certain background. Changes to achieve effects in the short term demand more dramatic exchanges of people but this can only be recommended in very special situations.

Means that can be used in order to influence the existing personnel are highly diversified. A common one is education through internal or external courses. Another one is internal communication campaigns where the management tries to spread both information and an attitude towards a certain market. A third means is the circulation of personnel, especially those people who are heading for senior positions. It is important to note that all these means can be used for personnel in the unit on the market as well as in the parent company.

Normally it is much easier to accomplish such changes in the unit in the market but often it is much more important that it is done in a systematic way at home.

*(b) Relationships.* In order to change the kind of relationships the company has with its customers it can choose between changing the existing customers for new ones (entering new relationships) or successively changing/developing the existing relationships. The company can in the first case direct its activities towards other segments of customers (more or less demanding, etc.). In the latter case its has to change its image and/or its technical or organizational features and performance. If it believes that it already has the right resources it can concentrate on changing the image. If not, it is more important to change the resources. This is also the normal case when the company wants to establish new kinds of relationships.

*(c) Marketing organization.* One means to influence the kind of relationship is to change the organization. But this can be done also for other reasons. It is too simplified merely to advocate changing the organization as this can be done in many ways. The structure can be changed by a higher degree of specialization or centralization. The organizational processes such as planning and control can be changed to give more standardization or formalization and so on. One important issue here is the function of the unit in the market as well as of its connections with headquarters. The ways in which the Swedish companies have solved these issues during the last ten years are possibly a little too static. Most companies have followed a standardized way by using sales subsidiaries as profit centres. This solution is certainly effective in some cases but is more doubtful in others. The organization must be adapted to the other aspects of the approach and especially to the kind of customers relationships the company wishes to establish.

In conclusion, this chapter has described a company's approach towards a market as multidimensional and time-related. Therefore, any approach is difficult to change as it is based on substantial investments in time and resources. These characteristics of the approach put great demands on the skills and abilities of the managers. The investment character, in combination with the stepwise development of the approach, requires persistency and consistency as well as an ability to see the long-term consequences of a lot of small and short-term decisions.

The multidimensionality of the approach requires the manager to be sensitive and creative in the use of means. Furthermore, he must be a generalist in the way that he must be able to use a lot of different kinds of means. In summary the manager must be a highly specialized generalist!

## NOTES

1. It is, of course, the personnel of the company that perceives, thinks, etc., so when the word "company" is used it should read as "company and its personnel".
2. For a discussion of the theoretical background see Chapter 2 of Håkansson (1982).
3. The term organizing is here used in the same way as in Weich (1969, 1974). Weich criticizes the use of the word organization. "The word, organization, is a noun and it is also a myth. If one looks for an organization one will not find it. What will be found is that there are events, linked together, that transpire within concrete walls and these sequences, their pathways, their timing, are the forms we erroneously make into substances when we talk about organizations" (1974, p. 358). Weich therefore uses the word organizing which is characterized by "repetitive, reciprocal, contingent behaviours that develop and are maintained between two or more actors" (Weich, 1969, p. 91).
4. There are certain exceptions to this assumption, e.g. if the country in which the company is situated is very heterogeneous, and also in the relationships with markets which border the country in question.
5. See Hallén (1980), Turnbull and Cunningham (1981), Perrin (1979) and Kutschker and Kirsch (1980).
6. The following statements were used to construct an index for each dimension:

   General problem solving
   (a) In . . . companies great attention is paid to product appearance (positively)
   (b) Consistent quality is closely watched by . . . customers (positively)
   (c) Buyers often tend to overemphasize product price and are thus not very susceptible to arguments about other less evident cost consequences (negatively)
   (d) . . . customers do not generally require detailed technical information (negatively)
   (e) . . . purchasers generally have to show their superiors and colleagues that they have negotiated a good price (negatively)
   (f) . . . companies are keen on new technical solutions.

   Adaptive problem solving
   (a) . . . companies are often interested in joint product development activities
   (b) . . . companies generally expect suppliers to make product adaptations.
   (c) . . . companies are usually unwilling to comply with international product standards
   (d) It is impossible to cooperate closely with . . . companies (negatively).

   General transfer
   (a) . . . customers often demand that we make very quick deliveries
   (b) Punctual deliveries are a necessary condition for keeping . . . customers
   (c) Immediate handling of complaints is a necessary condition for keeping . . . customers
   (d) We can always trust . . . customers to keep us fully informed of any developments that may affect us.

   Adaptive transfer
   (a) It is necessary to follow up how our products are used by . . . customers
   (b) We have to maintain close personal contacts with . . . customers
   (c) . . . companies often suggest that we jointly coordinate our production plans
   (d) . . . companies expect deliveries to be based on their production plans rather than ours
   (e) . . . companies expect foreign suppliers to conform to the usual ways of conducting business
7. The same does not apply to the research and development personnel on the seller side since they often do pure selling work.

## REFERENCES

Carlson, S. (1979) Swedish industry goes abroad. *Studentlitteratur*, Uppsala (1980).

Håkansson, H. Marketing strategies on industrial markets: a framework applied to a steel product. *European Journal of Marketing*, **14** (5/6), 365–76 (1980).

Håkansson, H. (ed.). *International Marketing and Purchasing of Industrial Goods – An Interaction Approach.* John Wiley and Sons, New York (1982).

Håkansson, H. and Wootz, B. Supplier selection in an international environment – an experimental study. *Journal of Marketing Research*, **XII** (Feb), 46–51 (1975).

Hallén, I. *Sverige pa Europamarknaden Asikter om inköp och marknadsföring* (Sweden in the European Market. Opinions about Purchasing and Marketing). University of Lund, Lund (1980).

Hornell, F., Vahlne, J. F. and Weidersheim-Paul, F. *Export och utlands etableringar* (Export and Foreign Establishment). Almqvist and Wiksell, Stockholm (1973).

Johanson, J. and Vahlne, J. E. The internationalization process of the firm – a model of knowledge development and increasing foreign market commitments. *Journal of International Business*, **8** (1), 23–32 (1977).

Johanson, J. and Weidersheim-Paul, F. The internationalization of the firm – four Swedish case studies. *Journal of Management Studies*, **2** (3), 305–22 (1975).

Lindblom, C. E. The science of muddling through. *Public Administration Review*, **19**, 79–88 (1959).

Thompson, J. *Organization in Action.* McGraw Hill, New York (1967).

# 7

# Russian Networks in Transition: Implications for Managers*

*Asta Salmi*

## INTRODUCTION

The network approach to markets has evolved over the past two decades. This holistic view focuses on the interdependence between economic actors and analyses systems of interorganizational relationships in industrial markets.[1,4,19,20] It differs considerably from the traditional ways in which markets and marketing management are seen.

Network research encompasses two main orientations. One considers networks as strategic arrangements set up by individual firms and focuses on relationship management.[9,20] This orientation is prescriptive in flavor and offers direct and operational implications.[2] The other orientation takes a more descriptive and metaphoric view of networks. This research tradition has been developed primarily in Europe and the Nordic countries, and has largely centred around the industrial marketing and purchasing (IMP) group.[1,4,8,15] The present article draws on the latter research tradition. Therefore, it begins by discussing the kind of managerial and strategic implications that the descriptive network view of markets can offer.

It has been argued that the holistic network perspective is useful for understanding the transition of the former Soviet Union from a planned to a market economy.[13,18] The fundamental process of change being experienced throughout the entire economy, including the industrial network, presents considerable challenges not only to researchers but also to Eastern and Western managers active on the market. Given that Russian managers are now asking questions like: "What is the market?" and "How should one act in market conditions?" this is the perfect time to discuss the network world view, and its implications, in the context of the transition process now in progress in the former Soviet Union.

The purpose of this article is to discuss the strategic implications of the network

*This is a revised version of the study presented at the 9th IMP Conference, Bath, United Kingdom, Sept. 23–25, 1993.

Reprinted by permission of the publisher from Russian Networks in Transition by A. Salmi in *Industrial Marketing Management*, Vol. 25, pp 37–45.

view in the context of Russia's transition to a market economy, the aim being to increase manager's sensitivity to network thinking. First, a brief review of the managerial implications in the network literature is provided. Central issues are the focal firm viewpoint, network position, and the strategic level of decision-making. Second, company positions in the changing Russian networks are inspected. Finally, implications for Eastern managers (the country's internal economy) and Western managers (the country's foreign trade) are explored.

## IMPLICATIONS OF THE NETWORK APPROACH

### Focal Firm Viewpoint

According to the research tradition established by the IMP group, industrial networks emerge as a consequence of interaction between economic parties; they are neither designed nor strategically created. Basically, the network approach examines a network from an aggregate, holistic perspective. The unit of analysis is the network of interorganizational relationships, not that of an individual firm or relationship. The primary aim of the network approach is not prescription; rather, the goal is description and understanding of network structures and processes.

It is clear that the network approach can provide an interesting tool for the industrial market analyst. But what kind of insight can it provide for managers?

In his review of the network research tradition, Easton[3] notes that "... normative implications ... are, in a sense, external to the industrial networks approach but provide an interpretation of it by taking a focal firm viewpoint" (p. 25). Thus, in addition to the basic holistic view, and in order to draw managerial implications, we can adopt a focal firm's view to networks. The goal, then, is to understand systems of relationships from a focal firm's perspective.

### Network Strategies

In the network literature, the concept of network position offers perhaps the most direct link to company strategies. In network terms, strategies are efforts by the actors to influence their network position.[11] Network position was first defined "as the roles that the organization has for other organizations that it is related to, directly or indirectly" (p. 266). Both micro and macro positions are discussed; the former refers to the actor's relation to one specific counterpart, whereas the latter reflects the role of the organization in its network.[8,14]

Position in the network determines the organization's strategic situation. Through its network position, the firm gains access to external resources controlled by other firms. Network positions are the result of investments in exchange relationships. Because network processes are cumulative, not only short-term profit but also the future network position in the long-term should be considered. Furthermore, earlier position investments – relationships with organizations and people – can be strategically used when establishing new positions.

A central strategic task is to establish, develop, defend, and maintain the network position by altering the patterns of relationships. The relationships, in turn, develop as a consequence of interaction among individuals. The network approach therefore pays much attention to the interacting personnel of the company and less attention to the top managers' decision-making. Managing is not seen to be "a unidirectional process controlled by, and ultimately derived from the top level but rather a multidirectional process covering every level and every corner of the organization" (pp. 15–16).[5]

The network approach directs strategic management to focus on two issues: the subjective nature of interpretation of the firm and its environment, and the interdependence prevailing in networks.[15] The first issue deals with very basic assumptions in our approach: the network is not transparent, and the context of the firm is enacted by management. The networks can only be learned about by acting in them, and relevant market information is gathered through interaction with other actors. Defining and interpreting the relevant network, or focal net, is therefore a major challenge to the management. The second issue emphasizes that positions in the network are dependent on earlier investments, and that these are interdependent: any change in one actor's position simultaneously means change in the position of the others.

The network view rejects the traditional planning view to strategic management, according to which strategy is a plan that is drafted internally and then implemented.[8] In essence, the network view to strategy stresses action more than planning. It recommends[6] that managers should "learn from what is happening, reflect from all reactions, instead of thinking out and planning everything beforehand" (p. 122).

The network view leads managers to focus on the organization's "relating" to the context. Effort should be directed not to managing the company's internal resources, but rather to managing the organization's relations with its environment. In some cases, of course, the use of internal resources may dominate company strategies.

## Managerial Implications

With respect to the focal firm's view of context and consequent managerial implications, the network literature tends to distinguish between two focus areas: the micro and macro view of network. Thus Håkansson[6] discusses both interaction between network actors and handling networks: Johansson and Mattsson[10] define micro-position as well as macro-position in the network; and Easton[3] discusses both management of relationships and the strategic position in a network.

These two areas of focus, or managerial orientations, call for, respectively,

1. explicit attention to individual relationships in their context, and
2. sensitivity to holistic network thinking.

Fundamentally, a holistic view is essential for network management, and these basic orientations are therefore tightly intertwined. Essentially, they reflect the development of the network approach; interest has shifted from interaction in individual relationships to total networks.[1,4]

The former managerial orientation concentrates on such issues as resource allocation between partners and management of individual relationships. It relates to the management of marketing and purchasing functions (even though the network view emphasizes a holistic view of the company and interdependence between company functions). Four key elements of relationships are stressed: mutual orientation, dependence upon others, various bonds, and investments.[3] This approach draws heavily on the interaction approach, but in addition, it considers each relationship in the context of other relationships. In essence, not only direct relationships but also indirect relationships are taken into account.

The latter managerial orientation involves a more holistic view of the network in which the company is embedded. Besides the concept of position, the concept of the company's strategic identity is defined.[7] These issues are clearly among the firm's general management tasks rather than its marketing management tasks. This is also more in line with genuine network thinking. The network approach is still in the early stages of development; this holistic strategic thinking, in particular, needs to be developed further.

In general, the managerial implications of the network view are rather vague. The aim is to "sensitize management to network thinking",[16] or to present "a new way of seeing the world".[1] Owing to the basic assumptions of the approach, it is questionable whether very precise recommendations can ever be derived.

To sum up, in order to draw managerial implications we must adopt a focal firm's viewpoint to the network. The managerial implications lie largely at the level of strategy, they relate to the concept of position, and they take into consideration interrelatedness and dynamics, features that characterize networks. Overall, the managerial implications of the network view boil down to rather vague recommendations concerning (1) explicit attention to individual relationships in their context and (2) sensitivity to holistic network thinking.

## COMPANY POSITIONS IN CHANGING RUSSIAN NETWORKS

Industrial activities can be controlled through different types of governance structures. Traditionally, i.e. before the economic reform process that started in the mid-1980s, the entire Soviet economy was controlled though a planned hierarchical arrangement. This article suggests that the transition to a market economy will mean the introduction of different governance structures: hierarchies, markets, networks. As in the Western economies, different kinds of relations will prevail between economic actors, ranging from pure transactions to long-term relationships.[16,18–20]

This article focuses on a situation where companies operate under network conditions (cf. reference 8). Therefore, we discuss features of the traditional Soviet "network" and the major changes taking place in that network. Moreover, changing company positions and foreign trade system are investigated. References to the traditional situation are essential, because present and future networks are necessarily a result of their own history.

### Changes in Industrial Networks

The traditional industrial network in the Soviet Union was tightly structured. The roles of different organizations were well defined, and interaction between actors was controlled by administrators. Industrial enterprises were responsible for production, whereas specialized organizations concentrated on foreign trade operations. Different planning organizations controlled resource flows between economic actors, and thus the planning system strictly limited business activities.

The economic reform process has caused considerable changes in that network. The once stable, or actually rigid, network is being transformed into a dynamic one. Relations between actors are no longer designed by planners and administrators, but are based on voluntary interaction between actors. Enterprise ownership is more diversified; in addition to state enterprises there are now joint ventures with foreign partners, cooperatives, small enterprises, and joint-stock companies. Moreover, new types of economic actors, such as independent banks, intermediaries, and advertising agencies, have appeared on the business network.

Despite the fundamental processes of change, the new exchange relationships and networks are not totally created from scratch. Instead, new networks seem to build on the old hierarchical arrangements of existing organizations and relationships.[13] There is evidence that small enterprises are often created from earlier departments within the state enterprises. These new entities characteristically continue with their earlier tasks and try to rely on their old relations.[12] An example can be found among the departments responsible for automatic data processing services within the state enterprises. Along with liberalization of Soviet foreign trade and relaxation of Western embargo regulations, several of these departments have been privatized. These newly created private businesses have started independent importation of foreign-made computers, which they supply not only to the company they were formerly part of, but also to new customers.

Essentially, the former coordination of industrial activities through a planning system is being replaced by new forms of coordination. In addition to market mechanisms, the interorganizational relationships and networks that seem to be evolving provide for a new type of planning of activities: planning that takes place between firms.

### Changes in Company Positions

Traditionally, Soviet enterprises produced goods from state supplies and aimed at meeting the quantitative output goals set by administrators and the planning system. The focus was therefore on the firm's production function and its internal efficiency in transforming input resources into output. Internal hierarchies were important, and all major decisions were made at the top level of management. Industrial enterprises were usually very large, because their production was specialized and they served entire national markets. Not only were the production goals clearly defined; each individual enterprise's suppliers and customers were assigned by administrators. Relations with business partners focused mainly on handling different logistical problems.

Consequently, industrial enterprises were largely isolated and had little, if any, genuine exchange. In that sense they were independent of each other, yet they depended to the highest degree on the planning system. Administrator's predetermination of each organization's role, tasks, and external relationships led to a notable absence of entrepreneurial activity. For instance, customer needs seemed to be of no concern to Russian managers. Traditional Russian enterprises, with their strict internal hierarchical structures and concentration on internal production problems, thus make a striking contrast to modern Western companies, which tend to employ network structures in both internal and external activities and emphasize strategic relating to the context.

At present, Russian enterprise managers are free to pursue their own strategies, which in network thinking means the establishment, development, and disruption of relationships in order to achieve favorable network positions. The new situation makes it important to understand the characteristics of the evolving network and the role the company plays in that network.

According to the network view, the role and strategic identity of the firm depend on its interaction with other parties. The enterprise's effectiveness becomes a key issue, and managers should focus special attention on the organization's external relations. In creating these relations, cooperative action is often more important than competition.

### Changes in the Foreign Trade System

Because of the foreign trade monopoly, external trade relations of the Soviet Union were the responsibility of special foreign trade organizations. Thus Soviet industrial enterprises were largely isolated from foreign markets and Western companies. For Western companies, doing business with the Soviet Union meant adaptation – in various ways – to the rigid foreign trade system. Companies were expected to relate in a specific way to certain counterparts, which were limited in number. Foreign trade organizations acted as gatekeepers and often restricted the entry of Western companies to the Soviet network. Moreover, access to end-users of Western products was restricted, one of the few possibilities to meet these being different trade fairs and symposia.

The economic reform process has made new options for relating to the Russian network available to Western companies. Legislation on joint ventures between Eastern and Western companies has advanced considerably since their introduction in 1987. Russia tries to attract more foreign investment, although the uncertainty prevailing in the country still curbs these investments.

Entry and exit of companies on the Russian foreign trade market is no longer restricted by the planning system. Instead of the earlier Moscow-centred trade, Western companies need to contract smaller and more numerous counterparts, which may be geographically dispersed throughout Russia; in addition, these Russian firms often lack competent foreign trade personnel. Clearly then, there is a need for Western companies to seek new ways to approach these new Russian entrants on the market.

## IMPLICATIONS FOR MANAGERS

### Eastern Managers

The new situation poses considerable challenges for all actors on the Russian market, but Eastern managers in particular are facing new issues. Consequently, the present analysis concentrates on the implications for Eastern managers. Picking up on the division made earlier, but beginning with a more general view, we shall first focus on issues raised by sensitivity to network thinking.

*Focus on relating to context.* According to the network view, a company is not surrounded by a faceless environment; rather, it is embedded in a context that includes multiple identifiable partners. Strategically, the key issue is how the company relates to this context; how it seeks potential business partners (suppliers and customers) and establishes relations with them. This is of special importance to Russian managers, who are used to focusing on internal issues within the enterprise.

*Defining the network and focal net within which the company is embedded is a difficult but essential task for management.* It is an especially difficult task today, as the Russian network is still undergoing dramatic changes. However, a manager with a network world view may perceive the interdependencies that prevail in networks. All actors in a network depend on each other and on each other's action. Definition of a sufficiently large net is therefore essential. This would mean, for instance, that not only customers, but their customers as well would be considered. Moreover, networks depend on their history. Suitable business partners may be found among those organizations with which the firm previously had contracts, whether informal or formal.

*The firm's position and role in the network is unique.* Each enterprise plays a certain role, and its activities form a link in the industrial network. Understanding this link improves the enterprise's ability to locate opportunities and threats that affect its position. For instance, an extensive information exchange with suppliers may help new product development. Better understanding how well the product meets the requirements of the customer, in turn, not only helps to develop the product further, but also helps to anticipate potential competition from other companies. A long-term relationship with extensive interaction is often needed in order to reach this understanding.

*Investments in network positions are required.* Network positions result from investments in relationships. These investments for future positions in Russian networks may be considerable, but they are unavoidable. Some Russian managers have jumped to new business possibilities, trying to proceed with numerous new firms and business ideas, while at the same time neglecting their existing business partners. Western companies, in particular, are sensitive to this type of "trying to do everything"; they prefer Russian partners who are clearly committed to the joint operation and who are consequently ready to invest money, time, and other resources in it. Fundamentally, network investments that have been made earlier should be employed to the full. Network processes are cumulative, being made up of previous interactions. Instead of disrupting all existing relationships or abandoning old practices, Russian managers should therefore build on their existing network positions.

To summarize, sensitivity to network thinking would lead Russian managers:

- to shift their focus to interorganizational relations with other companies,
- to analyse the characteristics of the surrounding business network, and
- to define the company's present and potential position in the network.

The following managerial implications centre around the issue of explicit attention to individual relationships in their context.

*Different types of actors control external resources.* The seller's market and the excess demand that have prevailed in Russia place suppliers in a special position. So far, enterprises have paid the most attention to ensuring their access to supplies. Marketing activities and customer relations will eventually be considered more carefully. But in addition to suppliers and customers, other actors in the network – such as banks, research institutes, and government agencies – may control important external resources and therefore require the company's explicit attention. For instance, a long-term relationship with a bank may help in arranging financing for new operations; or a working relationship with a research institute may introduce new opportunities for R&D and for the adoption of new technologies, undoubtedly a neglected area in Russian firms.

*Relationships provide access to important external resources and offer relevant market information.* In contrast to the traditional situation, Russian firms today must themselves establish relations with other organizations. Building up lasting relationships takes time and effort. Perception of partners and their resources is based on market information largely gained through interaction and exchange processes in relationships. Both the process and the underlying insight are in sharp contrast to the traditional Soviet planning system, where planning agencies gave companies specific production targets and other key information. The new circumstances place considerable demands on the manager's ability to gather and interpret the information relevant to their own enterprises. Therefore, managers should actively search for new information, especially new information concerning changes in the positions of other actors in the network.

*The prerequisite for a long-term relationship is mutual orientation.* Our approach emphasizes cooperative behaviour and mutual dependence between economic parties. Mutual orientation and consequent adaptation is important in receiving resources from other organizations. Adaptation may, for instance, concern products, production, and routines. Adaptation to other parties poses a major challenge for Russian enterprises; right now, they should adapt to individual partners instead of the overall planning system. This would lead, e.g., to understanding that, from the customer's point of view, not only the quantity but also the quality of products is crucial.

*New emphasis on personnel.* Interacting individuals, i.e. the entire personnel of an enterprise, deserve special attention, for several reasons. First, the old hierarchical arrangements within the Russian organizations are breaking down. Traditionally, almost all decisions were made at the top level of an enterprise, whereas at present, a decisive role may be played by people at different organizational levels. This applies to both the manager's own organization and the business partner. Second, interaction between organizations takes place at an individual level. Development of social bonds makes the interaction easier, and social bonds can even be important complements to or substitutes for written contracts, especially in the present period of great uncertainty. Social bonds are, however, person-specific rather than firm-specific, for which reason they are specific to interacting individuals. Finally, although the organizational structures and institutional arrangements of the traditional Soviet system are breaking down, in many cases the actual people involved in doing business remain the same.

In sum, a Russian manager who pays attention to individual relationships would realize that:

- well-handled relationships provide access to external resources and information.
- it is often useful to try to develop long-term, cooperative relationships with business partners, and
- interorganizational relationships evolve as a result of interaction between several individuals. Therefore, all people involved in business operations, and not only the top management, have an impact on their development.

### Western Managers

The discussion so far illustrates the present situation in Russian business networks. A few implications concerning the country's foreign trade, and thus implications relevant to Western companies, may be added. The first two issues relate to the more general sensitivity to holistic network thinking, and the latter two to management of individual relationships.

*Earlier investments can be a strength or a weakness.* Earlier investments in Russian markets seem to constitute both opportunities and constraints; their strategic use is a major challenge to Western managers. Two types of Western firms, with highly different strategic situations in East–West business, can be discerned: those who were already involved in the traditional business before the period of economic reform, and those entering the network for the first time. The key issue for the traditional traders is to utilize their earlier investments in network positions while still retaining flexibility of action. For instance, earlier contacts with local businessmen can be put to good advantage. New ways for relating to the changing network must, however, be considered instead of clinging to old solutions; at present there is, among others, the danger that existing partners may no longer be those with actual purchasing power within the country.

The main concern for the newcomers, in turn, is that they do not have earlier experience of Russian networks. Because social interaction is an essential part of economic exchange, there is little doubt that familiarity with Russian customs and the Russian language is a success factor for Western companies. Newcomers, however, are in a position to create genuinely new ways for relating to the network.

*Involvement in the network is crucial.* It is impossible to predict how the changing Russian networks will develop, and Western companies have been uncertain about how to proceed on these markets. Basically, the network approach emphasizes involvement. Getting involved in a network is an important means of receiving relevant information concerning it. The present lack of general market information, for instance, makes conventional market planning quite difficult, and places even more emphasis on the information received through interaction in interorganizational relationships. Moreover, by getting involved and being an actor in the network, the company will be in a position to influence network developments.

*Interaction involves teaching and learning.* Russian industrial enterprises used to be isolated from each other, and even more isolated from foreign partners. Establishing relationships with them requires a great deal of attention, and may even involve "teaching" them very basic Western business practices. It seem that the younger generation of Russian managers, in particular, has been eager and able to learn new ways of doing business.

Simultaneously, the Western actors themselves are experiencing important learning processes concerning the Russian counterparts and networks. Experiences of East–West joint ventures obtained thus far show that the actual operations and their management have proved to be difficult despite the good intentions of both partners in the initial phase. Clashes between two different management cultures have caused many misunderstandings, which can be corrected only over time as the partners begin to know each other and to understand each other's backgrounds. It is, of course, essential to understand that both partners in a joint operation should be ready to make concessions in order to reach a working compromise and true cooperation.

*Personal relations decrease uncertainty.* Since the transition period began, uncertainty and lack of proper information have been characteristic of East–West trade. Even the most basic general information, which is usually easy to gather from any market area, has been lacking. Resorting to earlier personal contacts has been one way of coping with uncertainty; earlier business contacts have been the best source of reliable information.[17] In this respect, the traditional East–West traders have a clear competitive advantage over the new entrants to the market. A further advantage of personal contacts is that personal relationships may be resorted to even though organizational structures are breaking down. When the company has dealt with certain people for a long time and trusts them, individual trust is usually maintained even if these longstanding contacts transfer to new organizations. This consideration is especially relevant to Russia's external relations: due to the earlier foreign trade monopoly, there are relatively few people competent in foreign trade activities.

To summarize, for a Western company the following aspects seem to be important:

- involvement in the changing Russian networks,
- building on earlier network relations but, simultaneously,
- sensitivity to the arising opportunities for establishing new relations, and
- paying special attention to the evolution and management of individual relations.

## CONCLUSIONS

This article suggests that, on the Russian markets, different kinds of relations – ranging from pure transactions to long-term relationships – will prevail between economic actors. Different governance structures, including hierarchies, markets, and networks, will emerge. This article concentrates on the implications for managers whose companies operate under network conditions.

Much of this inspection pertains to the interdependence that characterizes industrial networks. On the present Russian markets, this interdependence deserves attention from both Russian and Western managers. First, the easing of what used to be tight control has led some Russian managers to behave in an opportunistic way, which in the long run may not serve their best interests. Second, to the Western managers, it may be reassuring to notice that despite the great uncertainty now prevailing, a holistic long-term viewpoint is relevant.

In line with the basic aim and emphasis of the network approach, this article has not presented simple normative recommendations for managers. Instead, it recommends that managers be sensitive to holistic network thinking and explicit in considering relationships with different counterparts.

## REFERENCES


1. Axelsson, B. and Easton, G. (eds). *Industrial Networks – A New View of Reality*. Routledge, London (1992).
2. Cunningham, M. T. and Culligan, K. Competitiveness through networks of relationships in information technology product markets. In Paliwoda, S. J. (ed), *New Perspectives on International Marketing*. Routledge, London (1991).
3. Easton, G. Industrial networks: a review. In Axelsson, B. and Easton, G. (eds), *Industrial Networks – A New View of Reality*. Routledge, London (1992).
4. Ford, D. (ed). *Understanding Business Markets: Interaction, Relationships, Networks*. Academic Press, London (1990).
5. Forsgren, M. and Johanson, J. (eds). *Managing Networks in International Business*, Gordon and Breach, Philadelphia (1992).
6. Håkansson, H. (ed). *Industrial Technological Development: A Network Approach*. Croom Helm, London (1987).
7. Håkansson, H. and Johanson, J. Formal and informal cooperation strategies in international industrial networks. In Contractor, F. J. and Lorange, P. (eds), *Cooperative*

*Strategies in International Business*. Lexington Books, MA (1988).
8. Håkansson, H. and Snehota, I. No business is an island: the network concept of business strategy. *Scandinavian Journal of Management*, **5**, 187–200 (1989).
9. Jarillo, C. On strategic networks. *Strategic Management Journal*, **9**, 31–41 (1988).
10. Johanson, J. and Mattsson, L. -G. Internationalization in industrial systems – a network approach. In Hood, N. and Vahlne, J. -E. (eds), *Strategies in Global Competition*, Croom Helm, New York (1988).
11. Johnson, J. and Mattsson, L. -G. Network positions and strategic action – an analytical framework. In Axelsson, B. and Easton, G. (eds), *Industrial Networks – A New View of Reality*. Routledge, London (1992).
12. Johnson, S. and Kroll, H. Managerial strategies for spontaneous privatization. *Soviet Economy*, **7**, 281–316 (1991).
13. Lundgren, A. and Mattsson, L. -G. Industrial change and ecological consequences in the transition process of the Eastern economies – the dynamics of industrial network. Paper presented at the Future of the Baltic-Expert Seminar, Rostock, Germany, March 24–26 (1992).
14. Mattsson, L. -G. An application of a network approach to marketing: defending and changing market positions. In Dholakia, N. and Arndt, J. (eds), *Changing the Course of Marketing: Alternative Paradigms for Widening Marketing Theory*. JAI Press, Greenwich, CT (1985).
15. Mattsson, L. -G. Management of strategic change in a "markets-as-networks" perspective. In Pettigrew, A. (ed), *The Management of Strategic Change*. Basil Blackwell, Oxford (1987).
16. Möller, K. E. K. Interorganizational marketing exchange: metatheoretical analysis of current research approaches. In Laurent, G., Lilien, G. L., Pras, B. (eds), *Research Traditions in Marketing*. Kluwer, Boston (1994).
17. Salmi, A. and Möller, K. Business strategy during dramatic environmental change: a network approach for analysing firm-level adaptation to the Soviet economic reform. In Buckley, P. and Ghauri, P. (eds), *The Economics of Change in East and Central Europe*. Academic Press, London (1994).
18. Salmi, A. Business strategies in evolving Russian markets: a network approach. In Kaynak, E. and Nieminen, J. (eds), *Managing East–West Business in Turbulent Times*, Proceedings of the Second World Business Congress of IMDA, Turku, Finland, June 3–6 (1993).
19. Thorelli, H. Networks: between markets and hierarchies. *Strategic Management Journal*, **7**, 37–51 (1986).
20. Webster, F. E. The changing role of marketing in the corporation. *Journal of Marketing*, **56**, 1–17 (1992).

# Part IV

## Developing Purchasing Strategy

In the introduction to this book I made the point that the IMP group had emphasized the methodological importance of simultaneously studying both the buying and selling parties to a business relationship and the similarity in the management tasks facing both the buying and selling operations of a company. Both functions are involved in researching supply or customer markets. Each must plan, develop and manage relationships with a portfolio of customers or suppliers. This means that the value to buyers of understanding interaction and relationships is equal to its value to sellers.

The first reading in this section of the book by Campbell is chosen for two reasons. First, it provides a useful link between the more "traditional" analyses of business buyer-behaviour and an approach that emphasizes the *interaction* between buying and selling firms as a basis for analysis. Second, the reading provides a valuable framework for discussing the *choices* that face purchasing managers under different circumstances. In this way the reading highlights our view of business buyers as being strategically *active* in their markets. The second reading is taken from the most comprehensive of the works of group members in the purchasing area and develops these ideas further. In this reading, Håkansson and Gadde use a major study of purchasing activity to describe, categorize and analyse buyer–seller relationships from the perspective of the purchasing company. Also included in this reading are a number of illustrative case studies which deal with the relationship tasks facing the buying organization in the purchase of MRO (maintenance, repair and operating) supplies, new product development, supplier development programmes and subcontracting. The second reading by the same authors highlights three key issues facing buying companies: the question of make-or-buy, the structure of the company's supply base and the nature of its supplier relationships. The final reading in this section is by Hallén. He shows how the extent of internationalization in a firm's purchasing is not related just to the market conditions it faces, but also to its attitude towards buying from abroad and its managerial competence in international transactions.

This section of the book could justifiably have been expanded *if* suitable material had been available. There is a great choice of readings within the IMP tradition on marketing issues, but there is still a clear need for more empirical and conceptual research in the area of supplier relationships. For example, the previous edition of this book included an interesting paper by Kinch that described the development up to the early 1980s of the supply base of the retailer, IKEA. Unfortunately, there is a lack of more recent *conceptually based* work that examines the momentous changes occurring within networks that include major retailers and that analyses the strategic issues facing those retailers and the companies that supply them.

## CONTENTS

# 1

# An Interaction Approach to Organizational Buying Behavior

*N. C. G. Campbell*

Although interest in and research on organizational buying have increased over the past two decades, few empirical generalizations have emerged to provide specific guidelines for management action. This conclusion by Wind and Thomas[28] reinforces the view expressed by Wind[27] in the first edition of *Review of Marketing*. This paper attempts to fill this gap by developing the interaction approach associated with the International Marketing and Purchasing (IMP) Group.

The lack of empirical generalizations may be due to the complexity of available models.[17,22,23] The popular Webster and Wind model placed great emphasis on analysis of the buying center, the buying decision process, and the buying situation. In practice, this tripartite analysis has proved difficult to perform because the interpersonal process at work in a buying center are hard to unravel, the stages of the buying decision process are hard to distinguish, and even the distinction between "new buy" and "modified rebuy" is not always clear. Industrial marketing managers are well aware that their jobs are complex.

In order to guide marketing managers and resolve the research problems, attention has focused on discrete buying decisions. In consequence, research has concentrated on new buy situations in which discrete decisions are easy to identify. Routine response behavior, which Möller[17] claims is more common, has been neglected. In other words, the emphasis has been on the process of discrete purchase decisions rather than on the development of strategies for the management of a pattern of relationships over long periods of time.

In contrast, this paper stems from research in areas where long-term stable relationships are important, as attested to by many authorities.[2,9,11,26] In such situations, the study of discrete purchase decisions is less relevant than the study of the patterns of interaction between buyers and their supply markets.

This paper results from an intensive two-year research study designed to complement previous work carried out by the IMP Group. The original IMP research project[12] was an international, cross-sectional study aimed at understanding the

Reprinted by permission of the publisher from An Interaction Approach to Organizational Buying Behavior by N. C. G. Campbell in *Journal of Business Research*, Vol. 13, pp. 35 – 48.

nature of buyer–seller relationships. Some 300 companies covering 15 different industries in five countries were involved. The IMP researchers placed great emphasis on a comparative analysis of how suppliers and customers in various product technologies and end-use industries handled their relationships with counterpart companies in domestic and foreign markets. In contrast, the research study on which this paper is based focused on 167 trading relationships in the packaging industry in Europe. Both sides of the buyer–seller relationships were researched, and by examining one industry, the product technology variable in the relationships was held constant.

To understand the trading relationships, this paper classifies buyer–seller relationships and identifies the common strategies which buyers and sellers use in their interactions. This classification enables attention to focus on the critical variables which give rise to the different strategies. In addition, useful managerial guidelines are developed which assist sellers in choosing a strategy in response to the strategy being used by their counterpart.

## CLASSIFICATION OF BUYER–SELLER RELATIONSHIPS

The classification adopted is based on the three types of governance structure proposed by Williamson[25] for commercial transactions. Campbell and Cunningham[4] provide an extensive review of other approaches to the classification of buyer–seller relationships. Williamson's approach arises from his work on markets and hierarchies[24] and is linked to Ouchi's[18,19] concern with ensuring equity in relationships.

Equity is assured in many exchanges by the market mechanism. A fair price is established by competitive market forces, and the price itself contains most of the information needed by the parties. Such relationships are independent. However, where the exchange is contingent on uncertain future events, assessment of price is very difficult. Nevertheless, the requirement for equity remains and, for this reason, a bureaucratic, or hierarchical, relationship is preferred. The perception of equity depends on a social agreement that the bureaucratic system has the legitimate authority to decide what is fair. In these relationships, one party is dependent on the other.

Intermediate between the market and bureaucratic mechanisms is the clan mechanism, which Ouchi claims can also ensure equity. Equity based on clan control involves a long process of socializaton, which develops common value and beliefs. The evidence for long-term relationships and source loyalty suggests that the clan form, an interdependent relationship, is common in buyer–seller relationships.

Independent, dependent, and interdependent relationships arise in different situations. For example, independence arises when the buyer plays the market and the seller has plenty of potential customers. Marketing and purchasing strategies in these commodity-type markets are competitive. Independence also arises in a buyer's market, in which there are many competitive sellers, and in a seller's market, where there are many buyers. On the other hand, interdependence arises when both parties approach the relationship with a strategy of cooperation. They are both willing to establish a long-term relationship, to exchange information openly, and to trust each other. Finally, a dependent relationship results from the dominance one party exerts over the other.

Marketing or purchasing strategies which result when one party has a dominant position of strength are called *command* strategies. Thus, the independent, interdependent, and dependent types of relationships result from the interplay of interaction strategies, classified here as competitive, cooperative, and command. Campbell and Cunningham have described similar classifications developed by other researchers.[1,6,7,10,12] The interplay of these strategies leads directly to the nine-cell matrix in Fig. 1.

In Fig. 1 there are three cells with independent relationships, one with interdependent relationships, two with dependent relationships, and three labelled "Mismatch". The typical strategies and responses which apply to these different situations are discussed in the final section of this paper.

Thus, in place of the Webster and Wind classification of buying situations into new buy, modified rebuy, and straight rebuy, Fig. 1 proposes a new typology of buyer–seller relationships. In this typology, the buying situation is determined by the interplay or marketing and purchasing strategies, which are themselves determined by a variety of other factors. Therefore, a model is required which incorporates the interplay of marketing and purchasing strategies and identifies the conditions which determine their choice.

| Purchasing strategies \ Marketing strategies | Competitive | Cooperative | Command |
|---|---|---|---|
| Competitive | 1<br>Independent<br>Perfect market | 2<br>Mismatch | 3<br>Independent<br>Seller's market |
| Cooperative | 4<br>Mismatch | 5<br>Interdependent<br>Domesticated market | 6<br>Dependent<br>Captive market |
| Command | 7<br>Independent<br>Buyer's market | 8<br>Dependent<br>Subcontract market | 9<br>Mismatch |

Fig. 1. Classification of buyer–seller relationships.

## INTERACTION MODEL

Neither the Sheth[22] model nor the Webster and Wind[23] model fulfils the above-stated need to incorporate the interplay of marketing and purchasing strategies and their determinants. The Sheth model is mainly concerned with the psychological aspects of individual buyer behavior. However, in addition to individual factors, Sheth introduces product-specific and company-specific factors, as well as the outcome of previous decisions and situational factors, which he says are too varied and broad to analyze in detail. These factors converge in a "black box" called the *industrial buying process.*

Although it is more comprehensive and considers four sets of variables – environmental, organizational, interpersonal, and individual – the Webster and Wind model also poses problems. The desire for comprehensiveness leads to the inclusion of every possible influence, which makes the model difficult to use. Laczniak and Murphy[15] have cautioned against a "laundry list of possible influences."

Another disadvantage of both models is that they concentrate on the buyer's side. Scant attention is paid to the seller's influence on buyer behavior. By contrast, the interaction model developed by the IMP Group[12] stresses the interaction between two active parties, and the model proposed here (see Fig. 2) gives equal weight to buyer and seller characteristics.

This model goes beyond the work of the IMP Group by introducing the concepts of *interaction strategies,* whose interplay affects the interaction mechanisms and interaction atmosphere in a two-way exchange. Figure 2 also emphasizes a different set of variables from those in the IMP model.

Three groups of variables are shown – the characteristics of the buyer, the supplier, and the product. The characteristics of the buyer and the supplier are divided into three sets representing the industry, the company, and the individuals or buying center members. One could argue that the characteristics of the two industries should be separated from those of the two companies and the two groups of individuals. However, the strong inter-connection between company strategy and industry structure suggests the need to keep them together[20]. The impact of general environmental factors is presumed to take place through changes in the characteristics of the buyer's and/or supplier's industry. This has the advantage that the environment of both buyer and seller are explicitly considered, and it avoids the weakness of the IMP model, which includes only an aggregated environment.

A full list of the variables considered in the model is given in Table 1. There is no attempt to be comprehensive. Rather, variables are included which research indicates cause a particular buyer or seller to choose a strategy.

### Product Characteristics

Different writers have used different attributes in their attempts to classify products. Robinson, Faris, and Wind[21] proposed the three buy classes. Cardozo[5] suggests a classification by product use, degree of standardization, and the product's importance to the buyer. Other writers have also used characteristics of the product's importance to the buyer.[17,20] Homse[13] classifies products according to their

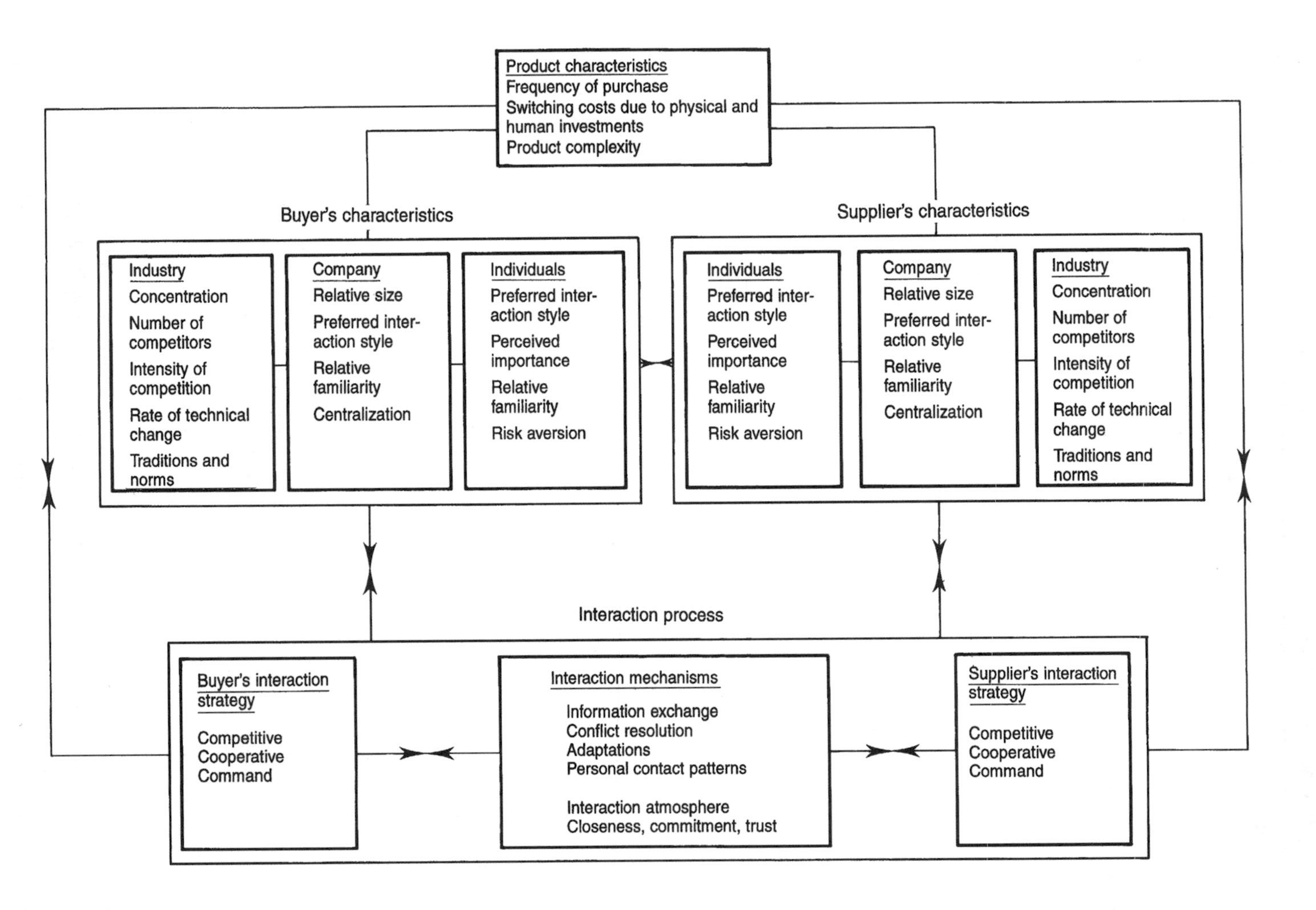


Fig. 2. buyer–seller interaction model.

Table 1. Interaction variables

| Buyer's side | Interaction variables | Supplier's side |
|---|---|---|
| Product | Frequency of purchase<br>Switching costs due to physical and human investments<br>Product complexity | Product |
| Industry characteristics | Concentration<br>Number of alternative partners<br>Intensity of competition<br>Rate of technical change<br>Traditions and norms | Industry characteristics |
| Company characteristics | Relative size<br>Preferred interaction style<br>Relative familiarity<br>Centralization of purchasing | Company characteristics |
| Individual characteristics | Relative familiarity<br>Preferred interaction style<br>Perceived importance of the purchase (sale)<br>Risk aversion | Individual characteristics |

complexity, and Williamson[25] concentrates on the three key dimensions of frequency of transaction, switching costs, and uncertainty.

Frequency of transaction distinguishes between the purchase of capital goods required infrequently and components and raw materials delivered more regularly. Where the transaction occurs frequently, the relationships are likely to be more interdependent. At the other extreme, the infrequent purchase of standard capital equipment is often dealt with by competitive tenders.

Switching costs are the costs incurred in changing suppliers. This dimension incorporates the ideal of standardization because standard products will normally have lower switching costs than customized products. The higher the switching costs, the greater the specific investments which each party has made in the relationship. Switching costs can result from human as well as physical investments. Salesmen and buyers invest in getting to know each other's business. Table 2 summarizes the main sources of switching costs between industrial buyers and marketers.

While switching costs are a function of the product in the sense that some products must be more closely adapted to the customer's needs than others, they also reflect the type of relationship that exists. In an independent relationship, a buyer pursuing a competitive strategy in a particular supply market will try to minimize switching costs to avoid being tied to one supplier. The aim is to standardize purchasers, and the buyer tends to have a technical staff to solve problems. On the other hand, a buyer pursuing a cooperative strategy is more ready to pay switching costs in return for joint efforts to find the best solution to his or her problem. Such a buyer has a relatively smaller technical staff, and is willing to cooperate on development work and to accept special products. In general, the

Table 2. Source of switching costs in buyer–seller relationships

| | Source of switching costs | |
|---|---|---|
| Activity | Supplier | Customer |
| Product introduction | Supplying prototype and test data<br>Training customer's staff | Testing a new product<br>Training own staff |
| Production | Changing materials, design, processing, or production equipment to meet customer's needs<br>Special quality control<br>Especially rapid production | Changing product, design, or production methods to accommodate the supplier<br>Special quality control |
| Logistics | Special stock-holding and delivery requirements | Special warehousing and handling |
| Product development and technical service | Time needed to get to know customer's problems and technical staff | Time needed to understand supplier's technical resources and staff |
| Buying, selling and administration | Time required to get to know the customer, his or her staff, and ways of doing business; special documentation and procedures | Time required to get to know supplier, his or her staff, and ways of doing business; special documentation and procedures |

higher the switching costs, the greater the tendency for cooperative or command strategies to be used.

The third dimension, product complexity, is preferred by Williamson's uncertainty Homse.[13] has identified six types of product complexity. A product has *functional complexity* when it consists of numerous parts and subassemblies. *Manufacturing complexity* is straightforward, but *specification complexity* refers to products which require extensive trial periods.[13] Products have a high *application complexity* due either to the extensive training required before the buyer knows how to use them or to the uncertainty inherent in the customer's pattern of demand. *Commercial complexity* refers to transactions involving complicated commercial arrangements, such as stage payments, penalty clauses, and performance bonds. Finally, *political complexity* applies to purchases which Lehmann and O'Shaughnessey[16] call "political problem products" – purchases for which different factions will be for and against. In general, the more complex the product, the more interdependent the buyer–seller relationships.

**Industry Characteristics**

The variables proposed in Fig. 2 are concentration, number of competitors, intensity of competition, rate of technical change, and traditions and norms. These variables are similar to those proposed by Robinson, Faris and Wind[21] in their discussion of the key characteristics of the supplying industry which influence buyer behavior. Their variables are the number of potential suppliers, the type of competition (whether price or nonprice), the threat of material or parts shortages, the traditional ways of doing business, social–political–economic conditions, and significant events such as technological breakthroughs.

The importance of concentration and the number of alternative partners was recognized by the IMP Group in their original formulation of the interaction model. They also included "dynamism" as a variable, referring to the heterogeneity of the supply market. Buyers in dynamic markets or buyers purchasing from dynamic markets, in which there is a high rate of technical change, tend to use competitive buying strategies to protect themselves from being tied to a partner who cannot keep pace. Most writers recognize that the traditions and norms of each industry have an important influence on buyer behavior, and these represent the final variable. Some industries, such as automobile manufacturing, have a reputation for using competitive buying approaches, which they are only now beginning to change.[3]

## Company Characteristics

The interplay of marketing and purchasing strategies and the mechanisms and atmosphere of the relationship depend on the characteristics of the parties involved. The IMP researchers proposed that the technology, size, structure, and strategy of the company be considered.[12] Some of these variables are included in Fig. 2.

The relative size of the two companies is obviously important; command buying is more likely to occur when the buyer is larger than the supplier. *Relative familiarity* refers to how well the two companies know each other relative to their knowledge of other partners. Familiarity resulting from many years of trading together, as found in mature markets, favors cooperative purchasing.

Familiarity is also important with respect to technology and the costs and ways of doing business. The buyer who is familiar with the technology of the supplier and knows the supplier's costs is in a powerful position. This buyer can either use a command strategy or, where several alternatives exist, adopt a competitive purchasing approach.

The interviews on which this paper is based also revealed that companies tend to have a preferred interaction style. One well-known US consumer company opening in Europe invariably uses a competitive purchasing strategy. In contrast, another US company has a policy of preferring interdependent relationships with one or two key suppliers for each class of purchase.

The last interaction variable covers organization. Möller[17] distinguishes between departmental and company organization, recognizing that the structure, managerial style, and organizational climate of individual departments, as well as those of the company as a whole, must be taken into account. Möller identifies many variables but does not indicate which ones he considers most important. Research in the packing industry suggests that the extent of centralization in the buying department is a key variable. For simplicity, this is the only variable included in the model.

**Individual Characteristics**

A relationship must ultimately depend on the interaction of the individuals who participate. In complex interactions, several members of a buying center interact with their opposite numbers in the supplying company.

Understanding of the patterns of behavior between members of a buying center is still rudimentary[14] and only recently has work been done on the interaction between the buying center and the sales team.[8,13] Cunningham and Turnbull[8] point out that interpersonal contacts fulfil different roles in different circumstances and that they vary widely in intensity and style. Indeed, individuals in some companies have preferred interaction styles. An individual's preference depends on his or her psychology. The IMP Group emphasizes motivation and experience. Möller includes all of these factors. In addition, he includes buying-related knowledge and interindividual behavior. Again, there are too many variables. In the interests of simplicity, only four variables are included in Fig. 2: preferred interaction style, perceived importance of the sale or purchase, relative familiarity, and risk aversion.

If the buyer has a number of alternatives and the product is perceived as important, then a competitive buying approach is more likely to prevail. High relative familiarity indicates the close, cooperative relationship of the buying center members with suppliers' sale teams.

**Summary**

Figure 2 develops the IMP Group's interaction model by introducing the interaction strategies of the buyer and seller. It identifies the main variables which determine the choice of strategy of the buyer or seller. Three groups of variables are discussed: the product and, for both buyer and seller, the characteristics of their industry, their company, and the individuals involved in the interaction. Table 1 identifies 16 variables of prime importance. Table 3 summarizes the above discussion and identifies the conditions favoring competitive, cooperative, and command purchasing strategies.

## MANAGEMENT IMPLICATIONS

Fig. 1 identified six common types of relationship. Marketing and purchasing managers can readily identify the type of situation they are facing. Table 4 indicates the typical strategies and responses used in these situations. In a buyer's market, there are normally many suppliers and only a few powerful buyers. The buyers request quotations or put out competitive tenders; their approach is to "play the market." Suppliers must submit quotes and try to gain a competitive advantage by obtaining cost leadership or buy differentiating.

In a seller's market, there are a few large suppliers and many small buyers. The sellers may see the advantage of forming a cartel to maintain prices. In this event, buyers may collaborate with other buyers and try to break the cartel, or at least exchange information to improve their bargaining position. Monopoly suppliers have different problems. Their marketing strategies are frequently directed at legitimizing their position and placating customers with elaborate complaint

Table 3. Conditions favoring different buying strategies

| | Competitive buying | Cooperative buying | Command buying |
|---|---|---|---|
| Product characteristics | Low or high frequency of purchase | High frequency of purchase | High frequency of purchase |
| | Low switching costs (standardized product) | High switching costs (customized product) | High switching costs |
| | Product performance can be precisely specified | Product performance difficult to specify | Products can be specified but is customized |
| Industry characteristics | Supplier's industry fragmented | Both industries are concentrated | Buyer's industry concentrated but supplier's industry fragmented |
| | Intense price competition among suppliers | Stable competitive situation in each industry | Average level of competition |
| | High rate of technical change | Low rate of technical change | Low rate of technical change |
| | Tradition of competitive buying | Tradition of cooperative buying | Tradition of command buying |
| Company characteristics | Buying company is larger than supplier | Both companies are similar in size | Buying company much larger than supplier |
| | Buying company prefers competitive buying | Both companies seek a cooperative relationship | Buying company prefers to dominate supplier's costs and technology |
| | Buying company lacks familiarity with the product (new buy) | Both companies are familiar with each other and respect each other's technical knowledge | Buying company is familiar with suppliers |
| | Centralized buying organization | Organizational structures are similar | Buyer has more professional organization than supplier |
| Individual characteristics | Product perceived as important by buyer | Product is perceived as important by both parties | Product is important to buyer |
| | Buyer is not risk averse for this purchase | Buyer is risk averse for this purchase | Buyer is risk averse for this purchase |
| | Individuals who interact do not know each other well | Individuals who interact know each other | Individuals know each other personally |
| | Buyer prefers competitive buying approach | Both buyer and seller prefer a cooperative relationship | Buyer prefers a command strategy and supplier accepts cooperative role |

Table 4. Marketing and purchasing strategies and responses in different types of markets

| | Typical strategies and responses | |
|---|---|---|
| Type of market | Marketing | Purchasing |
| Perfect market | Take it or leave it<br>Try to obtain lower cost<br>Try to differentiate | Play the market<br>Standardize requirements |
| Seller's market | Take it or leave it<br>Form a cartel<br>Legitimize, placate<br>Standardize the product | Accept gracefully<br>Buy jointly<br>Exchange information with other buyers<br>Complain, agitate<br>Encourage competitors |
| Buyer's market | Competitive bidding<br>Try to obtain lowest cost | Put out tenders<br>Play the market |
| Domesticated market | Customize, specialize, differentiate, innovate | Adapt, cooperate, work together |
| Captive market | Educate the buyer | Learn from the supplier |
| Subcontract market | Learn from the buyer | Educate the supplier |

procedures and information campaigns. Thus, at this general level, some management insights are possible. More specific guidelines for marketing and purchasing management now follow.

**Marketing Management**

First, the marketer must remember that buyers use more than one approach in a given supply market. Nevertheless, one approach usually predominates, and the marketer's own sales force can help to collect some simple data, such as those in Table 5, which will help to distinguish between competitive and cooperative buying strategies. Once the buying approach or strategy has been identified, clear guidelines for marketing strategies are available, as detailed in Table 6.

*Marketing Strategies for Cooperative Customers*

Cooperative customers require a lot of attention. They need reassurance that their decision to concentrate their purchases and put their faith in one or two suppliers is correct. To give this reassurance, senior management from the supplying company must visit these customers and take every opportunity to develop social changes. The service which cooperative customers receive needs to be excellent, and the supplier must stay ahead technically to justify this privileged position. Pricing is one of the most difficult areas with cooperative customers, since the marketer must recover operating costs but avoid overcharging lest this provide an opportunity for competitors to penetrate the account. The objective should be to use customers'

Table 5. Buying characteristics and buying strategies

| Buying characteristic | Buying strategy | |
|---|---|---|
| | Competitive | Cooperative |
| Number of suppliers | Many | Few |
| Proportion of purchases held by main suppliers | Low | High |
| Number of new suppliers taken on recently | Several | Few |
| Proportion of business given to new suppliers | Moderate | Low |
| Willingness to accept special adaptations | Unwilling | Willing |
| Desire for standardization of the product | High | Average |
| Technical dependence on suppliers | Low | High |
| Emphasis in buying | Price | Service, quality |

Table 6. Marketing strategies to match different buying approaches

| | Cooperative | Competitive | Command |
|---|---|---|---|
| Existing customers | | | |
| Pricing | Don't overcharge | Match market price | Negotiate prices |
| Customer service | Nothing is too much trouble | Competitive but no frills | At your service |
| Personal contacts | Frequent, including courtesy visits from senior managers | Regular visits | Ensure that personal relationships are maintained |
| Product development | Grasp all opportunities to work with the customer<br>Stay ahead technically | Do what is required<br>Beware of stealing of ideas | Work as required by the customer |
| New customers | Where competition is established, offer a major advantage, e.g. by innovation, or wait until there is a lapse by current competitors<br>Beware of being exploited by a customer who has no intention of changing | Offer comparable price, service, and quality, and stress benefits of multiple sourcing | Offer facilities to make whatever is required; propose trial order |

cooperation to find ways to meet their needs, preferably over time. This could lead to reduced costs, and enable a marketer to supply at a competitive price and make a good margin. Marketers who take advantage of a cooperative customer's loyalty and charge an elevated price run the risk of permanently ruining the relationship if the customer realizes that he or she has been overcharged. Such an occurrence breaks the feeling of mutual dependence and shared objectives on which this type of relationship depends. Derived of reassurance of equity in the relationship, the customer is likely to react sharply.

Knowledge of a customer's purchasing approach is very helpful when deciding which companies are the best prospects for future business. In mature markets, customers with cooperative purchasing strategies have, by definition, developed long-term relationships. These are difficult to penetrate unless the marketers can offer a significant price reduction or innovation which the existing supplier cannot match.

Marketers should be cautious about spending large sums in an effort to obtain business from such customers, who normally favor existing suppliers and are likely to give them an opportunity to match any new offers they receive. If the marketer has no significant advantage to offer, the only option is to wait until the customer is dissatisfied with the existing supplier or until there is a structural change such as a merger or takeover, which may sever existing links between personnel. The bonds with existing customers are also broken when there is a change in the customer's own market position. Such events provide good opportunities for the astute marketer.

### *Marketing Strategies for Competitive Customers*

Customers with competitive purchasing strategies require different handling. Marketing costs and contracts with competitive customers must be kept to a minimum because their prime concern is price. Many suppliers know the frustration of losing an order to a lower-priced competitor. A careful balance has to be struck between the advantages of differentiating the product by providing additional services and the disadvantage of a price which is out of step with the market price. Resources may be better deployed in searching for production economies which will lower the price.

Companies with competitive purchasing strategies may be the easiest to obtain as new customers. Their interest can often be gained by offering a comparable, or preferably better, price, quality, and service. The marketer should stress the benefits of multiple sourcing.

### *Marketing Strategies for Companies with Command Purchasing*

The company subject to a command purchasing strategy should also keep its marketing costs to a minimum. The supplier's role is to do the buyer's bidding, and the keys to success are flexibility, personal attention to the buying company's needs, and efficient production facilities. These are the points to stress in the search for new customers.

## CONCLUSIONS

This paper sets out to overcome the problem that research on organizational buying behavior has yielded few guidelines for management action.

Marketing and purchasing behaviors are classified into three interaction strategies. The buying decision process is modeled as resulting from the interplay of these strategies, which in turn are influenced by the characteristics of the product, the buyer, and the seller. A multitude of variables influence buyer and seller behavior. Sixteen variables relevant to both buyers and sellers are incorporated in the model because they seem to be the most important in influencing the choice of interaction strategy. Although useful guidelines have been developed, research has been conducted only in the packaging industry, and additional research in other industries is now required.

## REFERENCES


1. Blois, K. J. Vertical quasi-integration. *Journal of Industrial Economics*, **20**, 253 – 72 (1972).
2. Bubb, P. L. and Van Rest, D. J. Loyalty as a component of the industrial buying decision. *Industrial Marketing Management*, **3**, 25 – 32 (1973).
3. *Business Week*, pp. 62 – 3 (1982).
4. Campbell, N. C. G. and Cunningham, M. T. Interaction strategies for the management of buyer/seller relationships. *Journal of Marketing*, (1985).
5. Cardozo, R. N. Situational segmentation of industrial markets. *European Journal of Marketing*, April/May 222 – 38 (1981).
6. Corey, E. R. *Procurement Management: Strategy, Organization and Decision Making*. CBI Publishing, Boston (1978).
7. Cunningham, M. T. An interaction approach to purchasing strategy. In Håkansson, H. (ed.), *International Marketing and Purchasing of Industrial Goods: An Interaction Approach*. Wiley, Chichester (1982).
8. Cunningham, M. T. and Turnbull, P. W. Inter-organizational personal contact patterns. In Håkansson, H. (ed.), *International Marketing and Purchasing of Industrial Goods: An Interaction Approach*. Wiley, Chichester (1982).
9. Cunningham, M. T. and Kettlewood, K. Source loyalty in the freight transport market. *European Journal of Marketing*, **10**, January, 66 – 79 (1976).
10. Farmer, D. H. Developing purchasing strategies. *Journal of Purchasing and Materials Management*, Fall, 6 – 11 (1978).
11. Ford, D. The development of buyer–seller relationships in industrial markets. In Håkansson (ed.) *International Marketing and Purchasing of Industrial Goods: An Interaction Approach*. Wiley, Chichester (1982).
12. Håkansson, H. (ed.) *International Marketing and Purchasing of Industrial Goods: An Interaction Approach*. Wiley, Chichester (1982).
13. Homse, E. An interaction approach to marketing and purchasing strategy. Unpublished Ph.D. dissertation. University of Manchester. Institute of Science and Technology (1981), p. 150.
14. Johnston, W. J. and Spekman, R. E. Industrial buying behavior: a need for an integrative approach. *Journal of Business Research*, **10**, June 135 – 46 (1982).
15. Laczniak, G. R. and Murphy, P. E. Fine tuning organizational buying models. In Lamb, C. W. and Dunne, P. M. (eds) *Theoretical Development in Marketing*. American Marketing Association, Chicago (1982).
16. Lehmann, D. R. and O'Shaughnessy, J. Difference in attribute importance for different industrial products. *Journal of Marketing*, **38**, April, 36 – 42 (1974).
17. Möller, K. *Industrial Buying Behaviour of Production Materials: A Conceptual Model and Analysis*. School of Economics Publications, Series B-54, Helsinki (1981).
18. Ouchi, W. G. A conceptual framework for the design of organizational control mechanisms. *Management Science*, **25**, 833 – 48 (1979).
19. Ouchi, W. G. Markets, bureaucracies and clans. *Administrative Science Quarterly*, **25**, March, 129 – 39 (1980).
20. Porter, M. E. *Competitive Strategy*. Free Press, New York (1980).
21. Robinson, P. J., Faris, C. W. and Wind, Y. *Industrial Buying and Creative Marketing*. Allyn and Bacon, Boston (1967), pp. 119 – 212.
22. Sheth, J. N. A model of industrial buyer behavior. *Journal of Marketing*, **37**, 50 – 6 (1973).
23. Webster, F. E. and Wind, Y. *Organizational Buying Behavior*. Prentice-Hall, Englewood Cliffs, NJ (1972).

24. Williamson, Oliver E. *Markets and Hierarchies.* Free Press, New York (1975).
25. Williamson, O. E. Transaction cost economics: the governance of contractual relations. *Journal of Law and Economics,* **22**, October, 223 – 61 (1979).
26. Wind, Y. Industrial source loyalty. *Journal of Marketing Research,* **7**, November, 450 – 57 (1970).
27. Wind, Y. Organizational buying behaviour. In Zaltman, G. and Bonoma, T. (eds), *Review of Marketing,* American Marketing Association, Chigaco (1978).
28. Wind, Y. and Thomas, R. J. Conceptual and methodological issues in organizational buying behavior. *European Journal of Marketing,* **14**, May – June, 239 – 61 (1981).

# 2

# Supplier Relations

*H. Håkansson and L. -E. Gadde*

Our starting point is that there is a relationship, or connection, between a buyer and each of the individual suppliers. Also, a fundamental change is occurring, in which purchasing companies have gradually been making a transition from "looser" to "more solid" connections with suppliers. Because the concept of "solid" connections is far from simple or homogeneous, we devote this chapter to a discussion and analysis of some of its central elements. This chapter is divided into eight sections. The first section characterizes supplier relationships, and identifies six of their specific features, to each of which a subsequent section is devoted. The first of these features is the complexity of these relationships in terms of the multifaceted contacts between the companies. The second is the long-term nature of the relationship, which often stretches over decades, and the third is the scope of adaptation of individual relationships required, from both the technological and organizational points of view. A fourth main characteristic, because it emphasizes the informal nature of the relationship, is the low degree of formalization, indicating that the firms do their best to safeguard themselves against unpleasant surprises through reciprocal trust rather than through formal agreements. The fifth characteristic is the power–dependence balance in the relationship, and the sixth and final one is the simultaneous presence of conflict and co-operation, with one conclusion being that effective relationships must contain elements of both.

## GENERAL CHARACTERISTICS OF BUYER–SELLER RELATIONSHIPS

Business transactions between buyers and sellers may differ greatly from one another. At one end of the spectrum there are simple deals in which a person from the buying firm has a limited number of contacts with a person from the selling firm, and in which the products and conditions of their discussion are virtually standardized. At the other, a large number of officials representing several functions at the buying firm have contacts with officials in corresponding positions at the selling firm. In this

Reprinted by permission of International Thomson, Supplier Relations by H. Håkansson and L. -E. Gadde from *Professional Purchasing*, pp. 59–77, 101–121.

case a large number of technical, administrative, and economic problems are ventilated.

Every business transaction is an interesting phenomenon in itself. We use the term "episode" to define this type of event, limited in time. Many things which can happen between a buyer and seller such as a joint development project, testing a new product, or re-negotiating a long-term contract, can comprise an episode. How each episode is handled will depend first on how complex the episode is in itself, and second on the history of the previous relationship between the parties. They may already have met in many past episodes, and have developed an existing relationship.

The way the current episode is handled will depend largely on the past history. If the parties have come to trust one another, the situation will be handled differently from the way it will if the opposite applies. In other words, actions in given situations must not be seen in isolation, but must be viewed and understood in the light of previous occurrences.

For these reasons, it is important to base an analysis of upcoming actions on the complexity of past episodes, and the degree to which the relationship has already developed. Table 1 may be seen as a point of departure for discussing what happens when these two dimensions are combined. If there is no previous relationship, behaviour within the episode will be complete unto itself, and thus has to be judged and optimized as if it were to remain an isolated episode. If, as in case 1, the episode is a simple one, a typical market situation arises in which both parties are truly independent and may even be previously unknown to one another. Taking such an episode to its extreme, it may even be mediated via an exchange market. There is no past history and no likelihood that the transaction will lead to the initiation of a relationship.

Every company has purchases which fall under case 1. These may be highly standardized raw materials, or very simple products purchased in small amounts.

If the episode is a complex one in itself, a different situation arises (case 3). Complexity generates uncertainty. For this kind of business transaction to be completed, for example when a company is going to buy a non-standard product from a new supplier, the episode must be handled in such a way as to build up sufficient trust between the parties. The experience gained when a complex episode is carried out may lead to the creation of some kind of special interest, as a typical first episode which may lead to an established relationship, and which gives both parties a good opportunity to get to know one another.

Case 3 may also be a one-off purchase, for instance, when a firm buys a piece of equipment which is not normally part of its plant. Large investments also have these characteristics, even when the parties have been in contact previously. Such episodes

Table 1. Business transactions: four cases

| | No previous relationship | Well-developed relationship |
|---|---|---|
| Simple episode | Case 1 | Case 2 |
| Complex episode | Case 3 | Case 4 |

are so large and unique that the past relationship becomes relatively less significant. However, there are still rules applying to technical relationships which make it better for the purchasing firm to work with suppliers from whom they have bought in the past.

When there is an established relationship (cases 2 and 4), each individual transaction always has to be seen in relation to it. As a rule, the relationship facilitates individual episodes, which should be formulated so as to strengthen the relationship. In other words, how each episode is structured in relation to previous and anticipated episodes is more important than the fact that it is well formulated in itself. This is particularly important in relation to complex episodes. This connection between individual episodes and the long-term relationship means both considerable simplification of day-to-day work and the establishment of a dependency relation. One way in which the complexity becomes visible is that a number of officials at each firm are in contact with one another over time. In other words, the relationship consists of a number of intertwined, interdependent connections at the individual level, which require special efforts to handle.

A second important trait of relationships, as pointed out above, is that they are of long-term nature. A relationship comprises a number of episodes and, in some cases, has a protective, strengthening function, for instance when there are tensions among the parties involved. At the same time, in other situations, the existence of a relationship may impose limitations, for example when one of the firms wants to implement rapid changes. The very fact that a relationship is, by nature, a long-term undertaking, means that it has pros and cons. One way of elucidating this long-term characteristic is to see a relationship as an investment which, in terms of resources, makes it comparable to machinery or equipment used over a long period of time.

One vital aspect of the relationship being long term is that both parties adapt. Many adaptations are conscious and considered, while others happen more automatically, as a result of the complexity in the course of events described above. Handling of adaptations is important in several respects, as it can either give rise to blocks or enable skill and development potential to be used to advantage. Moreover, adaptations can be made in different dimensions: product and/or production technology, administration, knowledge, or economic aspects.

Furthermore, relationships are social processes in which different types of confidence-building activities are extremely important. It is impossible to cover all conceivable issues in agreements and contracts. There must be space in which informal, personal one-to-one contact takes over.

There are stages in the process of a relationship in which each party – the buyer and the seller – plays the key role in relation to the other, and in which situations of more or less strong dependence take over. Dependence carries power in its wake, and thus it is very important, and often extremely difficult, to handle a relationship in terms of power and dependence. The power–dependence relationship is often an asymmetrical one, and also shifts with time owing, *inter alia*, to the general state of the economy.

Finally, it is important to see that a relationship has other aspects to it besides co-operation. There will always be conflicting interests, which give rise to tension. One important attribute of effective relationships is that such conflicts are not suppressed, but allowed to surface and then to be handled constructively.

In the coming sections, the attributes identified above, the complexity, long-term nature, adaptability, informal social processes and power-dependence, as well as the existence of conflict and co-operation in relationships, will be discussed one by one. When we do this, it is important to keep in mind that relationships are entities, and their holistic nature implies that they do not easily succumb to being classified into different dimensions. We consider these classifications useful primarily from a pedagogical point of view.

## COMPLEXITY

In one of our studies, there was a supplier relationship in which roughly 600 people in the purchasing firm were in regular, significant contact with no fewer than 200 people in the selling firm. This extreme case gives some indication of the complexity of relationships in terms of sheer numbers of people involved. At another large mechanical engineering company, the purchasing manager admitted that he had held his position for a whole year before learning that two large meetings were held annually at which the technicians at his firm met with the technicians from one of their main suppliers and discussed technical issues. Apparently, since the technicians thought that "no commercial issues were discussed" at these meetings, they did not see any reason to involve the purchasing department. These examples indicate that, in many cases, there are extensive contacts with many officials from various departments on both sides meeting to discuss and solve more or less advanced problems. Even if these problems are solved independently of one another, though, this does not mean that they are independent. Rather, they are interconnected in many ways, and improved contacts between the firms would undoubtedly be very important. Fig. 1 depicts the complexity that may be found in an extensive relationship.

Thus it can be seen that a particular extensive relationship may be highly complex, and require substantial co-ordination of operations at the purchasing firm. One interesting solution, seldom applied today, is appointing a specific person to manage co-ordination of a given supplier relationship. At many firms the purchaser fulfils this function indirectly, but as he is concurrently responsible both for many suppliers and other tasks as well, it is often not possible for him to be an effective co-ordinator in practice.

The complexity of personal contacts and patterns of communication discussed above is, of course, attributable to complexity at a deeper level, relating to dependence with regard to each individual supplier relationship, and the interdependence among them. First, there is dependence in relation to the way the production technology, logistics and administration of the purchasing firm work. All supplier relationships have to be co-ordinated with regard to the technical and organizational resources of the purchasing firm. The solution found in relation to one supplier also affects this function in other relationships as well, which means that solving a problem with regard to one relationship may give rise to consequent problems in others.

Second, the relationship of the purchasing firm with supplier A may be contingent

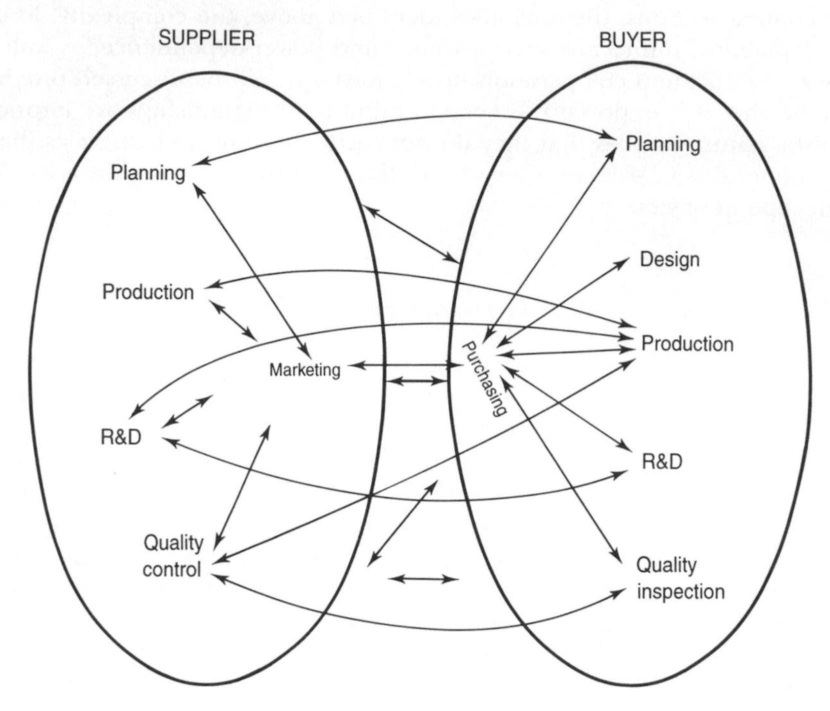


Fig. 1. Pattern of contacts in an advanced supplier relationship.

on how well relations with supplier B or customer C work, and vice versa, i.e. the purchasing firm may use its relationship with A to affect a third party. This means, for example, that the purchasing firm may discuss a technical development project with one supplier in order to get that supplier to behave in a certain way in relation to another party the buying firm wishes to affect. The more concentrated the network the individual firm works within, the more elaborate this type of behaviour has to be.

The type of complexity related to co-ordination of an individual relationship with others is considerably more difficult to handle than the type of complexity which arises with regard to co-ordination within one relationship. This is because there is an infinite number of ways of implementing the former type of co-ordination, and a conspicuous absence of simple solutions. It should be an appropriate first step to have the executives in the purchasing department identify the main connections and then, in systematic discussions with other executives, raise the awareness both of the current and the potential connections, so that they will both respect and take advantage of the opportunities arising from various situations.

Generally, we find that the complexity of the supplier relation can be explained by the fact that the "coupling" in the relationship is complex in itself from a technical, organizational and social point of view, i.e. a large number of officials are involved. This in turn creates a large number of problems of communication and co-ordination. Secondly, the complexity is attributable to the fact that there is dependence on other relations.

## RELATIONSHIPS AS INVESTMENTS – THEIR LONG-TERM NATURE

One very important element of relationships is that they are of a long-term nature. Deep relationships are often decades old. In other words, there is always a history which affects and is affected by the current interplay. Furthermore, there are often more or less overtly expressed expectations. Every action in a relationship must, therefore, be seen in a time perspective. Table 2 illustrates the relevant kind of time dimension by recapitulating the duration pattern of a number of supplier relationships for technical development (Håkansson, 1989).

One of the classic ways of accounting for the time dimension in economics is to examine activities with long-term effects as if they were investments. The difference between an investment and a cost, in principle, is that the revenue accruing from them is expected to take different courses in time. An investment is made on one occasion (in one period of time), and is expected to provide return over several periods, while a cost is associated with an activity the return on which is expected to come during the same period.

If we begin by examining the costs in a supplier relationship, we find that there are many items, and that they can mainly be divided into two groups: contact/information costs and adaptation costs. The contact/information costs of a relationship are high in the initial stages, when the buyer is getting to know the suppliers and their abilities and expertise, and these costs fall later. During certain later episodes contacts may need to be supplemented, which is associated with short-term additional costs, but generally the lower cost level may be maintained. Adaptation costs are all of a one-off nature, but as they arise successively, there is some natural adaptation over time, although there is a tendency for them to crop up early in a relationship. All the elementary adaptations necessary for the buyer to use the supplier must be made initially, which means that neither of the two main categories of costs is evenly distributed over time, and that the introductory period is liable to be a costly one.

We have discussed revenues which result from relationships above. Such revenues may include rationalization benefits or contributions to technical development. Some benefits (such as price benefits) may occur from the very first day, while many others, such as development benefits, take time. Studies made to date indicate that for two parties to venture to take the step of initiating joint development work, they need to have a long shared history. In other words, the return on a relationship also changes over time, but in the other direction, compared with costs.

Table 2. Duration of supplier relationships for technical development

| Duration | Proportion of relationships (%) |
|---|---|
| 0–4 years | 28 |
| 5–14 years | 41 |
| > 15 years | 29 |
| Weighted average | 13 years |

*Source:* Håkansson (1989), p. 112.

If we examine the cost and revenue aspects in overview, we find that relationships very clearly have some of the same characteristics as investments. The costs arise in an early stage (the investment), while the revenues are accrued over a longer period of time. Figure 2 illustrates this relationship from the perspective of a selling firm. The figure shows changes in customer profitability over time. In the first few years, costs are slightly in excess of revenues, which do not exceed costs until the fourth year. If

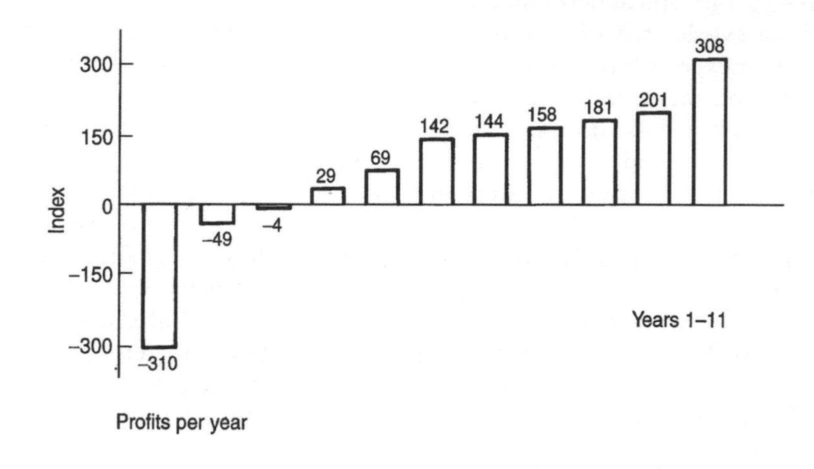


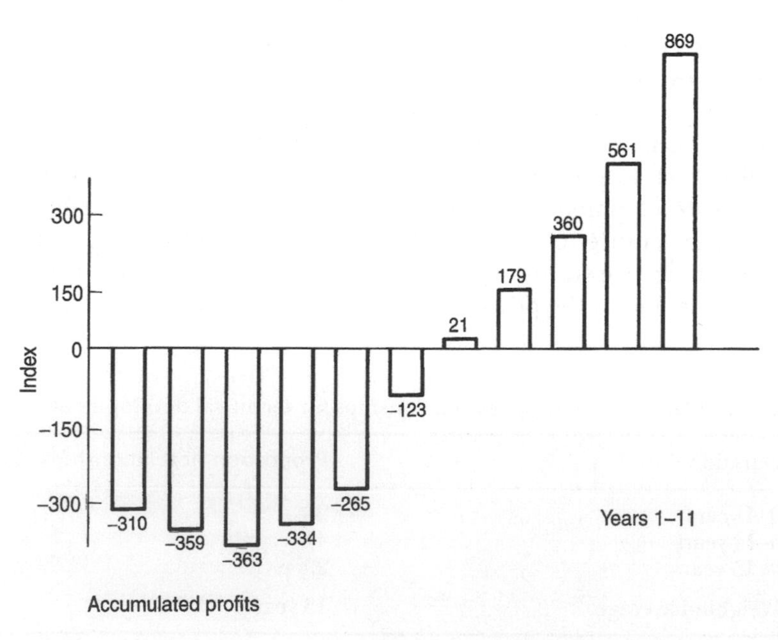


Fig. 2. Cost/revenue structure in customer–supplier relationships.

the figures are accumulated, it can be seen that the relationship is not profitable until year seven. According to this report, from an Italian consultancy firm, it appears to be more effective to retain and maintain old customer relationships than to seek out new ones. The cost/revenue distribution is probably similar for a purchasing firm.

Another way of seeing relationships with regard to investments is to ask whether a relationship is a resource which can be taken over. The answer is not completely clear. It is difficult to transfer a relationship to some other unit. If a firm acquires another firm, and somehow takes over operations, relationships may come along as part of the package. This is not necessarily simply an advantage, as it may pose an obstacle to implementing changes. If, however, the purchasing firm wants to take advantage of the established relationship it can easily do so, and this may be a cheaper way of getting into a new network than trying successively to build up new relationships.

One important corollary is how to maintain these relationships, and how much exploitation they can withstand. Maintenance is obviously important, and there are infinite examples showing how quickly a relationship is undermined when it ceases to develop. This means that day-to-day activities must remain at a relatively high level. This places demands in terms of creativity and continuity in day-to-day work with suppliers. With regard to exploitation, there are two possibilities. If, during a given period, a firm does not maintain its connections, it may still keep much of its position, thanks to inertia. If, on the other hand, a firm is experienced as systematically attempting to over-exploit its connections, the effect may be both very rapid and painful. In other words, having some problems and difficulties is acceptable, but consciously abusing one's established connections is not.

## ADAPTATIONS

Adaptation is one of the characteristic phenomena associated with relationships. In principle, adaptation in a relationship means that a certain supplier is handled in a unique way, either to give lower total costs or to give that supplier priority in relation to others. If all the parties involved – suppliers or customers – looked identical, purchased the same volumes and quantities, and had the same technological structure, adaptation would be irrelevant. Thus the degree of adaptation stands in direct proportion to the differences between the parties: the greater the differences the greater reason to make specific adaptations, and these may be seen as the means available to a firm to take advantage of the unique attributes of its supplier. By discovering and making use of these unique attributes, the purchasing firm may achieve a number of positive effects.

For instance, some specific attributes may be associated with the technology used by the supplier. Various suppliers may use the same technology and thus have some of the same attributes. Consequently, some adaptations may mean that a firm adapts not to a single supplier but to a certain category of supplier, with interchangeable members.

We now go on to discuss three particular aspects of adaptation. First we describe and exemplify various types of adaptation: technical, knowledge-based, administrative, economic and legal. Second, we analyse the way adaptations take place by distinguishing major adaptations occurring on isolated occasions from gradual, incremental adaptations over time. Third, we discuss some of the factors affecting the demand for and content of adaptations, primarily those relating to the technological structure of the firms and products concerned.

There are many types of adaptations. This has been shown in our previous discussions of effectiveness measures and elsewhere. One very important type is the technical ones. Buyers and sellers on industrial markets have plants and equipment with specific technical attributes, and their relationships are intended to bind them to one another effectively. Naturally, this places demands on and opens potential for technological adaptations, both in terms of the product sold by the supplier and the product manufactured by the buyer, as well as in terms of the production processes of each. In one large study we found that the purchasing firms primarily had technological co-operation with materials suppliers (Håkansson, 1989). In other words, materials adaptations appeared to be the most common type of adaptations, and we found this somewhat surprising. It may be explained by the fact that, from a production point of view, input goods are often the main cost factor. Of course we also found a number of adaptations regarding components and equipment.

Knowledge-based adaptations gain in importance the more development issues are emphasized in supplier relationships. In this respect as well, one may easily speak in terms of the necessity for a purchasing firm to market its needs. Buyers who encourage their suppliers to increase their knowledge of the buyer's application of technology, give themselves an important developmental boost. But in doing so the purchasing firm also commits itself, as it becomes better and better at using the technology of the supplier in question. Thus two bases of knowledge, that of the buyer and that of the supplier, proceed to approach one another, with reciprocal adaptation. Probably they should not be allowed to become too similar. There is some advantage in retaining a modicum of "friction", as the differences between them become a point of departure for future developments. This potential may be more positive if the two units remain separate. There may also be adaptations of administrative routines. Planning, supply and communications systems may need to be adapted so the firms can work together effectively.

Such adaptations take the form both of major one-off measures and small, successive steps over time. As a rule, major adaptations are highly visible ones which the parties involved consider strategic, while smaller adaptations are handled "locally" in the organization, and are considered natural measures necessary to facilitate collaboration. Frequently, such adaptations are substantial, although this may not be evident until one of the parties wants to implement a major change. The size and value of these successive adaptations are thus often difficult to overview, and there is a general tendency to underestimate their significance.

The need for adaptation will clearly depend on the attributes of the two parties. First, the need may arise because of specific characteristics of the seller, for example if the seller is a foreign company the buyer may demand local warehousing or some kind of local service. Second, the need may arise because of unique demands made by the purchasing firm. These may come up because the buyer is, in turn, subjected to unique demands from his customers or is working under special conditions for some other reason. Thirdly, the combination of seller and buyer and their interaction may create both demands and potential for specific adaptations.

The nature of these adaptations also depends on the type of product involved. Some products (such as some equipment) are routinely adapted, while others (such as material and standard components) tend to appear in standardized versions. Some customers purchase in such volumes that supply and inventory adaptations are important, while others (such as materials supplies) may be marked by considerable variation in both content and volume, making administrative adaptation of interest. This implies that product type and adaptation type are closely interrelated.

## RECIPROCAL TRUST RATHER THAN FORMALITY

One of the things that characterizes business deals is that they always contain uncertainty. Some of this is about the future, and is genuine, i.e. it can never be reduced, only handled with more or less sophisticated assessments. Other aspects of insecurity are directly related to the other party in the transaction. For example, there is often a time lag between the transaction itself and the delivery. In addition, it is impossible to specify or measure all the functions or characteristics of a product, even at a specific delivery. Instead, they become visible gradually. Unexpected events may also mean that the content of the business deal must be adjusted, and the technology may be both complex and difficult to assess in advance. Thus there are a number of factors which are difficult to overview at the point when the deal is made. These difficulties are so great that it is often pointless – or far too costly – to try to formulate agreements to cover all conceivable situations. Instead, the relationship has to provide the security. Table 3 demonstrates that the degree of formalization in a relationship is generally low and, even when the relationship has developed to include substantial technical development, this is only established to a limited extent through formal agreements.

Security in a relationship cannot be created on a single occasion, but must develop over time. The connection must be built up through a process of interaction in which reciprocal trust can successively be deepened. Interaction may lead to the development of a learning process in which both sides gradually get a better idea of the situations in which it is suitable to do business. The typical process follows a course in which the two parties first test one another through small business deals, and then move along to more complete deliveries. In addition to its being important to get to know one's counterpart well, it is also important to facilitate that party's learning about one's own operations. In other words, it is important to create different types of social situations in which the personnel in the functions needing contact with one another get to know their counterparts and their problems. There is even an example in which these contacts have been extended to comprise all personnel at a given unit. In one particular case, a supplier brought his whole staff to see a major customer so that all those involved

Table 3. Use of formal contracts in supplier–customer relationships involving technical development

| Type of relationship | Customer relationships | Supplier relationships |
|---|---|---|
| Formal | % | % |
| Annual contracts | 20 | 11 |
| Long-term contracts | 13 | 8 |
| Joint corporation | 2 | 22 |
| | 35 | 21 |
| Informal | | |
| Ongoing relationship | 51 | 67 |
| Other informal pattern | 14 | 12 |
| | 65 | 79 |
| Totals | 100 | 100 |

*Source:* Håkansson (1989), p. 113.

would gain understanding of the consequences of delays, and failure to meet quality standards.

The benefits of and the need for personal contacts in building up confidence cannot be too much stressed. This is often recommended from a marketing point of view, but it is certainly equally important for purchasing. We might even claim that the personal-contact network is one of the most important personnel resources, and that it should therefore be taken into consideration in recruitment of purchasers.

What happens, then, in situations in which one of the parties implements a measure which has a negative effect on the other? The answer will depend on how the other side sees that measure. If there are persuasive arguments for it, the dissatisfaction may be short-lived, but if the measure is interpreted as a long-term change of attitude, even a small shift may have grave consequences. This is where personal contacts between individuals at both firms become most important, as these may serve to give the other party a far more complete picture of why a certain measure is necessary. With such a personal network, a relationship can withstand substantial strain occasionally if the underlying policy remains the same. However, even small changes may impact greatly on the relationship if they are interpreted as shifting this underlying position.

## POWER AND DEPENDENCE

Power and dependence are important aspects of supplier relationships. At least for large firms, the most important supplier relationships always involve large volumes, and are thus the principal ones for both parties from an economic point of view. They also affect both parties in a number of indirect ways, which further increases their significance. Significance creates dependence, and the way in which the power–dependence issue is handled thus becomes an important aspect of purchasing work. In the past, it was recommended that purchasers should try to behave in such a way that dependence did not arise. Independence was a key objective. As purchasing has begun to work more systematically with long-term relationships, dependence is now more accepted, and the question has become how to handle the various dependence situations.

One of the problems associated with power–dependence relations is that they are seldom symmetrical. As a rule, they are unbalanced with regard to individual dimensions. For example, the relationship may be more important to the seller than to the buyer from a volume point of view, or vice versa. However, a certain amount of imbalance in one dimension may be set off against the equivalent but opposite imbalance in another dimension. If this is not the case, it is important for the buyer to attempt to create such imbalances. If a purchasing firm wishes to try to get priority from one supplier despite the fact that it is not one of that firm's major buyers, it must begin by trying to make itself interesting in some other way, for instance from a technical point of view. The firm must try to set off its volume disadvantage with some other advantage. This type of "balancing act" is an important aspect of handling suppliers.

Another characteristic attribute of the power–dependence relationship is that it usually varies with the general state of the economy. The seller may have more power during a boom, as may the buyer when supply exceeds demand. It may be tempting to exploit this variation for short-term gain, and there are examples from the Swedish steel industry of such behaviour between manufacturers and wholesalers (Gadde, 1978). But a firm which tries to take advantage of such opportunities runs the risk of reprisals. If a buyer abuses his position during a recession, his firm may very well suffer when an economic upswing ensues. Handling of pricing issues is very important in this respect. Klint (1985) describes how buyers and sellers of paper pulp built up reciprocal trust through their behaviour in different business cycles.

There are no simple solutions to recommend to the problem of imbalance in the power–dependence relationship arising, for instance, as a result of changes in the economy. It is not easy to say what the best strategy is in any individual case. Certainly, though, awareness of the problems and regular, systematic discussions are a first step towards learning to handle these questions better.

## CONFLICT AND CO-OPERATION

The parties in a business relationship have both contradictory interests and shared ones. If they do not learn to deal with the contradictory ones, conflicts arise. In the classic model of purchasing, relationships have been fraught with conflict. One typical example is this subcontractor, who characterizes his customers in the automotive industry as follows:

> They are nasty, abusive and ugly. They would take a dime from a starving grandmother. They steal our innovations, they make uneconomic demands, like "follow us around the

> globe and build plants near ours. We need good suppliers like you but if you can't do it we'll find somebody else." (Helper, 1986, p. 17).

There are an endless number of such examples, and both sellers and buyers have plenty of examples of dirty tricks they have played on one another, and they tend to blow their own trumpets about them. Needless to say, this type of behaviour does nothing to promote close relationships.

Reciprocal trust is a prerequisite for long-term relationships, adaptations, and joint investments. Realization of this fact led one representative of the automotive industry to make the following statement with regard to an essential change in existing relations:

> We need new relationships with what we have to think of as a family of suppliers. We need to throw off the old shackles of adversarial confrontation and work together in an enlightened era of mutual trust and confidence. (Berry, 1982, p. 26).

The description and aspiration is so heavenly that it almost makes one want to close with an "amen". At the same time, it is probably an erroneous appraisal of the ideal content of collaboration and conflict in a relationship. Unfortunately, there are altogether too many people who believe that elimination of all conflict in a relationship is a prerequisite for developing new supplier relations. It is important to point out that this is a misunderstanding. Of course effective relationships require some collaboration, but they require an equal measure of conflict. Fig. 3 depicts the ideal relationship.

The figure describes one dimension of collaboration and one of conflict. If the degree of both are low, the relationship will not be especially meaningful to either party – such relationships are characterized as marginal. If there is a high degree of conflict and a low degree of collaboration, the relationship will not work very well. Significant relationships come into being with a high degree of collaboration. A relationship with a low degree of conflict tends to be somewhat too "nice". The parties place too few demands on one another. Provided that it can be handled well,

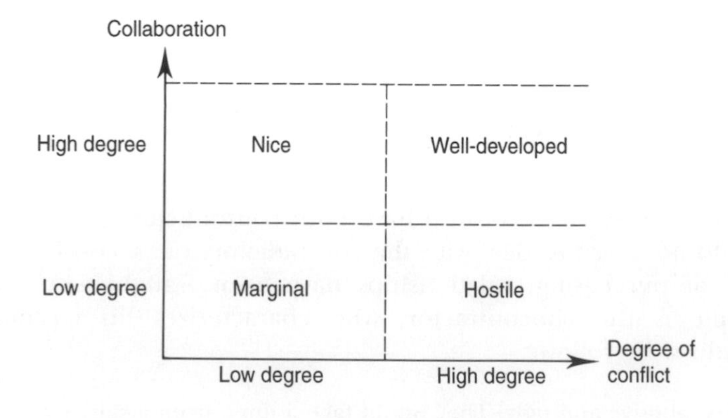


Fig. 3. Relationships with different combinations of collaboration and conflict.

raising the degree of conflict in such a situation enables a better climate for innovation and development.

It seems that the desirable type of relationship is one in which conflict is handled constructively. In this, we agree with Gemünden (1985, p. 405) who says that "buyer and seller should neither smooth over existing conflicts nor let them escalate". There will be conflict as long as both parties remain independent, because they will never have identical goals. There will always be conflicts of interest between buyers and sellers, because there will always be the distribution problem: the profits generated by their joint work will have to be shared. This problem of distributing profits is mainly accentuated when their shared processing value falls. For these reasons, collaboration must continually develop so as to keep shared revenues at least at a constant level. Continuous development of collaboration to achieve "mutual profits" or "mutual success" (Hay, 1988) is thus an effective way of preventing the escalation of conflict. Increased openness appears to be a prerequisite for this, particularly in relation to strategic issues. Expressions of this openness should include involving the supplier in the product-development process from an earlier stage than has previously been the case.

In conclusion, there is good reason to believe that there are many measures for improvement of the fundamental working climate between buyers and suppliers which can contribute substantially to future development of purchasing work. As indicated in the discussion above, this does not mean that a firm must neglect its own aims or interests. On the contrary, the only possibility for establishing long-term working relations is for all the parties involved to have the courage to work on the basis of their own ambitions at the same time as they accept the fact that their collaborators have different ones, and that these must also be taken into account.

## SUPPLIER RELATIONS – A CRITICAL RESOURCE

The main characteristics of a firm's supplier relations are summarized below. Our first conclusion is that relationships with suppliers are very important. They have considerable economic impact, because such a large proportion of the firm's activities are channelled through them. As a rule, more than half of the total turnover of the firm (sometimes up to 70 per cent) is handled within these relationships. They are important from a technical point of view, as they integrate the technology of the purchasing company with that of the supplier. Consequently, they also become central from an innovative point of view. They are one of the most important interfaces at which the knowledge possessed by the firm encounters other large bodies of knowledge.

Secondly, supplier relations comprise major investments. It requires a great deal of work both to establish a relation and to adapt the firm to it internally. Consequently, well-established supplier relations is one of the most important resources any firm has.

Supplier relations are built up through human effort and human contacts. Thus, their third characteristic is that they are "dynamic" in a number of respects. In order for them to survive, they must be under continual development. If they are not, there is a clear risk that one of the firms will develop the opinion that the other firm no longer considers the relationship important. The dynamic feature means both that all relations can be affected and that, in the long run, they are difficult to manipulate. Honesty is probably the word which recurs most frequently in our discussions with sellers and buyers of what characterizes good relations. Any sign of dishonesty has an immediately harmful effect on the relationship.

A fourth characteristic, to which we have thus far only alluded, is the fact that all the relationships a company has are interrelated and interdependent, and actually need to be seen as a network.

## THE CASE STUDIES

### Case 1: Procurement of MRO Supplies for Volvo

The first case study deals with mundane, everyday supplies – the customer is Volvo. The type of large-scale, mass production that characterizes the automotive industry made car companies aware from an early stage of the need to link their activities with those of their suppliers. In order to achieve more substantial rationalization benefits, they have to extend their analysis and involvement several steps backward into the supplier network.

#### *The "Change Project"*

Roos (1988) reports on a change project carried out at Volvo, the aim of which was to make operations more effective by closer co-operation with suppliers. The project was carried out at the procurement and purchasing department of the Volvo Car Corporation between 1984 and 1987. In emulation of the Japanese experience, efforts were being made to increase delivery frequency and decrease lot sizes purchased. To achieve this, a number of substantial changes were required. One was that purchasing decisions of a routine nature were taken directly by the operational units. In these cases, they made their requisitions directly to the supplier, via computerized communication, instead of via the purchasing department, as had previously been the case. This made it possible to decrease lead times from two weeks to twenty-four hours. A new purchasing strategy was also adapted. The previous strategy had been to have at least two suppliers of each individual product. In order to work with JIT deliveries and total quality control, the intended modification was to purchase all that was needed of a given product group from a single supplier, which was meant to lead to a tangible reduction in the number of suppliers. However, it proved to be difficult to reduce the number of suppliers in this way. Many articles had unique properties and were not interchangeable. Therefore, the new principle gradually became that of asking one firm to supply the entire volume of a given article. In a few cases it became possible to further reduce the number of suppliers by having others increase their product range.

*Effects at Volvo*

Three inventory units were affected by this project for change: tools and MRO supplies, uniforms and work boots. The change project went on for three years, with the following effects (see Table 4).

Stock reduction was particularly notable in warehouses 2 and 3, where it was cut back by substantially more than half, despite volume increases of 33 to 51 per cent. The number of articles kept in stock remained unchanged in one case, but increased considerably in warehouse 2 and decreased slightly in warehouse 3.

It was also found that the stock reduction could be combined with improvements in service level. There are no statistics from warehouse 1, but both the others indicate shortened delivery times and increased delivery reliability (a sharp decrease in the number of back orders).

Thus it can be seen that it was possible for the Volvo warehouses to increase their degree of service in spite of substantial reductions of the goods in stock, with a consequent reduction in capital costs. It is interesting to find that even greater savings could be made in relation to other costs in materials administration. The primary effects here were a result of it becoming possible to eliminate one warehouse, which meant a need for fewer facilities, less administration and handling, and shorter process times. Another considerable rationalization benefit was that, once the goods reception centre was moved, less quality-control work was necessary, and previous repetition of work was eliminated. The total effect of these cost reductions was nearly twice as great as the reduction of capital costs *per se*.

In the process of obtaining these effects, other costs increased. Improvement of in-house handling necessitated renovation of a warehouse, and investment in equipment for effective, flexible stock handling. The warehouses were also brightened up to increase personnel satisfaction and motivation.

Table 4. Effects of changes in purchasing behaviour

| | Warehouse | | |
|---|---|---|---|
| | 1 | 2 | 3 |
| Purchased volume (index) | | | |
| Before | 100 | 100 | 100 |
| After | 137 | 151 | 133 |
| Number of articles (index) | | | |
| Before | 100 | 100 | 100 |
| After | 100 | 540 | 81 |
| Inventory volume (index) | | | |
| Before | 100 | 100 | 100 |
| After | 65 | 30 | 44 |
| Delivery times (days) | | | |
| Before | | 21 | 12 |
| After | | 2 | 5 |
| Delivery reliability (no. of back orders/time unit) | | | |
| Before | | 1500 | 1800 |
| After | | 100 | 160 |

The estimates made of the total effect indicated that these changes resulted in annual savings corresponding to 25 per cent of the tied-up capital of the warehouse.

### *Effects on the Suppliers*

Roos also describes how the suppliers were involved in this process of change. One of his examples relates to deliveries of uniforms. The supplier (Tvättman) is situated in the immediate vicinity of Gothenburg, and supplies Volvo with new uniforms as well as laundering the ones already in use. This amounts to 85 000 articles per year, of which one-third are replaced annually. This clothing is manufactured by the Bergis company, which has three plants in western Sweden, which deliver 55 per cent of their production to Tvättman. One of Bergis' most important suppliers is an Italian cloth manufacturer (Klopman) (see Fig. 4).

In the introductory section of this case study we primarily analysed in-house effects at Volvo warehousing, and what happened in relationship A. Let us go on to examine effects on other relationships.

Volvo is one of Tvättman's main customers. For this reason, the changes initiated by Volvo had substantial effects when they were passed along via relationship B. The increased demand thus also meant that Tvättman had to change its purchasing behaviour. First, there had to be in-house changes with regard to its view of customer and supplier relations. Secondly, there had to be changes in actual working methods. To prevent Tvättman's stock from increasing owing to measures implemented at Volvo, it was necessary for Tvättman, in turn, to become more effective with regard to frequency of deliveries and lot sizes in relationship C. Ordering routines were changed so that Tvättman in Gothenburg submitted its orders directly to Bergis via telex. Previously, it had ordered by writing to its own head office in Malmö, which then placed the order with Bergis. This made it possible to shorten the lead time from two weeks to twenty-four hours.

For Tvättman, the effect was that stock volumes decreased by more than one third, despite the fact that the volume of uniforms handled increased by over one third during the three-year period. Service – in terms of delivery reliability – also improved from 85 to 97.3 per cent, in spite of the substantial increase in the number of items.

Tvättman's demands shifted down to the next link in the chain (Bergis). Bergis has not decreased its total stock of finished garments, because in conjunction with these changes Bergis began to serve as a central warehouse for special garments for

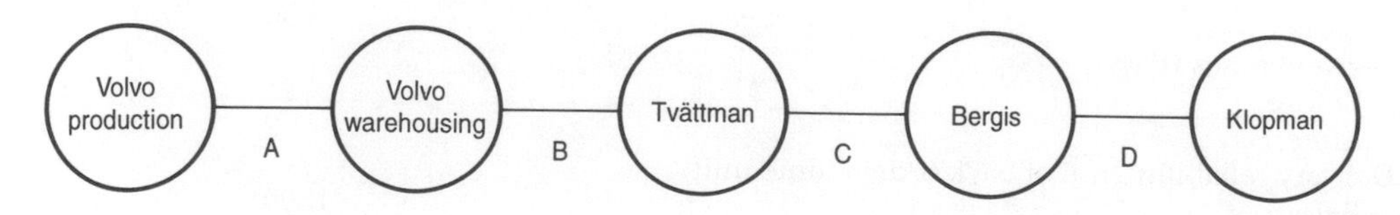


Fig. 4. The supply chain.

all 24 Tvättman plants. The result was that both volume and number of articles increased for Bergis. Relatively, therefore, its stock of the garments it previously supplied has dropped considerably, in part thanks to changes in its work organization.

Production workers previously performed only specialized parts of the process. In principle, this meant that twelve people contributed to every finished garment. Personnel received training to raise their competence, and today only one to three people are needed to sew each whole garment. The effects of this were that the production pipeline was shortened from nine to three weeks, and an estimated productivity improvement of 5 to 10 per cent. To make it possible to live up to the demands of JIT delivery and handling of the increased number of articles, the firm computerized its production, inventory and delivery follow-up and monitoring.

Bergis' orders, in turn (relationship D), also changed in the direction of increased frequency and smaller lots. The result of this has been a 60 per cent decrease in the stock of cloth on hand, and a drop in lead time from eight to three weeks. The firm itself claims that these changes in suborder routines have had no effect at all on the Italian cloth supplier, in whose total production volume Bergis is a marginal customer.

### *Case Comments*

The benefits of analysing the interface between the suppliers and the purchasing company's in-house activities is well illustrated by this case. Volvo is systematically trying to develop its supplier network for MRO supplies. The aim of these activities is not just to decrease costs, but also to improve the service level. The lesson to be learned is that the purchasing company must develop its own planning work and improve its execution of administrative and physical tasks to find out better ways of using its suppliers. Activities must be analysed step by step, through several links of companies, stretching from the buying firm, through the supplier, the subcontractor and eventually even the sub-subcontractor. For other products, such as components, this analysis should also be expanded forward to customers and their customers. This systematic analysis and co-ordination of the activity chain may show substantial potential for rationalization improvements whenever large quantities are handled. So when a company buys large quantities of any product (materials, components or MRO supplies) attempts should always be made to analyse the chain at least a few steps back.

The need to adapt resources to facilitate the close linking of activities can also be found in this case study. Volvo had to invest in order to implement its new way of using its suppliers, and so did the suppliers. This mutual investment process facilitates the interaction, but it also increases the mutual dependence of the counterparts.

The investments made in this case are small compared to what is needed when co-operation concerns the development of new products. Such a project is the theme of the next case study.

## Case 2: Biopharm's Use of Suppliers in Developing a New Product

Our second case study is an illustration of using suppliers in an active way in terms of technical development. The case deals with the development of a new system and the role the suppliers can play in developing different components of that system. The case illustrates the need for an actor analysis, in order to find suppliers who are both willing to be and are capable of being development partners. Other important issues are financial compensation for the suppliers and the need to involve the right personnel in the relationships. The data for this case study have been collected through interviews and from written documents, project documentation, etc. The interviews were made with four members of the project team, including the project leader and the product manager, and with two of the suppliers involved (Eriksson, 1989).

### *Biopharm and its Product*

Biopharm (disguised name) is a company which designs, manufactures and markets systems for the production of pharmaceuticals. It is a relatively large company, operating on a global basis.

In the early 1980s, Biopharm began manufacturing "The System". This system was used for the purification of pharmaceutical raw materials. It was produced in units or small lots, mainly for special orders, and the number produced and sold was about 30 units a year. Customer needs regarding quality and design were different, so the systems were often tailored to the buyer's requirements.

The production of the system was highly specialized, i.e. it was built mainly from components purchased from external suppliers. Purchased components made up about 85 per cent of the total production cost of the system.

Another characteristic of the original system was that only about 20 per cent of its components were technically adapted to the system, while 80 per cent were purely standard. This fact made supplier contacts easy to handle, not least from a technical point of view.

### *The Development Project*

In 1987, Biopharm decided to update and redesign the system to develop one single version. Biopharm wanted the system to be of high quality, as the buyers with high-quality requirements were growing in number. One important means of enhancing the quality was to obtain components that were well adapted to their functions in this particular system. In the original version, the large proportion of standard components led to a number of technical compromises in the system, or as one technician from Biopharm expressed the problem: "The system was a mish-mash of more or less well suited components, and badly documented."

Biopharm assigned a project group to redesign the system. The group started out by determining the functional standards of the system as a whole. Then every part was gone through carefully, and detailed specifications for individual components set. At this stage, some discussions and inquiries were carried out with component suppliers. It was not, however, until the specifications were ready and set, that a more systematic call for tenders was issued.

The companies that already supplied Biopharm with standard components for the original system then received inquiries concerning the new technical specifications. The majority of the old suppliers, however, turned out to be either unable or unwilling to meet the new requirements. Some of them were large companies and quite uninterested in adapting their standardized products just to satisfy a relatively small customer such as Biopharm. Actually, only two out of the approximately thirty former suppliers of major components (minor details excluded) turned out to be potential suppliers.

In effect, most of the components needed could not be obtained from the existing suppliers. This meant that much of the project work had to be devoted to contacts and discussions with a large number of potential new suppliers. Some 30–40 major components had to be purchased and throughout the project Biopharm was in touch with various suppliers of each one.

A number of suppliers presented samples and prototypes. An important task for Biopharm was to run tests on these in their own laboratory. These tests required competence within fields of knowledge related to the use of the system. Therefore the tests could not be performed by the component suppliers. This testing was time consuming, and progress in the collaboration with individual suppliers was often delayed, pending test results.

Many of the suppliers under consideration by Biopharm during the project, were either dropped or accepted but backed out after only a few contacts. During the process, however, a core of 12–15 especially interesting partners crystallized. An intensive discussion with these suppliers then evolved. Many people from each side were involved and engaged in frequent contacts, technical discussions, visits, etc. Among these innovative relationships, the two remaining old suppliers were found. Not surprisingly, they both had 20–25 year connections with Biopharm, and each of them supplied components that constituted a large proportion of the total system value.

The technical specifications demanded by Biopharm were sometimes perceived by the suppliers as being nearly impossible to fulfil. One example was a valve manufacturer who was asked to make a new type of valve, cast in one piece. To begin with, the supplier found the whole idea absurd and rejected the proposition. However, after a lot of involvement on the part of their own technicians, Biopharm eventually made the supplier see the point of the proposed design. The supplier began to see the idea more as a "new way of thinking" and decided to give it a try. The new type of valve was not completed by the time of the launching of the new

Table 5. Supplier structure of "The System"

| | |
|---|---|
| Total number of suppliers | 60 |
| Suppliers of major components | 30 |
| Old suppliers of major components | 2 |
| New suppliers of major components | 28 |
| Suppliers with close collaboration during the project | 12–15 |

system in the fall 1989, but the first delivery was expected by the end of the year.

Biopharm's persistence – and sometimes "absurd" requirements – made the company quite a fussy customer to deal with. Nevertheless, their demands and ideas also made them an interesting and stimulating partner. Some of the suppliers perceived their interaction with Biopharm as an opportunity to develop their own field of competence.

Biopharm's relationships with its two former suppliers developed even more during this project, and assumed a somewhat different character. Both suppliers were foreign companies, whose sales to Biopharm had previously been handled entirely through local agents. During this project, however, technical matters became too complex to handle via intermediaries. Therefore a direct dialogue between Biopharm and the manufacturers was established. In other words, the earlier standardized, routine ways of handling these relationships were not adequate when the product was no longer standardized. Both the social and technical exchange between the companies was extended, as was the number of people involved in the relationship.

The financial side of the collaboration was managed in different ways in different relationships. Some of the suppliers were very small firms, not able to finance development costs themselves. Such firms also saw very little possibility of benefiting from the outcome in other areas. In some of these cases Biopharm either paid for the whole or part of the cost and thereby obtained exclusive rights to the product. In other cases, however, the supplier was large enough to bear the expense and also saw possibilities in other areas. Some of these companies were offered financial support by Biopharm, but refused it, since Biopharm required exclusive rights in return.

Not all collaborative attempts in this project were successful. One of the 12–15 promising relationships mentioned earlier was with a domestic manufacturer of electronic instruments. This was a very small company, specialized in a narrow niche. The instrument Biopharm wanted them to design was unique. The supplier seemed receptive to Biopharm's technical instructions, and at the beginning of the collaboration both parties were quite optimistic. The supplier began working on the product, and over the next 4–5 months the firms had frequent contact. The supplier behaved as if everything was working out as planned. When the first delivery arrived, however, the product was not at all satisfactory. Technical discussions continued. The supplier still wanted to proceed with the project. One year later, Biopharm had major doubts about the outcome of this collaboration, and was seriously considering dropping the supplier. It was discovered that the supplier had considerable problems connected with the establishment of a production unit in Southeast Asia. According to Biopharm, the supplier had not been frank about the scope or impact of its internal problems.

In the successful cases of collaboration, i.e. where a satisfactory component was obtained, Biopharm's efforts and active participation in the suppliers' development work seems to have been of great importance. First, especially in the completely new relationships, Biopharm's commitment was necessary to reinforce the suppliers' faith in the project. In this way resources could more easily be mobilized. Second, the input of Biopharm's knowledge about the function of a supplier's component in this particular application was important to the supplier. Third, because Biopharm's expertise was mainly in a different field than that of the suppliers, "absurd" – but also innovative – solutions were suggested and new ways of thinking could sometimes be found.

*Results*

When the project was completed, the outcome was a system that fulfilled Biopharm's expectations with regard to quality and design. Proper documentation had also been accomplished. The original version of the system had consisted of 20 per cent specially designed or adapted components and 80 per cent standard components. In the new version these proportions were reversed. These results could to a large extent be considered as products of the close collaborations between Biopharm and the suppliers.

The outcome of the project could, however, be seen in other respects besides the quality of the system developed. First, because of the technical adaptations in the new components and also because of the documentation produced for the components, Biopharm's new supplier relationships are much tighter than were the old ones. For most of the components there is now only one supplier, which would be rather difficult to replace quickly.

Second, the social bonds with suppliers have become rather strong since a lot of people got to know each other during the development process.

Third, indirect technical dependencies between different suppliers have been created as their components are all adapted to fit the system. In effect, one supplier cannot change his component without affecting the functioning of other components.

Fourth, new ways of thinking and developed knowledge within supplier companies could open new possibilities for them in other networks.

*Case Comments*

It is interesting to compare Biopharm's supplier network for its earlier system with its new one. In producing the first system, Biopharm was in contact with a group of suppliers with no connections between them. The relationships were not especially developed, i.e. Biopharm simply bought products, standardized items, that had been developed for other applications. It was easy for Biopharm to change suppliers, because there were always other suppliers who could offer them the same products. All units were relatively independent.

The new structure moves Biopharm to the other end of the spectrum, with all the relationships, and thus also the companies, much more dependent on one another. The products are much more specialized and they fit together in a much more integrated way than before. There are even dependencies among suppliers. Today, it is quite difficult for Biopharm to change a single supplier. Such a process takes time and means a loss of investments. On the other hand, all the suppliers are under pressure. If the final system becomes too expensive there will be no sales, which will affect them all, independently and as a whole. They could, of course, use extortion upon one another, but only for a short time because there is still the opportunity to exchange any part of the system. If a supplier has to be changed, it will never be given a second chance. The new network thus contains much more tension than the first. As long as this tension can be used constructively, however, it will be beneficial to most of them. But there may always be a loser. If the costs of making the adaptations are larger than the revenues accrued from Biopharm or some other complementary relationships, the supplier will operate at a loss. As is shown in this case study, a number of the previous suppliers decided that this might be the case for them when they chose not to participate.

The necessity of interplay between the competence of the purchasing company and that of its suppliers for development of an effective network is thus brought into focus. This is further elaborated on in the next case, where a purchasing firm works systematically to educate its suppliers in order to make them better partners.

## Case 3: Motorola and a Supplier–Development Programme

Our first case dealt with purchasing problems in terms of how to develop individual relationships or how to develop a supplier network for a certain type of purchased products. The second case extended the problems into the development of products and knowledge. In the last two cases, we extend the analysis one step further and look at the whole company's supplier network. The first case study shows how Motorola has developed a general training programme in an attempt to develop more or less all of its suppliers. This case provides us with a good illustration of the need to make long-term purchasing strategy very clear, in order to communicate it effectively to suppliers. Even then, however, complementary activities must be undertaken to stress the importance of this issue.

### *Supplier Involvement*

Motorola, Inc. is one of the world's leading manufacturers of electronic-equipment systems and components. During the 1980s, the company has become a well-known example of a promoter of total quality. Our case description is based on Cayer (1988).

Of every Motorola sales dollar, between 30 and 60 per cent (depending on the business group) goes to suppliers. This alone makes it quite clear that suppliers have a heavy impact on the quality of Motorola products. Company representatives think that suppliers "affect quality more than any other factor in the equation" except for design. Owing to increasing foreign competition, Motorola is committed to accelerating its quality-improvement programme. For this process to be successful, considerable supplier improvement is vital.

Supplier involvement is known to be a major source of potential for improving competitiveness. One company representative states that all the Motorola factories have made tremendous efforts and gains in product quality, reduction of cycle times, and cost reductions. Although some suppliers have played important roles in these improvements, the majority of the supplier base is considered not to have kept up with the pace of Motorola.

Four demands on suppliers that are part of the Motorola improvement process are stated. Motorola needs suppliers who:

- keep pace in attaining perfect quality
- are on the leading edge of technology
- use JIT manufacturing
- offer cost-competitive service.

According to the company, stating the requirements is the easy part – the difficult thing is implementing them. Motorola has worked with supplier development for a number of years. The major problem has been to change the culture associated with the relationships – from the old adversarial type to "win-win" partnerships. After observing good examples at other companies (such as Rank Xerox and Ford) Motorola has been able to improve supplier relations through a series of programmes carried out with their suppliers.

*Training and Education of Suppliers*

Training and education were very important factors in the internal quality programme at Motorola. They estimate that they invested 40 million dollars annually in training in more sophisticated manufacturing, design and management techniques. In the beginning, the programmes were open only to the employees of Motorola. Then, through an analysis of best-practice firms Motorola found that one significant difference between itself and Ford and Rank Xerox was that these companies had extended their training to suppliers as well. Motorola considered that fact to be an important key to its subsequent success.

This was the starting point for the supplier-training programme established in 1988, with the aim of training suppliers to keep up to par in efficiency and productivity. The reason Motorola provided this programme was that its training courses had already been proved to work internally, and it had gained a great deal of hard-earned experience when developing them. Another reason was that only a small part of the supplier base would have had the resources necessary to develop the kind of training needed.

The benefits of the partnership training programmes are mutual. Motorola, of course, has a vested interest in improving supplier performance as they are a part of the assembly line. But suppliers also stand to gain, as the training provided by Motorola will strengthen their overall competitive power. They will be able to broaden their customer base to include other companies striving for zero defects.

The Motorola training programme provides us with an illustration of the structural role of purchasing. By increasing their strength and capabilities, suppliers become more competitive. In the US a trend has developed in that many domestic suppliers have encountered difficulties because foreign competitors are more efficient. According to one Motorola representative, there are several component categories for which there are no longer any domestic suppliers. An increasing dependency on foreign suppliers is not considered a desirable future by Motorola. Therefore it is in its own interest to help develop and promote the capabilities of domestic suppliers so that they will be able to make significant quality improvements.

*The Programme*

Motorola began by establishing a "partnerships for growth advisory board", which initiated a programme with three courses. These training courses covered SPC (statistical process control), design for manufacturability and short-cycle management (where the JIT concept is introduced).

Suppliers were made aware of the courses in a letter signed by the general managers of the Motorola divisions concerned, with a brochure enclosed describing the Partnership for Growth Training Series. Response was limited and suppliers were encouraged again, and were also reminded of the fact that the completion of the three courses was a condition for ongoing business. Even then reactions were slow in coming. Many suppliers felt they didn't need the training. Others were so established that SPC appeared to them to be a basic technique. After almost one year Motorola increased the pressure on suppliers and insisted that suppliers had to take all three courses if they were interested in doing business in the future. The reason for this increasing pressure was the findings presented in a five-year study conducted by the Automotive Industry Action Group, which indicated that suppliers implemented technology, JIT and other viable programmes only to the extent enforced by their customers, and that they did not take opportunities to improve their own productivity.

Motorola considered this a serious drawback to the future competitiveness of suppliers, and intensified its pressure on them. After five months, 167 of the 500 suppliers intended for the programme had completed courses. The results achieved were considered very substantial by Motorola representatives. Within some weeks of basic SPC training, suppliers had made dramatic leaps towards better quality.

The supplier-training programme is only one of a number of activities undertaken to encourage partnership in relationships. Another is promotion of early supplier involvement in new product development. In a number of commodity-product areas, the suppliers' technicians are considered to be the true experts. Therefore, a growing interest has been shown in many of the divisions of the company in facilitating participation of supplier technicians in new product development from a very early stage.

The Communication Sector, Motorola's largest business, encourages supplier participation by focusing on four formalized functions – the supplier advisory board, annual conferences, annual technical symposia and the supplier show. The supplier advisory board was formed to improve two-way communication between Motorola and a core of selected suppliers. The annual supplier conferences provide an exchange of information and insights into various business activities. Conference speakers are always top managers at Motorola. This is an indication to the suppliers of the importance the corporation attaches to the conference and to the development of supplier partnerships. The technical symposia and supplier shows provide Motorola's engineering, manufacturing and purchasing people with an awareness of a broad range of products and technologies available from suppliers. The symposia take the form of in-depth technical seminars on topics presented by technical experts from supplier companies.

*Case Comments*

It might appear relatively uncomplicated to change a purchasing strategy. However, doing so requires a complete change in the way relationships with suppliers are handled. Only when there are no previous relationships to have an influence, might it be easy to change one's own strategy, but in all other cases a change has a substantial effect on how the suppliers should work. Making this type of change takes a long time and is extremely demanding on resources, as can be seen in the case of Motorola. Even for such a very large buyer, it proved difficult to get the suppliers to take an active part in development work.

There is some resistance to change in all networks. This makes it necessary to work with systematic mobilization strategies. Nothing will be accomplished without the support of the counterparts, and all changes must, accordingly, be seen from the other actors' point of view. Neither purchasing nor marketing strategies can be formulated only from the point of view of one's own company. For changes to be accepted by other actors, therefore, both purchasing and marketing must be analysed and structured so as to create business opportunities for other parts of the network as well.

This type of network strategy can be seen in the last case study, of Nike.

## Case 4: Nike's Network Strategies for Subcontracting

One of the keys to a successful network strategy for purchasing is making the different suppliers systematically interrelated. One of the aims is to mobilize the suppliers for development and production in what the buying company considers the right way. In this last case study, Nike's purchasing strategy stands as an illustration of how this can be done.

### *Nike's Supplier Network*

Nike is a major US athletic footwear producer. The case study deals with their supplier network structure and strategy. It is based on information in an article written by Donaghu and Barff (1990).

Nike's supplier network is structured in two layers (Fig. 5). The first thing to observe is that Nike's current production system is almost entirely based on outsourcing to independent suppliers. First-tier suppliers are considered "production partners", rather than subcontractors. Many of their supplier relations are of a long-term nature (eight to ten years) and suppliers are given various kinds of responsibilities within the Nike production system.

### *The Subcontracting System*

Three groups of first-tier suppliers can be identified. One is "developed partners". These firms are responsible for the production of Nike's latest and most expensive products. Their factories are located in Taiwan and South Korea. In these countries, production costs have risen substantially during the late 1980s, and so production of price-sensitive products has been moved to factories elsewhere. The shoes produced by developed partners are characterized by rather low price elasticity, however, which means that they can absorb increasing production costs. Nearly all the developed

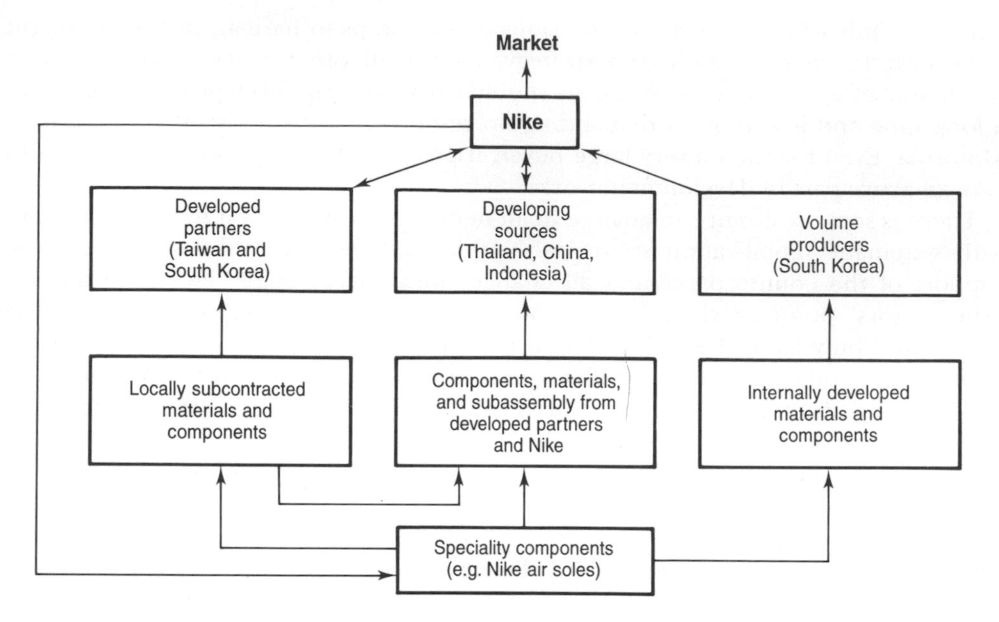


Fig. 5. Nike's system of first- and second-tier subcontracting (Donaghu and Barff, 1990, p. 545).

partners manufacture Nike shoes on an exclusive basis. These relations are therefore characterized by strong mutual dependence, making it important for both parties that stability and trust are promoted. These firms are typically characterized by a lack of vertical integration. Their factories are usually supplied by local subcontractors.

"Volume producers" are suppliers of more standardized footwear. They generally manufacture a specific type of footwear (e.g. football boots, athletics shoes, etc.). They tend to be more vertically integrated than developed partners. They often own leather tanneries, rubber factories and assembly plants. Volume producers have a production capacity four or five times that of developed partners. Their customer relations are not exclusive. Instead, they have ten or more separate buyers purchasing shoes from them. Therefore, Nike does not develop or manufacture any of its up-market and innovative products in these plants. Nor do the competitors manufacture their newest footwear in these volume factories, where other brands are produced at the same time. Rather, volume producers are used to balancing demand and supply in various phases of the business cycle. The cyclical variations in demand can only be marginally absorbed by developed partners, owing to their limited capacity.

Consequently, variations in demand can be considerable. Monthly orders to individual volume producers may fluctuate by 50 per cent or more. Therefore Nike makes only limited efforts to stabilize and deepen its relationships with the volume producers as the strategy is to utilize them for cyclical subcontracting.

The third supplier group is represented by "developing sources". Producers in this group are attractive owing to their low costs (especially labour) and their potential to diversify assembly location. Presently, these firms are located in Thailand, Indonesia and China. Almost all of the development sources are exclusive Nike manufacturers. Due to their limited expertise, Nike is very active in assisting these firms in their development. At the beginning of the collaboration, the product and production standard of these firms can be compared to the situation forty years ago in the United States. One important thing for Nike, therefore, is to increase the production capability of these factories to meet the global production standard of Nike. The long-term goal is that a significant proportion of the developing sources over time will become developed partners.

*The Management of Supplier Relations*

We can see that Nike's supplier network is a mixture of different kinds of relations. Some are long-term while others change from year to year. Some are characterized by deep commitment while others are of an arm's-length nature.

Long-term, intimate partnerships with suppliers must somehow be promoted by customers. Nike uses three main strategies to do this:

1. Nike operates what it calls an "expatriate programme" wherein Nike expatriate technicians become permanent personnel in the factory producing Nike footwear. While at the factory, they function as liaison between Beaverton's headquarters and R&D to help insure a smooth product development process and maintain quality control.
2. Nike encourages its partners (particularly the older ones) to participate in joint product development activities. Most basic research is performed at Nike's Beaverton facilities, but the responsibility for the development of new footwear is shared with its production partners. The partners are especially important in the search for new material inputs and the implementation of improved production processes, but these close ties also serve to keep the production partners abreast of the directions Nike intends to take in the marketplace.
3. With those factories that manufacture only Nike products (over half of all the partners), Nike places a monthly order, preventing production from varying more than 20 per cent per month. These efforts to stabilize the production of Nike shoes take place with those factories that have been with Nike for many years as well as with newer producers (Donaghu and Barff, 1991, p. 542).

It is interesting to observe the activities undertaken by Nike to increase the capability of their developing sources, but the developed partners also participate in this process. The establishment of developing sources often takes the form of joint ventures between local factories in China or Indonesia and a Nike exclusive developed partner in South Korea or Taiwan, which means that the developed partners have a financial interest in the development of the new sources, and will be interested in transferring their sharing capabilities with these partners.

In this way all three actor groups benefit from deeper co-operation. Developed partners are able to move production of the price-sensitive part of the product programme to locations where cost is lower. They concentrate their own manufacturing activities on the more expensive, image-creating products, where price is less important. Developed partners will also be able to supply developing sources with both components and materials.

Developing sources will clearly be able to benefit from the joint venture. The transfer of various capabilities (from Nike and the developed partner) will accelerate the development of these firms as compared with a situation without these links with the larger network. Advantages will be obtained in terms of manufacturing techniques, owing to the demands from competent customers and the availability of important input resources.

Finally, Nike also stands to benefit from the new structure of the production system. The diversified structure of production hedges against currency fluctuations, tariffs and duties. The joint venture arrangements seem to be an efficient way for a natural transfer of capabilities which must be efficient for the entire network. But the system also keeps the pressure on the developed partners at the first tier. They need to keep production costs low as developing sources might otherwise mature into full-blown developed partners.

### *Case Comments*

Nike's way of organizing the production system is an excellent example of a network strategy. It is an extreme case, as the whole production process is out-sourced, but similar tendencies can be found in almost all types of production. Suppliers are becoming more important from a volume point of view, and efficiency is more and more determined by how different production units – internally and externally – are systematically interrelated. In this kind of co-ordination, the activities as well as the resources of the different units must be co-ordinated, and a key issue is to find and develop points of complementarity. For the same reasons, the selection of companies to include in the network is very critical. Nike seems to do this in an excellent way. Their ability to do so is probably attributable to their marketing position in relation to the end market, and to two important knowledge bases. Their position in relation to the end market – the image and the distribution network – is their major asset. In the long run it might not be sufficient, however, and should be supplemented with at least two knowledge bases. The first base is the product knowledge and a need for continuous development regarding individual components, as well as the interaction between different components. This knowledge of how to create good footwear must be kept centrally, in order to keep up the central position within the network. There is always a risk, otherwise, that the developed partners, or the volume producers, might be able to take over. The second base is knowledge of potential suppliers. The development of the production network will never be finalized. There will always be both possibilities of and needs to increase efficiency in terms of finding better activity structures as well as better resources constellations. Every network can, and must, be developed in order to be sustainable.

## Conclusions

Our four case studies have clearly illustrated the potential for increasing efficiency and effectiveness in purchasing activities. With systematic development of individual supplier relations and supplier networks, significant improvements can be made.

It has also been shown, however, that the potential benefits can be quite difficult to attain. Companies have to change their internal activities, as well as change the suppliers in various ways. Such a process means that a number of critical issues are raised. The major one is that companies need to facilitate co-operation, as their own activities will be increasingly dependent on other actors. For such a division of work to be efficient, two major issues must be dealt with. One is the organization of the companies. Certain types of organizational structures might increase the opportunities for an efficient linking of the actors, activities and resources. The other issue is communication. A critical aspect of supplier relations and supplier networks is the exchange of information. As activities undertaken by suppliers are dependent on (and affect) the activities of the customer, there is a strong need for information exchange.

## REFERENCES

Berry, B. Is Detroit prompting a shake-out in the supplier network. *Iron Age*, 14 July, 25–8 (1982).

Cayer, S. World class suppliers don't grow on trees. *Purchasing*, 25 August, 45–9 (1988).

Donaghu, M. and Barff, R. Nike just did it: international subcontracting and flexibility in athletic footwear production, *Regional Studies*, **24** (6), 537–52 (1990).

Gadde, L. -E. *Efterfrågevariationer i vertikala marknadssystem*, Business Administration Studies, Gothenburg, (1978).

Gemünden, H. G. Coping with Inter-Organizational Conflicts. Efficient Interaction Strategies for Buyer and Seller Organizations, *Journal of Business Research*, **13**, 405–20 (1985).

Håkansson, H. *Corporate Technological Behaviour – Co-operation and Networks.* Routledge, London (1989).

Hay, E. It takes more than low bid to be world class, *Purchasing*, 10 November, 50–80 (1988).

Helper, S. Supplier relations and technical progress: theory and application to the auto industry. Department of Economics, Harvard University (1986).

Klint, M. *Mot en konjunkturanpassad kundstrategi.* Department of Business Administration, University of Uppsala.

Roos, L. -U. *Kapitalrationalisering i varulager – kan japansk management och japansk syn på inköp untnyttjas?* Handelshögskolan i Göteborg, Företagsekonomiska institutionen.

3

# The Changing Role of Purchasing: Reconsidering Three Strategic Issues

*Lars Erik Gadde and Håkan Håkansson*

During the last 20 years a new view of purchasing has gradually emerged. From being considered a clerical function – with the ultimate purpose of buying as cheaply as possible – it is today regarded in many companies as a major strategic function. This new attitude towards purchasing is responsible for more than half the total costs in many companies. Nevertheless, the scale of the recent change is so considerable that an analysis of its development is of interest. This paper draws on our own research and that of many others. Our focus is manufacturing and assembly industry.

Let us begin with a quotation that gives a representative statement on the traditional view of efficiency in purchasing:

> Price has been the principal yardstick by which manufacturers have traditionally selected their suppliers. By spreading their purchases among several suppliers, it is argued, manufacturers can achieve the cheapest price and the greatest assurance of a secure flow of material (Dillforce, 1986, p 3).

Such purchasing behaviour does not allow for making direct use of the total resources of the suppliers. This can be a considerable drawback, according to the analysis provided by, for example, Axelsson and Håkansson (1984) and Spekman (1985). During the last decade, however, many companies have changed their behaviour in the directions proposed (see for example Carlisle and Parker, 1989; Gadde and Håkansson, 1993; Lamming, 1993).

In 1987, Morgan observed a tendency among customers to move from an arm's-length relationship (a number of competing suppliers) towards single sourcing and even to "alliances". The last type of relationship involves a deepened cooperation between the customer and a specific supplier. Similar frameworks have been presented by Frazier *et al.* (1988) and Lamming (1993). Frazier *et al.* have developed a conceptual model where the traditional view is called *market exchange.* The deeper relationships are then characterized as *relational exchange* and *just-in-time exchange.* Lamming's discussion is based on empirical observations from the automobile

Reprinted from *European Journal of Purchasing and Supply Management,* Vol. 1, No. 1. L.-E. Gadde and H. Håkansson, pp. 27–35, with permission from Elsevier Science Ltd, The Boulevard, Langford Lane, Kidlington, OX5 1GB, UK.

industry. This model takes a dynamic view and identifies a four-phase development process from the traditional model (prior to 1975) to the partnership model (after 1990).

The strategic purchasing context for the partnership model is very different from that of the traditional model, and similarly for just-in-time exchange versus market exchange. The aim of our contribution, therefore, is to analyse the changing role of purchasing in terms of purchasing strategy and purchasing behaviour. We shall discuss the impact of the new view in three dimensions of purchasing strategy.

The major strategic decision is always whether to buy or to rely on in-house production. Consequently, the first strategic issue is related to the question of *make or buy*. If the role of the purchasing is changing, the nature of the make-or-buy decision might be affected.

The second strategic choice is to decide on the *supply-base structure*. This issue regards the number of suppliers to use, as well as how the suppliers should relate to one another. The third strategic aspect deals with the nature of the *customer-supplier relationship*. When buyer–seller relationships turn into alliances, partnerships or just-in-time exchanges, the suppliers become more or less parts of the customer's production system. We discuss the benefits that can be obtained from this kind of close relationship.

## MAKE OR BUY

The first strategic issue deals with the decision of whether to make or to buy. This question has been a major topic ever since industrial activities were established but it does not seem to have been considered as a strategic problem by manufacturing firms. Culliton (1942) concluded that most managers, when they were asked about their make-or-buy problem, said they had none. According to Culliton, however, that answer should be considered as representing a lack of insight into strategic issues, rather than the absence of the problem. The relevance of this aspect seems to have been neglected even in more recent times: see for example Janch and Wilson (1979), Leenders and Nollet (1984), and Ford *et al.* (1993). These authors conclude that make-or-buy problems have generally been ignored by top management. Where they have been considered, they seem to have been handled by purchasing departments and based on short-term cost criteria, rather than on strategic analysis.

In spite of the perceived absence of strategic decisions, it is possible to identify a clear trend over time towards the increasing importance of "buy". In 1942 Culliton argued that, in general, it seemed that "buying is preferable to making". The reasons for his conclusion, however, appear to be the disadvantages associated with a "make" strategy, owing to rapid changes in the market, and the lack of flexibility that characterizes in-house production. Hayes and Abernathy (1980) agree with Culliton in advocating a "buy" strategy. Their main reason is the risks associated with being locked into a specific technology, which might be challenged by new developments. A company with asset-specific investments, they argue, may have problems in maintaining its innovativeness. The authors therefore warn companies against too high a degree of vertical integration. Dirrheimer and Hübner (1983) analysed the vertical integration in the automobile industry and discovered a considerable variation between different companies and different countries. For all manufacturers analysed, however, vertical integration had decreased during the previous five-year period.

In total, therefore, as the levels of vertical integration have increased, suppliers appear to have become more and more important as sources of resources. This is illustrated by examples in Gadde and Håkansson (1993). In a study of four large multinationals in the Swedish engineering industry, it was shown that components and systems purchased from outside suppliers accounted for about two-thirds of the turnover. In the construction industry, it was found, the proportion is even higher. The situation also seems to be familiar for small and medium-sized firms. In a study of 123 Swedish companies, purchasing accounted for more than 40% of the turnover for 70% of the companies. For almost every fifth firm, the proportion extended to 70% (Håkansson, 1989).

The figures also seem to be representative for a general trend in other countries (Ford *et al.* 1993) and other industries (Kumpe and Bolwijn, 1988). These findings show that many manufacturing companies are increasingly relying on competent suppliers, which have been able to contribute to the customer's efficiency in production as well as in R&D.

It is possible, therefore, to identify a decreasing rate of vertical integration. A strategic shift of this kind can lead both to advantages and to disadvantages. One interesting question is whether this trend will continue. Miles and Snow (1986) predict that it will. In their opinion, the changing environmental conditions and new competitive forms will result in industries being characterized by completely new organizational forms in the future. They suggest that the functions necessary in an industrial system (such as design, production and marketing) will be performed by specialized companies, each one undertaking separate functions. Such dynamic networks are supposed to be fairly loose coalitions intertwined by "brokers" responsible for the integration of the functions. In this integration, exchange of information will be a crucial determinant of efficiency and effectiveness, as the network governance is based on market mechanisms. Such an industrial system is characterized by a lack of vertical integration.

Kumpe and Bolwijn (1988), in contrast, argue that the degree of vertical integration will increase in the future, because value chains today are characterized by an imbalance in the distribution of profits. Enterprises in the final stages of the production chain (assembly and marketing/distribution) usually tend to be profitable, while profits in the earlier stages (such as component production) are generally substantially less profit-making. For the value chain as a whole to be competitive, however, there is a great need for investments in these stages as well. There is an obvious risk, then, that the investments necessary for long-term competitiveness (in design, product development and component production) will never be undertaken, because suppliers might be unable to raise the necessary financial resources. Therefore, Kumpe and Bolwijn argue, firms in the final stages of the value chain will be forced to integrate backwards and provide these resources; otherwise suppliers might be driven out of business, implying severe problems for the customer. A strategy aiming at an even lower degree of vertical integration, which might be efficient in the short term, is therefore considered to be a disaster in the long run.

We have thus been able to identify two contradictory views of the future of vertical integration. The divergent opinions can partly be explained by their focus on the formal degree of integration: that is, on ownership ties. As we have seen, vertical integration in this respect has decreased over time. It has been replaced, however, by informal arrangements that keep the industrial networks together. This is what is usually called "quasi-integration" (Blois, 1972). Quasi-integration can take various forms and include, among other things, customer investments in production tools, joint product development and various forms of financial support. It is apparent that these informal mechanisms are increases in importance over time. Therefore, the divergent opinions held by Kumpe and Bolwijn and Miles and Snow need not be as conflicting as they appear at first sight. Through quasi-integration arrangements customers can provide suppliers with support, without moving back to ownership relations. However, buying firms will not be free to change suppliers as easily as indicated by Miles and Snow. Investments undertaken on either side of the dyad will restrict the opportunities to change supplier.

We do not foresee any major strategic shift in the view of make-or-buy decisions. Our opinion is that the observed tendency – towards buying more from outside suppliers – will continue. The driving forces towards increasing specialization will still be strong in the future, and will favour outsourcing not only of components but also, at an increasing rate, of systems of components, design and product development. One important implication following from our discussion, however, is that make-or-buy decisions should be given more strategic attention than in the past. When most of the resources of a company are provided by outside suppliers it is necessary for these decisions to be given top priority. This need is heightened because make-or-buy decisions are increasingly characterized by technical complexity. Venkatesan (1992) has found that the aim of preserving jobs has been one important determinant of make-or-buy decisions. The effect, in many cases, has been insourcing of parts that are easy to manufacture and outsourcing of components and systems that are more complicated. In the long run, such a strategy might erode the capability of the firm. According to Venkatesan, therefore, the management challenge is to identify the really strategic components among the thousands of parts that they know mostly in terms of cost, rather than function or importance to the product.

## DESIGN OF THE SUPPLY-BASE STRUCTURE

The issues regarding the supply-base structure can be divided into two strategic aspects. One has to do with the *number of suppliers*, the other with the *way suppliers are organized*. The number of suppliers has always been an important aspect of purchasing strategy. As mentioned above, the traditional view of purchasing meant that there was a group of suppliers eagerly competing with one another – mainly in terms of price: thus the more suppliers a company had in its supply base the better. We know that this view of efficiency has been increasingly questioned and we discuss the implications below. One of the reasons for the changing view is the insight into the advantages that can be obtained from more cooperative relationships with a reduced supply base. Activities that deepen individual relationships will also have an effect on the supply-base structure as a whole. In fact, many companies today have clear strategic aims for the shape of the supply-base structure. This is a growing dimension of purchasing strategy.

### Number of Suppliers

The choice between single sourcing and multiple sourcing is a classical issue in purchasing strategy. The established criterion of efficiency has often resulted in multiple sourcing, as supplier competition has been given priority. By promoting competition among suppliers, customers are expected to be given better control of price levels as well as more reliable supply through diversification of risks.

It is obvious that purchasing strategies have undergone considerable changes in this respect during the 1980s. Newman (1988) has identified a clear trend towards single sourcing. The significance of the changes differ between industries. It seems to be most obvious in the automotive industry. The North American motor manufacturer Chrysler decreased its number of suppliers of wiring harnesses from fourteen to three and its paint suppliers from five to two: one for the US plants and one for the Canadian plants (Raia, 1988). General Motors reduced its supplier base for its Quad-four from 140 to 69 through single sourcing (Offdile and Arrington, 1992). A US survey of more than 1000 suppliers showed that the average number of firms competing with the average supplier to produce the same product for a given customer decreased from 2.0 to 1.5 in five years (Helper, 1991).

Such changes for specific components and firms have substantial effects on the supplier structure as a whole. Considerable changes in the total number of suppliers have been reported for Ford US, from 3200 in 1981 to 2100 in 1987 (Burt, 1989), and Chrysler, from 3000 suppliers on the roll only a few years ago to just over 1000 today (Raia, 1993). Similar changes are evident in other industries and companies: in 1981 Rank Xerox had almost 5000 suppliers, but six years later the number had been reduced to just over 300 (Morgan, 1987).

These observations contrast sharply with the traditional view of purchasing efficiency. Newman (1988) states that only a decade ago a purchasing strategy relying on single sourcing would have been characterized as an "invitation to disaster". At that time customers implementing single sourcing were expected to lose opportunities for price control, as well as diversification of risks. The reason for looking at this trade-off through other glasses is the changing role of purchasing. Today it is possible, in fact, to argue that single sourcing leads to an increase in the reliability of supply. Purchasing firms that reduce the number of suppliers and try to strengthen their relationships with the remaining ones might be able to establish very efficient logistical systems together with their suppliers. We discuss this below when dealing with the quality of supplier relations. Regarding price control, Newman (1988) argues that the price competition perceived when dealing with multiple sourcing can often be illusory. Price is only one of the costs affected and changed, when purchasing activities are handled differently. A number of indirect costs are also affected, as discussed below.

### Organization of the Supply-Base Structure

The second dimension of the supply-base structure has to do with organization of suppliers. The effects of various organizational forms are illustrated in a study of supplier relationships in the automobile industry (Gadde and Grant, 1984). The number of suppliers dealing directly with automobile manufacturers showed substantial variability. General Motors, in their US operations, used around 3500 suppliers, while Volvo Car Corporation relied on 800 suppliers. The difference between GM and Volvo can be explained by scale factors such as number of plants and number of cars produced. The corresponding figures for manufacturers from Japan, however, did not fit into this pattern. Only around 200 suppliers delivered directly to Toyota and Nissan in spite of the fact that the production output of these companies was closer to that of GM than that of Volvo.

The main reason for these deviations was shown to be the different ways that companies organized the supply-base structure. GM and Volvo, in fact, had no organization at all. The strategy of supporting competition among suppliers through multiple sourcing had resulted in fairly "wild" structures. Toyota and Nissan had organized their suppliers in hierarchies. Only the suppliers on the first level delivered directly to the customer. These first-tier suppliers were made responsible for just-in-time deliveries. They had also become more "system" than "component" suppliers over time, and were to an increasing extent responsible for product development. Furthermore, they were responsible for the activities of the suppliers on the other levels in the structure. Nishiguchi (1987, 1993) provides a detailed discussion of these systems and their characteristics.

The first analysis of the Japanese supplier structures concluded that customers were relying on single sourcing. More recent research, however, has shown that this is true for large complex systems that require massive investments in tools. In other supply situations, however, two or more vendors can be used (Womack *et al.* 1990). The same observation is further elaborated by Richardson (1993) who characterized the purchasing strategy used by Japanese auto-manufacturers as *parallel sourcing*. This system is observed when the car manufacturer produces a number of models at different plants using a sole source for a component of one model at one assembly plant, while another source is used at another plant. A second aspect of parallel sourcing is that some components can be common to various models and may have multiple sources, while they may still be sole sourced for a particular model.

When the number of suppliers is reduced, the customer becomes more dependent on individual suppliers. The traditional view of efficiency recommends that customers avoid such dependencies. In spite of this we have seen firms turning in this direction. The underlying reason is that reducing the number of counterparts is a prerequisite for improved and deepened supplier relationships.

## THE NATURE OF CUSTOMER – SUPPLIER RELATIONSHIPS

The main reason for reducing the number of suppliers has been to provide opportunities for deeper cooperation with selected individual firms. Two driving forces can be identified in this process. One is reduction of costs: the potential for rationalization through a close relationship. The other is the possible exploitation of supplier resources in order to improve technical development: that is, development through a close relationship. We shall now discuss these two dimensions of increasing quality in supplier relations.

Cost rationalization effects can be obtained in several ways. A number of indirect costs can be affected through a deeper cooperation with suppliers. We shall discuss these effects in terms of administrative costs, production costs and costs related to the material flow. Costs of R&D and product developments can also be affected. These are discussed in the section on development cooperation.

### Rationalization of Administrative Costs

The flow of administrative information between customer and supplier provides substantial potential for rationalization. In Gadde and Håkansson (1993) a number of examples are presented. One of the them deals with a customer whose ambition was to decrease the paper flow in one of the supplier relationships. By eliminating purchase orders and introducing daily deliveries with monthly invoicing, it was possible to decrease the number of documents per transaction from seventeen to three. Another illustration of the substantial administrative costs is a big Swedish company in the construction industry that receives around 1.2 million invoices a year. Internal calculations indicate that the cost for handling one invoice is more than 300 SEK (about US$40). Clearly, the administrative costs represent an enormous potential for rationalization.

A powerful tool for attacking these costs has been obtained through the development of information technology. Enquiries, orders and invoices can be transmitted today, very quickly and accurately. In addition to reducing administrative costs, such arrangements provide purchasing officers with more time for working with strategic questions. An analysis of the impact of information technology on purchasing is presented in Dubois *et al.* (1989).

### Rationalization of Production Costs

One way of affecting production costs is to combine in-house production capacity and capability with the corresponding supplier resources. This is the general make-or-buy problem as already discussed. By moving production activities from one firm to another it is possible to increase efficiency. It is clear, however, that such changes in the division of labour can be handled in a more sophisticated way within more intimate customer – supplier relationships. In long-term relationships successive adaptations will enhance performance. Another effectiveness measure may be coordination amongst suppliers: for example, by increasing the cooperation between them. Marler (1989) exemplifies this by illustrating how Ford told all their suppliers of door components that they were no longer interested in purchasing individual components. The suppliers were encouraged to do what they could to form alliances and then tender for complete door systems.

The Ford example illustrates the increasing interests of many automotive firms in purchasing complete systems rather than separate components. One implication of this general trend is a development towards networks of highly specialized production units. As shown by Dubois and Håkansson (1993) the activity structures of such networks can be combined in a number of different ways. This is another reason why the make-or-buy decisions must be given increasing strategic attention.

## Rationalization of Material Flow Costs

Costs related to material flow include the costs of handling goods, costs of keeping inventories, and costs of capital. A reduction in these costs is probably the most significant advantage that can be obtained through closer supplier relationships. Many firms have achieved substantial improvements in efficiency by reducing stocks of input goods and work in process. Activities of this kind were originally inspired by observations from Japan:

> It only takes 10 minutes inside an assembly plant in Japan to realize that relationships with suppliers are very different. The visitor accustomed to the loading docks, the large storage areas and the large incoming inspection area, typical of US plants, is likely taken aback by the stocking of Japanese assembly lines. Trucks from suppliers back up through large bay doors right to the assembly line; supplier personnel unload a few hours of parts, clean up the area and depart. There is no incoming inspection, no staging area, not expediting of material, just a seemingly continuous flow of material (Hervey, 1982, p. 6).

This just-in-time philosophy is generally considered to be one of the major factors underlying the competitive power of the Japanese auto industry over the past three decades. It is natural, therefore, that competitors in other parts of the world have tried to neutralize this competitive edge. Raia (1988) claims that Chrysler's early extensive JIT initiatives were one of the main factors contributing to the recovery in the mid-1980s. The tied-up capital could be reduced by one billion dollars by improving material flow efficiency.

The major changes when adopting JIT deliveries are a decrease in lot sizes and an increase in delivery frequency. In the Honda plant in Ohio there is no tyre inventory at the assembly plant. A local tyre supplier makes 136 deliveries each day by truck. The supplier is responsible for ensuring that the tyre specified is loaded on the conveyor belt connected to the assembly line, according to the schedule decided by the purchaser. This system then works in the same way as the Japanese system discussed above: no storage, no inspection, and no extra handling (Offodile and Arrington, 1992).

## Development Through Supplier Relations

Purchasing companies can benefit in a number of ways from cooperation with suppliers in technical development regarding their products and processes. Two of the most frequently mentioned issues deal with increasing and activating the resource base and shortening lead times in technical development projects.

In close relationships, it is possible to identify and activate complementary resource bases. Many products are characterized by the need for deep knowledge in several areas of technology. Owing to increasing specialization, it is not possible for one company to cover all these areas. It is necessary, therefore, to find suppliers who are willing and able to contribute to technical development. One positive effect will be an extension of the total resource base. Another is that interactive effects might emerge. In the active confrontation of two resource bodies innovative sparks can arise (Håkansson, 1987).

It is no surprising, therefore, that suppliers have, over time, been increasingly used as a resource in product development. Eriksson and Håkansson (1993) describe two interesting examples of supplier involvement. They deal with development of a robotized system and a piece of medical process equipment. A large number of suppliers are activated in the development processes. In both cases suppliers are responsible for the most innovative parts of the new system.

The other main reason for activating suppliers in development processes is to shorten lead times (see for example Takeuchi and Nonaka, 1986; Burt, 1989; Raia, 1991). Raia presents a number of interesting examples. One is that of Xerox, which has managed to reduce lead times for new products by more than half as a result of increasing supplier involvement. Ingersoll-Rand introduced several suppliers to a project when the new product only was "a gleam in the eye of the marketing manager. In this way it is possible to shift certain development activities to suppliers, making it possible to reduce lead times substantially. One important prerequisite for successful implementation of programmes with such aims is that suppliers are involved in the development processes much earlier than they have previously been allowed to be.

## IMPLEMENTATION OF CHANGES

New forms of supplier relations provide customers with opportunities for rationalization as well as development activities. It is important to observe, however, that such effects do not follow automatically from a concentration to fewer suppliers and policy declarations. On the contrary, a lot of hard work is needed to attain the potential benefits. A number of problems can arise when changes are implemented.

The advantages associated with JIT deliveries can be substantial, but the transition to JIT is far from simple. This is shown by an observation from a purchasing company that could demonstrate that supplies arrive precisely on schedule. On the shopfloor, however, the impression was entirely different.

> But when I walked through the plant I saw weeks of stampings, acres of work-in-process, and subassemblies strewn around the body-shop. Boxes of parts were stacked so high on the chassis and trim lines, that it was difficult to see what was going on in these areas. In fact, the inventory took up so much room that they could have put five major press lines in the same space. This is JIT, I wondered? (Harbour, 1986, p. 14).

It is interesting to compare this observation with the attitudes of the American whilst visiting the Japanese company, described earlier. It is very clear that JIT must not be regarded only as a purchasing strategy affecting lot sizes and delivery frequencies. In fact, JIT is a basic determinant of the efficiency of an integrated production system. Activities and requirements directed towards suppliers therefore have few positive effects if they are not followed – or rather preceded – by changes at the buying firms. If this is not done, subdeliveries of the JIT type might increase problems when delivery frequencies are increased.

When JIT was first introduced into the West, the effect seems to have been that inventories were moved to an earlier stage in the production chain. This was found in a comparative study of JIT in Europe, Japan and the USA (Nishiguchi, 1989). In the US automotive industry it was observed that suppliers increased their delivery frequencies. However, these deliveries often came from newly established warehouses. The inventory business in Detroit was booming; one company even picked the name "JIT Warehousing" (Raia, 1988).

In a major survey of US automotive suppliers, Helper (1991) concluded that suppliers implemented JIT mainly because customers demanded it, but that no major effects were attained in the production processes of suppliers. The prevailing attitude to JIT was that it only transferred responsibility for inventories. Less than one-third of the respondents were of the opinion that JIT decreased the inventory levels for the chain as a whole. The major reason stated for the shortcomings was that customers did not provide suppliers with stable delivery schedules.

The conclusion to be drawn is that efforts to increase efficiency in material flow are major undertakings requiring a number of changes both from suppliers and from the purchasing companies. Therefore it should not be surprising that progress takes time. To establish the links of a total JIT system is a highly demanding process. Toyota began experimenting with its system in 1948. Not until 1965 was a fully synchronized system between Toyota and its first-tier suppliers completed (Nishiguchi, 1987, 1994).

Regarding development cooperation with suppliers, several problems can be identified. One is related to the knowledge of the potential in such collaboration. Burt and Sukoup (1985) concluded that suppliers, at that time, were rather neglected as resources relating to product development. Most customers did not seem to understand the potential available, which the authors considered a major strategic defect. A study of a large number of small and medium-sized firms in Sweden showed that more than one quarter of them had had no cooperative development projects with any supplier during the preceding three-year period (Håkansson, 1989).

What is the explanation for this reluctance towards using supplier resources? One important reason could be a lack of insight into the actual potential. Another reason can be identified as a reluctance on the supplier side. Increasing cooperation should also be of interest to suppliers: through such activities they might be able to strengthen their ties to customers. In spite of this potential advantage, suppliers often appear to hesitate to enter into deeper relations with customers. The reason is that market investments of this type have a cost side that must be compared with the benefits. Suppliers have to invest in specific resources in order to be attractive partners. These resources may be difficult to obtain, as the costs associated with them may be substantial. Furthermore, they sometimes create a very strong dependence, as they might have no alternative use if they are very specialized solutions.

It is also clear that suppliers who are used to customer behaviour such as playing suppliers off against one another will think twice before entering into a close relationship. One prerequisite for increased involvement is some kind of confidence in a long-term business relation. The usual adversarial relationship must be changed to a more symbiotic one. Before this can be achieved, customers themselves have to change their attitudes. Communications of long-term strategic ambitions must be undertaken at the buying company as well as towards the supplier company. It is obvious that changing attitudes is a very time-consuming activity in a large company, especially if the new attitudes deviate substantially from the old ones. Only after these changes within the companies is it possible to change the relationship between them.

## IMPLICATIONS

Our analysis of the changing role of purchasing indicates the following tendencies regarding the three strategic issues identified:

1. An increasing importance of "buy" as compared with "make" – i.e. reducing the degree of vertical integration and because the make-or-buy problems are becoming increasingly complex, they deserve more strategic attention;
2. Systematic attempts to structure the suppliers, including a reduction of the supply base, and improvement of coordination among suppliers;
3. Deeper cooperation with individual suppliers to achieve benefits regarding rationalization and technical development.

These changes have naturally brought with them related changes in purchasing and marketing activities. The most dramatic ones have certainly taken place on the purchasing side. The most significant changes have to do with the relationships with individual suppliers, but this has also had important implications for the way purchasing strategies have been formulated and the ways in which purchasing activities have been organized. The marketing function within selling companies has also had to make substantial adaptations but these changes have been easier to integrate into already existing strategies and organizational forms. These changes have also affected the general industry level in terms of production structures and degree of innovativeness. Our final section, therefore, deals with implications for marketing, purchasing and the aggregate industry level.

### Purchasing Implications

The first and most important implication is that purchasing strategy has become an issue for top management. Never before have so many companies discussed, analysed and formulated offensive strategies for purchasing. The analyses are directed towards finding efficient supplier structures, forming alliances with key suppliers, developing training programmes together with suppliers and activating suppliers in technical development projects. This is a considerable change from the earlier concentration on formulating procedures for efficient purchasing, such as the number of bids that had to be asked for. These changes reflect a new view of purchasing efficiency, which is further analysed in Gadde and Håkansson (1993).

A second implication is related to the organization of purchasing. The major shift has been towards a decentralization of purchasing activities away from the centralized purchasing departments that used to characterize large manufacturing firms. There are two main reasons for this change. The first is that the purchasing decisions must be made by people who are close to the problems to be solved. They must have a good knowledge of the use of the products and about the problems regarding logistical and administrative routines, to be able to capture the potential for rationalization and development. The second reason is that decentralization of purchasing has been well in accord with general organizational trends towards independent profit centres with decentralized responsibility. If purchasing costs account for more than half of the total costs, then each profit centre must be given the right to make its own decisions regarding purchasing and suppliers. Decentralization makes it generally easier to develop close relationships, while also making it more difficult to coordinate the relationships of the whole company.

A third implication, following the organizational change, is a trend away from functional specialization. The changing role of purchasing will call for a shift towards more integrated problem-solving. Purchasing today is much more focused on technical and logistical matters than before, when strictly commercial issues dominated. Developing supplier relationships means finding efficient solutions, considering the trade-offs between direct costs (mainly price), various indirect costs (in production, administration, material flow, for example) and other strategic benefits from the relationships. This aspect will also affect the role of individual purchasers. Highly specialized purchasers will be replaced by more general problem-solvers. Before, a purchasing officer was often regarded as a rather isolated person responsible only for the commercial aspect of procurement and sometimes considered only as an executor of decisions taken by others. Today, a purchaser must be a member of a team, working closely together with, and coordinating, specialists from other functions. In some companies this change has been so considerable that the purchaser as a functional specialist no longer exists.

### Marketing Implications

The changes described from the purchasing perspective have, of course, also affected and involved the selling companies. Some suppliers have been very actively involved and have even been change agents, while others have taken part more reluctantly or have even tried to counteract the changes. Those who have considered the transition of purchasing as an opportunity have had to learn a new way of dealing with customers. One characteristic of this new role is the development of mutual relationships, which have two consequences, both contradictory to established marketing traditions. The first is that reaction is as important as action. This means that strategic marketing decisions should increasingly be based on adaptations to the changing purchasing strategies of customers.

The second consequence is that departments other than sales and marketing have to be much more involved in developing the relationships. Direct contacts have to be established between technicians in the two companies, as well as between departments taking care of material and information flows. Furthermore, issues regarding technical development must be discussed between R&D people on both sides. Sometimes even the purchasing department of the selling company needs to be involved in the process, as the customer might have requirements regarding which subsuppliers to use, especially for critical components and materials.

Owing to these conditions, marketing will be much more of an organizational problem than has been previously recognized. The main issue will be to handle the development of individual customer relationships. Developing these relationships will call for coordinating activities from the selling company. The first is that the internal activities of the supplier must be coordinated with those of the customer. The second is that the various customer relationships have to be considered in several dimensions. The third, finally, is that the customer relationships have to be coordinated with the selling companies' other external relationships, such as suppliers and technical consultants.

## Implications on an Aggregate Level

The new purchasing philosophy also has effects at a more aggregate level. The development of relationships and networks increases the potential for further specialization. Consequently, companies become increasingly specialized production units, within a network structure. In the future, various production activities will be undertaken by highly specialized companies, which are bound together through close relationships into efficient production structures. As pointed out by Richardson (1993), the combination of a high level of relatonship-specific investments and single sourcing might lead to problems with supplier performance, but it is also possible to say that close relationships will increase the pressure on supplier performance. Deepened customer–supplier relationships will be characterized by clear, directed, individually based pressure, as the counterparts are mutually dependent. This also means that the pressure can be expressed in much more detailed and specific terms than is possible in market-mediated pressure. Our conclusion is thus that production structures based on deepened relationships need not be less flexible *per se*.

The transitions in purchasing and buyer–seller relationships also influence the nature of innovation and innovativeness. At an increasing rate, innovations will be developed in the interactions between users and suppliers. In general, this will shorten lead times in product development, which is considered to be an important strategic issue in most industries today.

Another consequence is that innovations will be more in accordance with the needs of the established network structure. It is reasonable to believe that such a change will have positive effects on the failure rate in product innovation. Conversely, a potential negative outcome might be a decrease in the number of revolutionary innovations.

Purchasing's concern for innovativeness is a far cry from its former role. The strategic role of purchasing will emerge naturally as the competitive pressures on businesses increase.

## REFERENCES

Axelsson, B. and Håkansson, H. *Inköp för konkurrenskraft.* Liber, Stockholm (1984).

Blois, K. Vertical quasi-integration. *Journal of Industrial Economics,* **20**, (3) 33–41 (1972).

Burt, D. Managing suppliers up to speed. *Harvard Business Review,* July–August, 127–35 (1989).

Burt, D. and Sukoup, W. Purchasing's role in new product development. *Harvard Business Review,* September–October, 90–7 (1989).

Carlisle, J. and Parker, R. *Beyond Negotiation, Redeeming Customer–Supplier Relationships.* John Wiley and Sons, (1989).

Culliton, J. *Make-or-buy.* Harvard University Graduate School of Business Administration, Boston (1942).

Dillforce, W. Purchasing – a singular way to increase competitiveness. *Financial Times,* 24 October (1986).

Dirrheimer, M. and Hübner, T. Vertical integration and performance in the automotive industry; paper presented at the Future of Automobile Forum, Boston, MIT (1983).

Dubois, A., Gadde, L.-E. and Håkansson, H. The impact of information technology on purchasing behaviour and supplier markets. Working Paper No. 1989:11, Gothenburg, Institute for Management for Innovation and Technology (1989).

Dubois, A. and Håkansson, H. Relationships as activity links. *Proceedings of the conference: Forms of Interorganizational Networks: Structures and Processes.* European Science Foundation, Berlin (1993).

Eriksson, A.-K. and Håkansson, H. Getting innovations out of supplier networks. *Journal of Business-to-Business Marketing,* **1** (3), 3–34 (1993).

Ford, D., Cotton, B., Farmer, D., Gross, A. and Wilkinson, I. Make-or-buy decisions and their implications; *Industrial Marketing Management,* **22**, 207–14 (1993).

Frazier, G., Spekman, R. and O'Neal, C. Just-in-time exchange relationships in industrial markets. *Journal of Marketing,* **52** (October) 52–67 (1988).

Gadde, L.-E. and Grant, B. Quasi-integration, supplier networks and technological cooperation in the automotive industry. *Proceedings of the International Research Seminar on Industrial Marketing.* Stockholm School of Economics, Stockholm (1984).

Gadde, L.-E. and Håkansson, H. *Professional Purchasing.* Routledge, London (1993).

Håkansson, H. *Corporate Technological Behaviour – Cooperation and Networks.* Routledge, London (1989).

Harbour, J. What is just-in-time manufacturing? *Automotive Industries,* January, 14 (1986).

Hayes, R. and Abernathy, W. Managing our way to economic decline. *Harvard Business Review,* July–August, 67–77 (1980)

Helper, S. How much has really changed between US automakers and their suppliers? *Sloan Management Review,* Summer, 15–28 (1991).

Hervey, R. Preliminary observation on manufacturer–supplier relations in the Japanese automotive industry. The Joint US – Japan Automotive Study, Working Paper series No. 5, University of Michigan, Ann Arbor (1982).

Janch, L. and Wilson, H. A strategic perspectives for make or buy decisions. *Long Range Planning,* **12** (December) 56–61 (1979).

Kumpe, T. and Bolwijn, P. Manufacturing: the new case for vertical integration. *Harvard Business Review,* March–April, 75–81 (1988).

Lamming, R. *Beyond Partnership. Strategies for Innovation and Lean Supply.* Prentice-Hall, Hemel Hemptead, UK (1993).

Leenders, M. and Nollet, J. The grey zone in make or buy. *Journal of Purchasing and Materials Management,* Fall, 10–15 (1984).

Marler, D. The post Japanese model of automotive component supply: selective North American case studies: IMVP International Policy Forum, MIT, Boston (1989).

Miles, R. and Snow, C. Organizations: new concepts for new forms. *California Management Review,* **18** (3), 62–73 (1986).

Morgan, I. The purchasing revolution. *The McKinsey Quarterly,* Spring, 49–55 (1987).

Newman, R. Single source qualification. *Journal of Purchasing and Materials Management,*

Summer, 10–17 (1988).
Nishiguchi, T. "Competing systems of automotive components supply: an examination of the Japanese "clustered control" model and the "Alps" structure. First Policy Forum, International Motor Vehicle Program, MIT, Boston (1984).
Nishiguchi, T. Is JIT really JIT? Third Policy Forum, International Motor Vehicle Program, MIT, Boston (1989).
Nishiguchi, T. *Strategic Industrial Sourcing: The Japanese Advantage.* Oxford University Press, New York (1993).
Offodile, F. and Arrington, D. Support of successful just-in-time implementation: the changing role of purchasing. *International Journal of Physical Distribution and Logistics Management,* **22** (5) 38–46 (1992).
Raia, E. JIT in Detroit. *Purchasing,* 15 September, 68–77 (1988).
Raia, E. Taking time out of product design. *Purchasing,* **4** (April 4), 36–9 (1991).
Raia, E. The extended enterprise. *Purchasing,* 4 March, 48–51 (1993).
Richardson, J. Parallel sourcing and supplier performance in the Japanese automobile industry. *Strategic Management Journal,* **14**, 339–50 (1993).
Spekman, R. Strategic supplier selection: understanding long-term buyer relationships. *Business Horizons,* July–August, 75–81 (1985).
Takeuchi, H. and Nonaka, I. The new new-product development game. *Harvard Business Review,* January–February, 137–46 (1986).
Venkatesan, R. Strategic sourcing: to make or not to make. *Harvard Business Review,* November–December, 98–108 (1992).
Womack, J., Jones, D. and Roos, D. *The Machine that Changed the World.* Rawson Associates, New York (1990).

# 4

# International Purchasing in a Small Country: An Exploratory Study of Five Swedish Firms

*L. Hallén*

## INTRODUCTION

Discussions of issues dealing with foreign markets are often supposed implicitly to refer to questions of marketing and exports; moreover it is quite clear that success or failure in foreign markets is crucial for many firms, particularly from countries with small domestic markets. The handling of foreign markets is not, however, merely a matter of conducting sales. An efficient use of sources of supply that are available in foreign markets is often very important for industrial firms. Efficient purchasing – that is, efficient use of the productive resources and product development resources of other firms – is a condition for profitable sales no less than is the efficient use of the buying firm's own productive and development capability. Efficient purchasing requires also that suppliers from abroad are exploited adequately.

Three groups of factors that influence the extent of international purchasing[1] in relation to the total purchases of the firm will be dealt with in this article; these are: the market conditions, the attitudes towards buying from abroad, and the ability to execute purchasing transactions in foreign markets. These aspects constitute the basis for the questions that will be discussed herein: does the firm need to, does the firm want to, and is the firm able to, buy from abroad?[2]

The purpose of this article is, thus, to explore some of the factors underlying international purchasing by going beyond the macroeconomic theories of international trade, and, instead of using aggregate data, employing data from specific firms that are involved in international purchasing. The author intends to avoid focusing merely on cost differences between supplier countries (as in the theory of comparative advantage). Data from five Swedish industrial firms should help to account for other major factors that affect purchasing decisions in international trade. The primary purpose is thereby exploratory, but there is also a secondary one: to describe some important aspects of international purchasing strategies in Swedish industrial firms. Although they do not constitute a sample from

Reproduced by permission from the University of Western Ontario, International Purchasing in a Small Country. An Exploratory Study of Five Swedish Firms, by L. Hallén from *Journal of International Business Studies*, Winter 1982, pp 99–112.

a statistically defined population, the five selected firms still represent typical aspects of purchasing in a small country because they are among the most prominent in the highly concentrated Swedish industry.

The three aspects upon which the analysis is based do not comprise a total explanatory model of importing. As mentioned previously, the purpose is to shed some more light upon the factors that lead to buying from abroad. Nevertheless, the three aspects can be referred to conventional theories of international trade. By means of the classical analysis of the theories of relative advantage (Cateora and Hess, 1979, p. 53 ff.), the first aspect – the market conditions and the ensuing need to import – can be referred to the fundamental idea of the classical model; that is, the existence of domestic demand for products that are more profitably manufactured abroad. The domestic supply of the required product may, in addition, be non-existent or insufficient, for example for the use of parallel suppliers.

The applicability of the classical model, however, is restricted by a number of conditions that must be fulfilled if actual trading is to take place. Cateora and Hess (1979, p. 57) present the following restrictions:

1. The production gains must be greater than the costs of trading and shipping.
2. Products must be identical or equally acceptable in the minds of middlemen and consumers, regardless of national origin.
3. There must be a sufficiently effective market information network so that traders in both countries are aware of cost differentials.
4. The differential must be sufficient to interest an entrepreneur in trading.
5. Tariffs must not exist or must not exceed the differences in cost after transportation and profit are considered.
6. No other governmental or financial restrictions inhibit the products and trading of these products.

The second and third aspects of international purchasing that will be discussed in this article can be referred to specific restrictions in the classical model of relative advantage. As we consider the attitudes toward buying from abroad, the analysis will be extended beyond the second restricting assumption of the classical model because we must now assume that there may be a prejudice against foreign products and foreign suppliers. When we discuss the ability to carry out purchasing transactions in foreign markets, we recognize explicitly that an entrepreneur must not only be attracted by a cost differential (assumption no. 4 of the classical model) of which he is aware (assumption no. 3), but he must also master the specific skills of dealing with international trade.

## DATA

The data were collected within the framework of the IMP Project – a joint research project involving researchers from Sweden, Britain, France, West Germany, and Italy, which studies about 1000 relations between buying and selling firms in five West European countries. Product and information flows together with social relations and national attitudes are mapped as seen by both the purchasers and the marketers.[3] For the analysis in the present article, however, only a small part of this data base is used. Most of the following analysis is based on a subset of the Purchasing section of the Swedish part of the project. A total of 35 supplier relationships (and the 35 supply markets connected with these relationships) that were recorded in five Swedish industrial firms constitute the basis for most of the discussion. This approach can be characterized as a case study method.

In order to illuminate some aspects of the attitudes to international purchasing, a larger part of the data base of the IMP Project is used here. The discussion that is centered on Table 4 uses data from all the studied markets in Britain, France, West Germany, and Sweden.[4] For this purpose, data describing 368 output markets and 464 input markets are used, and the approach is consequently of a more general character.[5]

The extent of the involvement in foreign markets may vary considerably between firms in the same line of business. The firms that will be considered in this article are in different industry branches, but all are internationally oriented in the sense that at least half of their sales go to foreign markets. Two firms are large and dominate the Swedish economy; two are medium-sized, and one is somewhat smaller. The turnover of the five firms is in the 0.5 billion to 5 billion Swedish kronor bracket – that is, between US$0.1 billion and US$1 billion. In an international list of the biggest firms these would consequently rank low if included at all; however, in a small country like Sweden they are considered to be big and important firms. The domestic demand for their products is clearly insufficient for economic production volumes; therefore, big shares of their output are sold to customers abroad. The firms are also highly internationalized in the sense that they have international sales organizations. (They have sales subsidiaries in many important customer countries, and sales agents represent them in many countries that are of secondary importance as export markets). All of the five firms also have production subsidiaries in a few foreign countries. Nevertheless, most of their products are made in Sweden, where the headquarters, including the central marketing and purchasing functions, are located.

Two of the five firms are among the biggest in Sweden. They are both engineering firms but employ different mixtures of production technologies. Firm 1 uses a mass-production technology of an assembly character; that is, a major production task is the large-scale assembly of purchased or internally produced components – hence, components constitute an essential share of the purchases of this firm. Firm 2 uses a similar technology for parts of its production; however, important shares of its production volume are made up of big, complex, and, often technically advanced, products or systems assembled as single units or in small batches. Component parts and component materials are important inputs that are acquired externally by Firm 2.

Firms 3, 4 and 5 are smaller than Firms 1 and 2 but nevertheless are very important in their respective lines of business. Firm 3 converts component materials to products of rather low complexity by means of a mass-production technology; hence, materials form rather low complexity by means of a mass-production technology; hence, materials form a large part of its purchases. Firm 4 assembles capital equipment and converts component material to special operating supplies used with the equipment it makes; therefore, this firm buys both component parts and materials and employs

Table 1. The five firms

| | Firm 1 | Firm 2 | Firm 3 | Firm 4 | Firm 5 |
|---|---|---|---|---|---|
| Turnover[a] | Big | Big | Medium | Medium | Small |
| Export share of sales | 80% | 50% | 50% | 80% | 75% |
| Import share of purchases | 50% | 15% | 20% | 40% | 70% |
| Number of supply markets studied | 9 | 9 | 5 | 4 | 8 |

[a]"Small" turnover: $0.1–0.25 billion; "medium" turnover: $0.25–0.5 billion; "big" turnover: $0.5–1.0 billion.

both small-batch and mass-production technologies. Last, Firm 5 is a process industry, which converts raw and component materials into finished products.[6]

In Table 1 some descriptive data about the five firms are summarized. As is shown in this table, the degree of internationalization on the purchasing side – that it is, the share of the bought goods that is procured from abroad – differs far more between the firms than the share of the sales that goes to customers abroad. The lowest share of inputs acquired from abroad for the five firms' production units in Sweden is 15% and the highest, 70%. Basically, this variation reflects the market conditions, or, the supply of goods in demand domestically and abroad.

In all, 35 supply markets are studied. These supply markets often comprise both domestic and foreign suppliers. The "market" concept, thus, does not refer to "country markets" (the British market, and so on) but to sets of suppliers offering solutions to certain problem categories. The buying firm's definition of required functions delimits these supply markets. In order to make possible comparisons between domestic and foreign sourcing, such supply markets have been selected where the major supplier for the buying firm in question is Swedish (seven cases) and from four of the Common Market countries (28 cases). Table 2 indicates how these supply markets are distributed with respect to product categories and national origin of the major supplier used by the buying firm.

Of the 28 international relations, 17 cases involve "direct purchasing" from the supplier's headquarters. In the remaining 11 cases both the seller's representative in

Table 2. The 35 supply markets

| | Product category | | | |
|---|---|---|---|---|
| Origin of major supplier | Materials | Components | Equipment | Total |
| Sweden (domestic) | 2 | 5 | 0[a] | 7 |
| Britain | 4 | 2 | 2 | 8 |
| France | 3 | 4 | 1 | 8 |
| West Germany | 2 | 3 | 2 | 7 |
| Italy | 3 | 0[a] | 2 | 5 |
| Total | 14 | 14 | 7 | 35 |

[a]Although there are no supply markets in the data material, where the major supplier of equipment is Swedish or the major supplier of parts is Italian, there are indeed Swedish and Italian firms involved as actual (though minor) suppliers in these markets. See for example Table 6 ("Equipment B").

Sweden (agent or subsidiary) and the marketing department of the headquarters participate actively. In the cases of direct purchasing, too, the seller often has a representative in Sweden but with only insignificant or no involvement in the studied business relations.

To summarize: the "markets" studied are sets of suppliers offering to fulfil different kinds of functions that the buyers require. These functions are categorized as conventional product categories – raw materials, components, and capital equipment. Fourteen of the 35 are supply markets for materials, 14 are markets for components and parts, and seven are markets for capital equipment. The distinction between international and domestic purchasing is made within each of these markets, which were selected in order to provide examples of supply markets where the major supplier is Swedish as well as markets where the major supplier is a Common Market firm.

## THE MARKET CONDITIONS

### Supply Markets

When there are no domestic suppliers, it is inevitable that the goods must be procured from abroad. The structure of the supply markets – that is, the distribution of alternative suppliers (sources that are equal regarding supplier services) – between different countries may vary widely from product to product. For instance, often there are only very few potential suppliers of many important raw materials catering to the whole world. This limitation is also the case for many kinds of capital equipment.

The "supply market," remember, is not considered to be the same as the "country market". The supply market concept is rather difficult to handle; and it is not possible to give an "objective" description of the structure of a supply market; in a way it is a perceptual construct.

One way to define a supply market is to use the supplied product as the delimiting factor, but in many cases different physical products (or "functional solutions") may be used for the same purpose by the buying firm. Different products may compete with each other as they satisfy the same need. A purchaser of automotive components may regard products from different industries, for example: plastics and metals, as alternatives within the same supply market. Thus, a supply market is delimited not by the production technology of the supplying firm but by the needs of the buying firm – needs which are to be satisfied by products of one kind or another. The functions of the product and the buying firm's needs are decisive for the delimitation of the supply market.

Further, the functions that the buyer requires from the supplier are not confined to aspects of the product's performance – for example: adequate levels of quality, durability, or adaptability to the buyer's production process. Aspects of the supplier's performance with respect to his ability to offer required volumes, maintenance services, and so on, are also factors that delimit the size of the supply market and thereby reduce the number of possible alternative suppliers.[7]

A definition of the supply market and functional need concepts thus necessarily builds upon subjective judgements; but even if these perceived needs are approximated by products, difficulties remain because the official production and trade statistics are based upon the traditional industry categories. These are, in turn, based on the production technologies of the supplying firms, a situation which hardly conforms to the supply market concept as defined earlier.

The market conditions are a relevant determinant of purchasing behaviour only to the extent that they are observed by the decision-makers of buying firms. For an analysis of international purchasing, therefore, it is not the abstract "absolute" availability of supplier alternatives that is relevant but the purchasers' knowledge of such alternatives.

### Market Structures

The market structure of the 35 supply markets as perceived by purchasers of the five Swedish firms is shown in Table 3. The markets are defined by the purchasers themselves because they have mentioned viable alternatives to their present suppliers of a certain product.

Two observations can be made directly from the data presented in Tables 3A and 3B. First, the number of perceived potential suppliers in the world is not very large. In only six of the 35 cases are the purchasers aware of more than 50 alternative suppliers, which is only to be expected if the proposed definition of supplier alternatives is used. An alternative source must be able to offer not only the product but also other required supplier services, which certainly limits the number of potential suppliers. Second, in small countries there are often no domestic suppliers. In more than half of the cases the purchasers have no knowledge of domestic supplier alternatives.

Although the domestic supply markets are normally familiar to the purchasers one cannot exclude the possibility that some alternatives have been overlooked. But, for

Table 3. The structure of 35 supply markets

| Number of suppliers | Markets for raw materials | Markets for components | Markets for capital equipment | Total |
|---|---|---|---|---|
| A. The perceived number of potential suppliers in the world | | | | |
| 1–10 | 9 | 7 | 6 | 22 |
| 11–50 | 1 | 5 | 1 | 7 |
| 51 + | 4 | 2 | 0 | 6 |
| Total | 14 | 14 | 7 | 35 |
| B. The perceived number of potential suppliers in the home country | | | | |
| 0 | 9 | 4 | 5 | 18 |
| 1 | 2 | 3 | 2 | 7 |
| 2 + | 3 | 7 | 0 | 10 |
| Total | 14 | 14 | 7 | 35 |

this analysis, only the perceived markets matter. In another seven cases, too, the availability of domestic suppliers is extremely limited because the purchasers are aware of only a single Swedish supplier within the supply market concerned.

Differences prevail between the market structures of the raw materials, component, and capital equipment markets. The markets for raw materials and capital equipment seem to be more dominated by foreign suppliers than the markets for components. There are no domestic suppliers available in 64% of the selected raw material markets or in 71% of the selected markets for capital equipment, whereas the corresponding percentage for the markets for components is 29. The most likely reason for these structural differences is that the total number of raw material producers as well as capital equipment producers is smaller globally than the number of component producers, and consequently the nearest supplier is more often to be found at a greater distance from the buying firm. Another reason for the higher relative availability of component suppliers in the home market may be that – at least with respect to certain components – the dominating element of the supplier services is not the product *per se*, but the suppliers' flexibility and ability to cooperate. These requirements are particularly pronounced in the case of continuous deliveries – for example: of subassemblies to buyers with varying demands of volumes and specifications. Domestic suppliers may have advantages in offering such current adaptations.[8]

Naturally a buying firm must turn to foreign suppliers when there are no domestic supplier alternatives, but even when there are such alternatives, the buyer may have to turn to foreign suppliers.

The establishment of a supplier relationship may be intended to promote the acquisition of a physical product, but it also serves as a channel for exchange of information regarding technical issues, new materials, new applications, and so on. In many cases such information is available in the open market only to a very limited extent. Another purpose for the establishment of a relationship is a wish to avoid becoming too dependent on one single source, at least as far as important inputs are concerned.

Both these circumstances make firms turn to several parallel suppliers in a supply market; moreover, because the number of domestic suppliers is often limited, it is necessary to turn to foreign suppliers. The firms' production and the need for inputs derived therefrom determine the supply markets the firm will use. The structure of these markets determines the need to use foreign suppliers.

## ATTITUDES TOWARD BUYING FROM ABROAD

### "Buy Domestic" Versus "Active Market Orientation"

In the preceding section some objective reasons for firms' foreign purchases were specified. The market conditions may imply that the firm's needs – in quantity or quality – cannot be met satisfactorily within the home country. These objective conditions are, however, seldom so obvious as to indicate comprehensively which supplier alternatives are superior because the situation may be perceived in different ways by separate firms and by separate purchasers. In those cases where there are several equal supplier alternatives – hence, real choices – the general attitude to buying from abroad versus buying from domestic producers also influences purchasing behavior.

In many countries in Western Europe there is a great debate about the drawbacks (and also sometimes the advantages) of buying from abroad or importing. The arguments against imports are well known. They can be traced back to mercantilistic lines of thought. Particularly when they are exposed to unfavorable balances of trade, nations are subject to "Buy Domestic" campaigns. "Buy British" is an often heard slogan in Britain; French firms are frequently accused of operating in a protectionistic system (at least by their foreign competitors); and in Sweden, too, arguments have been raised about expansion of the industry producing for domestic sales and a reduction of the dependence on foreign markets. Of course, purchasers also listen to these arguments dealing with the dependence on foreign suppliers, but the arguments refer to national problems, and it is very uncertain if this ambition to reduce total imports influences actual decisions about national versus foreign sources.

There is another line of argumentation in the debate, however, which focuses upon the connection between efficient purchasing and the general performance of a firm. This reasoning refers, thus, to problems on the firm level, not specifically problems on the national level. An active market orientation of purchases and efficient purchasing influences the attitude toward buying from abroad. According to this perspective the "best" supplier alternative is to be used – disregarding the possible undesirability of buying from abroad.[9] Hence, the extent of the involvement of a firm in buying from abroad depends also upon purchasing policy or general opinions about what purchasers should do.

Table 4 illustrates both tendencies. These figures are derived from a larger data bank than the 35 Swedish purchasers who supplied the information about the supply markets of this analysis. The percentages in the table are compared from the responses of 464 marketers and 368 purchasers distributed over four Western European countries.[10] The first two columns of the table show that a higher proportion of buyers "like dealing with" domestic suppliers than with suppliers of the

Table 4. Opinions about buying from abroad

| Buyers | Percentage of buyers who "like dealing with": Domestic suppliers | Foreign suppliers | Percentage of foreign suppliers who consider purchasers to have "favorable attitudes to foreign suppliers" |
|---|---|---|---|
| British | 100 | 79[a] | 54[a] |
| French | 87 | 64[b] | 40[b] |
| West German | 100 | 59[c] | 38[c] |
| Swedish | 85 | 76[d] | 70[d] |

[a]Suppliers from France, West Germany, and Sweden
[b]Suppliers from Britain, West Germany, and Sweden
[c]Suppliers from Britain, France, and Sweden
[d]Suppliers from Britain, France, and West Germany.

four foreign countries; however, this preference for domestic suppliers cannot be interpreted as an aversion to imports. The figures should be seen, instead, as evidence that it is easier to do business at home with people who speak one's own language and understand the same culture and behaviour patterns.[11] Because the percentage of buyers who "like dealing with" foreign suppliers is also fairly high – although lower than in relation to domestic suppliers – this can be seen as a demonstration of the preparedness of buyers generally to buy from the "best supplier" without undue preconceived aversion to foreigners.

The data of Table 4 can, however, be used also to support the idea that purchasers do indeed have certain reservations against foreign suppliers. The third column of the table shows the opinions of the marketers regarding what they consider to be the attitude of their customers against foreign suppliers. There the percentages are lower: for example, less than half of those exporting to West Germany or France consider their customers to have a "favorable attitude to foreign suppliers". As a matter of fact, of the four selected countries only Swedish purchasers seem to be reasonably free of reservations against buying from abroad according to the marketers' opinions.

## Using Domestic and Foreign Suppliers

The reported opinions indicate that domestic suppliers would be preferred when a domestic and a foreign supplier would offer the same supplier services[12]; however, this tendency would be less pronounced in Sweden. An analysis of the actual behavior of the Swedish buying firms in those of the studied supply markets where there is a real possibility of choice can therefore be expected to reveal interesting patterns. Such real choice exists in 17 of the 35 supply markets as no alternative domestic supplier was known to the purchasers in the remaining 18 supply markets where foreign suppliers must necessarily be selected. The use of potential domestic suppliers in those 17 markets where alternatives exist is shown in Table 5.

Table 5 shows that the preference for domestic suppliers is reflected in actual behavior in the sense that the domestic suppliers are normally used when such domestic alternatives exist: in 12 of the 17 supply markets the buyers use the

Table 5. The use of potential domestic suppliers in 17 supply markets

| | Domestic suppliers | | | |
|---|---|---|---|---|
| Company | Are not used | Are used together with foreign suppliers | Are used exclusively | Total |
| 1 | 3 | 3 | 1 | 7 |
| 2 | 2 | 1 | 1 | 4 |
| 3 | 0 | 2 | 0 | 2 |
| 4 | 0 | 3 | 0 | 3 |
| 5 | 0 | 0 | 1 | 1 |
| Total | 5 | 9 | 3 | 17 |

potential suppliers of the home market. The data also illustrate, on the other hand, that Swedish buyers are not particularly reluctant to buy from abroad: in only three supply markets do the buyers rely exclusively on domestic suppliers. The typical situation is that several suppliers originating both from abroad and from the home market are used simultaneously.

In seven of these 17 supply markets with potential domestic supply, the buying firm is aware of just one domestic supplier. By looking more closely at the selection of suppliers in these seven cases, the reasons for buying from abroad can be illustrated. Is the domestic supplier considered to be a sufficient supply source? If not, why?

As can be seen from Table 6, the sole potential domestic supplier is used in five out of seven cases, but in only one of these are foreign suppliers not used simultaneously. This single case concerns Firm 5, who buys the specialized raw material A from a semi-dependent supplier who sells this product only to Firm 5. No other supplier alternatives are available for Firm 5 because the foreign suppliers of this raw material are more or less integrated with their major customer – that is, with the competitors of Firm 5. In this case buying from abroad is not a viable alternative.

Two other cases oppose Firm 5's procurement of this specialized raw material in the sense that only foreign suppliers are used; however, in these cases one option has been excluded – that is, the potential domestic supplier has not been used. One of these cases deals with the purchases of components by Firm 1. Here the somewhat paradoxical situation exists that the Swedish supplier is perceived as more "distant" than the foreign suppliers that have long been used.[13] The well-established connections with the foreign suppliers make these seem more "domestic" than the Swedish supplier of the goods in question. The other case in which the potential domestic supplier is not used is that of equipment purchases by Firm 2. This kind of equipment is bought infrequently. Only one supplier is required for this low volume and intermittent purchases, and this has become the foreign one.

In the four remaining cases both domestic and foreign suppliers are actually used. One of these deals with purchases of equipment by Firm 4. This situation is quite similar to the equipment purchases of Firm 2. The equipment is bought only infrequently, but Firm 4 has found that new equipment from competing suppliers proved to be superior to the one bought previously from other suppliers.[14] Thus the

Table 6. Supplier relations when only one domestic supplier is available

| Firm | Product | No. of actual suppliers | | | Major reason for buying from abroad |
|---|---|---|---|---|---|
| | | Domestic | Foreign | Total | |
| 5 | Raw material A | 1 | 0 | 1 | No buying from abroad |
| 4 | Raw material B | 1 | 2 | 3 | Avoidance of supplier dependence |
| 1 | Component A | 0 | 3 | 3 | Better contacts with foreign firm |
| 1 | Component B | 1 | 2 | 3 | Avoidance of supplier dependence |
| 1 | Component C | 1 | 3 | 4 | Access to technical information |
| 2 | Equipment A | 0 | 1 | 1 | Better offer |
| 4 | Equipment B | 1 | 2 | 3 | Better offer |

latest purchases have been made from a single firm – one of the foreign suppliers – and the others including the domestic supplier are used "simultaneously" only in the sense that the equipment they have delivered is still in use. But the next repeat purchase will probably be made from the foreign supplier who made the current delivery.

Two of the cases are typical examples of purchases made from abroad in order to avoid too high a dependence on the domestic supplier. This is the situation for Firm 4's purchases of a raw material B and Firm 1's of component B. The domestic supplier is used as the main supplier in both cases, and the foreign firms are used in order to secure deliveries in the event of problems that arise in relation to the Swedish supplier or in order to get leverage in negotiations with the domestic firm.

The remaining case is Firm 1's purchases of component C. Firm 1 acquires most of its needs (95%) from its major supplier, which is the domestic firm; hence, the quantities bought from the three foreign suppliers are fairly small, and the reason for maintaining the relations with these firms are not connected primarily with security in obtaining required volumes. Instead, the prime reason is to maintain contacts with these technically advanced firms in order to be able to obtain information regarding technical progress and innovations.

The analysis of these examples of supplier relations in situations where only one domestic supplier exists shows that the attitudes toward purchasing from abroad do not seem to influence the decisions – at least not so far as these situations have been described by the purchasers. The market conditions seem, instead, to be of major importance together with the requirements of the company policy. When parallel suppliers are required, at least one foreign supplier must necessarily be used in these situations; when contacts are required with technically advanced firms, purchases are made from abroad because these advanced firms are often foreign; and "one-shot" deals with equipment producers are made with foreign firms if their goods are deemed to be superior. Thus, the attitude toward buying from abroad does not seem to counteract efficient purchasing in the sense that it would prevent the "best" supplier in a total sense to be selected. In a way this is, of course, a very clear-cut effect of attitudes toward international purchasing.

## THE COMPETENCE FOR INTERNATIONAL BUSINESS

Three areas of competence can be identified: Market Knowledge, Cultural Awareness, and Trade Techniques.

So far the discussion has dealt with the need for buying from abroad and the prosperity for or willingness to do so. Last, the ability of the firm to handle relations with foreign suppliers will be considered.

A basic precondition for successful international business relations is the market orientation of the firm's purchasing function. An active market orientation of purchases means that the purchasing function not only connects the firm with its suppliers but also actively seeks and develops new supplier alternatives, where "alternatives" means new products – better functional solutions to problems – as well as new sources with superior supplier services in a total sense.

Such an orientation of the purchases must be based upon market knowledge: how can the firm's needs be met, and where are the suppliers who are able to satisfy these needs? In other words, it is necessary to enlarge and sharpen the image of the structure of the supply market in the different supplier countries and to become aware of the possibilities within these markets. This kind of ability is acquired primarily through experience of such active purchasing. General experience of purchasing is therefore one of the bases for buying from abroad as well as from the domestic suppliers.

When the firm is buying from abroad, however, other kinds of problems are added to those that affect domestic purchasing. Business practices, social habits, language, and so on – all of which fall under the heading "culture" – vary between different supply countries, and these differences may be considerable. An ability to handle these different environments is required. Of course, the representatives of the selling firm often handle the bridging of the cultural gap between the buying and the selling firm, for example by the establishment of a sales agent or a sales subsidiary in the buying country. A supplier relationship with a satisfactory level of supplier services can often be developed only over time through direct interaction between the selling and the buying firms. This is why this need to handle direct relations within other cultural environments is important also for purchasers.

International purchasing requires not only market knowledge and an ability to handle foreign cultural patterns but also an understanding of the special transaction problems in international trade. The latter ability refers to knowledge of trade techniques, such as customs and non-tariff obstacles to trade, currency problems, and other aspects of international payments, quota systems, international chartering, and so on. In these cases, too, the seller is often competent to shoulder these difficulties; but again the largest potential benefits for the purchaser can be reaped from active development by the buying firm of contacts with the supplier on several levels.

It is not possible to state in detail what is the required competence for international purchasing, but the three areas mentioned previously are undoubtedly of central importance: market knowledge, ability to handle other cultural environments, and a certain competence in trade techniques.

## Individual Competence: The Knowledge of Languages

Competence in the three areas mentioned is required both on an individual and organizational level. The individual's competence determines basically how a relation with a foreign supplier can be handled, but this individual competence can be favored differently in different company environments. The competence is developed by means of personal experience, and the company can be a more or less advantageous setting for such a learning process.

A mastery of foreign languages is one of the components of the purchasers' ability to handle foreign cultures. Other aspects of cultural awareness are knowledge of the business practices and social habits of the foreign country. The linguistic competence is of great importance for the said active market orientation of purchasing. Table 7 summarizes the 35 Swedish purchasers' knowledge of English, German and French.

As can be seen in Table 7, almost all purchasers consider themselves to have a

Table 7. Knowledge of foreign languages[a]

| Company | English | German | French |
|---|---|---|---|
| 1 | 2.6 | 2.6 | 0.6 |
| 2 | 2.9 | 2.4 | 0.0 |
| 3 | 3.0 | 2.3 | 0.8 |
| 4 | 3.0 | 2.7 | 1.0 |
| 5 | 2.8 | 2.0 | 0.2 |
| Average | 2.8 | 2.4 | 0.4 |

[a]Competence rated by purchasers themselves on four-point scale: 3 = able to discuss and negotiate; 2 = able to discuss technical matters; 1 = some knowledge but with little value for the job; and 0 = no knowledge.

good working knowledge of English. Behind the average rating of 2.8 lies the fact that 86% of the interviewed purchasers of the five firms considered themselves to be able both to "discuss and negotiate" with suppliers in English (level 3). The rating for knowledge of German is not much lower (2.4), but the distribution is rather different: here 48% of the questioned purchasers rated themselves on level 3, and 45% on level 2. Knowledge of French seems, however, quite limited: 69% of the purchasers rated themselves on level O – that is, no knowledge of French, and no purchaser rated himself on level 3 with respect to knowledge of French. It can be concluded from Table 7 that the purchasers are, thus, very competent at English and German, the business languages in many supplier countries for Swedish firms; however, an active market orientation of the purchasing from France may be hampered by the Swedish purchasers' very limited knowledge of French.[15]

Knowledge of foreign languages is just one element of the individual competence for doing international purchasing, but in many ways it is typical for this international competence. To some extent this individual competence is general, but other elements of this competence are company specific. This is particularly so regarding market knowledge, but also parts of the language competence and the trade techniques are company specific. The organizational setting is of great importance for the development of competence of this company specific kind. The organization must give possibilities for the accumulation of learning from experience. This is one of the links between the company's organization and its ability to purchase from abroad successfully.

## CONCLUSION

One of the most striking points regarding the choice between domestic and foreign suppliers is that this choice seems to be very restricted. The number of potential domestic suppliers is still more limited. In most of the cases analyzed here, there are just a few or even no domestic suppliers available. Consequently, for firms in a small country like Sweden the need to buy from abroad is often self-evident.

It seems that this need to use foreign suppliers is connected with low "national myopia", as the Swedish firms are considered by their suppliers to have "a favorable attitude to foreign suppliers" to a greater extent than firms from three other larger European countries. The Swedish buyers have a more positive attitude toward their own domestic suppliers than toward their foreign suppliers, but this preference for domestic suppliers is less pronounced with the Swedish buyers than with buyers from the three other larger countries. This is reflected in the actual supplier relationships in the manner that the domestic suppliers are almost always used, but mostly together with foreign suppliers.

This international orientation is reflected also in the Swedish buyers' competence in international business. The earlier discussion about active market orientation of the purchasing activities may be adjudged an attempt to use experience from the marketing side of the firm for the development of purchasing. Such parallels can be drawn also with respect to organization. On the selling side it is well known, for example, that market knowledge is acquired through experience, and the market orientation is reflected in the organizational structure. It is considered important to collect and make available the experience from new markets. The internal structure of a sales department often reflects the need for the specialization. There are special units for different markets, for market research, for shipping, and so on. The sellers often specialize in certain products, and this specialization facilitates learning.

This does not mean that purchasing should imitate marketing with respect to internal organization, but it is of great importance that the organization allow learning, and this requirement has implications for purchasing organization.

Type of product is still the most common basis for specialization within purchasing departments; but many of the effects of market orientation are not visible in the formal organization. Only a minority may take the form of formal reorganization, as in the establishment of market research for purchasing. Some big companies establish their own purchasing offices abroad with the task of monitoring the market and keeping contact with suppliers. These offices may be either informally a part of the company's sales organization in the foreign market or they may be autonomous units connected only with the purchasing function.

A firm's ability to draw benefits from foreign supply markets is largely dependent upon its capacity to use its innate experience of international business. Thus, of the three questions put initially – does the firm need to, does the firm want to, and is the firm able to buy from abroad – the question of competence is crucial for the extent of actual purchasing from abroad. The sections of the supply markets that are composed of foreign firms can be fully used only by firms that have sufficient competence in international business. Last, this competence is linked to the firm's organization and the conditions for making use of the experience of doing business abroad.

## NOTES

1. "International purchasing" refers to such cases of imports where the negotiations are carried out directly with the supplying firm abroad or indirectly with its representative in the buyer's country, if there are also some direct contacts between the buying firm and the supplier abroad. These distinctions between imports and international purchasing are discussed more extensively in Hallén (1982).

2. These three aspects of influences on international purchasing are also discussed by Hallén and Snehota (1978).
3. The International Marketing and Purchasing Project (IMP Project) has been conducted in collaboration between researchers from Britain (D. Ford, University of Bath, and M. Cunningham, E. Homse, and P. Turnbull, University of Manchester); France (J.-P. Valla and M. Perrin, Ecole Supérieure de Commerce de Lyon); West Germany (M. Kutschker, Universität München); Italy (I. Snehota, ISVOR-FIAT); and Sweden (L. Hallén, H. Håkansson, J. Johanson, and B. Wootz, University of Uppsala). The major report of the project is Håkansson (ed., 1982).
4. The Italian data are excluded from this particular tabulation because of some missing data.
5. Further analyses of the attitudinal data of the IMP Project are made by Kutschker (1979), Perrin (1979), Hallén (1980a), and Cunningham and Turnbull (1981).
6. The production technologies are defined according to a taxonomy suggested in Hallén (1980b). It is derived from Woodward (1965, 1970) and Perrow (1967).
7. In many cases there are no actual alternatives because the buyers and sellers by means of mutual adaptations have developed relations to each other that included some features of bilateral monopoly. The study of processes creating these situations is fundamental to the interaction approach to the analysis of industrial markets. (See for example: Håkansson and Östberg, 1975.)
8. The degree of adaptation of market strategies to customer demands is found to be related to the cultural affinity of the seller's and the buyer's countries in an analysis of the opinions of 416 West European purchasers. (See Hallén and Johanson, 1981.)
9. Melin (1977, p. 69) defines "market orientation" as one of a set of purchasing strategies. "The evaluation behind market orientation is that the company increases its flexibility through continuous monitoring of different supplier markets . . . [M]onitoring may also come about through the building up of a specialized market analysis function which collects and processes information from both primary and secondary sources concerning market development among suppliers."
10. These opinions of purchasers and marketers are collected within the framework of the IMP Project. (See Note 3.) The Swedish purchasers, who are the data source of the analyses in this article, are included in the total group of West European purchasers and marketers, whose opinions form the data source of Table 4.
11. A conceptual model for the analysis of the effect of cultural differences ("psychic distance") is presented in Hallén and Wiedersheim-Paul (1979).
12. Håkansson and Wootz (1975B) have shown that Swedish purchasers actually have such a preference for domestic suppliers.
13. According to the terminology used in Hallén and Wiedersheim-Paul (1979) this would mean that the interfirm distance is more relevant than the intercountry distance because of the development of interfirm trust.
14. Reasons for the replacement of suppliers are discussed in Mattsson and Björkroth (1978).
15. In another study of supplier selection by Swedish firms (Hákansson and Wootz, 1975a) an assessment is made of factors contributing to the selection of culturally distant suppliers. From their analysis one can see that the education and experience of the purchasers are the principal factors. The knowledge of foreign languages is ranked sixth and last. This low impact of the language competence indicates that language is just not a bottleneck for international purchasing in internationally oriented Swedish firms.

## REFERENCES

Cateora, P. and Hess, J. *International Marketing.* Irwin, Homewood, IL (1979).

Cunningham, M. and Turnbull, P. *International Marketing and Purchasing: A Survey Among Marketing and Purchasing Executives in Five European Countries.* Macmillan, London (1981).

Håkansson, H. (ed.) *International Marketing and Purchasing of Industrial Goods: An Interaction Approach.* Wiley, Chichester (1982).

Håkansson, H. and Wootz, B. Risk reduction and the industrial purchaser. *European Journal of Marketing*, **9**, 35–51 (1975a).

Håkansson, H. and Wootz, B. Supplier selection in an international environment – an experimental study. *Journal of Marketing Research*, February, 46–51 (1975).

Håkansson, H. and Östberg, C. Industrial marketing – an organizational problem? *Industrial Marketing Management*, **4**, 113–23 (1975).

Hallén, L. *Sverige på Europamarknaden – Åsikter om inköp och marknadsföring* [Sweden in the European Market – Opinions of Purchasing and Marketing]. Studentlitteratur. Lund (1980a).

Hallén, L. Stability and change in supplier relationships. In Engwall, L. and Johanson, J. (eds), *Some Aspects of Control in International Business*. Acta Universitatis Upsaliensis. Studia Oeconomiae Negotiorum, 12, pp. 83–101 (1980b).

Hallén, L. *International Industrial Purchasing. Channels, Interaction, and Governance Structures*. Acta Universitatis Upsaliensis: Studia Oeconomiae Negotiorum 13, Uppsala (1982).

Hallén, L. and Johanson, J. *Industrial Market Strategies as a Matter of Environments*. CIF Working Paper 1981/1, Department of Business Administration, Uppsala University (1981).

Hallén, L. and Snehota, I. "Företags internationella inköp" [International Purchasing by Companies]. In Håkansson, H. and Melin, L. (eds), *Inköp* [Purchasing]. Norstedts, Stockholm (1978).

Hallén, L. and Wiedersheim-Paul, F. Psychic distance and buyer–seller interaction. *Organisasjon, Marked og Samfunn*, **16**, 308–24 (1979).

Kutschker, M. and Kirsch, W. *Industriegütermarketing and Einkauf in Europa – Deutschlandstudie*. Planungs-und Organisationswissenschaftliche Schriften, Munich (1979).

Mattsson, L.-G. and Björkroth, G. Varför byter man leverantör – och varför inte? [Why are supplier replaced – and why not?]. In Håkansson, H. and Melin, L. (eds), *Inköp*. Norstedts, Stockholm (1978).

Melin, L. Strategisk inköpsverksamhet – organisation och interaktion [Strategic Purchasing Actions – Organization and Interaction]. Ph.D. Dissertation. Ekonomiska institutionen vid Linköpings universitet, Linköping (1977).

Perrin, M. *Les enterprises Françaises face à la concurrence sur cinq marchés Européens*. Centre Français du Commerce Extérieur. Paris (1979).

Perrow, C. A framework for the comparative analysis of organizations. *American Sociological Review*, April, 194–208 (1967).

Woodward, J. *Industrial Organization: Theory and Practice*. Oxford University Press, London (1965).

Woodward, J. *Industrial Organization: Behaviour and Control*. Oxford University Press, London (1970).

# Part V

## Technology and Networks

Technology is a major factor in the relationships between companies in business markets and in the structure and evolution of business networks. The bringing together of the skills or technological resources of companies provides the logic for business relationships to exist and for their connection together in a wider network. For this reason technological issues have formed an increasingly important focus of attention for members of the group in the recent past and justify a separate section in this edition.

The first reading by Ford and Saren is intended to set the scene for a strategic approach to technology. It is written on the basis that the task facing the business marketer can usefully be conceived as that of matching the company's technological resources to those of its customers. The marketer's products or services are the vehicles by which the value of its technology is delivered to the customer – technologies that the customer does not have to develop for itself. For the buyer company, the task is to use the technological assets of its suppliers to complement its own and to manage these "external technologies". This clearly involves strategic choice about what technologies the company will seek to develop in-house and for which it will rely on others for. It follows that managers operating in business markets will need to take a technological perspective in developing an approach to relationship partners and to their network position. Further, decisions on their own technological development will need to relate current and prospective technological assets to those that exist or are emerging around them.

The second reading, "Product development in networks", uses a case study to illustrate many of these technological issues. In particular, it emphasises that the task of product development, which may superficially be seen as the individualistic "core" of a company's activities, is most likely to be an interactive process between the company and others in the surrounding network. The next reading does not take the perspective of the individual company. Instead, Lundgren takes as his unit of analysis an individual technology: digital imagery. He examines the interplay between the evolution of the technology and the emergence of a new network surrounding it. He sees this interplay as three parallel processes: genesis – the creation of novelty and variety; coalescence – the formation of a community or network for establishing the emerging technological system; and dissemination – establishing the technology in relation to complementary industrial networks.

The fourth reading, by Hallén, Johanson and Seyed-Mohamed, uses IMP1 data. It is concerned with the *production* technology of the *customer* company in relationships. The authors describe how differences in these technologies affect the nature of the demands made on suppliers and the nature of the relationships between the two companies. Further, they suggest that a reverse causality between inter-firm social structure and inter-firm adaptation means that technical change may be a *consequence* of how relationships are organized. The final paper is by Biemans, who has written extensively on technical innovation using a network perspective. At the start of this reading he echoes an argument made in both this and the previous edition of this book – that much of the work on networks and the interaction in them has tended to focus on the formulation of theory and hypothesis and there has still not been enough work that focuses on recommendations of value to managers. Biemans seeks to address this issue through a study of seventeen cases of product development in a specific industry and he draws from this a list of eight critical success factors related to ''networking''.

This is perhaps a suitable paper to end this edition with. The first paper in the book tried to provide a general model of buyer–seller interaction in business markets. The last one tries to use some of these ideas developed by the original group and by many others to provide some directly practical managerial recommendations. The process from first to last is not straightforward, nor are the papers linearly related. Each can be criticized in numerous ways. However, both of these papers, and the ones inbetween, illustrate an immensely enjoyable experience – which hopefully is also of some value to the reader.

## CONTENTS

# 1

# First Steps in Technology Strategy

*D. Ford and M. Saren*

## INTRODUCTION

In this chapter we first examine three different views of the relationship between technology and strategy. This leads to a definition of technology strategy which will form the basis of the remainder of the book. We examine the technological interdependence that exists between companies and provides a categorisation of three generic types of technology which will be used in subsequent chapters. We believe that a strategic approach to technology is as much about attitude as about plans, and as much about ideas as about structure. A strategic view of technology is more likely to emerge slowly through careful thought and self-analysis, rather than be produced by a conscious, deliberate strategy development programme. This means that we should not start our discussion with a view that ''strategy'' means the same as ''plan''. Instead, we see company strategy more as the formation of perspective[1] and this book is about the development of that perspective.

## THREE VIEWS OF TECHNOLOGY AND STRATEGY

It is important to make clear the exact relationship between technology strategy and the more general concept of corporate strategy and hence the precise area of our attention in this book. We can think of three aspects of this relationship. First, there is a technological dimension to overall corporate strategy in the same way that there is a financial, production or marketing dimension to it. Each dimension is an area to which attention must be devoted, each provides ingredients for the strategy development process and each is a way in which strategy is implemented and through which the effects of strategy become apparent. Thus, a corporate strategy to achieve a low-cost position can be implemented through process technology improvements to achieve lower production costs. This strategy also has a product technology element as design improvements can lead both to product cost reductions and a smoother

Reprinted by permission from the publisher, First Steps in Technology Strategy by D. Ford and M. Saren from *Technology Strategy for Business*, pp. 41–52.

production flow. Further, a low-cost strategy will affect the brief given to the purchasing department on the types of components which should be bought and the product technology on which they are to be based.

Second, technology can be used as a unit of analysis in evaluating a company's behaviour and performance as a basis for strategy development. This is similar to the way in which we could evaluate a company in terms of its financial or market performance. Thus, if we have the tools of analysis we could consider such factors as technological leadership, exploitation performance, technology share, etc. In this book we are involved with questions of evaluation of a company's overall technological position and performance. We argue strongly for the value of an analysis in technological terms as a basis for strategy building and suggest that this is particularly important in today's conditions of rapid technological change and uncertainty.

Third, we can consider the development of strategy for the acquisition, management and exploitation of the company's technology. This is the view of technology strategy with which we are mainly concerned in this book. The elements of technology strategy are illustrated in Fig. 1.

The acquisition of technology includes far more than conventional R&D. Technology can be acquired internally, through the company's own R&D, or externally, by licensing from other companies, or from contract research houses, or via joint ventures with others or from suppliers of products, etc.

Similarly, technology can be exploited internally, by incorporating it in the company's own products, processes or market offerings or externally, by licensing it to others, by turnkey deals, by contract manufacturing for others, by designing or marketing products for them, or by joining in joint ventures with them.

Finally, technology management includes a variety of activities:

- the development of long-term strategy for technology;
- the co-ordination of different means of acquisition and exploitation of technology;
- effectively transferring technologies between different operating units within the company;
- efficiently inserting new technologies where they are needed;
- integrating the different technologies which are held by the company and those around it to meet the requirements of any chosen customer.

Our approach to technology strategy is not confined to the issue of technological innovation, because introducing innovative technology may be irrelevant to a company at any one time. Instead, it may be vital for that company to concentrate on strategy for the fullest exploitation of its existing technology. This exploitation may involve difficult choices between a variety of different means such as new product introduction, licensing or joint ventures, all of which can have both short- and long-term consequences for the company. Perhaps even more importantly, we would argue that a strategic approach to technology is vital even for companies that may see themselves as being low-tech or would never think of being involved in innovation. These companies also need a clear understanding of the technologies on which their companies are based, their

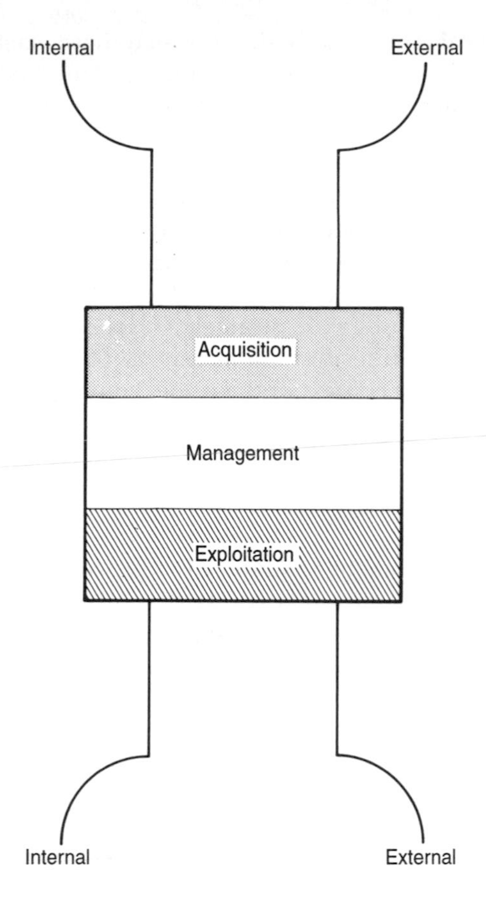


Fig. 1. The elements of technology strategy.

respective positions in these technologies and their performance in exploiting their technological assets.

## TECHNOLOGY STRATEGY

We use the following working definition of technology strategy: Technology strategy is the tasks of building, maintaining and exploiting a company's technological assets, no matter what their level or newness when compared to other companies in the same or other industries.

This definition emphasises that technology strategy is central to a company, whether it is a ''high'' or ''low'' technology company, a product or service provider, a technological ''innovator'' or a ''follower''. This means that in order to make sense of technology strategy we cannot simply concentrate on what is to be the content of that strategy. Instead, we must look at technology strategy in its wider organisational and corporate strategical contexts, both of which have such an impact on the outcome and success of strategy. For example, collaboration between different functions in the company is vital for success in the technological innovation process.[2,3]

A company's technology is the sum total of its abilities – including that which exists inside the heads of all its staff. Technology strategy is not something which can be separated out as the responsibility of a single department. It cannot be relegated to a terse request from marketing or elsewhere for R&D to produce "something new and quick". Nor is technology a question of detailed implementation and hence beneath the dignity of those with strategic responsibilities. On the contrary technology is a thread which runs through *all* aspects of a company and hence it can only be understood within the context of the whole company and its culture.

## BASIS OF ANALYSIS: TECHNOLOGY AS ASSETS

A prerequisite for the development of strategy is a process of self-analysis to establish current position. This analysis must be expressed in a language which is appropriate to the subject of the strategy. Thus our language must be about technology and not about products or markets. Technology is embodied in products or services and these are the final outputs from technology strategy, not its ingredients. Technology strategy is not just about managing R&D, or the process of introducing new technology into the company. Nor is it just about new ventures or new products. An approach to technology strategy must start with the following questions:

1. What are the technological assets on which the past, present and future success of the company depend?
2. Can these assets be divided into those which are core and those which are more peripheral?
3. How can we assess the strength of our assets, relative to those of our competitors, how can we maintain them and how can we grow them?
4. How can we ensure that we achieve the best possible return on the investment we have made in these assets?

Our view of technology strategy looks at least one level behind a conventional listing of strengths in terms of products and markets. Instead of taking these products and markets as the units of analysis, we believe that we must examine and evaluate the underlying technologies which form the basis of its products and processes: "The core of a company is not its products or its markets, but what it knows and what it can do".[4]

### Internal and External Technologies

The distinction between internal and external technologies is important in the development of technology strategy. Internal technologies are those which the company owns or controls, possibly because they were developed by the company itself. External technologies are those from which the company benefits but does not own, such as those that have been developed by companies which supply it with products or services. The management task in developing technology strategy includes decisions on which areas of technology the company wishes to develop internally. It also includes decisions on which technologies it should not develop for itself, but on which it will continue to depend. These external technologies are increasingly vital as the cost and range of technologies needed to operate in any market escalate. Therefore, relationships with product or service suppliers must increasingly be seen in technological terms, rather than as routine, cost-reducing, fail-safe activities which are labelled as "purchasing".

Ideas such as those concerning partnership purchasing, if properly conceived, can tie together the existing and potential technologies of both buyer and seller companies. But a failure by a company to effectively use and develop the technologies of its suppliers means that the sum total of the technology which the buying company has available is restricted to its own internal "stock", or that which it is able to develop internally. The value of external technologies was illustrated by Kenichi Ohmae when he spoke of "the heart of IBM's accomplishment with the PC is its decision – and its ability – to approach the development effort as a process of managing multiple external vendors".[5]

---

*Example*

*Externalising technology: The interrelationship between distinctive and external technologies over time*

This example shows how the technologies controlled by the firm can change in value and lose their distinctiveness as technical change elsewhere impacts upon them. In this case the development of microprocessor technologies for applications in other industries made redundant some of the central skills of the company.

This datacommunications firm manufactured and sold a range of products, services and systems to business users. One of its core product groups, modems, was traditionally supported by substantial R&D expenditure, particularly on system software. The ability to use standard circuitry, adapted to differing product and customer needs by varying software configurations, was considered a key distinctive skill.

Within the microprocessor industry, however, major investments were being made in the development of integrated circuits aimed at specific applications. In this way, manufacturers sought to counter the growing "commoditisation" of chips. In due course the communications industry was targeted with the development of the "modem on a chip". Much of the functionality of earlier combined hardware and software could now be integrated on to a single microprocessor.

The result for the company was that many of its product technologies based on its own design skills in this area became obsolete. In response it elected to rely on external sources of product and process technology rather than invest heavily in updating its own. The company concentrated on maintaining its market skills and developing new skills in managing critical supplier relationships (marketing technology). It accepts that a key technology is now external to the firm and gains access to this technology through a purchasing relationship.

---

*Example*
*Externalising technology: Massey Ferguson*
Snowballing development costs have led to rationalisation in the tractor market. Survivors have had to reduce development resources and activities, and learn to rely more on specialist suppliers.

Massey Ferguson, a long-established tractor maker has, along with its competitors, faced hard commercial times over the last ten years. It used to make a full range of tractor models and related equipment such as combine harvesters.

Now, under the same sustained competitive pressures which led Ford and Fiat to merge their tractor operations in 1992, it makes two middle-market tractor ranges in the UK and France respectively, and fills in its product range by selling badged models sourced mainly from Japan. More fundamentally, it is re-examining its engineering and development activities and deciding which areas of tractor design should remain inhouse and which should be left to suppliers. In future Massey Ferguson aim to compete by "maintaining a core tractor knowledge and utilising outside resources as and when appropriate for specific design tasks".

To this end a major reorganisation has taken place at the two manufacturing locations. At the UK factory in Coventry, tractor assembly and marketing is now separate from the manufacture of components and subassemblies. Internally manufactured parts consist of gears and driveshafts, major chassis castings and the linkages to towed implements such as ploughs. Towed implements are to be outsourced, in line with a strategy to produce only transmission and associated castings internally. While the logic underlying this simplification of business philosophy is clear, it creates new management tasks and changes priorities both within and between functional areas.

For engineering, a major task now is the overseeing and co-ordination of design activity within suppliers and contracted design houses. In general, a more modular overall product design philosophy has had to be adopted to allow components and subsystems to be effectively integrated.

More specifically, intense design collaboration is needed. For example, in developing a new range of tractors to replace its current basic models (which derive from a 1950's design), Massey Ferguson decided that even in the core area of transmissions, specialist design input was desirable for four-wheel drive models. A four-wheel drive firm was contracted to provide leading edge knowledge in this area. Because the bulk of this firm's experience was in road and rally cars, considerable joint activity was needed to link these skills to Massey Ferguson's knowledge of tractor performance, reliability, operating conditions, etc. As a result a team of Massey Ferguson engineers has been sited with the supplier for the duration of the project. In a similar example for engines, the need to trim external designs to specific requirements has led Massey Ferguson to "do more engine design in the last 12 months than in the last 20 years".

For the purchasing function, a routine order management role has been transformed by the need to manage these critical supplier relationships. For bought components such as fuel injection systems, tractor firms represent a small niche market in comparison to mass-production car makers. A major challenge for Massey Ferguson will therefore be persuading suppliers to meet its particular technical requirements. Skill in choosing co-operative suppliers, and in carefully managing relationships with them, will be a key to its future competitive success.

## TECHNOLOGIES AND INTERCOMPANY NETWORKS

We have already emphasised that an understanding of technology and its management needs to take place within the context of the network of competing and co-operating companies within which all firms are enmeshed. A technology in itself has no value. It is simply a passive resource which is only activated when its owner interacts with another company which places some value on it – either because the other company wishes to acquire the technology for its own use, or because it wishes to buy products or services based on the technology, or plans to combine this technology with its own skills to provide something of value to others in the network. The value of a technology is specific to the other company and will be related to that company's own technologies and to its view of the technologies of other companies in the surrounding network.

A company which seeks to meet the requirements of its customers will use its own technologies and those which are embodied in the products and services of other companies which supply it. In order to meet customer requirements it may also seek to acquire other technologies directly, from licensors, contract research houses or those with which it has a joint venture. In this way it builds a "bundle" of technologies suitable for its own customer (Fig. 2). It may also use the services of other companies that provide the means by which the bundle of technologies can reach the customer, such as distribution companies or subcontract manufacturers, etc. Of course the company will not control this bundling process entirely. Other companies will have their own ideas of the importance of the company and its customer, and their own role in the network. Thus for example, a component maker may seek to influence how its components are used and who the final products are sold to.

The interaction between a company and those that surround it is not simply to acquire the use of their technologies. This interaction is not a zero-sum gain; both sides benefit by the exchange which takes place and by the learning which occurs from each other through the interaction, perhaps over many years. In this way the technological resources of both parties can grow through that interaction.

### Interaction and Product Development

This brings us to a second reason for emphasising the interdependence between companies. A large proportion of new products are not developed by suppliers alone or by buyers, but interactively between them. Because of this, our ideas of the nature of the product development task in industrial firms may need to be revised and the question of intellectual property rights becomes much more complicated. Additionally, companies will need to think very carefully about how the product development task carried out with any one partner will affect its dealings with others. Even more importantly, interdependence between companies means that a nationally independent company is not surrounded by a solid boundary, but by one

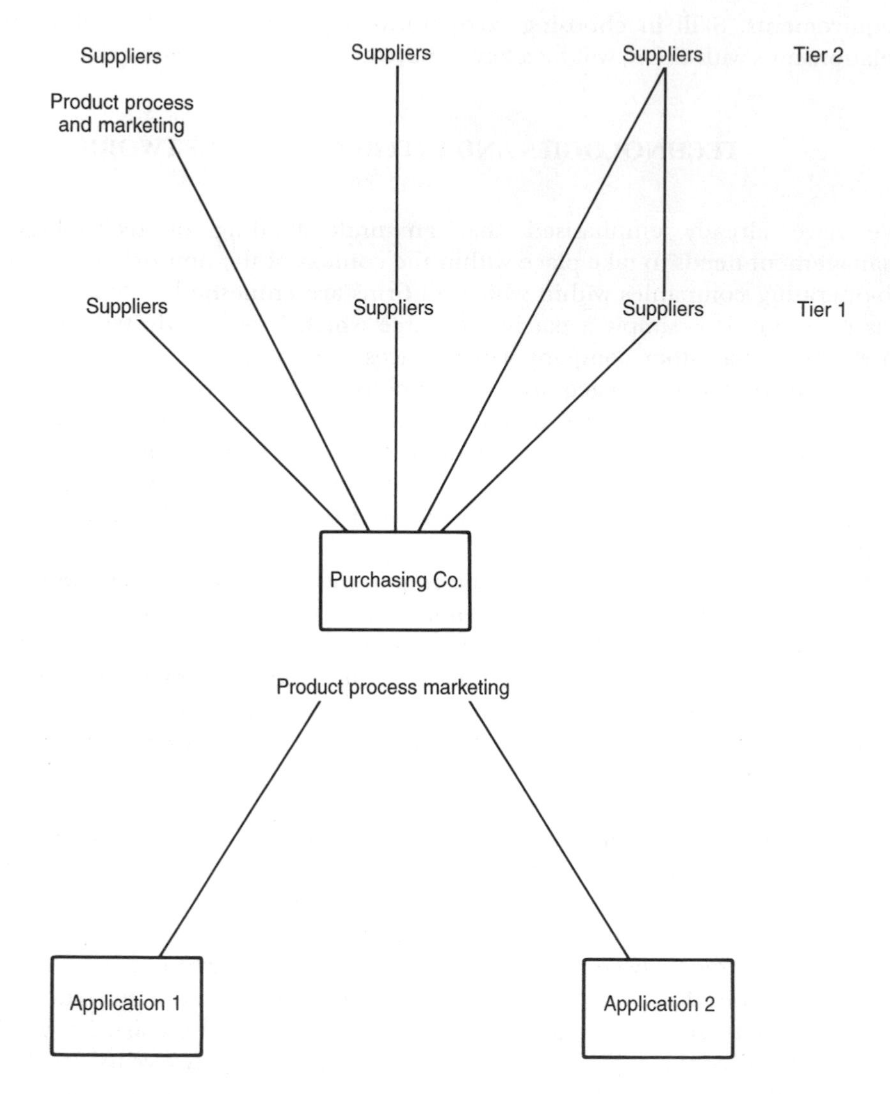


Fig. 2. Technologies and networks.

which is permeable. In fact, when we look at many companies which buy and sell from each other or develop products together, it is rather difficult to identify the boundary between them or where the areas of each company's responsibility, ownership or even culture start and finish. The extent to which a company will allow others to influence its nominally internal activities and will seek to involve itself within others is an important issue of managerial decision-making and control. For example, when a company is developing a new product it will often be influenced in that activity by the product development departments of a customer or its own suppliers. Similarly, the production plans for a new product will often be largely determined by the quality specifications of a main customer. Lake and Trayes[6] describe this interaction as occurring across "discretionary boundaries" and this is illustrated in Fig. 3.

## TECHNOLOGY STRATEGY, PRODUCTS AND PROCESSES

A technological perspective on analysing a company may give a different view of the activity of buying products or services. For example, a customer may appear to choose a supplier because it wishes to buy its particular products. However, that supplier's products may be absolutely standard and unremarkable. Instead the buyer may have chosen the supplier because of the distinctive way in which it produces these standard products, which provides greater consistency of quality. In this way the purchase is actually determined by the process technology of the product supplier. The customer values these skills of the supplier, either because of its own lack of production capacity or because it does not have the necessary process technology itself. This may mean that if it produced the product itself its costs of production would be higher or its quality lower. In this way the company is treating these process technologies as "external".

In some cases the importance of the supplier's process technology is reinforced because the customer may be buying to its own product design. Even when this is not

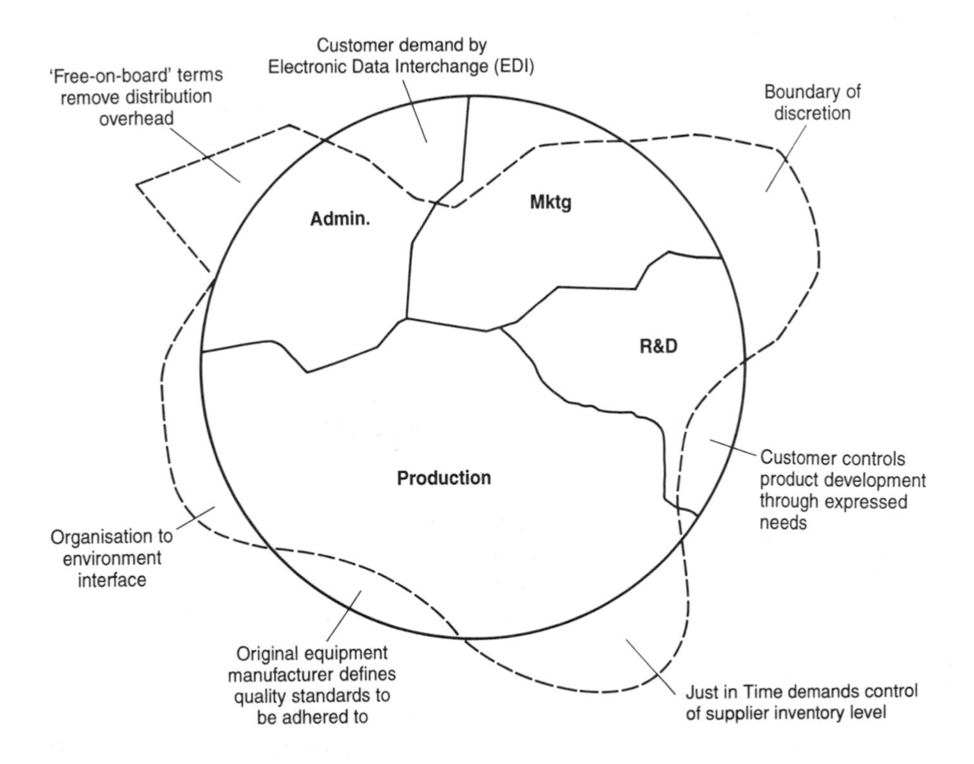


Fig. 3. Discretionary boundaries.

the case and the product is designed by the seller (based on their product technology), the customer may not be prepared to pay a premium for those technologies and will decide between suppliers on the basis of competing process strengths.

On the other hand, a buying company may not be primarily interested in either the product or process technologies of a supplier. It may seek to take advantage of the supplier's Marketing technology. Marketing technology includes the skill of market analysis, the ability to tailor product and process technologies to the particular requirements which have been analysed and skills in logistics, advertising and selling. These skills are necessary in order to transfer a package of product and process technologies to a particular application. In many cases it is the marketing technologies of the seller which are critical in meeting the buyers' requirements. For example, the functionality may be very similar between many proprietary software packages used in such areas as business logistics. In these circumstances, success comes to the software company which is best at tailoring its offering and its sales presentations to the requirements of its potential clients. Similarly in many consumer markets it is often the distinctive marketing technology of a manufacturer which enables it to build the appeal of its product for a particular group of customers, even though its product is functionally identical to others in the market.

Marketing technology requires similar investments to develop as product and process technologies. It is also exploitable in a number of different ways, such as when a company uses its skills to market the complementary products of another company on an agency basis. More importantly, a bundle of product, process and marketing technologies is needed to meet any set of customer requirements. For example, many companies have the product technology suitable for a particular group of customers, they may also be able to develop the process skills to manufacture for that application. But, they also need the appropriate marketing technology to determine those customers' requirements precisely, tailor, package and communicate their offering, and transfer it to the customer at an appropriate price. Without this marketing technology they will fail, or have to use the services of someone else who has these skills or form a joint venture with another company to assemble a package of the requisite technologies. For example, when Arm and Hammer decided to introduce their baking-powder toothpaste internationally they obviously had the necessary product and process technologies. However, they did not have the skills or marketing resources to support the launch of the product in unfamiliar markets. For this reason, in the UK, they used the resources of the marketing agency Food Brokers to provide the necessary marketing technologies.

Definitions of the three types of technologies are given below:

1. Product technology is *knowledge* of the physical properties and characteristics of materials and the *ability* to incorporate these into the design of products or services which could be of value to another company or individual.
2. Process technology is *knowledge* of ways of producing products or services and the *ability* to produce these so that they have value to others.
3. Marketing technology is *knowledge* of ways of bringing these product and process technologies to a particular application and the *ability* to carry this out. This involves the skills of market analysis, branding, packaging, pricing, communications and logistics.

## THE INTERDEPENDENCE OF COMPANIES

The second major issue of technology and interaction centres on the interdependence of companies. It is a false picture to see a company as the master of its own destiny, building its independent strategy and trying to get a favourable reaction from the market – such a view is more appropriate to the rather colourful newspaper accounts of the lives of famous industrial "barons" than it is to an understanding of industrial reality.

There are a number of reasons for this. It is difficult to imagine a company which is able to meet any application in a modern market solely on the basis of its own technologies. A hundred years ago, railway companies brought-in raw timber and billets of iron and created locomotives, carriages and wagons using their own skills and abilities. Nowadays, the products of most companies depend to a great extent on the technologies of others, whether they are supplying technology in its "pure" form via licence etc., or whether the technology is incorporated in the products or services which the company buys. Increasingly, both the pace of technology change and the escalating up-front cost of R&D mean that it becomes more and more difficult for a company to maintain a position in even a relatively narrow technological area, much less in a wide range of technologies. A company is faced with the difficult question of which technologies it should continue to devote its resources to maintaining and developing internally and which it should regard as external technologies it has the benefit of, such as when the company buys products based on external technologies but does not own them.

## CONCLUSIONS

This chapter has introduced the idea of technology strategy as three interrelated tasks of acquiring, managing and exploiting technology. The tasks are interrelated because the process of technology acquisition takes place with the specific purpose of, and frequently in parallel with, the exploitation of that technology. The task of managing technology has both short-term and longer-term strategic aspects. It involves managing a set of resources, only some of which are tangible, and many of which exist in the form of the knowledge and abilities of the company's employees and, indeed, in the culture and collective experience of the company. A good analogy for this management task is that of the farmer who seeks to exploit the assets of his land, but at the same time seeks to replenish those assets and leave the land "in good heart" for his successors.

Although some technologies are individually important, a bundle of product, process and marketing technologies are needed to meet the requirements of a company's markets. In some cases it is prowess in only one or a subset of these technologies which makes for competitive advantage. In other cases none of the company's technologies will be distinctive when compared to other companies. But it is the company's skill in assembling the appropriate bundle of technologies to deliver the requirements of its customers which is distinctive. No company has all of the technologies which are needed to satisfy the requirements of a market. A company must work with others around it and use their skills as external technologies so as to assemble the required bundle of technologies. This bundling will involve many companies; the process of bundling may be more or less controlled by all the companies in a wide network ranging from component manufacturers to retailers. The management of a company's position and interactions in that network is a major issue of strategy. Through those network interactions its technological resources acquire their value to other members of the network and to final customers.

## REFERENCES

1. Quinn, J. B. and Mintzberg, H. *The Strategy Process: Concepts, Contexts and Cases,* Prentice-Hall, Englewood Cliffs, New Jersey (1991).
2. Ford, D. (ed.) *Understanding Business Markets,* Academic Press, London (1990).
3. Nonaka, I. Redundant, overlapping organization: a Japanese approach to managing the innovation process, *California Management Review,* Spring: 27–38 (1990).
4. Ford, D. Develop your technology strategy, *Long Range Planning,* **21** (5): 85 (1988).
5. Ohmae, K. *The Mind of the Strategist – the Art of Japanese Business,* McGraw-Hill, New York (1982).
6. Lake, K. and Trayes, A. Technology and networks, unpublished MBA project report, University of Bath (1990).

# 2

# Product Development in Networks

*H. Håkansson*

## THE IMPORTANCE OF STUDYING PRODUCT DEVELOPMENT

Product development has received substantial attention during the last two decades. There are hundreds of studies and articles devoted to models, analyses, and recommendations regarding this concern. However, the main body of research concerned with product development has been criticized for applying an overly narrow perspective – see for example Gold (1979) and Teubal (1979). The aim of many studies has been to attempt to isolate and analyse individual phenomena instead of relating the development issues to broader and more general processes or structures. The law of reductionism has been applied.

This can be explained, at least partly, by the fact that the research has been oriented towards a specific actor – usually the producer – which has been seen as the innovator. The "Newton Syndrome" was in other words operative here. Another explanation is theoretical which we will come back to later.

The high level of interest for new product development can largely be explained by two interrelated factors. One of these is the increased professionalism among managers leading to a belief that companies can and furthermore need to be managed by some kind of central unit. Taking this perspective new products have been seen as the means to secure the future of the company. During the strategic wave of diversification this interest was especially strong. The second and interrelated factor is a belief that everything is developing more quickly, implying an increased uncertainty and, among other things, shortened product life cycles. Thus, as a consequence there is an increased need for the continual development of new products. It will not be discussed here whether these two factors are based on solid empirical ground or are simply beliefs, This is, however, an interesting question with no self-evident answer.[1]

Thus, our interest in product development is not based on arguments such as a lack of earlier studies or that this issue has become more important for management. Instead our argument is that product development must be looked at in a new way.

Reprinted by permission of International Thomson, Product Development in Networks by H. Håkansson from *Industrial Technological Development: A Network Approach*. Edited by H. Håkansson, pp 84–198 abridged version.

Before presenting our view we will briefly describe earlier studies. It is possible to categorize the studies of product development in a number of ways – for recent reviews see Kennedy (1983) and Golding (1983). Taking a network analysis perspective it is interesting to see which actor is perceived to take the initiative in product development. For example, is it the producer, the user or some other actor? These perspectives are examined further in the following three subsections.

### Product Development Initiated by the Producer

The overwhelming majority of studies focus on the producer as the initiator of the product development process and a lot of attention is devoted to determining new methods to increase the success rate of new products or at least reduce the failure rate. The reasons for this concentration on the producers is related to the two earlier mentioned factors – active management and increased degree of change. This focus is so established and self-evident that, for example, the previously mentioned review articles (Kennedy, 1983; Golding, 1983) take it for granted.[2]

The main conclusions from all these studies are recommendations to producers to use a rational, straightforward product development process. The process consists of a sequence of activities such as information gathering, screening, business analysis, product design, market test, and commercialization. During the whole of this sequence the producer is believed to take the initiative and, for example, make the external contacts that are necessary. Much is said about actions and very little about reactions.

### Product Development Initiated by the User

A few studies have perceived the user as the active party. Von Hippel's studies are the most well-known, but there are also others, e.g. within the field of industrial purchasing. Von Hippel (1978) and (1982) has developed a "customer-active" paradigm which he contrasts to the old "manufacturer-active" paradigm. His main argument for this new paradigm is that it better suits (a) industrial buying behavior, and (b) the engineering problem-solving process. The customer-active paradigm is supported by empirical studies of, for example, semiconductors, electronic sub-assembly processes, and scientific instruments.

Results showing the same tendencies can also be found in certain industrial purchasing studies (see for example Axelsson and Håkansson, 1984. And it would be very surprising if such was not the case, since users such as GM, Toyota, General Electric, Volvo, IBM and others, who are themselves large manufacturing companies, invest heavily in product and process efficiency.

### Product Development as an Interaction Process Between Users and Producers

In the preceding sections the initiative has been seen as located in one actor only. An alternative is to combine these two and see both the producers and the users as taking an active part in interaction processes. In the IMP study (Håkansson, 1982) company case analyses revealed that in a majority of situations joint development activities could be identified.

The three types of product development studies that we have described are complementary but to some extent also overlapping as is shown in Fig. 1. Together, they could cover the whole spectrum of product development but as will be seen in the next section serious criticism can be directed against all of them.

## PRODUCT DEVELOPMENT IN A NETWORK PERSPECTIVE

One criticism toward the main body of earlier research regarding product development is, as was mentioned earlier, its focus on one or a few actors. If we, for example, consider the three groups of studies described in the previous section, the first two are oriented toward one specific type of actor and the third to the interplay between two actors. Thus, in all these studies the focus has been restricted to very few actors with accompanying types of analysis variables.

It is also possible to identify a theoretical explanation associated with how the relationship between individual events and the total technical development process is perceived. If the total technical development is believed to be composed of a lot of small and independent events then it is perfectly correct to study individual events or factors in an isolated way. But there is an interesting alternative. If the individual events are simply indicators or expressions of the total technical development process then there is a need to use an approach that takes as its starting point the total process. A number of studies have tried to do this in different ways. For example, Utterback and Abernathy (1975) relate individual events to the product life cycle, Baranson (1978) studies the development within a whole industry, Sahal (1980)

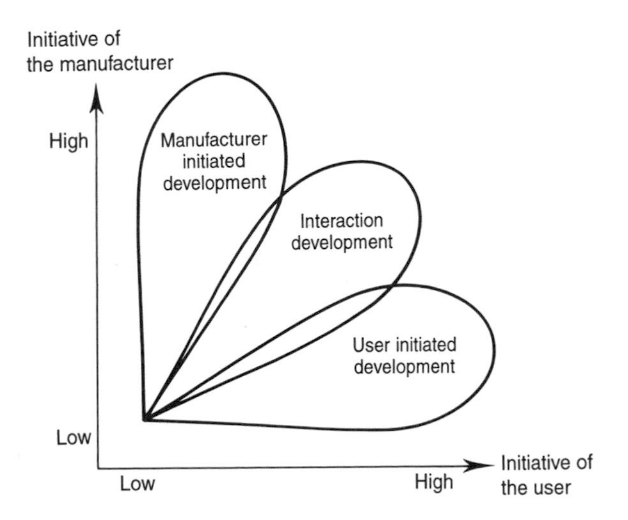


Fig. 1. The initiator of product development.

studies technical development as a learning process, and Stindl (1980) perceives it as an evolutionary process.

In this chapter the network perspective will be used as a tool to relate individual events such as product development to the total technical development within some technical fields. The network constitutes the frame to each individual episode but is at the same item built up by these episodes.

The network perspective means focusing on relationships between actors, activities and resources. In the network perspective a specific product becomes a question of relationships. It itself constitutes a relationship between certain activities, resources and actors. A product is produced through certain transformation and transaction activities – and is consumed through others. Some resources are used when it is produced or during the transaction and others when it is consumed. Some actors control these activities and resources. Thus, a product relates these activities, resources and actors to each other in a specific way.

In this way product development becomes a network issue in terms of how the new product will affect the activities, the resources and thereby the relationships between the actors. The response is furthermore related to how this new product is connected to other types of change that occur at the same time within the network. It can not be isolated from other technical changes nor from economic or power structure changes. In summary, individual product development activities must be seen as part of a total technical development process which in turn must be regarded as an integral feature of the specific network.

## Technical Development as a Combined Political and Random Process

In order to obtain a better understanding of the total development process we have to start with the network. Several network features are important to the technical development process. These can be summarized as follows:

1. The existence of activity cycles and transaction chains. Different activities are systematically related to each other and constitute repetitive activity cycles which in turn are combined to build up transaction chains. The repetitiveness is important as it is a prerequisite for efficiency. The border between different activities is always arbitrary and can be changed.
2. The instability and imperfection of the networks. The terms optimality or balance can never be applied to a network as there is no single evaluation criterion or reference point. The role of the network is different for all its members and also in relation to all other networks connected to it. Thus, there are always both possibilities and reasons to change it. Existing transaction chains can be developed, new ones can be created, and so on. A network is in this way always alive and adaptable. But, at the same time there is no guarantee whatsoever that the development is positive from, for example, society's point of view. There is no "invisible hand" creating a situation of efficiency and health. Instead there are several "visible hands" that try to create situations that are beneficial to themselves.
3. The network structure creates limitations. The technical changes that occur

must be performed within a certain structure. The existence of activity cycles and the combination of activity cycles in transaction chains are built on certain fixed combinations or resources. Thus, the relationships between different activities, between the activities and different resources, and as such between different actors, are based on specific technological concepts. The latter are expressed in the combination of products and the use of products and must be considered as a feature of the network.

The network characterized by the above three features develops over time. The second feature gives the reasons and possibilities and the first and third the limitations and directions. Three types of technical change activities can be identified:[3] investments in real capital, day-to-day rationalizations, and product development. Investments in real capital include development of equipment or new production processes thereby changing the transformation activities. Day-to-day rationalizations are all those thousands of minor changes that increase the efficiency of the transformation, the transaction activities or the connection of those two types of activities. Product development, lastly, always means changes in the transaction activities and, at least to some degree, changes in the transformation activities. It is clear from the above description that there are close connections between these three types of technical development, and in many situations they cannot be clearly separated.

Together these three types of activities, performed by the actors of the network, constitute the total technical development process. This can be regarded as a learning (Sahal, 1980) or as an evolutionary (Steindl, 1980) process. It can also be regarded as a "muddling through process" (Lindblom, 1959). Lindblom uses this concept to characterize the method of formulating policies (which he regards as synonymous to decision-making). He writes:

> This might be described as the method of "successive limited comparisons". I will contrast it with the first approach, which might be called the rational-comprehensive method. More impressionistically and briefly they could be characterized as the branch method and root method, the former continually building out from the current situation, step-by-step and by small degrees; the latter starting from fundamentals anew each time, building on the past only as experience is embodied in a theory, and always prepared to start completely from the ground up (Lindblom, 1969, p. 44).

Although the muddling through process was originally developed for the purpose of describing and explaining decision-making, it can also be used to characterize the total technical development process within a given network. The muddling through process indicates the simultaneous existence of consciousness and experience of the actors and the presence of random situations. Consciousness is present via the actor who more or less systematically acts in a purposeful way based on earlier experience. The random variable is due to the large possibilities of different combinations and the genuine uncertainty connected with consequences in the future. Let us take a closer look at these three characteristics.

Consciousness gives the actors a direction or purpose to try to do what is best in each situation, and they will always try even if the results of the previous steps have not been as expected. However, consciousness of the actors is restricted by the lack of capabilities to survey the network and to estimate consequences in more than just a few dimensions. The existence of consciousness is important in another way as it indicates that technical development is never neutral – it is always biased towards the interests of those involved. Technical development is therefore a political process.

Experience is an essential ingredient of the process. Obviously, the actors perform and evaluate activities in relation to their experience. But the actors are also sensitive to the existence of others' experience. If others have used a specific product for some time this can be seen as a reassurance in terms of aggregated experience. The accumulation of experience is by no means a simple straightforward process. Experience gained in earlier unsuccessful products can suddenly become vital in a new project. Other experiences that beforehand are perceived to be important inputs in a project can during the process prove to be of little or no value.

The random factor is due to the interplay between several actors, alternatives and knowledge. This means that it is not possible to predict which ideas will be realized nor which of these will develop into useful products or processes.

Some ideas – alternatives – are tried and some of these successively become the standard solution. The reason for this may not be that they are better from a technical point of view but more that resources have been mobilized to make them useful. An alternative might have been better but as no resources have been put into the development of it this will never be known. The random factor is limited by the existence of earlier investments in resources (plants, equipment relationships). This limitation will be further discussed in the next subsection.

### Network as a Control Mechanism

Both the consciousness of the actors and the random factor are integrated aspects of the network. The actors' perspective, and thereby their consciousness, are often influenced by the network which logically relates different actors and aspects to each other. The structure of the network will also give the random factor a non-random (systematic) character. The structure of the network, thus, will act as a control mechanism of the development process. It makes certain changes easier and others more difficult. The resources are structured in relation to the network and they are more easily mobilized if the development is in accordance with the structure of the network compared to the case when the development implies structural changes. In summary, we believe that in order to understand the technical development process one must understand the network in terms of structure and processes.

## TECHNICAL DEVELOPMENT FROM AN ACTOR'S PERSPECTIVE

In the previous section the technical development of a network has been discussed in general. Here the problems at the actor level – mainly companies – will be examined.[4] In other words, we will take an individual company as a starting point and discuss how the processes and phenomena dealt with in the preceding section will look from this actor's perspective, especially in respect to the company's product development.

One starting point is the actor's ambition to improve his position, and the various ways to do this. One way is to develop the product. The network can be used in a positive way but can also be a very important limitation factor. This will be further discussed in the following three subsections.

### The Network as an Obstacle to Change

The network consists of many relationships, as well as other types of interdependence relations. As we pointed out earlier, the product is one of these interdependencies. If a product is changed other relationships might also have to be changed. This can only be done at a certain cost. Thus, when dependencies have to be altered, this always entails the cost of such a change.[5] The most common types of dependency which may be obstacles are

- Technical dependencies;
- Knowledge dependencies;
- Social dependencies;
- Logistic or administrative dependencies.

Each of these will be discussed in more detail below.

Technical dependencies are due to the fact that individual products are used together with other products or within technical systems. Successively related products are developed to better fit together. In a mature technology this integration of products is usually quite extensive (Utterback and Abernathy, 1975). In a study of "the hydraulic network", we found, for example, that the fittings between valves, pistons and packings, despite the fact that they were produced by different companies, had developed in a very extensive way. To introduce a new product within such a network requires that the producers of complementary products adapt to the new product. All these kinds of fittings are important from an efficiency point of view but they are certainly obstacles to new products. A new product does not usually fit as well from the start; not does it use the capabilities of the other products in such an extensive way as the old products do. Thus, it takes both time and great effort before a new product can merge into the network.

Knowledge dependencies occur because the user needs certain product knowledge in order to use a product. This knowledge must be spread within the buying company to all those coming in contact with the new product. How many these are and how difficult this is depends both on the characteristics of the product and the buying company. The time between the introduction of a product and the full use of all its features by a buying company can be quite long. During that period there can also be a need to dispose of old knowledge.[6]

The network is a social construction and as such built upon social relationships between the actors. This creates social dependencies which are difficult to break into for new actors. The normal social process of groups in terms of values, norms, legitimization, etc. are relevant.

Logistic and/or administrative dependencies can also create problems for a new product. These types of dependencies have become more important during the last decades as companies have grown internationally. Production units united together into international groups are often exposed to different coordination attempts, such as standardization of components or raw materials.

The following case illustrates this point. Ten years ago the Swedish bolt company Bulten AB attempted to introduce a new range of bolt products called HIGRIP. This new type of bolt was featured by a new configuration giving better technical performance. Bulten realized from the beginning that they needed to cooperate with a tool manufacturer. This cooperation was easily established as the largest Swedish tool manufacturer Bahco AB is situated just 50 km from Bulten. In tests made by customers – mainly car manufacturers – the new products gave better production results in terms of decreased costs for the tools, shorter production time per unit and increased quality of end-product.

However, the car manufacturers were still reluctant to buy new bolts because they wanted to have at least dual sourcing of all products. As a consequence Bulten and Bahco approached Britool and GKN in the UK and Kamax and Hazet Werk in West Germany. Together these six firms formulated a cooperation agreement. Despite these network activities and the superior technical features of the product, the endeavour failed. The main reason, according to the responsible manager at Bulten, was an important administrative/logistic dependency. As long as the cars with the new bolts are in the hands of the car manufacturer there are no problems. The problems arise as soon as the car is sold. It can be sold anywhere in the world; consequently spare parts and tools must be distributed world-wide. Furthermore, the storing of both the old and new version of bolts would be required for some 20–30 years (until all previously produced cars have been taken off the road). The international nature of the market in combination with the long lifespan of the end-product became obstacles impossible to overcome. Thus, a simple bolt has important dependency effects.

Together, the four types of dependencies can create strong barriers for new products. It is important for the individual actor to have a comprehensive and multifarious picture of these dependencies before launching a new product. They are also the main reasons why incremental development steps are more common than dramatic changes. The total strength as well as the distribution of these types of dependencies varies between different networks. We will come back to this variation later on in this chapter.

## Network as Idea Generator and Resource Source

As described earlier, the network consists of a number of relationships between actors, activities and resources. But there are also a number of potential interdependence relationships. Usually the number of the latter type exceeds the number of the former. Each potential relationship can be regarded as a possibility. Each actor is furthermore a potential cooperation partner and in this way a potential resource source. Partners can be used both as a means of attaining ideas and to receive direct development assistance. Lastly, there are numerous ways to conduct cooperation. Together these factors often give rise to a large number of combination possibilities of ideas, partners and cooperation forms.

Potential relationships can exist between activities, actors and/or resources, between different networks or activities, resources or actors in one network and some other activities, resources or actors in another network. Thus there is no limit to the number of ideas.

A difficulty for the actor is to know if a certain product will be accepted by the network. The only way to find out is to test the idea on some of the actors. The interplay within the network can in this way be used as a means of evaluating ideas. Ideas which fit into the network will be more or less accepted and the others will be more or less rejected. It is important to notice the "more or less" of both acceptance and rejection. The network is seldom so uniform that only one type of solution will be accepted. A certain differentiation will be retained because different actors mobilize in favour of different solutions. A completely new idea, however, will usually not be accepted because it often changes the entire network structure. Thus, a network consisting of actors from previously different networks has to be built around the new idea. This takes time and demands a lot of resources.

The existing network can be used in different ways; there can be cultural differences in this use as illustrated by the following case from a Swedish company in a high-tech industry. A new product idea had emerged in the marketing department from a relationship with a large customer. The marketing department put forward a proposal and the research and development department was asked to give an estimate of the time and resources needed for the development of the product. The research and development department answered that it would take 24 months and the cost would be one million Swedish crowns. The managing director realized that if the research and development department estimated 24 months it would probably take 36 months and that would be too long. The managing director asked a Japanese company if they could develop the product and if so in what time limit and price. The Japanese company replied that they could do it in 9 months and for three quarters the cost estimated by the internal research and development department. The company chose to buy from the Japanese company. But how could the Japanese company do it so much faster and at a lower cost? The managing director explained the difference in the following way:

> When our R&D department made their estimation they thought of a completely new product. The Japanese company divided the new product into different technical functions and chose existing solutions for most of these. Then they directed their development resources towards the design of the remaining components. In this way they utilized the existing suppliers much more effectively than we did.

The Japanese company used the network in a much more effective way. But in this case the Swedish company adapted by using the Japanese company as a supplier! The important lesson, however, is that there are many reasons for utilizing the existing network in all possible ways in the development work. In some situations it can be done by procurement of advanced products or systems.

### Network as an Information Transmitter

The network can be regarded as a communication system. In a well structured network everybody knows what is happening. In a few hours news of a positive or negative event spread throughout the network. A less structured network is not as effective or fast, but nevertheless has a communication function.

The actor can use the network to spread and/or to collect information. The actor does not in this way have to have direct contact with all other actors. He can use the network as an intermediate. The information reaching different actors, however, is influenced by the structure of the network. The content is perceived in accordance with a network logic. Each link absorbs and distorts to some degree the information. The information is formulated in the language of the network which in turn is related to the basic technology and the structure of the network.

The network does not merely transmit information about events that happen within it, but also information related to other networks. This gives an individual actor an opportunity to obtain an understanding of what happens within a large number of technical areas, without having to invest in direct relationships with each of them.

## PRODUCT DEVELOPMENT WITHIN NETWORKS – AN EMPIRICAL ILLUSTRATION

Having discussed the theoretical implications of the network model, this section will be devoted to a presentation of an empirical study that we have carried out using this theoretical frame of reference. Product development within a specific network will be analysed as an integrated part of the total technical development process. The analysis will be done in the following sequence.

1. Identification of the main actors within a network.
2. Characterization of their activities and resources.
3. Description of the technical development for each of these actors for a certain period in terms of:
   (a) investments in real capital (plants, equipment, etc.);
   (b) day-to-day rationalizations (all the minor activities that increase productivity);
   (c) product developments.
4. Analysis of how the characteristics of the product development are related to the total technical development as well as to the characteristics of the network. The description includes many technical details which, however, must be known in order to fully understand the later analysis.

## THE METAL DRILL NETWORK

This network is defined by the function of making holes in metals. First, the actors and the basic structure of the network will be presented, then the technical development within it will be summarized. The description is made in general way giving just enough information to make it possible to understand the conclusions.

## The Network

Five main types of actors can be identified within this network.[7] These are the users – mainly the mechanical engineering industry, the producers of the bench drilling machines, the tool producers. Each of these will now be described in more detail.

The users are many and varied. The largest users are the automotive and aeroplane industries. In Sweden this includes companies such as Volvo and Saab. But other large engineering companies such as ASEA, Alfa-Laval, Atlas Copco and Sandvik are also large users. The users differ in terms of production technologies as well as in other aspects. Important features of the drilling operation is speed, exactness, surface finish, and noise conditions.

Most of the users buy their equipment and drill tools from distributors. The latter represent about three quarters of the total market for bench drill machines. They are usually local trade companies specializing in selling different types of machines and supplies to the industry.

There are four producers of bench drill machines in Sweeden: Arboga Maskiner, Solberga Mekaniska Verkstad, Strands Mekaniska Verkstad, and Widmek. The largest is Arboga Maskiner which furthermore is highly international. More than 70% of this company's turnover is exported. The product manufactured consists of components such as columns, work tables, drill chucks, and power drives. The production equipment is partly standard engineering machines such as lathes, drills, milling cutters, etc. Another major part of the production consists of foundry equipment.

There are only two tool manufacturers: SKF Tools and Wedewågs Bruk. The first of these two is highly international and is believed to be the largest producer in the world of these products while the other is basically oriented towards the Nordic countries. Both of them started to produce drills during the first two decades of the 20th century; thus, they are well established in this area. Between 60 and 80% of their sales are sold by distributors.

The drills are made of high-speed steel. There were three such producers in Sweden: Fagersta, Uddeholm Tooling and SKF Steel. The last to these started production of high-speed steel during the 1970's, while the two others have a long history. Both of them are among the eight leading high-speed steel producers in the Western Countries, which together represent 50% of the market. The three Swedish producers are highly international and export 80–90% of their production. In order to be competitive these companies need to have a production characterized by large batches of the same product. The customers' demands on the steel concern the straightness, the quality of the surface, and high and even internal features. The requirements have increased during the last decade due to the increased production automization of the customers.

The main structure of the network is given in Fig. 2. The structure of this network is basically very similar to that of the wood saw network. There is one "equipment chain" and one "tool chain".

## Technical Development Within the Metal Drill Network

The major technical developments for the different types of company, divided into capital investments, day-to-day rationalizations and product developments, are summarized in Table 1. Here some additional comments will be made.

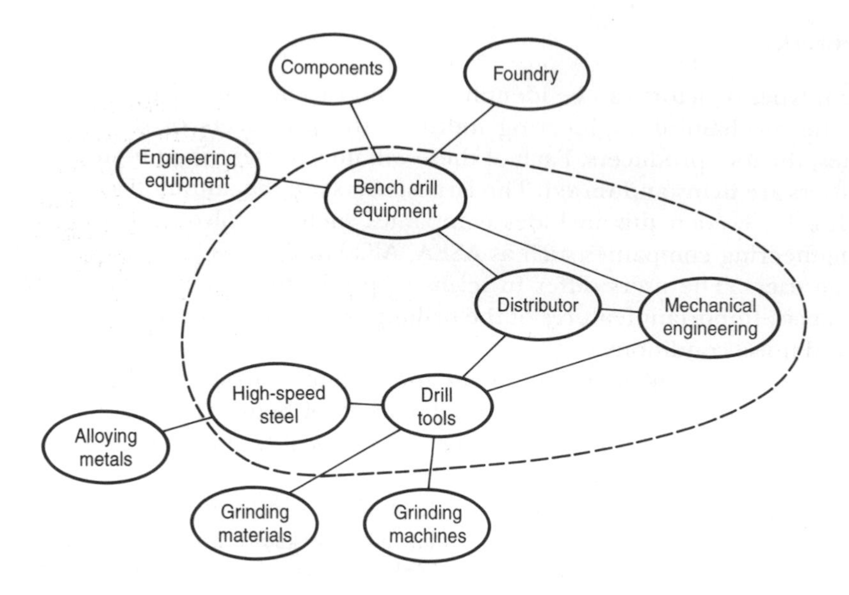


Fig. 2. The metal drill network.

The most important capital investments from the network's point of view have been made by the drill manufacturers. The largest of these changed production philosophy in the 1960s and then again in the 1970s. This has demanded large investments. The other types of company have also made investments; for example, one of the producers of high-speed steel has developed a new type of steel which has demanded large investments. This new steel, however, is only used to a limited degree in drill production. A disinvestment has been made by one of the bench drill producers. This company has closed its foundry and instead buys this product from a supplier.

There have been important day-to-day rationalizations in all units. Among the high-speed steel producers there have been important developments within each production step. The content of these has been partly influenced by the need for the steel companies to change their product mix due to the change in production philosophy of the tool manufacturers. Another important change is a new way of organizing production in order to keep the width of the product mix and still reduce the capital invested in stocks.

Among the drill manufacturers there have also been important day-to-day rationalizations. The exchange of production philosophies has opened up large potential for rationalization. There have not been any major changes in the product mixes but some "exchanges" of products between competitors have occurred.

The producers of bench drill equipment have increased their product mixes. However, due to standardization of components and subsystems this has not resulted in shorter production runs. The rationalization of production has been very important as there has been substantial price press on the product. Product adaptations in order to achieve more efficient production have been of major importance.

Table 1. Technical development within the metal drill network

| | High-speed steel producers | Drill manufacturers | Bench drill producers | Distributors | End-users |
|---|---|---|---|---|---|
| Capital investments | Small within strip steel production. Large in the general production of steel and for one producer a new type of steel | Large due to changes in production philosophies, first in the 1960s and then during the 1970s | In NC-machines and in computerization of production | Computer facilities | Increased automatization, increased use of multipurpose machines |
| Day-to-day rationalizations | Substantial, especially in the product mix; specialization of high-speed steel. New production methods have decreased capital investment in storing | Substantial, especially in production methods | Important both in production methods and in the product mix. Increased standardization of components and subsystems | Large in storing and distribution | Substantial, varied |
| Product development | Incremental changes are dominant, better internal properties. One of the producers has launched a new type of steel | Incremental changes most important. Higher and more even quality. New applications of special uses | Incremental changes in terms of lowered noise level, increased speed, and increased life length. New multipurpose machines (produced by specialists) | Increased software – storeless buying, etc. | Varied |

Product development has been dominated by successive improvements in the three groups: steel, drill and equipment producers. There have also been some major changes. One of the steel companies has developed a new type of steel, one of the drill manufacturers has complemented its product mix with a drill edge grinding machine, and so on. This has, however, merely resulted in a minor change in the total network.

**Analysis of the Technical Development**

Two major transaction chains can be identified. One connects the steel producers, drill manufacturers, distributors, and end-users with each other. The other does the same with bench drill producers, distributors and end-users.

In the first of these two chains there have been two major changes during the last 20 years. During the 1960s there was an increased use in rolling as the main production type of the drill manufacturers. The major advantage with this was cost efficiency when producing large quantities. This type of production was chosen by all the larger producers while some smaller ones, exemplified in the case of the smaller Swedish producer, retained a previous production form. The use of rolling required use of tungsten as one alloying metal; this metal gives the steel the right properties while at the same time it makes the steel possible to roll. However, problems were caused by fluctuations in tungsten prices during the 1970s. Tungsten can be substituted by molybdenum but then the steel cannot be rolled. Instead the production must be built up around grinding operations. The larger producers were once again forced to change their production philosophy. For the largest Swedish producer this took five years. This change was important to the high-speed steel producers, who had to change product mix, which in turn required certain capital investments but mostly rather large day-to-day rationalizations. All these changes had very little effect in relation to the distributors and the end-users. There, the major changes have been related to decreasing total storing without decreasing the total availability of the tools. By increased use of computers and better planning of stocks and transports this task had been fulfilled. The products have been successively improved due to better properties of the steel.

The first transaction chain is in general characterized by repetitivity high interdependence, and routinization. However, there have been two major changes in this chain.

These changes have been important to several actors (the producers of alloying metals, the steel mills, and the drill tool manufacturers) and have resulted in new transformation and transaction activities. A condition was that the end-users should not be affected. Thus, there were major changes but within very clear limitations. As soon as the major changes occurred – which took quite a bit of time – all activities were directed towards incremental changes in order to increase the efficiency. The impetus for the change was an uncertainty factor causing extra costs – the price of tungsten. The fluctuation of the price of this product caused severe problems both to the steel producers and to the tool manufacturers. The only possibility to get away from this problem was to change production technology.

Thus, it appears that the tight transaction chain is built on a combination of certain resources. If the supply of these resources is changed in some way the transaction chain has to be redesigned. The changes are done in such a way that as few of the actors as possible have to be involved. The changes are done in a "surgery" form – to change as little as possible and to make the change as local as possible.

The second transaction chain (bench drill equipment producers–distributors–end-users) features a rather high degree of standardization. The manufacturers of bench drill equipment have specialized in some types of machine which they attempt to produce in large numbers. Other producers have specialized in multipurpose machines. The standardization in the chain is an effect of the standardized characteristics of the material machined in the production operation. This has made production specialization on an international basis possible. Furthermore the drill operation is, in most of the cases, simply one operation among others. This has caused an increase in the use of combined machines. One of the Swedish manufacturers has developed such a machine but the usual case is that one specialist takes care of each type of product. One end-user described their procedure for purchasing this type of equipment by saying:

> We buy the more simple bench drill machines and combined drill and milling cutters from Swedish suppliers, special drill machines are often bought from the U.S.A., and Italian suppliers are normally used when buying multipurpose machines.

Thus, the use of the machines are so similar that the producers can sell them worldwide. But the high degree of internationalization increases competition and requires cost efficient production. This in turn must be met by standardization and large batch production which is best combined with product development in incremental steps.

A comparison between the case outlined here and others we have investigated gives an indication of the complex and multidimensional connections between the technical development process and the characteristics of the network. Here we will limit our main conclusions to the connections between the characteristics of the transaction chain and the product development. These can be summarized as follows.

A tight transaction chain often gives rise to incremental product development, but the changes can be much greater if some basic conditions in terms of used resources are changed. Such change opens up the transaction chain or parts of it and creates opportunities for new technical solutions. As soon as one major solution has been accepted by most of the actors the transaction chain goes back to the tight and closed structure. One important feature of the chosen solution is probably that it should change as little as possible and affect as few actors as possible.

A loose transaction chain creates opportunities for flexibility and problem solving with accompanying openness to new solutions. This is because there are fewer restricting technical dependencies, as well as other dependencies, within the loose transaction chain. As loose and tight transaction chains normally intersect in certain actors, the former will often be dominated by the latter in terms of product development. The openness of the loose chain is in fact restricted by the influence of the more established "tight" transaction chain. The product development becomes in these situations open to larger changes in respect to the internal characteristics of the product, as long as the performance of the product from the user's point of view is not changed.

However, a loose transaction chain can also give rise to standardization of solutions (products) which can be sold world-wide. This creates new dependencies in technical, knowledge and administrative/logistic dimensions and tightens the structure in terms of the positions and roles between competing companies. Product development once again takes on an incremental character in respect to the various solutions.

## The Process of Technical Development

The process of technical development was at the start of this chapter characterized as a muddling through process combining both political and random factors. It was also suggested that this process takes place within a network featured by:

- Existence of activity cycles and transaction chains;
- Instability and imperfection;
- Specific structure creating limitations.

The case has illustrated and supported this theoretical description in several ways. It has been easy to identify activity cycles and transaction chains and also to see their importance for technical development. These phenomena are without doubt important considerations in all technical development.

The instability and imperfection of the networks, as well as how these are used by different actors, can also be seen in the cases. The drill manufacturers tried to increase their control (power) through an exchange of one raw material for another. In other cases responsibility for system design shifted over time between different actors as a result of perceived changes in the power distribution. The network can in these respects be seen as a social melting-pot continuously confronting different interests. By combining the word "social" with the technical concept "melting pot" we wish to indicate firstly that the results of the process are perceived by the social actors with accompanying variation in judgement, and secondly that most of the power bases are technically oriented in terms of control of resources (raw materials, knowledge, etc.) or activities (transformations and/or transactions). Together the social and technical dimensions create the conditions for exchange and thereby for technical development.

The network structure in terms of dependencies between different activities, different resources and different actors, as well as between combinations of all these, allows for little freedom in action. One actor can do very little if the actor is not able to mobilize others in the network. If the actor succeeds in doing the latter almost anything is possible. Thus, the structure is the result of interactions (it is interacted) and must be changed through interactions.

## MANAGEMENT IMPLICATIONS

This last section will be devoted to what all this means in relation to the individual company. Earlier in this chapter we discussed some implications in terms of the network as an obstacle to change, as an idea generator, and as an information transmitter. Here the discussion is centered on four issues. The first concerns the question of how generally applicable this type of analysis is; e.g. can it be used in both mature and new technological fields? The second issue concerns the strategic implications as regards the company. Can the networks be managed? This leads to the third issue which concerns the ability of networking; in what ways can a company improve its ability to survive in a network? The fourth issue concerns one such possibility, namely the company's ability to handle functional interdependence which to a large extent is an organizational problem.

### Applicability of the Approach

The case presented can be characterized as representing mature technologies. We have however, with encouraging results, used the network approach for analyses of individual as well as groups of companies in relation to their development within other technological fields.

One such field is the marine engine network. This highly international network consists of actors such as separator producers, engine producers, oil companies, shipyards, and ship-owners. The analysis described the technical collaboration between the separator producer Alfa-Laval, the engine producer Sulzer and the oil company Shell, as well as the accompanying problems of protecting individual product development.[8]

Another study examined the development of a block tool system by Sandvik. The actual network is highly international. One strategic issue for Snadvik was to establish close contacts with some of the producers of lathes without offending others.[9]

A third study examines how a company, one which is well established within one network (the pulp and paper network), tries to establish itself in a consumer product network through product development and later by means of a merger.[10]

The birth of a high-tech network was the object of a fourth study. The network approach proved to be highly useful when describing and analysing the early development of a technological field.[11]

All of the above studies, as well as others which have been conducted, indicate that the network approach is not just a research tool but can also offer useful and stimulating insights for management. Furthermore, the approach is not limited in its application but can be used in quite different areas such as new advanced technologies as well as more established, mature technologies.

### Strategic Implications

We started this chapter by indicating a certain scepticism about the possibility of managing large companies in a more direct manner.[12] One important reason for this is the existence of networks. The company is interlocked with others – it is not a free and independent unit. Thus, in our perspective management is often involved in wrestling with dependencies in order to create an alternative, in finding a way, rather than of choosing among existing alternatives. The "muddling through process" can once again be used as a means of identifying important strategical issues. Broadly speaking two issues emerge. The first can be labeled "get into the mud" and the second "get through the mud".

A network must be learnt through working within it. The reaction pattern is namely affected by the entrance of a newcomer, which makes previous in-depth studies of it more or less obsolete. This does not mean that managers should not analyse and think, but only that such activities do not compensate for the necessary experience gained by working within the network. Our recommendation is to learn from what is happening, reflect from all reactions, instead of thinking out and planning everything beforehand. It is more important to gain experience than to attempt to do things exactly "right" from the beginning. The development of a new product can be used as a means to get into a new network, as a way to test the other actors, and to learn how they react. In these situations product development is more of a reconnaissance than a commercial project.

Another interesting effect of membership in the network is that by getting into it, the network will also entrap the new-comer. There will be investments made by the company trying to get in but there will also be investments made by those letting the new-comer in. The larger those investments are the more unwilling the others will be to let the new-comers slide out again.[13]

The second issue – to get through the mud – again points to the need for power of endurance. A research and development manager in a successful Swedish company in a speech concluded that:

> If I should point out one single most important individual factor for success in product development, I would choose power of endurance without any doubt. It is never the question of how good, useful or profitable the idea is from the beginning but how to make it useful and in this way profitable by hard work. Thus, product development without endurance is worth nothing!

The strategic implications are obvious. It is important to have enough resources to force projects through, thus it is better to back up a few projects more heavily than trying to work with several projects. Another implication can be that it is important to find ways to "mummify" projects instead of completely abandoning them in situations when it is impossible to go any further. The mummifying facilitates a restart when the network has changed in such a way that earlier impossibilities have become possibilities – new materials, equipments, knowledge, etc. The mummifying is in other words a tool for increasing the company's power of endurance.

There are also some other more specific network issues that can be of importance both when getting "into the mud" as well as when one is working one's way through it. These are the cooperation, the neutrality, and the protection issue. All of these are related to each other which have been exemplified in the cases presented earlier.

Cooperation with others is an important tool both in order to mobilize resources and to use existing resources in a more efficient way. But cooperating with others in product development creates problems in respect to neutrality and protection of in-house knowledge. Working together with one customer can have as an effect that other customers questions the neutrality of the company. It is in this way easy to be seen as allied with certain actors. This can have negative consequences and therefore needs to be carefully handled. One way to deal with it is to be open and take part in several different cooperation projects so as to appear neutral in respect to product development. Another way can be to avoid having too clear a policy in these questions. This can be used as an excuse for inconsistencies when dealing with similar customers.

Another related issue is how to protect in-house ideas or knowledge in cooperation projects. The involvement of other companies always implies a certain risk in terms of getting weakened rather than of being strengthened. Although there is no simple solution to this, one important step is to be aware of it. In our case studies we have seen examples where companies have begun cooperation projects but later, when the project moved too close to the unique technical core of one of the companies, this company has taken over the project and continued alone. Another way is to divide the cooperation project; to separate out subprojects which can be completed internally.

### Networking Ability

Our empirical studies have convinced us that there are substantial differences between companies in their ability to handle the network. Some become highly talented and stable practitioners while others are quite simple "amateurs". One aspect of the networking ability concerns that position of the company within the network. The position is defined by the actual combination of resources and activities. Product development means, as we have stated earlier, that these combinations change. In order to strengthen its position the company needs to systematically build further, firstly to improve the integration of its resources and activities, secondly in terms of fusing its resources in new activities and thirdly by using new resources in the existing activities. These three types of product development are quite different in character from the network point of view. Thus, one critical networking ability is to be sensitive to these differences and organize and judge the different types of resources accordingly.

Another important networking ability regards the handling of individual relationships. Earlier we have given many examples of how relationships can be used in product development. But the opposite can also be important. Product development can be used as a means of showing mutuality in the relationship with an important customer. In this way product development can be utilized in order to secure the selling of other established products.

### Functional Interdependence

The network approach points out the interdependence between company functions. In this chapter we have covered marketing, purchasing, research and development, production, and economic issues. We have indicated the need to actively use technical factors in marketing and purchasing as well as using suppliers, customers, and other external actors in the company's technical development. This interdependence must be captured by the organization of the company. It can also be formulated as to reflect the network in the organization. In doing this there are two critical aspects which must be considered. Firstly, the organization should not function in such a way so as to underestimate the complexity of the network.[14] It is easy to see the effects on product development if the organization fails in this aspect. Secondly and related, the complexity can easily lead the company to increase the planning and the analysing to such an extent that it more or less replaces activities towards different counterparts. As we have concluded earlier, networks relate activities and actors to each other in such a multifarious way that they require learning by experimental means, thus the company has to "get into the mud".

The functional interdependence can be seen in the product development itself. Product development is dependent on a combination of different factors, as shown above, but it also has effects in several dimensions. It can be a means of finding new markets but it can as well be a means strengthening established relationships, to show mutuality or power in relation to certain actors, or to increase the interest of, for example, suppliers. It is in other words a genuine network issue.

## NOTES

1. Scott (1982, pp. 175–77) is as one example critical to both these and we very much support his view. If, for example, the change process is looked upon from an investment point of view it seems quite obvious that the speed is decreasing. As the total stock of investments is much larger today, new investments even if they are large become more and more marginal. The belief of the need of an active management is very much dependent on an assumption about the possibility of rationality in decision-making. This assumption has been criticized by several researchers; for a recent review see Brunsson (1982). Littler (1984) has given the same kind of opinion in regard to product development.
2. This can also be seen in the use of concepts and models as adoption and adoption processes. One explanation to this focus can be that the economic consequences of a new product usually are of much larger magnitude to the selling company compared to the buying company.
3. This division of technical development into three subgroups is taken from Carlsson *et al.* (1979).
4. In every network some main actors can be identified. In our cases they are usually companies or other organizations (e.g. research units).
5. An early discussion of cost of change can be found in Carlson (1970). Another related concept is source loyalty – see, for example, Wind (1970) and Cunningham, and Kettlewood (1976).
6. This has by others been called unlearning – see Hedberg (1979).
7. The data collection was done by two students under our supervision – Björk and Edwall (1982). Companies in all categories were interviewed.
8. Kostiainen (1984). This network consists of actors such as separator producers (Alfa-Laval, Mitsubishi, Westfalia and some small producers), engine producers (Sulzer, Buhrmeister and Wein, Mitsubishi and some small companies), oil companies, shipyards, and ship-

owners. The need for product development was caused by technical changes in the production of oil products. The network is very well structured and the companies have known each other for many years. Technical development in this case was initiated by Sulzer (the largest engine producer) by a proposal for a cooperation project with Alfa-Laval. The latter responded favourably and furthermore asked SHELL to partake. The product development was one of the results from this cooperation project. One important issue for Alfa-Laval in this case was to balance the need to cooperate in order to get access to necessary resources (for example an engine lab on a ship) with the need to protect the results in order to acquire a patent. Furthermore, working closely together with some partners without being perceived as being joined too closely by other important actors was another objective.

9. Axelsson and Lövgren (1984). Sandvik Coromant is the world leader (25% market share) in the area of cemented carbides for cutting tools. The tools are used in different types of lathe. During the last decades there have been increasing automatization which as one consequence has caused an increased interest in the tool holders. The block tool system developed by Sandvik is one attempt to solve this problem in a new way. Development was started in 1976 and very early (after just 2 months) Sandvik tried to establish close contact with four lathe producers: Heyligenstaedt in West Germany, Cincinnati in the USA, Wickman in the UK, and SMT in Sweden. One reason for choosing four was that Sandvik did not want to favour any one lathe producer. In other words, Sandvik did not want to offend any producer. A cooperation agreement for 2 years was signed with all of the above-named producers, but the contacts with Cincinnati and Wickman soon died out. In the period 1978–80 Sandvik continued development work but mainly without external contacts. One important exception was ASEA (an end-user) that actively took part in some field tests.

   The product was introduced at the Chicago fair in 1980 and that was also the starting point for several minor projects in cooperation with lathe producers as a means of ensuring compatibility. Another group of actors that must be influenced are the end-users (e.g. automotive companies). To change to the block tool system is most interesting for the users when they change the equipment, i.e. make larger investments. In these situations both the lathe producers and the tool system producers are actively influencing the users which can cause triangle dramas.

10. Waluszewski (1985). The study is focusing on technical development in regard to products and production processes in SCA, the largest Swedish producer of pulp and paper. One product development studied regards the introduction of a customer product which became a commercial failure. However, the process had opened up contacts with customer oriented companies using paper as an important raw material. In this way the project led to a merger between SCA and Mölnlycke, the latter being the largest and most powerful of the customer oriented companies.

11. Lundgren (1985). The automization of image analysis has become of increasing interest partly due to the enormous number of pictures that are produced today by satellites, in hospitals, in the control of processes, etc., but also because of the need of giving robots and other automatic processes an ability to "see". In Sweden several research teams, as well as some other organizations and companies, interested in different but related research issues have successively, over the last 10 years, built up what can be called an "automatic image analysis network". The birth process includes both the creation of new companies such as Context Vision and the involvement of established companies like ASEA (Robotics) and Hasselblad. The new companies have mainly universities or other research centres as their origin. For example, there have been a whole series of companies created around the University of Linköping.

12. See note 1.

13. This type of barrier to exit can in many situations be larger than investments in production facilities. From the individual level it is well known, for example in relation to gangs of criminals.

14. This can be compared with Weick's (1969, p. 40ff) discussion of organizing as directed toward removing equivocality from the informational environment.

## REFERENCES

Axelsson, H. and Lövgren, L. Externa relationers betydelse för producent-varuföretagets tekniska utveckling - Block Tool System, En fallstudie. (The importance of external relationships for the technical development of a producer company – the block tools system. A case study). *C-report, Department of Business Administration, University of Uppsala,* (1984).

Björk, L. and Edwall, Å. Teknisck utveckling och marknadsföring inom borrstålsområdet (Technical development and marketing of drill steel). *C-report, Department of Business Administration, University of Uppsala,* (1982).

Brunsson, N. The irrationality of action and action rationality; decisions, ideologies and organizational actions. *Journal of Management Studies,* **19** (1), 29–44, (1982).

Carlson, S. Some notes on the dynamics of international economic integration. *Swedish Journal of Economics,* **72** (1), 21–39, (1970).

Carlsson, B., Dahmén, E., Grufman, A., Josepsson, M. and Örtengren, J. *Teknik och industristruktur – 70-talets ekonomiska kris i historisk belysning* (Technology and Industry Structure – The Crisis of the 70s in the Light of History). IUI, IVA, Stockholm (1979).

Cunningham, M. T. and Kettlewood, K. Source loyalty in freight transport buying. *European Journal of Marketing,* **10** (1), 60–79 (1976).

Hedberg, B. How organizations learn and unlearn. In Nyström, P. and Starbuck, W. (eds), *Handbook of Organizational Design,* Vol. 1. Oxford University Press, Oxford, (1979), pp. 3–27.

Kostiainen, T. Teknisk utveckling genom samarbete – en fallstudie av en ny separeringsprocess (Technical development through cooperation – a case study of a new separation technique). *C-report, Department of Business Administration, University of Uppsala,* (1984).

Littler, D. A. Organization of new product development. Paper presented at the International Research Seminar on Industrial Marketing at Stockholm School of Economics, August 29–31, (1984).

Lundgren, A. Datoriserad bildbehandling i Sverige (Computerized image processing in Sweden). *Working Paper, EFI. Stockholm School of Economics* (1985).

Scott, R. W. *Organizations. Rational, Natural, and Open Systems.* Prentice-Hall, Englewood Cliffs, NJ (1982).

Waluszewski, A. SCA-fallet: tekniska utvecklingsprocessor inom ett företag (The SCA-case: technical development processes within a company). *Working paper, Department of Business Administration, University of Uppsala,* (1985).

Weick, K. E. *The Social Psychology of Organizing.* Addison Wesley, Reading, Mass. (1969) (2nd edn, 1979).

Wind, Y. Industrial source loyalty. *Journal of Marketing Research,* **VIII**, 433–6 (1970).

# 3

# Technological Innovation and the Emergence and Evolution of Industrial Networks: The Case of Digital Image Technology in Sweden

*Anders Lundgren*

## INTRODUCTION

Digital image technology is slowly invading the prevalent structures of western technology. Digital cameras are becoming more readily available, the first Sony Mavica was presented in 1981 and Canon recently introduced a still-video camera on the consumer market. Our everyday newspapers are turning into color magazines, exhibiting more and more color pictures of excellent quality. An ordinary night in front of the television is filled with computer generated images. Even picture phones, first presented in the mid-1960s, are re-appearing as the future of telecommunication. Digital technology is gaining headway in the battle of systems between analog and digital image technology. This technological shift can also be observed beyond the scope of our everyday lives. Radiology departments of hospitals are turning into veritable computer laboratories with CAT-scanners, magnetic resonance imaging, digital image archives and image processing computers. Computer processed satellite images are increasingly being used in the production of maps. And in industrial production robotic and machine vision is writing a new chapter in the development of industrial automation.

It began nearly 30 years ago when groups of researchers, independently, began to experiment using computers to analyze data contained in images. Since then the path to image processing technology of today has been filled with successes and failures and surrounded by futile attempts and unexplored routes. The technology that stands before us is neither optimal nor conclusive. It plainly is and whatever is, is right.

Digital image technology is comprised of a combination of technologies – computer technology, electronics, telecommunications and others – moulded into a

Reprinted with permission from *Advances in International Marketing*, Vol 5, pp 145–170.

technological system of interconnected technologies. The present state of the development of image processing does not result from the work of a single heroic inventor or from a single grand invention. True, some innovations and the deeds of some great men stand out as being pioneering contributions: the work at MIT on perceptrons and on parallel processor computer architecture; the development, at Bell Laboratories, of light sensitive semiconductors; the work of Godfrey Newbold Hounsfield on computer aided tomography and the development of magnetic resonance imaging technology. But, more importantly, behind these more spectacular contributions, we can find series of small interrelated innovations produced by individual actors in different countries and industries. As these actors pushed the frontier of digital image processing they paired with other proponents of the technology, not randomly or according to the pre-existing structures, but according to the emerging logic of the new technological system.

Thus the study of the emergence and evolution of industrial networks necessitates an appreciation of the intricate relationship between technological innovation and social action. The purpose of this article is to develop a framework for the understanding of the emergence and evolution of new industrial networks: the emergence of a new technology, digital image processing, and the emergence and evolution of a Swedish industrial network developing, supporting and producing the emerging technology. Knowledge about the interaction between technological innovation and social action is essential in the formulation of public and business policies concerning technological development.

## TECHNOLOGY IN CONTEXT AND HISTORY MATTERS

Technological innovation cannot be fully understood in isolation. Technologies depend upon and interact with one another in intricate ways. The smallest unit of observation is therefore not a single innovation but interrelated clusterings of innovations (Rosenberg, 1982). Technologies are combined into technological systems of complementary products of different technologies and pieces of knowledge. Only in school do technologies appear in their pure and simple forms. The concept of system suggests that these technologies are combined, not randomly, but according to a specific logic set by the historical development of the system. This logic of a system is by itself a powerful driving force for further development. Innovation is the mother of even more innovation (Kranzberg, 1986). An innovation which solves a problem in one part of the system creates a new problem, a bottleneck, in another part, inducing even further innovation to balance the system (Schumpeter, 1975, 1983; Rosenberg, 1976; Dahmén, 1988; Hughes, 1989).

Without descending into simplistic technological determinism we must still acknowledge the fact that technological development is a prime mover shaping society. But technology is not autonomous. It is the result of human endeavor: the researcher's pursuit of a solution, the businessman's hunt for profit, the politician's quest for power. Thus technology is also socially constructed, laden with the attitudes and values of the society that promotes it (Hughes, 1987). Every innovation is embedded in a specific context, social as well as technological. The development of ploughs cannot be separated from the technique of ploughing, the quality of the soil, the social organization of the community, the holding of draught animals, the nature and quality of available raw materials or the skills of the producers and users of ploughs (White, 1962). Hence, if we are to understand technological development, we must combine insights into the nature of technology with an understanding of the social structure fostering, inventing, changing and using it. In modern dynamic economics the process of change is often perceived as the dynamic interplay between technical and institutional change (Dosi *et al.*, 1988). Hence our primary interest is not in technical and/or social change as such, but in the dynamic interplay of technological change and social action.

The focus is upon the emergence and evolution of new industrial networks defined as technological systems and networks of relationships between actors. Pre-existing technological systems result from the combined historical efforts of different actors acting, independently or jointly to solve locally defined problems. Each actor acts within historically defined boundaries. No actor can efficiently control the complexity of a full technological system. But, as the pay-off of collaborating with an actor controlling complementary technologies is often higher than abstaining from collaboration, individual actors are encouraged to join forces with others, thus forming a community or network of interrelated actors. Actions and interactions undertaken by interrelated actors set the conditions for future development of the technological system. Thus the development of technological systems cannot be separated from the network of actors prompting, supporting and applying the changing technology. The fruitfulness of applying a network perspective on technological development has been shown in several studies (Håkansson, 1987, 1989; Laage-Hellman, 1989; Waluszewski, 1989).

The embeddedness of innovation creates a decisive momentum forcing future development into the same direction as the historic. History really matters. Technological and industrial development chisels a path, historically determined and seemingly inescapable. Yet, the order of things change, obsolete technologies are replaced by new technologies presumably better adapted to the social pattern. Typewriters were replaced by word processors which were replaced by personal computers. The replacement is seldom complete; here and there you will find pockets where the older technology persists. Attributes of the older technology, efficient or not, are often incorporated in the replacing technology. The qwerty-keyboard, developed for the first typewriters and proved inefficient already for the second generation typewriters, is with minor modifications still the dominant design used for computer keyboards. Yet, changes do occur; new technologies emerge and succeedingly replace older technology, but not as suddenly and completely as suggested by revolutionary theory.

The time between original invention and successful implementation of new technology is usually very long. In image processing the original ideas turned up nearly 30 years ago and it is, still, to early to say that the technology is successfully implemented in today's society. Social and technological momentum is accumulated in technological systems and industrial networks. The development is path-dependent (David, 1988). The past holds a stronger grip over the development process than all the future opportunities combined (Håkansson, 1989). Small historical events, such as previous investments in particular technological solutions or a long history of successful interaction between two actors, can lock the evolution of industrial networks into particular paths.

To summarize, it has been argued that technological innovation must be set in its particular context of time and place. It was suggested that the emergence and evolution of new industrial networks resulted from the dynamic interplay of technological systems and networks of exchange relationships. Finally it was proposed that technological and social change are continuing processes of accumulation and change pushing the process into path-dependent evolution. In the next section the nature of industrial networks is further elaborated.

## INDUSTRIAL NETWORKS – TECHNOLOGICAL SYSTEMS AND NETWORKS OF EXCHANGE RELATIONSHIPS

Industrial networks are sets of interrelated actors performing interconnected activities by employing interdependent resources. Industrial networks can be perceived as unions of technological systems and networks of exchange relationships. (The concept networks will in the future be used as an abbreviation for networks of exchange relationships.)

Technological systems are globally defined and characterized by technical interrelatedness and prospects of economic benefits from system integration (David, 1987). Technological systems are more than the interdependence between physical artifacts, such as generators, transformers, transmission lines, consumption measuring devices, and light bulbs and electrical apparatus in the electric light and power system (Mayntz and Hughes, 1988). Embodied in technological systems is an industrial logic of the nature of the production and consumption activities of the system; knowledge of product technology, production methods and natural resources (Hughes, 1987; Johanson and Mattsson, 1992). Technological systems are reflected in locally defined networks of exchange relationships. Inherent in these networks is also institutional structures of government agencies, laws and regulations and common rules of behavior.

Due to the historical pattern of interaction within local networks, a technological system can be reflected differently in different local networks. Local in this context do not suggest that the networks are primarily demarcated by geographical boundaries. They can be extended over several different countries or several local networks can co-exist within the same country. The fact that networks are locally defined simply implies that they can be separated from other networks reflected by the same technological system.

Technological systems can be used to set the boundaries for a specific industrial network. Actors, especially large multi-product firms, are often engaged in several different networks of exchange relationships. The concept of technological systems enables us to delimit industrial networks to focus on particular networks of exchange relationships. But the concept is also essential when it comes to the understanding of the complex interplay between technological innovation and changes in the pattern of interaction in networks. Actors perform acts of innovation to resolve perceived imbalances in the technological system or imbalances in their relationships to other actors. If reproduced, the innovation will be preserved in the technological system, functioning as a driving force for further changes in other parts of the network in focus, as well as in other local networks.

The development and subsequent implementation of radical technological innovation and the emergence and evolution of new industrial networks, thus, embodies two sets of interrelated issues. Firstly, we have the emergence of a new technological system, adapting and integrating the parts of the system to one another. Secondly, we have the emergence of a new network of exchange relationships, coordinating specialization and division of labor between actors, routinizing transactions and distributing the economic surplus, setting the scene for further integration within the technological system. The emergence of new industrial networks will thus neither be purely cumulative nor purely revolutionary. It will most likely be the result of a combination of change and accumulation, where previously independent technological systems and networks become united.

As new industrial networks, through different acts of social and technological innovation, diverge from the path of established technological systems and networks, the innovators – the newly established firms and the different research and development departments – will attempt to accumulate resources to transform the innovations into self-sustaining economic enterprises (Van de Ven and Garud, 1987). Simultaneously, new infra-structures and new industrial networks which connect the interrelated parts of the emerging technological systems must evolve. A new industrial network cannot function in isolation and eventually it must be integrated with the structure from which it emanated. The emergence of a new industrial network can thus be perceived as a continuous process transforming the industry from one structure to another, conveying new technological systems and new networks of exchange relationships.

## A Framework for the Understanding of the Emergence of New Industrial Networks

Evolutionary processes in industrial networks are the subject of several recent studies (Håkansson, 1989, 1992; Lundgren, 1992; Hertz, 1992). In these studies different concepts are used to depict network processes. Yet they share a common view in that they present industrial networks as living, ever-changing, organisms. From these studies we can conclude that the evolution of industrial networks, basically, is composed of two complementary, but contradictory processes; the generating of variety and the organizing of everyday life. Both processes are embedded in the pre-existing network and are thus bound by their historical evolution. The organizing of everyday life refers to the process through which activities and components of everyday life are coordinated, integrated or adapted to one another. The organizing of everyday life is constantly disrupted by the generating of variety; the inducing of innovation or the establishing of new network relationships, motivated by perceived problems. Organizing of everyday life primarily increases the degree of integration within the network while the generating of variety induces heterogenization and disintegration. Specific evolutionary patterns result from these two parallel processes. As these are likely to be dominant in different periods of time we can expect the evolution of a network to move from integrative to disintegrative back to integrative, conveying a transforming network structure.

Two different metaphors would be conceivable in the study of the emergence of new industrial networks. First of all, we could perceive it as a biological life-cycle, where the conditions and the interconnectedness of the complex system is set from the beginning. When properly fostered and nurtured, industrial networks will move through the stages of birth, adolescence, growth, maturity, declining years bent with age, and eventually death, bringing prosperity to the society. The policy implications are rather obvious; the state should provide support during birth and adolescence, it should facilitate and balance the death process. The state should accumulate resources to do this by collecting taxes during growth, maturity, and declining years. The individual actors should strive to decrease the time span and cost of birth and adolescence, extend the time and increase the profits of growth and maturity, and manage the decline, thus exhausting final profits and timing the dismantling of the dying system. A modern expression of this metaphor is technological trajectories (Dosi, 1988).

Against the biological life-cycle we can put another more action oriented metaphor, where we do not assume that the conditions and interconnectedness of the complex system are set from the beginning. In fact we assume that this is what evolution is really all about: the creation of the environment through individual action, the incessant formation, establishment and adaptation of the interconnectedness of the technological system and the interdependencies of the industrial network (Gherardi, 1991; March, 1981). Not in consecutive order, but simultaneously, constantly expanding and contracting the industrial system, changing, integrating or disintegrating it. The emergence of a new industrial system is thus not characterized by a sequence of life, but by life itself: with ascending growing, maturing declining and dying elements constantly co-existing. Here, policy implications do not come as easily.

The study of the development of digital image processing in Sweden suggests that the emergence and evolution of a new industrial network can be described as consisting of three parallel processes: genesis, coalescence and dissemination. Genesis represents the creation of variety: the independent, initiation of several different research and development projects and the origination of the new technological system. These projects were initiated within different technological systems and in different networks of exchange relationships and the actors of the emerging network were scattered geographically, functionally and technologically. As the projects deviated from their origins the proponents of image processing initiated search processes for support and complementary resources outside the specific centers of origin. As the proponents of image processing commenced to interact with one another, the emerging network coalesced into a close-knit community of complementary and competing image processing firms, who all strived to develop image processing to a multi-purpose technology. As the industrial network coalesced, the parts of the new technological system were adapted to one another, the technological system of digital image processing was integrated, and several different image processing systems were produced. Hence, coalescence represents an integrative process in the emergence of industrial networks. In adapting the technology to the specific needs of different users, thereby inducing processes of learning by using and exploiting complementary investments made outside the close community of image processing firms, the image processing network disseminated. Dissemination represents a disintegrative process and it refers to the extension of the industrial network backwards and forwards connecting it with the industrial networks of suppliers and users.

To summarize this discussion, the emergence of new industrial networks is treated as a combination of three parallel processes of genesis, coalescence and dissemination. Even if these processes are omnipresent, each one can dominate in different periods of time. In the emergence of the image processing network it has been found that they dominate in consecutive order. For a graphic representation of the model see Fig. 1. A remaining question is: what determines the shift from the domination of one process to another?

Changes in this structure can be analyzed by using a variety of techniques. In the next section two techniques – graph theory and social network analysis – are presented.

## Network Analysis

Networks, industrial as well as social, are complex and messy. Almost any empirical study of networks puts extremely high demands on the analytical skill and effort of the observer. These demands increase with increased size of the network in focus. For very large networks, analysis becomes nearly impossible. Seemingly simple, basic questions, such as which actors and relationships are to be included or excluded, produce lengthy and imprecise answers, discouraging researchers from further inquiry into the nature of total network structure. Maybe, this explains why studies of dyadic relationships by far outnumber total network studies or why the number of conceptual network studies by far exceeds the number of empirical. Nonetheless, total network studies can provide important insights into the dynamics of industrial change and into the attributes of industrial networks, technological systems and networks of exchange relationships.

Graph theory and its progenies of social network methods offer sets of different methods through which the structure of networks can be unravelled (Sprenger and

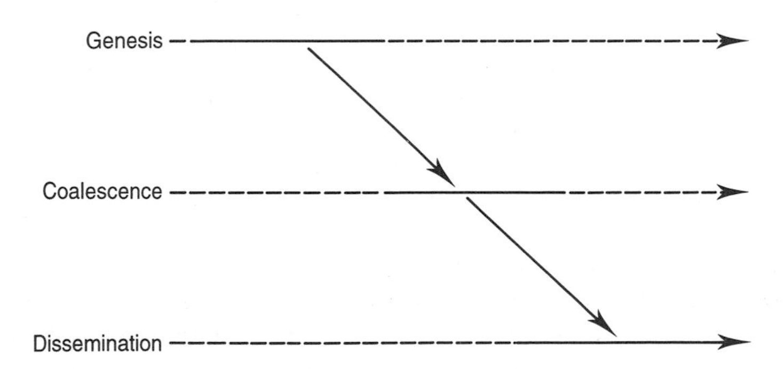


Fig. 1. A framework for the understanding of the emergence of new industrial networks.

Stokman, 1989). Social network methods can be used both to illuminate features of the total network structure and to comprehend particular components of the whole. Most commonly network analysis is employed on three different levels of analysis. First, it is used to characterize the structure of the total network. Second, it is used to identify and characterize subgroups within the total network. Here two different approaches can be distinguished: one in which subgroups of actors are more closely related to each other than to outside actors; and one in which a subgroup is defined as sets of actors holding similar network positions. Finally, network analysis is applied to characterize the specific network positions and roles of individual actors (Knoke and Kuklinski, 1982).

Network analysis, by itself, seldom produces conclusive answers to specific research questions. It is most often applied to provide new insightful descriptions of networks or to increase understanding of already existing, often thick, descriptions of network processes. In this article network analysis is employed to study the outcome of network processes as changing network structures. Centrality analysis and EBLOC-analysis (Everett, 1983), a form of cluster analysis, will be used to generate representations of the structures of the emerging industrial network in different periods of time.

## THE EMERGENCE AND EVOLUTION OF A NEW IMAGE PROCESSING NETWORK IN SWEDEN

Digital image processing is an example of a high technology where Sweden has been able to build a strong reputation in spite of the lack of an electronics industry, and the fact that the technology was developed simultaneously with the decay of the once so promising Swedish computer industry. Sweden is today one of the leading nations when it comes to developing, producing and applying digital image processing.

### Digital Image Processing

If we are to study technological innovation in image processing we must have, at least, a basic understanding of the technology in focus. Digital image processing is a multi-purpose technology, enabling the computer processing of information contained in natural images. It emanates from the progress within computer technology, opto-electronics and telecommunications. Using the taxonomy suggested by Freeman and Perez (1988), digital image technology can be characterized as a combination of radical and incremental innovations, constituting changes in a technological system. Digital image technology is furthermore one part of a technological revolution – the battle of systems between analog and digital technology.

In general an image processing system consists of an image reading instrument, a computer and an output unit. Within this general system we can observe a high degree of variation. The image reading instrument can be both analog or digital, varying from a video camera to nuclear magnetic resonance. The output can be produced as a yes or no decision, an instruction to an industrial robot, or a digitally processed image. The computer used to perform the actual image processing, connecting input and output, can be anything from personal to specialized image processing computers. Four basic technological problems of digital image processing can be identified. First, the images must be digital or converted from analog to digital. Second, the output must be adapted to the specific application. Third, as the information content in an image by far exceeds the information content in symbols, image processing requires much faster computers with larger memory than what is offered by ordinary computers. Fourth, these three parts must be integrated into a well-functioning system. A schematic picture of image processing technology is presented in Fig. 2.

Let us now take a closer look at technological innovation and the genesis, coalescence and dissemination of the image processing network in Sweden.

## Genesis

Image processing emerged in the late 1950s and early 1960s as the development of solutions to specific problems around five centers of origin: optical character recognition, satellite reconnaissance, radiology, the analysis of images in different research laboratories and picture telephones. As the capabilities within these technologies were developed in different countries, digital image processing emerged in different forms in different countries.

Sweden did not exhibit equal strength in the five centers of origin of digital image processing and all the problems which propelled the acts of innovation were not equally immediate. In Sweden image processing emerged around five centers, the most important being the National Defence Research Institute (FOA) which initiated research on satellite reconnaissance and remote sensing in 1966. The research at

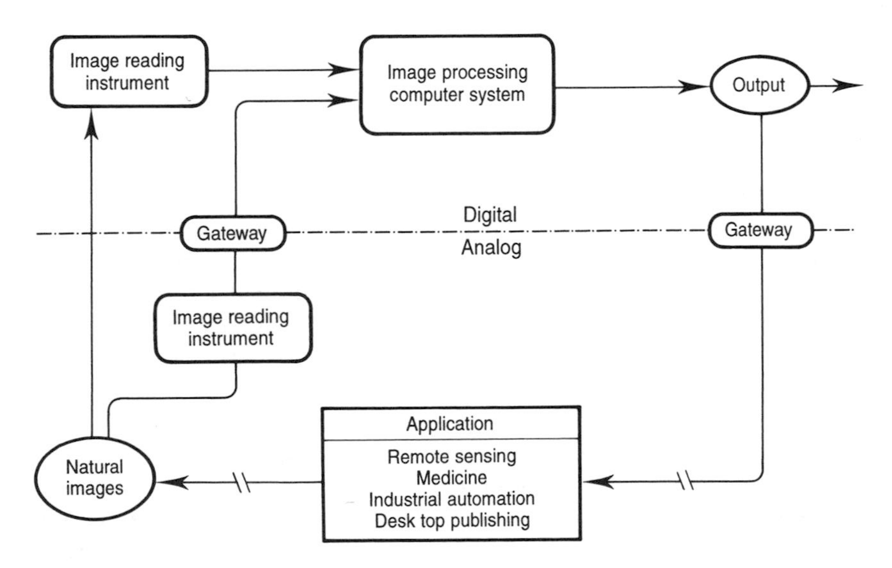


Fig. 2. A schematic representation of digital image technology.

FOA was not provoked by a pressing military need to improve the analysis of reconnaissance images. Rather, knowledge of the problems spurring the development in the United States and other countries motivated FOA to develop image processing addressing civilian problems. Two centers, one based in the chemistry institution at Gothenburg University, and the other in a physics institution in Stockholm (Physics IV), developed image reading instruments to mechanize the previously manual feeding of image data into computers. The fourth center consisted of the research laboratories in the steel industry using an image processing system of English origin to measure non-metallic inclusions in steel. The fifth center comprised of cooperative efforts of L. M. Ericsson and Swedish Telecom to develop a picture telephone.

The fact that image processing emerged from multiple centers of origin should not come as a surprise. After all, the social and technological momentum accumulated in different countries and different industries are rather similar, and it would be more surprising if we were to find only a single center of origin of a new technology.

The processing of images in computers entail two sets of basic problems. First of all the information contained in images must be registered in digital form and secondly the huge amount of information contained in images requires computers with higher processing capacity and larger memories (Dyring, 1984). The first wave of research and development primarily addressed the problem of digitalization of images. As solutions to this problem became available, the problem of inadequate computer processing capacities turned more critical. In 1972 a second wave of image processing development emerged primarily addressing this problem. The second wave, in Sweden, was spurred by the research at FOA, the introduction of mini-computers and micro-processors, the launching of the ERTS1-satellite producing digital images, and the erection of the new university in Linköping.

Swedish industry participated willingly in different projects related to the development of image processing. Especially important was the emerging computer industry, which manufactured most of the image processing systems developed at this time.

The independent initiation of a cluster of related research projects, combining new technologies with previous experience and hence slowly departing from their source of origin, describes the genesis of the Swedish image processing network. The genesis can neither be associated with a single point in time nor with isolated activities of technological change. The genesis of a new industrial network is a process over time, involving complex sets of transfer of technology, innovation, diffusion of innovation and adaptation of innovation to local settings. And as we can see from the developments within FOA, the transfer of problems can be of equal importance to the generation of new technologies as the transfer of the technology itself.

Genesis represents the creation of variety and thus it induces heterogeneity. Creation of variety – radical and incremental innovation and changes in the network of exchange relationships – transpires continuously in industrial networks. What characterizes then the emergence process dominated by genesis? First of all, it is marked by the concentration in time of a number of interrelated innovations. Secondly and more importantly, it is characterized by the identification of a new technological system; of the interconnectedness of components in the pre-existing structure and a number of radical and incremental innovations being something different from the pre-existing technological systems. In studies of the development of individual products, invention or innovation is commonly regarded as the starting point. When we turn our eyes towards the evolution of technological systems we, however, often find that the existence of a single individual innovation is hardly enough to push the evolution of a whole system. Rather it is the identification of the technological system itself that pushes the genesis of the industrial network. Identification by itself, however, is not enough. The identification must furthermore be shared by a sufficient number of actors.

In the emerging image processing network in Sweden, FOA played a decisive role in identifying the technological system and spreading this to other actors. The emerging network was, in the beginning of 1975, a loosely interconnected network of a heterogeneous group of actors, performing a wide range of activities. The most central actors were FOA, representatives of the Swedish computer industry, and Physics IV.

## Coalescence

The genesis process initiated a range of research and development related to image processing. Combined, the emerging research and development activities in Sweden represented the essential parts of the technological system of image processing: image reading, computer systems and software for image processing, image transmission and application specific experience. Individual research groups could neither control nor beget the development of the underlying technologies, nor were they able to incorporate and stay on the scientific and technological frontier in all of the essential parts of image processing. The technological system of a country is forged by the accomplishments of the individual actors. Simultaneously, the outcome of each individual research and development endeavor is to a large extent dependent on the overall development of the technological system. The outcomes of different development activities are thus interdependent and each actor can increase the probability of success or decrease the risk for failure by cooperating with other actors within the same technological system. Cooperation between actors undertaking complementary research and development induces increased integration within the system. As actors within the technological system begin to cooperate to get access to complementary research and development and to adapt the parts of the technology to each other, the emergent network will coalesce.

The existence of a critical mass of similar and complementary research and development activities is a necessary condition for the evolutionary process to transcend from the domination of genesis into coalescence. In digital image processing, a critical mass of activities was accumulated during the 1970s; in other fields, such as image scanner technology, it was not. The presence of a critical mass suggests an availability of potential partners with whom it was possible to cooperate. As some of the actors of digital image processing began to cooperate, the emerging network coalesced; attracted by a common set of solutions, the involved actors deviated from the industrial networks of their origins. Thus they coalesced into a recognizable network resembling the technological system of digital image processing. Not all early research ventures were attracted to the core of image processing development. The growing computer industry was addressing other pressing problems and image processing was left to others.

As the image processing network coalesced, the actors grew closer to other actors engaged in the development of digital image processing and further away from their origins. The coalescence process implies contraction and contains a tendency towards isolation. This process is to some extent reflected in the fact that more image processing systems were sold in Sweden between 1960–1970 than between 1970–1980. For the network to coalesce and the actors to deviate from their origins, the actors must attract new resources: research and development must be legitimate to ensure continuing evolution of the network. Coalescence is thus a dual process of forming a new industrial network and legitimizing the activities of the network to the outside world.

Digital image processing was legitimized in Sweden through the existence of several actors pursuing similar and complementary research and development and in 1976 they all joined forces and instituted the Swedish Association for Automatic Image Analysis. As digital image processing technology was legitimized and the industrial network coalesced, an increasing amount of resources was devoted to continued development. Public policy previously assumed a passive role; it now actively supported the rise of what was thought to have the capacity to become a new Swedish frontline technology. In 1979 the National Swedish Board for Technical Development (STU) initiated a five-year special program concentrated on the development of image processing technology. The program prompted the researchers to take their projects to the industry, and in the beginning of the 1980s several image processing firms spun-off from the university research.

In the coalescence phase, an industrial network containing the basic elements of the technological system emerged. As the actors strived to adapt the parts of the system to one another, the network was structured accordingly, and it became more integrated. At the end of the coalescence phase, the spin-offs induced a heterogenization within the network. Actors developed specific positions in the network and FOA lost its central position to a group of university research actors. Public policy also assumed a central role in the evolution of the network by legitimizing and supporting the development of digital image technology.

## Dissemination

The coalescence phase involved a minimum of specialization and division of labor which was the major ingredient of the dissemination phase. The critical problem was no longer to adapt the parts of the primary technological system of image processing to one another. Instead the challenge was to adapt the whole system to the surrounding technological systems, thus connecting the investments made in image processing with complementary investments made in other fields, such as cartography, computer aided design and newspaper production.

When the image processing firms established exchange relationships with actors outside the focal network, they faced other needs than purely technological. This did not come as a surprise; most of the firms had adapted their systems to their perception of the needs of the users. The use of the image processing system under normal conditions induced processes of learning by using, requiring further adaptation, integrating previously unrelated technological systems, but also extending the applicability of the new technology to the specific usage. These processes required concentrated interaction and as the actors were only able to handle a limited number of exchange relationships, a concentration towards specific applications was induced. The firms abandoned the vision of general machine vision and the instruments were adapted to specific applications. As different firms concentrated their efforts on different and more specific applications of image processing, the network disseminated towards other networks. The path dependency of technological innovation is obvious in that the Swedish network of image processing acquired a relative strength in the fields from which it originated: remote sensing, industrial automation, image transmission and the development of image processing computer systems.

The image processing actors did not only engage in exchangeable relationships with users. As they engaged in exchanges with suppliers, a pattern of exchange relationships evolved where the suppliers assumed a greater responsibility in the production of image processing equipment.

Following a line of reasoning similar to the above, we might conclude that an existence of a critical mass of complementary investments in related industrial networks is a necessary condition for coalescence to transcend into dissemination. Previously the problem had been to legitimize digital image technology as such. The problem during dissemination was primarily to legitimize specific applications of the technology.

The development of image processing technology, the introduction of new products in the field and evolving standards, enabled actors to focus specifically upon parts of the technological system. The technological system could be integrated through exchange relationships. The actors assumed certain roles and positions in relation to other actors controlling complementary resources. Thus as the network disseminated backwards to suppliers of components and forward to users, the suppliers and users were connected through specialization and division of labor. Where the network previously had been horizontally structured, it became increasingly vertically integrated. The dissemination phase was dominated by heterogenization, integrating the industrial network vertically. This vertical structuring was, however, balanced by the merger, in 1988, of three of the largest image processing firms in Sweden, Context Vision, Imtec and Teragon Systems. The network took the final leap from research and development to industrial production. During the 1980s the industrial firms accumulated strength and in 1989 they held the most central positions in the image processing network.

## STRUCTURAL ANALYSIS

The emergence of a digital image processing network in Sweden has been treated as an evolutionary process comprised of three parallel processes: genesis, coalescence and dissemination. Genesis represented the identification of the new technological system and the mobilization of resources to solve specific problems. Coalescence embodied the formation and legitimation of the new technological system and the structuring of the existing resources to solve more general sets of problems. Finally, dissemination involved the adaptation of digital image processing to other technologies coordinating sets of technologies into functioning systems.

The structure of the evolving industrial network supporting the development and application of digital image processing can be assumed to have emerged as a heterogeneous set of loosely connected actors. As the network evolved it became more tightly connected as the actors were attracted to each other by their common interest; the network contracted into a homogeneous core consisting of the prime proponents of Swedish digital image processing. The homogeneous image processing network was dissolved through the extension of the connections backwards to the suppliers and forward to the users, producing a more disseminated network.

How do then these general observations compare to the network of exchange relationships in different periods of time? Social network analysis of the structure of the image processing network in 1975, 1983, and 1989 confirms the above assumed pattern of evolution. In Table 1 some traditional network measures are presented. And we can see that the image processing network becomes increasingly integrated over the three phases of genesis, coalescence and dissemination. In 1989 the network density has decreased suggesting the dissemination of the network. This interpretation is consistent with the changes in the mean and variance of point centrality.

Social network analysis is not unproblematic. Graph centrality measures are highly dependent on the number of actors. The point centrality measure used, degree, does not portray the full magnitude of actor centrality. So, even if both the graph and the point centrality measures are pointing in the same direction, the interpretation of the analysis can at best be suggestive.

Table 1. Point and graph centrality of the Swedish image processing network 1975, 1983 and 1989

| | 1975 | 1983 | 1989 |
|---|---|---|---|
| Number of actors | 40 | 57 | 80 |
| Point centrality[1] | | | |
| Mean | 2.25 | 3.193 | 2.65 |
| Variance | 2.188 | 7.384 | 2.65 |
| Graph centrality | | | |
| Density[2] | 0.058 | 0.057 | 0.034 |
| Integration[3] | 90 | 182 | 212 |

*Notes*: [1]The measure used for point centrality is degree, that is the number of direct connections to other actors a specific actor has.
[2]Density is a measure of the connectedness of the network, where the number of actual connections is divided by the total number of possible connections.
[3]Integration is a measure of the distance between all actors in the network.

To take the structural analysis of the network further we can perform different types of cluster analysis: here EBLOC-analysis has been used to analyze the structure of the relationships. In EBLOC-analysis actors are clustered into blocks, where actors within a block are more connected to each other than to actors outside the block. The analysis also distinguishes the relationships or actors connecting different blocks. The Swedish image processing network in 1975, delineated in Fig. 3, exhibits some interesting features. The network is comprised of five loosely connected blocks that, together with some peripheral actors, represent the major components of image processing technology: image reading, image processing, image communication and different areas of application. The five blocks exhibit a relatively high degree of internal heterogeneity.

In 1983 the network had coalesced (see Fig. 4) forming a core of proponents of image processing technology. Some actors or groups of actors did not coalesce with the community of image processing proponents, and these, the metallurgy block, Semyre Electronics and ASEA assumed a more inferior position in the future development of the technology. We can also observe how the core block consisted of both research organizations and business firms.

In 1989 (see Fig. 5) the coalesced network had disseminated, exhibiting a more complex structure of blocks and groups of actors. Contrary to the blocks of 1975, these blocks were homogeneous to a greater extent. We can also see the total separation of research organizations and business firms.

Looking at individual actors in the network it can be seen that different actors have played important roles in different stages of development. Fig. 6 exhibits different patterns of change in the importance of actors. We can see that the most central and significant actor in the denomination of genesis, FOA, assumes a less significant role in the domination of coalescence and dissemination. Inferior actors in the early development are gaining strength in the later stages. This suggests that actors are not

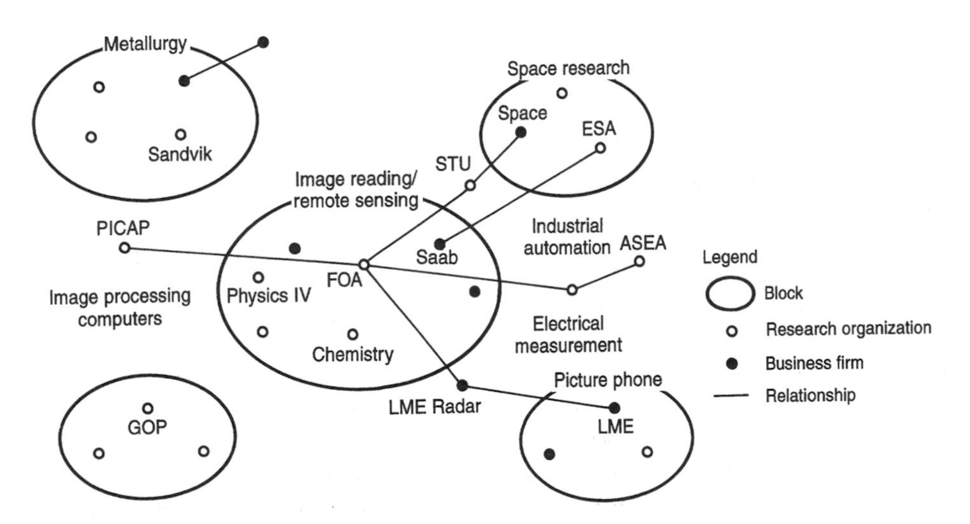


Fig. 3. The image processing network in 1975. (Note that the graphical representation is not intended to depict the centrality of individual actors.)

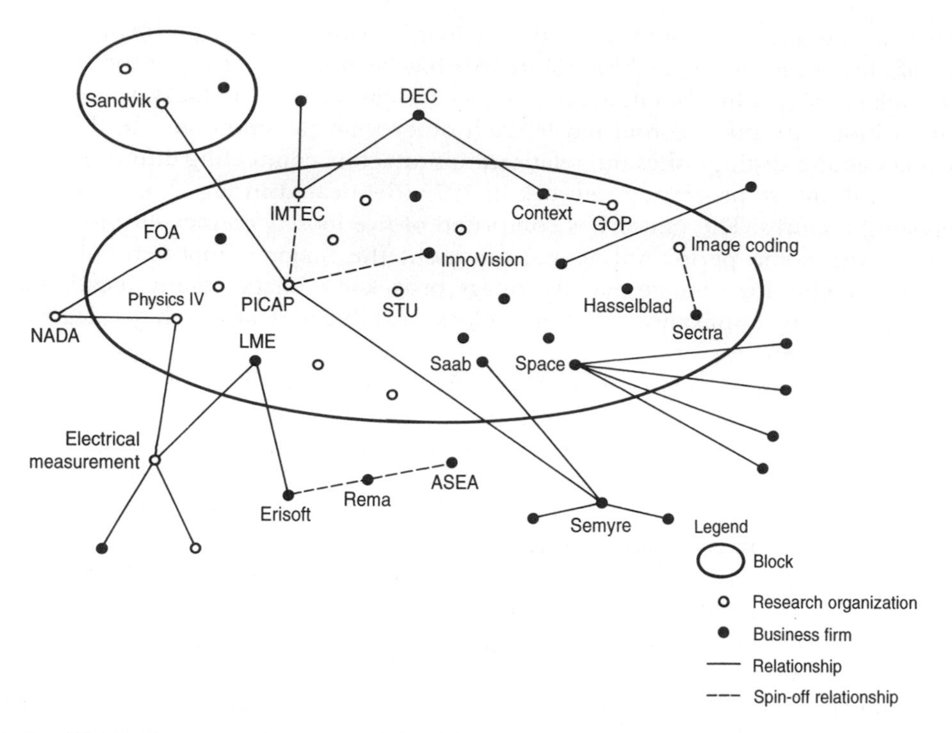


Fig. 4. The image processing network in 1983. (Note that the graphical representation is not intended to depict the centrality of individual actors.)

only complementary in terms of technological systems, but that they also perform complementary roles in the emergence of new industrial networks. It furthermore indicates the problem of picking winners in research and development games.

## CONCLUSIONS

The study of digital image technology in Sweden suggests that the emergence of a new industrial network is a doubly dynamic process of creation of an environment which can be understood as an interplay between networks of acting and interacting actors and technological systems. The emergence of the image processing network is comprised of three parallel processes: genesis, coalescence and dissemination. Genesis represented the creation of novelty and variety; coalescence portrayed the formation of a community, a network, for the establishing of the emerging technological system; and dissemination depicted the establishing of image processing in relation to complementary industrial networks.

Genesis, coalescence and dissemination were suggested to correspond to three processes in the emergence of new technological systems: identification, legitimation and adaptation. Even if it was stressed that these processes were parallel, we could observe how they dominated the evolution in consecutive order. If the technological

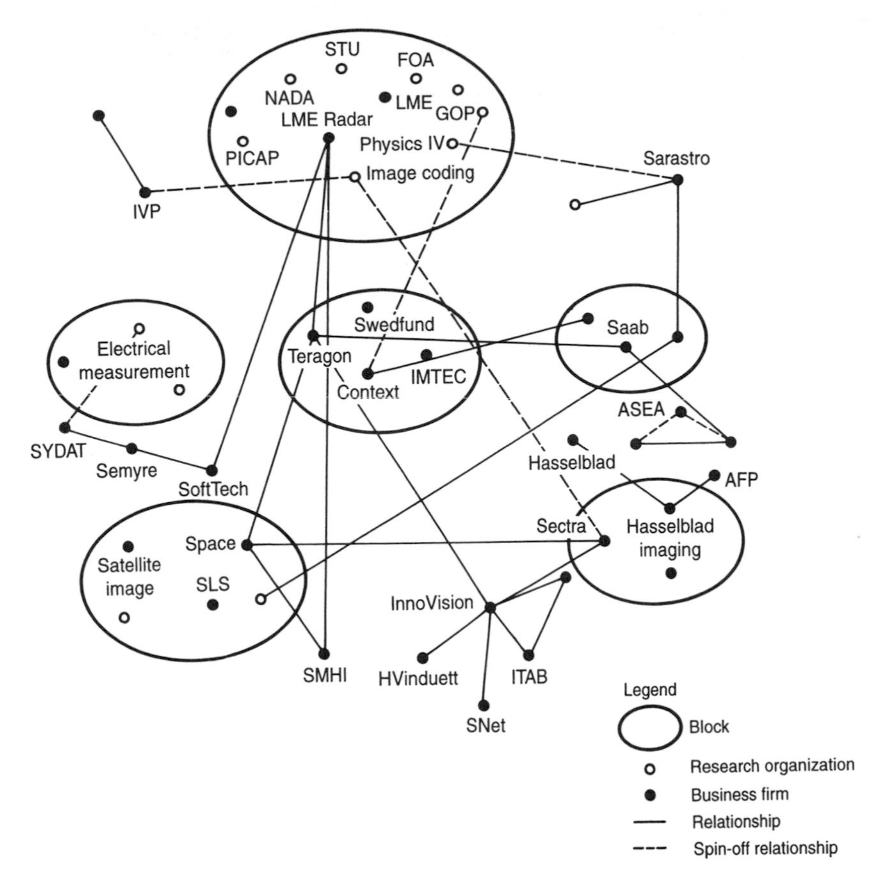


Fig. 5. The image processing network in 1989. (Note that the graphical representation is not intended to depict the centrality of individual actors.)

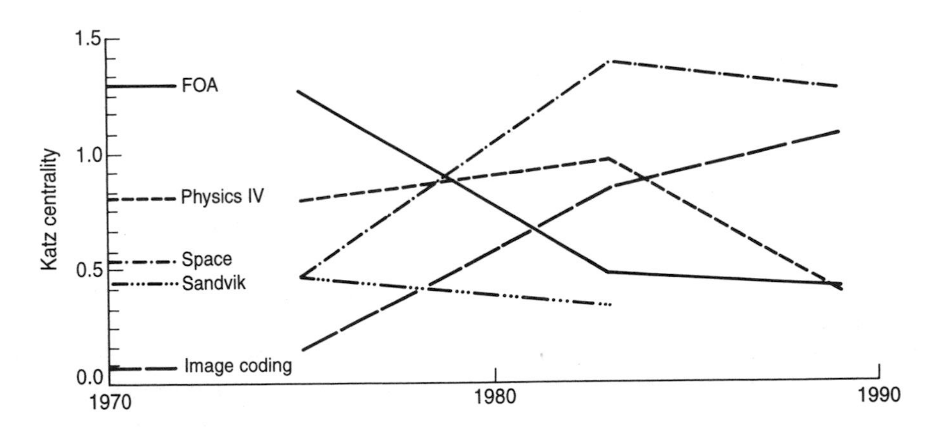


Fig. 6. Patterns of changes in centrality of actors.

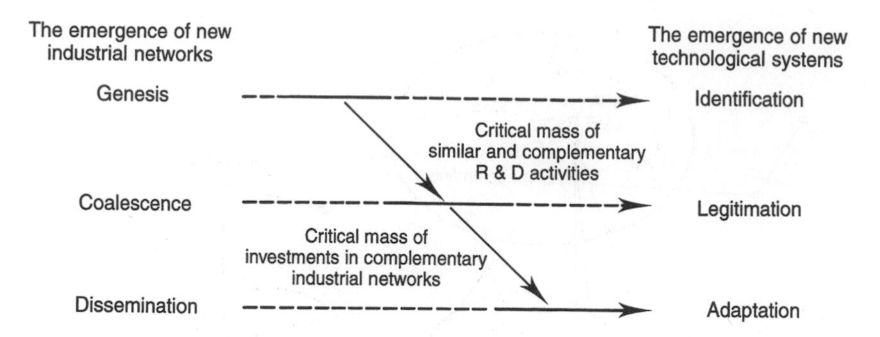


Fig. 7. A framework for the understanding of the emergence of new industrial networks and technological systems.

system were not continuously identified or legitimated, there would be no force holding the industrial network together in the adaptation of the technological system to complementary technological systems and the industrial network would be dissolved or abandoned. Critical masses of similar and complementary research and development ventures and of investments in complementary industrial networks, were necessary conditions for the domination of one process to transcend into the domination of another. For a summary of the suggested framework, see Fig. 7.

The suggested framework is based upon the empirical observation of the development of digital image processing in Sweden. It does not imply that this is an optimal route. It would probably be more efficient if these processes occurred simultaneously, but as people often proceed sequentially in solving problems, this might be the only available route. Neither does this imply that all emergent networks will follow similar paths. It is however plausible that most cases of the emergence of new industrial networks will unfold in a manner similar to that of digital processing in Sweden.

The emergence of new industrial networks has been perceived as a process where the industrial network is created through the acts of individual actors. Hence, individual actors must build a strong position of their own at the same time they have to participate in the evolution of the industrial network as a whole. Since different problems are critical in different phases of development, the interaction strategies of the actors must vary accordingly. Public policy should not only be geared towards the support of individual projects, but also towards the structuring of the network as a whole. This would, however, require a higher degree of flexibility of public and private policy towards new technology than is normally the case.

As was discussed earlier, digital image technology is slowly invading the prevalent structures of western technology. We have not yet reached the state where the predominant analog image technology has been made completely obsolete. Digital image processing is not yet fully established in our society and the actors of the Swedish network have not yet reached a position where self-sustained growth can be taken for granted. But this study shows that even in a small country like Sweden, high technology can emerge. The emergence of an image processing network in Sweden was partly a result of the interaction between the emerging new technology and the emerging new network. It was also partly the result of the barriers to develop image processing within the computer industry. As the barriers to developing image processing in the computer industry are dissolved, it might be expected that the networks of digital image processing will continue to be restructured.

## REFERENCES


Dahmén, E. Development blocks in industrial economics. *Scandinavian Economic History Review*, **1**, 3–14 (1988).

David, P. A. Some new standards for the economics of standardization in the information age. In Dasgupta, P. and Stoneman, P. (eds), *Economic Policy and Technological Performance*. Cambridge University Press, New York (1987), pp. 206–39.

David, P. Path-dependence: putting the past into the future of economics. *Institute for Mathematical Studies in the Social Sciences, Stanford University, Technical Report, No. 533* (1988).

Dosi, G. Sources, procedures and microeconomic effects of innovation. *Journal of Economic Literature*, **XXVI** (September) (1988).

Dosi, G., Freeman, C., Nelson, R., Silverberg, G. and Soete, L. (eds) *Technical Change and Economic Theory*. Pinters Publishers, London (1988).

Dyring, E. *Nolla etta bild – Den nya bildrevolutionen* (The Zero One Image – The New Image Revolution). Prisma, Stockholm (1984).

Everett, M. EBLOC: A graph-theoretic blocking algorithm. *Social Networks*, **5**, 323–46 (1983).

Freeman, C. and Perez, C. Structural crises of adjustment, business cycles and investment behaviour. In Dosi, G., Freeman, C., Nelson, R., Silverberg, G. and Soete, L. (eds), *Technical Change and Economic Theory*. Pinters Publishers, London (1988), pp. 38–66.

Gherardi, S. *Development and Decline in Organizational Analogies – A Critical Review*, Working Paper, Dipartimento di Politica Sociale, Universita' Degli Studi Di Trento (1991).

Hertz, S. Towards more integrated industrial systems. In Axelsson, B. and Easton, G. (eds), *Industrial Networks – A New View of Reality*. Routledge, London (1992).

Hughes, T. P. The evolution of large technological systems. In Bijker, W. B., Hughes, T. P. and Pinch, T. J. (eds), *The Social Construction of Technological Systems*. MIT Press, Cambridge, Mass (1987), pp. 51–82.

Hughes, T. P. *The American Genesis*. Viking Penguin, New York (1989).

Håkansson, H. Evolution processes in industrial networks. In Axelsson, B. and Easton, G. (eds), *Industrial Networks – A New View of Reality*, Routledge, London (1992).

Håkansson, H. *Corporate Technological Behaviour – Co-operation and Networks*. Routledge, London (1989).

Håkansson, H. (ed.). *Industrial Technological Development*. Croom Helm, London (1987).

Johanson, J. and Mattsson, L.-G. Network positions and strategic action – an analytical framework. In Axelsson, B. and Easton, G. (eds), *Industrial Networks – A New View of Reality*. Routledge, London (1992).

Kranzberg, M. Technology and history: "Kranzberg's laws". *Technology and Culture*, **27**, 544–60 (1986).

Knoke, D. and Kuklinski, J. H. *Network Analysis*. Sage Publications, Beverly Hills, CA (1982).

Laage-Hellman, J. *Technological Development in Industrial Networks*. Department of Business Studies, Uppsala University (1989).

Lundgren, A. Coordination and mobilization processes in industrial networks. In Axelsson, B. and Easton, G. (eds), *Industrial Networks – A New View of Reality*. Routledge, London (1992).

Lundgren, A. *Technological Innovation and Industrial Evolution – The Emergence of an Image Processing Network in Sweden*. Doctoral Dissertation, Stockholm School of Economics, Stockholm (1991).

March, J. G. Footnotes to organizational change. *Administrative Science Quarterly*, **26**, 563–77 (1981).

Mayntz, R. and Hughes, T. P. (eds) *The Development of Large Technical Systems*. Campus Verlag, Frankfurt am Main (1988).

Rosenberg, N. *Perspectives on Technology.* Cambridge University Press, New York (1976).
Rosenberg, N. *Inside the Black Box: Technology and Economics.* Cambridge University Press, New York (1982).
Schumpeter, J. A. *Capitalism, Socialism and Democracy.* Harper, New York (1975).
Schumpeter, J. A. *The Theory of Economic Development.* Transaction Books, New Brunswick (1983).
Sprenger, C. J. A. and Stokman, F. N. (eds). *GRADAP, Manual, Version 2.0. iec ProGAMMA.* Groningen, The Netherlands (1989).
Van de Ven, A. H. and Garud, R. A framework for understanding the emergence of new industries. *Discussion paper N66, Strategic Management Research Center,* University of Minnesota (1987).
Waluszewski, A. *Framväxten av en ny mekanisk massateknik* (The Emergence of a New Pulp Technology). Department of Business Studies, Uppsala University (1989).
White, L., Jr. *Medieval Technology and Social Change.* Oxford University Press, London (1962).

# 4

# Dyadic Business Relationships and Customer Technologies

*Lars Hallén, Jan Johanson and Nazeem Seyed-Mohamed*

## INTRODUCTION

While technology has a prominent role in organization theory, its absence in marketing theory is conspicuous. This is particularly surprising in business marketing as the marketing concept so strongly stresses the need of the customer and the lesson from organization theory is that technology is one of the main factors determining the needs of the industrial customer.

Moreover, research reported on the role of technology in marketing deals typically with issues related to the marketing of high technology, diffusion of technology and buyer acceptance of new technology (Capon and Glazer, 1987; Fiocca and Snehota, 1989; Gatignon and Robertson, 1989; von Hippel, 1978; Robertson and Gatignon, 1986; Shanklin and Ryans, 1984). Although one line of organization research correspondingly concerns the development and introduction of new technology, mainstream research on organization and technology focuses on the organizational consequences of different technologies (Gerwin, 1981). The underlying assumption is that the technology poses demands on the organization so that firms with different technologies need different organization structures. Although the issues regarding new technology are interesting, there is reason to assume that much marketing takes place within fairly stable technological structures and that the marketing implications of such structures are highly relevant.

Studies of business markets have shown that suppliers and customers in such markets often establish and develop lasting relationships with each other (Arndt, 1979; Carlton, 1986; Gadde and Mattsson, 1987; Jackson, 1985; Wind, 1970). It has

The authors thank the researchers of the international IMP Group, who conducted the empirical study with them, and Docent Dag Sörbom, Department of Statistics, Uppsala University, who offered valuable methodological help.

Funding was provided by the Swedish Council for Research in the Humanities and Social Sciences and by The Bank of Sweden, Tercentenary Foundation.

Reprinted by permission from the publisher, Dyadic Business Relationships and Customer Technologies in the *Journal of Business-to-Business Marketing*, Vol 1, No 4, pp 63–90.

been argued that such relationships have strong managerial implications (Levitt, 1983). From a managerial point of view it seems to be important to differentiate between different conditions that may have a bearing on the management of relationships. The objective of this paper is consequently to investigate whether the technology of the customer firm has an impact on business relationships between suppliers and customers in business-to-business markets. By a business relationship we mean an exchange relationship between two firms doing business with each other.

The first section focuses on interaction in business relationships between suppliers and customers and posits some connections between exchange and adaptation processes in such relationships. Against that background the second section discusses some relevant parts of the contingency theory of organization and derives a structural model for the analysis of customer technology and interfirm business relationships. After a description of the empirical basis the model is tested empirically in four steps. In a final section the results are discussed and some implications for research and marketing are elaborated.

## CUSTOMER–SUPPLIER INTERACTION IN BUSINESS RELATIONSHIPS

It has been shown that business relationships between actors in business markets can be analyzed fruitfully by using a social exchange framework (Anderson and Narus, 1984, 1990; Dwyer, Schurr and Oh, 1987; Håkansson and Östberg, 1975; Håkansson, 1982; Hallén, Johanson and Seyed-Mohamed, 1991; Webster, 1979). This framework focuses on the social interaction between two interdependent actors over time as they exchange benefits with each other (Blau, 1964; Emerson, 1962; Homans, 1958; Thibaut and Kelley, 1959). The interdependence between the actors is based on the abilities, needs, and evaluative criteria each actor brings to the dyad as well as the ways in which these are related to each other (Kelley and Thibaut, 1978).

According to this view dyadic business relationships can be analyzed as interconnected exchange and adaptation. Exchange is the core concept in marketing and does not need any explication (Bagozzi, 1975; Kotler, 1972). Adaptation, defined in this interfirm perspective, concerns the ways in which the interacting firms, by modifying their ways of performing their activities, bring about match between their respective needs and capabilities (Hallén, Johanson and Seyed-Mohamed, 1991; Newcomb, Turner and Converse, 1952). Thus, in a dyadic business relationship, where the two firms bring to the dyad efficiency and profitability criteria, needs and capabilities rooted in complex systems of interrelated products, production processes, logistic as well as administrative procedures, an important element in interaction entails adaptations of those systems by one or both of the parties so as to achieve a better fit and more efficient exchange. The interfirm adaptations coordinate the activities of the two firms, but they also tie the parties to each other. In a business context adaptation can be regarded as enabling the more primary product exchange. Very generally, it can therefore be expected that adaptations are conditioned by product exchange requirements.

The social exchange framework implies that an ongoing relationship between two firms evolves towards becoming a solitary dyad (Dwyer, Schurr and Oh, 1987). This is clearly demonstrated in the model of Hallén, Johanson and Seyed-Mohamed (1991), in which the parties mutually adapt to each other in a trust forming process. Thus, a loose interorganizational relation develops through the social exchange process into a distinctive interorganizational dyad that can be viewed as an organizational unit having its own organizational characteristics. Moreover, in this process the social interaction between the firms is a critical element enabling both interfirm adaptation and product exchange (Kelley and Thibaut, 1978). It can therefore be expected that social interaction is conditioned by product exchange and interfirm adaptation requirements. The social interaction affects and is affected by the interfirm social structure, which is expressed in terms of interfirm contact patterns.

## TECHNOLOGY AND CUSTOMER–SUPPLIER INTERACTION

Ever since Woodward (1965) published her seminal work on technology and organization structure, technology has had a prominent role in organization theory. A steady stream of research results has been published on the topic, most of it under the heading of the contingency theory of organization (Galbraith, 1973; Lawrence and Lorsch, 1967; Thompson, 1967; Perrow, 1972; Pugh *et al.*, 1969). This theory posits, as confirmed in several studies, that technology and organization structure are closely interrelated (Fry, 1982; Gerwin, 1981; Scott, 1990).

Technology represents the conversion processes, by which the task of an organization is accomplished. Most technology definitions have tended to be broad, encompassing not only the machinery and tools but also devices, knowledge, or techniques that mediate between inputs and outputs (Tushman and Anderson, 1986). Organization structure is the pattern of relations among people facilitating the accomplishment of the task. While earlier studies considered formal organization structures, subsequent research (Barley, 1990; Burkhardt and Brass, 1990) has adopted a social network perspective on organizational structure according to which structure is viewed as a patterned, repeated interaction among social actors (Mintzberg, 1979; Weick, 1969). The term task refers to the products or services rendered by the organization.

The general argument is that in order to carry out the task the organization needs a suitable technology and structure and to operate the technology an appropriate structure is required as well. The underlying, and more precise, argument most widely adopted is that because of complexity, uncertainty, and interdependence, task and technology give rise to a need for information processing, which, in turn, is handled by the organization structure (Galbraith, 1973, 1977).

To the extent that customer–supplier relationships evolve into dyadic business relationships it seems reasonable to draw on an analogy using the technology–structure framework of organization theory. Given this framework, product exchange can be viewed as the task of the dyadic relationship. This task requires that interfirm adaptations are made in order to achieve fit between the firms' products, processes, and procedures. Moreover, the interfirm social structure has to be organized so that problems and issues associated with product exchange and interfirm adaptation can be handled.

In the contingency theory the task is often characterized in dimensions that directly, or indirectly via the technology, are supposed to affect structure because of information processing requirements. Important aspects of the task of product exchange, influencing the requirements on interfirm information processing, are the complexity of the product and the frequency of the deliveries. If the products exchanged are complex involving a multitude of relevant characteristics, it will be possible to raise the efficiency of the dyad by adapting products, processes, routines, and procedures of the firms to each other.

*Proposition 1a.* In dyadic business relationships, the more complex the product exchanged between the firms, the more extensive the interfirm adaptation is.

Likewise, when the delivery frequency is high there will be opportunities for raising the efficiency of the exchange between the parties by interfirm adaptations of processes, routines, and procedures. Consider, for instance, just-in-time production systems (cf. Frazier, Spekman and O'Neal, 1988).

*Proposition 1b.* In dyadic business relationships, the higher the delivery frequency, the more extensive the interfirm adaptation is.

In the same way, we expect that the two product exchange dimensions have separate, direct impacts on the interfirm social structure. Thus, an exchange of complex products with multiple properties requires more information processing than the exchange of simpler products, which leads to a tighter interfirm social structure involving more people with more frequent interpersonal contacts in both firms. This may, for instance, occur in connection with the software or services that are frequently associated with the exchange of complex products.

*Proposition 2a.* In dyadic business relationships, the more complex the product exchanged, the tighter the interfirm social structure is.

A similar relation can be expected between delivery frequency and interfirm social structure. A high delivery frequency, requiring a greater amount of current problem solving and delivery systems handling, gives rise to a tighter interfirm social structure than the case of low delivery frequency.

*Proposition 2b.* In dyadic business relationships, the higher the delivery frequency, the tighter the interfirm social structure is.

Furthermore, the analogy implies that the interfirm social structure is organized so that it can handle the interfirm adaptations. Adaptations require information processing. In particular, it can be expected that adaptations are associated with problem solving necessitating personal contacts between different managers in the firms.

*Proposition 3.* In dyadic business relationships, the more extensive the interfirm adaptation, the tighter the interfirm social structure is.

Proposition 3 corresponds to the technology–structure causality in the dominant contingency paradigm. Some newer contributions, however, have suggested the reverse causality: that social structure influences technology (Scott, 1990). In a similar way it can be expected that close contacts between two firms make it possible to discover new ways of adapting operations in the two firms to each other. This is in accordance with observations of the importance of customer contacts as sources of innovation (von Hippel, 1988; Laage-Hellman, 1989). It is consistent with a view that the social relationship can be a basis for the development of the technical systems of the parties.

Moreover, from a theoretical perspective different from the contingency theory, another view on interfirm adaptation and social structure could be advanced. It could be argued that they are two alternative means of tying the two firms to each other. The interfirm adaptations forge a technical tie and organization structure a social tie. In this perspective social structure would be developed as a compensation for a lack of technical ties based on adaptation.

Two counter-propositions to Proposition 3 could thus be formulated: one based on newer contributions to the contingency paradigm and specifying a reverse causality between interfirm adaptation and interfirm social structure, and another one, outside the contingency paradigm, specifying a negative correlation between these two variables. Although not explicitly included in the structural model, these possible counter-propositions are nevertheless addressed in the discussion.

Proposition 4 takes into account that both interfirm adaptations and interfirm social contact patterns can be expected to be time dependent, as business relationships evolve over time as a consequence of social exchange processes. Thus, irrespective of task it takes time both to realize interfirm adaptations and to develop interfirm social structures.

*Proposition 4a.* In dyadic business relationships, the older the relationship, the more extensive the interfirm adaptation is.

*Proposition 4b.* In dyadic business relationships, the older the relationship, the tighter the interfirm social structure is.

The causal structure of the set of propositions according to the dominant contingency framework is illustrated in Fig. 1, which is the basis of a structural model used in the empirical analysis. In the figure each proposition corresponds to an arrow, denoted by the number of that proposition. The contingency theory of organization distinguishes between contingencies on organization and job levels, where it is generally assumed that the interdependencies are more specific on the lower level (Gerwin, 1981). The organization provides the framework for the job level contingencies. In the present context the specific dyadic business relationship corresponds to the job level and the overall organization of the firm with its technology constitutes the framework of the relationship. Thus we expect that the causal structure outlined above is conditioned by the technology of the customer firm.

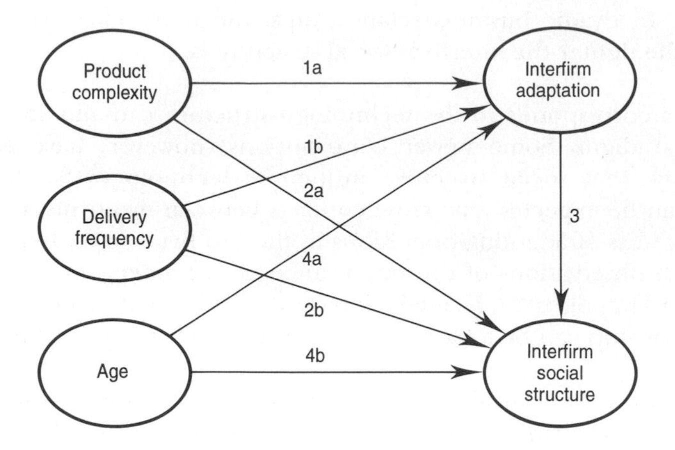


Fig. 1. Product exchange, interfirm adaptation, and interfirm social structure in dyadic business relationships: a structural model. *Note*: Numbers at arrows refer to proposition numbers in the text.

Technology conceptualizations on the organization level are usually based on Woodward's (1965) research, in which manufacturing firms' technologies are categorized according to the dominant type of production process (Child and Mansfield, 1972; Hickson, Pugh and Pheysey, 1969; Khandwalla, 1974; Lincoln, Hanada and McBride, 1986). Woodward distinguishes three major technological categories: (1) unit and small batch production, (2) large batch and mass production, and (3) process production. This classification has the advantage of corresponding closely to classifications among engineers. Although a number of technology classifications have been advanced by other researchers (Perrow, 1967; Thompson, 1967), the main basis of the classification, the continuity of the production process, is common both to theirs and to Woodward's.

Process continuity is related to the rigidity of the production systems. The unit production systems are flexible. System and product changes can be carried through quite easily and the planning horizon usually includes only a few orders. New orders often bring with them new problems, which have to be resolved as they arise. The organization is characterized by close, extensive and informal interaction between different managerial functions.

The process production systems, in contrast, are often extremely rigid – they cannot be used for anything but the inputs and outputs for which they were originally designed and constructed. Changes are only made in connection with plant erections. The organization is characterized by formal organization structure and a wide gulf between different managerial functions.

Large batch and mass production systems are also rigid, but usually they can be reorganized so that new products or at least new models can be produced. Still, many of the problems which arise in the relationship are of a recurrent character, which allows routinization of the exchange processes. Decisions about changes are taken on a higher level in the managerial hierarchy than in the unit production system and the managerial functions are clearly separated from each other.

Thus, high production rigidity makes it difficult to employ interfirm adaptation to resolve current problems associated with the task of product exchange. Consequently, in such situations, the interfirm social structure is not involved in facilitating adaptations, nor is it developed further as a result of such adaptations. Therefore, the higher the production rigidity and the more centralized the business decision-making, the weaker the impact of current tasks is on interfirm adaptations and interfirm social structures. Correspondingly, if production rigidity is high and decision-making is centralized, the weaker the impact of interfirm adaptations is on the interfirm social structure of the business relationship.

Against this background we assume that there are structural differences between business relationships with unit production, mass production, and process production customers.

*Proposition 5a.* In dyadic business relationships with unit production customers, there is a stronger causal relation from product exchange to interfirm adaptation than in relationships with mass production customers, and the causal relation is weaker still in business relationships with process production customers.

*Proposition 5b.* In dyadic business relationships with unit production customers, there is a stronger causal relation from product exchange to interfirm social structure than in relationships with mass production customers, and the causal relation is weaker still in business relationships with process production customers.

*Proposition 5c.* In dyadic business relationships with unit production customers, there is a stronger causal relation from interfirm adaptation to interfirm social structure than in relationships with mass production customers, and the causal relation is weaker still in business relationships with process production customers.

The empirical analysis is carried out by testing and refining the structural model when analyzing it with respect to business relationships in three technological categories, involving customers with unit production, mass production, and process production technologies. The whole model is used with respect to each category to determine how the customer's technology differentiates between the three groups.

## THE EMPIRICAL BASIS

The empirical analysis is based on a subset of the data base established in the European International Marketing and Purchasing Project (Håkansson, 1982). The data concern 237 business relationships of industrial suppliers in Germany (79), Sweden (102), and the United Kingdom (56) with their most important customers in France, Germany, Italy, Sweden, and the United Kingdom. The firms are internationally oriented companies in the manufacturing sector.

A quota sample was used in the data collection to ensure that a similar number of relationships concerned materials, components, and equipment. The sample was also designed to include a similar number of relationships with customers with unit production, mass production, and process production. Finally, it was designed to comprise the same number of relationships to customers in each of the five country markets, including the domestic market. The objective was to eliminate biases due to differences with regard to product type, customer technology, and customer country. Out of the 237 customer–supplier relationships 64 concerned unit production, 113 mass production, and 61 process production customers.

The customer relationships to be studied were selected by marketing executives in the companies. Personal interviews were held with marketing managers who were required to have extensive individual experience of business with the customer in question. Interviewer bias was checked by using members of the research team as interviewers and by employing detailed coding manuals. Both in-depth and standardized data were collected.

## MEASURING THE CONCEPTS

The endogenous variables are interfirm adaptation and interfirm social structure. Adaptation variables include adaptations made by the customer and the supplier and are indicated by six items: adaptation of product, adaptation of production process, and adaptation of stock-holding (in the case of the supplier) or adaptation of production planning (in the case of the customer). The adaptation variables are expressed on a three-level scale indicating the extent of adaptation undertaken as estimated by the interviewer on the basis of extensive accounts of the adaptations by the respondent.

The interfirm social structure variables are continuous variables describing the interfirm social contact pattern, indicated by four items based on direct numerical estimates by the respondent: the number of people involved from the supplier and customer firms who had had contacts with the counterpart firm during the past two years, and the number of meetings per year in the customer's and the supplier's offices. The variables used are summarized in Table 1. Product complexity and delivery frequency represent two different aspects of product exchange and are two separate exogenous variables. Product complexity is estimated by the interviewer in a three-level scale based on the respondents' descriptions. Delivery frequency is a direct numerical estimate by the respondent. The third exogenous variable, relationship age, is also a direct numerical estimate by the respondent.

The sample and its three technology groups are characterized in Table 2 on the basis of the thirteen measurement variables. The table shows relatively small differences between the technology groups. However, concerning the exogenous variables, it can be seen that product complexity and delivery frequency in general are somewhat lower in business relationships with unit production customers than in the other groups. The average age of the relationships in the three groups is almost the same, viz. 14–17 years. The differences between the technology groups are relatively small as far as the adaptation variables are concerned. On average, the customer firm makes large adaptations in 7–10 relationships and small in 14–18 relationships. Correspondingly, the supplier makes large adaptations in 12–19 relationships – 12 in unit production and 19 in process production relationships –

Table 1. Variable and operational measures

*Interfirm Adaptation*: 3-level scale based on detailed product description by the respondent

Customer adaptation of product
Supplier adaptation of product
Customer adaptation of production process
Supplier adaptation of production process
Customer adaptation of production planning
Supplier adaptation of stockholding

*Interfirm Social Structure*

The number of persons involved from the customer's firm in the past 2 years
The number of persons involved from the supplier's firm in the past 2 years
The number of meetings per year in the customer's office
The number of meetings per year in the supplier's office

*Product Complexity*: 3-level scale based on detailed description of product and product use

*Delivery Frequency*: the number of deliveries per year

*Age*: the age of the relationship

and small adaptations in 24–28 relationships. Considering the size of the sample these differences are too small to give reason to further comments. The same holds for social contact patterns, which are slightly less tight in the process production relationships.

The analysis of the variables and the model was carried out by PRELIS and LISREL, two statistical packages for the study of structural equation models. PRELIS, which is a preprocessor to LISREL, is a software package that can provide a first descriptive look at the raw data before testing them in a model. Furthermore, with this program it is possible to compute the appropriate data matrix used as input for structural equation models. PRELIS was used for this sample and the distribution properties of the individual variables were jointly scrutinized. Polyserial correlations were computed for pairs of ordinal and continuous variables, and product moment correlations were computed for pairs of continuous variables. Polychoric correlations were computed for pairs of ordinal variables. The assumption in LISREL is that the ordinal variables and the pairs of ordinal variables have an underlying continuous distribution, and the computation of the matrix is based on these continuous variables.

The PRELIS data screening and the computed joint distribution of the variables did not provide reasons to eliminate any of the variables. The computed correlation matrix (Appendix 1) was used as input in the LISREL model and tested with the Maximum Likelihood Method. A weight matrix would have been preferable since it provides better fitting conditions and does not assume normal distribution of the variables (Jöreskog and Sörbom, 1988). This would have given lower $\chi^2$ values. But the method demands a large sample size and eliminates observations with missing values. Because of the sample size it was not possible to compute such a weight matrix.

$\chi^2$ values, however, must be interpreted carefully and are very sensitive to sample

Table 2. Distribution of the model's variables

| Production technology | Percentage distribution of ordinal variables Unit (n = 64) | | | Mass (n = 113) | | | Process (n = 61) | | |
|---|---|---|---|---|---|---|---|---|---|
| | None | Small | Large | None | Small | Large | None | Small | Large |
| Supplier adaptation of product | 69 | 21 | 10 | 73 | 16 | 10 | 87 | 10 | 3 |
| Customer adaptation of product | 46 | 37 | 16 | 40 | 33 | 17 | 46 | 29 | 25 |
| Supplier adaptation of production process | 76 | 11 | 13 | 73 | 16 | 11 | 66 | 21 | 13 |
| Customer adaptation of production process | 80 | 14 | 6 | 70 | 18 | 12 | 72 | 21 | 7 |
| Supplier adaptation of production planning | 82 | 18 | – | 70 | 22 | 8 | 74 | 21 | 5 |
| Customer adaptation of stockholding | 62 | 24 | 14 | 52 | 32 | 16 | 54 | 23 | 23 |
| Product complexity | 30 | 39 | 31 | 43 | 32 | 25 | 40 | 30 | 30 |

Mean distribution of continuous variables

| Production technology | Unit (n = 64) | Mass (n = 113) | Process (n = 61) |
|---|---|---|---|
| Persons involved from supplier | 7.5 | 7.7 | 5.2 |
| Persons involved from customer | 8.5 | 9.2 | 6.3 |
| Meetings per year in customer's office | 7.1 | 6.2 | 4.1 |
| Meetings per year in supplier's office | 2.6 | 1.6 | 1.9 |
| Deliveries per year | 28.1 | 46.8 | 37.9 |
| Age of relationship | 14.5 | 16.0 | 16.8 |

size and departures from multivariate normality of the observed variables. Two other magnitudes, the goodness-of-fit index and the root mean square residual, can be used to study how the data fit the specified model. Unlike $\chi^2$, the goodness-of-fit index is independent of the sample size and relatively robust against departures from normality. The root mean square residual can be used to compare the fit of two different models for the same data, whereas the goodness-of-fit index can be used to examine the fit of the model for different data (Jöreskog and Sörbom, 1988).

## TEST OF THE MODEL

The test of the model is performed in four steps. In short, step 1 tests whether the observed interfirm adaptation and interfirm social structure variables are valid indicators of the two corresponding latent variables. In step 2 it is investigated whether the two latent endogenous variables are correlated and whether this correlation is invariant over the three technology groups. Since it is shown that the process production relationships are structurally different from the others, the test of structural models is performed separately on unit and mass production (step 3) relationships on one hand, and on process production relationships on the other (step 4).

In the first step of the empirical analysis of the model it is tested whether the six observed interfirm adaptation variables as well as the four observed interfirm social structure variables are indicators of the single endogenous constructs interfirm adaptation and interfirm social structure in all the three technological categories. It is also verified whether the indicators are significant estimators of the underlying constructs (Appendix 2). It can be concluded that interfirm adaptation and interfirm social structure are valid constructs characterizing dyadic business relationships. Thus, the indicators form constructs characterizing the dyad rather than each business partner as such. It can also be concluded that the quality of the indicator variables differs between the technology groups. In particular, one of the indicator variables is not significant in the process technology group. Finally, although the adaptation variables refer to the behaviour of the parties they are good indicators of one common relationship construct. Both interfirm social structure and interfirm adaptation are properties of relationships rather than of the parties involved.

In the second step it is tested whether interfirm adaptation and interfirm social structure are significantly correlated. This is the case in the unit and mass production groups but not in the process production group, where there is no significant correlation (Appendix 3). It can be concluded that business relationships with process production customers are structurally different from those with unit or mass production customers. The results also indicate that there is an invariant structure pattern between these two groups.

In the third step, the structural model is tested on the unit and mass production relationships. The test shows that the correlation between interfirm adaptation and interfirm social structure is not due to the two constructs having product complexity, delivery frequency and age as common causes (Fig. 2). Statistically, this is done by testing whether the partial covariance between interfirm adaptation and interfirm social structure is significant. It also demonstrates that the relation between interfirm adaptation and interfirm social structure, on statistical grounds, should be regarded as one-way from interfirm adaptation to interfirm social structure rather than reciprocal or one-way from interfirm social structure to interfirm adaptation. This is in accordance with the relation specified in Proposition 3 on the basis of the contingency theory. Neither of the two latter relations can, however, be rejected.

The test shows, moreover, that the three exogenous variables have significant influences, albeit different, on interfirm adaptation and interfirm social structure. Product complexity has a significant influence on adaptation in both technology groups. The age of the relationship has a significant influence on interfirm social structure in both groups. Delivery frequency has a significant influence on interfirm adaptation in the mass production group and on interfirm social structure in the unit production group. Thus, there is a difference between relationships with unit

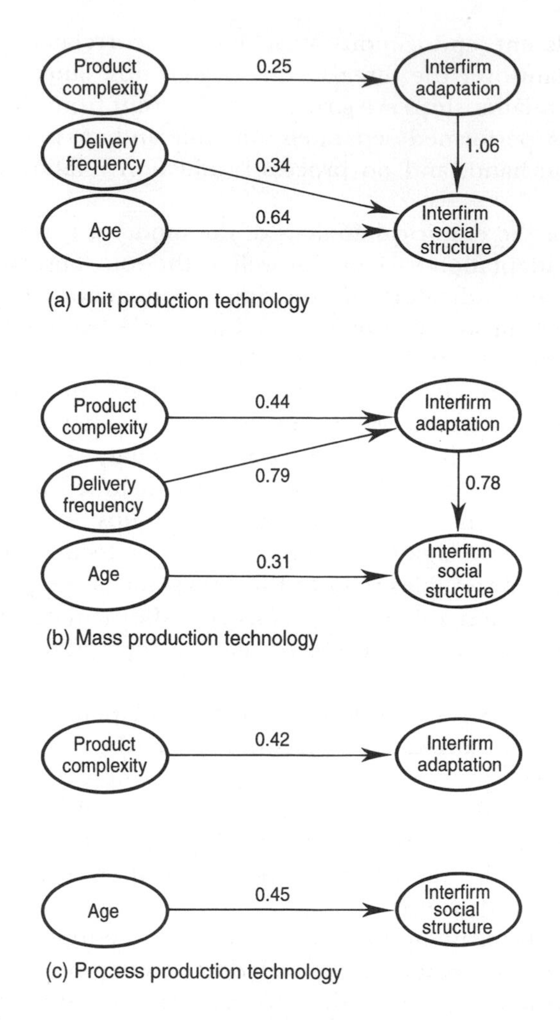


Fig. 2. Product exchange, interfirm adaptation, and interfirm social structure in dyadic business relationships: empirical results in three technological categories.

production customers and those with mass production customers.

When the model is tested for the unit and mass production technological groups, the tests show that certain associations between the constructs are not statistically significant. After subsequent refinement the structural model is strongly supported in the case of unit production customers and supported, although less strongly, in the case of mass production customers. For the unit technology group we obtain a $\chi^2$ value with 59 degrees of freedom equivalent to 79.78 (p-value = 0.037), a goodness-of-fit value of 0.86, and a root mean square residual of 0.08. For the mass production group the $\chi^2$ equivalent is 139.71 (p-value = 0.000), the goodness-of-fit value is 0.82, and the root mean square residual is 0.122. These measures, which are measurements that evaluate the overall fit of the structural model, indicate that the data from the unit production group fit the specified model well and better than the data from the mass production group.

In the fourth step, the structural model is tested and refined on the process production group, in which the endogenous constructs interfirm adaptation and interfirm social structure are not correlated. Here further tests show that adaptation is significantly influenced by product complexity. They show, in addition, that interfirm social structure is significantly influenced by the age of the relationship, but that delivery frequency has no significant influence on either of the two endogenous variables. The $\chi^2$ value with 61 degrees of freedom is 262.9, the goodness-of-fit index is 0.723, and the root mean square value is 0.148. These values indicate that the fit of the data to the specified structural model is poor.

## DISCUSSION

The empirical analysis shows that the analogy from organization theory to interfirm business relationships is supported in the sense that the complexity dimension of product exchange has an influence on interfirm adaptations in all three groups of customer technology. It is interesting to observe that there is no direct effect of product complexity on interfirm social structure. Thus, the task variable product complexity influences the interfirm social structure only to the extent that the technology variable interfirm adaptation influences the interfirm social structure.

The second dimension of product exchange – delivery frequency – has a less uniform effect. In unit production relationships it influences the interfirm social structure; however, in mass production relationships, adaptation, and in process production relationships, neither are affected. This means that in the case of unit production customers, the interfirm social structure is sensitive to differences in delivery frequency. The interpretation according to the contingency theory is that many interfirm social contacts are needed in business relationships with unit production customers, when the delivery frequency is high. This can be understood against the background of the non-repetitive characteristics of dyadic business relationships in this case, which precludes the setting up of routinized systems to handle intensive deliveries. The required short-term flexibility must be ensured through personal interaction within an interfirm social structure.

In relationships with mass production customers the higher standardization possibilities allow highly frequent deliveries to be handled by interfirm adaptation, e.g. by setting up just-in-time or other routinized delivery systems. The recurrent characteristics of the technology make long-term solutions feasible. Nevertheless, indirectly via the interfirm adaptation, this also creates tighter interfirm social structures.

With regard to the effect of delivery frequency there is thus a clear difference between short-term flexibility requirements and social interaction in relationships with unit production customers and long-term, standardized solutions in mass production relationships.

The third exogenous construct, the age of the relationship, has a reinforcing effect on interfirm social structures in all three technology groups, implying that interfirm social contacts increase with increasing relationship age. The explanation is that social structures, and consequently, social ties are, as expected, built over time.

The characteristics of the relation between the two endogenous constructs separate process production relationships from the two other technologies. Thus, while the technical ties in the form of interfirm adaptation and the social ties within the interfirm social structures are closely interrelated in the case of unit and mass production customers, they are not at all related in the case of process production customers. There seems to be a reinforcing effect between the technical and social ties in the relationships in the former two groups, which is totally absent in the third. The lack of correlation between interfirm adaptation and interfirm social structure in the relationships with process production customers reflects a separation between long-term investment and short-term business interaction.

Although the hypothesis derived from organization theory of a one-way causal relation from interfirm adaptation to interfirm social structure is indeed supported, the statistical analysis also indicates a possible reciprocal relation between the two variables. This gives reason to believe that there is a strong reinforcing effect in the unit and mass production relationships. The mutuality of this mechanism indicates that conditions are present for continuous interfirm learning in unit and mass production relationships, which are absent in process relationships, as it implies that over time interfirm adaptations may be made as an indirect effect of increasing social ties between the parties.

Thus, depending on the technological category, there is either a positive or a non-existing correlation between interfirm adaptation and interfirm social structure. In no case is the correlation between the constructs negative. There are consequently no indications of a compensatory function of one tying mechanism, when the other mechanism would be unavailable.

The overall finding of the analysis is that in terms of the structural model there is a basic difference between relationships with process production customers and those with unit and mass production customers. There is also a difference between unit and mass production relationships – although less fundamental – with regard to the influence of the task, in terms of delivery frequency, on the two endogenous relationship variables corresponding to technology and structure.

Thus, although there is a difference between the customer technologies in the direction expected on the basis of theory, it is not the exact one we had expected. We expected a more gradual or stepwise difference so that interfirm adaptation and interfirm social structure would be more closely related in the unit production technology than in the mass production technology and even more than in the process technology. As it turned out, no such difference between unit and mass production technologies was observed, but these two differed fundamentally from the process production technology. One explanation of this can be that unit and mass production usually, and in contrast to process production, are dominated by assembly which implies a need for coordinating several supplier relationships both as regards interfirm adaptation and interfirm social structure. There is no such coordination need in process production where usually just one or a few inputs are fed into the production process. This type of explanation gains some support from the fact that delivery frequency does not have any influence on the endogenous variables in the process production group.

## CONCLUSION

The findings have several implications. From a managerial point of view the basic message is that the customer's technology matters. Customer technologies differ with respect to the demands put on supplier flexibility and consequently on the possibilities to handle relationships through long-term interfirm adaptations or short-term problem solving requiring more personal interaction with interfirm social structures. Moreover, it should be recognized that the conditions for building and maintaining relationships seem to be different when the customers are firms employing process technologies. When interacting with a unit or mass production customer the supplier can, at least to some extent, rely on a socio-technical mechanism reinforcing the relationship (Clark, 1972). That mechanism is absent in the process technology. This implies that the technical and social ties can and perhaps should be handled as separate managerial issues.

The study also shows that technology is not just a factor which merely influences business. It is a central element in important business relationships. There is a need for recognizing it as a relationship management issue. The indication of a reverse causality between interfirm social structure and interfirm adaptation suggests that technical change may be as a consequence of how relationships are organized.

With regard to research implications the study demonstrates the relevance of technology as an important contingency factor when analyzing business relationships. Evidently, more research is needed about this factor. Thus our analysis stresses the difference between the technologies with regard to continuity. If the critical difference between the technologies is assembly or process production rather than production continuity, studies should be performed explicitly taking into account the customers' needs to coordinate their supplier networks and how this affects the relationships with single suppliers. Obviously corresponding managerial problems may exist on the supplier side indicating the need for analyzing how single customer relationships are connected to each other. A vast field of research about the embeddedness of business relationships in wider networks of connected business relationships is opened.

## REFERENCES

Anderson, J. C. and Narus, J. A. A model of the distributor's perspective of distributor–manufacturer working relationships. *Journal of Marketing*, **48** (Fall), 62–74 (1984).

Anderson, J. C. and Narus, J. A. A model of distributor firm and manufacturing firm working relationships. *Journal of Marketing*, **54** (January), 42–58 (1990).

Arndt, J. Toward a concept of domesticated markets. *Journal of Marketing*, **43** (Fall), 69–75 (1979).

Bagozzi, R. P. Marketing as exchange. *Journal of Marketing*, **39** (October), 32–9 (1975).

Bagozzi, R. P. *Principles of Marketing Management.* Maxwell Macmillan, New York (1986).

Barley, S. R. The alignment of technology and structure through roles and networks. *Administrative Science Quarterly*, **35** 61–103 (1990).

Blau, P. M. *Exchange and Power in Social Life.* John Wiley & Sons, Inc., New York (1964).

Burkhardt, M. E. and Brass, D. J. Changing patterns or patterns of change: the effects of a change in technology on social network structure and power. *Administrative Science Quarterly*, **35**, 104–27 (1990).

Capon, N. and Glazer, R. Marketing and technology: a strategic coalignment. *Journal of Marketing*, **51** (July), 1–14 (1987).

Carlton, D. W. The rigidity of prices. *American Economic Review*, **76** (4), 637–58 (1986).

Child, J. and Mansfield, R. Technology, size, and organization structure. *Sociology*, **6**, 369–93 (1972).

Clark, P. A. *Organizational Design*. Tavistock, London (1972).

Dwyer, F. R., Schurr, P. H. and Oh, S. Developing buyer–seller relationships. *Journal of Marketing*, **51** (April), 11–27 (1987).

Emerson, R. M. Power-dependence relations. *American Sociological Review*, **27** (February), 31–41 (1962).

Fiocca, R. and Snehota, I. High technology and management of the market differential. In Hallén, L. and Johanson, J. (eds), *Networks of Relationships in International Marketing*. JAI Press, Greenwich, Connecticut (1989), pp. 199–209.

Frazier, G. L., Spekman, R. E. and O'Neal, C. R. Just-in-time exchange relationships in industrial markets. *Journal of Marketing*, **52** (October), 52–67 (1988).

Fry, L. W. Technology–structure research: three critical issues. *Academy of Management Journal*, **25**, 532–52 (1982).

Gadde, L.-E. and Mattson, L.-G. Stability and change in network relationships. *International Journal of Research in Marketing*, **4**, 29–41 (1987).

Gatignon, H. and Robertson, T. S. Technology diffusion: an empirical test of competitive effects. *Journal of Marketing*, **53** (January), 35–49.

Galbraith, J. R. *Designing Complex Organizations*. Addison Wesley, Reading, MA (1973).

Galbraith, J. R. *Organization Design*. Addison Wesley, Reading, MA (1977).

Gerwin, D. Relationships between technology and structure. In Nystrom, P. C. and Starbuck, W. H. (eds), *Handbook of Organizational Design*, Oxford University Press, Oxford (1981).

Håkansson, H. (ed.). *International Marketing and Purchasing of Industrial Goods: An Interaction Approach*. John Wiley & Sons Ltd, Chichester (1982).

Håkansson, H. and Östberg, C. Industrial marketing – an organizational problem? *Industrial Marketing Management*, **4**, 113–23 (1975).

Hallén, L., Johanson, J. and Seyed-Mohamed, N. Interfirm adaptation in business relationships. *Journal of Marketing*, **55** (April), 29–37 (1991).

Hickson, D. J., Pugh, D. S. and Pheysey, D. C. Operations technology and organization structure: an empirical reappraisal. *Administrative Science Quarterly*, **14**, 378–97 (1969).

von Hippel, E. A. Successful industrial products from customer ideas. *Journal of Marketing*, **42** (January), 39–49 (1978).

von Hippel, E. A. *The Sources of Innovation*. Oxford University Press, Oxford (1988).

Homans, G. Social behavior as exchange. *American Journal of Sociology*, **63** (May), 597–606 (1958).

Jackson, B. B. Build customer relationships that last. *Harvard Business Review*, **63** (November–December), 120–8 (1985).

Jöreskog, K. G. and Sörbom, D. *LISREL 7: A Guide to the Program and Application*. SPSS Inc, Chicago (1988).

Khandwalla, P. N. Mass output orientation of operations technology and organizational structure. *Administrative Science Quarterly*, **19**, 74–97 (1974).

Kelley, H. W. and Thibaut, J. W. *Interpersonal Relations: A Theory of Interdependence*. John Wiley & Sons, Inc., New York (1978).

Kotler, P. A generic concept of marketing. *Journal of Marketing*, **36** (April), 46–54 (1972).

Laage-Hellman, J. *Technological Development in Industrial Networks*, Acta Universitatis Upsaliensis, Comprehensive Summaries of Uppsala Dissertations from the Faculty of Social Sciences, 16, Uppsala University (1989).

Lawrence, P. R. and Lorsch, J. W. *Organization and Environment*. Graduate School of Business Administration, Harvard University, Boston (1967).

Levitt, T. *The Marketing Imagination*. The Free Press, New York (1983).

Lincoln, J. R., Hanada, M. and McBride, K. Organizational structures in Japanese and US

manufacturing. *Administrative Science Quarterly*, **31**, 338–64 (1986).
Mintzberg, H. *The Structure of Organizations*. Prentice-Hall, Englewood Cliffs, NJ (1979).
Newcomb, T. M., Turner, R. H. and Converse, P. E. *Social Psychology: The Human Interaction*. Routledge and Kegan Paul, London (1952).
Perrow, C. *Complex Organizations*. Scott, Foreman, Glenview, Ill (1972).
Pugh, D. S., Hickson, D. J., Hinings, C. R. and Turner, C. The context of organization structures. *Administrative Science Quarterly* **14**, 91–114 (1969).
Robertson, T. S. and Gatignon, H. Competitive effects on technology diffusion. *Journal of Marketing*, **50** (July), 1–12 (1986).
Scott, W. R. Technology and structure: an organizational-level perspective. In Goodman, P. S. and Sproull, L. S. (eds), *Technology and Organizations*. Jossey-Bass, San Francisco (1990).
Shanklin, W. L. and Ryans, J. K., Jr. *Marketing High Technology*. D.C. Heath and Co., Lexington, MA (1984).
Thibaut, J. W. and Kelley, H. H. *The Social Psychology of Groups*. John Wiley & Sons, Inc., New York (1959).
Thompson, J. D. *Organizations in Action*. McGraw-Hill, New York (1967).
Tushman, M. L. and Anderson, P. Technological discontinuities and organizational environments. *Administrative Science Quarterly*, **31**, 439–65 (1986).
Webster, F. E., Jr. *Industrial Marketing Strategy*. John Wiley & Sons, Inc, New York (1979).
Weick, K. E. *The Social Psychology of Organizing*. Addison-Wesley, Reading, MA (1969).
Wind, Y. Industrial source loyalty. *Journal of Marketing Research*, **7** (November), 433–6 (1970).
Woodward, J. *Industrial Organization: Theory and Practice*. Oxford University Press, London (1965).

## APPENDIX 1

### Correlation Matrices

(a) Unit production technology

| | CAP | SAP | CAPP | SAPP | CAPL | SAS | MC | MS | CC | SC | PC | Age |
|---|---|---|---|---|---|---|---|---|---|---|---|---|
| CAP | 1.00 | | | | | | | | | | | |
| SAP | 0.16 | 1.00 | | | | | | | | | | |
| CAPP | 0.18 | 0.28 | 1.00 | | | | | | | | | |
| SAPP | 0.17 | 0.38 | 0.26 | 1.00 | | | | | | | | |
| CAPL | 0.13 | 0.02 | 0.17 | 0.20 | 1.00 | | | | | | | |
| SAS | 0.15 | 0.19 | 0.34 | 0.20 | 0.23 | 1.00 | | | | | | |
| MC | 0.33 | 0.37 | 0.18 | 0.26 | 0.06 | 0.17 | 1.00 | | | | | |
| MS | 0.38 | 0.34 | 0.08 | 0.21 | 0.11 | 0.21 | 0.77 | 1.00 | | | | |
| CC | 0.35 | 0.32 | 0.26 | 0.18 | 0.07 | 0.32 | 0.61 | 0.80 | 1.00 | | | |
| SC | 0.06 | 0.26 | 0.31 | 0.20 | 0.01 | 0.33 | 0.57 | 0.63 | 0.70 | 1.00 | | |
| PC | 0.14 | 0.08 | 0.48 | −0.05 | −0.01 | −0.02 | 0.22 | 0.19 | 0.36 | 0.38 | 1.00 | |
| Age | 0.14 | 0.05 | 0.19 | −0.11 | 0.10 | 0.06 | 0.33 | 0.38 | 0.54 | 0.34 | 0.37 | 1.00 |

*Appendix 1 continued on next page*

*Appendix 1 continued*

(b) Mass production technology

| | CAP | SAP | CAPP | SAPP | CAPL | SAS | MC | MS | CC | SC | PC | Age |
|---|---|---|---|---|---|---|---|---|---|---|---|---|
| CAP | 1.00 | | | | | | | | | | | |
| SAP | 0.30 | 1.00 | | | | | | | | | | |
| CAPP | 0.13 | −0.09 | 1.00 | | | | | | | | | |
| SAPP | 0.13 | 0.49 | 0.12 | 1.00 | | | | | | | | |
| CAPL | 0.14 | 0.10 | 0.26 | 0.29 | 1.00 | | | | | | | |
| SAS | 0.19 | 0.39 | 0.12 | 0.33 | 0.11 | 1.00 | | | | | | |
| MC | 0.09 | 0.35 | 0.12 | 0.27 | −0.04 | 0.30 | 1.00 | | | | | |
| MS | 0.32 | 0.45 | 0.16 | 0.30 | −0.07 | 0.35 | 0.66 | 1.00 | | | | |
| CC | 0.02 | 0.32 | 0.02 | 0.33 | −0.06 | 0.15 | 0.52 | 0.50 | 1.00 | | | |
| SC | 0.14 | 0.32 | 0.25 | 0.25 | 0.09 | 0.19 | 0.51 | 0.54 | 0.43 | 1.00 | | |
| PC | 0.33 | 0.01 | 0.26 | 0.03 | 0.25 | 0.18 | 0.10 | 0.21 | 0.02 | 0.16 | 1.00 | |
| Age | 0.13 | 0.01 | 0.16 | 0.11 | 0.14 | 0.14 | 0.28 | 0.28 | 0.08 | −0.01 | 0.22 | 1.00 |

(c) Process production technology

| | CAP | SAP | CAPP | SAPP | CAPL | SAS | MC | MS | CC | SC | PC | Age |
|---|---|---|---|---|---|---|---|---|---|---|---|---|
| CAP | 1.00 | | | | | | | | | | | |
| SAP | 0.61 | 1.00 | | | | | | | | | | |
| CAPP | 0.13 | 0.48 | 1.00 | | | | | | | | | |
| SAPP | 0.48 | 0.53 | 0.19 | 1.00 | | | | | | | | |
| CAPL | −0.12 | 0.11 | 0.12 | 0.26 | 1.00 | | | | | | | |
| SAS | 0.37 | 0.06 | 0.14 | 0.41 | 0.47 | 1.00 | | | | | | |
| MC | −0.09 | 0.23 | 0.40 | 0.27 | 0.13 | 0.07 | 1.00 | | | | | |
| MS | 0.10 | 0.20 | 0.03 | 0.32 | 0.25 | 0.07 | 0.40 | 1.00 | | | | |
| CC | 0.27 | 0.06 | 0.11 | 0.11 | 0.12 | 0.20 | 0.43 | 0.17 | 1.00 | | | |
| SC | −0.11 | 0.18 | 0.34 | 0.12 | −0.05 | −0.11 | 0.69 | 0.45 | 0.42 | 1.00 | | |
| PC | 0.38 | 0.50 | 0.10 | 0.51 | 0.11 | 0.00 | 0.16 | 0.26 | 0.15 | −0.05 | 1.00 | |
| Age | −0.03 | −0.05 | −0.08 | 0.26 | 0.01 | −0.03 | 0.22 | 0.23 | 0.08 | 0.24 | −0.03 | 1.00 |

CAP, customer adaptation of product.
SAP, supplier adaptation of product.
CAPP, customer adaptation of production process.
SAPP, supplier adaptation of production process.
CAPL, customer adaptation of production planning.
SAS, supplier adaptation of stockholding.
MC, meetings per year in customer's office.
MS, meetings per year in supplier's office.
CC, persons involved from customer.
SC, persons involved from supplier.
PC, product complexity.
DF, delivery frequency.
Age, age of relationship.

## APPENDIX 2A

### Estimates for the Measurement Model for Interfirm Adaptation (3 groups)

| | Customer's production technology | | |
|---|---|---|---|
| | Unit | Mass | Process |
| CAP | 0.32 (2.2) | 0.34 (3.0) | 0.69 (5.5) |
| SAP | 0.51 (3.3) | 0.72 (6.0) | 0.84 (6.9) |
| CAPP | 0.57 (3.7) | 0.26 (2.0) | 0.47 (3.4) |
| SAPP | 0.55 (3.6) | 0.65 (6.0) | 0.66 (5.1) |
| CAPL | 0.30 (2.0) | 0.27 (2.4) | 0.13 (0.9) n.s. |
| SAS | 0.48 (3.1) | 0.51 (4.9) | 0.29 (2.0) |

n.s., Not significant.
t-values for the estimates presented within brackets.

The overall fit of the model:
Unit production technology: $\chi^2$ with 9 d.f. = 5 (p = 0.79);
Mass production technology: $\chi^2$ with 9 d.f. = 24 (p = 0.01);
Process production technology: $\chi^2$ with 9 d.f. = 65 (p = 0.00).

CAP, customer's adaptation of product.
SAP, supplier's adaptation of product.
CAPP, customer's adaptation of production process.
SAPP, supplier's adaptation of production process.
CAPL, customer's adaptation of production planning.
SAS, supplier's adaptation of stocks.

## APPENDIX 2B

### Estimates for the Measurement Model for Interfirm Social Structure (3 groups)

| | Customer's production technology | | |
|---|---|---|---|
| | Unit | Mass | Process |
| MC | 0.79 (7.4) | 0.81 (9.3) | 0.82 (6.6) |
| MS | 0.94 (9.7) | 0.82 (9.5) | 0.50 (3.8) |
| CC | 0.85 (8.1) | 0.63 (6.9) | 0.49 (3.7) |
| SC | 0.71 (6.3) | 0.65 (7.1) | 0.85 (6.9) |

t-values for the estimates presented within brackets.

The overall fit of the model:
Unit production technology: $\chi^2$ with 2 d.f. = 9 (p = 0.01);
Mass production technology: $\chi^2$ with 2 d.f. = 0.5 (p = 0.77);
Process production technology: $\chi^2$ with 2 d.f. = 0.9 (p = 0.63);

MC, meetings per year in customer's office.
MS, meetings per year in supplier's office.
CC, persons involved from customer.
SC, persons involved from supplier.

## APPENDIX 3

## Estimates for the Measurement Models for the Production Technologies

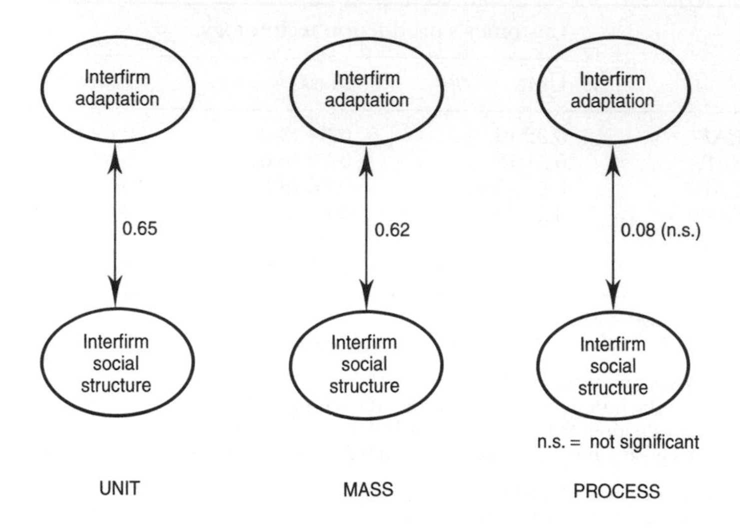

# 5

# The Managerial Implications of Networking

*Wim G. Biemans*

Marketing can be seen as relationship management: creating, developing, and maintaining a network in which the firm thrives (Gummesson).

## DISCREPANCY BETWEEN THEORETICAL THOUGHT AND MANAGEMENT PRACTICE

Academic researchers have shown an increasing interest in studying interorganizational interaction and the functioning of networks. The large majority of these studies relate to the area of developing innovations (mostly for industrial markets). Traditionally, product development has been regarded as the sole province of the manufacturer. The process is typically divided into a series of subsequent stages and specific recommendations to the manufacturer are formulated.

The manufacturing firm is regarded as the party that both initiates and controls the product development process. However, the famous studies by von Hippel demonstrated the involvement of users in the generation of new product ideas in a number of specific industries. Based on these investigations he developed a customer-active paradigm (CAP) in contrast to a manufacturer-active paradigm (MAP) (von Hippel, 1978). Von Hippel's findings were confirmed by a number of other researchers who demonstrated user involvement in product development processes in areas as diverse as industrial machinery (Foxall and Tierney, 1984; Vanden Abeele and Christiaens, 1987), medical instruments (Shaw, 1986; Vanden Abeele and Christiaens, 1987), applications software (Voss, 1985) and machine tools (Parkinson, 1982). Gradually, the focus of research shifted from characterizing the product development process as being either manufacturer-active or customer-active to determining the role of customers during the whole process of product development. Thus, the initial concept of CAP evolved into a broad range of supplier–customer interactions. During the second half of the 1980s, the Swedish branch of the international IMP Group started to criticize the perspectives outlined above. Their main criticism was that each of them focuses on only one or a few

Reprinted with permission from *European Management Journal*, Vol 8, No 4, W. G. Biemans, The Managerial Implications of Networking, pp 529–540.

actors. These views were argued to be too narrow in their approach; the development of innovations should be seen as an interplay between a number of actors and thus as taking place within networks (Håkansson, 1987). These networks consist of a number of different organizations linked together by means of individual interactive relationships of varying nature, strength and duration.

However, the further advancement of theoretical thought by academic researchers seems to have created a discrepancy with the direct interests of management practice. Whereas academics construct their new and exciting theoretical concepts on the basis of scientific evidence, they typically fail to accompany their analyses with detailed attention to the managerial implications. Thus a significant gap arises between the knowledge accrued by academics and the knowledge needed or wanted by managers.

This article presents some results of an investigation designed especially to remedy this situation (Biemans, 1991). Product development was studied from a network perspective with the express purpose of getting operational guidelines for management practice. Thus, by linking the latest theoretical ideas with traditional objectives, the observed chain of theoretical thought has come full circle again. We will start by briefly sketching the research methods employed. The main body of the article is devoted to presenting the most relevant findings in the form of eight critical success factors accompanied by their managerial implications. For illustrative purposes some of the observations are illustrated by brief case descriptions. The main conclusions are summarized by *The Five C's of Innovation Management.*

## SOME REMARKS ON METHODOLOGY

During the years 1985–1987 we conducted a preliminary investigation into the development practices of industrial firms through in-depth study of five cases taken from various sectors of Dutch industry. The results led to the initiation of a detailed follow-up investigation, carried out during the next two years by investigating seventeen cases of new product development within thirteen firms in the Dutch medical equipment industry. This particular industry seemed best suited for our purposes because of the ubiquity of networks and innovations, as well as its strategic relevance from the perspective of national industrial policy. The results presented in this article refer to the investigation into networking practices by Dutch manufacturers of innovative complex medical equipment.

The investigation was conducted along the following lines. First of all, on the basis of publications, newspaper clippings, expert interviews and chance contacts a fairly representative sample of thirteen firms was selected. Typically, either a marketing manager or R&D functionary was contacted and asked to take part in the investigation. Next, the basic information was gathered by means of semi-structured in-depth personal interviews with one or more persons at the manufacturer, while the majority of these people were interviewed more than once. Each interview took between two and four hours. Interviewees were asked to describe in general the process of product development at their company and to give a detailed description of the most recent innovation project. The results were written down in comprehensive reports and reviewed with the persons interviewed, thus inviting them to correct errors of fact and supply additional information. The information thus obtained was supplemented by (a) the incidental study of documents (e.g. schematic representations of the product development process, written down review procedures, market introduction brochures, product information leaflets, articles and books) and physical artefacts (e.g. the innovation, mock-ups, test models and stimulation devices), and (b) direct observation (e.g. of the testing of developed software, discussions between the manufacturer and major customers, and the functioning of prototypes at test sites). Subsequently, potential users and various third parties (such as competitors, suppliers and research institutions), insofar as they contributed substantially to the product development process, were interviewed in order to obtain additional information and cross-check the information provided by the manufacturer. Typically, one interview of two hours, supplemented by a limited number of phone conversations, proved to be sufficient to obtain the needed information. Based on all interview reports, comprehensive case descriptions were drawn up, that were subsequently reviewed by the manufacturers. Finally, all individual case descriptions were compared and analysed in order to formulate general conclusions and implementable guidelines.

Naturally, the procedure outlined above presents the ideal situation. In some cases deviation from this extensive data collection procedure was inescapable. For seven of the thirteen manufacturers of medical equipment investigated, the comprehensive procedure was followed, sometimes resulting in conducting as many as ten in-depth interviews involving eleven different persons. In the remaining six firms (five of which were small and one of medium size), however, the managers operated under extreme time pressure and had only a limited amount of time available. In these cases, the desired information had to be gathered by means of only one personal interview, complemented by few follow-up inquiries by telephone to obtain additional information. However, this presented no special problems because (a) all these cases were studied at the end of our investigation, (b) the innovation processes in question were relatively simple, and (c) we benefited from the experiences gained previously.

## CRITICAL SUCCESS FACTORS

Successful innovation can only be achieved by carefully addressing all essential factors influencing the course of the product development process. Our investigation into innovation practices in the Dutch medical equipment industry identified a set of eight critical success factors that guide the functioning of firms within networks. This section discusses them consecutively with strong emphasis on their managerial implications.[1]

### Critical Success Factor 1: Integration of Marketing and R&D

All managers were asked to describe their firm's overall product development strategy. (1) Only two of the thirteen firms responded by characterizing it as being a *balanced mixture of R&D and marketing.* (2) Five firms maintained that they based their new product development predominantly on *future oriented R&D* activities. Three of these firms were quite small in size, very much technology-oriented and lacked any formal marketing department. Whereas in two of them marketing activities were practically absent, the remaining firm had the marketing activities carried out by engineers with some commercial knowledge. Two (medium-sized) firms were in transition from basing the development of new products on research and development activities alone to founding it on a careful balance between directed research and development activities and a clearly formulated marketing strategy. (3) Six of the firms investigated let *marketing considerations* guide their product development efforts. However, only a minority of them employed a formal marketing plan. Instead, most firms relied on an explicitly stated market introduction strategy.

Traditionally, Dutch manufacturers of medical equipment emphasized the technological aspects of product development and neglected to pay marketing the attention it warranted. The marketing department only became involved when the moment of launch came into view. Such a strategy is doomed to fail; firms should pay attention to marketing-related issues during all stages of the product development process instead. Networking through established relationships with major customers provides a means to achieve this end. However, this does not imply that the strategy of having a *balanced* mixture of marketing and R&D (in the sense of paying equal attention to both factors) should always be considered the ideal one. Individual cases illustrate that the best strategy strongly depends on the situation involved.

Mijnhardt is the only Dutch firm specialized in the development, production and marketing of lung function diagnosis equipment. As technological developments have slowed down considerably in this particular industry, Mijnhardt has adopted the strategy of combining available technologies to develop new products that offer the user an improved solution with distinct advantages. Marketing is clearly involved in all stages of the development process: potential users comment on new-product ideas, well-known specialists criticize initial prototypes and several groups of widely different users test prototypes under actual user conditions.

Marketing can only provide meaningful contributions to product development when it is in a position to do so. This implies that the marketing function should be taken seriously by the manufacturer; a matter often found wanting in the firms investigated. In addition, integration of marketing and R&D necessitates good cooperation between both departments. Although significant differences may exist between representatives of both departments, they may often be easily solved. Marketing and R&D functionaries can obtain a better knowledge and understanding of each other's situation by having them jointly work on projects or visit a number of customers.

The case of Sentrex* underscores the need for good cooperation between the marketing and R&D departments. The geographical distance between the marketing department on the one hand and the departments of R&D, production and quality control on the other, formed a serious impediment for the successful development of new products.

Whatever the situation, marketing should be given its legitimate position within the organization. For many manufacturers this means that they should rely on experienced marketing managers, rather than sales managers bearing the title, but lacking the expertise. Naturally, this advice only makes sense for medium- or large-sized firms, as most small ones lack the financial resources to employ experienced marketers. Acquiring the necessary marketing expertise is a prerequisite for integrating marketing with the product development process. Often this integration can be accomplished effectively in very simple ways.

Philips Medical Systems had an extensive user manual drawn up before even the actual development of the prototype began! This obliged the people involved to consider the product specifications both carefully and in detail, leading to better specifications, reduced problems during actual development, improved internal communication, shorter duration of the development process and therefore early market introduction.

To sum up: Successful product development necessitates effective integration of marketing and R&D, while the exact nature and extent of the integration depends on the situation involved. However, this integration presupposes an effective marketing–R&D interface. Even small firms with limited resources may achieve this end through creative management.

### Critical Success Factor 2: Performance of Predevelopment Activities

The proficiency with which the predevelopment activities (i.e. the initial stages of the product development process, consisting of idea generation and evaluation, preliminary assessment and formulating and testing the product concept) strongly influences the course of the product development process. Even when the manufacturing firm is approached by university researchers or users who have developed a functioning prototype and used it under real-life conditions, the manufacturer still needs to carry out said predevelopment activities.

Eye-Tech*, Holland's leading manufacturer in the field of ophthalmology, was approached by university researchers who had developed a functioning prototype. Enthusiasm on the part of the managing director carried the firm directly, that is to say, without performing a preliminary assessment, into actual product development. Only after quite some resources had been spent on redevelopment activities, was a market assessment undertaken and it was discovered that a broader (and profitable!) market did not exist for that particular innovation.

Insufficient performance of the predevelopment activities was typically caused by one or more of three major factors. (1) Involving only one type of cooperation partner: in six cases manufacturers confined themselves to acquiring information from their major customers and neglected to use other potential sources of relevant information. (2) Involving a limited number of cooperation partners (per type of partner): in three cases the firm relied on the information provided by just one major customer. In four other cases the information gathered by questioning just one customer was supplemented by interacting with one or more third parties. (3) Neglecting to apply well-considered selection criteria: in only eight cases were potential users selected on the basis of such well-considered criteria as representativeness and the available expertise.

About a quarter of the firms investigated combined these deficiencies in quickly and superficially carrying out the predevelopment activities. The predevelopment activities can be characterized as having been performed only perfunctorily in four cases, reasonably in five cases and well in seven cases. Inadequate performance of the predevelopment activities typically resulted in the actual development of the prototype taking much longer than expected, increased development costs, a prolonged product development process and a postponed market launch, thus giving competitors ample opportunity to catch up with their own development efforts.

The recipe for improving the performance of the predevelopment activities is quite obvious, considering the nature of the shortcomings. In all situations, the manufacturer should undertake the predevelopment activities and undertake them well by considering three major questions related to his networking efforts.

### *(1) What Type of Cooperation Partners Should be Involved?*

While users are frequently employed during the predevelopment stages, much specific information can be provided by other potential cooperation partners, such as distributors (broad view of the market), industry experts (general technological and market trends), inspection agencies (product specifications), research institutes (state-of-the-art technology) and competitors (product specifications and production techniques). As each partner offers different information, the choice of a partner depends on the specific predevelopment stage.

Although potential users, distributors, universities and research institutes are frequently employed during the predevelopment activities, other less obvious parties are frequently overlooked. For instance, one manufacturer commented on the use of competitors during these critical stages: "Because of existing good personal relationships and, by using subtle interview techniques, competitors can be induced to provide significant market and technical information".

### *(2) How Many Cooperation Partners Should be Involved?*

The optimal number of partners to interact with strongly depends on the category of partners involved. For example, in the whole world there may be only two or three renowned international industry experts (often termed *gurus*) as regards the specific medical subdiscipline involved, but thousands of potential users of the new product.

### *(3) How Should the Cooperation Partners be Selected?*

In selecting cooperation partners, the manufacturer should determine the partner's representativeness, knowledge, objectivity, willingness to cooperate, market position, ability to keep confidential information and ties to major competitors. For example, because of close contacts with a major competitor, a key user may be questioned in a roundabout manner, so as not to divulge the exact nature of the new-product idea.

To sum up: In carrying out the predevelopment activities, manufacturers need to address three basic issues: what type of partners to use, how many to use of each category and what criteria to use in selecting them. Competitive advantage can be gained through innovative use of available options.

## Critical Success Factor 3: Allocation of Resources to Actual Development Activities

Firms may direct their networking activities to involve all kinds of external organizations in their product development efforts. For instance, by maintaining weak ties (Granovetter, 1973) with specific departments at universities (e.g. through the sponsoring of experimental research), manufacturers can keep up with state-of-the-art research in many areas without incurring large expenses of time and money. The weak ties serve as communication channels and may at all times be transformed into strong ties, e.g. by converting the sponsoring agreement into a joint development project. Another strategy involves the conscious and continuing scanning of the scientific community to identify researchers that have come up with innovative ideas in the form of functioning designs, combined with a receptive attitude towards any such researchers that should contact the manufacturer.

Medlab*, a medium-sized Dutch subsidiary of a large American industrial firm, distinguishes three types of cooperation that differ in their degree of intensity: (1) half-yearly contacts with universities and hospitals in order to stay in touch with important developments, (2) sponsoring of research projects through the provision of services and/or the payment of salaries, and (3) intensive collaboration by means of joint research projects.

Whatever networking strategy is followed, there are important consequences for a number of issues as regards the internal organization of the innovation process. One of them concerns the allocation of resources to the actual development activities, that is the employment of technological resources, such as R&D, engineering and industrial design, to the transformation of product specifications (the product concept) into a prototype.

Take, for instance, the case of a manufacturer who is approached by university researchers who have developed and built an original design. Even in this situation, adequate resources must be allocated to the redevelopment activities. The findings of our investigation clearly show that in these cases the developed device typically needs to be considerably modified before it is suitable for large-scale industrial production and satisfies more universal user requirements.

In cooperation with a physician of the Groningen University Hospital, a number of researchers from the University of Twente developed a prototype of a measuring instrument for use in obstetrics and proved its value through use in practice. Applied Laser Technology, a small manufacturer specialized in laser applications, was asked to manufacture and market the innovation. Because of various technical problems it took about a year and a half to redevelop the product and get it ready for introduction.

Typically, the firms studied tended to underestimate the time, money and resources needed for the actual development activities. The majority of the managers interviewed admitted that the actual development activities had taken longer than planned. In general, they stated that both the experienced risks and total costs involved were considerably larger than anticipated. Product development processes (from idea generation till market launch) that took up twice as long as planned proved to be the rule rather than the exception.

In general, the frustrations caused by exceeded budgets and deadlines can be prevented in two ways. One obvious strategy is improved (and realistic!) planning coupled with meticulous execution. Particularly to small firms, the introduction of (some of the principles of) project management may prove beneficial. Another strategy, in line with recommendations made previously, consists of improving the way the predevelopment activities are carried out. As Leiva and Obermayer (1989) put it: "Do your homework, especially early in the product development cycle... More work at the definition phase of the project always translates into savings of both time and money as the project nears completion". In the specific case of cooperation with a university, detailed and timely communication may prevent many misunderstandings, problems and delays.

To sum up: Manufacturers should not underestimate the time and other resources involved in actually developing a prototype, even when external parties have done part of the job. Experience shows that budgets exceeded by 100% are the rule rather than the exception. Improved planning, meticulous execution and elaborate attention to the predevelopment activities may remedy this situation.

### Critical Success Factor 4: Testing Prototypes with Users[2]

The majority of the firms investigated reported to interact predominantly with potential users during the process of product development, with strong emphasis on the testing and launch stages. In three quarters of the cases studied the manufacturer employed potential users to test a newly developed prototype. In this context, we need to distinguish between testing a prototype internally (in-house tests) and externally (tests with potential users). While the in-house tests mainly concern the innovation's technical functionality, the clinical tests with users serve a totally different purpose. These are generally undertaken as a last check on the match between product characteristics and user requirements and to discover any problems that may arise in actual use of the product in a clinical environment. Despite the manifest importance of undertaking clinical tests, many manufacturers pay insufficient attention to this critical activity.

(1) Four of the thirteen innovations that actually reached the market were introduced without ever having been clinically tested by potential users. In all cases the firms in question displayed an excessive amount of confidence in their own technical abilities and the product's functioning. Although, by skipping the clinical evaluation stage, a firm may manage to stay ahead of the competition, it is at the same time running the risk of launching an imperfect product.

> Medsound* decided against having prototypes tested by potential users as a matter of principle. The decision was based on prior negative experience with gynaecologists who were afraid to injure their patients by using unsafe new products and tested a new prototype only superficially on themselves. However, these negative experiences could possibly have been prevented by providing better instructions and exerting tighter control over the external tests.

(2) Due to pressure of time, caused by an important trade show or sales meeting, in two cases the firm involved conducted the clinical tests prematurely and carelessly and launched the new product too early. (3) In four cases the firm relied on feedback provided by only one user. (4) Potential users were mainly selected on the

basis of their reputed know-how, their perceived commercial potentialities and an existing relationship, rather than their representativeness for the market segment in question. Reputable physicians or institutes that have tested the prototype may subsequently assist in launching the product, thus lending additional credibility to the manufacturer's claims and confirms the user's reputation in the medical field. Nevertheless, the firms investigated typically failed to capitalize on these opportunities. (5) A successful external test includes such elements as formulating objectives, instructing the users, executing the test, providing support and control, and registrating and evaluating the results.

Numerous examples from actual practice illustrate how relationships with major customers may be impaired because of mistakes made during external testing. However, careful design of this critical activity provides the manager with a veritable wealth of essential information.

> Mijnhardt, a manufacturer of lung function diagnosis equipment, had a prototype tested extensively by four groups of potential users: (1) a barracks, with military athletes in top condition to test the functioning at the upper end, (2) a hospital, with real patients to obtain clinical information, (3) a business firm, that intended to measure large numbers of employees, to test the durability and user friendliness of the device, and (4) healthy young children to test the prototype's functioning at the bottom end. Furthermore, at the time of investigation additional tests were planned with very young sick patients to test the product under even more extreme conditions.

The evidence demonstrates that manufacturer–user relationships in the context of testing newly developed prototypes frequently display symptoms of ossification. Once relationships are established and strengthened by good personal contacts, they tend to function during a number of successive development projects. Long-term relationships with a limited number of high-quality specialists/hospitals are established in which the very existence of a relationship, rather than the characteristics of the project, determines the cooperation. Needless to say, this need not represent the ideal situation: a well-functioning personal relationship is no guarantee for good results (in this case: high-quality information).

To sum up: Having prototypes tested by potential users is not only a logical, but also a very critical part of the product development process. While it offers the manufacturer various opportunities to obtain strategic information, its full potential can only be realized through careful planning and meticulous execution.

### Critical Success Factor 5: Timing of Market Launch

As regards complex medical equipment, the right time to introduce a new product may be strongly determined by a limited number of annually organized (inter)national trade shows. Many firms commented on the need to be present at certain selected trade shows, while launching a new product between two important trade shows is considered to be less effective and to require substantial additional support of promotional effort. In four of the cases studied, an annual trade show or sales meeting greatly influenced the scheduling of the product development efforts. In three of these cases the resulting tight schedule led to an untimely product launch. This goes to show that networking by means of conforming to established communication patterns may be necessary but should not be detrimental to the overall quality of the development efforts.

> In response to a new-product introduction by a major competitor, Eye-Tech* developed an improved version with distinct additional user benefits. The developed prototype was tested in-house, demonstrated at an important annual trade show for end users and tested by a local hospital. Based on the positive results, the product was subsequently launched during an annual sales meeting and clinically tested by a number of hospitals in the Netherlands and abroad. After modifying some details of the product's design, the first production run of 25 units was started. One of these units was tested by an evaluation centre in Germany. While the first orders generated by the enthusiastic dealers arrived, some essential defects were uncovered by the German centre. This necessitated (1) stopping delivery, (2) taking back and modifying all units already delivered, and (3) discouraging further demand generated by the dealers.

Firms may hasten the moment of market launch by consciously skipping the clinical evaluation stage. This was actually done in four cases because of (a) confidence in the firm's technical abilities, (b) confidence in the product's functioning, or (c) lack of confidence in the ability of physicians to meaningfully evaluate prototypes. However, this strategy appears only to be feasible when the firm is very familiar with both the market and the product involved (as is often the case with minor innovations rather than major ones). In all other situations, the critical importance of networking by having users perform clinical evaluations can hardly be overstated. One of the firms referred to above learned this the hard way when its product, which was completely new to the firm, failed in the market. There was nothing left to do but to start from scratch by reformulating the product specifications.

The initiation of joint development projects with competitors is frequently mentioned as one of the major strategies to shorten the duration of the product development process, and thus advance the moment of market launch. However, due to the typically small number of competing firms per category of complex medical equipment, this strategy would only result in fierce price competition and is therefore not feasible in this particular industry. As an alternative, various firms devised innovative solutions to this problem.

For instance, the increasing importance of software needed to control and direct the product's operation, allows a firm to advance the time of market launch by means of a *basic package introduction*.

> Philips Medical Systems developed and introduced their Digital Cardiac Imaging (DCI) system according to the following strategy. First, the firm developed and introduced the hardware and the basic software, consisting of (1) the operating software, and (2) software to perform the innovation's most basic functions, that is the "basic package". Next, additional software (various clinical programmes) was developed and introduced in a number of subsequent releases.

The most significant advantage of following this strategy is obvious. The hardware plus the accompanying basic software (i.e. the basic package) can be introduced relatively early, resulting in market penetration at an early stage, a distinct competitive advantage and confirmation of the firm's innovative image (thus establishing a prominent position in the minds of leading physicians). However, this strategy entails some potential disadvantages, too. Although most of the software is launched in future releases, they must be compatible with the previously introduced hardware and therefore be specified quite early in the development process, which calls for detailed planning and coordination. Despite these efforts, the firm may run into problems in developing the clinical programmes that were already announced when the basic package was launched. Delayed introduction of announced releases may give customers the impression that the manufacturer does not live up to his promises, thus impairing the firm's reputation. In addition, the development of certain clinical programmes found to be of interest to physicians, but that were not foreseen at the time of designing the basic package, may have to be postponed until it is time to develop a second updated version of the hardware.

To sum up: A manufacturer may employ several strategies to advance the moment of market launch and thus gain a competitive advantage. However, all of them require careful planning as well as realistic estimation and evaluation of their probable consequences.

### Critical Success Factor 6: Employing Users as References During Market Launch

It was noted before that the firms investigated interacted predominantly with potential users during the testing and launch stages. This is quite logical and reflects a conscious strategy, as users who have tested a prototype can be employed for promotional purposes during market launch. For this reason, these users may be referred to as *launching customers* and some manufacturers do speak of *luminary sites* when selecting users to test prototypes.

> In addition to potential users, manufacturers sometimes have specialized research institutes test their newly developed prototypes. Naturally, these test results may also be used for promotional purposes during market launch. An example is provided by Enraf-Nonius, which frequently cooperates with The Netherlands Organization for Applied Scientific Research (TNO) in the development of specific components and the testing of new products. The

evaluative reports of TNO are used by Enraf-Nonius during market launch as support from an independent research institute. At the same time it offers TNO the opportunity to increase its reputation/prestige in international markets.

As has been shown previously, the reputed know-how, an existing relationship and the perceived commercial potentialities were by far most frequently mentioned as criteria in selecting test users. This particular combination of criteria appoints to point to the use of reputable physicians or institutes which, mostly due to their repeatedly proven medical expertise, occupy central positions in the medical community. However, the results of our investigation do not fully support this observation.

The findings show that ten of the thirteen innovations that actually reached the market were clinically evaluated by users, while just six of these (i.e. 60%) were actually introduced with the help of these users. This number is surprisingly low, even more so, as informal communication and opinion leadership have often been said to be of great importance in institutional markets (Schiffman and Gaccione, 1974). Apparently, manufacturers do consider the commercial potentialities in selecting test users, but fail to capitalize on the opportunities thus generated during market launch. This is further illustrated by the fact that those manufacturers who do employ users during market introduction only do so marginally. Typically, they employ users by only using the name of the physician or institute involved in promotional material and during sales presentations (e.g. by incorporating such remarks as "...extensively tested and approved by..."). However, test users may be employed in a variety of ways during market launch.

- Having the physician or institute demonstrate the new equipment to other potential buyers.
- Having the test user publish scientific articles about the innovation. Especially articles that compare the innovation's performance with that of competing products are suitable for promotional purposes.
- Stimulating the test user to deliver talks or present papers at trade shows and scientific conferences.
- Employing the test user to distribute the innovation.

Oldelft, a medium-sized manufacturer of optical instruments, collaborated with researchers of Erasmus University in Rotterdam in developing a new piece of medical equipment for monitoring heart action. In May 1988 representatives from both parties gave a joint presentation during an important national trade show. Rather than using the time for an extensive discussion of the product's unique features, they focused on the problems encountered in the course of the cooperation project and the measures taken to solve them.

To sum up: Employing users during market launch is a logical consequence of having them test newly developed prototypes. Nevertheless, manufacturers typically fail to fully capitalize on the available opportunities.

### Critical Success Factor 7: Cooperation with Universities

In general, universities are frequently involved in the development of innovative medical equipment. The results of our investigation corroborate this observation. In four out of the seventeen cases studied university researchers developed the original design or contributed substantially to the development of the prototype. In three of them, both university researchers and physicians from a university hospital were involved in the development project through intensive interaction. In addition, there were numerous instances where industrial firms interacted with universities in order to have the latter develop parts of the product, test prototypes or solve technological problems. Due to the essentially different nature of industrial firms and universities, such cooperation may be accompanied by a number of problems. While these are partly of a general nature, some of them are specific to industry–university cooperation. The collective experiences of the firms involved led to the formulation of the following recommendations.

- At the outset of the cooperation project, both partners need to state their objectives, expectations and criteria for evaluating the project. Essential differences concerning these issues may cause serious misunderstandings, frustrations, delays and excessive development costs.
- The cooperation partners need to make clear-cut agreements about the publication of results, division of activities to be undertaken as well as the accompanying responsibilities, time schedule, etc.

> The cooperation between Oldelft and Erasmus University was characterized by substantial problems, frustrations and misunderstandings. These were largely caused by essential differences in perspectives. While Oldelft was interested in acquiring some basic technological know-how, the university's interest went out to developing an innovative piece of medical equipment. These differences led to lack of commitment, unclear agreement and delays and inefficiencies during the development process. However, despite this bad start the ultimate product was quite successful.

- The cooperation should be started at an early stage of development to prevent problems and the waste of time and money.
- A manufacturer needs to conduct a detailed market study to evaluate a product's commercial potential; also when a fully developed original design is being offered by university researchers.
- A manufacturer must allocate sufficient resources to transform an original

design developed by university researchers into a commercially viable industrial product.

- A manufacturer needs to participate in the development activities carried out by the university researchers in order to stay fully informed, identify and solve problems at an early stage, demonstrate commitment and ascertain that its own objectives are being met.
- Both parties need to establish and maintain properly functioning personal relationships. Despite all formal agreements, the ultimate success of the cooperation project largely depends on the people involved.
- The parties involved need to demonstrate and accommodate for flexibility, so that changed circumstances can be met by appropriate actions.

> In developing a quite complex medical equipment innovation Medlab* closely cooperated with researchers at a university. However, at a certain time the firm had acquired so much knowledge that the university could no longer be expected to contribute additional relevant information. The cooperation project with the university was more or less terminated and Medlab initiated its own development project, this time in collaboration with a competitor.

In discussing the allocation of resources to the actual development activities we mentioned that firms may maintain weak ties with a number of universities, for instance through the sponsoring of experimental research. As soon as the research proves to be fruitful, the limited sponsoring may be replaced by a contract for a joint development project. Thus, weak ties are considered to be potential strong ones. However, the example above illustrates that the intensity of cooperation may be changed in the other direction as well. A cooperation contract should provide enough flexibility to allow this kind of action.

To sum up: Because of their specialized knowledge, universities may contribute in various ways to the development of innovations. Essential cultural differences are frequently the underlying cause of critical problems. They may be prevented through timely communication and detailed agreements.

### Critical Success Factor 8: Management of Internal Networks

The results of our investigation demonstrate that networks vary in complexity. At the one extreme we found *simple networks* consisting of a single interactive relationship between the manufacturer and e.g. a user, university or inspection agency, while at the other extreme we discovered *complex networks* in which the manufacturer interacts with a number of widely different parties. Complex networks were found to be necessary when (a) the development process involved a very complex innovation, (b) the manufacturer lacked knowledge or expertise with respect to some relevant areas, or (c) unanticipated problems arose during product development which necessitated the hiring of specialized organizations.

The analysis of complex networks in particular leads us to conclude that networks should be considered at two different levels. While each of the major parties involved in the product development process is part of a large *external network*, every one of them has its own *internal network* as well.

> The development of an innovative piece of medical equipment for monitoring heart action illustrates the intricacies of complex networks. The original design was developed by researchers of Erasmus University and subsequently transferred to Oldelft. This manufacturer of optical instruments translated the design into an industrial product which was then delivered to an original equipment manufacturer. The OEM incorporated the product in a complete monitoring system, which was being sold to hospitals. While these three main parties constitute the heart of the external network, each of them has its own internal network. The successful development of the original design necessitated close cooperation between engineers of the university and physicians at the university hospital. The successful translation of the original design into an industrial new product by Oldelft was made possible through effective communication and coordination between the departments of marketing, R&D, production and quality control. Finally, the purchasing and marketing departments of the OEM had to coordinate their activities.

The distinction between external and internal networks is crucial, since the functioning of each of the internal networks directly influences the efficiency and efficacy of the external network. Thus, the old saying "a chain is no stronger than its weakest link" proves to be relevant to innovation management as well.

To sum up: Successful product innovation frequently necessitates cooperation with external parties. However, the critical importance of such cooperation does nothing to dispel the need for effective management of the internal network.

## MANAGERIAL IMPLICATIONS: THE FIVE C'S OF INNOVATION MANAGEMENT

Based on the results of empirical investigations into innovation processes, numerous academics have demonstrated the need for cooperation within networks and commended its beneficial consequences. However, the critical success factors discussed in this article demonstrate many potential problems and pitfalls that may confront a firm functioning within a network. The findings can be summarized by *The Five C's of Innovation Management* (see Fig. 1). This theoretical concept captures the following train of thought.

Particularly in industrial markets, a number of trends can be observed. Technological developments have accelerated to a level where product life cycles

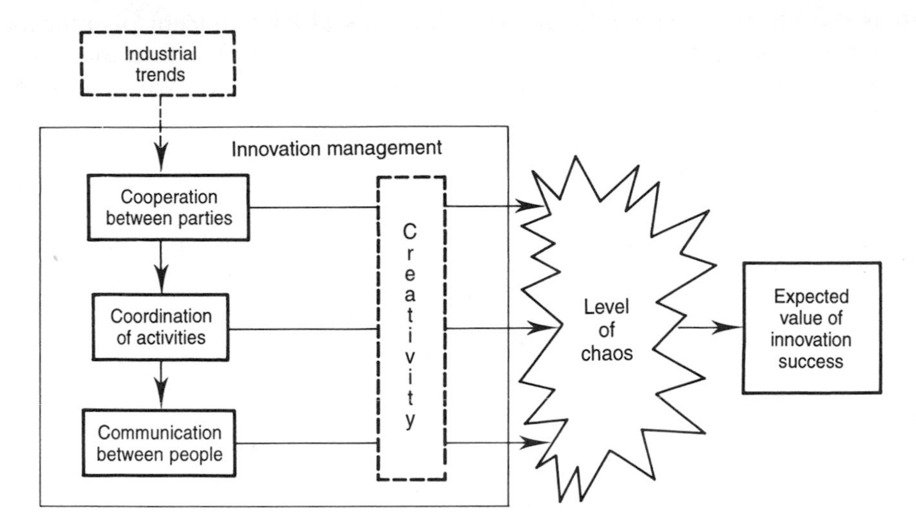


Fig. 1. The five C's of innovation management.

have shortened considerably. This implies that a manufacturer must continually and actively be searching for innovative products to succeed the existing ones, while the time available to reap the benefits has been significantly reduced. In addition, industrial new products are becoming increasingly complex and their development necessitates the combination of different areas of knowledge. This growing complexity fuels a demand for standardization. To further complicate matters, competition is growing and becoming more and more global. New products need to be aimed at international markets, which may not always be easily accessible to the manufacturer. Typically, these trends combine to make new product development an expensive and high-risk endeavour.

More often than not, one or more of these factors force a manufacturer to develop industrial innovations through *cooperation* with other organizations, such as users, competitors, research institutes, suppliers and distributors. New product development is no longer considered to be the sole province of the manufacturer. Instead, many parties may contribute in various ways to the product development process. This has the obvious advantage that each party can do what it does best. For example, a selected group of potential users may supply the necessary application knowledge, a university may incorporate the latest technological know-how and a specialized agency may be hired to provide the industrial design. In addition to this external cooperation, management needs to organize for internal cooperation by setting up multidisciplinary project teams that take the new product from its inception to market launch (Takeuchi and Nonaka, 1986).

The benefits of cooperation may only be enjoyed when the parties involved establish effective and efficient *coordination* of the various activities to be undertaken. Key activities need to be divided among the partners involved and the accompanying responsibilities must be assigned to the right people. However, subdividing the problem like this should not preclude parties from providing creative contributions to areas outside their assigned tasks (cf. Nonaka's (1990) concept of information redundancy). Having a product champion at a high level in the firm may facilitate coordination and prove to be very beneficial in supplying the necessary commitment. Firms may employ several mechanisms to achieve coordination of activities, for instance, periodic job rotation, joint customer visits, physical proximity of work places, project teams, seminars, regular joint review meetings, social interactions, and joint development contracts.

While activities need to be coordinated, the outcome of the innovation process is largely determined by the people involved. Effective and efficient coordination can only be achieved when the cooperation partners involved create and maintain an atmosphere that encourages good and timely *communication*, not just externally (with cooperation partners) but internally (at a departmental, functional and personal level) as well. However, it should be noted that interaction with external cooperation partners is a means by which strategic information may be disseminated as well as gathered. This calls for greater self-discipline and even greater emphasis on individual responsibility for relationships and for communications (cf. Drucker, 1988).

Whereas many investigators have attempted to formulate recommendations concerning the management of innovation processes, we need to mention that some authors question the value of such guidelines. According to them, innovation processes are not rational and ordered, but to a large extent better described by *chaos*. For example, Quinn (1985) argued in an article that "Innovation tends to be individually motivated, opportunistic, customer responsive, tumultuous, nonlinear, and interactive in its development. Managers can plan overall directions and goals, but surprises are likely to abound". However, the article's revealing title "Managing innovation: controlled chaos" captures the essence of our argument: even though innovation processes are very much characterized by chaos, in the sense of surprises and unexpected changes, they can still be controlled *to a certain extent*. The three C's of cooperation, coordination and communication are key elements in successfully developing innovations through reduction of the level of chaos. A reduced level of chaos serves to increase the expected value of innovation success at a project level, which is a product of (1) the probability of developing and introducing a successful innovation, and (2) the returns in terms of money, competitive advantage, reputation, etc. However, this should not be taken to imply that in the ideal situation chaos is eliminated entirely. Nonaka (1988) acknowledges the beneficial potential of a certain level of chaos by arguing that a firm may use chaos as a catalyst for the creation of innovative solutions.

The extent to which the three C's of cooperation, coordination and communication are able to reduce the level of chaos may be significantly enhanced through creative use of management practices. Thus, the fifth C of *creativity* serves as a critical intermediary variable. Successful innovation is not achieved through routine adherence to prescribed detailed procedures, schedules and measures. Instead, a firm should strive to enhance its competitive advantage by applying creative management to devise innovative solutions. Experimentation and the principle of trial and error have proven to indicate the right direction on the route to success.

The presented concept of *The Five C's of Innovation Management* acknowledges that cooperation with other parties may be essential in developing innovations. However, cooperation with external parties is nothing like the purely beneficial strategy it is often made out to be. Instead, it may pose numerous unexpected problems and requires a lot of serious effort and commitment of the people involved to make it work.

## NOTES

1. In some of the cases that serve as illustrations, the name of the firm and the product involved have been disguised for reasons of confidentiality. In these cases, the name of the firm has been marked with *.
2. A detailed discussion of this particular stage of the product development process can be found in Biemans (1990).

## REFERENCES

Biemans, W. G. Manufacturer–user relationships in testing newly developed prototypes. *Research Developments in International Industrial Marketing and Purchasing, Proceedings of the 6th IMP Conference*, September 24–25, Milan (1990).

Biemans, W. G. *Innovative Networks.* Routledge, London (1991).

Drucker, P. The coming of the new organization. *Harvard Business Review*, January–February (1988).

Foxall, G. R. and Tierney, J. D. From CAP1 to CAP2: user-initiated innovation from the user's point of view. *Management Decision*, **22** (5) (1984).

Granovetter, M. S. The strength of weak ties. *American Journal of Sociology*, **78** (6) (1973).

Håkansson, H. (ed.) *Industrial Technological Development: A Network Approach.* Croom Helm, London (1987).

Leiva, W. A. and Obermayer, J. W. Commonsense product development. *Business Marketing*, **74** (August) (1989).

Nonaka, I. Creating organizational order out of chaos: self-renewal in Japanese firms. *California Management Review*, Spring (1988).

Nonaka, I. Redundant, overlapping organizations: A Japanese approach to managing the innovation product. *California Management Review*, Spring (1990).

Parkinson, S. T. The role of the user in successful new product development. *R&D Management*, **12** (3) (1982).

Quinn, J. B. Managing innovation: controlled chaos. *Harvard Business Review*, May–June (1985).

Schiffman, L. G. and Gaccione, V. Opinion leaders in institutional markets. *Journal of Marketing*, **3** (1974).

Shaw, B. *The Role of the Interaction Between the Manufacturer and the User in the Technological Innovation Process.* PhD Thesis, Science Policy Research Unit, University of Sussex (1986).

Takeuchi, H. and Nonaka, I. The new new product development game. *Harvard Business Review*, January–February (1986).

Vanden Abeele, P. and Christiaens, I. De Klant als Generator van Innovatie in "High-Tech" Markten – Een Conceptuele en Empirische Studie (The Customer as Generator of Innovation in "High-Tech" Markets – A Conceptual and Empirical Study). *Economisch en Sociaal Tijdschrift* (1987).

Von Hippel, E. Successful industrial products from customer ideas. *Journal of Marketing*, **42**, January (1978).

Voss, C. A. The role of users in the development of applications software. *Journal of Product Innovation Management*, **2** (1985).

# Conclusions: Managing in Business Markets

## EVOLUTION

The second edition of this book of readings comes to a stop at a very different position to the first. Up to that time, the majority of our empirical work and conceptual development had been directed towards understanding what happened in the relationships between companies in business markets. The first edition of this book was intended to show that a relationship perspective was not only fruitful from a research point of view, but that it could also help managers to see their task more clearly and help to raise the level of the debate in both the purchasing and marketing functions in companies. The first edition also illustrated how members of the IMP group and other researchers had turned their attention to particular aspects of inter-company relationships. Examples of this were research on the impact of technological resources on relationships as well as the study of relationships that were international, or involved distributors or consultants. The first edition also included early ideas on portfolios of relationships; some of these have been retained in this book because of their clarity of approach.

The final part of the first edition was entitled "Networks". In retrospect, this seemed to show them as a sort of separate extension to the basic ideas on relationships. I suggested at the time that some of the network concepts had "run ahead" of their empirical base and that we needed "to improve our understanding of the complexity of multiple inter-company relations in the context of higher and more rapidly changing technology". The IMP2 project, in which we were engaged at the time of the first edition, was aimed at the need which I identified for "large scale, long-term and very detailed empirical work to firmly ground... network concepts in reality". That project is now complete and many of the papers in this edition owe much to it.* In this edition, the readings on networks are included early in the book,

*Much of the conceptual and empirical output of this project was published in Håkansson and Snehota (1995)—see reading II.4.

to emphasize their importance as a basis for understanding business markets and the management tasks in them and also to show how central they have become to our work.

## INTERACTION AND RELATIONSHIPS

Throughout this book we have emphasized that management in business markets is not a process through which the seller acts independently *on* its market, but where a number of interdependent companies each act *in* a network. Furthermore, we have argued that business sales and purchases do not exist as individual events and hence cannot be understood fully if each one is examined in isolation. Each interaction between companies, whether for product, service, financial, social or information exchange is an episode within the relationship between the companies. This relationship may be close or distant, complex or simple, and each episode within it is affected by the relationship and in turn may affect the relationship itself. The relationship between the companies consists of learned rules and behaviours that provide the atmosphere within which interaction takes place. Individuals will approach each episode on the basis of their experience within the relationship and elsewhere, and on the basis of the values that they hold, both in general and with regard to the particular relationship. For the majority of companies in business markets, a small number of suppliers and/or customers tend to be responsible for large volumes of their purchases or sales. In these cases, relationships tend to be close, complex and long term. These relationships evolve over time and this evolution is often described as a series of stages characterized by increasing mutual adaptation, reduced "distance" between the companies and increasing commitment as discussed in reading I.3. However, we have to take care to avoid thinking that there is any inevitability in this process of development. Business relationships can of course decline, become inert or die (readings I.4 and I.5). Companies in business markets will have a number of relationships with more or less significant suppliers, customers and other partners. These relationships will be surrounded by many more relationships, including some with which they have no contact. Despite this, these third-party relationships will indirectly affect and be affected by the company's own interactions and together they constitute the network of which the company forms part. This is the manifestation of what Håkansson and Snehota (reading II.3) call the "connectedness" of the business relations of a company.

## MANAGEMENT PRACTICE

The readings in this edition of the book are perhaps more managerial in approach than those in the first edition and they emphasize the *use* of some concepts as well as simply explaining the concepts themselves. This orientation has stemmed from a concern that despite 20 years of research and teaching about business relationships, management practice does not seem to have changed in many companies. Many marketers still fail to see the importance of taking a long-term view of their relationship investments. Many buyers fail to develop a clear idea of the tasks involved in using the resources of their suppliers effectively and integrating them with their own. There are very good reasons for this: the inherent complexity of inter-company relationships and networks means that it is unrealistic to imagine that they can be wholly "designed" by any one party, still less that their evolution can be solely the result of conscious one-sided *plans*. An interaction approach to the study of business markets also makes it clear that the *state* of the relationship between two companies at any one time is the result of the actions of many individuals in both companies and elsewhere, based on their respective motivations and the interactions between them. Similarly the *outcomes* of particular decisions taken within a relationship are subject to the actions of the relationship partner, some of which may be more or less predictable. Outcomes are also likely to be affected by the actions of other companies and organizations elsewhere in the network, which may be unknown to the decision-taker.

## STRATEGY IN BUSINESS MARKETS

Nevertheless, despite this complexity, managers *have* to take decisions within relationships and some of them *do* try to develop a strategic approach to them. The readings in this book show the complexity of the potential outcomes of relationship decisions and the unpredictability of external actions in a network. This means that *effective* decision-making by managers is likely to be based at least as much on analysis of experience of what has happened previously within their company's relationships, as it is on explicit planning. The importance of this experimental analysis, or what is now fashionably called "corporate memory", was expressed by Håkansson and Snehota (reading II.3) as follows: "purpose-directed behaviour...calls for the adoption of behavioural rules that do not necessarily derive from a cognitive elaboration of the specific situation as it is met, but rather from an individual elaboration of past experience". This view of "emergent" strategy is illustrated in a number of the readings in this collection, in which the idea of satisfaction in a relationship is "on-going" and the possibility of modifying an approach to a relationship is ever present.

A conclusion from the readings in this book is that the strategy process in business markets is not one that is wholly amenable to explicit or detailed *planning*. Despite this, we argue that decision-making in relationships must take place in the context of both the longer-term and the wider network issues involved in each relationship. Without this view managers face two problems. The first is that they will restrict their orientation towards short-term issues and to existing ways of acting, within individually significant relationships, at the expense of the company's overall network position. Second, that they will take an approach based on an overly rigid plan, so that neither the plan nor the company itself has the flexibility to take account of the possible actions of others elsewhere in the network or of its inability to predict them.

This view of the strategy process has evolved through the group's work over the past 20 years. It is noteworthy that some of the earlier writing in both this and the previous edition of the book is much more confident of a company's ability to plan and "strategize" in its relationships than much of the later work. Readers may find it interesting to compare some of the earlier and later readings in this book and draw their own conclusions on whether our thinking about the nature of relationship strategy has evolved.

## THE MANAGEMENT TASK

The group's research and the readings in this book contribute to a view of the task facing the manager in a business market and it is perhaps worth trying to encapsulate these as a conclusion to this edition.

Managers in a business market have to cope with the complexity that surrounds them, and with restrictions on their ability to act independently and to make strategy. The outcome of any decision taken by a company in a business market will be mediated by the actions of those in surrounding companies. Each company will be dependent for success and its continuing operation on the resources of both its suppliers and customers, and of others with which it does not deal directly. All of these companies have their own agenda to follow and business relationships comprise a combination of choices by the companies involved, some of which will be intended to achieve mutual advantage, some that will be at the expense of another company and some that will merely take the other into account. Any decision that managers take about their relationship with another company will have effects on a number of levels. For example, a straightforward decision to increase price to a particular customer will have an immediate effect *in* that relationship. But it could also have an effect *on* the relationship itself by altering the customer's longer-term attitude. The same decision could also affect the company's relationships with others in its *portfolio* when they think of its implications for them; and, finally, the single decision can also have an effect on the wider *network*, if other suppliers follow the company's lead.

Managerial decisions must take into account both these wider and longer-term effects and the manager must balance the value of a continuing relationship against both its short- and long-term costs. This requires the company to develop a clear view of what it seeks from each major relationship, the investment it needs to make to achieve those things and how the relationship relates to its wider portfolio. It must also take a view of where that relationship fits within the portfolio of its counterpart. A further complication for the manager is that many business relationships are both complex and long term. This means that the manager will need to deal differently with each major relationship as it develops. Each relationship is made up of the detailed interactions of many individuals in different functional areas and they are often based on formal or informal rules of conduct that have been developed by those involved over many years. The successful manager is much more likely to be an integrator or a conductor of these many interactions than to be a director.

The interactive nature of business markets means that strategy for those markets must also be interactive. It is not enough simply to take account of the surrounding world, nor to spell out the company's view of its own direction. A company's strategy in a business market will emerge from the pattern of decision-making by its members on a continuing basis that will not fit neatly with 3-year or annual planning cycles. Its strategy is likely to be based on an individualistic approach to important relationships. Strategy will not only have to be responsive to the moves of others, but often must be developed with them. Finally, those who have had experience of trying to develop strategy in business markets will also be aware that it must be based on a realization that much of what happens there cannot realistically be anticipated or controlled. Under these circumstances the business manager is not someone who simply manages his or her own business, but also someone who copes with and tries to manage in interactions, relationships and networks.

*D.F.*

# Index

Page numbers in *italics* refer to illustrations and tables; page numbers in **bold** refer to main discussion.